# INDO-CENTRAL ASIAN RELATIONS
*From Early Times to Medieval Period*

# Indo-Central Asian Relations

*From Early Times to Medieval Period*

MANSURA HAIDAR

MANOHAR
2004

First published 2004



ISBN 81-7304-508-9

*Published by*

Ajay Kumar Jain for
Manohar Publishers & Distributors
4753/23 Ansari Road, Daryaganj
New Delhi 110 002

*Typeset at*

Digigrafics
New Delhi 110 049

*Printed at*

Lordson Publishers Pvt. Ltd.
Delhi 110 007

*Dedicated*
*to*
*my Friends*
*in*
*Central Asia*

# Contents

# Acknowledgements

It is a pleasant duty for me to thank all such persons who have contributed in some way to the completion of this volume.

Having already been introduced to the late Professor Bobojan Ghaffurov through my supervisor at Aligarh, I received considerable help from him. He took keen interest in the progress of my work during my stay in erstwhile Soviet Union. My supervisor at Tashkent University Professor Goga Abrarovich Hidayatov, who happened to be the Dean and Chairman of the Department of History was very generous about extending all possible assistance in my academic pursuits which facilitated my access to the relevant libraries throughout the country.

I recall with gratitude and with a deep sense of personal loss now about my association with (late) Professor Mrs. Sabahat Azimjanova (the then Director of the Oriental Institute at Tashkent) whose affectionate care and concern for my welfare as well as the studies has always been a great source of encouragement to me. I learnt much through useful discussions and long scholarly discourses with academicians like Professor Bori Ahmedov of the Oriental Institute, Tashkent, Professor Razia Muqminova of Institute of History (Tashkent), Professor Mrs. Davidovich, the then Director of the Oriental Institute (Moscow), Professor Olga Chekhovich, Professor Hamid Sulaimanov, Professor Mrs. Razia Sulaimanova and Professor Pugachenkova. Their keen academic advices proved to be very useful in my work.

Grateful thanks are due to Professor Orinbaev, the Director of Abu Raihan Alberuni Institute of Oriental Studies, Tashkent. The (late) Professor Hashimov and Professor Khairullaev of the Institute of Oriental Studies, Tashkent for their kind academic assistance. My boundless gratitude to Professor Ahror Mukhtarov of Dushambe, Tajikistan continues to this day as he was gracious enough to ensure constant supply of newly published works to me which assisted enormously to update my knowledge about the latest developments in Central Asia. My acquaintance with Professor Mansur

Bobokhanov, the then Chairman, Department of History, Dushambe and the (late) Professor Abdullaev of Institute of History at Dushambe though for a short period had further confirmed my belief about the amicability and generosity of the Central Asians.

Having enjoyed the fulsome hospitality of my Central Asian friends for many months at a strech during my stay made the alien land seem like a 'second motherland' to me. Amongst the galaxy of my personal friends were included: Dr. Mrs. Farida Salimova (an Indologist at the Oriental Institute, Tashkent, a great friend of India and a niece of the famous poet Ghaffur Ghulam, herself a well-known scholar and writer of several works on Indian customs and traditions and the author of monographs on Indira Gandhi, Aruna Asaf Ali and others); Dr. Shirin Jahlova, another reputed Indologist at the Oriental Institute, Tashkent who happens to be well-versed in Hindi language and has contributed tremendously towards popularizing Indian languages in Central Asia and strengthening the bonds of friendship between the people of the two countries. Mrs. Sorkina—the Russian teacher at Tashkent and Dr. Yulduz Teshabaev—a well-known Indologist at the Oriental Institute. Their constant and active support sustained me during those lonely days in a foreign land. I also cherish the numerous friends like Gulsara, Sewar, both from the Institute of Oriental Studies, Mariam Yuldashaev (French language teacher at Samarqand University), her aunt Borchhin Opa and Ninel Ghaffurova, the daughter of (late) Professor Bobajon Ghaffurov and presently Reader in the Oriental Institute, Moscow.

My special thanks are due to the librarians in Tashkent particularly to Mr. Munirov, the then librarian of Abu Raihan Alberuni Institute of Oriental Studies and Anwar Apa at the Fundamental Library, Tashkent.

Back in my country and particularly at Aligarh, I have very fond memories of assistance I received from the librarians and the library staff of Maulana Azad Library. The three successive librarians namely, Professor M.H. Rizvi, Professor Nurul Hasan and Professor Shakeel Ahmad have always accorded whole hearted assistance not only to me but also to all the seekers of knowledge by providing the required material for research. My very sincere thanks are due to the librarians at the departmental library of the Centre of Advanced Study in History at AMU, Aligarh and particularly to Mr. Yusuf

Siddiqui who is not only a devoted caretaker of books but is also willing to offer all possible assistance to the scholars.

I am grateful to the University Grants Commission for providing me some financial grant for competing this work.

Finally, I wish to record my grateful thanks to the persons who had done the typing of the script, namely Mr. Badar Afroz, Mr. Hamid, Mr. Bahauddin and Mr. Sajjad Abbas.

MANSURA HAIDAR

# Introduction

Due to geographical proximity and a close cultural affinity and for reasons of a long history of exchange of ideas between India and Central Asia, there is enough ground to promote serious research on a variety of subjects connected with Central Asia. While undertaking an indepth study of their relationship through the ages, it may be prudent to keep an eye on future developments in India's relationship with Central Asia.

The study of Central Asian history and culture has been important for Indian scholars for many centuries. In the modern context, however, this has become rather compulsive due to a variety of political and economic reasons. With the emergence of separate Republics in Central Asia, the region has acquired an added importance even in the global context. India, as one of its closest neighbours, cannot avoid the responsibility of assimilating the ethos of the times and making vigorous attempts at cementing the bonds with each Republic in a new fashion. The task calls for a consistent and deep study of this relationship. Many of the tensions have been inherited as a historical legacy. A study of the past connecting the minutest details of the old and new socio-economic and religio-political systems is likely to facilitate a better appreciation, understanding and moulding of the present-day bilateral relations.

Being India's immediate neighbours, Central Asian states have had an age-old association and multidimensional contacts with India from the time of the *Rig Veda*, the *Zend-Avesta* and Buddhism to the influx of medieval conquerors and fortune seekers from the north-west with the dawn of Sufism in its wake. By and large, the people of India have remained unaware of their contribution to the glory of their neighbouring countries. The Indo-Central Asian exchanges in the sphere of fine arts cannot be fully understood and examined unless the then contemporary trends prevalent in the neighbouring regions and having a bearing on the concerned areas of this study are also taken into consideration. Unlike Turkey, the countries of Central Asia and Iran have no geographical barriers to afford them an isolated culture. The continuous invasions, emigrations and immigrations, however, had drawn Turkey within the same orbit of culture in which it was ecologically located. Similar traits and common characteristics are thus observed in the belt stretching from Mongolia to Central Asia, Iran and Turkey. The available works on Indo-Central Asian relations largely lack the authenticity of a kind supported by the sources. An appraisal of the sources and particularly a study of hitherto unexplored Persian and Turkish manuscripts is, therefore, the most fruitful part of this research.

The main purpose of this indepth quest is to prepare an authentic, first-hand report material on the social and political structure—its socio-economic and religio-political aspects highlighting the direction, nature, need and pattern of multifoliated and multidimensional facets of a real exchange of ideas and associations existing in the past which would be quite beneficial for bilateral and mutual negotiations in the future.

In the process, the study critically examines the writings of scholars from Central Asia and other parts of the world and analyses conclusions drawn by other scholars. Critical enquiry becomes necessary as some scholars (like G. Wheeler) have dubbed the pre-Russian Central Asia as the 'Dark Ages' or others have glorified the independent Central Asia beyond reality. A balanced study without any preconceived notions or ideological compulsions and following an analytical approach was urgently needed and is therefore being attempted here.

Scholars who are not well informed about the Central Asian past or are not fully acquainted with the ethos and the historical background of society and culture of a particular people cannot really distinguish between myth and historical reality. They are likely to study modern institutions and events necessarily in the context of the Islamic world and within the framework of those ideas and customs prevalent elsewhere or perhaps examine the problem with preconceived notions drawing conclusions first and then looking for fitting in suitable supporting facts. Similarly, a person who is not sufficiently proficient in the languages of region (e.g. Uzbek, Persian and Russian) cannot be expected to provide an appropriate interpretation of the terminologies used in the region. Such mistakes have frequently been seen in the works of modern researchers, e.g. Suniti Chakroborty defined the two etymologically different (though phonetically somewhat similar) terms—'But' (statue) and Buddha as having the same origin though actually the two are markedly different from each another. The institutions and posts are often misunderstood and misinterpreted. For example, the term '*ataliq*' is invariably used in India and elsewhere in respect of a guardian or the tutor of a minor—a regent. In Central Asia, however, *ataliqs* signified the Centre's nominee for keeping a check on the provincial rulers' activities who functioned like governors of the Centre and prime ministers of the provinces. Some scholars have described the Jats of India as the ancestors of the Jetas of the Central Asian Semireche regions, though the two were vastly unidentical and even entirely different from each other in racial and ethnic characteristics. The term '*suyurghal*' (rendered as subsistence allowance in the Mughal empire, would more often denote *iqta* in Central Asia and would refer to a military grant or provincial rulership in the Timurid Empire.

To understand and interpret the actions and reactions of the Central Asian people and to provide a correct reappraisal of and approach to Indo-Central Asian relations and development of a mutually beneficial programme, it is imperative to overcome the drawbacks stemming from the communication gap and the lack of lingual proficiency and knowledge about the region. Since adequate acquaintance with the region and lingual proficiency for closer personal contact were the two prerequisites of this study and since the knowledge of Central Asia's past history and culture was an added advantage, the present scholar can safely claim to be in a position to handle the subject better than many others.

This study, the first of its kind, aims to be comprehensive and thoroughly researched with a careful analysis of facts and is presented lucidly.

## I. Manuscripts—An Evident Emblem of Indo-Central Asian Contacts

The rich collection of valuable manuscripts (in various libraries of India, e.g. Rampur, Hyderabad and the Maulana Azad Central Library of Aligarh Muslim University) is a tangible proof of active contacts existing between India and Uzbekistan through the ages. These manuscripts comprise not only scriptures, documents and chronicles of Indian origin, but also the valuable works acquired by the Mughals—the lovers of fine arts, from various far-off regions (including Turan). This collection includes a rare assortment revealing the medieval multidimensional heritage which is a witness to some common and composite culture. It is very difficult to pick and choose manuscripts from the rich collection the library offers and it would take too long to describe the excellence of each of these. It is, therefore, best to adopt Abul Fazal's method to 'pluck a flower from every meadow, an ear from every sheaf'.

Akbar's 'response to his heritage' was somewhat different from that of Babur and Humayun. He was brought up in India and 'thought of the subcontinent as his home'. Although Babur was at times nostalgic and criticized the new and unusual environment of India, Akbar felt at his best in Indian surroundings. Like Babur, Akbar highly admired the Indian world. Akbar's deputy Abul Fazl reflected Akbar's deep felt appreciation for India: 'Shall I portary the beauty that charms the heart or sing of purity unstained? Shall I tell of heroic valour or weave romance of their vivacity of intellect and their lore? The inhabitants of this land are religious, affectionate, hospitable, genial and frank. They are fond of scientific pursuits, inclined to austerity of life, seekers after justice, contented, industrious, capable in affairs, loyal, truthful and constant. The soil of India is for the most part arable and of such productive power that the same land is sown each year and in many places three harvests and more are taken in a single twelve month and the vine bears fruit in its first year.' While enjoying the fruits of his newly found paradise, Akbar continued to cherish notions of an inherited cosmopolitan bliss. With the customary adaptability of a Turco-Mongol ruler, he not only preached but also practised the concept of *Sulhi Kul* which in many ways had its parallel in Sankara's ideal of *Vasudhaiva Kutumbkam* (the world family). Ties with the ancestral lands were not severed and even his descendants had a sentimental attraction towards the lands beyond the Hindukush. Rarities from Central Asia were often brought to India by those seeking gains. Such subtle reminders must have heightened the Mughal passion for Central Asian lands. Once Yadgar Khwaja of Samarqand brought a rare *muraqqa* from Balkh. Among the rarities carried by the Khan-i Khanan was a valuable and rare copy of *Yusuf wa Zulaikha* in *belles-lettres* of Mir Ali, the renowned calligrapher of the times, which was gift wrapped in a beautiful binding. Emperor Jahangir paid 1,000 *muhars* for it.

Like Timur, Akbar was also fond of books and is credited with the love of books as is revealed by the following comments: 'among books of renown there are few that are not read in His Majesty's Assembly Hall; and there are no historical facts of the past ages or curiosities of science, or interesting points of philosophy, with which Akbar "a leader of impartial sages" is unacquainted'. Thus, books like the *Akhlaq-i-Nasiri*, the *Kimia-i Saadat*, the *Qabus Nama*, works of Sharif Maneri, the *Gulistan*, the *Hadiqa* of Hakim Sanai, the *Masnavis* of Shaikh Nizami, the works of Khusrau and Maulana Jami and the *divans* of Khaqani, Anwari and several works on history were read by Akbar. These works were popularized both by Akbar and his deputy Abul Fazl. Akbar's *Dastur-al Amal* issued to his officers as well as Abul Fazl's letters to various persons (particularly to the Khan-i Khanan), include instructions that these books should be read by all so as to get acquainted with the higher values of life.

The philologists were engaged in translating the relevant works. Mir Fathullah Shirazi translated a part of the *zich-i jadid Mirzai*. The book is available in the Maulana Azad Library at Aligarh. It is only in the sphere of fine arts that Abul Fazl's eulogy of Akbar finds support in the accounts of his (Akbar's) bitter critics like Badauni. Abul Fazl describes Akbar as an 'excellent judge of form and thought' and describes the letter which is 'the tongue of the hand' the instrument of *belles-lettres* as a 'magical power—a spiritual geometry emanating from the pen of invention'—and a portrait painter of wisdom. Of the eight calligraphical systems current in Iran, Turan, India and Turkey, the eighth character *nastaliq* was patronized by Akbar. The Maulana Azad Library, has specimen of the works of men like Mulla Mir Ali, Maulana Abdurrahim of Khwarazm, Mir Abdullah, Maulana Jamshed and Maulana Sultan Ali of Meshed.

Babur describes Samarqand as a centre which often produced jurists and theologians. Numerous works on jurisprudence *sharia* and *tasawwuf* were written and were read and quoted by scholars everywhere. Many books on this subject are available in the Central Library of Aligarh. Fazlullah Ruz Bihan Isfahani, the famous jurist of the sixteenth century, was well known in India and his work the *Adab-i Zikr-i Tasawwuf* (Munir Alam Collection, Box 3, no. 15/4 B *farsiya*) is available in the library. Abdulla Samarqandi's *Bustan ul sharia* (Abdus Salam 766/86 f. 10) and *Muqaddam-us Salwat* (282 fiah Abdus Salam), Alkashghari's *Manbat-ul Mussila* (Sulaimani 44/14), etc., are some of the other works found in the library.

Seemingly the works on *fiqh*, *mazhab*, *tasawwuf* and *malfuzat* were ordered and acquired in various languages and in abundance. Khwaja Kalam Ubaidullah b. Khwaja Muhammad Baqi Billa's *Mublaghul Rijal* (Univ. Coll. 19/f. *Mazhab-o Tasauwuf* written in 1066 in *nastaliq*; Khwaja Muhammad Parsa bin Muhammad Hafiz Bukhari's (d. AH 822) *Tahqiqat* transcribed in 1082 in *nastaliq* by Katib Muhammad Yusuf Ismatullah Alhusna; Abdul Khaliq Ghujdwani's *Jawami ul Kalam* (Habib Gunj Coll. 21/359, *farsiya tasawwuf*); the *tafsir* of the work of Yaqub Charkhi written in *nastaliq*; and Khwarazm Ali Muhammad bin Ali's *Fatawa-i Shaibani* (Habib Gunj Coll. 17/28 f. *fiqhi Hanafial usul-i Naqshbandiya* of Alkashifi Univ. Coll. 3) were often copied by famous calligraphists. The Naqshbandi order was popular in India, particularly in Kashmir. A large body of the *malfuzat* literature on the Naqshbandis is available in India. The library has a wealth of these MSS including the *Rashhat-i ainul haywat* (Habib Gunj 6, 41/75 f.), the *Tazkira-i Khwaja Ubaidullah Ahrar* (Habib Gunj 22/81 *farsiya*), the *Tuhfat-ul Ahrar* of Jami (Abdus Salam 1008/104 f. *tasawwuf* also Habib Gunj 22/81); Ibn-i Shaikh's *Miftahuttalibain* (Subhanullah 2977/13 f. *tasawwuf*); the *Tazkira-i Hazrat Makhdumi Azam* (Subhanullah Shamil no. 891, 5514/73); Abdulqasim Muhammad bin Masud's *Muqamat-i Khwaja Bahauddin Naqshband*, the *Fiqrat-i Ubaidullah Ahrar* (Shefta, Collection f. 801/105 I) and Abdul Ghafur Lari's *Taliqat-i Nafhat ul uns* (Habib Gunj 22/27 f).

Apart from Abdul Khaliq Ghujdwani's *Jawami-ul Kalam* (21/399 f.), the other valuable works include the *Tarikh Nigaristan* of Qazi Ahmad Ghaffari (d. 975), the famous poet and calligrapher. This work is important particularly because it was copied by Abdullah Al Husain in AH 1018 in his specialization, i.e. the art of *nastaliq*. The manuscript bears the seal of Al Husain and Nuruddin Muhammad along with the dates. The Central Asian scholar Ahi Quli Beg Chaghatai translated the *Ramayana* under the title of *Nargistan*. According to Abul Fazl, Akbar was greatly interested in the art of calligraphy and in the different systems of writing, a large number of skilful calligraphists adorned his court. *Nastaliq* in particular was encouraged. Numerous works on calligraphy were written in India. The library has many works on Khattati, e.g. one of which the *Adabulkhat* (Box 5, no. 18f.) deserves to be mentioned.

Valuable works on different fields and varied spheres of administration are available. These include documents, manuals, etc. Works like *Asar-ul Wuzara* of Saifuddin Haji bin Nizamul Aqih (Box no.

5718), the *Tuhfat-ul Muluk* (Aftab Coll. 28/7 *adab nasr*) transcribed in 1239 by Muhammad Abdul Hakim and translated into Turkish by Muhammad Munib Darvesh Zada (Univ. Coll.128 *farsiya* transcribed in 1265) and the *Tuhfatul wuzara* (Habib Gunj 21/142 f. *tasawwuf*) are also available.

The valuable manuscript *Dasturul Siyaq—Parwanajat, Dastak hisab-i karkhanajat* (Univ. Coll. *ulum* 401) is a collection of important general notes, etc., with miscellaneous tables of the *karkhanas* of the Mughal rulers mainly from Shahjahan down to the later Mughals in the eighteenth and nineteeth centuries. In the preface, the author explains that this manual was prepared by him for those Persian knowing individuals who are less acquainted with or ignorant about the Hindu terms, hence the translation into Persian. The work describes the method of accounting and arithmetical calculations, ways to write '*hindisa*', tables, names of days, months and provides details about crops and workshop rates of various cereals. The signatures of Mir Bakhshi (p. 48) along with the date 2 Rabi II 1217 and that of the *nazim* with signatures on the *nishans* (f. 47-8, 52) indicate that these were either included as specimen or added to augment the authenticity of these documents. Incidentally, the weights have been given with suffixes as *Wazan-i Akbari* or *Shahjahani* or *Alamgiri* or *Farrukhsiyari*. A portion of this work was translated by one Buddh Prakash and was affixed to this manuscript.

Gourmets may find works like the *Kitab-i Khwan-i Neamat* (University Coll. 11/11) interesting which contains instructions and recipes (*dastur-i pukhtan*) of the dishes cooked for Emperor Shahjahan in the contemporary *matabkah* (kitchen). These include different types of *kebabs* and *nans*, *qaliyas*, stewed dishes, *murabba jughrat*, *pilav*, *khaginas* and the right proportion in which each spice has to be added and other ways to enhance the appetising appearance of the food (e.g. making the oil multicoloured).

It seems that the later Mughals were not well versed in Turkish language. Several works on Turkish lexicography, grammar, literature, dictionaries and glossaries are available in the library which confirm that the interest in Turkish language continued not so much for emotional reasons as for practical need. Some of these works include a dictionary of Arbaic, Persian and Turkish, i.e. in three languages (MS 1037/10 AS Coll.). Two important works in the rich collection of Turkish manuscripts in the library, are the *Lughat-*

*i Turki Lissan us Salatin* prepared for Aurangzeb's son Muhammad Shah Alam Ghazi, dated end of *shuhur* AH 1145 /22 December 1894 (Ahsan Coll. 1042/15) and the *Lughat-i Turki* prepared from the *Risail* of Abdur Rahman Jami, Ali Shir Navoi, Muhammad Mehdi and Mirza Hasan (117/310 Qutubuddin Coll.). Sometimes Indians also undertook this, e.g. Kashi Lal Kayasth prepared a Turkish *Lughat* the *Haft Akhtar* (*farsiya* 53/28 Habib Gunj). *Lughats* of other languages are also available, e.g. the Lughat in Dari by Yusufi Shirwani (Subhanullah 89135529/20).

There are works on grammar as well, for instance the *Sharh-i Mait Aamil* by Muhamed Darvesh Alhalwai Alsamarqandi (Firangi Mahal 1114/100; also Ahsan Coll. 492/75/2). *Sharahs* (explanatory notes) on varied Central Asian works are also available in the library. Ibrahim bin Mir Muhammad Khujandi transcribed the *Jami-ul Muamma* (Univ. Coll. 5/2; *farsiya ulum* 3). Among the works on geography with valuable discussions on the flora and fauna are a sixteenth-century Central Asian work *Ajaib-ul Makhluqat* and Ali Shah b. Muhammad's *Alashjar Walasmar,* etc. The library has a collection of manuscripts on astrolab (*usturlab*) including the *Haiyat-i Usturlab* of Muhammad bin Muhammad Kashghari (Habib Gunj 44/6 f.) and the *Risala dar ilm-i Usturlab* of Jafar b. Umar Alusturlabi copied in *nastaliq* (Sulaiman Coll. 538/17). Mustafa bin Ali's *Risala-i Usturlab* copied in 1055 in Turkish language (Univ. Coll. f. *ulum* 128) is rare and probably the earliest. There are various Central Asian works on astronomy as well. The MS *Rasad-i Sitaragan-i Ulugh Begi* (f. Subhan 520/17) reveals the eagerness of the ruler to acquire each new work. The continuing interest in scientific learning is reflected in the *Jawahar-i Faridiya dar sanat-i Usturlab* (Univ. Coll. 42/1 f. *ulum* and Sulaiman Coll. 534/13) written in *nastaliq* by Dabiruddaula Khwaja Fariduddin, the maternal grandfather of Sir Saiyid. It is interesting to note that some Central Asian works bear not only the *Bismillah* and 786 on the front page but also the name of Tingri (Mongol God). Several copies of Zichi Gurgani are available. One copy of the *Zichi Ulugh Beg* transcribed in 1643 contains the horoscopes (*Zaicha-i tale*) of Dara Shukuh and predictions relating to Shah Abbas. The MS bears several seals one of which has Shahjahan's name on it (Univ. Coll., *farsiya ulum* 29). The commentaries written on the *Zichi Ulugh Beg* (like the one by Abdul Ali b. Muhammad Husain) are available (Univ. Coll. 27f. *ulum*). *Taqvims* were also acquired, e.g. *Tuhfa-i shahi* of Haider b. Muhammad Almunajjam (Univ. Coll., 61 *farsiya ulum*). Although most of the valuable illustrated collections are housed in other places (e.g. the Royal Asiatic Society, Philip Hafer Collection, British Museum, Walter Art Gallery, Chester Beatty Library, etc.) some are available in India including in the university library.

The Subhanullah Collection (no. 891.5514/51) contains a rare and valuable masterpiece (*nuskha-i nadir ul wujud o jalil ul qadr*), an old copy of *khamsa* of Nizam-i Ganjavi (d. 598 or 999/1202 or 1203) copied by Husain Abdullah in Zilhijja year AH 873 as mentioned on the last page (442). In addition to its marvellous gold work, it contains beautiful illustrations on several pages (19, 52, 57, 67, 81, 98, 107, 115, 155, 168, 208, 217, 225, 234, 238, 240 and 294). Surprisingly this *nuskha* contains three different seals—one of which bears the name of Sultan Sulaiman with the date AH 1012/1503, the second is that of Abdul Khaliq and the third is unintelligible. An illustrated MS Khusru Shirin of Nizami (Univ. Coll., f. 891 5514/79) does not mention the name of the transcriber as the last page carries a prayer to God 'and shower of *durud* on Prophet and his descendants and request forgive the sins of one who copied this work and pray to bestow paradise upon him' (p. 249).

Another exquisite piece of calligraphy and illustration is the *Khumsa* of Nizami transcribed in AH 963 (the name of transcriber has been erased). The second part *Haft Paikar* contains seven paintings. The first page is richly decorated with azure and golden designs. The paintings depict Bahram Ruz in his white, green, red (Aftab Coll. 44/5 *farsia nazm*), blue and other palaces. Several places have been left blank for proposed miniatures. Another *Khumsa* of Nizami contains the signatures of Muhammad Ali al Husaini on the first page though it is illustrated and well written. Jami's *masnavi* '*Yusuf Zulaikha*' (Univ. Coll. 88/2) copied by Sultan Husain Ibn-i Jamshed Haravi in 963 has beautiful illustrations on pages 55, 77 and 114.

The library has in its collection many pocket book or large copies of illustrated and dainty *divans* of the famous poet Hafiz Shirazi. The romantic and wine drenched poems of Hafiz were a source of pleasure and fascination for Jahangir who himself was a winebibber and afflicted by perpetual pangs of love. Jahangir's love for seeking auguries from the *divan* of Hafiz is well reflected in his memoirs. It is little wonder that several ordinarily illustrated or richly decorated volumes were made available. The two *divans* of Hafiz Shirazi—one copied by the famous Sultan Ali Meshedi (d. 919) preserved in Abdus Salam (817/54) and another transcribed by the renowned Mulla Mir al Husaini in 1585 (Univ. Coll. 251 f I) are among its richest possessions. Both these calligraphers are mentioned in nearly all the works on Khattati. Another *divan* of Hafiz containing 19 illustrations (University Coll., *farsiya* I, no. 138) and an eulogy of the emperor (*dar midh-i Padshah*) does not mention the name of the transcriber. (It has illustrations on pages 11, 17, 21, 26, 32, 33, 39, 51, 57, 64, 72, 77, 87 and 93.) These paintings, however, are not extraordinary as they depict certain scenes similar to the ones found in the other collections. It is possible that this pocket book edition may have been prepared at Jahangir's or behest by some amateur painter in search of employment, none of the paintings bear the name of the artist. Another copy of the *Divan-i Hafiz*, copied by Abdur Rahman and illustrated in AD 1563, bears the signature: Banda-i Shahjahan (Univ. Coll., f. 124) as well as the name of Mullah Muhammad Salih (dated 16 Khurdad) and at another place 32 regnal year and the name of Munim Beg. Yet another was copied by Kamaluddin Husaini in 1018 (Univ. Coll. 816/53). A *divan* of Hafiz Shirazi prepared at Khwarazm in AH 766 and transcribed by Muhammad bin Yusuf Al-Zahir in *nastaliq* (at times dotted with *naskh*) bears a square on the last page which has been erased. Hafiz Shirazi's *qasida* in praise of Amirul Muminin Hazrat Ali, copied in the twentieth century (dated 1910), is written in the peculiar style of *Khatti nakhun* (Univ. Coll., f. I 148). Another rare *divan* of Hafiz copied by Matulub Qari in AH 766 (in *nastaliq*) at Khwarazm bears an erased seal and contains miniatures (124 Univ. Coll., f. I *nazm*). The tazkiras of poets and the collection of *divans* comprise the works of external and internal artists. Apart from the well-known *tazkira* of the sixteenth century—Bahauddin Nisari's *Muzzakkira-i Ahbab* (several copies of which are available though the MS Habib Gunj 980 or 974 f. 51/1) is considered more valuable as it was transcribed by Mirak—there are several other *tazkiras* of immense value, e.g. *Tazkira-i Daulat Shah Samarqandi* transcribed in 994 (Habib Gunj 51/47 f.).

Abdurrahman Jami was one of the most respected, and talented author whose works *Lawaih Jami* (Subhanullah 891 552/9 *nasr* f., *Laila Majnun* (Univ. Coll. 2/4 f. 2), *Yusuf Zulaikha* (Univ. Coll. 88 f. 2), *Lawami, Kunz-ul Asrar, Haft Aurang, Sab'saiyyar, Makhza-*

*nulasrar, Majmua-i Bisto do Risael-i Jami* and *Etiqad Nama* (179 *farsiya* 2, Univ. Coll.) are available in the library. One of the collections of poems of Jami (Univ. Coll. 986/81 f. *tasawwuf*) has a couplet written by the poet himself. Similarly, the *divan* of Sultan Husain Mirza of Herat (in Turkish) is also a rare possession (891/551/1 Subhan).

The *divan* of the Uzbek ruler Ubaidullah Khan Uzbek 'Ubaidi' in Turkish (Univ. Coll. 891/ 5526/1 f.) and another collection of such *ghazals* bearing the name *Risala 'Hikmat-o nasihat'* of Ubaidi are rare works. The *Majmua-i Ashaar* (891/551/1) containing poems of Central Asian poets like Babur, Kahi, Khwarazmi, Badi, Shahi and Khanzada Begum (Babur's sister) is another valuable work in the library.

Rare historical works includes Qazvini's *Tarikh-i Guzida Nusrat Nama* copied in AH 843 and bears the square seal of first and second page with the seal of the ring of Nasiruddin Mahmud (Habib Gunj, f. Tarikh 32/2). Akbar's love for hunting is clearly revealed in the work *Shikar Nama* of Saiyid Arab Balkhi dedicated to Akbar (429 Jf.).

## II. Central Asia and the Compilation of Treatises and Encyclopaedic Literature in Mughal India (Sixteenth Century)

The Mughal rulers of India had inherited a legacy of love for fine arts and scientific learning from their Central Asian ancestors whose homeland was once part of the empire of one of the most innovative, imaginative and adventurous people—the Arabs. Central Asia was a land without geographical barriers and its open frontiers not only invited military invasions and subsequent cultural fusion, but also facilitated a brisk exchange of ideas, scientific knowledge and technological skills. The emphasis on the acquisition of knowledge in Islam encouraged the growth of learning and the emergence of multifarious literature. Being in the neighbourhood of advanced nations like China and Persia and having continuous contacts with distant lands either through war or commerce, Central Asia was both an imbiber of new influences and a vector of the most novel trends. India, on the other hand, maintained its aloofness and splendid isolation supported by its economic security and sustained by its spiritual and intellectual strength. Whereas the Central Asian lands produced and received men of pen (*ahl-i-qalam*) and talent almost continually, Indian Mughals only acquired the windfall of men of parts during periods of upheaval in the lands beyond the Hindukush or else had to look forward to the trickling of fortune seekers during peace times. The numerous letters sent by Faizi and others document Akbar's eagerness to ensure a constant influx of such talented men for whom arrangements for advanced payments were made even in Iran and other countries on Akbar's behalf. The Mughals kept in constant touch with their homeland to enrich their intellectual sphere.

In Central Asia, the historical raw material was varied, comprising not only the chronicles but also the *tazkiras* of poets, geographical works, *malfuzat* literature, administrative documents and manuals both in the form of practical and theoretical or even advisory suggestions. For the benefit of higher and middle-class bureaucrats exclusive *dasturs* and collections of specimen *manshurs, farmans*, etc., were written. *Risalas* were prepared for each branch of the fine arts and handicrafts, and encyclopaedic literature was produced with finesse, precision and clarity. Fully aware of the worth of such works, the Mughals (particularly Akbar) decided to follow the age-old tradition of hiring and transplanting talents whenever possible. However, the system had certain inherent problems. Outstanding talents were expensive to hire and were not permanent as being uprooted from their homeland meant a painful experience and they therefore preferred a sojourn. The only class which was happy to settle down in India was that of the Sufis and saints some of whom gave up their spiritual pursuits to enjoy worldly charms and even enrolled in the state services. Nevertheless, men of arts of Central Asian and Persian origin wistfully looked towards India and yearned for it; not for its wealth or better prospects but for its other charms as is substantiated by the verdict of poets like Kahi and Mahmud.

The Mughals of India, therefore, had no option but to accept the terms dictated by the poets. Jahangir's persuasions and rich offers were turned down by Mutribi but this was preceded and followed by similar such incidents during the sixteenth century. The Central Asian sources document show various poets, physicians and men of arts visited the Mughal court and returned with a pocket heavier than their hearts. The biographical sketches found in the *Ain-i-Akbari*, the *Muntakhab-ut Tawarikh*, the *Tabaqat-i-Akbari* (and at a later period the *Maasir-ul-Umara*, *Zakhirat-ul-Khawanin*) and other sources confirm the arrival and sojourn of most of the renowned men of talent from Turan and Iran. Akbar's efforts to encourage various branches of learning was a follow up of the Central Asian trend. Trade in books was the most lucrative business bringing in rich dividends. Efforts were made to acquire the best productions through toytrade.

Even diplomatic missions were not spared from the pleasant task of acquiring valuable works available on various subjects in the host country. (Hakim Abul Fath Gilani's valuable works have been discussed elsewhere.) There were interesting works on varied subjects like chess and *chaupar*, cuisines, calligraphy, account keeping and mathematics (e.g. *Dastur-i Hisab-i Navisandagi* see, Aligarh MS 624), *risalas* providing information on revenue records, e.g. *Tahqiq-i Salaha-i Falahat* by Rafiuddin (Univ. Coll., *farsiya ulum,* no. 25/5) and the details of crops, etc. In the sphere of handicrafts, the Central Asian collection of treatises was, however, far richer than that seen in India though a few works on various handicrafts are extant here also. The depth, detail and intricate complexities of a particular art or handicraft are lucidly discussed in the Central Asian works, most of which are available here even today. It is interesting to note that whereas Indian handicraftsmen were illiterate and merely engaged in their trade on a family basis, the Central Asian handicraftsmen were members of *futuwwa* (or *akhi*) organisations, spent their evenings in lively intellectual discussions or merely acquiring knowledge through verbal discourses during their 'night's sports'. The Central Asian scholars made immense contributions to the enrichment of various kind of literature and were invariably present in the court of Akbar. The Central Asian literary pattern often paved the way for Mughal literary production.

Banai, the famous poet of Central Asia, wrote The *Shikar Nama* (Subhanullah 6001/891 *Farsi*). The *Qanuni Shikar* (Jf. *mutaffariq* no. 688) on the same subject added to the series and augmented the information. At Akbar's behest, the *Shikar Nama* (Jf. 429 *Funun-i Mukhtalfa*, M.A. Library, Aligarh) was produced. However, the works on astronomy, *zij, taqvim*, astrolabe were not really original in content as Ulugh Beg's work was still valued highly and was widely studied and scribed with much fanfare. The *Qaida-i Ramal* (Habib Gunj 44/25 *farsiya* Aligarh) or the *Raml Ahkam nuqat* (Aligarh MS no. 80/17 Qutubuddin Collection) was another work. In Central Asia, the art of calligraphy was widely appreciated and a number of *Tazkira-i Khattatan* were available. Several works like the *Qaida-i Khuttati* by Mir Ali (Abdus Salam, no. 1126/6187 *Muttaffarriqat; Adabavkjat*) were produced at the Mughal court though the Central Asian pattern dominated.

Inspired by the Indo-Central Asian trends, *risalas* were compiled on the *shamsi* and *qamari* (solar and lunar) calendars; there were works on inscriptions and coins; Turkish language and grammar textbooks (for the benefit of later generations of Mughal princes). Several books dealt with the problems of routes and their easy approach (such as Berdi Beg bin Bairam Beg's treatise on *Rahahai Kabul az Iran o Turan* (Abdus Salam 1043/16B) and Abdul Qadir's *Halat-i Manazil az Shahjahanabad ta Kabul* on the Central Asian pattern and as part of pre-war preparations.

Numerous works were produced on the art of warfare, arms, armaments and tactics of war. Beginning with Fakhri Mudabbir's *Adab-ul-harb wa Shujaat* or *Phenk* (Aligarh MS Habib Gunj Collection, 55/281 Urdu *Muteferriqat*) the Delhi sultans and the Mughals tried to establish their continued interest in this medieval form of chivalry. Yet, these works lacked as much conviction as the scenario here negated the necessity for warfare.

Apart from *risalas*, the Mughal collection includes some valuable encyclopaedic literature as well. Encyclopaedias and treatises were produced in the Islamic world much earlier, e.g. Alkashi's treatise 'The Key to Arithmetic', Fakhruddin Razi's *Jami ul ulum,* Alidrisi's *Kitabi Nuzhat al Mushtaq fi ikhtiraat Afaq*, Alkashani's *Arais-ul Jawahir,* Hunyan Ibn-i Ishaq's 'Book of the Ten Treatises on Eye' (an adaption of the galenic theory of optics), or a more original work of Ibn-al Haython's 'Optics' are more specialized treatises. During the Mughal period concise and detailed encyclopaedias were compiled either at the emperor's behest or by some fortune seeker, e.g. the *Jawahir-ul ulum-i Humayuni.* The author claims to have referred to important works like the *Nafais-ul funun fi araisuluyun* and the *Satin-ul Asar wa hadaiq-ul anwar* and even consulted learned men and expert officers of his times do so as to prepare a concise thesaurus or encyclopaedia. Apart from the description of prophets, the work offers a short account of the Mughal emperors (pp. 79-178) and a brief survey of places and tombs of the Khwajas of Naqshband (pp. 206-30). The wide gamut of subjects commented upon by the author include *fiqh*, grammar, *tib*, *hikmat*, literature, calligraphy, religions, prayers, the art of *kimia*, *simia* and *limia*, logic, the art of discussion, hunting, flora and fauna, wise sayings, chess, *ilm-i jufar*, mathematics, astronomy, physics, chemistry, medical art and treatment, different diseases and various kinds of fevers, riddles, *fatwa*s, etc.

Other books credited to Muhammad bin Ali Katib Samarqandi include the *Qissa Sindbad Jahazi* (Subhanullah 89135527/13) and the *Sirat-ul Hufaz wa Faidat-ul Waaz* (Habib Gunj 27/12, etc.). The *Jawhir-ul Ulum* was presented to Humayun whose interest in novelty was well known as is revealed by the compilation of the *Qanun-i Humayuni*. In this voluminous work, the author has discussed 120 different branches and disciplines of knowledge. Nowhere does the author Alqazi Samarqandi mention that the book was written at the behest of the emperor thus indicating that he may have compiled it on his own. He stresses the fact that 'if someone spent only one day of his time in the acquisition of knowledge, it is better than the prayer of thousand years in the eyes of God'. The encyclopaedia offers a variety of information on every branch of catechism. Its scope is as varied as the extent of investigative talent of its compiler. One of the most interesting part of the work is the portion where the author has copied the *tallqiat* and *manshurat* selected from the *Musadaat* of Maulana Husain Alwaiz Alkashifi, Khwaja Abdullah Marwarid and Maulana Abdul Wasey. The *nishans* bestowing Shaikhul Islami, *naqabat, sadarat, tadris, qaza, wazarat, imarat, ihtisab, khitabat,* etc., provide information on the duties and obligations of these officials. Similarly, the *nishans* on *tauliyat, mauqufat,* exemption from taxes in part or whole, *suyurghal* and the system of issuing passes to pilgrims to Mecca are equally informative. The letters exchanged between medieval potentates containing discussions on the intricate issues of *suluk,* Sufism and *politie* provide as much information as the anecdotes relating to personalities like Shahab-uddin Suhrwardi and Khwaja Hasan. The section dealing with the Mongols is rather sketchy presumably to avoid any controversy and also because enough information was already available. Equally rich in information are the comments on the various dynasties along with the names and biographical sketches of the rulers. In this connection, events which had an impact on the Islamic world have been described in greater detail. For instance, there is more focus on Timur and his descendants for obvious reasons. Details are given about various sufis and their cells, tombs and *mazarat*. Similarly, the four schools of thought have been discussed at length. A separate section is devoted to the description of norms of good behaviour, social commitments, responsibilities, righteous living, duties and obligations of men and women, regulations for inheritance, accountability in marriage, rules governing separation, divorce and alimony, another short section on the preparation of agreements and bonds, on the maintenance of registers, records of court of judicature, minutes and attestations of notary.

Apart from the political chronology and important events, other spheres have been discussed by different scholars. Both secular and religious topics have been discussed; there are chapters on *fiqh*, a section on zodiac signs, some pages devoted to the metres, the art of innuendo, musicology and architecture. The section dealing with the science of different kinds of ordinary and extraordinary diseases, diagnostics, virus, pollution, infections, contagious epidemic, plague, pestilence is particularly important. A cursory description of sickness, infirmity, loss of health, different disorders, invalidism, pathology, therapeutics, various diseases and their cure, common psychological or mental disorders, forgetfulness, morbidity, paralysis, tuberculosis, epilepsy, etc., has also been provided. The most useful section, however, is the one on medieval assessment of nutritious food, drinks, intoxicants, digestives and appetisers, etc. Another section discusses herbs, *serbats*, elixirs, home-made medicines, recipes for preparing marijuana, etc. Medicines have been prescribed for changing moods and varying temperaments. Perhaps, this most urgently needed antidote for kings and commoners alike was long overdue.

# The Central Asian Contribution in the Sphere of Indo-Persian Literary and Historical Sources

The tradition of Indo-Persian historiography owes much of its development to the traditions established and the trends set by their Central Asian predecessors who had so laboriously built up the historical foundations of this discipline. History comprises most diverse and mutually incomparable spheres of learning and embraces them all in one singular, fixed, and balanced survey. Whether it is other such subjects, each has its own place as an ancillary discipline and an auxiliary science in the purview of history.[1] With the advent of the Turks in India, the Persian language gained prominence and a basic difference in the presentation of history began. Historiography which dealt not only with one more or less confined and homogeneous sphere of man's communal life but with the whole of it flourished during the Middle Ages. After the conquest of India by the Mughals, further developments in Indo-Persian historiography took place. Although valuable studies have been produced on medieval Indo-Persian historiography, the Central Asian contribution to its enrichment has not yet been fully realized and appreciated. This chapter is an attempt in this direction.

Historiography developed in Central Asia as a literary art. Being exposed to various external influences and due to their innate love of learning, the Central Asians fully realized the importance of history as a subject. Although the Central Asians were not entirely above the pitfalls of prejudices and parochialism, they were modern enough to believe that 'a society without history is like a man without memory and perception'. The Central Asian scholars have always appreciated and valued the 'science of history' or 'historiography'. They were keen to 'preserve the memory' of their predecessors and recognized that history demonstrates the direction of a society. Although Haidar Dughlat was conscious of the fact that 'the rank and dignity which historians attain is not so high that one should have a craving for it',[2] he had never underestimated the importance of this subject. In his Prologue to *Tarikh-i-Rashidi*, Haidar Dughlat records the significance of historiography in the following words:

> Let it not be concealed from the minds of the wise that the Koran, which is the greatest of the miracles of Muhammad, is divided into three sections. The first contains the declaration of the unity of God; the second the statutes of the Holy law of Muhammad, and the third historical matter, such as the lives of the Prophets. Thus, we see one-third of this book (none but the clear shall touch it) is intended to teach the history of past generations; and therein lies the clearest proof of the excellence of the science of history. Moreover, all are agreed concerning the utility of this science; and most nations, nay, all the peoples of the world, have studied it, and have collected and handed down the traditions of their forefathers, of which they give ample proofs and upon which they rely.[3]

The *Tarikh-i-Guzida*, which was (compiled in AH 730) and dedicated to Khwaja Rashiduddin Fazlullah, also expresses similar views. Describing the benefits which accrue from the study and compilation of history, Qazvini says that the advantages of the study of the science of history cannot be overestimated. It is through historiography that knowledge about the thinking, faiths, and beliefs of the past and of by-gone generations can be acquired and transmitted to the present and future generations. History provides information about the conditions of people; their experiences in military expeditions; their modes of war and peace; the causes of the rise and fall of nations; the reasons for their adversity and suffering; and the factors contributing to their fortunes or misfortunes.

Another significant feature of the science of history is that it generates polemics, as after an intermission the same history is written again. Starting from the time of Adam, each important and big event (like Noah's tempest, Ibrahim's fire, Pharaoh and Moses, the founding of Kaaba, Greek and Roman stories, the reign of Alexander) which happened in the past becomes a part of the earlier history of the Turks (*Tarikh Peshin-i-Turks*). How could the Turks then forget history?[4] 'Similarly the author of *Miraz-ul-Ansab* says in AH 830 that it is evident and clear to the men of wisdom (*ululalbab*) that the science of history and traditions have been appreciated in every religion. In every religion and nation, this fact carries significance that the history of a people's ancestry and progeny should be intact and preserved. Hence the dynasties of the Turks and the Mughals and their tribes also desired that the history of their *urugh/uruq* should be secure and the studies of their genealogies should be carefully prepare'.[5] Haji Salim, an eighteenth-century writer, records that he prepared his work *Silsilat-us-Salatin* with the view that the readers who would go through his historical narrative may be acquainted with the rules of good conduct, be informed of the right path, be warned of the vagaries of fortune and the vicissitudes of life; that the book may serve as a light-house for showing the way to imparting justice, and the proper method of administering the sultanate.[6] The then prevalent standards and traditions of history writing had been clearly underlined by Haidar Dughlat in his prologue. He writes:

It is fitting that the opening of a royal history, and the beginning of a book of victory and good fortune, should be the praise and glory of that Monarch, the length and breadth of whose Kingdom, (according to the words: 'Say verily God is the holder of the Empire'), is defended and preserved from change and decay, and whose palace is securely guarded from the evil of destruction and ruin. 'He settles upon the throne whomsoever he will' is a testimony to this glorious unity; 'And all that is twixt earth and sky, the sun and moon, the east and west; from India to far Turkistan, the mighty conquerors of the earth have girt the belt of service and are prepared to do their Lord's behest.[7]

Nevertheless, the traditions and tenor of history writing kept on changing over the years and Central Asians continued to produce histories of all kinds. In Central Asia, each historian was a researcher who thoroughly studied the works of his predecessors and either accepted and transmitted the same contents or criticized them after sifting them carefully, the former being the more commonly adopted technique. Central Asian historiography possessed all the features of Perso-Arab traditions and contributed the same traits to enrich the Indian art of history writing. Shaikh Ali has best summarized the Central Asian contribution to the sphere of Indo-Persian historiography:

Unlike the Christian chronicles which were written by monks, it was written by men of affairs, often by contemporaries, who had witnessed the drama, and sometimes taken part in it. It is too much to expect that Muslim historiography of the medieval period could stand the test of twentieth-century standards in terms of treatment, technique, and approach, but judged from what prevailed at that time, it was quite far ahead of its age. From the mythological, theological, and legendary phase of ancient Indian historiography emerged a more rational, secular, and authoritative phase under the Muslims.[8]

In different Indian libraries, there are innumerable works on history, *fiqh* (jurisprudence), logic, grammar, eloquence, *haiat* (astronomy), *tazkira* (biography), mathematics, theology, *hadis* (traditions), epistolary, mysticism, *kimia* (alchemy), *tafsir* (interpretation of the Koran), morality, literature, faith, medicine, *hikmat*, physics, philosophy, all of which testify to the valuable contribution of Central Asian scholars and chroniclers in varied fields and diverse branches of learning.

The commonly found traits in medieval Central Asian sources are best reflected in the Indo-Persian chronicles of the same period. It would be far from the reality if Central Asian chronicles are seen as being connected to the Asharite school of thought. It was perhaps due to the impact of the Mutazalite school of thought that most of the Central Asian chroniclers often went deeper into the causes and consequences of historical events, which is an unusual trait in Persian historiography. The Central Asian chronicles seem to bear the influence of Arabic historiography. It was due to Arab influence that the Central Asian scholars became fond of producing works on geography. Several works such as *Ajaib-ul-Gharaib* or *Ajaib-ul-Makhluqat*, *Jughrafia-i-Hafiz Abru*, and others were produced. The urge to check the veracity of statements (the *usual-i-Isnad*) and the emphasis on the truthful presentation of facts were ideas again borrowed from Arabic historiography and were always followed. The king who was supposed to be the shadow of God on earth and the one divinely appointed, divinely protected, and divinely guided was to be depicted not necessarily as a paragon of virtue but as a practising Muslim who offered prayers regularly, visited holy saints and their shrines, showered, lavish gifts, grants, and endowments, waged *ghazawat* (holy wars), propagated the *sharia*, and governed the empire in accordance with the rules laid down in the works prepared by experts in jurisprudence following the Hanafite school of thought especially for the guidance of kings. Books on statecraft, Hanafite regulations, and *dasturs* were, therefore, frequently ordered by the rulers. Certain kings who were not 'puritans' or 'believers' and who ignored the *sharia* were treated as condemned souls bound to beget evils and reap the rich harvest of calamities.

Central Asians were usually erudite and learned men who excelled in the use of the pen. Central Asian sources represented history not as a 'concatenation of events', one following upon another, and supposedly 'manipulated by some superhuman, mysterious, and uncontrollable force and hence supposedly working independently from an individual. Instead, they emphasized the process of historical inevitability, and avoided the usual formulae or syndromes known as the 'Church', transcendentalism, and fatalism which were characteristic features of *Malfuzat* lietrature only. Chroniclers did not always surrender their critical judgement to contemporary trends nor did they put their faith in divine acts, interventions, and the immutability of the writing of moving fingers. They believed in the actions and reactions of individuals caught in the whirlpool of historical forces. Facts which are said to be the backbone of history and the data of experience were well presented, and in the form of raw material which could serve as food for thought. It would not be correct to presume that medieval Central Asian history was merely a bulletin of campaigns or 'a succession of events, deeds, and episodes', as some Central Asian chroniclers did possess a clear conception of causation in history. In the sources, a random jumble of economic, political and, ideological explanations of each event, long-term and short-term causes, or at times 'chance' in history is found. The interpretation may sometimes be totally biased or may be partially absent due to a lack of vision and objectivity, but these values were seldom missing. It is undoubtedly true that the court historians often ignored the 'spirit of the age', 'social forces', or the process of causation in history, but the *tazkiras* of varied types, *Malfuzat* literature, and geographical works contained a great deal of information about the life of lesser mortals and discussions over the causes and effects of historical events.

Some Central Asian chroniclers, however, had a particular idiosyncrasy of treating history as a preeminently spiritual discipline. A striking instance of this kind is noticed in the *Malfuzat* literature which forms an integral part of historiography. Every action or reaction of a king is judged through the myopic criterion of his relations with saints and dervishes. The downfall or disgrace of any king was inevitable if the ruler was not kindly disposed towards the dervishes and saints or if he had ever humiliated them. Consequently, this predilection is also frequently reflected in the Indo-Persian sources. Before passing any value judgement it should be remembered that the medieval historians were as much a part of their society as any one else and therefore their angle of vision was bound to be affected by the spiritual atmosphere in which they lived. For example, genocides, *ghazawat*, were a regular feature in the sixteenth century and were recorded faithfully in the sources. For some chroniclers, the imperialistic wars of the sixteenth century had the religious significance of the *ghazawat* because sectarian bigotry was a value acquired from his social environment which could easily be exploited by ambitious rulers.

Despite such flaws, the contribution of Central Asian scholars was sufficient enough and can be classified under two broad categories. In the first place, Central Asians had given direction to Indo-Persian literature and historiography. They enriched it by introducing manifold forms and broadened the scope of knowledge. Second, Central Asian texts, whether general histories or court chronicles, added immensely to and supplemented the already available information in Indo-Persian sources. Sometimes they even contradicted the information supplied by the Indian sources. As will be discussed later, the Central Asian contribution to the enrichment of Indo-Persian sources and in the augmentation of knowledge about the Indian Turks and the Mughals was not negligible.

The Central Asian scholars and chroniclers opened the sphere of historiography to its multifarious ancillary disciplines and auxiliary sources. It is interesting to note that these chroniclers often assessed, previewed, and examined history with all its concomitant aspects though usually in the context of the Turks. But this attitude did not arrest their access to and interest in non-Central Asian history. The modern concept of 'intellectual history' seems to exist in a theological form in propagating or transmitting ideas about political and socio-religious developments, ranging from liberalism, egalitarianism, and eclecticism. Sufi ideology with all its metaphysical and ethical views provided the grounds for socio-religious movements and even prepared the atmosphere for intellectual evolution. The *Malfuzat* literature so commonly prepared in Central Asia paved the way for the introduction of such a form of literature in India also. Thus, works such as *Munis-al Arwah*, *Khair-ul-Majalis*, *Gulzar-i-Abrar*, *Mirat-ul-Asrar*, and others were prepared in India.

The Mughal rulers were particularly keen to develop all branches of knowledge. An attempt to enhance the efforts for the transfer of knowledge and the exchange of ideas which had continued for many centuries increased, and produced remarkable results. For example, Indian astronomy had almost always attracted the attention of Central Asian scholars. The attempts of Aryabhatta had been so overwhelmingly appreciated that his works were translated into Persian. The works of Ulugh Beg further added to the knowledge on the subject. Not only did Shahjahan order the preparation of a work entitled *Zijishahjahani* but a number of other works on the same subject were also written by various writers. Some of these are: *Rasad-i-Sitaragan-i-Gurgaon*; Jafar b. Umar al Ustarlabi's *Risala dar ilmiusturlab*; Abdul Ali bin Muhammad Husain Barjandi's *Tasmail Zijis Ulugh Beg Mustafa bin Ali Risalai usturlab*. A valuable contribution in this category was made by Sir Saiyid Ahmad Khan's maternal great-grandfather, Khwaja Fariduddin, whose work *Jawahir i Faridia dar sanati usturlab* is famous. Although astronomy is not directly connected with historiography, it does throw light on cultural and intellectual aspects of history and is, therefore, indirectly connected with history. Many Central Asians were engaged in translation work and prepared valuable reproduction which facilitated the Indo-Central Asian exchange of knowledge. Abdur Rahim translated a number of works, including the *Baburnama*. Ali Quli Beg Chaghatai translated the *Ramayana* into Persian and named it *Nargistan-i-ahi*, Rup Narain Khatri's *Sirajut Tariq* included Sumrit Puran's stories (*Hikayat-i-Naskit*). Abul Fazl records that philologists were 'constantly engaged in translating Hindi, Greek, Arabic, and Persian books into other languages'.[9] A long list of translated works is given in the *Ain-i-Akbari*. *Risalas* were compiled on methods of warfare, archery, astronomy, languages (Turkish, Persian, Arabic), mysticism, physics, medicine, khatati, sports, jurisprudence, and such other subjects.

Apparently, encyclopaedic works in India were not in vogue and the Central Asian trend of producing such capsules of knowledge was only gradually adopted by the Turks in India. A number of encyclopaedic works on the pattern of those in Central Asia such as Razi's *Jawami-ul-Ulum*, and Awfi's *Jawami-ul-Hikayat* were produced. Muhammad Fazil Samarqandi's *Jawahir-ul-Ulum* is one such example. Sultan Muhammad Darvesh Albalkhi compiled *Majma-ul-Gharaib* and Alauddin Alaulmulk b. Muhammad Juvaini's work *Tasalliul-Ikhwan*. The work *Tajarib-ul-Salf* of Hindu Shah Naklichiwani was another important contribution.

In medieval Central Asia, the general practice was to prepare books on statecraft and methods of administration. Kautilya's *Arthashastra* had many parallel specimens in which the principles of the Hanafite ideals of kingship and administrative machinery were frequently compiled. Muhammad b. Ali bin Muhammad Hasanul Katib Samarqandi's *Araz-us-Siyasat fi ghraz-ul-Riyasat*; *Suluk-ul-Muluk* of Ruz Behan Isfahani; *Majma-ul-Arz*, *Tuhfat-ul-Muluk*, and such other works were prepared in Persian after the Central Asian fashion. The Mughal chancellory work had been appreciated by chroniclers. Shahjahan himself boasted of its excellence and even advised the Ottoman sultan to borrow one such expert from the Mughal court to improve the standard of their letter writing. In this context, the Central Asian contribution is also worth mentioning. Babur had invited Khwand Mir who had prepared specimen orders, *manshurs*, etc. The *Nama-i-Nami* of Khwand Mir in the *nastaliq* is still extant. The practice of compiling the history of rulers as well as their *wazirs* was perhaps borrowed from Arabic historiography. The *Tajarib-ut-Salf dar Tawarikh Khulfa wa Wuzra-i-Islam* compiled by Hindu Shah b. Sanjar in 724 was an attempt in this direction as the author himself says he had been 'impressed by the book *Maniat-ul-Fuzala fi Tawarikh-ul-Khulfa wal Wuzara* written by Safiuddin bin Altiqtiqa and had made some additions in his own version which gives it the appearance of a translation (*aslan tarjuma manindi*).[10] The *Dastur-ul-Wuzara Tahafat-ul-Wuzara* and such other works were compiled to serve as guide books for the wazirs. The *Asar-ul-Usuzara* of Saifuddin Haji b. *Nizam Fazli* was transcribed by Shaikh Faizullah on 1 Muharram 1240 AH in the twenty-fifth regnal year of Muhammad Akbar Shah.[11]

The literary and religious works also had their own historical and intellectual dimensions. The *tazkiras* of poets have immensely enhanced our knowledge about the civil and cultural life, the ethos, and the socio-economic conditions of the period in which these particular works were compiled. Since these *tazkiras* had almost always included Indian, Persian, and Central Asian poets, they add to our historical knowledge. Hasan Nisari's *Muzakira-i-Ahbab* and Sahab's *Tazkirat-ul-Ashab* included many Indian rulers and literary figures and offered solutions to many complex socio-religious problems. Bibliographical sketches and couplets threw light on the inner recesses of the social structure and assist us in understanding and reconstructing the prevalent customs, traditions, and conventional. The *Tazkira-i-Daulatshah Samarqandi* records several incidents which throw light on the plight of taxpayers and the high-handedness of government officials. Following the examples of *Habib-us-Siyar* and such other sources, Mughal historical works like *Muntakhab-ut-Tawarikh*, *Tabaqat Akbari*, *Badshahnama*, and such other works also included the biographies of important persons.

In Central Asia, the development of lexicography greatly enriched the sphere of historical knowledge. The Mughal sources frequently referred to Indo-Persian, Perso-Islamic, and Turco-Mongolian terms, expressions, and words which had become obsolete. Many multilingual dictionaries had, therefore, to be compiled to facilitate the understanding of the Turkish language. The Dictionaries like *Siraj-us-Subiyan Lassan-us-Salatin*, *Risala dar lughat-i-Turki*, and such other works were prepared in India till the eighteenth and nineteenth centuries. The dictionaries proved to be a great help in comprehending the various Turco-Mongol words and customs. Works on jurisprudence were specifically ordered by the sultans to serve as guide books. Indian libraries are full of such volumes. The *Fatawa-i-Shaibani* prepared by Khwarazmi Ali tib Muhammad Ali, written in *nastaliq* by Khairullah at *tasdiqi*, or *Sulk-ul-Muluk* of Ruzbihan are some examples. The mystic literature produced in Central Asia is available in Indian libraries. These include the valuable work *Nafhat-ul-Uns*. The Ahsan Collection (920-2) of the Aligarh Muslim University library has many copies of this *magnum opus* but the oldest and the best copy available is the one scribed by Qasim bin Ibrahim in a style in which *nastaliq* and *nasq* have been mixed together. The year of its compilation is 883 and that of its transcription is 964. Apart from this, the Aligarh library has a vast collection of mystic literature, which has already been discussed elsewhere. The Indian Sufis had their own devotees who compiled the *Malfuzat* and mystic accounts in the Persian language in the same style as that of Central Asia.

According to Central Asian traditions, wars were always preceded by full-fledged preparation, which included the drawing of maps and the compiling of descriptions of the most convenient route to be taken towards the enemy country. Many of these maps and works have survived. The diaries written during the expeditions to the far-off regions provide interesting information. In India, the Mughals also followed these practices. The *Ruznama-i-Ghazawat-i-Hindustan*, written by Ghiyas Ali, is a diary of Timur's Indian expedition. It contains a detailed description of India's geographical features, and provides an account of the routes lying between India and Central Asia. Accordingly, in Mughal sources accounts of the states invaded (for instance, Kashmir) are given in detail. Before the Balkh and Badakhshan campaigns, Shahjahan had ordered the preparation of certain works on the Indo-Central Asian routes. One such work, Berdi Beg bin Bairam Beg's *Rahahai Kabul az janib-i-Iran wa Turan* is still extant.

Many general histories written in Central Asia provide information about India. Abu Nasr Ahmad b. Ahmad Al Bukhari's famours book *Tajul Basar* consisting of 405 pages and scribed in the sixteenth century (KBL, Patna MS. no. 34) is also an important contribution on the history of India. The *Rauzat-ul-Ahbab* is another valuable and informative work. Sirajuddin Bukhari's travelogue gives extremely useful material for research. The manuscript *Tajut Tawarikh* presents many interesting aspects of Indian and Central Asian history. *Asar-us-Salatin* has a very interesting account of Indo-Uzbek conflict. The *Kashkul-i-Salimi* provides additional information on tripartite relations (India, Persia, and Central Asia) during the seventeenth, eighteenth, and mid-nineteenth centuries. Abdullah Kabuli's *Tazkirat-ut-Tawarikh* has a very short but useful account of tripartite relations.[12] There are sources like *Abdullah Nama*, *Bahrul Asrar*, *Tazkira-i Muqim Khan*, *Tarikh-i-Saiyid Raqim*, *Mirat-ul-Alam*, *Tarikh Qipehaqi*, and such other works which add to our information regarding bilateral relations. There are interesting and informative references to India's relations with Central Asia and Persia in the *Muntakhab-ut-Tawarikh* of Hakim b. Tura.[13] Although the author extensively quotes and refers to the points which he has borrowed from *Tazkira-i-Muqim Khani*, there are many interesting episodes in the source which have not been included elsewhere. Almost all the general histories written by the Central Asian chroniclers contain chapters on the past and contemporary Indian history. These include works like *Tarikh-i-Wassaf-ul Hazrat*, *Jami-ut-Tawarikh, Tarikh-i-Banakiti*, *Rauzat-us-Safa*, *Habib-us-Siyar*, and other works, each of which had a separate section on the description of India, its people, and its history. Even details about the learned of that country were provided. *Matla-us-Sadain* of Abdur Razzaq Samarqandi who visited the Vijayanagar empire gives an extremely useful account of India. Similarly, Muhmud bin Wali also presented an eye-witness account of Orissa and other places which he visited during his sojourn in India.

Books were written on hobbies and pastimes. Muhib Ali Barlas prepared *Baznama* (Book of Sports) and Aminuddin compiled *Hidayat-ur-Raml* (The Archer's Guide). Similarly, Saiyed Arab Balkhi compiled *Shikar Nama* on the orders of Akbar. Another work on the same theme was prepared by Binani. There are few manuscripts that are either reproductions or abridged forms of some large history already compiled, for instance a book entitled *Chiragh-i-Tur dar Sharh Ahwal-i-Timur* seems to be a reproduction of the *Habib-us-Siyar*, vol. II, part III. Khairullah Haji's *Dastur-i-Jahankusha* is a history of the Mughals. The *Tarikh-i-Jahangir* and the work by Bindraban Rai, son of Rai Bharmal, *Lubbut Tawarikh* also come under the same category. The history of Timur both in prose and poetry for instance, the Aligarh manuscript *Timur Nama Manzum Sirat Farsi, Timur* and the *Mirat-ul-Waridat* (also known as *Kitab-i-Tarikh-i-Chaghatai*) written by Muhammad Shafi Warid bin Sharif in 1100 AH on the orders of Inayatullah Atufat Khan and other works corroborate and supplement Indian sources. Even the names were frequently borrowed by Indian or Central Asian writers from each other, for example, *Badai-ul Waqai* by Anand Ram Mukhlis *Lubbut Tawarikh*, *Muntakhab-ut-Tawarikh*, etc.

Like Mahmud bin Walis and Haji Mir Muhammad, Salim Haji, the author of *Silsilat-us-Salalin*, was also fond of travelling far and wide. He left Transoxiana in 1123/1711 and happened to meet certain dignitaries somewhere near the borders of Iran. This group of high officials and amirs of Turan, who were on their way to the court of Shah Sultan Husain of Iran (1194/1722) as envoys, later on told the latter about the arrival of Muhammad Salim. The Shah offered warm and extremely lavish hospitality to the author, who left for Mecca in 1128/1716 and from there he reached India. During his journey, he visited Isfahan, Baghdad, Aleppo, Damascus, and Istanbul. He was a widely travelled person. On reaching India, he joined the service of Muhammad Shah and lived with him for some time. He dedicated his book to Muhammad Shah (1719-98).[14]

Strangely enough, Storey in his *Persian Literature* records that the only manuscript extant is marred by lacunae and is 'defective at both ends'.[15] It opens with the year 1468 and ends in 1711. The Bodleian MS to which he refers, however, comprises the full work, starting with the author's deep desire to travel, his sojourns in various places, and finally his arrival in India. The first twelve pages deal with the history of Adam and various prophets, ending with a description of the Prophet Noah, the ancestor of the Turks, from where the author picks up the threads of his narration of the history of the Turks. There is a short and sketchy account of Yafis Turk, Alanja Khan, and Mughal Khan. The history of the Turco-Mughals, traced from Oghuz and the Chingizide sultans, continues up to the Timurids of Central Asia and India. The author had consulted many books, a list of which was provided by him. These included: *Maasir-ul-Muluk*, *Tarikh-i-Wassaf*, *Jahankush Juvaini*, *Ajaib-ul-Taboat*, *Majma-ul-Ajaib*, *Zafarnama*, *Makarim-ul-Ikhlaq*, *Tuhfat-ul-Gharaib*, *Rauzat-ul-Ahbab*, *Habib-us-Siyar*, *Rauzat-us-Safa*, *Khulasat-ul-Akhbar*, *Tarikh-i-Rashidi*, *Dastur-ul-Wuzara*, *Majma-ut-Tawarikh*, *Jahan Ara*, *Akbar Nama*, *Tarikh-i-Alamgiri*, *Alam Ara*, and others. Although opponents of Mughal authority like Ajit Singh were called Ajit-i-Khabis, praises and soft words and titles were showered upon members of his patron's dynasty. The first fifty pages deal with the history of the early Mughals and their ancestors. The account of Muhammad Shah starts from p. 68 and comprises merely a few pages. It is interesting to note that the pages of the manuscript are so jumbled that once the account of Akbar abruptly ends, but the history of this great Mughal reappears all of a sudden after a few pages when the account of the downfall of the Mughal Empire has already ended. With complete ease, the author forgets about his Indian patron as his history conveniently switches over to a narrative about the Khans of Turan (i.e. the Shaibanids and the Ashtarakhanids) to whose account the remaining pages (over 250 pages out of 340) are dedicated. The history comes to an end with the reign of Abul Faiz Khan. Yet the information available in this work has its own unique characteristics.

## NOTES

1. It is generally surmised that since history is based on facts, it differs from the humanities which are supposedly based on imagination and feeling. Yet the information supplied by literature and the arts is an essential ingredient of an all-round and comprehensive knowledge and understanding of history.
2. Haidar Dughlat, *Tarikh-i-Rashidi*.
3. Ibid.
4. Muhammad bin Muhammad bin Abu Bakr bin Hamid bin Nasr Hamdullah Mustaufi Qazyini, Aligarh MS, *Tarikh-i-Guzida*, *Farsiya Tarikh* 32/20, transcribed in Rajab 843, compiled in 730 AH, ff. 2-5.

5. Ibid.
6. *Muizz-ul-Ansab*, Aligarh MS, *Farsiya Akhbar*, ff. 1-2.
7. Haji Salim, *Silsilat-us-Salatin*, MS Bodleian, no. 169; MS Ouseley, pp. 1-7.
8. B. Shaikh Ali, *History, its Theory and Method*, Mysore, 1987, p. 309.
9. Abul Fazl, *Ain-i-Akbari*, vol. I, Eng. tr. by Blochmann, New Delhi, 1977, pp. 110-13.
10. Hindushah Abbas Iqbal, Tehran, 1313 AH, Shamsi year, Introduction.
11. The work is extant see Aligarh MS, Box 5/18, p. 282.
12. *Kahskul-i-Salimi*, ff. 245-60. *Taj-ut Tawarikh*, ff. 90-6; *Ansar-us-Salatin*, ff. 40-67; *Tazkirat-ut-Tawarikh*, f. 227.
13. Hakim b. Tura, *Muntakhab-ut-Tawarikh*, ff. 180-200.
14. *Silsilat-us-Salatin*, MS Bodleian, no. 169, MS Ouseley, pp. 1-7, 269.
15. A. Storey, *Persian Literature: A Bibliographical Survey*, vol. I, pt. I, sec. II, pp. 380-1, nos. 5 to 20, *Silsilat*, f. 7.

# Evolution and Expansion of Buddhism in Central Asia

Buddhism, a religion of humanity, fraternity, and equality, was one of the world's greatest unifying forces which transcended the barriers of regional diversity. The introduction, evolution, and expansion of Buddhism in the lands beyond the Hindukush and its survival in alien territories is an amazing story. Apart from the factors which accounted for its popularity in India, there were some additional reasons for its spread and growth abroad. Whether it was asceticism, self-penance, *arya ashtang marg*, *ahimsa*, or any other precept, the golden mean (*majjhim paripada*) was always preferred by the Buddha. The democratic functioning of the *sangh* was ensured through the decisions of parish members, even through *chanda* (communication). Buddhism approached the common people through their own speech (*sakaya niruttiya*); it taught the equality of the sexes and of human beings; it stressed wildlife protection; it emphasized the open door policy of the *sangh* for monks from all quarters; it rejected the widely prevalent notion of *noblesse oblige*. The concept of universal brotherhood in all its multifarious forms (be it peace upon all, *Vasudhaiva Kutumbkam*, *umma*, or *la hilfa fil islam*) was the key principle which sustained humanity through the ages. Buddhism directly appealed to the sentiments of the people and established direct communion between the devotee and the Almighty. On a mundane level, Buddhism played a very important role in spreading Indian languages, scripts, philosophy, religions, and ideas to the farthest corners of Asia and opened and exposed India to foreigners.

Although Buddhism was born in India, for some curious reason it was to survive outside its borders. Every country where Buddhism was adopted nurtured it in its own fashion and adapted this philosophy to suit the needs of its own spiritual search and material well-being. Thus, Buddhism evolved in accordance with the historical background, of each place, in its own form and with completely novel religious experiences, though in consonance with the traditions of its nursery. In India and China, Buddhism branched out into many sects, though in Mongolia and Transoxiana it was confined more to a specific school. The concentrated devotion to Tara was the hallmark of Buddhism in Mongolia. The *yogabhyas* provided Buddhists with the much needed physical prowess to cope with the demands of their *natura maligna* region which was characterized by a harsh and difficult terrain. In the desert, a life of abnegation was as much a rule for the 'nomads' as it was for the saintly Buddhist monks who voluntarily abstained from the luxuries of life and preferred a simple and ascetic existence. The open air atmosphere was another advantage for the dwellers of Central Asia. It is interesting to note that the wandering life adopted by Buddhist saints also attracted the Central Asians. Incidentally, the ancestors of the Turks and the Turko-Mongols, known as the 'Oghuz', prescribed a life of constant movement, 'to be like a pawn in the chess game', saying 'Be always on the move, never to settle down.' The search for greener pastures was as much a necessity, although an inconvenient burden, for them as fighting the wars which were considered to be a money-generating device in these regions. For the harassed souls who were forced to raise swords for their masters (whose main source of surplus revenue was booty) and who also looked forward to serene moments, Buddhism provided the answer to their problem. The policy of non-violence at once turned them into disciplined scholars, averse to gluttony and somewhat resilient to reckless ruthlessness. Moreover, in Mongolia and in other parts of Asia, the Tantric school of Buddhism flourished mainly because it was closer in its externals to Shamanism, the religion of the majority in the region. The Tantric school and the secret practice of yoga 'taught the magic observance in Buddhist practices'. These were far from the rigours of philosophical, esoteric, and fundamentalist doctrines of the original *Bahusrutiyas Mahasanghika*, *anityata*, *duhkha*, *sunyer* (transitoriness, suffering, absence of attributes). The concept of gender equality was another common factor. Like the Bhikshunis of Buddhism, the Turkish and Turko-Mongol women enjoyed freedom as well as equal responsibility in fulfilling life's demands.

The religious books discovered at Tun Huang stress the fact that the Soghdians were above all Buddhist Manichaeans or Nestorians but the frescoes depicted them as Zoroastrians. It was concluded from these contradictory statements that there it was a 'somewhat unorthodox Zoroastrianism mixed up with the purely local Central Asian cult of the Anahita'. The information gleaned from the sources, however, reveals that there were many centres of Buddhism in the heart of Asia as well.

There is a controversy regarding the exact date of the introduction of Buddhism into various parts of Central Asia although the expansion of Buddhism into these regions is attributed to the patronage and zeal of various rulers such as Asoka. It is surmised that the Sakas and the Kushanas as well as Indian merchants had carried elements of Indian culture along with Buddhism to the different states of eastern Turkestan at least a century before the beginning of the Christian era,[1] and that small Indian colonies had sprung up on the southern part of the region from Khotan up to the Lapnor region before the Christian era. Other scholars date the introduction and spread of Buddhism to the reign of Asoka, who deputized a group of monks to Gandhara to propagate the *dharma*. It is believed that the first missionary who took Buddhism to Central Asia was Vairochana, a Kashmiri scholar, who built the first monastery at Khotan. When Buddhism spread in Central Asia, it came to the notice of Xiongnu, an ancient Mongolian tribe, which had direct relations with Central Asia. Soon conversions took place. Khan Ogedei (1229-41) supported Buddhism and began to build Buddhist monasteries and a big *stupa* in his capital Karakorum. Equally zealous was Mongke (Monkh) Khan who had appointed the Kashmiri monk Namu to the newly created position of state teacher for whom he used the word guru.[2]

It is also opined that since there is an absence of images of the Bodhisattvas, these monuments presumably belonged to the Hinayana or the Little Vehicle School, in which the Bodhisattvas did not appear. But this theory must be treated with some reservations as there is a lack of concrete evidence to support it. Besides, it should be noted here that Kucha had long been converted to Buddhism but it had not always been Hinayanist, as we read of one of its former kings being a devoted Mahayanist. Nevertheless, the Buddhist priests had a special position in Kucha. Ta-Tang Siyuki says that twice in a month (i.e. on the fifteenth day and on the last day of the month) the king of the country and his ministers discussed administrative matters among themselves but it was only after 'taking the counsel of the chief priests that they published their decrees', which shows that these saints in Kucha played a role in state matters also. Turfan too was 'one of the chief centres of Buddhists in the earlier centuries of the Middle Ages'.[3] The Arab invasion did not bring about any change in the religion of the inhabitants of Chinese Turkestan (except in the case of the Qarakhanids). In the central and eastern parts, the Uighurs retained their faith in the Red Sect of Buddhism.

The spiritual radiance and fervour of Buddhism had left an indelible stamp on the soil of Central Asia, though its signs dimmed in the land of its birth. Buddhism was, more widespread in the four important states in north Chinese Turkestan, namely, Bharuka (Aksu), Kucha, Agnidesa (Kara Shahr), and Kaochang (Turfan). Of the four states, Kucha had been the stronghold of Buddhism ever since, the first century AD and had played a key role in the propagation of Buddhism, facilitating its rise and evolution in the northern states and also in China. There were said to be one thousand *stupas* and temples in Kucha around the third century AD.

Kucha has been mentioned in various other sources under different names (such as Kuitze in the Han histories; Kutze in the Tang period; Kuchi in Hieun Tang's account in the seventh century; Kuche in Chinese maps, and so on) as a well-known centre of Buddhism. Incidentally, there is some controversy regarding this place Kheecha which 'had not been clearly identified'. Remuset mistook the word for Kashmir. Klaproth thought it was Skardo. Beal described it as Kartchou, and Eitel called it Khasa. In Legge's view, it was Ladakh or some other well-known place in it.

It should be noted that Siyuki specifically refers to the name 'Kheecha' and explains the reason why this name had been given to the Kucha monastery. According to Siyuki, a former king of the place worshipped the 'three precious ones', i.e. the Buddha, *dharma*, and *sangh*, and leaving the state to his brother, he departed on a pilgrimage. The younger brother, having received this order, mutilated himself in order to prevent the rising of any evil passion, fearing the circulation of slanderous reports that might harm him. His fears came true as some mischief mongers spread false stories about the king designate to his elder brother on his return. Since the ruler knew about his brother's action and the truth and since his brother was thereafter cured through some heavenly magic, the king was happy and looked on his brother as a prodigy (*khiteh*). From this circumstance the convent took its name, which he built to honour the conduct of his brother and to perpetuate his name.[4] When Siyuki visited the place, 'there were about one hundred convents (*sangharamas*) in this country; with five thousand and more disciples' belonging to the 'Little Vehicle of the School of Sarvastivadas (*shwo yih tsai yu po*). Their doctrine (teaching of the *sutras*) and their rule of discipline (principles of the *vinaya*) were stated to be like those of India, and those who read them used the same (originals). They especially clung to the custom of the gradual doctrine and partook only of the three pure kinds of food. They lived purely and provoked others by their conduct to lead a religious life.[4]

Towards the north of this desert city, there were two convents close together on the slope of a mountain, but separated by a stream of water, both named *Chau-Hu-Li* because they were situated east and west of one another and hence the name. Here a statue of the Buddha was seen by Siyuki who found it to be 'richly adorned and carved with skill surpassing that of men'. The monks of the place were 'pure, truthful and diligent in the discharge of their duties'. Siyuki found that the style of writing literature was 'Indian with some differences'. In the hall of the eastern convent, called the Buddha pavilion, there was a jade stone with a foot trace of the Buddha on its surface, which emitted a bright and sparkling light. On the right and left sides of the road of the western gate of the chief city also there were (one or two) erect figures of the Buddha, about 90 feet high. In front of these statues, there was a place erected for the quinquennial assembly. In all the convents Siyuki found highly adorned images of the Buddha, richly decorated with precious substances and covered with silken stuffs which were carried in idol cars on stated occasions called the 'procession of images', which attracted people who flocked by the thousands to the place of assembly. The convent Oshelini (extraordinary or unique) was situated in the north-west of the meeting place and across the river. Here also the hall of the temple was open and spacious, and the image of the Buddha was beautifully carved. The disciples also were grave, decorous, and diligent in their duties, though rude and rough men also came. The aged priests were talented, scholarly, learned, and very well read, hence most eminent seekers of law came to 'acquire just principles'. The king, ministers, and the elite also offered to these priests four sorts of provisions and their celebrity spread farther and farther.[5]

Buddhist assemblies and ecclesiastical conferences were frequently organized in the Oshelini convent at Kucha. Fa-Hien (AD 399-414 ) has described at length the Great Panch Parishad (quinquennial assembly) of monks and *sramanas* from all quarters held at Kheecha for which the saints arrived 'as if on clouds'. The place of session was richly decorated with silken streamers, canopies were hung, and golden and silver water lilies made and fixed behind the places where the delegates were to be seated. The kings and ministers made special offerings of precious things. Fa-Hien was impressed by the rules observed by these *sramanas* which were 'remarkable and too numerous to be mentioned in detail'. At that time there were two sacred things at Kheecha. The first was a tooth of the Buddha for which the devotees had constructed a tope with which were associated more than a thousand monks and their disciples, all of whom were students of Hinayana. The second sacred object was a spittoon which belonged to the Buddha; it was made of stone and its colour was like his alms bowl.[6] Further, Siyuki mentions that in the hall erected for the quinquennial assembley, every year at the autumnal equinox, during ten days, the priests assembled from all over the country. The king and all his people, from the highest to the lowest, on this occasion abstained from public business, and observed a religious fast. They listened to the sacred teachings of the law, and passed the days without weariness. Fa-Hien gives a picturesque description of a four-wheeled carriage, the procession of images, seven precious substances grandly displayed, with silken streamers and canopies hanging all around, and with the chief image in the middle of the car, with two Bodhisattvas in attendance on it, 'all brilliantly carved in gold and silver, and hanging in the air'. Each monastery had its own distinct carriage, brilliantly decorated and displayed. Such was the great veneration and regard shown by the king to this procession of images that even when the carriage was 'a hundred paces from the gate, the ruler removed his crown, put on other clothes and with bare feet went out to meet the images'. When the images were brought inside the gate, the queen and the brilliant ladies showered flower petals. Every effort was made to promote the dignity of the occasion. Strict discipline seems to have prevailed in these monasteries. Fa-Hien describes how the monks received their food from the common store and how the funds were procured. While describing the method of this mess, he records that these monks were called to their meals by the sound of a bell. When they entered the refectory, their demeanour was marked by a reverent gravity, and they take their seats in regular order, all maintaining a perfect silence. No sound is heard from their alms bowls and other utensils. When any of these pure (*vimala*) men require food they are not allowed to call out (to the attendants) for it but only make signs with their hands.[7]

In Suyuki's time and also in his own estimation, Aqsu (Baluka) was a sufficiently well-known centre of Buddhism, having ten *sangharamas* and over one thousand priests and monks, all of whom followed the teachings of the school of the Little Vehicle and who belonged to the School of the Sarvastivadas. In Tirmiz, there were ten *sangharamas* and a thousand monks. Here the *stupas* and the images of the honoured Buddha were said to be 'noted for various spiritual manifestations'. In Chaghaniyan, there were five *sangharamas* with a few monks. Similarly, Sumana and Kulab had two convents and a few monks. Kubadian had three convents and five hundred monks; since there were many Buddhist sites in the neighbourhood of Balkh, it was generally called 'Little Rajagriha'. There were a hundred convents and three hundred monks who were all followers of the Hinayana sect and who studied the religious teachings of the Little Vehicle School. Outside the city, Siyuki saw a convent called Navasangharama built by a former ruler. The masters of Buddhism, who used to live to the north of the great snowy mountains and who were the authors of the *shastras*, stayed only in this convent and consistently worked hard. There was a figure of the Buddha studded with sparkling precious stones and gems. The hall was also decorated with expensive and rare pieces of silk. Lured by this rich and elegant setting, many rulers of the neighbouring countries often raided it as they were 'covetous of gems'. While Siyuki mentions that it 'has often been robbed', he quickly adds that there was a statue of Pishamen (Vaisravana) Deva by whose spiritual influence, in unexpected ways, protection was afforded to the precincts of the convent. To support his statement, he cites the example of the conquerer-king Khan Yeh-hu's (She Hu's) son who came with the intention of plundering it. Before he could do so, he saw Vaisravana Deva in a dream, who reprimanded him and hurled his lance and transfixed the aspirant with it. The king's son later went to the convent to confess his crime to the priests, but before he could receive an answer he died.[8]

Apparently, imitation relics of the Buddha were also provided in the southern hall to make it more sacred. There was a washbasin (which the Buddha had used) of varied colours so dazzling to the eye that it was difficult to name the gold and stone of which it was made. There was also a tooth of the Buddha, about an inch long and about eight-tenths or nine-tenths of an inch in breadth. Its colour was yellowish-white but it was pure and shining. Another object was the sweeping brush of the Buddha, made of the plant kashe (*kasa*), 2 feet long and 7 inches round, with an ornamented handle studded with gems. These three relics were presented with the offerings on each of the six fast days by the assembly of lay and clerical believers. Those who perhaps were blind followers and watched everything with deep devotion found these 'objects emitting a radiance of glory'. In the northern part of this *sangh* was a *stupa*, 200 feet high, plastered with a hard stuff shining like a diamond, and decorated with a variety of precious substances. It 'enclosed a sacred relic (*she ti*) and at times this had reflected a divine splendour'. There was a *vihar* also, constructed many years before. People assembled here from distant quarters. Apparently, the zealous pursuance of *dharma* had started dwindling. When Siyuki happened to pass through this monastery, there were a hundred priests there, 'so irregular were some of them morning and night in their duties that it was hard to tell saints from sinners'. He adds , however, that there were also 'a large number of men of conspicuous talents. As it was difficult for the several possessors of the four different degrees (fruits) of holiness to explain accurately their condition of saintship, therefore, the Arhats (*lohans*) when about to die, exhibit their spiritual capabilities (miraculous powers) and those who witnessed such an exhibition founded stupas in honour of the deceased saints. These are closely crowded together here to the number of several hundreds. Besides these, there were some thousand others who had reached the fruit of holiness (i.e. Arhatship), yet having exhibited no spiritual changes at the end of their lives, have no memorial erected to them.[9]

Some historians point out that one of the chief monks of Kucha was Mokshgupta who had acquired learning in India for over two decades and who enjoyed a great reputation in Kucha especially for his knowledge of commentaries and etymology. But Hieun Tsang 'exposed the ignorance' of Mokshgupta to such an extent that 'the latter came to treat him as his master in religion'.[10]

The Indo-Persian and Central Asian contemporary and later sources do not so frequently refer to Buddhism. The book *Dabistan-i-Mazahib* exclusively deals with various religions, and its author

(Muhsin Fani?) had allocated over eighty pages mainly to the description of different Indian religions starting from the Vedic age to the rise of the Sikhs. He gives a detailed description of Brahminism, the cult of Mahadev, Shakti, Shiv, Vishnu, and Krishna, stories of the Kauravas and the Pandavas, Gosain, Bhartrihari, *sanyasis*, Gobindpanthis, *jogis* of the Gorakhnath sect, with notes on Sankhyan, the four *varnas*, *trishul*, etc. There are, however, some references to a faith which resembles Buddhism. For instance, the sixth chapter entitled '*Dar Maqasid-i-Jog*' has references to the eightfold path (*Arya ashtang marg*), the *dukh*, *samudai*, and *dukh nirodh*, yet the three *ratnas*, the Buddha, *dharma*, and *sangha* have not been mentioned.[11] Similarly, while covering the portion on Indian religions in his general history *Tarikh-i-Banakiti*, its author Fakhruddin Banakiti does not refer to the religion of the Buddha. Surprisingly, a section of his book deals exclusively with Hindus and Brahminism (the information being drawn mostly from Alberuni and some geographical works), Krishna, and lastly with the sultans of Delhi. Since Banakiti was associated with the court of Uljaitu Khan (in whose reign he compiled and completed his book in Shawal 717), the fact that he ignores Buddhism, then the religion of the ruling family and the elite, is surprising. Besides, the author himself claims to have a penchant for providing information on all religions and omits the state religion, which is indeed inexplicably strange. In the eighth chapter on China, however, he notes that the inhabitants of China were all idol worshippers and infidels belonging to varied kinds of faiths. In the sources, the followers of Buddhism had either been mentioned as idol worshippers (*sanam parast* or *but parast*), infidels (*kafir*), or occasionally confused or bracketed with other non-Muslims such as Christians called *tarsiyan*. There is a short legendary description of Lord Buddha who had also been described as Shakyamuni or Shakmoni. Shakyamuni, a future prophet, was born from Lady Moya Nojin (wife of a young Kashmiri man) from a beam of light. His extraordinary intelligence; his prayers and his six years of meditation on a mountain; and his subsequent rise to the position of an apostle who invited people to accept his prophethood; and his followers who hailed from Kashmir, India and China, and who became subservient to him and acknowledged his godhood have all been described in detail.[12] This provides a parallel historical source of reference to the Buddha. Works such as *Hudud-ul-Alam*, *Nuzhat-ul-Qulub*, *Jami-ut-Tawarikh*, *Tarikh-i-Wassaf*, and others do not (or only casually) refer to Buddhism. There are numerous references to Kucha, Kizil, Khotan Kara, Qara Shahr, and other places in various other Persian and Central Asian sources, but Buddhism has seldom been described under its proper name. If ever mentioned, the Buddha was referred to as Shakyamuni and the Buddhists as idolators.[13]

Buddhism deeply influenced the minds of the people not merely as a spiritual or religious sect but also as a way of life. It is no wonder that it has engaged the attention of specialists from Russia, France, Britain, and Germany for the last two centuries—particularly after opening up of the monuments of Buddhism in Xinjiang. Over the past 40-50 years, some significant progress has been made in this direction thanks to the archaeological excavations in Bactria-Tokharistan, Soghdiana in Ferghana, Jutake (archaeological expedition in Turkmenistan) by people such as Girshmatt, Harmata, Masson, Litvinski, G. Koselenko, and others. The archaeological material evidence and inscriptions in Kharoshti found in the Karatepe, Fajaz Tepe, and Tirmiz shrines and the ancient statue found in Dalverzin Tepe (in the Kuchean Empire in Bactria) have also provided enough material for further study.[14]

There were hurdles faced by Buddhism in its expansion. The 'politics of repression which the Sassanid kings often took up from time to time hardly changed'. Usmanova says that under Shapur II (309-79), who was well known for his policy of religious intolerance, the Christians of Iran were cruelly persecuted and the Kuchean territories were also conquered. Shapur undertook campaigns against Bactria and particularly against Tirmiz merely because these were centres of Buddhism. Nevertheless, archaeological evidence suggests that Buddhism continued to flourish in the north till the eight century AD. Even when these states had disintegrated and declined, Buddhism was patronized by the Uighur Turks till the eleventh and twelfth centuries, and their capital Turfan also became a centre of this faith in the early thirteenth century.

The influence of Buddhism was quite strong in Kashghar and Khotan. For example, when Kuchluq (Guchluk, Kushluk) defeated and killed the Chinese Gurkhan and occupied Kashghar, he

> changed from the religion of Jesus to the practice of idolatry of Buddhism and the rest of the people he caused to abandon Hanifism and to become fire worshippers. They did everything to encourage idolatry and no one was able to prevent them. They next went to Khotan which they captured

and compelled all the inhabitants of the surrounding districts to abjure the religion of Muhammad, giving them the choice of adopting either Christianity or the idolatrous creed or to don the garb of Khitayans. Since it was difficult to switch over to another religion, by reason of hard necessity, they clad themselves in the dress of the Khitayans. The mosques were closed and the schools abandoned. One day they conducted the imams of Khotan out into the plains and began to argue with them. Imam Alauddin of Khotan was asked questions to which he gave answers, and at length they crucified and hung him up over the door of a college. After this the faith of Islam having lost its splendour, the darkness of evil spread .... When Chingiz sent Noyon Chebe with a body of 20,000 men in 1218, the conquest of Kashghar and Khotan was made easy as the Mongol ruler Chingiz's generals 'sanctioned the call to prayers (*takbir* and *azan*) and they issued a proclamation in the town that every one might practice his own religion. The advent of these people was held to be an act of mercy and bounty from the Almighty.'[15]

If ancient Khotanese traditions are to be believed, Kustana, a son of Asoka, had established the kingdom 234 years after the *nirvana*, i.e. about 240 BC. His grandson Vijiyasambhav had introduced Buddhism in Khotan. A Buddhist scholar, Arya Vairocana, from India soon became the king's spiritual guide. Thus, the first monastery in Khotan was built in 211 BC. Throughout the 56 generations of this Indian dynasty which ruled Khotan, Buddhism continued to be the state religion. There were four thousand different religious centres of Buddhism, such as temples, chapels, monasteries, etc. From Khotan spread the precepts of Buddhism and influenced the states in the south such as Niya, Calmadana (Cherchen), Kroraina (Loulan), and also to Cokkuka (Kashghar). In the middle of the shifting sands of the Great Desert lying between Niya and Cherchen lived a variety of people such as the Tibetans, Turks, Uighurs, Tukuhuns, Chinese, and others in the province called Tangut (which was also the name of a tribe). Here Marco Polo visited Sachiu and found that people were 'for the most part idolators', though there were some Nestorian Christians and Saracens also. These Buddhists had a 'great many abbeys ... full of idols of sundry fashions to which they pay great honour and reverence, worshipping them and sacrificing to them with much ado'. For example, they will feed a sheep in honour of the idols, have it slaughtered and cooked, present it before the idols and leave it there while they pray for the idols' blessings. And if one will believe them, the idols feed on the meat that is set before them. After these ceremonies they organize a dinner.[16] Marco Polo, however, found that the people of Khotan were 'all worshippers of Mohammed'.[17]

While travelling through Khotan and other Buddhist lands between AD 399 and 414, Fa-Hien noticed that all the inhabitants of the region of Khotan 'professed Buddhist law, and joined together in its religious music for their enjoyment' a fact confirmed by Hsian Chwang and others. The Buddhist monks 'numbered several thousand, most of whom were students of the Mahayana'. Such was the popularity of Buddhism in this region that throughout the country the houses of the people stood apart like separate stars, and each family had a small tape reared in front of its door. The smallest of these was twenty cubits high or a little more. Monasteries were built 'for monks from all quarters'. The 'travelling monks are provided with whatever else they required'. Fa-Hien and others were 'lodged' comfortably by 'the lord of the country' in one such monastery called 'Gomati' (of the Mahayana school) where their 'wants' were 'supplied'. There were three thousand monks attached to this one monastery alone. Fa-Hien says that 'there were four (some say 14) great monasteries not counting the smaller one'. Fa-Hien was particularly impressed by the grandeur of the king's new monastery which he says was '250 cubits in height' with elegant carvings and inlay work, covered above with gold and silver, and finished throughout with a combination of all the precious substances. Behind the tope there was a Hall of Buddha of the utmost magnificence and beauty, the beams, pillars, doors and windows being all overlaid with gold leaf. Besides this, the apartments for the monks were also imposingly and elegantly decorated, 'beyond the power of words to express'. No wonder the construction of this monastery took eight years and extended over the reigns of three rulers. The resources for this monastery were generously provided. It was said that: 'Of whatever things of the highest value and preciousness of the kings in the six countries on the east of the (T'sung) range of mountains are possessed, they contribute the greater portion (to this monastery) using but a small portion of them themselves.'[18]

Indeed, the most sincere efforts for the dissemination of Buddhism were made by scholars who translated the books from Sanskrit, Tibetan, and Uighur into Mongolian and other Central Asian languages. By the fourteenth century, most of the major works on Buddhism had been translated and printed. A Mongolian scholar,

Choiji Odzer, played a key role and not only translated the sacred texts but also provided elaborate commentary on the subject. The last Mongol, Khan Ligdan (1604-34), undertook the difficult task of completing the single largest translation project. The compilation of the Mongolian *Ganjur* and *Danjur,* comprising 333 large volumes, represented translations from various Indian languages first into Tibetan and then into Mongolian. *Ganjur* is attributed to the Buddha, while *Danjur* is a collection of thousands of works by other Indian pandits and saints. The Mongolian *Danjur* is said to be 'far richer than its Tibetan counterpart because it included many Indian texts translated both from Sanskrit and Chinese that are not included in the Tibetan *Danjur*'. Besides Bogdo Jebtsundamba Hutukhtu, Zanabazar, a well-known artist, created a special script called *Soyombo* (*Svayambhu*) exclusively for religious purposes. This script was derived from Devanagari or Landza with certain additional symbols and markings to suit their Khalkha dialect. The significance attached to this script is well reflected through its '*soyombo phoneme om*' on Mongolia's national emblem.[19]

In the southern part of Central Asia, where the Khotanese language was spoken, several Buddhist texts were translated into the Khotanese language. These included: *Vajra echedika*, *Aparimitayuh Sutra*, *Bhadra Caryaesana*, *Suvarnaprabhasa-Sutra*, *Maitreya Samiti Nahka*, etc. Apart from this '*Maitreya samiti-nataka*', *Suvarnaprabhasa Sutra* of Kalyanankara and Papankara were translated into the Tukharian language, from which they were again translated into Higher-Turkish. *Suvarnaprabhasa-Sutra* was also translated into the Kuchean language. There are Tukharian manuscripts testifying to the close spiritual ties. With the spread of Buddhism in Central Asia, more extensively in the first millennium AD, Sanskrit language also became popular. The compilation of bilingual dictionaries such as the '*Sanskrit-Tukharian Vocabulary*' c. AD 700, in the Kucha area and a Sanskrit-Chinese lexicon prepared by a Kuchean scholar in the seventh century AD) further affirm the view that Sanskrit texts were extensively read in this region. The full text of the Sanskrit work *Udanavarga* (presumably compiled by a Sarvastivadin teacher called Drasmatrata who happened to be a contemporary of Kanishka I) was discovered from Chinese Central Asia by Grunwedel and Pelliot, and its fragments were found by Stein. This work is similar to the *Dhammapada* whose Prakrit version was also available from the Khotan region. *Chandoviciti* is a work on metres known to have been used in the northern area of Central Asia.[20]

Hieun Tsang confirms that the Sarvastivadins of Agnidesh and Kucha had for long laid emphasis on learning the *Sutra* teachings and the *Vinaya*[21] regulations. Several excerpts and fragments from many Sanskrit manuscripts have been discovered in different parts of Central Asia. The complete Sanskrit *tripitaka—Sutra Pitaka, Vinaya Pitaka, Abhidamma Pitika* of the Sarvastivada School—was evidently once available in the Central Asian region. The *Dharani* (magical formula of the later Mahayana school) text was also discovered in Central Asia which indicates that perhaps the Mahayana canon was 'seriously studied in Central Asia'. Apart from *Chandragarbha Sutra*, several other texts of the Mahayana school were found in Central Asia. A Prakrit recession and fragments of the Chinese translation of the manuscript of Dhammapada (*Dharmapadavadana Sutra*) (I 1892 and 1897) and *Karmavachana*, a text of Mulsarvastivada Vinaya, were discovered in Turfan. Similarly, its fragments were found in Shorchuq (near Turfan) and Tumshuq (near Maralbashi). The manuscript of Sangitiparyay of *Abhidhamma Pitika* was also discovered in the Turfan oasis area and in a cave in Bamiyan in Afghanistan. Matreeta (possibly Asvaghosh) was very much loved by the people of Chinese Central Asia and his hymns (*Anaparaddha-stotra*) were also popular. The Agnean language was used in the northern areas of Chinese Central Asia and the Agnean versions of *Punyavanta Jataka*, *Saddanta Jataka*, *Aranemi Jataka*, and *Maitresamiti Natak* were available. Certain portions of *Pratimoksha Sutra* were discovered in Kucha. A manuscript of Mulasarvastivada Vinaya was found in the Turfan area. The followers of Mani who lived in certain parts of Central Asia used the Parthian language, which was also affected by the Buddhist literature in a major way. In Indo-Central Asian exchanges, special importance is attached to Manichaean Parthian texts which contain certain Indian Buddhist terms. It is surmised that 'clearly there is evidence revealing a strong impact of the literature of northern Buddhism on Manichaean-Parthian literature'. Similarly, the Parthian texts seem to have borrowed and twisted certain terms to suit their accent, for instances, Shakyamuni Buddha came to be known as *sh'qmn bwt*; *Sramana* as *Shmn*; *bhikshu* as *byxs*; *maitreya* as *mytrg*; *nirvana* as *nybr'n*. The list of *yakshas* given in the amuletic text in Parthian has a striking resemblance to the Buddhist *Dharani* texts.

Many Indian scholars of Buddhism were popular in the Central Asian region. There were innumerable manuscripts of hymns, such as *Satapancasatika* and *Varnanha Varna Stotra* (*Varnanha Varna*, *Buddha Stotra*), which were discovered in the areas of Tumshuq, Kucha, Shorchuq, Turfan, and Tunhuang and which are said to have been compiled by Matreceta. A palm-leaf manuscript written in the Kushana Brahmi script discovered from the Kucha area comprises excerpts from three Sanskrit dramas. One of these, entitled *Sariputra Prakarana* (compiled by Asvaghosh) of which a later manuscript discovered in the Kucha region has not been found at any place outside Central Asia. The two important works of Asvaghosh, namely, *Buddha Charita* and *Saundarananda Kavya*, were discovered in the ruins of Shorchuq. It seems that such works on Buddhism found in Central Asia had their own peculiar significance. The *Pratimoksha Sutra* which 'represented' *Vinaya Pitaka* and certain parts of *Bhikshuni Pratimoksha* were found at Duldur Aqur in Kucha. *Vinaya Vibhanga* was also discovered in the Turfan region. *Varnanha Varna Strota* (*Varnanha Varna*, *Buddha Stotra Catuh Satakam*), a collection of hymns, was recovered from the areas of Tumshuq, Kucha, Shorchuq, Turfan, and Tunhuang.[22]

Several Buddhist texts were written in Gandhari Prakrit as is well proved by the Kurram inscription of the year 21 (AD 99), wherein the Prakrit version of the *Pratitya Samutpada* formula is mentioned. It appears that the Buddhist literature introduced in Sinkiang by the Sarvastavadins must have been in Prakrit. The Gandhari Prakrit written in the Kharoshti script was prevalent in Khotan up to the sixth century AD, after which it was replaced by the Brahmi script between the periods of Sung Yun (early sixth century AD) and Hiuen Tsang (seventh century AD). It is surmised that since there were colonies of Soghdian merchants in different parts of Chinese Central Asia, the Soghdiana language had become the *lingua franca* in ancient Central Asia. Almost all the Sanskrit texts of Buddhist literature were translated into the major local languages of Central Asia (including Kuchean, Agnean, Khotanese, and Soghdian). The books translated into Kuchean included *Pratimoksa*, *Udanavarga*, *Udanastotra*, *Udana Lankara Karmavibhanga*, and *Suvarna-prabhasa Sutra*. The most talented and renowned scholar of Kucha was Kumarajiva, the son of an Indian father and a Kuchean mother. He had thoroughly studied Buddhist literature and philosophy, first in Kashmir and then in Kucha, and later also spent a long time in China. He translated a number of Sanskrit works into the Chinese language since he was 'admirably suited to interpret Indian Buddhist thought'. He had translated *Pratimoksha Sutra* into Chinese in AD 404. Asvaghosh's *Sutralankara* was also translated into Chinese in the early fifth century which 'agrees with a poetical work in Sanskrit, recovered from Kucha and Turfan. In the colophon of the work concerned, the name of the book is given as *Kalpana-mandika* or *Kalpanna Mandika drstata pankti* and that of the author as Kumaralata'.[23]

The city of Bamiyan formed a part of a splendid district of the same name and touched the eastern part of Ghur. Here the remnants of a lost civilization suggest that Bamiyan was a centre of Buddhism. In the beginning of the thirteenth century, Yaqut had appreciated the magnificently sculptured statue of Buddha. According to Yaqut, there was a beautifully constructed chamber up above the hill peaks. On the walls of this chamber, which were supported on columns, there were excellent sculptures of birds of every kind, 'most wonderful to see'. Outside the gate, there were two mighty idols cut in the rock of the hillside, from base to summit, and these were called the Surkh and the Khing (red and grey) Buddhas and 'nowhere else in the world is there any to equal these'. Qazvini also describes a 'Golden House' at Bamiyan and the two pretty statues of the Buddha. Baladhuri describes the idols of Al Budd (Buddha) near Qandahar.[24]

With the onset of the Gonanda dynasty, Buddhism, which had flourished in Kashmir from the Asokan era to the Kushan period, started gradually declining. Although Hiuen Tsang who sojourned in the place (*c.* 63-3) noticed this change, the coexistence of Buddhism and its institutions *stupas* and *viharas* side by side with the resurgence of Hinduism and its shrines of Shiva and Vishnu was a fact. Consequently, Oukong (759-63) who followed Hiuen Tsang still found Buddhism flourishing in Kashmir though it was overshadowed by the worship of Shiva who occupied the first place. Kashmiri rulers such as Husain Shah of the Chak dynasty had allocated Saturday for his discussions and religious discourses with Hindu and Buddhist priests. With the arrival of Shamsuddin of the Nur Bakhshia order, Buddhism suffered a setback in Baltistan where missionary activities had led to the conversion of Buddhists who were already troubled by spiritual unrest as well as dissatisfied with Rinchana and Lall Ded.[25]

It is generally assumed that it was by the northern route through Central Asia and over the Silk Road that the first really important Buddhist missionary reached China, and that these missionaries were from Soghdiana, Bactria, and Khotan. In the lands where multi-religious and multilingual people lived and where the Hindu god

Shiva, Helois or Selene, Mani, the sun god Mithras, the moon god Mah, the god of waters Artoasp, and the Semite goddess of fruitfulness known as Nanaia had secured their positions, the appearance of a new lord, Fo (a Chinese designation for Gautam Buddha), and the widespread doctrine of Buddhism and its most marked advance in Bactria, Soghdiana, and Khwarazmia was really very amazing. It was due to this extraordinarily extensive and popular appeal to the common people through charms and magical *tantra* that Buddhism rapidly made its advance 'socially in Taoist circles and geographically in those trading centres and colonies where diverse populations resided'. One of the most noteworthy monks who brought *Amitabh Sutra* to China from Central Asia in AD 1478 again was a Parthian related to the Arsacids, he founded an important Buddhist school in Loyang. Along with bouquets, Buddhism also received its share of brickbats. While Confucians criticized the doctrine of celibacy for monks which 'clashed directly with the social duty of procreation'—Grouset has denounced this doctrine as 'metaphysically negative'—Confucian historians always criticized the Chinese empress for squandering the wealth of her people on a Buddhist enterprise; still there were many people appreciative of this canon. Boulnois expresses the thoughts and opinions of many when he says that Buddhism (as well as Christianity)

> caused a breakdown of the social order and of the accepted conventions. They replaced the destiny of the family with the destiny of the individual; their doctrines were universal rather than national and they recognized no distinction of race or sex. Instead of inexorable justice and inflexible gods, they raised up the revolutionary ideal of infinite mercy and universal charity. Both, in times of war, poverty and misfortune offered a safe refuge from the world and the promise of a future life in which there would be no suffering and to which all men, even sinners might be admitted.

## NOTES

1. P.V. Bapat, *2500 Years of Buddhism*, pp. 65-8; P.C. Bagchi, *Expansion of Buddhism*.
2. For the spread of Buddhism in Mongolia, see *Buddhism in Mongolia*, Ullan Bator, 1983. Also see Oidot Nyamdovaa, 'Insights with the Mongolian crescent of India', New Delhi, 1999, pp. 16-19.

3. Samuel Beal, *Siyuki, Buddhist Record of the Western World*, Delhi, 1969, pp. 18-24, 78, 313-14. See also pp. 18n11, 67n. James Legge, *A Record of Buddhist Kingdoms*, New York, 1965, pp. 10, 16, 17, 18n.2.
4. James Legge, op. cit.; see also *The Travels of Fa Hien*, New York, 1965, pp. 22-3; *Siyuki*, pp. 22-4.
5. Samuel Beal, op. cit.; Bretschneider, *Medieval Researches*, vol. II, no. 44, pp. 244-5.
6. *The Travels of Fa Hien*, pp. 22-3.
7. Ibid. See Chapters 16 and 34; Legge, op. cit., pp. 16-19.
8. Haidar Dughlat, *Tarikh-i-Rashidi*, New Delhi, 1973, pp. 96-7. Also see Introduction, p. 113; *Records of Western Countries*, Book I, pp. 24, 38-9, 44-6.
9. *Records*, pp. 44-6.
10. Watters, p. 64.
11. *Dabistan-i-Mazahib*, ed. Newal Kishore, Kanpur, AD 1321, pp. 177-9. For *jogis*, for general references to Hindu sects, see pp. 135-96.
12. Fakhruddin Banakiti, *Tarikh-i-Banakiti*, Tehran, pp. 1, 3, 311, 314-26, 376.
13. Ibid., pp. 348-52; *Hudud-ul-Alam*, ed., Ahrar Mukhtarou, Dushambe, 1983, pp. 45, 52.
14. Margarita I. Filanoic et Zamira Usmanova, 'Les frontieres accidentales dela diffusion du Bouddhisme en Asie Centrale, *CAHIERS O'Asie Centrale*, nos.1-2, *Inde Asie Centrale, Routes du Commerce et des idees*, Tashkent, 1996.
15. Guchluk, the son of Taiyang Khan of Naimans, who had been driven out by Chingiz Khan, joined hands with Tukta Khan of Merkits in 1208, only to be defeated again near the river Dgem. Guchluk took refuge with Gurkhan, married his daughter, usurped his kingdom, and killed his benefactor. He was himself a Nestorian Christian and a persecutor of Islam. After his marriage to Gurkhan's daughter, he embraced Buddhism.

    Juvaini, *Tarikh-i Jahan Kusha* I, Manchester, 1958, pp. 65-8, 70-5; *Tarikh-i Rashidi*, pp. 291-3; Rashiduddin Fazlullah, *Jami-ut-Tawarikh*, Tehran edn., pp. 17, 55.
16. *The Book of Ser Marco Polo*, ed. Henry Yule and Henry Cordier, vol. I, New Delhi, 1993, pp. 196-205.
17. Ibid., vol. I, p.188. See also vol. II, p. 44.
18. Fa-Hien, pp. 18-19.
19. Nyamdovaa, op. cit., p. 18.
20. Krishnamurthy, *A Dictionary of Buddhist Literature and Literary Personalities*, Delhi, 1994, pp. 49-61.
21. There were *Vajracchedika, Ratna Sarisutna, Ratandhvaj Sutra, Chandrapala Sutra, Mahaparinirvana Sutra, Saddharma Pundarika Sutra, Dashbumika Sutra, Dharmacaria Sutra, Gandavyuha Sutra, Satsahastrika Prajnaparamita, Suvarna-prabhasa Sutra*, and *Samadhiraja Sutra*. K. Krishnamurthy, *A Dictionary of Buddhist Literature and Literary Personalities*, Delhi, 1994, pp. 49-58.
22. Krishnamurthy, pp. 54-6.
23. Ibid., pp. 50-6, 160-2.
24. Yaqut, vol. I, p. 481; Qazvini, *Nuzhat-ul-Qulub*, p. 103. For illustrations of Buddhist sculptures at Bamiyan, see Talbot and Maitland in *JRASS*, 1886, p. 323; Baladhuri, pp. 434-45.
25. Muhibbul Hasan, *Kashmir under the Sultans*, pp. 39, 158, 234, 237, 286.

# Indo-Central Asian Political Relations in the Sixteenth and Seventeenth Centuries

The nature of diplomatic relations between Akbar and Abdullah Khan has already been discussed in several monographs.[1] It is, therefore, possible now to acquaint oneself with the details of the exchange of embassies and the circumstances shaping the policy of Akbar towards the Uzbeks at various times. However, since the accounts so far offered have been mainly based on Indian and Persian sources without any detailed study of the Uzbek sources, their entire emphasis is on presenting the attitude of Akbar towards his closest neighbour and contemporary monarch. The picture will remain incomplete till a study is also undertaken of the factors which influenced the polices and attitudes of Abdullah Khan towards Akbar. As the history of the Uzbeks in the second half of the sixteenth century was earlier rather obscure, scholars have tended to interpret the purpose of each embassy of Abdullah Khan in the light of the Uzbek-Persian conflict. It is, therefore, necessary to analyse the facts and highlight the various factors that shaped the policies of Abdullah Khan towards Akbar.

With the expulsion of Babur from Central Asia, the traditional hostility between the Mughals and the Uzbeks was suspended for the time being, probably due to the fact that there was no bone of contention between the two powers, as in the case of the Persians and the Mughals over the issue of the Qandahar. Kunchum and the other Uzbek sultans had sent an embassy in 1528 to India to congratulate Babur upon his conquest.[2] Notwithstanding this amicable gesture on the part of the Uzbeks, the Mughals never forgot the loss of their ancestral kingdom. Despite a persistent and wistful desire on the part of the Mughals to conquer Transoxiana, it was probably apparent to them that their ambition itself was an impractical proposition. When the defence of the north-western frontier had become a constant problem and when even the conquest of Qandahar was still a dream, how could they plan to conquer Transoxiana. How could they hope to exercise an effective control over these remote 'ancestral land'. Both Uzbek and Mughal rulers could not venture to expand the horizon of their ambition at this stage. A new chapter begins in the history of Mughal-Uzbek relations with the emergence of Abdullah Khan Uzbek (1560-98), who tried to establish contacts with Akbar. The entire policy of Abdullah Khan towards Akbar can be discussed in three phases.

The first embassy from Abdullah Khan arrived at Akbar's court in 1572.[3] As the letter sent by Abdullah Khan along with this embassy is not traceable, it is presumed by certain historians that the proposals contained in this letter were 'directed against Persia'.[4] This assumption is purportedly based on 'subsequent developments' and circumstantial evidence from Persia itself. Both Islam and Verma seem to have drawn their conclusions from the fact that since the second embassy sent in 1577 contained proposals for an invasion of Persia, the first one was also presumably despatched for the same purpose. Explaining the 'circumstantial evidence' about the situation in 1572, Verma informs us that Shah Tahmasp was growing old and that a civil war was imminent in Persia. According to him, this could give an opportunity to the Uzbek sovereign to occupy Khurasan, but since Akbar was not likely to tolerate it, an envoy was despatched so as to arrive at some understanding with the Mughal emperor over the question of the partition of Persia between the two rulers. The Soviet historians K.A. Antonova and Illias Nizamuddinov only mention the Badakhshan civil war as being the main reason for sending the embassy. Illias Nizamuddinov, however, refers to the apprehension of Abdullah about the conquest of Balkh by the Badakhshan rulers and the subsequent declaration of independence by the Balkh ruler.[5]

While discussing a proposal from the Uzbeks for a holy war against the Persians, it would be worthwhile to examine whether Abdullah himself was in a position to initiate a war against an external power at this time. Soon after acquiring the *de jure* rulership of Transoxiana in 1560, Abdullah found himself confronted with a challenge from a group of hostile kinsmen who were not prepared to accept his supremacy. The interregnum lasting from 1510 to 1560 had considerably undermined the authority of the *khaqan*. Due to inter-state feuds and the frequent depositions and assassinations of sultans, chaotic conditions prevailed in the country at this time. The nobility and the *mullahs* had not only increased their political power but had also appropriated the revenues which were even larger than those of the Khan himself.[6] Thus, the financial condition of the state also required the immediate attention of the ruler. Against this background, it may be seen that Abdullah could hardly afford to accept additional responsibilities by involving himself in external matters. It may also be noted here that while Abul Fazl mentioned the proposal for an invasion of Persia in connection with a later embassy from Abdullah in 1577, he did not make even a casual reference to any such intention behind the embassy of 1572. An important proposal like this would have provoked an answer from Akbar. Moreover, in 1572, Shah Tahmasp was still alive and ruled over the country effectively. The internal situation itself was quite secure at the time and a threat to the stability of the Persian empire did not exist after the successful reigns, extending for about seventy-four years, of the two Persian kings, Shah Ismail (1502-4) and Shah Tahmasp (1524-76). The civil war started in Persia only in 1575-6, and there is no mention of extreme turbulent conditions existing prior to this date.[7] Besides, the Persians were sufficiently strong in 1572 to repel the attack on Khurasan and Qandahar by Abdullah and Akbar respectively. Thus, the embassy of 1572 would have had nothing to do with the Persian empire. It was probably due to his internal circumstances that Abdullah had been prompted to send an embassy to Akbar, which was a probing as well as an appeasing mission. This is proved by the following facts:

Although the Uzbek sources do not mention anything about the despatch of an embassy by Abdullah in 1572, Abul-Fazl offers a fairly clear account of the arrival of this embassy, which was led by Haji Iltatmish. According to him, the purpose of this embassy was to:

> Recall ancient relations and to renew friendship in order that, by the help of such divine glory, he might act vigorously against the princes of Turan. Another object was that he might repose in peace and be without apprehension of the strokes of the world-conquering (i.e. Akbar's) armies. For greater security and success, he sent presents to Munim Khan and Mirza Koka Khan-i Azam in order that they might exert themselves to lay the foundation of friendship.[8]

This statement of Abul-Fazl is further corroborated by circumstantial evidence. In 1572, Abdullah Khan laid siege to Balkh which was ruled by one of his cousins, Din Muhammad. When the other sultans of Transoxiana noticed the expansionist proclivities of Abdullah, they became suspicious about his intentions and decided to collaborate with each other to thwart his designs. Shah Sulaiman of Badakhshan also proceeded to join the Uzbek sultans to extend support to Din Muhammad. Although Shah Sulaiman of Badakhshan was defeated in the battle of Jam by Abdullah even before the former could join Din Muhammad,[9] the attempt must have alarmed Abdullah, particularly in view of Sulaiman's past connections with Babur, and also because of the cupidity of the Mughals themselves for Transoxiana which could drag the Indian ruler into the affairs of Central Asia. To add to his discomfiture, Khudabanda (son of Shah Tahmasp) sent his envoy to Akbar at this time. It may be mentioned that Abdullah had crossed swords with him in 1565. Although the purpose of the embassy was not to make an alliance against Abdullah, the fear of Indo-Persian friendship was still frightening for him. During the campaign of Balkh, a large number of the inhabitants of Balkh fled to India to take shelter in this country.[10] The condition of anarchy in Transoxiana as well as the external and internal pressures must have terrorized Abdullah Khan. In these circumstances, it was necessary to seek friendship with Akbar. Hence, Abdullah Khan sent the embassy to ensure Akbar's neutrality and non-involvement in the affairs of Turan as well as to protect his own borders against the pressure from an external army, and if possible to secure some assistance from Akbar to subdue his kinsmen. It appears that in view of his policy of non-involvement, Akbar did not want to encourage Abdullah to undertake further correspondence. Having seen the fall of his father, he had now learnt to give the foremost importance to the question of establishing his position in the empire and to be content with the minimum possible relations with external powers. Hence, Akbar did not despatch a return embassy to Abdullah Khan Uzbek.

Despite the lack of a proper response or a return embassy from Akbar in 1572, Abdullah despatched a second embassy after only five years. Although the Uzbek sources do not speak of this second embassy, and the letter from Abdullah to Akbar is also not traceable, Abul Fazl informs us that in this letter a joint invasion of Persia had been proposed. The statement is corroborated by the contents of the reply sent by Akbar to Abdullah.[11] The situation existing in Persia at that time also makes this very likely. Soon after the death of Shah Tahmasp in May 1576, the empire had been plunged into a civil war. Notwithstanding the professed motive, a careful examination of the situation in Transoxiana reveals that Abdullah could not have sent his second embassy only for the sake of organizing a joint attack on Persia. In spite of his having conquered Balkh (1573) and Hissar (1574), the internal situation was not so secure as to permit him to launch an offensive against Persia.

In view of the circumstances at this time, it was more profitable for Abdullah to concentrate on Badakhshan rather than to take an interest in Khurasan. Due to the existences of the two rulers in Badakhshan, internal dissensions and disturbances had broken out which made the eastern borders of Abdullah Khan's territories very insecure. The territory also offered asylum to the rebels and fugitive sultans from Abdullah Khan's kingdom. Besides, Shah Sulaiman had joined hands with the Uzbek sultan against Abdullah Khan on two occasions in the past. Abdullah was, therefore, not quite willing to help him in spite of the supplicant attitude he conveyed through the embassies.[12] In vies of the vacillating loyalties of Shah Sulaiman, Abdullah was not prepared to risk the possession of his newly conquered territories of Balkh and Hissar. He was also afraid that external powers might intervene in the affairs of Badakhshan which could even extend up to his own territories. If Badakhshan remained in the hands of an unfriendly power, this would be a great hindrance in his future operations against Persia. Incidentally, the conquest of Badakhshan was not an easy task since Shah-Rukh's mother had sent envoys to Akbar in 1577, offering the hand of her son Shah-Rukh for Akbar's daughter.[13] Consequently, the support of Akbar to Shah-Rukh could also be expected. On the other hand, Sulaiman had secured military assistance from Shah Ismail II for defeating Shah-Rukh.[14] Perhaps this alliance had prevented Akbar from making a prompt commitment to extend any help to Shah-Rukh. In any case, Abdullah was apprehensive that the intervention from either of the two great powers would seal his fare in Badakhshan for ever. At this juncture, therefore, Abdullah was not wiling to open hostilities against Persia immediately as he was aware that the consequences of this act might not be very advantageous for himself.

By this time, Abdullah must have learnt of Akbar's policy of non-involvement, which was first seen in his indifferent attitude towards

Abdullah's problems in 1572, and then revealed by his attitude to Sulaiman of Badakhshan in 1574.[15] Even in 1577 it is very doubtful whether Akbar would have liked to involve himself in a holy war or other such enterprises. The nature of Indo-Persian relations during the last few decades also indicates a mutually helpful and friendly attitude between the two empires, in spite of certain differences. If a 'holy war' had to be fought at all by Abdullah Khan, a more natural ally would have been the Ottoman Sultan, Murad III, as the Ottoman rulers were generally hostile towards Persia and had remained on friendly terms with the Uzbeks. Although Tahmasp had died and anarchic conditions prevailed in Persia, the empire was still sufficiently strong. Presumably due to this, Abdullah did not attempt to invade Khurasan in June-July 1576, immediately after the death of Shah Tahmasp, when the situation was comparatively more favourable for him. Instead, he preferred to attack Hazarasp and its environs rather than initiating hostility against Persia. The new Persian ruler, Shah Ismail II (1576-7), had a liberal and tolerant attitude towards the Sunni population.[16] It was thus out of the question for Abdullah even to play upon the religious sentiments of the local population for achieving his political ends. Besides, there is no indication of Abdullah's intention to invade Khurasan.

Thus, it was neither the expectation of some military assistance from Akbar nor a question of exploring the possibility of making an alliance against the Persian empire which had prompted Abdullah to send a second embassy in 1577. Actually, this action was dictated by the necessity of having to establish cordial relations with Akbar so as to ensure his neutrality in all matters concerning external relations. With his designs on territories like Badakhshan and Qandahar, it was only natural that Abdullah should strive to develop friendly relations with Akbar and thereby try to ward off the danger from this side. Thus, the second embassy was also a continuation of the same old probing and appeasing mission. It is possible that Abdullah may have sent this embassy for the following purposes: to ascertain Akbar's attitude towards Persia and Qandahar; to assess the real strength of the emperor; to find out his general policy in relation to Badakhshan; and, if possible, to misled Akbar about his own designs on Badakhshan. This matter having been settled, if friendly relations could be established with Akbar through persistent supplicatory gestures, Abdullah could easily wield his sword elsewhere to extend his influence at the expense of the other powers.

At this point, it will be interesting to examine the attitude of Akbar towards Abdullah. The envoy from Abdullah arrived some time preceding the month of September 1577 and was graciously received at Akbar's court.[17] Now at this stage Akbar sent a return embassy under Mirza Faulad along with a letter. Although the exact date of the embassy is not know, Abul Fazl has recorded this fact before mentioning the events of September 1577. The Uzbek sources say that the embassy reached Abdullah Khan's court in July 1578,[18] and was received by Abdullah at Zamain, where he was engaged in suppressing the uprisings in Samarkand and Zamain. The immediate response to Abdullah's embassy exhibits a great change in Akbar's attitude towards Abdullah.

Verma concludes that this change was necessary since Akbar was planning 'to bring about the settlement about Badakhshan' and apprehended an alliance between Sulaiman and the Uzbeks, and that he was only anxious to help Shah-Rukh and had, therefore, taken steps to organize an army under Yusuf Khan and Raja Bhagwan Das.[19] In this connection, it will be interesting to examine certain facts.

Akbar had received the embassy from Shah-Rukh some time before the month of September 1577, almost concurrently with the arrival of Abdullah's envoy at Akbar's court. At this time, Shah Sulaiman had enlisted the support of Shah Ismail II and did not maintain very cordial relations with Abdullah. Till 1578, Akbar had not given a categorical reply or an assurance to Shah-Rukh. Even after the death of Shah Ismail in November 1577, when Shah Sulaiman had been left alone, Akbar still did not care to reply to Shah-Rukh nor did he attempt to interfere in the affairs of Badakhshan. It may be noted here that the army under Bhagwan Das was sent much later, some time towards the end of 1579,[20] and not immediately after the despatch of the envoy in 1577. From 1577 to 1579, there is no mention of Akbar's intentions to conquer Badakhshan nor of despatching an army in support of Shah-Rukh. The letter sent by Akbar to Abdullah in 1577 does not contain even a causal reference to Badakhshan. This, it seems that, at this time, Akbar's attention was not fixed on the Badakhshan problem.

The view that a rapid increase in Abdullah's power had compelled Akbar to send a return embassy[21] is also not supported by the facts of the situation, which show that Abdullah had continued to be in a difficult and insecure position till 1577. The assumption that Akbar was trying to explore the possibility of an alliance with Abdullah in the event of the dissolution of Persia also needs careful examination since it is very doubtful that the Persian Empire had reached the brink of ruin only one year after the death of Shah Tahmasp. Nor was the conquest and division of Persia very easy owing to the independent territories of Siestan, Makran, and Takhta among others on the Indo-Iranian borders.[22] Moreover, due to his own problems, Akbar was not in a position to secure the maximum benefits from this alliance.

Akbar seems to have been alarmed by the development on his north-western frontier. He personally visited Punjab in 1577-8 raised an army to suppress the Baluchis, and sent Sakina Begum to persuade Mirza Hakim to render obedience. The attitude to Mirza Hakim had given rise to great apprehension in his mind. Shah Ismail II was not only giving assistance to Shah Sulaiman but had also sent a letter to Mirza Hakim, addressing him as an independent monarch and requesting from him regular correspondence.[23] With the rebellious attitude of Mirza Hakim, and with Akbar's own inability or unwillingness to become involved in external affairs, the possibility of the emergence of a triple alliance may have necessitated a friendly attitude towards Abdullah. The Uzbek ruler could exploit the situation by encouraging Mirza Hakim or even by establishing contacts with Sulaiman. Thus, the dangers threatening Akbar on his north-western frontier seem to have compelled him to sent a return embassy to Abdullah.

In his reply, Akbar rejected the proposal for a joint attack, not so much to restrain the Khan from any aggressive designs on Persia, but to maintain his own policy of non-involvement and also because he realized that he would not gain much from this venture. By expressing his regard for the Persian ruler, and showing his disapproval of Abdullah's insulting references to the Shah of Persia, he simply desired to utilize this opportunity to frighten Abdullah by conveying veiled threats over the issue of Qandahar. Referring to Abdullah's advice that Akbar should not leave his hereditary territory of Qandahar in alien hands and that he should occupy it, Akbar retorted that not only Qandahar but certain other territories (the reference is naturally to the land of Transoxiana) had also been conquered in the past and had thus belonged to his ancestors, but in view of the continuance of the norms of submission and friendship, the maintenance of the safety of roads, and the regular despatch of presents and supplications, there was no harm in allowing the Persians to hold Qandahar. If, however, they decided to give up this old practice after the death of Tahmasp, the Mughal armies could easily occupy Qandahar.[24] These words were equally meant for Abdullah Khan. In this letter Akbar also mentioned that pilgrims to Mecca could proceed from the Gujarat side. He further emphasized that he was engaged in a holy war against the infidels in India and intended to launch a crusade against the Portuguese.

The court historian of Abdullah Khan records that the Indian envoy obtained an audience with the Khan in the vicinity of Samarkand through the good offices of Latif Khwaja, and having presented valuable gifts, he conveyed the message of obedience and submission.[25] It seems that the reaction of Abdullah to this letter was not quite favourable since no further embassies were sent to Akbar for about a decade.

From 1577 onwards a shift is noticeable in the respective positions of Abdullah Khan and Akbar, which also brought about a change in their policies towards each other. By 1583, Abdullah had conquered all of Transoxiana, and had also eliminated all his kinsmen, one after the other. When his father died in 1583, he became the *khaqan* and could now compete with his other counterparts in the Muslim world. In 1584, Abdullah conquered Badakhshan, and the two *mirzas* had to leave the territory. Abdur-Rahim's view that Akbar had tried to save Badakhshan from Abdullah is not supported by any action on the part of the Mughal emperor. To say that Abdullah had instigated Jalala also does not seem to be very convincing. The Uzbek sources do not mention anything about the Raushanais, and Abul Fazl does not refer to any links or alliance between Abdullah Khan and Jalala. In the *Akbar Nama*, it is simply recorded that 'Jalala went to Turan and returned unsuccessful'.[26] There is a possibility that Jalala might have attempted to secure assistance from the Urukzais or some other tribal populations. The boundaries of the empires of both Akbar and Abdullah Khan had come closer, and the pressure of Abdullah's increasing power was being felt by Akbar. While Abdullah had improved his position and was now adopting a bolder and more demanding attitude towards Akbar, the attitude of Akbar himself had become more conciliatory.

By this time, the difficulties of Akbar had increased still further.

There were troubles in Kashmir and Gujarat, and tribal commotions in Kabul, Zabulistan, Sawad, and Bajur.[27] Even the escorting of Turani ambassadors had to be arranged by Akbar who sent his own officers for fear of the Raushanais.[28] The frontiers of Akbar's empire had become even more insecure, due to the growing friendship between Mirza Hakim and Sulaiman. Mirza Hakim had exchanged embassies with Abdullah Khan and Khwaja Kalan in 1579-81,[29] and had attempted a rebellion in 1585. When Mirza Hakim died in 1585, Akbar was immediately confronted with the internal problems of Kabul, apart from the task of organizing the defence of the north-western frontiers. Abul Fazl mentions that after the death of Mirza Hakim the soldiers of Kabul 'were wickedly thinking that they would become wanderers in the desert of failure and would go to Turan'.[30] Due to such developments, Akbar had personally proceeded to Kabul in August 1586.[31] For ensuring the safety of his frontiers, Akbar was anxious to occupy Qandahar and to save Kabul from the designs of Abdullah Khan, so that he could protect the remaining portions of his north-western frontiers since Badakhshan had already been lost to Abdullah.

To add to Akbar's worries, the Persian empire had also become weak under the reign of the incompetent and half-blind ruler Khudabanda from 1577 to 1588. The empire had also been completely shattered by the invasions of the Ottomans (1580-1) as well as by internal rebellions of the nobles. In these circumstances, it had become necessary for Akbar to maintain a more conciliatory attitude towards Abdullah Khan.

After a lapse of several years, Abdullah sent another embassy to Akbar in 1586. Although the letter of Abdullah Khan is available,[32] its contents do not reveal the real purpose of this embassy. In this letter, he refers to the delay in sending an envoy due to his own problems and not because of any lack of regard for Akbar. Proceeding further in this letter, Abdullah justifies the conquest of Badakhshan on the ground the Shah-Rukh had invaded his territory, and finally refers to the despatch of certain pigeons and the master pigeon-flier Habib.

Abul Fazl writes:

> The arrival of Akbar at Kabul, the construction of roads in the Khaibar Pass, and the construction of a bridge over the Indus have frightened Abdullah, as the design of marching to Zabulistan became conspicuous, and from fear of a rapid march of the lord of the world, the gates of Balkh

were generally kept closed. Abdullah Khan tendered supplications, sent an affectionate letter and pulled at the chain of friendship.[33]

While describing the events of 1585-6, the author of the *Rauzat-ul-Tahirin* states that Abdullah sent a letter to Akbar saying that Shah-Rukh had attacked and plundered his villages, and so the troops had been sent to restrain the Mirza who, out of suspicion, fled to Akbar. Since Abdullah Khan thought that his action would hurt Akbar's feelings, he apologized by claiming that it was not his fault and assuring the Mughal emperor that 'this faqir (Abdullah) has acted out of friendship'.[34] While referring to this embassy in his letter of March 1586 to Khan-i Khanan, Akbar also mentions that Abdullah had sent the pigeons of Husain Mirza in the cause of unity.[35]

The Uzbek sources, however, give an entirely different picture of this embassy. Hafiz Tanish records that one Amir Quresh, a Saiyid and a trusted Amir of the Khan, was sent as an ambassador to Akbar. A large number of hunting birds valuables, and suitable presents were sent to the Khan. The object of the mission (*Mazmum-i-risalat*) was that:

The Persians had been occupying the wilayats of Iran for a long time and were practicing tyranny, creating commotion, and committing sins. Having given up the Sunni religion, they had deviated from the laws of the Prophet and were heading towards utter confusion and destruction. The extermination of such a group is the duty of all Muslims including ourselves. So far, we have not attempted their expulsion owing to certain problems. Now, with the favour of God, the circumstances are favourable: all the places had been subdued and there were no external factors to obstruct the plan. So it was decided that early in spring we should proceed with [the] our extermination of that misguided group and try our utmost to destroy them. If Emperor Akbar could extend material or moral support in this venture, it would be better. In case, however, this was not possible, protection must not be given to those who fled from our sword to your side.[36]

In one of the collection of letters found in Tashkent,[37] however, there is another letter addressed to Akbar and sent by Abdullah Khan through Nazar Be Dadkhwah. Illias Nizamuddinov believes that the missive was delivered as a personal letter to Akbar by Nazar Be who was received in audience earlier than Mir Quresh.[38] Although the *Akbar Nama* mentioned that Nazar Be got an audience earlier than Mir Quresh, there is no reference to any personal letter delivered by him.[39] It is difficult to explain why Abdullah chose to send two separate letters simultaneously, particularly when one of these was sent through an expelled noble of Abdullah, that is, Nazar Be. Nevertheless, neither of the two letters can be dismissed as spurious since Akbar's reply contains answers to the questions raised separately in both letters.

The purport of the letter sent through Nazar Be is also confirmed by other Uzbek sources. In his letter, Abdullah recalls the old friendship, refers to the embassies already sent, congratulates Akbar on his coronation, and sends him good wishes for a successful reign. Informing Akbar that all the 92 Uzbek tribes and the Qazaq, Kirghiz, and Kalmuks have been subjugated, Abdullah expresses his intention to teach a lesson to the 'heretic Shias' who were putting obstacles in the path of pilgrims to Mecca and Medina, so as to prevent them in future from doing such things and to bring them back on the right track (i.e. Sunnism). Nazar Be had already been sent to them but they had declined to accept the terms. Abdullah thereupon asked the Khwarazm ruler to invade Meshed, Astarabad, and Nishapur, and ordered the Manghits and the Turks to cooperate with him from the direction of Merv. With the same end in view and on the advice of high-ranking officials, Abdullah also proposed to Akbar that he take part in the struggle against the Shia heretics. 'If these two pearls of the mine of valour support and assist each other, marching together, they can overrun and topple these groups of heretics and turn them to Islam.' It is quite probable that a written message had also been given to Nazar Be to be conveyed only verbally to Akbar. This is also supported by the account given in the *Abdullah Nama*. The facts are also corroborated by the reply sent by Akbar to Abdullah in response to the embassy of 1586. From the evidence noted above it is also clear that the purpose of this embassy was not to seek the co-operation of Akbar for an attack on Persia, but to prevent him from sending any assistance to the Persian ruler. It was thus intended to cause him to adopt a neutral attitude in these proposed wars and to act in a friendly manner towards Abdullah.

The Uzbek sources say that Abdullah did not have very cordial relation with Akbar even before 1586, presumably because he suspected that Mirza Shah-Rukh and Shah Sulaiman had received help from Akbar in 1584 to make a raid on Badakhshan to recover their lost territory. Abul Fazl, however, records that Mirza Sulaiman was assisted by Mirza Hakim and Shah-Rukh was supported by the Hazara tribes. Since the two *mirzas* had arrived at Akbar's court only in 1585, it is highly improbable that the attack could have been organized with Akbar's help. It was also stressed that Abdul Momin had suspected the hand of Akbar behind the rebellion of Muhammad Zaman Mirza. Form all this, it appears that these events had created a presumption in the mind of the Uzbek ruler that Akbar had certain designs on Central Asia. Not only does Abul Fazl mention the intention of Akbar to conquer his 'ancestral domains' but Jahangir also seems to have nurtured the same longing for reclaiming the hereditary territories of the Mughals, irrespective of the considerable obstacles and undeterred by the practical difficulties preventing any such move from taking a practical shape.[40] The author of the *Silsilat-us-Salatin* notes:

> In spite of the vast dominion of India, Akbar still possessed the desire to occupy Samarkand and had once even written a couplet that without these, a valuable life is being spent in deprivation and sorrow. When the couplet was received by Khaqan Abdullah, he sent an emphatic reply saying that Akbar should try his strength if he so desired, but his own suggestion was that he should give up the idea and be content with his empire. He was advised to forbid his army from advancing towards Badakhshan and also to leave the territory of Qandahar to Abdullah's servants, or else the Uzbek armies led by the Chingizide sultans would be mobilized for the conquest of India.[41]

The same historian further informs us that:

> A group of saints and learned men, being distressed by Akbar's heresy, arrived at Abdullah's court and reported that, having been misled by certain mendicants, Akbar had adopted the religion of Metempsychosis (Tanasukhia) and the behaviour of Jogis and had deviated from the religion of the Prophet. As the Khaqan had discontinued all correspondence with Akbar from 1578 to 1585 and was planning in 1585-1586 to invade India, he sent Maulana Mirza Jan, a distinguished scholar and learned man, to investigate the actual truth about Emperor Akbar's beliefs and also about the real state of affairs in his empire.[42]

Mirza Jan went with Abdullah's envoy Mir Quresh and reached India in 1586. The account is confirmed by Akbar's reply to Abdullah. In a letter sent to Abdullah, Akbar referred to Abdullah's explanation regarding the discontinuation of correspondence as 'due to the reports which had reached Abdullah about Akbar'. Akbar called this 'the fabrications and absurd accusations of certain disaffected and expelled persons from India to flatter Abdullah Khan' and stressed that friendship demands the search for truth. He pointed out that:

Though Maulana Mirza Jan was an accomplished man, a great scholar and a theologian, it was obvious that he could not claim equality with rulers in the matters of insight and wisdom, and that the rulers should utilize this quality while managing the affairs of the two worlds and while dealing with persons who misinterpret the world of God communicated by his Prophet in order to gain advantage for themselves.[43]

While certain extraordinary developments were taking place on the north-western frontier, Akbar's fears were further deepened by the arrival of the embassy of 1586. An immediate return embassy was despatched under the leadership of Hakim Human in 1586. Their journey started on 28 August 1586. It is reported that the:

Mughal envoys arrived at Abdullah's court in September 1587, and as they had brought with them a large number of presents for which many camels had to be hired, they made a sojourn at Shibarghan, and only Mir Quresh proceeded to Abdullah's court where he spent the whole night describing the details about his stay at Akbar's court. Three persons, namely Haji Muhammad Mirza, Haider Munshi and Aban Shughawal, were deputed from Abdullah's court to receive the Mughal envoys and to escort them to the madrasa of Mirza Husain where great festivities were arranged. The envoys performed Kornish twenty-seven times and delivered presents through Abdullah's Diwan Qulbaba Kukultash. Gifts were distributed among all the nobles and courtiers, and then the envoys were taken to Abdul Momin. After staying at the khan's court for some time, they received a large number of presents consisting of foodgrains, horses, camels Turkish slaves, etc. from the nobles and courtiers. Later on, they were escorted by Mir Quresh to Bukhara, where magnificent arrangements were made by Qazi Nur Muhammad for their stay. The envoys were asked to stay on till the Heart campaign was over.[44]

After conquering Heart in 1588, Abdullah granted leave to the Mughal envoys to proceed along with his own ambassador, Ahmad Ali Ataliq. Abul Fazl records that Hakim reached the Mughal court in September 1589 and conveyed the praises and supplications from the ruler of Turan. Abdullah also conveyed the news of the capture of Khurasan which was 'due to his devotion to the lord of the world and that one of his confidants, Ahmad Ali Ataliq, was being sent along with the gifts and compliment'.[45]

But Riazul-Islam and Abdur-Rahim state that as a result of the embassy of Hakim Human, some sort of an alliance had been formed between the two rulers.[46] In this connection, Abdur-Rahim quotes a letter from Abdul Momin to Shah Murad III which, according to him, makes a reference to the actual formation of an alliance. In fact, in this letter, Abdul Momin simply says 'the ruler of India strengthened friendship and sincerity with this magnificent house and sent Hakim Human with gifts and a letter expressing concord, friendship and unity (*Izhar-i-ittehado yagangi-o mawaddat namud*)'.[47]

There is, however, sufficient evidence in other contemporary and later sources to prove that an alliance had been made between the two rulers during the period 1588-90. Abul Fazl records that Akbar had refused to help Muhammad Zaman Mirza, saying the, ' I have made a treaty of concord with the ruler of Turan, and my greatness does not allow of my fighting him'.[48] Abdullah expressed a similar view in his letter to Din Muhammad.[49] Notwithstanding the fact that Abul Fazl sent a letter to Hakim Human (dated October 1587), urging him to arrange for some sort of an agreement or a treaty of peace with Abdullah,[50] the contents of Akbar's letters suggest that the proposal for a concord had been initiated by Abdullah Khan himself. Apart from a letter of Akbar to Abdullah in which it is clearly stated that the question of 'ways of peace'[51] had been raised by Abdullah Khan, the same impression is conveyed through other letters also. In one of his letters sent to Shah Abbas in 1594, Akbar mentions that:

> Abdullah Khan sent time after time loving letters referring to and confirmatory of affection by the instrumentality of skilful ambassadors and set in motion the chain of concord and devotion, and laid the foundation of affection. As to go to war with one who is disposed to be peaceable is contrary to the Divine Decrees and is disapproved of in the balance of lofty reason, our head turned away from this project.[52]

In his letter of 1591, also addressed to Raja Ali Khan, Akbar conveyed that his plans for the conquest of Badakhshan were being postponed because 'the envoys of Abdullah had come to his court along with presents, and as for himself since noting is more important than sincerity and friendship, he returned to Lahore'.[53] Nevertheless, a formal acceptance of this offer of peace was confirmed by Akbar only in 1596 after the conquest of Qandahar.

The despatch of Ahmad Ali Ataliq from Abdullah's court marks the beginning of the third phase in Uzbek-Mughal relations. Through the letter sent with this envoy, Abdullah initiated talk of friendship, and sent counsel for 'exerting ourselves to strengthen the foundation of peace and to purify the foundations of concord and make this Hindukush the boundary between us'.[54] There were certain plausible reasons behind this overture. Mirza Shah-Rukh had taken shelter at the Mughal court, and the sons of Mirza Hakim were also brought there. From 1588 to 1589 Akbar himself remained at Kabul which might have caused Abdullah to apprehend a possible invasion of Badakhshan.[55] Abdullah's fears were not entirely unfounded as Akbar mentions in one of his letters to Raja Ali Khan of Khandesh dated September 1591 that on reaching Kabul in 1588, he had proposed to recover Badakhshan and to assign it to Shah-Rukh.[56]

When the situation in Persia started showing signs of improvement form 1589 onwards, Abdullah had no choice except to maintain friendly relations with Akbar. In 1588, Shah Abbas ascended the throne after the abdication of his father, Khudabanda. The young prince was so enthusiastic that he immediately wanted to take action to save Herat from the onslaught of Abdullah.[57] The internal conditions of his empire, however, did not permit him to proceed in the matter. Shah Abbas attempted to solve the internal problems of his country with an energetic attitude. Having seen this change, Abdullah could not afford to take an aggressive attitude towards Akbar. Although displeasure had been shown by him over the grant of asylum to Shah-Rukh as 'a cloud on his heart', the letter largely contained friendly remakrs.[58] Since Abdullah already had his eye on the territories of Qandahar, Farab, Siestan, Zamindawar, and Garmsir, and was planning to undertake an expedition after the completion of the Khurasan conquest, it was necessary for him to ensure Akbar's neutrality.

The envoy from Abdullah had been granted leave when another person came from Abdul Momin with a demand for the return of the Aimaqs of Badakhshan (who had fled to Akbar's court due to Abdul Momin's tyranny). Abul Fazl records that this envoy was drowned in the Jhelum. At this point, Akbar's silence and the insolent letter addressed to him by Abdul Momin caused much worry to Abdullah Khan.[59]

It seems that developments elsewhere at this time also did not favour Abdullah Khan. The strained relations with the Qazaqs had acquired new dimensions, as the diplomatic relations of the Qazaqs with the Russian Czars which began under the Timurids in the fifteenth century were very actively pursued between 1550-99.

Notwithstanding the 25 embassies sent by the Uzbek rulers and the six return embassies, one under, to the *khanates* and the Qazaqs, relations were no better than what might be termed a 'diplomatic-economic offensive'.[60]

After the conquest of Kazan, Astrakhan, and Siberia by Russia, the main intermediary commercial centres and the brisk trade between the two states established earlier by Timur were destroyed. Similarly, the rivalry over the Qazaq region between the Czar and the Khan turned the balance in favour of the Qazaqs, whose ruler Tawakkul's envoy, Qul Muhammad, sent to Russia in 1594, not only brought troops with firearms but also the assurance of full diplomatic protection. A provocative message, in July 1589, to Abdullah was also sent by Boris Godunov, demanding that communications from Bukhara to Russia thereafter be prefaced with the Czar's full name and entire lengthy titles, and that similar respect be shown to Godunov himself. In 1595, two Central Asian envoys, Qutluq Adam and Isen Gildey, were kept in detention.[61] To make matters worse, in 1590, Shah Abbas concluded a humiliating treaty with the Ottoman sultan so as to be able to deal with the Uzbeks,[62] and he also sent a letter to Akbar through Yadgar Sultan Shamlu to seek his assistance against the Uzbek ruler. The author of *Silsilat* informs us that Abdullah had learnt about the despatch of this embassy beforehand and was extremely frightened when the contents of the messages, given below, were reported to him:

> In view of the past relations between their ancestors, Abbas desired that military assistance be sent to him under capable generals via Qandahar. Since the Shah was personally proceeding with his Qizilbash armies, it was hoped that the vast land would be conquered soon. The Shah further expressed the hope that if unity and friendly relations were established between him and Akbar, it would not only be beneficial for both the kingdoms but would also be a cause of degradation for the enemies of the two states.

To cause further provocation, Shah Abbas pointed out that: 'If the Uzbeks acquired greater strength, they would even aspire for the territory of Emperor Akbar. In this situation, if open help was not possible, at least moral support must not be avoided.'[63]

Alarmed at these developments, Abdullah immediately appointed his nephews, Din Muhammad, Baqi Muhammad, and Wali Muhammad, to conquer Farab, Siestan, and Qandahar which had been detached from Persia after the occupation of Khurasan by the

Uzbeks. Din Muhammad occupied Zamindawar, Siestan, Garmsir, and the territories up to the river Helmand, and halted at the banks of the Urghandaq, from where he sent letters to the *mirzas* of Qandahar in 1590-1, persuading them to surrender the territory to Abdullah's forces. In order to save their territory, the *mirzas* decided to reveal their alliance with Akbar. They sent a reply stating that Qandahar belonged to the Mughal empire and that they were holding the town only as the governor of Akbar. Only if the Uzbeks wanted to begin a war with Akbar were they at liberty to besiege Qandahar. The territory of Qandahar had lately become a source of trouble for Abdullah since the Persian nobles, Sultan Ali Khalifa and Sulaiman Khalifa, had also been tying to instigate the *mirzas* of Qandahar against Abdullah and were attempting to use them as tools for creating several problems for the Khan.[64] Abdullah had no intention of provoking a war with Akbar. He also believed that Qandahar in the hands of the Mughals would be far less dangerous than if it were in the hands of the Persians. Apprehensive about confrontations with the Mughals, Abdullah sent another letter to Akbar through Maulvi Husain Khurasani, who reached the Mughal court in January 1591. Although the letter was purportedly written to apologize for the misdemeanour of Abdul Momin, the actual purpose of this embassy was to confirm the friendship with Akbar and also to assess his intentions regarding the territory of Qandahar. This is quite apparent from his words 'that certain campaigns had been postponed till the return of Ahmad Ali Ataliz'.[65]

Akbar did not send a reply to this embassy immediately. Under the changed circumstances, he felt emboldened. He was also aware of the aggressive designs of Abdullah Khan due to which he had personally come to the Punjab, and was also panning to occupy Qandahar as well. In February 1591, immediately after the arrival of the Uzbek envoy, he appointed Khan-i Khanan to lead the forces for the conquest of Qandahar so as to save it from Abdullah. Since the Persian envoy had been staying at the Mughal court, the possibilities of a Mughal-Persian alliance still existed. Thus, it seems that Abdullah was frightened by several events. In 1592, he sent *nishans* to Din Muhammad, advising him to give up the idea of conquering Qandahar since an understanding had been reached with Akbar that the Hindukush and Qandahar should form the boundary line between the two kingdoms.[66]

Notwithstanding these pronouncements, Abdullah had not given up the hope of acquiring Qandahar and tied to establish friendly relations with the *mirza* of Qandahar sometime in 1593. In this letter sent by Abdullah, there were expression of affection for Muzzaffar Husain and assurances that, although the enmity between the Persians and the Turanis was quite old, the *mirza* need not have any apprehensions regarding Abdullah's intentions and was urged not to leave his paternal kingdom of Qandahar. It is interesting to note that almost immediately after these assurances has been given, the Uzbeks again invaded Qandahar, describing it as a retaliatory measure against the Persian nobles.[67]

From 1589 onwards, Akbar entertained designs upon Qandahar and was finally successful in persuading the *mirzas* to come to India. Although Rustam Mirza arrived in 1573, Muzzaffar only sent his consent to proceed to India. It seems that the letter of Abdullah had an influence on him, as a result of which he was not quite willing to go to India. The Mughal officers, however, forced him to leave Qandahar.[68]

With the conquest of Qandahar in 1595, Akbar felt the need to revive his contacts with Abdullah Khan. While the Shah of Persia quietly reconciled himself to the loss of Qandahar to the Mughals, it was unlikely that the Uzbeks would accept the position so easily. Since after the occupation of Qandahar, the Mughal forces had engaged themselves in an armed conflict with the Uzbeks over the possessions of Garmsir and Zamindawar, it had become all the more necessary to pacify Abdullah Khan. Moreover, in 1594, the Ottoman Sultan Murad III had sent a letter to Abdullah proposing a joint attack on the Persian territory. The fear of an Ottoman-Uzbek alliance probably also alarmed Akbar. However, no military alliance could take place at this time, as the Uzbek envoy was still on his way to the Ottoman court when Shah Murad died in 1595. The fear of the Uzbeks still continued, particularly in view of the fact that Abdullah Khan had opened correspondence with the new Ottoman ruler Muhammad and had even proposed a joint attack on Persia.[69] After the occupation of Qandahar, Akbar realized the urgency of sending an embassy to Abdullah through Khwaja Ashraf Naqshbandi, and showed his willingness to accept the Hindukush as the boundary line between the two kingdoms. The envoys carrying these messages received an audience with Abdullah in September 1579 at Qarshi. For the return embassy, Abdullah sent Mir Quresh with the Mughal envoy, but before they could reach India, the Uzbek ruler died in 1598. The Indian ambassadors returned, though Mir Quresh was not able to accompany them.[70]

## NOTES

1. Abdur Rahim, *Mughal Relations with Persia and Central Asia*, unpublished dissertation; Riazul Islam, *Indo-Persian Relations*, Iranian Culture Foundation, Tehran, 1970; A. Verma, *Foreign Policy of the Great Mughals*, Agra, 1967.
2. *The Babur Nama*, English trans. by A.S. Beveridge, London, 1922, pp. 351-3, 357.
3. Abul Fazl, *Akbar Nama* (hereafter: *AN*), 2 vols., Calcutta, 1879, 1886 (coll. *Bibliotheca Indica*, text, p. 138), English trans. by A.S. Beveridge, II, p. 368.
4. Riazul Islam, op. cit.; A. Verma, op. cit., p. 48.
5. Illias Nizamuddinov, *Iz istorii sredne-aziatsko-indiiskikh otnoshenii*, Tashkent, 1969, pp. 51-2; K.A. Antonova, *Ocherki obshchestvennykh otnoshenii-i politicheskogo storia Mogol' skoi Indii vremena Akbara*, 1952.
6. A. Jenkinson, *Purchas and his Pilgrims*, James Macklihouse University Press, 1906, vol. XIII, p. 23; R. Haklyut, *Principal Navigations*, I, p. 456.
7. Iskandar Beg Mirza, *Alam Ara-i-Abbasi* (hereafter: *AAA*), Tehran, 1313, I, pp. 58-91.
8. *AN*, III, pp. 211-12.
9. Hafiz Tanish, *Abdullah Nama* (hereafter: *AbN*), MS, India Office Library, London, 3, no. 574, ff. 192-3.
10. *AbN*, f. 196a.
11. Munshi Bhagchand, *Jam-i-ul-Insha* (hereafter: *JI*), British Museum MS, OR, 1702, Rieu III, 984 a, ff. 196-9.
12. *AbN*, ff. 192b-193a, 199, 231-4, 315; *AN*, pp. 153-4.
13. *AN*, III, pp. 210-11.
14. *AAA*, pp. 153-60; *AN*, III, p. 423.
15. *AN*, III, pp. 157-8.
16. *AAA*, pp. 153-7.
17. *AbN*, III, pp. 211-12.
18. *AbN*, III, p. 233.
19. A. Verma, op. cit., p. 52.
20. *AN*, III, p. 288.
21. Abdur Rahim, op. cit., p. 169; Riazul Islam, op. cit., pp. 52-3.
22. I. Nizamuddinov, op. cit., p. 56.
23. Riazul Islam, op. cit., pp. 52-3.
24. *JI*, ff. 199-204; Ibadullah al Fayyaz, *Fayyaz-ul-Qawanin*, I, O, 3901, ff. 177-81; *Majmaul Insha*, f. 196; Calendar, BM, OR, Tx 327, f. 1559.
25. *AbN*, p. 223.
26. *AN*, text, p. 607; trans., pp. 810, 928.
27. *AN*, pp. 715-37, 792, 802, 957.
28. *AN*, p. 721.

29. *AbN*, ff. 284, 315; Badr-al-Din Abdussalam Kashmiri, *Rauzat-ul Rizwan*, MS Oriental Institute Library, Tashkent, no. 2094, f. 333.
30. *AN*, p. 466.
31. *AN*, p. 467.
32. *JI*, ff. 199-204; *Fayyaz-ul-Qawanin*, op. cit., ff. 181-5; *Munshaat-i-Namkin*, Aligarh, MS Farsiya Nasr, pp. 3, 26.
33. *AN*, III, p. 487.
34. Tahir M. Sabzwari, *Rauzat-ul-Tahirin*, I-II, British Museum, MS, Rieu 119b; I, f. 569.
35. Abul Fazl, *Mukatabat-i-Allami* (hereafter; *Mukatabat*), Harsi Daftar, Lucknow ed., pp. 33-4; also see Mansura Haidar, *Insha-i-Abul Fazl; Mukatabat-i-Allami*, New Delhi, 1988.
36. *AbN*, p. 460.
37. *Collection of documents and letters*, MS, no. 289, Ivan, Oriental Institute Library, Tashkent; I. Nizamuddinov, op. cit., p. 62.
38. Ibid., pp. 62-5.
39. *AN*, III, p. 735.
40. Jahangir, *Tuzuk-i-Jahangiri*, English trans. by Rogers, New Delhi, 1978, I, p. 26.
41. *Silsilat-us-Salatin* (hereafter: *Silsilat*), MS Bodleian Liberary, no. 269, f. 134.
42. *Silsilat*, ff. 138-9.
43. *Mukatabat*, pp. 17-21; *Munshaat-i-Namkin*, op. cit., pp. 251-2.
44. *AbN*, pp. 479-85.
45. *AbN*, p. 566.
46. Riazul Islam, op. cit., pp. 52-3; Abdur Rahim, op. cit., pp. 78-9.
47. Muhammad Yusuf Munshi, *Tazkira-i-Muqimkhani*, MS Royal Asiatic Society, no. 161, ff. 28-30.
48. *AN*, III, p. 571.
49. *Silsilat*, pp. 138-9.
50. *Mukatabat*, pp. 197-8; *AN*, III, p. 705.
51. Ibid., pp. 3, 74.
52. Ibid., pp. 4, 11, 21.
53. *AN*, p. 473; *Mukatabat*, p. 48.
54. *Mukatabat*, p. 4.
55. *AN*, p. 473.
56. *Mukatabat*, p. 48.
57. *AAA*, pp. 277-8.
58. *AN*, p. 578; Muhamad Khan, *Iqbal Nama*, Newal Kishore edn., p. 416; *Mukatabat*, p. 5; *Munshaat-i-Namkin*, op. cit., pp. 251-2.
59. *AN*, III, p. 876; *Mukatabat*, p. 5; *Iqbal Nama*, op. cit., p. 416.
60. E. Allworth, ed., *Central Asia: A Century of Russian Rule*, New York, 1967, pp. 22-3, 37-40.
61. '*Kazakhsko-russkie otnosheniia* v XVI-XVIII vekakh', iz *Sbornik dokumentov-i materialov*, Alma Ata, Izd. AN Kazakhskoi SSR, 1961, pp. 3-9; '*Dopolneniia Nikonovskoi letopisi*', iz *Polnoe sobranie russkih letopisei*, Leningrad, XIII, 2, pp. 313, 318, 385; Sbornik kniazia Khiltova, St. Petersburg, 1879, pp. 487-8; *Materialy za istoriiu Uzbekskoi, Tadzhikskoi-i Turkmenskoi SSR*, I, 66, pp. 400-7; E. Allworth, op. cit., pp. 22-3, 37-40.

62. Faridum Bey, *Munshat-us-Salatin*, Istanbul, H 1274, I, ff. 157-62.
63. *Silsilat*, ff. 138-9.
64. *AAA*, pp. 326-34; *Silsilat*, ff. 138-9.
65. *Mukatabat*, p. 7; also see *AN*, III; tr., pp. 856-7, 885; text, p. 583.
66. *Silsilat*, ff. 138-9.
67. *Silsilat*, ff. 146-8.
68. *AN*, III, pp. 654-6, 670-1; *Rauzat-ut-Tahirin*, op. cit., f. 577; *AAA*, pp. 331-3.
69. Faridun Bey, op. cit., ff. 157-62, p. 484.
70. *AN*, III, tr., p. 1103; *Mukatabat*, p. 4.

# Linkages and Interactions between the Mughal Rulers and the Lands Beyond the Hindukush in the Sixteenth Century

India's linkages and interactions with other Asian countries go back to several thousand years. Notwithstanding the diversity in Asia's lingual landscape and socio-religious conditions as well as the heterogeneity of its people, one also finds similarities of ethos and culture and a cohesive sense of commonness and regional affinity, which is obviously due to geographical and geo-political determinants and the result of overlapping Marches and contiguous frontiers. As a result of human migration over the centuries, there was a continuous process of cultural diffusion and exchange of ideas, commodities, and technology. Frequent mass migrations in response to different stimuli, such as war, fear of genocide, famine, or the search for employment, fame and fortune and brisk commercial relations reduced the differences between nations, while at the same time removing the barriers to communication in Asia. These medieval states frequently faced war, which could be both terribly devastating while they could also provide opportunities for the generation of wealth and for ushering in revolutionary trends. Still, such political or domestic reasons for the sealing of frontiers against certain unwanted commercial transactions could not prevent the diffusion of technology across the borders. The transfer of technology and active cultural exchanges through irregular and unofficial channels have continued unabated. As these exchanges were multifaceted and diverse and since they served vital interests, the relations between India and Central Asia have been more tenacious than India's relations with other remoter and farther off regions. In this chapter an attempt is made to study the nature and other aspects of India's relations with its immediate neighbours (mainly Iran and Turan) during the Middle Ages.

Central Asia (used here in a much broader sense to include Mongolia, part of China, Kashghar, Turan, Iran, and the regions up to Turkey) presented a chequerboard of geographical and climatic differences. The entire Eurasian region was intersected by deserts and agricultural zones. Consequently, there were both nomads and sedentary regulations, with equally large numbers of people living in states of quasi-urbanity and semi-nomadism. Despite the wide differences in the topography, Central Asia shared many cultural similarities, characterized by a degree of uniformity in the biological, psychological, linguistic, and socio-religious spheres.

Ethnographically speaking, majority of the population of Eurasia is said to be 'of one stock'.[1] The Mongols (who created an empire in Mongolia in the beginning of the thirteenth century), the Turks (who established their sway over the regions of Turan and Turkey) and the Turcomans, a corruption of the word '*Turk-manand*' meaning 'like the Turk', who resided and ruled over the region near the Caspian Sea and in the north of Iran were all Turkish-speaking peoples and had become Turkicized by the thirteenth century. Wittek refers to the 'origin of the Ottoman Turks in Mongolia, their admixture with Iranian tribes in Central Asia and their advent into Asia Minor where they gradually displaced and absorbed their Seljuqid cousins'.[2] Bernard Lewis in his illuminating chapter 'Egypt and Syria' in the *Cambridge History of Islam*, notes: 'Though Turks and Mongols are probably not related peoples, they had a great deal of shared background and experience.'[3] The Ottoman and Uzbek chroniclers (both contemporary and later) as well as modern historians such as Gibbon, Wittek, Niyazov and others offer various interpretations and descriptions of Ottoman, Uzbek and Mongol genealogies.

A careful study of the historical sources in various languages (Uzbek, Persian and Turkish) confirms the fact that the Mongols and the Turks were of one stock (*min jins-i wahid*). It is interesting to note that various dynasties of the Turks or the Turco-Mongols, namely, the Ottomans, the Uzbeks and the Timurids, all trace their lineage to the maiden Alonqova who was ravished by the Moon-beam. In all these genealogies, the name of Yafis bin Noah also appears as one of the later ancestors of the Eurasian peoples. Two brothers, Turk and Munsak, are said to be the ancestors of the Turks and the Mongols respectively. This fact was known to their progeny, who frequently exploited the myth of their common origin to suit their purposes. In a letter addressed to Amir Fazil, Timur stressed these consanguineal ties existing between the Turks and the Tartars (Mongols):

> Your nobility is also mine, and your race joined with mine and our countries with yours; we have the same ancestors, we are all shoots and branches of the same tree; our father long ago in the past grew up in one nest and gradually occupied countless others; you are, therefore, truly one shoot from my stock, a branch of my branches, members of my members, my own marrow and my own intimates.[4]

This was not merely a literary flourish (emanating out of political expediency) but it was a fact that Timur belonged to a Turco-Mongol tribe named Barlas. Babur and his descendants were also Turco-Mongols (Turks from the father's side and Mongols from the mother's side). In a letter written to Imam Quli, the Uzbek ruler of Turan, at a very crucial moment, Aurangzeb emphasized this kinship and common origin by using the epithet '*Samar-i Shajar-i Chingiz Khan*' (fruit of the family tree of Chingiz Khan) for the addressee. Similarly, on the eve of the battle of Syr, Mahmud Khan, the Mongol ruler of Moghulistan, won over the loyalty of Shaibani Khan Uzbek (then a hireling of the Timurid ruler, Sultan Ahmad Mirza) simply by reminding him of their common ancestry. Furthermore, it should be remembered that the Turks resided around Mongolia even before the rise of Chingiz Khan. The Uighur state which preceded Chingiz Khan's rule in Mongolia was a Turkish state in the eighth and ninth centuries. When Chingiz Khan invaded Turan, his forces comprised the Turks in such vast numbers that the invading army could safely be designated as Turco-Mongol. The Mongol cataclysm in the thirteenth century dispersed the Turkish population of Turan which spread far and wide all over the Eurasian region. One such group of fugitives from Merv (in Turan) reached Erzi Rum at a time when Sultan Alauddin bin Kaikhusaru was fighting a desperate battle. The timely assistance given by these fugitives earned for them not only the gratitude of Alauddin but also a few small territories. From this nucleus emerged the Ottoman Empire which replaced the Seljuqids of Konya. For several centuries, the various branches and clans of the Turks ruled over Turkey, Turan, India, Egypt, and several other places. The Qara Quyunlu and Aqquyunlu dynasties of the Turks also had the same origin. Even the traditional theory of the origin of the Arabs (though discarded by Hitti) stresses the fact that the Semites

(Arabs) too had descended from Yafis, the son of Noah, who happened to be the ancestor of the Uzbeks, the Ottomans, and other Turkish peoples. According to the genealogical tree of the theories of origin, therefore, various Eurasian peoples were of one stock and were racially homogeneous. Ferishta gives a very detailed account of this common heritage and kindered relationship:

> All the human beings of this world are the children of Adam. After the tempest, prophet Noah had sent his three sons, namely Sam, Yafis and Ham, to three different directions of the world. Ham who happened to be the eldest of the three had 99 sons. All the Arabs were said to be their progeny. Yafis had a region extending between east and north. As his eldest son was named Tura, all the inhabitants of the region were assigned to him (Mughal, Uzbek, Turcoman, Iran, Chaghatai, Osmanli [Ottomans] Turks). The second son of Yafis was Chin after whose name the country of China had been named. The third son of Yafis was Arades whose territory was expanded by his descendants from northern borders upto Zulmat . . . and all the Tajiks and the people of Ghaur and Saqlab are stated to be his descendants. The third son of prophet Noah was Sam whose six sons were called Hind, Sind, Habsh, Afrang, Hurmuz, and Boya. The eldest son Hind gave his name to India. Thus all the inhabitants living between Mongolia and Turkey had one common ancestor, Yafis bin Noah.[5]

There was a continuous movement of peoples between Mongolia, China, Turan, Iran, Turkey and India. Ever since the much traversed Silk Road have provided the opportunity for frequent intercourses and exchanges of commodities and ideas, emigrations and immigrations had become common phenomena, and people migrated in waves and new settlements sprang up. In this context, some enthusiasts have even gone to the extent of suggesting that the Tajiks were one such group of Persian traders who had settled in the heart of Turan instead of returning to their Iranian homeland at the end of their commercial adventure through the Silk Road. However, the sources do not support this view, and no definite or specific information regarding the Tajiks being an external element is available anywhere in the sources. Incidentally, the power of the Safavids was also based on the Turcomans, with many common ancestral ties to vouchsafe for their consanguineal affinity.

The similarities of geographical features naturally had a bearing on social and historical developments within the Eurasian region, imparting to it a cultural homogeneity which was further augmented by the development of a common literary language (*Hochsprache*), followed by the Pax Turcica. The Arabic script, used in more than half of the Asian countries for several centuries, was another binding factor; the Arabic language was employed in *belles-lettres*, buildings, coins and documents. Arabic terminology and administrative phraseology travelled far and wide through the Asian lands and were extensively used side by side with Turco-Mongol and Persian terms. The bilingual population living between Turan and Turkey and between Iran and Arabian Sea could understand each other only too well. This facilitated their close contacts and the communication, leading to cultural diffusion and assimilation. Throughout the Middle Ages, lingual fusion in Central Asia was a prominent feature of the cultural landscape. Arabic, Turkish, and Mongol words crept into Persian, thus enriching it. While studying the Central Asian polity, society, and culture, therefore, one is struck by the remarkable similarities existing in political institutions, social structures, administrative terminology, and cultural patterns and ethos. A nice amalgam of the Perso-Islamic and the Turco-Mongol traditions took place.

The study of the history of political relations among various states has much significance as it helps in constructing the edifice on the right foundations and in shaping future relations in the proper direction. Historical signals could thus hardly be ignored and were generally taken as the lessons of history. The medieval sovereigns, while relying on divinations from the Holy Book, also drew conclusions from the precedents in the past. Being forced by political necessity to broaden their vision, medieval rulers (even the illiterate ones), therefore, allocated some time to acquaint themselves with the historical annals, either through direct study or by appointing readers specifically for the purpose. Even the potentates and nobles were advised to study this literature for their own enlightenment and political awakening.

For a proper understanding of the political relations between India and its neighbouring countries and also for a correct appraisal and appreciation of Mughal diplomacy, the epistolary collections provide the best evidence. The drafting of diplomatic letters was an art in which the Mughal *munshis* excelled. At Akbar's court, men of intellect and learning such as Abul Fazl and Abulfath Gilani were engaged in this task. The glowing compliment paid to Abul Fazl by Abdullah Khan Uzbek is fair evidence of the widely acknowledged excellence of the Mughal *munshis*. Abdullah Khan had once even admitted that he 'feared Abul Fazl's pen more than Akbar's sword'.

It was no wonder, therefore, that the casually drafted and crudely worded letters sent by the Ottomans often irked the Mughal rulers. Shahjahan had once, even offered rather caustically, to send some Mughal *munshis* to the Ottoman court to teach the art of drafting letters to the Ottoman munshis.

India, which has been described as 'a league of submerged nations and a cockpit of rival religions' with its heterogeneous population, was sure to have many cross currents of contacts with its neighbours.

While discussing the various aspects of the political relations between India and the Central Asian lands, it should be remembered that the Mughals had come to India on the rebound since they had been exiled from their ancestral domain of Turan by the Uzbeks led by Shaibani Khan. Before the establishment of the Mughal dynasty in India, two new states, namely, Iran (or Persia) and Turan (or Transoxiana or the five Central Asian republics of the erstwhile Soviet Union), had emerged under the Safavids (1502) and the Uzbeks (1505) on the ashes of the Timurid and the Turcoman states respectively. The expulsion of Babur from Central Asia had involved both the states of Iran and Turan, although in entirely different capacties. The Uzbeks of Turan had been instrumental in ejecting Babur from his homeland, whereas the neighbouring. Safavid ruler Shah Ismail (1502-24) of Iran had provided assistance to Babur to enable him to reconquer his lost territory. Babur was so annoyed that even after he had conquered India and the congratulatory embassy sent by the Uzbeks arrived, he did not care to send a return embassy. Babur's criticism of India and his comparison of India with Central Asia reveals his dislike of the newly acquired land, permeated by a strong sense of nostalgia and homesickness. Still, with all its natural beauty and immeasureable wealth, India did satiate the Mughals as seen by Babur and Akbar's appreciation of this country as revealed by the comments of Abul Fazl. Akbar's response to his Central Asian heritage differed somewhat from that of Babur and Humayun. He was brought up in India and 'thought of the subcontinent as his home'. Although Babur was at times nostalgic for his homeland and criticized the new and unusual environment of India, Akbar's deputy Abul Fazl revealed Akbar's deeply felt appreciation for India:

> Shall I portray the beauty that charms the heart or sing of purity unstained? Shall I tell of heroic valour or weave romance of their vivacity of intellect and their lore? The inhabitants of this land are religious, affectionate,

hospitable, genial and frank. They are fond of scientific pursuits, inclined to austerity of life, seekers after justice, contented, industrious, capable in affairs, loyal, truthful, and constant.

The soil of India is for the most part arable and of such productive power that the same land is sown each year and in many places three harvests and more are taken in a single twelve months and the vine bears fruit in its first year.

Although Akbar proudly boasts in one of his letters that the land revenue from the newly conquered territory of Ahmadnagar alone exceeded those of Transoxiana, Turkestan and Khwarazm, a nostalgic love for the unseen world of his ancestral domain evidently continued to haunt him and his successors. Whenever there was turmoil in Turan, the Mughal rulers in India were always eager to seize the opportunity to wrest any slice of their lost ancestral domain, as is clearly evident in the wistful desire and ambitious plans of Babur. In his letter to Humayun written in 1528-9, Babur expressed his joy at the opportunity provided by Shah Tahmasp's victory over the Uzbeks. Babur instructed Humayun to proceed to Hisar, Samarqand, Herat or 'to whatever side favours fortune' since 'in many decades comes such a chance as this.' . . . [6] Informing Humayun that the 'Kamran and Kabul begs have orders to join him', Babur exhorted his son to 'risk life and slash swords' so that 'if through God's grace, Balkh and Hisar countries be won and held, put men of thine in Hisar, Kamran's men in Balkh. Should Samarqand also be won, there make thy seat. Hisar, God willing, I shall make a crown domain. Should Kamran regard Balkh as small, represent the matter to me; please God, I will make its defects good at once out of those other countries.'[7] But Babur's high hopes were belied as Turan could never be reconquered. In the later years of Mughal rule, the longing for the lost 'ancestral domain' continued to linger. Akbar's circumspection and expedient policy made him concentrate the extension and consolidation of his empire within India rather than involving himself in non-productive ventures beyond the Hindukush. His successors, however, were drawn into the whirlwind of a reckless imperialist ambition, and hence in many ways the Mughal empire had to pay the price for the adventures of the north-western frontier campaigns under Shahjahan and Aurangzeb.

As has already been discussed, in the first decade of the sixteenth century, the Timurid and the Turcoman states fell apart and two new states came into existence in West Asia and Central Asia. The borders of the two states, Turan and Iran, ruled by the Uzbeks and the Safavids respectively, were contiguous, except that the river Amur separated the two lands. Mutual rivalry and persistent hostility between the two were, therefore, inevitable as their imperialistic adventures could only succeed at the expense of each other's territorial possessions. Although these new states had earlier formed the provinces of a large empire (those of the Umayyads and the Abbasids) and therefore for this and many other reasons, they shared many common features, they became two separate and distinct entities in the early sixteenth century. They came to differ from each other in their racial, lingual, sectarian, and to a great extent even in their socio-cultural formations and traditions. The upsurge of the Shia 'warriors of faith', who zealously organized their co-religionists into political force, established a Persian state, emerging as a rival (though inadvertently) to the Sunni empires of the Ottomans and the Uzbeks. Large-scale migrations (whether voluntary or forced) resulted in the reshuffling of populations. The Sunni Muslims trickled from the Shia Persia of the Safavids to the Sunni Transoxiana of the Uzbeks and vice versa. The three states in the region, namely, the Uzbek Turan, the Ottoman Turkey and the Mughal India, happened to owe their allegiances to the Sunni faith, and had no bone of contention between themselves (except Qandahar between the Mughals and the Safavids) to embitter their relations. While the Uzbeks could, therefore, rely upon their Sunni neighbours like the Ottomans, the Safavids had no such reliable and permanent allies bound to them by ties of a 'common faith' (so extensively exploited in the sixteenth century for political ends).

Apart from 'sectarian differences', Persia had several other serious differences with the above-mentioned states which led to discord. Due to geographical proximity, the extension of the Uzbek empire was possible only at the expense of Persia, which was geopolitically important, commercially prosperous, and fertile. As the Ottoman empire was keen to control all the maritime trade routes, its interest in the flourishing part of Hormuz, the Red Sea trade, and the Indian Ocean was sure to bring it into conflict not only with the Persians but also (at times) with the Portuguese; and the Portuguese particularly in the Indian Ocean, were a constant threat to the Ottomans who wanted to eliminate them. The occasional case of Portuguese-Persian friendship, therefore, was not surprising. The commercial and strategic significance of Persia and its carpet and silk industries and the fertility of its soil always excited the cupidity of its neighbours. Thus, Persia had to face alternately and almost continually the ambitions and the expansionist ventures of the Ottomans and the Uzbeks. Since the czars of Russia had their eye on Transoxiana, they not only instigated the Qazaqs to invade Uzbek Khan but they also sought friendly relations with Persia. Thus, Persia could manage to win the temporary support of the Portuguese, the Russians, and later on of the English, each of whom had their own vested interests and wanted to use Persia only as a counterpoise to their respective rivals. It is interesting to note that the Uzbeks and the Ottomans had, awaited with much anticipation, the dissolution of Persia (and its subsequent division between themselves) in the sixteenth century in the same way as Russia and England had dreamed of having their share in its territories and had looked forward to its disintegration in the nineteenth century.

With India, the Persians had a bone of contention. The disputed territory of Qandahar led to situations ranging from a cold war to armed struggle. Nevertheless, the Persians almost always responded to every call of help from the Mughals as and when necessary. Not only had Shah Ismail assisted Babur against the Uzbeks but Tahmasp (1524-76) had also ensured the restoration of the lost empire of Humayun. Shah Abbas (1588-1629) maintained friendly relations with Akbar and Jahangir, and keenly responded to the call for help from the Deccan Shia states of Golconda and Bijapur and even pleaded their case with Akbar.

Indo-Persian relations were far more complex and complicated than Indo-Uzbek relations where the bonds of kindered and kinship relations still existed. Babur's appraisal of the Iranians and the Turanians offers fair evidence of how the Mughals in the early sixteenth century evaluated their neighbours' characters. The views expressed by Babur in his letter (dated April-May 1526) to Kamran are indicative of his opinion about these two different peoples. The letter is written in the Uzbek language and offers the following comment regarding the Turanis: 'The people of Tansoxiana (Turanis) are simple but when they have brains, they are worthy of trust and office.'[8] An appreciation of the services rendered by the Uzbeks (other than the ruling dynasty) in the consolidation of Akbar's regime is acknowledged by Abul Fazl in the *Akbar Nama*. As against this, the attitude towards the Iranis smacks of prejudice. Babur comments:

> Though the Khurasanis are a pleasant folk, and there can be no question about their cleverness, there is doubt about their religions and their principles, and they are a nation of . . . agitators. The sons are alienated from the fathers and the fathers from the sons. Do not be deceived by their plausible ways and for your own safety's sake, do not let them go out of control.[9]

Humayun had also warned Shah Sulaiman of Turkey that he 'should not put faith in the Qizilsah'.[10] Indeed, Babur had his own reasons, and very genuine ones, for his hostile attitude. Notwithstanding the assistance offered by Shah Ismail to Babur for the reconquest of Turan, the very terms and conditions on which this help had been granted carried with them the seeds of Babur's expulsion from Turan. The orthodox Sunni population of Turan hated seeing Babur in Persian attire and listening to the *khutba* with the names of the twelve Imams and that of Shah Ismail inserted in accordance with the demand of Shah Ismail. In order to dissociate himself from the 'Shia heretics' and to extricate himself from the mire of religious controversy surrounding his own faith, Babur was vociferous in criticising Shiism as well as denigrating the Iranians.

As the luck would have it, Babur's own son Humayun also had to fall back upon the mercy of the Persians when he was expelled from India by Sher Shah. Shah Tahmasp could appreciate Humayun's difficulty as he himself had faced 'similar troubles' due to his (Tahmasp's) rebellious brother Alqas Mirza.[11] Tahmasp offered a regal welcome to Humayun, assuring the fugitive king that 'so much good fortune and success would ensue that the high and low of India, Turkestan, Iran and Turan will see and wonder and these will be talked [about] for ages and that [the] Emperor's enemies will be reduced to dust and darkness of Kufr (heresy)'.[12] Even when some misunderstanding did crop up, Shah Tahmasp did not hand over Humayun to Kamran as this could 'obliterate the sacred heritage of Sultan Safi'. All these assurances, however, soon evaporated and Qandahar was captured by Tahmasp's forces as soon as Humayun managed to reconquer India with the help of the Persians. It is interesting to note that the Mughals did not even spare their traditional supporters, i.e. the Persians, when the question of Qandahar was involved. Such was Akbar's anger over the loss of Qandahar that the umpteen embassies sent by Shah Tahmasp and Shah Abbas remained unanswered until Akbar managed to wrest Qandahar from the Persians. There was certainly a rupture in their relations and this did not go unnoticed. In one of his letters, Shah Abbas emphasized that friendly relations had existed between the two dynasties ever since the days of Timur. The same cordiality continued up to the reigns of Babur and Humayun. Shah Abbas attributed the coldness of their relationship to Akbar's attitude. Even the hopes of Daniyal that the conquest of Ahmadnagar and Asirgadh and the proximity of Gujarat and the Deccan to the Persian ports of Hormuz and Bahrain were likely to promote closer relations between the Mughals and the Persians were belied.[13] The embassy sent by Khudabanda under Ali Quli Sultan Hamadan Oghli[14] and the subsequent embassies sent by Shah Abbas were cordially received but no return embassy was sent until 1596, that is after the occupation of Qandahar by Mughal forces in 1593. During these years of Akbar's silence, Shah Abbas had continued to maintain friendly relations with Prince Salim.

Akbar preferred to play it safe in the game of regional politics. In response to Abdullah's veiled threats (as conveyed through his letter of 1586) warning Akbar against giving any possible material or moral support to the Safavids, Akbar resorted to a policy of conciliation and shock therapy. On the one hand, Akbar expressed his intention of proceeding to Iraq and Khurasan to offer military assistance to the Shahs of Persia who were the descendants of the Prophet and were also closely connected with the Timurid dynasty by ancient ties. On the other hand, an incessant stream of letters were sent by Akbar's confidantes (including Abul Fazl and Abulfath Gilani) exhorting Hakim Humam (Akbar's envoy to Abdullah Khan) to expedite the arrangements of a treaty (*Sulh Nama*) acceptable to Akbar.[15] Almost simultaneously, the envoys of the Persian Shahs were warmly received and given the *congé* without any letter or response from the Mughal side. It was only after his own conquest of Qandahar that Akbar confirmed Abdullah's proposal that the 'Hindukush should form the boundary between the two Kingdoms'.[16]

After the death of Abdullah Khan, the north-west frontier of India became insecure and consequently turned into a source of constant trouble and anxiety. Border politics with its promising prospects now attracted his attention. In his letter to Baqi Muhammad of Transoxiana, Akbar asked him to refrain from undertaking hostile actions against Mirza Badi-uz Zaman who had recaptured Badakhshan in 1601 and who had read the *khutba* in Akbar's name. But the prince was defeated, captured, and killed.[17]

Akbar's policy of *Sulh-i-kul* (peace with all) and his relations with external powers (particularly with the neighbouring countries) were the result of a well-thought-out and carefully considered action plan evolved keeping in mind the needs of the political situation in India. The policy of *Sulh-i-kul* was as much a modified version of the Hindu philosopher and religious teacher Shankar's motto '*Vasudhaiv Kutumbakam*' as it was an echo of '*Lahilfa fil Islam*' (there are no confederations in Islam). Whatever be its origin, the policy of *Sulh-i-kul* was the harbinger of the principle of co-existence and a precept heralding the present-day policy of non-alignment. A monarch of Akbar's stature and political acumen could indeed initiate high-level diplomacy and maintain active foreign relations, but he continued to pursue a policy of circumspection abroad and consolidation at home which paid him dividends in the long run. In response to the many letters and envoys which he received from the rulers of Persia, Turan, and other places, Akbar sent only two letters to Abdullah Khan of Turan, one to Shah Abbas I of Persia, and one or two each to the rulers of Kashghar, Tibet and Spain, and one to the Sherif of Mecca. From the very beginning, therefore, he wanted to retain Kabul and Qandahar under his sway as a bulwark against external invaders. While Kabul remained a part of India, Qandahar proved to be a problematic possession as both the Safavids and the Mughals wanted to retain it. Explaining his attitude towards the Uzbeks, Akbar affirmed 'that he was never willing to wage war against one who seeks peaceful and friendly relations'.[18]

Apart from conflicting ideologies, Akbar also had a number of other points of disagreement with Abdullah Khan. Indeed, the loss of the Timurid domain of Badakhshan and the flight of Mirza Shah Rukh to India was a bitter reminder of the expulsion of Babur. In his letter to Raja Ali Khan of Khandesh, Akbar stated that during his sojourn in Kabul, he had toyed with the idea of 'liberating' Badakhshan from the Uzbeks and handing it over to Mirza Shah-Rukh but he gave up the idea on the repeated entreaties of Abdullah Khan.[19] Abdul Momin's misdemeanour over the question of the *aimaqs* of Badakhshan; Abdullah's threatening attitude as reflected in his two letters of 1586; the suspected Uzbek designs on Kabul and Qandahar; and the annoying incursions on the Indian borders only added fuel to the fire.

The Uzbeks considered the Mughals as an important balancing power whose slightest tilt towards Persia could disturb the prospects of Uzbek peace and progress in the region. The Ottomans had no enmity with the Uzbeks, and their sectarian affinity, common interests, and shared enmity against Persia brought them even closer to each other. Thus, the Persians had to face alternately and almost continually the ambitious and the expansionist ventures of the Ottomans and the Uzbeks.

The Deccan factor was also quite important in Indo-Persian political relations. Sectarian affinity brought the rulers of the Deccan and the Safavids closer to each other and they both often shared common views on many matters. Shah Abbas I wrote to Sultan Muhammad Qutb Shah that the 'excesses and tyranny perpetrated by the Chaghatai forces on the frontiers of the Qutb Shahi kingdom and the forces being collected by the Mughal nobles for invading the Deccan must be prevented and nipped in the bud'.[20] In a letter to Shah Abbas, one of the Deccan rulers insisted that the main 'reason[s] for this harassment are the religious and political bonds which this kingdom has firmly established with the Safavids'.[21] In later years also, letters with sectarian overtones were written by Sultan Abdullah Qutb Shah (1626-72) to Shah Abbas II. Referring to Safavid support and sanction for the past 170 years, the Golconda ruler implored that sectarian regard and solidarity should be the cementing force and a guarantee for Safavid cooperation. It is interesting to note that the Deccan rulers always managed to wrest enough support and recommendations from the Safavids.[22] In 1613 or earlier, Shah Abbas had recommended that Quli Qutb Shah 'who was devoted to Shah Abbas be forgiven as there existed traditional bonds of attachment and devotion'[23] between the rulers of the Deccan and Safavid Persia. Moved by sectarian affinity, the Persian rulers often pleaded on behalf of the Deccan rulers. Shah Abbas I recommended in 1616-17 that the 'faults and blunders of the Deccan rulers may be forgiven. If any transgression is noticed, their chastisement should be left to the Shah. Let the world appreciate the mutual regard and accord existing between the two dynasties.[24] At times the Safavids recommended certain persons for better prospects and certain posts. Surprisingly, such recommendations almost always met with a curt reply by the Mughal court, that stating appointments were made not through recommendations but on the basis of merit. The Safavids, interference in the political affairs of the Deccan further inflamed Akbar, who viewed the extra-territorial relations of the Deccan rulers with suspicion.

With Jahangir's accession, however, Indo-Persian relations took a new turn. Jahangir had almost always liked the Persians better than the Uzbeks. Whether it was due to the influence of his Persian wife Nurjahan and the much publicized *junta* or because of recurring Uzbek revolts during his father's reign and the resultant disenchantment with the Uzbek nobility, Jahangir preferred Persians, who now dominated the Mughal court at all levels owing largely to their own inherent efficiency as *ahl-i-qalam* (men of the pen) as much as to the two factors mentioned above. The change did not go unnoticed. In his letter to Jahangir (dated 1612), Mirza Aziz Kuka complained that 'for fifty years under Akbar the Chaghatais and the Rajputs flourished and multiplied. They were always loyal to the Emperor. When Jahangir ascended the throne he ignored and bypassed both these communities and enlisted all power and privileges into the hands of Persians and Indian Muslims who excelled in nothing but mischief mongering and treachery.'[25]

Presumably Jahangir's emotional bonds and political liaisons with the Persians within Indian environs emanated from fear. Initially, he wanted to use the Persians as a counterpoise to the then unreliable Turani nobility. But these men of the pen, with all their medieval efficiency, soon made themselves indispensable to the ease-loving Jahangir. This fraternity proved to be dangerous when it extended to an extra-territorial relationship. In the numerous letters sent to Jahangir by Shah Abbas, there was an emphasis on cultivating mutual concord and cherishing a friendship based on hereditary sanctity and continuity. To Shah Abbas, even Jahangir's purchasing missions seemed to smack of 'indifference'. Jahangir could follow the example of his father or else he could directly ask for the desired commodities from his 'dearest brother'. Shah Abbas's soothing words had always boosted the morale of the young disheartened prince who was then desperately fighting for his rights. The political myopia of Jahangir enabled the enterprising Abbas to fulfil his imperialist ambitions of conquering Qandahar.

During Jahangir's reign, however, Akbar's careful, studied, and calculated foreign policy and his the realpolitik were replaced by inertia and indifference. Jahangir's penchant for Persians his love for, their culture and art, made for a 'full and complete unison' exclusively with the Persians. He had been drawn to them ever since the days when his accession to the throne was not guaranteed. The letters of Shah Abbas I to Prince Salim brim with exaggerated expressions of amity, such as 'the friendship between Shah Abbas and Prince Salim is spiritual and cannot find full expression in material ways'.[26] In order to ratify the long-standing friendship between the two dynasties, Shah Abbas had even sent a copy of the document of the region to Timur (found during excavations at the village of Khwaja Dukohak during one of Shah Abbas's campaigns at Andkhud), confirming Timur's friendship with the ancestors of the Safavids. When Khwaja Burj Ali Nakhchwani brought a list from Salim containing the names of certain rarities which were to be procured from Iran, Shah Abbas supplied all the articles from the imperial stores and complained that Salim had taken the trouble to send merchants and insisted that in future Salim should write to him directly.[27] Such was the cordiality between Jahangir and Shah Abbas that the former grew complacent and withdrew most of the Mughal forces from Qandahar during Khurram's rebellion. This enabled Shah Abbas to reoccupy Qandahar without much trouble, though Jahangir was stunned by this breach of trust. Thus, outmanoeuvred by the Shah, Jahangir reacted very sharply and soon after in his *nishan* (dated December 1622) to Mir Baraka, Jahangir used denigrating language for the Shah, branding him as 'ill-natured, ungrateful' (*Abbas-i bad asas-haq na shinas*).[28] Recalling how Shah Abbas had almost always professed sincerity to him and that he himself had shown favour and honoured him (Abbas) with numerous valuable gifts, Jahangir stressed that the Shah had played false because of religious differences (*Mukhalafat-i Mazhab wa taassub*) and his own fanatical views. It had, therefore, become obligatory on him to chastise the Shah. The amicability thus turned into bitter enmity, and once again religious and sectarian beliefs which then both shared threats of a common political foe were emphasized to win over allies and sympathizers in the region.[29] In his letter to Imam Quli sent through Mir Baraka, Jahangir once again played the same old tune of sectarian similarity and predicted the victory of Sunnism if Shah Abbas, the emblem of heresy and Shiism, was not removed from the scene. Jahangir also persuaded the Uzbeks, not Imam Quli Khan, to rise against the Persians. In his letter of 1628, he emphasized that the 'mutual accord of the two dynasties concealed for long became manifest' and in this way, the Khan could also settle his old scores (*intiqam-i derina*) against the Safavids.[30] Reminding Imam Quli of the fact that Akbar used to address the Khan as his son, Jahangir emphasized these brotherly relations between them. Certain secret proposals were conveyed through the Khwaja (Mir Baraka). The common creed of the Mughals and the Uzbeks was also highlighted and 'for the sake of their religion and community', the Khan was requested to 'wholeheartedly cooperate in attaining their common aim'.[31] In the *nishan* to Mir Baraka Jahangir also emphasized, 'Thank God, he (the Emperor) and the Khan are of the same faith and, therefore, duty bound to cooperate'[32] in the proposed war against the Persians.

Fully aware of these proposed bilateral agreements, Shah Abbas too started seeking allies. Immediately after the conquest of Qandahar in June 1622, he wrote to the Ottoman Sultan, Usman II (1618-22), about his conquest of Qandahar and the adjoining areas and requested the Sultan 'to inform him whenever the Sultan intended to proceed against the firangis so that he [the Shah] may also come forward to assist his co-religionists and send [the] Persian army to take part in the holy war against the Portuguese under the banner of the Ottomans'.[33] Nevertheless, the Ottoman Sultan's letter to Jahangir, sent in 1625, shows that the Ottomans were still unmoved as by this plea, shown by the comment that 'the Ottomans have been engaged in extirpating the misguided sect. Ottoman commanders and armies will be sent against Shah Abbas, the most mischievous of men, in case he attacks and ravages any part of the Indian territory. If the Emperor also attacks from the Indian side, the destruction of the Shias is certain.' A similar fate awaited Jahangir as the Uzbeks had not forgotten the cordial Indo-Persian relations in the past; her had they overlooked the fact that Jahangir's relations with Shah Abbas had soured only when Qandahar was lost to the Persians. The Uzbek ruler Imam Quli of Turan, however, seized this opportunity and exhorted Jahangir to support the cause of the Uzbeks in the same way as Akbar had done. In his letter (written in 1625), Imam Quli showed his eagerness to avenge the murder of his own father Din Muhammad but stressed the fact that

> the object (of the reconquest of Turan) cannot be achieved without securing the obedience and allegiance of royal princes and nobles. It is, therefore, strongly recommended that [the] prince [Shahjahan] who had strayed onto a rebellious path on account of sanguine youthfulness and immaturity be pardoned and given full assurance of royal favours. Thereafter, an army should be sent to collaborate with the Uzbeks in reopening the passage to Mecca for the benefit of pilgrims of all lands.[34]

These attempts at persuasion did not have any effect, presumably because the conditional offer and recommendations made on behalf of Prince Khurram had infuriated Jahangir.

Incidentally, this was an opportunity to establish a tripartite alliance, and the two bitter enemies (the Ottomans and the Uzbeks) of the Persians were to wage war against the Shah. Encouraged by the capture of Baghdad, the Ottoman Sultan now dreamed of exterminating the Persians. Playing upon the grievances of the Uzbeks, Sultan Murad III instigated them in 1624 to wrest Iran from the Persians. Simultaneously, the Sultan also prompted Jahangir to recover Qandahar. But no agreement seemed to be forthcoming. Curiously enough, the three major powers in the region, namely, Turkey, Turan and India, never undertook a joint venture against Persia though the epistolary records prove that an exchange of letters to this effect had taken place.[35] The Uzbek rulers explored the possibility of an alliance with Akbar against the Persians. The Ottoman rulers like Salim the Grim and Sulaiman had invited Uzbek cooperation before fighting the Persians. Shahjahan's overtures to the Ottoman Sultan and the Astrakhanid rulers for a combined operation against Persia met with a similar fate. Thus, the relations between these states were determined mainly by the exclusive and individual interests of a particular country. As the political situation changed, attitudes also shifted. These fluctuating views and perceptions were as frequent and rapid as the vicissitudes in the fortunes of the rulers themselves and the shifting frontiers of their states.

While still a prince, Shahjahan had written letters to Shah Abbas I convincing the latter that he (Shahjahan) had obtained permission from Jahangir to open correspondence with the Shah. In his letter to Shah Abbas, Shahjahan expressed his sincerity and requested the Shah to indicate if he liked anything from the samples of things available in India and which were being sent by the Mughal ruler as *yadbud*.[36] The Shah sent his reply only after the Persians had conquered Qandahar. Explaining that the delay was due to the fact that he was waiting for permission from Jahangir to open correspondence with the prince, the Shah asserted that the bonds of Persian amity and friendship with the Mughal dynasty were too strong to be broken by 'petty mundane affairs'.[37] The claim was true at least in one context, when Prince Khurram (Shahjahan) had rebelled against Jahangir and asked the Shah for help in 1622, reminding the Shah of his promised support in case of need and also of the fact that 'it was the hereditary practice of Mughal emperors to seek assistance from the Safavid rulers',[38] the Shah failed to send succour. Instead, he advised the prince to be obedient to his father.[39] Shahjahan did not appreciate this gesture. Like Akbar, Shahjahan too refrained from writing to Shah Abbas though the latter sent him a number of letters. It was only after the accession of Shah Safi that Shahjahan despatched the embassy. Shahjahan was conscious of his own power and boasted in his letter to Jahangir that 'there is none like me in warfare from India to Iraq',[40] and added further that 'if I had been on the battlefield, Qandahar would not have been lost'.[41] Once the conquest of Qandahar by the Mughals had removed the rancour, all military plans of aggrandisement were directed against Turan. When Qandahar was conquered by the Mughals, Qalich Khan, the Mughal governor of Qandahar, on hearing the news of the Uzbek raid on the frontiers of Qandahar, offered to send the Mughal army and its officers to assist the Persians in 1639.[42] The Uzbek incursions on Merv and Maruchaq and an attack on Khurasan by Abdul Aziz, the Uzbek ruler, in 1639 encouraged Shahjahan to plan a return to Kabul and send the Mughal forces to conquer Badakhshan since Transoxiana (Turan) happened to be the *gorkhana* (cemetry) of his ancestors and also because the Uzbeks had invaded the Kabul marches during his first regnal year. Shahjahan was keen to chastise the Uzbeks and to recover his ancestral lands. At this juncture, a number of letters written by Hasan Khan of Herat assured Shahjahan that if he intended to march against Turkestan, the Persian forces in accordance with the standing orders of the Shah would come forward to help him.[43]

Thus, the policy of reconciliation and peaceful coexistence with neighbouring countries took a new and aggressive turn under the enterprising and energetic Shahjahan who was keen to undertake reconquest of Qandahar, the occupation of Turan, and the subjugation of the Deccan. Fluctuations in his relations with the Shahs of Persia and the Khans of Turan were, therefore, inevitable.[44] Shahjahan's letters written to the Uzbek rulers confirm that the Mughals needed the cooperation of the Uzbeks (or at least their neutrality) in affairs relating to Qandahar and that they wanted to use the Uzbeks as a counterpoise against the Persians. The three letters sent to Nazar Muhammad in 1647 by various persons from Shahjahan's court reveal the undercurrents of apprehension and fear generated by the concern that the growing Uzbek-Persian closeness would result in Mughal isolation. These letters refer to the following points: the Shah of Persia had committed an act of gross fraud (*ghabn-i-fahish*) by not delivering the cordial letters sent by Shahjahan to Nazar Muhammad during the latter's sojourn in Persia. A copy of the same letter was, therefore, enclosed; expressions of regrets over the misdemeanour of Rustam Khan (who had entered the fort when Nazar Muhammad happened to be inside), and his own inability to show due respect to the Khan; the letter takes a strong view of the fact that the Khan should have approached Shahjahan (in the face of such provocations) instead of proceeding to Iran and returning from there 'empty handed'.[45] In 1636, Shahjahan had even proposed a tripartite treaty (between India, Turan and Turkey) against Persia. Reasons were not wanting for a vendetta as Imam Quli of Turan was keen on avenging the murder of his father. Sultan Murad of Turkey was equally eager for war against the Persians but the situation was still not ripe for a joint venture. In his letter of June 1650, Shahjahan offered generous help for ventures in the present and in the future, and bestowed a sum of one lakh rupees to encourage the Khan to undertake anti-Persian activities. Although Shahjahan explained that 'he has no motive in doing so except to earn a name and lasting fame', his criticism of Shah Abbas indicates his other interests in this matter. Shahjahan criticized Shah Abbas for his short-sightedness and improper conduct in seizing Qandahar, as well as describing his own recent withdrawal from the attempted conquest of Qandahar due to the approaching winter and the shortage of fodder.[46] All these exercises were, however, futile as the Uzbek Khan died the same year (1650).

The Turco-Mongol rulers and their descendants in India (i.e. the Mughals) eschewed bigotry and sectarian chauvinism, and anticipated in many ways the philosophy of Anabaptists of sixteenth-century England. The religious persecution and genocide then going on in the region was, therefore, neither understood nor appreciated by the pantheist Akbar.

In his letter to Humayun, Tahmasp claimed that 'this similarity in temporal circumstances (of exile and [his] brother's rebellion) is fully matched by their mutual identity in spiritual and religious beliefs'. Similarly, Shah Abbas I also claimed that 'the same wine from the same divine tavern was poured in the tumblers of both of them (i.e. Akbar and Abbas)'. The surroundings and circumstances in which the Mughals and the Persians were placed evidently dictated the adoption of entirely different philosophies of life religious policies. While appreciating Akbar's high qualities and recalling the abiding amity and age-old ties of friendship between the two dynasties, Shah Abbas discarded Akbar's policy of *Sulhikul*, brushed aside Akbar's criticism of genocide, and finally asserted that 'each one of the Prophets urged war on the *ashqiya* (tyrants or criminals)'. Such a reaction is understandable from a person who had helplessly watched as his territory was conquered by his adversaries, the Uzbeks and the Ottomans. Elsewhere the Shah gave a somewhat modified version of his attitude. Once Shah Abbas I had strengthened his position and managed to recover his lost territories, he even played an important role in the internal politics of Turan. By 1611 the two rulers of Turan, namely Imam Quli and Nazar Muhammad, with their centres of power at Bukhara and Balkh respectively, maintained friendly relations with Persia. In his letter (1621) to Husain Khwaja Juibari (son of Abdurrahim Khwaja and grandson of Khwaja Kalan), Shah Abbas expressed a solidarity of view with the Khwaja over the subject of the elimination of the causes of strife between Iran and Turan. While professing his solicitude for the welfare of the people and his own preference for peace and amity over war and hostility, the Shah further assured the Khwaja that he himself 'stands pledged to preserve mutual peace and would do everything to strengthen it'.[47] Furthermore, in response to Khwaja Abdurrahim's pleas that the Persian Shah should follow a lenient policy towards the Uzbek rulers, ignoring the errors, committed by the latter, Shah Abbas I asserted in his letter of August 1622 that he himself 'prefers *Musalaha* (mutual peace; reconciliation) to *munazara* (strife)'. Imploring that the Uzbeks should also abide by a mutual agreement and giving the assurance that 'no breach of its arkan (terms, elements) would occur', Shah Abbas promised to (and in fact did) confer 'favours and bounties on Uzbek rulers in deference to [the] Khwaja's entreaties'.[48]

During the following two decades, the Persians continued to assure the Mughals of their cooperation if and when they wanted it against the Uzbeks. Shahjahan's campaigns in Balkh and Badakhshan were, however, fought without Persian cooperation. Shahjahan justified the action on the part of the Mughals because the 'Uzbeks disobeyed their rulers and the lawlessness that ensued resulted in large-scale massacres in which even the Saiyids were not spared.' In his reply to Shahjahan's letter, Shah Abbas II adopted a patronizing tone and in a way retaliated by offering the same explanations that were usually given by the Mughals in response to Persian demands for help. Shah Abbas's claim that 'in the absence of any hostilities and due to [the] weak condition of the Uzbeks, it was not thought proper to interfere in their internal matters' seems to be an echo of Akbar's explanations to Shah Abbas I for not offering him assistance. With a big brotherly attitude, Shah Abbas II wrote to Shahjahan (in 1647) regarding Nazar Muhammad's arrival in Iran: 'The emperor Shahjahan's recommendation to show due respect to the Khan and provide him with regal hospitality was uncalled for as there was never a denial of hospitality for a guest at the Safavid Court.' Referring to Uzbek Khan's sole aim of seeking succour to take revenge and liberate his country, he explained that, 'all the advice given to him to avoid hasty action and to wait until a Persian envoy could go to India and recommend his case to the Emperor and arrange terms, proved futile'.[49] On hearing about the withdrawal of the Mughal forces from Balkh and Badakhshan, Shah Abbas II stated that he appreciated this 'generosity' and requested, in 1648, that a similar benevolence also be shown by bestowing Qandahar on the Safavids, though ultimately Qandahar had to be wrested from the Mughals by force of arms.

Akbar also maintained diplomatic relations with the rulers of Little Tibet and Great Tibet. Ever since the conquest of Kashmir by Akbar, the Tibetan rulers 'had continually made supplications'.[50] Abul Fazl would have us believe that Akbar had his eyes on Tibet but had to postpone his plans due to scarcity as it was difficult to provide soldiers with the necessary provisions for forty days.[51] Although no other information in the Tibetan sources is presently available in this regard, a casual reference to Indo-Tibetan relations pointing to the fear of the Tibetan rulers can be gleaned from the sources. In 991 AH, Haji Mirza Beg Kabuli brought the daughter of Ali Rai (ruler of Little Tibet) to be betrothed to the eldest prince.[52] The matrimonial alliance was formed probably to ward off the ominous possibility of Akbar's advance towards Tibet. The Tibetan sources confirm that when civil war broke out in 1727-8, 'Po-tha-nas tried to destroy lum-pa-nas, the Na'ris and g-Tsan begged Po-tha-nas to retire to Na'ris and return with a large army. If, however, this was too difficult Po-tha-nas could always bribe the Emperor of Delhi and the job could be done in ten days.' But they also deliberately raised the bogey of religion in order to frighten those looking to the Mughals for support, saying, 'To call in the Mughals from India would mean the end of Buddhism in Tibet.'[53] It is interesting to note that Akbar's contacts with the lamas of Tibet and his own eclecticism were not a secret. Abul Fazl writes 'Lamas of Tibet broke my peace.'[54] Akbar held long discussions on the night of Shivratri not only with the Yogis of India but also with the lamas of Tibet and the hermits of Cathay; following their practices, he abstained from meat and curtailed his consumption of food and drink. Akbar's keenness to know more about Tibet is clearly evident from the fact that a treatise was written concerning the manners, customs, and religious sects of the Tibetans based on the accounts of Mirza Beg and Mulla Talib Isfahani who had visited the place twice in their capacity as ambassadors.[55]

Tibet also offered certain commercial possibilities, as walrus teeth and sables were much in demand in the rest of Asia. Gold was also found in abundance in the region.[56] If Badauni's account is to be trusted, all the products of the country of Tibet could be had in Wajrai (near Ajmer). [57] Since *cowries* were the staple currency, the shells were imported from India.[58]

The rulers of Kashghar and the Mughals had established diplomatic relations. Both Humayun and Akbar sent letters to Abdur Rashid Khan of Kashghar. Khwaja Abdulbari Naqshbandi, sent by Humayun on a mission to Kashghar, returned only after Akbar's accession. Akbar's letter to the ruler of Kashghar had two main points. In the first place, Akbar insisted that 'all contemporary monarchs keep on sending embassies in order to cultivate cordial relations with Akbar and he expected the same from the ruler of Kashghar'. Second, Akbar showed his keenness to know everything about Kashghar 'out of his usual curiosity', though he admited that 'after the conquest of Kashmir (by Akbar), the distance between the frontiers of Mughal India and Kashghar had been reduced'. The ruler of Kashghar was especially requested to supply to Akbar detailed information about the ruler of China, as well as information on wars, administration of justice, religious beliefs, men of learning, artists and craftsmen. The professed reason for this curiosity about China was that a certain world-roving merchant named Fattaha at Akbar's court wished to visit China.[59] The cordial relations between the two states continued even during the reign of Jahangir who not only wrote letters to Shujauddin Ahmad of Kashghar but also sent some of the choicest Indian products as *yadbud*.[60]

Protected by natural barriers on three sides, through the Himalayas and the Indian Ocean, India was exposed to external threats only from its north-west frontier. Invaders came at frequent intervals from the lands beyond the Hindukush mountains, that is from Persia, Kabul, and Turan (Transoxiana). Apart from the Greeks, the Huns, the Turks, and other invaders, the Mughals themselves had arrived in India by the same old route and were, therefore, always vigilant to guard their north-western frontier. From the very beginning of their rule in India, the Mughals had emphasized the importance of Kabul and Qandahar as the 'twin gates' to India, a description which was also echoed, by Abul Fazl, Sujan Rai Bhandari and others. The Mughals wanted to bring Kabul and Qandahar under their sway and keep them as buffer states or as bulwarks against foreign invaders. While Kabul remained a part of the Mughal empire, Qandahar was occupied alternately by the Safavids and the Mughals through stratagems or by conquests. Although some of the letters (for instance, Shah Abbas's letter to Shahjahan and Hasan Khan's letter to Qilich Khan) do emphasize that the 'occupation of Qandahar by one party or the other has never led to [the] termination of friendship between the two dynasties', a complete though temporary rupture in relation or a diplomatic silence always followed such aggressive ventures. The frontiers of each of these regions remained exposed to danger, and the bordering territories had fluctuating frontiers and ever changing masters. While Khurasan, Meshed, Isfarain, Nishapur, Keraili and Sabzwar were often wrested from the Persians by the Uzbeks, the territory of Qandahar long remained a bone of contention between India and Persia. For the Ottomans of Turkey, the Baghdad-Aleppo and the Tabriz-Bursa Silk Road was a major attraction, and Diyari Bakr, Tabriz, and Baghdad bore the brunt of the Ottoman invasions. The Afghans, Hazaras, Baluchis, Raushnais and other tribal populations created trouble for all the four powers alike. The Badakhshan rulers, given their past connections with the Mughals, were a constant disturbing factor for the Uzbeks. Externally, Imam Quli received presents from the rulers of India and Istanbul, but internally the Qazaqs and the Qalpaqs created trouble for him,[61] presumably at Russian instigation. Since the days of Akbar, the Raushnais under Jalala, having failed to receive help from Abdullah Khan Uzbek of Turan, stirred up the Afridis and the Urukzai Afghans.[62]

In their relations with their neighbouring countries, the medieval sovereigns were as adept in counting the enemies of their enemy as friends (and using them as countervailing forces) as any modern nation-state would do. Thus, the Ottomans gladly utilized the services of the rulers of Sind and Gujarat, Egypt and Turan, setting them as counterweights against their own sworn enemies (i.e. the Portuguese and the Persians). The Ottomans were not satisfied merely with direct confrontations with their enemies and also supplied the munitions, arms and armaments, artillery and soldiers to those who could wage war against the Persians and the Portuguese. For instance, the Turkish Admiral Sidi Ali Reis was despatched to Turan and Gujarat (along with war equipment and soldiers) and convoys were sent to the Mumluks of Egypt. Although the medieval kings belonged to warlike tribes and martial races, they were neither bellicose nor recklessly gallant like Don Quixote. Their relations with the external powers were usually based on well-thought-out strategies and sound statesmanship. Expressions of amity and friendship as noticed in the epistolary records were not matched by circumstantial evidence and political actions on the ground. The exigencies of the situation, political pressures, and regional and global factors all influenced their foreign policy, despite the expressions of cordiality and amity. Pragmatism was the keynote in the conduct of foreign relations, and external relations were almost always dictated by expediency and realpolitik. Imperial interests were paramount during the medieval period. Proposals for a tripartite treaty and for joint ventures were as feverishly and enthusiastically discussed as the need for mutual support (both material and moral) was considered. But a combined operation against any one power was never attempted as each state had to safeguard its own aims and objectives and each sought to pursue its own course of action.

Another permanent feature of foreign relations among these states was a continual concern for the well-being of the nation. Whatever be the status and standing of these states in the regional or global context (whether they were satellites under the spell of a big power or whether they fell within its sphere of influence; whether they were active allies of weaker states; or whether they were engaged in open and bitter hostilities, they were not prepared to sell their freedom. Their deliberately assumed stance of inert passivity and pregnant silences was ready to change very quickly on any sensitive issue. However, in the external relations of these states in the medieval period there seems to have existed some sort of a consistency based on careful consideration of important factors due to which yesterday's enemies could not quickly be turned into tomorrow's allies. The regional scenario in medieval Central Asia had, therefore, remained static. For example, the Ottomans and the Uzbeks were as friendly with each other as they were both consistently hostile towards Persia throughout the period under review (the sixteenth to the eighteenth centuries). The Mughals and the Persians had been uneasy allies; the Persians generously helped the Mughals in the hour of crisis, though the Mughals always reacted sharply to the seizure of Qandahar by the Persians. Akbar, ever the diplomat, desisted from sending condolences on the deaths of Shah Tahmasp and Hamza Mirza (elder brother of Shah Abbas), the crown prince.[63]

Thus Mughal relations with Persia and Central Asia were determined partly by internal political developments and partly by their own mutual tripartite needs and partly by global and regional perspectives and considerations. Yet there existed an *entente cordiale* between the two blocs—a very close and clear concord between the Ottomans and the Uzbeks and a more conventional understanding between the Mughals and the Persians.

Examined retrospectively in the light of some very reliable historical records (i.e. the epistolary collections), supplemented by official and private chronicles it is clearly evident that regional political relations (existing between Iran, Turkey and Turan) during that period and the diplomatic games of power politics were all played with same cunning and foresight as seen in present-day geopolitics.

In medieval times, religion was a vague form of nationalism, a unifying and binding factor. Sometimes religious sentiments were exploited for the gratification of political ends. Wars were inevitable due to regional rivalries and imperialist ambitions but they became 'holy' when clothed in the cloak of religion. Timur, a Sunni Muslim ruler, declared a 'holy war' against Turkey, a universally acknowledged Sunni state. The opening of the pilgrimage route to Mecca was a burning topic which was discussed in all the letters exchanged between the Ottomans, the Uzbeks, and the Mughals. The need to secure a protected and safe route for pilgrims to Mecca and also for traders was demanded with much vehemence and urgency by the later Mughals particularly when they were themselves eager to pursue a vendetta or to undertake expansionist wars. Akbar consistently reminded the (imperialist) 'zealots' that the conquest of Gujarat and the subjugation of the Afghans had made the Hajj pilgrimage easier as now the pilgrims could come from Turan, Khurasan, Iraq and other places to India and go to the holy places by the sea route which was cheaper and more convenient, but these reminders were ignored by the rival parties eager for war. This concern for the safety of routes to Mecca was heightened whenever the political differences between the Mughals and the Persians grew serious, and as relations with Persia deteriorated during the seventeenth century. The letters exchanged between Jahangir, Shahjahan, Imam Quli and Nazar Muhammad dwelled on the same theme. In his letter of 1687 to Aurangzeb, Subhan Quli, the Uzbek ruler of Turan, also expressed his resolve to 'destroy the Shiite power in Iran' merely 'in order to ensure complete freedom of access through Iran to Mecca so that the Muslims can go there. This intention is further strengthened owing to the proposed holy war by the Mughal rulers against the Shia heretics. If the two great powers jointly undertook the venture, the destruction of this sect was inevitable.' Subhan Quli added that 'for Muslims in general and in particular for the sovereigns who are like the limbs of the same body, it is essential to be zealous and united in such ventures'.[64]

In his letter to Islam Khan, the Wazir of Shahjahan (1639-45), the Ottoman Grand Wazir (1639-43) also emphasized the religious affinity between the two rulers. 'The bond of [the] Sunni faith ensures their mutual accord', that 'the absence of a royal reply is at variance with the need of solidarity between the Hanafi rulers.' The letter refers to the extent of the vast and powerful empire of the 'mighty' Ottomans and also stresses the fact that 'all the monarchs of the world acknowledge that the Sultans of the Ottoman family are the greatest monarchs of the earth'. It also carries the assurance that 'there existed no ground for enmity between the Mughals and the Ottomans'.[65]

In the first ever letter of the Mughal ruler to the Ottoman Sultan, Murad III (1623-40), Shahjahan had also affirmed the 'strong bonds of faith (*din*) and sect (*mazhab*)' existing between the Ottomans and the Mughals, both of whom were 'followers of Mazhab-i Hanafi'. Shahjahan further added.

> Extirpation of these heretics is an obligation on the Padshahs of Islam. It is imperative to liberate Iraqi Arab especially Baghdad. If the Sultan settles all his affairs (at the capital, and stays at the frontier for two or three years

> with two well-equipped armies, one operating in the north and the other in the south, the desired end can be achieved. God willing, his (Shahjahan's) own armies will soon be marching on Qandahar and thereafter on Khurasan. The wali of Transoxiana and the hakim of Balkh too will make a move (against Iran) when asked to.[66]

Murad IV also expressed his solidarity with the Mughal ruler. In his letter of 1639 sent from Mosul, he professed his desire 'to cleanse the earth of the polluted existence of the people of "*rufzoilhad*" (Shia heresy)' and requested Shahjahan also to be 'firm and steady' in his proposal to cooperate for the extermination of the Persians.[67] The Ottoman Sultan Muhammad Khan (1648-87), however, categorically stated that 'God raised the Ottomans to power in order to succour the friends of the faith and protect and help the weak', and showed a partisan attitude towards the Uzbeks.[68] The same ruler had addressed Shahjahan as the 'supporter of the dominions of the Sunnis and the breaker of the heads of the Shias'.[69]

The rulers frequently levelled charges of heresy against each other. In his letter to Sultan Sulaiman II of Turkey (1520-66), Shah Tahmasp criticized Humayun for the following acts: 'misled by Satan, Humayun grew vain and conceited and aspired for divinity. His occasional appearance before the people came to be called divine effulgence (*jalwai quddusi*). The Shariat was abolished in his entire dominions and in his army, prayers ceased to be offered and heresy (*ilhad*) became as rampant as in Rum (the Ottoman Empire).'[70]

This common feature of almost all the Eurasian religions was *Plenitudo potestatis*, i.e. the struggle for supremacy between the spiritual and the temporal heads. In Turan, Turkey and other places, the increasing power of the spiritual and ecclesiastical groups was both a support and a threat to the king's authority. To safeguard against such encroachments by the ecclesiastics on king's authority, political thinkers like Rawandi, Imam Ghazali and Ruzbihan Isfahani had specifically asserted the divine rights of a sovereign who was divinely appointed, divinely guided and divinely protected. Akbar's *mahzar* was, therefore, not his (or his coterie's) innovation. A continuation of the age-old conflict between the two rivals for power and a subsequent attempt to ward off a headlong collision between the king and the superficial *mullahs* almost always ended in such experiments though their forms may vary. Akbar's *mahzar*, therefore, seems to be an echo of Rawandi's ideas. As late as the twentieth century, an attempt in this direction is seen in the Kemalist reforms in Turkey, Kemal Pasha's views are well reflected in the term 'laicism', which emphasizes that there should be a complete depoliticization of religion though within the purview of a rationalized, humanized, and enlightened Islam and without any 'anti-religious' activity.[71]

The most effective and convincing explanations and justifications were put forward by the medieval chroniclers for imperialist adventures. Aggrandizement was often justified under the pretext of 'establishing peace and law and order for the safety of mankind'. Shahjahan bitterly criticized Nazar Muhammad (in his letter of November 1628) for the latter's reckless folly in invading the Kabul Marches 'due to which the ancient relations between the two dynasties might have been spoilt by the younger Khan's folly but for the consideration shown by Shahjahan'.[72] It is interesting to note that Shahjahan in his letter to Nazar Muhammad on the subject of his raids on Kabul described these inroads as 'deplorable', particularly because they were directed against a Sunni Muslim state.[73] On the contrary, the aggressive policy towards Turan and the conquest of Balkh and Badakhshan were justified by Shahjahan on the grounds that the Turanian ruler was in a difficult situation, having lost his authority every where except in Balkh. Since the excesses of the rebels and their lawlessness and violence had resulted even in the Saiyids being massacred, Shahjahan's 'sense of duty to community and religion, compassion for the Muslims of Turan and mutual friendship with the ruler of the place' led him to rise to the occasion.[74] Similarly, Aurangzeb also justified the campaign, saying that there was no breach of faith or friendship on the part of the Mughals as they were simply subduing the rebels of Transoxiana.

In matters of external relations money was lavishly spent for political planning and diplomatic gains. When Hakim Humam was sent as an envoy to Turan, he had been informed by his brother Hakim Abulfath Gilani, on 3 June 1588, about the repayment of all the money borrowed by Hakim Humam in connection with his sojourn in Turan and the despatch of additional sums through Mulla Sulhi. Some more money was to be sent to him again and he was instructed not to worry as there were no financial constraints. The same letter further states that 'without any concern on account of funds, he should continue to entertain people in a manner to attract them to his side. There is absolutely no need for him to be close fisted in such matters.'[75]

Similarly, in one of his letters to Mir Safiuddin Ahmad Kashi (dated November 1584), Akbar had requested that the Mir 'will keep Akbar informed about the members of the Tabaqai Illiyai Umana in Iran'. The Mir had also 'offered to perform any service in Iran'. But these activities ultimately proved disastrous for the Mir as he was blamed for misguiding the Iranians and was executed by the Shah of Persia. In his letter to Abdurrahim Khan-i Khanan, Abul Fazl had categorically advised the former to win over the Baluch and the Afghan *zamindars* 'by the tongue of assurances and the hand of generosity' and to march towards Qandahar as the conquest of this city would be a preface to the conquest of Iran: he tells him to borrow money, if necessary, even at 50 per cent and 100 per cent rates of interest and spend lavishly on the campaign.[76]

Apart from the alert envoys who were always watchful in collecting relevant information for their masters, the presence of secret agents, spies, and informers is often noticed in the sources. A Persian spy was once caught in Merv.[77] Another Persian spy was arrested and thrown to his death from a minaret in 1549.[78] Some other Persian secret agents were found at Surat, Thatta, and other places. Many of these spies were well versed in Indian languages. Since they faced almost certain death in case they were caught, these spies often demanded much higher emoluments than was their due. The news about the political conditions of the neighbouring regions was acquired from traders, refugees, fortune seekers, or directly from the rulers of the nearby territories. In one of his letters Faizi reports the arrival of three ships from Hormuz at Chaul (a port in the Nizam-ul-Mulk's territory) in which certain Qizilbash (including Husain Quli Asfshar and Hasan Beg Lashkar Newis) had also come to work under Akbar. They had provided a lot of new information about the state of affairs in Iraq, Fars and Rum and particularly about Shah Abbas.[79]

In addition to the diplomatic relations, contacts between India and its neighbouring states were also pursued through other channels. The Mughals sent purchasing missions and agents for 'toy trading' to the neighbouring regions. Ample evidence is available to show that specimens of luxury goods, medicines, and other valuables were frequently ordered from places outside India. The custom of combining political missions with state trading was also not uncommon. Private enterprises (for instance, of the Khwajas of Naqshband) were further encouraged and officially recognized. The letters exchanged between Shah Abbas I and Jahangir and the *nishans* of Shahjahan issued to merchants and preserved in the libraries confirm the fact that the kings often sent their deputies to make such purchases. Sometimes the local potentates or kings were requested to help in making the purchases. On several such occasions, Shah Abbas had complained that Prince Salim had not written to him directly and had instead sent merchants. Similarly, the Khwajas of Naqshband were also often requested to assist in this matter. For example, Aurangzeb wrote to Khwaja Abdul Ghaffar requesting him to guide and assist his nominee Ibrahim Beg in the purchase of horses, valuables, and rare commodities. In another letter, the same Khwaja was directed to help Mirza Quli (an imperial servant being sent to Balkh) to procure Turkish horses.[80]

The exchange of gifts and the supply of required rarities on request was also not uncommon. In return for the rare *qutubnuma* (compass) sent by Shah Abbas I through Haji Rafiq Saudagar, Jahangir sent him a Venetian wine cup (Karivendik). In 1617, Shah Abbas had promised to fulfil Jahangir's wish 'to have the astrolabe of Ulugh Beg' and assured him that 'a group of astronomers and mathematicians have been ordered to prepare a replica of the astrolabe so that the original of the same may be sent to Jahangir'. In his letter of 1611 to Jahangir, Shah Abbas also demanded certain 'specialities' of India to 'serve as an abiding reminder of the friendship of the two monarchs' and requested Jahangir to send:

> *amla* (myrobalan tree) and Malila, alongwith a horticulturist [who] specialised in dressing these plants; *resha-i zanjabil* (ginger root). *Tukhm-i birinji* Bengal (Bengal rice seed); indigo with an indigo planter and indigo dye maker; *gaobahl* (a wagon drawn by oxen) and the long horned *gaomesh* (buffalo), for the purpose of their horn being used for bow making. It would be considered a special favour if a quiver made of the same material could be sent.[81]

Shah Abbas I sent the desired articles to Jahangir, including the rubies which belonged to the pious foundation of the shrine at Najaf (one of which had the names of the Timurid ancestors inscribed on it) and for which Abbas took pains to convince the *ulama* and the *sadrs* in releasing them from the Waqf.[82] Similarly, Jahangir's desire for an agate rosary (*tasbihi-i aqiq*) was also fulfilled as Shah Abbas procured for him one each from the royal stores and from Mecca in 1615.[83] Among the other things which Shah Abbas sent to Jahangir at different times were a watch made from crystal and a white falcon.

Having learnt about Jahangir's dire need, Mumyai Shah Abbas immediately sent him 14 *tolas* of a medicine.

The Shah was particularly interested in the enamel work (*mina-kari*) of India and had sent vessels of pure and less pure gold for the purpose. Although the vessels of pure gold had to be returned in their original form as these cannot be enamelled, those containing less pure gold were handed over to the artisans for the early completion of the task and were returned in batches by Jahangir. In the meantime, Jahangir sent a water drinking cup along with a saucer and a *sarposh*, and a wine drinking cup, all especially enamelled for the Shah.[84]

Even a cursory survey of the various Islamic states would in Central Asia show the extent of similarity in the methods of war, tactics of battle, military organization, and siege warfare. The slave system was also a common feature in most of these states. Similarities are noticed not only in the 'cult of the garden' but also in its

> extension to architecture, pottery, tiles, textiles, carpets, calligraphy and decoration of manuscripts. The celebrated knots used in the ornamentation of books (placing a large shield in the centre and small ornaments in the corner) adopted by the Timurids in the mid-fifteenth century were borrowed from Herat by Turkey where it became a very popular motif towards the end of the same century.[85]

A continuous movement of artists from one state to another further facilitated the exchange of artistic expertise, skill, and knowledge. Haji Mir Muhammad Naqqash, who belonged to the painting studio-cum-school of Shah Tahmasp at Tabriz, went to Turkey during the reign of Sulaiman and was given a warm welcome. Sultan Sulaiman visited him frequently and assigned to him a pension of 100 *aspers* per day, and a studio was reserved for him.[86] In his letter to the ruler of Kashghar (dated 1552-3), Humayun informs him of the arrival of a group of 'celebrated artists' from Iraq and Khurasan whose talents had impressed Humayun even during his sojourn in these places. They joined the Mughal service in September-October 1552. One of these was the outstanding painter Mir Saiyyid Ali, who had once painted a polo field showing several *sawars* in different positions on either side of a grain of rice. There were two goal posts, one couplet, and the name of the painter along with the date (959 AH) inscribed in the same place.

The saints and the Sufis, being in closer proximity to the common folk were seen to play a greater role in bringing the people and the nations together. Akbar tried to utilize their good services for his own purposes. In one of his letters to Mir Saifuddin Ahmad Kashi (dated November 1584), Akbar stated that 'love for the people of Iran is deeply embedded in the imperial heart of Akbar and it is his desire that this exalted community (*guruh-i-wala*) should be drawn nearer to him both spiritually and materially and the high and the low (i.e. all classes) thereof should partake of imperial favours'. This Mir Kashi was, therefore, despatched to carry out these tasks and to further Akbar's laudable objectives of peace with all. Akbar was himself delighted at Mir Kashi's activities and wrote to him:

> It is, therefore, fortunate that Amir Ahmad is present there so that he can guide the community on the right path. The Mir should constantly report his spiritual experiences to and seek guidance from him (Akbar) who is indeed the solver of problems both spiritual and universal (*hallat-i Mushkilat-i rumuz-i anfas; wa afaq*). Akbar had not only invited Sadiduddin Darwesh Khusrau (whose excellence had been brought to Akbar's notice by Abul Fazl) but also requested Saiyid Ahmad Kashi that he will keep Akbar informed about the members of the tabaqai illiyai Umana in Iran.[87]

In his letter to Abul Fazl, Mir Kashi expressed his nostalgic love for the company and society of Abul Fazl and offered to perform any service in Iran. But these activities ultimately proved disastrous for the Mir as he was blamed for misguiding the Iranians. Charges of heresy were levelled against him and he was executed by the Shah personally at Kashan in 1594.[88] There were perhaps several such persons in Akbar's pay. Abul Fazl's *manshur*, discovered among the papers of Darvesh Khusrau Qazvini, the leader of the Nuqtavi cult in Persia, offers evidence of these mutual contacts. Akbar's pantheistic and eclectic approach towards religion was undoubtedly misunderstood and confused with latitudinarian (*wasil-ul mashrab*) thinking or metempsychosis (*tanasukhya*) both by the Iranian and Turanian rulers.[89] The cosmopolitan Akbar was also disgusted with the division of humanity along religious and sectarian lines and he criticized and condemned the genocide going on in Persia, Turan and Turkey.[90]

The Safavid rulers also maintained active religio-political bonds with the Indian Shias. In a letter addressed to Shah Tahmasp, a certain Shah Tahir Husaini referred to his 'work of organization and propagation of religious learning' in India. Informing the Shah about the compilation of *tafsir* showing the triumph of the Shia philosophy over that of the others, he emphasized that the work would be of much use for the *sadrs* and requested some financial assistance for himself.[91] Tahir Husaini's correspondence with the highly-placed officials, religious personages, and saints proves that the Safavid rulers also followed the policy of using the good offices of saints for spreading goodwill. The Shia rulers of Indian territories like Ibrahim Qutb Shah (1550-80), ruler of Golconda, also claimed that he (Qutb Shah) was the first to 'raise the standard of [the] Shia religion and to recite the Khutba of the Isna ashariya'. Ibrahim Adil Shah II (1580-1627) went to the extent of saying that the Deccan territories form as much a part of the Safavid empire as Iraq, Khurasan, etc., and that the *khutba* is being read in the name of the Safavid Kings who look upon themselves as 'mansabdars of the Shah's Court'. The fear of the Deccan rulers is understandable. The Hanafite school of jurisprudence had been most commonly followed in Asian countries (including Turan, Turkey and India) ever since the Abbasids accorded it an 'official status'.[92] The Safavids and the Deccan rulers were followers of Shiism. Ibrahim Adil Shah II, therefore, confirmed that they would not allow the Mughal rulers to occupy an inch of their territory which belonged to the Shah. They invited the Shah to come and assist them. A well-equipped army from Qandahar, supported by the Afghans, could easily occupy 'invaluable Mughal treasure'. Assurances of assistance from the rulers of Golconda and Ahmadnagar were also given. While the Sunni Hanafite rulers (Ottomans, Uzbeks and Mughals) constantly spoke of destroying the Safavids in order to clear the path to Mecca, Shah Abbas I persuaded Sultan Muhammad Qutb Shah (1612-26) to believe that his 'military intervention' in the Kij Makran region was merely an attempt to 'facilitate the land travel between the two lands'.[93] In one of the letters of Shah Abbas, Mir Muhammad Mumin described himself as being 'in the Shah's own employ, for the rulers of this Qutb Shahi dynasty are hereditary devotees of the Safavid family'.

The Timurid rulers of Central Asia were devotees of the Naqshbandi saints. Haidar Dughlat says that each Timurid prince had his own spiritual guide. Even when the Mughals had established their sway in India, their attraction to Sufi saints continued. In his letter to Kamran, Babur instructed the prince to respect the saints

> By the incitement of that orb of the night, that cradle of light and majesty, that eloquent nightingale of [the] flower garden, Hazrat Khwaja Ubaidullah who has rendered help through them (people of Turan) you have become a

disciple of and a companion and been called the son of Padishah. See that you do them due honour and that you make no shortcoming in this.

The Naqshbandi saints of Bukhara followed the motto '*Khidmat-ul Mulk Nisfulsuluk*' (i.e. service to the sovereign is half the way to the path of God/Sufism/Salvation). In Turan, therefore, the Naqshbandi saints dominated the political scene and were the power behind the throne. The Naqshbandi order found adherents in Turkey and also in India. It is interesting to note that some affinity existed in the religious sphere also. Thus, not only in Turan and India but also in Turkey the Sunni Hanafite school prevailed. The order known as Ishqiya (spiritual successors to Shaikh Abu Yazid Ishqi) in Central Asia and Iran was famous as Bistamiya (after the name of Abu Yazid Bistami) in Turkey. The same order founded by Shah Abdullah of Transoxiana in India was known as 'Shattari' after the title 'Shattar' given to its founder for his 'claims to make his disciples perfect by the shortest and quickest means'.[94] The Bektashi or Bektashia order, one of the most popular and strongest orders which 'reveres' the Caliph Ali, was apparently a 'sect rather than a Sufi fraternity' on the Naqshbandi pattern. Hitti included this order awaking the 'ultra Shiite sects',[95] which seems improbable keeping in view that the Janissari (Yenicheri) soldiers acquired under Devsherma were all converted to the Bektashia order and that too in the purely staunch Sunni Muslim state of Turkey. Hitti further suggested that 'besides inheriting the old religion of Asia Minor the dervish orders of that country have preserved traces of Shamanism which the early Turks brought with them from Central Asia'.[96]

Amidst the whirlpool of worldly politics, the most glorious and constructive role was played by the intellectually inclined members of the Futuwwa organizations. The peculiarities of Futuwwa (also known as Akhi or Fityan) organizations indicate how the common folk and lesser mortals in medieval times, propelled as much by their gregarious instincts and *esprit de corps* as well as being motivated by the feudal notion of universal brotherhood and their invoke generosity, showered hospitality on visiting learned men or foreigners the name of humanity. This institution, not so commonly known and not properly understood in its true perspective, existed in Turan, Iran, Turkey, and several other places. These Akhi organizations were 'corporations' of unmarried young artisans who entertained the social purpose of 'providing a structure of solidarity and mutual aid in the urban environment'. These associations were usually headed by an

Akhi who was a man of considerable worth, enjoying the confidence and respect of people in general. They performed a 'crucial civic function of helping to maintain urban cohesiveness and defense and were expected to lead lives approaching these ideal qualities. As for demonstrations of generous hospitality to visiting strangers, Ibn-i Battuta had enjoyed this warm, refined, 'lavish and enthusiastic' hospitality in more than twenty-five cities. In the sixteenth century, Wasifi recorded the literary assemblies and hospitable social gatherings of these Akhi organizations. For initiating new members (Fityan), a special ceremonial initiation was organized which was attended by members in formal initiation dress. Presumably each AKHI group had its own costume (white cap and a special pair of trousers) and held regular meetings of their clubs.

Ibn-i Battuta explained the term '*akhi*' in its Arabic sense (*akhi* or *akhw*) of 'brother' though the word also denotes 'a good work, manly, generous'. The words '*futuwat*' (liberality or bountifulness), '*fatiy*' (singular), and '*fityan*' or '*fatayan*' (youth, young men) stood for 'knightly' or 'noble' in the Turkish and Uzbek languages.[97]

Apparently, these Fuluwwa organizations along with all their concomitants appeared in Asia Minor either from Iran or Turan where they were already active. During the caliphal regime of Al-Nasir (1180-1225), the 'special order of [the] sworn brotherhood Futuwwa' acquired royal patronage and developed as 'a sort of Knighthood of Chivalry' and invigorated the brotherhood. This 'fraternity' was said to have originated at the time of the fourth Caliph Ali ibn-i Abi Talib, and was composed of distinguished high-born men mostly from amongst the Prophet's descendants. Although Ali may have been devoid of political acumen or diplomacy, he was an 'ideal Arab'—valiant, wise, eloquent, truthful and magnanimous—and became 'the paragon of Moslem nobility and chivalry (Futuwwa)'. Hitti nicely sums up the situation as follows:

> The later Fityan movement, which developed ceremonies and insignia savouring of medieval European chivalry and the modern scout movements took Ali for its first 'Fata' and model. Regarded as wise and brave by all the Islamic world, as idealistic and exemplary by many Fityan and dervish fraternities, as sinless and infallible by his partisans and even held to be the incarnation of the deity by the Ghulah (extremists) among them, he whose worldly career was practically a failure has continued to exert a posthumous influence second only to that of the Prophet himself.[98]

It is surmised that the Fuluwwa organization in which 'Moslem Arab chivalry sought to express itself' took among the Turks and the Turco-Mongols a new form, that of the Akhis. Hitti's view that originally these Akhi organizations may have been economic guilds[99] has been contradicted by R.E. Dunn, who states that 'they were not synonymous with trade guilds'.[100] Although these clubs were often organized along 'occupational lines', the members could belong to different professions. They held regular meetings of the club in the lodge especially built for the purpose or in the homes of their Akhis where they enjoyed food, fun, and frolic. Ibn-i Battuta[101] mentions a cobbler who was the Akhi of a club or hospice comprising about two hundred men of different trades. In their own small way, therefore, the Sufi saints and the Akhi organizations contributed to the strengthening the ties of brotherhood among the various nations.

## NOTES

1. Rashiduddin Fazlullah, *Jamiut Tawarikh*, Tehran edn., p. 100.
2. Philip K. Hitti, *History of the Arabs*, London, 1949, pp. 475, 478, 489, 702; Wittek, pp. 1-100.
3. *The Cambridge History of Islam*, vol. I, edited by P.M. Holt et al., Cambridge, 1970, p. 214.
4. Ibn-i Arab Shah, *Ajaibul Maqdur*, Eng. tr. by Sanders, *Life of Timur*, p. 278.
5. See Mansura Haidar, 'Sovereign in the Timurid Empire', *Turcica*, vol. VIII, no. 2, 1976, The eldest son of Sam was said to be Arfakhshad, who was the ancestor of Hud, Saleh, and the Prophet Ibrahim. The second son of Arfakhshad, Kiumars, was the ancestor of all the kings of Ajam. His six sons, namely Siamak, Fars, Iraq, Tur, Sham, and Damghan, gave their own names to the respective territories where they were sent to govern. Some say that one of the sons of Noah was called Ajam and that all the Muluks of Ajam, were his descendants. Abulqasim Farishta, *Gulshan-i Ibrahimi* or *Tarikh-i Farishta*, Newal Kishore edn., pp. 9-10.
6. Babur, *Babur Nama*, text, pp. 348-50; Eng. tr., pp. 624-5.
7. Ibid.
8. A letter from Emperor Babur to his son Kamran, *JASB* (NS), vol. XV, 1919, pp. 329-34.
9. Ibid.
10. Riazul Islam (*Calendar II*, pp. 295-6) argues that the letter is not genuine.
11. *Munshaat-i-Tusi*, 2338, Blochet, ff. 132, 293-5; *Afzal-ut-Tawarikh*, BM OR 4678, ff. 161-3.
12. Ibid., *Munshaat-i-Tusi*, f. 250.
13. *Munshaat-i-Tusi*, p. 250.
14. *Ruqqat-i-Abulfath Gilani*, pp. 117-20; also see *Silsilat*, f. 214.
15. *Mukatabat-i-Allami*, Lucknow, 1280/1863, pp. 17-26; *Mukatabat*, pp. 196-8;

Abulfath Gilani, *Ruqqat* or *Chahar Bagh*, Lahore, 1968, pp. 90-2; also see Mansura Haidar, *Insha-i Abul Fazl*, Delhi, 1988.
16. *Mukatabat-i-Allami*, pp. 1-14.
17. *Calendar* II, p. 228, no. 338; also see *Akbar Nama*, III, pp. 792, 817.
18. *Insha-i-Abul Fazl*, Lucknow edn., Akbar's letters to Shah Abbas and Raja Ali Khan of Khandesh.
19. *Insha-i-Abul Fazl*, p. 121.
20. *Jamiul Murasalat*, pp. 230-1
21. *Munshaat-i-Tusi*, Blochet, 2338, ff. 165-6.
22. *Naskha-i-Jamiul Murasalat*, Add. 7688, ff. 229-30.
23. Shaikh Jalal Hisari, *Arzdasht*, BM Add. 16, 859, ff. 17-19.
24. *Nuskha-i-Jamiul Murasalat*, BM OR 3482 ff. 223-6, 235, 238, 242-5.
25. Ibid., pp. 223-6, 235, 238, 242, 246. Shaikh Jalal Hisari, *Arzdasht*, BM Add. 1685, ff. 17-19. *Tahmas Nama*, Ethe 2067, f. 63.
26. For other such letters of friendship, see *Jamiul Insha*, BM OR 1702, ff. 226-69; *Gulshan-i-Balaghat*, Ethe 288, ff. 74-7. Riazul Islam speaks of the 'low esteem' in which Jahangir held the Uzbeks and refers to his abiding interest in furthering Mughal-Persian friendship. Riazul Islam, *Calendar of Persian Documents*, II, no. 340.
27. Ibid. *Mukatabat*, Ethe 2068, ff. 45-6.
28. *Mukatabat*, Ethe 2068, ff. 321-2.
29. Ibid.
30. *Silsilat*, pp. 195-6; *Amali Saleh*, I, pp. 315-18; Lahori, I, pp. 234-7.
31. *Silsilat*, Bodleian 169, ff. 189-92.
32. *Mukatabat*, Ethe 2068, ff. 321-2.
33. *Nuskha-i-Jamiul Murasalat*, BM Add. 7688, ff. 174-5.
34. Faridun Bey, II, 1849, pp. 142-3; 1858, pp. 234-5.
35. Lahori, *Badshah Nama*, vol. I, pp. 232-3; Kamgar Husaini, *Maasir-i-Jahangiri*, Bodleian MS, ff. 220-5; *Insha-i Abul Fazl*, pp. 1-24, also see appendix.
36. *Majmua*, Tehran Univ. MS 2591, pp. 89-90.
37. See *Nuskha-i-Jamiul Murasalat*, BM Add. 7688, ff. 226-7; *Tahmas Nama*, Ethe, 2067, ff. 73-4.
38. *Nuskha-i-Jamiul Murasalat*, ff. 227-8; *Tahmas Nama*, pp. 88-90.
39. *Munshaat-i-Tusi*, Blochet 2338, ff. 247-9; *Nuskha-i-Jamiul Murasalat*, ff. 227-9.
40. *Majmua*, MS 2465, Tehran University Central Library.
41. Ibid.
42. *Bahar-i-Sukhan*, BM OR 1789, ff. 48-51, pp. 36-42.
43. *Bahar-i-Sukhan*, BM OR 1789, ff. 45-8; Shamlu letters, BM Add. 7802, ff. 76-9, 81-3.
44. Chandra Bhan Brahmin, *Chahar Chaman*, BM 1892, ff. 49-50.
45. *Mukatabat-i-Saadullah Khan*, Lahore edn. 1968, pp. 18-19, 23-5; *Tarikh-i-Badia*, Bodleian MS, ff. 259-61; *Silsilat*, III, pp. 5-12.
46. Lahori, I, pp. 232-3; *Maasir-i-Jahangiri*, pp. 220-5; Waris, *Badshah Nama*, BM Add 6556, ff. 433-5.
47. *Mukatabat-i-Tusi*, MS, Blochet, 2338, ff. 272-4; *Alam Ara-i-Abbasi*, pp. 982-3.
48. *Alam Ara-i-Abbasi*, pp. 963-78; Muhammad Salih, *Majmua-i-Makatib-i-Mukhtahfa*, MS Majlis Library (Tehran), MS 2247 (Ca.) 3349, pp. 423-5.

49. Abul Fazl, *Akbar Nama,* III, text, p. 603, Eng. tr., p. 921.
50. Ibid., text, pp. 730-2, Eng. tr., p. 1091.
51. Badauni, *Muntakhab-ut-Tarwarikh*, Eng. tr., Lowe, II, pp. 325-6, 376-88. Also see *Akbar Nama*, III, Delhi, 1973, text, p. 603, Eng. tr., p. 921.
52. L. Petech, *China and Tibet in the Early 18th Century*, Leiden, 1950, p. 114.
53. *Akbar Nama*, III, p. 117.
54. Badauni, Eng. tr., Lowe, II, pp. 325-6, 376-88; also see *Akbar Nama*, Delhi, 1973, text, p. 603, Eng. tr., p. 921.
55. *Travels of Manuel Komraff and Witald Gordon*, New York, 1926, p. 189; also see Richard Hambly, *Marco Polo*, London, 1975, p. 151.
56. Badauni, Eng. tr., Lowe, II, pp. 125-6.
57. *Travels*, op. cit., p. 189; Richard Hambly, p. 151.
58. *Insha-i-Abul Fazl*, Lucknow edn., p. 57; Ibadullah Fenyyaz, *Faiyyazul Qawanin*, BM OR 9617, II, f. 171, BM OR, pp. 702, 765.
59. *Mukatabat*, pp. 33-4, 57.
60. *Faiyyazul Qawanin*, BM OR 9617, II, f. 171; BM OR 1702, f. 265; *Mukatabat*, p. 57.
61. *Kashkul-i-Salimi*, f. 246.
62. *Ain*, I, Eng. tr., p. 452.
63. See Shah Abbas I's letter to Akbar (1591) for such complaints. *Nuskha-i-Jamiul-Murasalat*, BM Add. 7688, ff. 202-5. Nasrullah Falsafi, *Zindagani-i-Shah Abbas*, I, p. 226; Jahangir, *Tuzuk-i-Jahangiri*, pp. 16, 37.
64. *Silsilat*, Bodleian MS. no. 169, ff. 300-12.
65. Abdullah Effendi, *Dastur-ul-Insha*, Flugel, 316, ff. 127-9; Faridun Bey, *Munshaat us Salatin*, II, 1849, pp. 59-61; 1858, pp. 153-5. *Insha-i-Tahir Waheed*, BM Add. 7690, ff. 1-3.
66. Faridun Bey, II, 1849, pp. 67-9; 1858, pp. 161-3; Lahori, II, p. 185.
67. Abdullah Effendi, *Dastur-ul-Insha*, Flugel 316, ff. 123-6. Also see *Calendar* II, pp. 314-15. For other such letters see Faridum Bey, p. 275.
68. Faridun Bey, II, 1849, pp. 65-71; 1858, pp. 159-65.
69. Faridun Bey, II, pp. 276-9.
70. *Tahmas Nama*, Ethe 2067, ff. 397-430; Riazul Islam, *A Calendar of Documents on Indo-Persian Relations*, Karachi, 1982, vol. II, p. 294.
71. Adnan Menderes, 1952.
72. *Silsilat*, ff. 195-6; *Amal-i Saleh*, I, p. 318; Lahori, pp. 234-7.
73. Lahori, pp. 466-9; *Silsilat*, pp. 205-8; *Silsilat*, Bodleian MS no. 169, ff. 195-6, 223-5; Lahori, pp. 530-3.
74. *Silsilat*, Bodleian MS no. 169, ff. 223-5; Lahori, II, pp. 530-3.
75. *Ruqat-i-Abulfath Gilani, Chahar Chaman*, Lahore, 1968, pp. 117-20.
76. *Mukatabat-i-Allami*, Lucknow edn., 1863, pp. 128-31.
77. *Rauzat-ur-Rizwan*.
78. *AAA*, pp. 260-7.
79. *Latifa-i-Faizi*, Ethe 1479, ff. 17-38.
80. *Adab-i-Alamgiri*, Lahore edn., pp. 617, 632-3.
81. *Mukatib-i-Mukhtalifa*, Majlis Library, Tehran, MS 2247, Cat. X, 3349, ff. 265-6; *Tahmas Nama*, Ethe 2067, ff. 56-8; Jung, Majlis MS no. 3455, p. 205.
82. *Tahmas Nama*, Ethe 2067, ff. 141-3; *Nuskha-i Jamiul Murasalat*, BM Add 7688, ff. 215-16.

83. *Nuskha-i-Jamiul Murasalat*, BM 3482, f. 236.
84. *Tahmas Nama*, ff. 54-6; *Tuzuk*, p. 116.
85. *Majmua*, Tehran University Central Library, MS no. 2591, ff. 109-10.
86. F.R. Martin, *The Miniature Painting and Painters of Persia, India and Turkey*, vol. I, London, 1912, pp. 90 onwards.
87. F.R. Martin, *The Miniature Paintings and Painters of Persia, India and Turkey*, pp. 117-18.
88. *Majmua,* Tehran University Central Library, MS no. 2591, ff. 152-3; Muhammad Salih, *Majmua-i-Mukatib-i-Mukhtalifa*, ff. 195-6.
89. *Çalendar* I, p. 103.
90. *AAA*, pp. 473-7.
91. Nasrullah Falafi, *Zindagan-i Shah Abbas*, I, p. 226; Jahangir, *Tuzuk-i-Jahangiri*, pp. 16, 37.
92. *Nuskha-i-Jamiul Murasalat*, BM Add 7688, f. 124a.
93. Athar Abbas Rizvi, *Wonder that was India*, II, p. 8.
94. *Alam Ara-i-Abbasi*, pp. 866, 941.
95. Rizvi, *Wonder that was India*, pp. 261-2.
96. Hitti, *History of the Arabs*, London, 1949, pp. 43, 70, 438, 449.
97. Hitti, p. 481; Dunn, p. 146.
98. Franz Taeschnev, *Islamica*, vol. IV, 1929, pp. 1-47; vol. V, pp. 285-333; Deny, *Journal Asiatique*, ser. II, vol. XVI, 1920, pp. 182-3; Hitti, p. 183.
99. Hitti, *History of the Arabs*, London, 1949, pp. 183, 479.
100. Ibid.
101. Ross E. Dunn, *The Adventures of Ibn-i Battuta*, Kent, 1986, pp. 146-7.

# Central Asian Heritage in the Mughal Polity

The history of any country is very closely related to the development of its people. Civilizations of different regions also influence each other due to geographical proximity or close cultural relations. Sometimes, this hastens the process of cultural amalgamation, as in the case of India and Transoxiana. Political instability, social unrest, natural disasters, or the search for work compel, people to leave their homes. Invasions aimed at empire building or to secure booty, and the arrival of mystics and men of letters whether individually or in delegations adds to the population movement. The movements of people and the exchange of ideas from the prehistoric period down to our own times has been the hallmark of this region.

The 'Indianization' of thought and art and the deep impact of Indian culture on Central Asian spiritual and material culture was as apparent as the Central Asian influence on Indian culture, art, architecture, language, and socio-religious movements. The multi-dimensional contacts existed in the literary sphere, and the pursuit of learning ranged from literary styles, artistic modes of expression, religious ideas and thoughts, to trade in books and raw materials, and the visits of scholars and poets.

Almost all the invaders who have profoundly influenced the history of India came from or through the Central Asian regions. Apart from the Huns, the Shakas, the Greeks, and later on the Arabs, there were the Turks, the Afghans, the Mongols, and the Turco-Mongols. The sultans of Dēlhi and the Mughals governed India for over eight centuries and introduced a vast range of institutions, customs, traditions, and loan words. All this changed the political and cultural life, of India, resulting in the birth of a composite and syncretic culture. The process was not confined to a few decades or to a few centuries but persisted through the ages. People from Transoxiana continued to trickle into India as fortune seekers, militiamen, traders, men of letters, poets, artists, exiles and refugees, or men of influence. Migrations were a regular feature of Central Asian and Indian history. These movements were voluntary emigrations of martial men or literary talents in search of better opportunities or were the consequence of an exodus during wars. There are stray references indicating that the process was particularly strong from the eleventh to the seventeenth centuries. Such a movement of people had its own socio-economic and religio-political influence. Owing to the frequent interactions and the continuous movement of peoples and trade and commerce between India and Central Asia, the exchange of ideas was possible at all levels and at all times. Common elements of culture and a fascinating similarity in ethos can be seen in numerous forms.[1]

As will be subsequently discussed, Central Asia has played an important role in the history of the world through the ages, both as the creator and the carrier of civilization and culture. While the influence of Central Asian culture has been noticed and recognized in various spheres in all periods of history in neighbouring and remote areas, the extent and depth of this impact or even the nature of the cultural fusion has not so far been adequately analysed, estimated, and determined. Starting from the Aryans, we find a certain commonness between the *Rig Veda* and the *Avesta*. Similarities are also noticed between the neolithic and chalcolithic cultures of the two regions. Commercial contacts have continued through the ages. During the Kushana period, the lands between the Oxus and the Ganges were joined together; Gandhara art represented the fusion of the two cultures. Ever since the last quarter of the sixth century BC both the north-western part of India and certain areas of Transoxiana (like Soghdiana and Sali Sarai) have had much in common as they formed, intermittently, a part of one and the same empire (as under the Achaemenids, the Bactrians, the Greeks, the Kushanas, and the Sasanids).This ensured the free movements of people, facilitated the exchange of ideas, and encouraged brisk commercial transactions. Indications of the presence of Indians are said to have been found in various statues of a somewhat south Indian type excavated at Toprak Kala (Uzbekistan).[2] The transit and terminal trade between India and Central Asia flourished through the ages, particularly under the Kushanas and the Mughals. The graffiti on rocks at various places (such as Ziarat, Khamar, and Hunza) in the north-western frontier suggests the familiarity of Soghdian merchants with the Gilgit route.[3] It is also surmised that the historical movement of the sub-groups that affected India can be traced with fair certainty to two great waves of pastoral tribesmen originating in the Khwarezm region. The first started about the beginning of the second millennium BC, the second towards the end.[4] Kosambi writes:

> The conquest by Darius towards the third quarter of the sixth century brought the land of the seven (or by then only five) rivers into chronological history. His inscriptions list Kambujiya, Gandhara Hindus among the provinces which therefore extended through Afghanistan to the Indus, over previous Aryan settlements. Recruits and levies from the West Punjab (Hindus) fought in the armies of Darius and Xerxes against the Greeks. Just at the margin, perhaps subjected to a normal tribute by the Persians (when they could collect it), was the city of Taxila, a great centre of the overland trade between two economically powerful regions, namely the static Persian empire and a growing kingdom in the Gangetic valley.[5]

In his grave inscription (486 BC), Darius I of Persia declared himself to be a Persian, son of a Persian, an Aryan of Aryan descent (Parsu, Parsahya, Puthra, Arya, Aryamithra). The Arioi occupied some areas of Iran (Ariana) and Afghanistan extending to the Indus at the time of Alexander's invasion (Strabo 15.2.9). The Aryans settled under that name over a vast region on the west bank of the Indus, extending through parts of Afghanistan and eastern Persia—to which last country they gave the name Iran (Ariana).[6] Romila Thapar writes: 'The impact of Indian ideas in Western Asia can also be traced to the period 100-150 AD. In particular the doctrines of the Manichaeans, Gnostics and Neo Platonists constitute an interesting study from this point of view.'[7] Under the Achaemenids, towards the fifth century BC, several forms of early Indian art started spreading into Western Asia. For instance, the presence of rock architecture is well established by the similarities and the 'singular family resemblance' as seen between the facade of the tomb of Darius at Naksh; the tomb of Rustam near Persepolis; and that of the Lomas Rishi 'chapel' in Bihar. Although 'the latter is on a much smaller scale, the textural properties of the three sites have not a little in common'.[8] The brisk 'intercourse known to have been maintained between the Sasanian court and India is further proved by a form of brick arching which was employed at Bodh Gaya and the Pettuk Pagoda of Pagan in Burma'. It is also opined that 'the idea of making rock inscriptions may have come to Ashoka after hearing about those of Darius'. Even the opening forms of address resemble each other. The Ashokan inscriptions found in the north-western region were written in the Kharoshthi script, which is derived from the Aramaic script used in Iran and Central Asia.[9]

In ancient days, Central Asia had been opened to trade, with routes traversing the oases and valleys of the vast region One of these routes later became famous as the Old Silk Route. Indian traders had established trading stations and merchant colonies in places such as Kashghar, Yarqand, Khotan, Miran, Kuchi, Qarashahr, and Turfan, all remote regions which were soon opened up not only by Indian merchants but also by Buddhist missionaries. As a result of this activity in Central Asia, communication with China improved. In the process, the inhabitants of the Central Asianoases at which the missionaries halted were converted to Buddhism, and monasteries grew up at places such as Yarqand, Khotan, Kashghar, Tashkent, Turfan, Miran, Kuchi, Qarashahr, and Tun Huang.[10]

Khotan was said to be a part of the Mauryan empire and Ashoka's visit to the region is recorded in the Tibetan sources.[11] D.N. Jha writes that under the Mauryan kings 'Different parts of the country were now connected by trade routes, some leading to Western and Central Asia.' Taxila was connected by a highway with Kabul, from where roads went in different directions. The northern route passed through Bactria (north Afghanistan), the Oxus region, the Caspian sea and the Caucasus to the Black Sea. The northern route was from Kandahar and Herat to Ecbatana (later Hamadan in Persia); from there traders travelled overland to the eastern Mediterranean coast. A highway also ran from Kandahar to Persepolis and Susa in Persia. Foreign invasions may have disrupted some of the land routes connecting India with Western and Central Asia. But they also gave an impetus to trade. The conquest of north-western India by the Indo-Greeks, the Kushanas and Shakas promoted closer contacts with Western and Central Asia. Through Central Asia passed the Silk Road which connected China with the West Asian provinces of the Roman empire. The Indian merchants participated as intermediaries in the Chinese silk trade. Central Asia, therefore, acted as a link between India and China. The merchants of north-western India mostly traded with these regions.[12] In ancient times, Afghanistan and Persia were 'the other likely sources' of gold. Silver was imported from Afghanistan and Iran. Lapis lazuli was rare in Harappan archaeological material and came from Badakhshan (in north-east Afghanistan), and turquoise from Iran.

The Hun kingdom extended from Persia to Khotan, with its capital at Bamiyan in Afghanistan. Kanishka, who ruled India from Sanchi to Benaras any where between AD 78-144, was undoubtedly of 'Central Asian origin since he is depicted as such in one of the portraits of the Kushana kings discovered near Mathura'. It has been noted that the 'history of northern India under the Kushanas was closely associated with events in Central Asia. Buddhist missionaries were sent to Central Asia. Kanishka himself is believed to have died fighting in Central Asia.'[13]

In medieval times both Abul Fazl and Sujan Rai Bhandari referred to seven routes between the two lands, traversed by all kinds of fortune seekers, artists, traders, warriors, and refugees. The Chinese, Latin, and Greek records mention that the Kashmir route was the most difficult of all these routes (through Takla Matiar, Gilgit, Khaiber Balari, Sinkiang, Agsi, Yarqand, and Balkh-Lamghanat).

Between 602-54, Hieun Tsang found a great centre of original Buddhist studies at Batha and noticed the Brahmi script in use in Qarashahr, Kucha, Yarqand, Kashghar, and Khotan. The Afghan immigrants (referred to by Hieun Tsang as Pokien and by Varah Mihra as Vokkaan) continued to arrive in India as soldiers of fortune or as the defenders of borders. Certain documents found in Qunduz, Qaratepe, and Tirmiz were written in an early form of Prakrit mixed with Sanskrit, and often contained loan words from Soghdian, Iranian, Greek, and Tibetan. The ceramics at Afrasiyab resemble those found in the Purana Qila, the Adilabad excavations, Champanir in Gujarat, and Golconda in Andhra Pradesh. Alberuni[14] supposedly wrote his book to 'provide necessary information for any one who wants to converse with the Hindus and to discuss with them question of religion, science or literature on the basis of their own civilization, which reflects the search of the curious medieval mind. Abul Fazl beautifully sums up this yearning for knowledge and the difficulties involved in such cross-cultural encounters. Although Abul Fazl's ideas were expressed in a different context, they throw valuable light on contemporary events:

> the distance that separates the learned men of Hindustan from scientific men of other nationalities who thus are unable to meet, and if chance should bring them together, the need of an interpreter would preclude any practical result. An accomplished linguist capable of mastering the intricacies of science and the abstract speculations of philosophy among various nations and competent to give them luminous and efficient expression is very rare.

Even at the present time when through His Majesty's patronage of learning and his appreciation of merit the erudite of all countries are assembled and apply themselves with united effort in the pursuit of truth so proficient a person is not to be found. Such as those who thirst after the sweet waters of wisdom and who leaving their native land undertake the wanderings of travel and with diligent assiduity employ their energies in the acquisitions of various languages only are indeed uncommon. It needs a seeker, such as Anushirwan, who amidst the pomp of empire, should yet search for the jewel of wisdom, and again this sagacious personage, making no distinction between the absence or presence of his employers, must be diligent in his inquiries and succeed in the accomplishment of his desire through the frankness in his demeanour and his largesse of gold. Or, the occasion would demand an indefatigable and lofty intellect like that of Tumtum the Indian who, to receive the instruction of the divine philosopher Plato, passed from Hindustan into Greece, set himself to face the changes of seas and deserts and perfected his spiritual health and the harmonious balance of his soul. Or, a powerful mind and vigorous body such as Abu Maashar of Balkh, enamoured of wisdom, who holding exile of his native country and toil and ease . . . travelled into India from Khurasan and gathered a store of knowledge at Benares and carried it as a priceless gift to the learned of his own land.[15]

It is pertinent to note here that the need to collaborate and exchange ideas between the two regions was no less keenly felt by the medieval sovereigns as it is being realized by present-day political leaders. A movement to bring about peace and stability in the region exists, whose aim is to create an understanding for a better tomorrow. In the medieval period, however, the rulers sometimes sought to justify their military conquests on the grounds that these were undertaken 'in order that your people and mine may have easy access to one another through land routes and without difficulty and we may be aware of our mutual conditions and circumstances'.[16] The proposed military ventures (beyond the Hindukush) so wistfully or ambitiously desired by medieval Indian rulers could hardly materialize (as in the case of Muhammad bin Tughlaq or the early Mughals). When they did succeed (for example, in the case of Shahjahan and Aurangzeb), these conquests always proved to be cumbersome if not completely abortive. Nevertheless, the cultural winds and spiritual breezes continued to move between the two lands, crossing the tall mountains and the extensive oceans. Buddhism made a deep impact on the lands beyond the Hindukush. Similarly, the mystical philosophy of Central Asia delivered the message of love and peace in India. The Sufis came to India as frequently as the Buddhist saints had earlier crossed the Hindukush.

The medieval age in India was heralded by the arrival of the Turks of various tribes, most of whom were from the Central Asian heartland. The Mongol invasions, though shortlived, continued throughout the Sultanate period and have left some indelible marks on the history of the Indian subcontinent. In many ways, Iltutmish had tried to introduce Central Asian features in India. Thus, the *tanga*, a Central Asian currency, and the *iqta*, were two of his most important imported administrative devices. Even the settlements of the '*nau* Muslim' Mongols in Delhi's vicinity under Jalaluddin Khilji should not be treated as an insignificant factor. Alauddin Khilji's much appreciated market controls and agrarian reforms owe their origin to the Central Asian custom of fixing the market prices by the state. Alauddin's measures, which reduced marketmen to abject poverty (and which had been bitterly criticized by Barani), seem to be a continuation of the tax imposed by the Turco-Mongol rulers in their military-oriented command economy. The system had also been followed by Timur. Muhammad bin Tughlaq's attempt to recruit into his service many foreigners from Central Asia and other countries indicated his own appreciation of their capabilities. The adoption of Persian in India, which ultimately led to the emergence of a soldiers' apost and a traders' dialect like Urdu, is a prominent example of lingual fusion. Indo-Persian literature was produced in the medium of the Persian language but dealt with Indian ideas and motifs and was narrated against an Indian background.[17]

Cultural interchange followed as the political interests of the two regions were so closely linked to each other. The balance of power was maintained in the region through a series of rather strange and non-committal 'friendly' embassies. On the one hand, the Safavid rulers of Persia created hope of support among the 'tribute-paying' and '*duniyadaran*' Deccani Shia rulers who willingly read the *khutba* in the name of the Shah of Persia and who complained against the Chaghatais who were being wooed by the Shah through assurances of moral support whenever necessary, notwithstanding the Qandahar affair. On the other hand, the Ottoman-Uzbek alliance often tempted rulers like Sher Shah and Bahadur Shah of Gujarat to join the coalition against the Safavids though the reasons for this alliance were different. Shah Rukh's close contacts with Vijayanagar, Bengal, and Calicut are elearly reflected in Abdur Razzaq

Samarqandi's accounts. The epistolary records confirm the existence of active relations between the rulers of the two countries in the medieval period.[18] The exchange of innumerable and apparently innocent courtesy embassies between the rulers of these countries ranged from probing missions to proposed defence alliances. Some of these were, diplomatic missions, seeking assistance from the Central Asian rulers during turbulent periods in India. Examples of these were: Firuz Shah Bahmani's letter to Timur, letters of Afghan and Rajput chiefs, the letter from Bahadur Shah to Babur, and the letters of the Deccani rulers to Shah Abbas.[19] Other embassies despatched during the heyday of the Mughals carried messages of 'peace with all', and comments on the existing political situation along with declarations of policy regarding religious toleration and non-alignment (as professed by Akbar in his letter to the rulers of Iran and Turan).[20] Apart from such letters between the rulers, others like the Khwajas of Naqshband and the men of letters also exchanged letters with their counterparts and even with the rulers. Included in this category are the letters of Jami and Novoi expressing feelings of love and friendship for India; the letters of Indian rulers sent to the Khwajas of Naqshband; and the letters from Ali Sher Navoi to an Indian ruler, Sharif Khan.[21]

After the Arab conquest of Central Asia, the exchange of ideas between the two lands continued as the Barmakids and the Abbasids played a significant role in promoting cultural exchanges. Not only were Indian mathematicians, scholars, and physicians honoured by extending invitations to them but their works were also translated. A Balkhi astronomer and mathematician is said to have sojourned in Benaras during his study tour.[22] The arrival of such persons as Hieun Tsang, Won Kang, Alberuni, Ibn-i Battuta, and others provide evidence of the increasing interest among foreigners in Indian culture and scientific learning. Ibn-i Battuta refers to the visit of Nasiruddin Waiz Tirmizi.[23] An additional attraction for the Muslims was that they often proceeded for the Haj pilgrimage through Indian routes.[24] Sportsmen like Barkai Hindi also went from India to Tabriz to compete with Amir Ali, an expert at chess.[25] Physicians, poets, learned men, philosophers, and men of letters came to India seeking patronage or employment. Their names are recorded in the biographical notes given in the *Ain-i-Akbari*, *Tabaqat-i-Akbari*, *Muntakhab-ut-Tawarikh*, as well as in the *tazkiras* of poets like *Muzzakkira-i-Ahbab*, *Tuhfa-i-Sami*, *Lataif Nama-i-Fakhri*, and the autobiographies and memoirs of poets like those of Mutrabi. The Timurid prince, Baisunghar Mirza, is said to have collected 12,000 couplets of Khusru. Babur himself despatched a copy of his memoirs to the learned men of Transoxiana for their comments.[26] Not only did Akbar invite learned men from Shiraz and other places[27] but his large and valuable collection of books also contains all kinds of works on science, philosophy, and literature, which included the *diwans* of Jami, Khaqani, Anwari, and others.[28]

## India and Central Asia: Consanguinity and Kindred Connections

While the Mughal rulers of India were not very favourably inclined nor kindly disposed towards the Uzbek sultans and Khans, their attitude towards the people of Transoxiana reveals of their deep sense of fraternal belonging. Babur's criticism of those responsible for his exile is understandable. Nevertheless, the sentiments of kinship, racial identity, and territorial affinity seem to have exercised a potent influence. Even a careful court chronicler like Abul Fazl reveals Akbar's deep longing for and his designs on reclaiming Central Asia (a view confirmed by other sources). To realize this unfulfilled dream of conquering this unseen ancestral domain, both Jahangir and Shahjahan were determined to 'chastise' the Uzbeks and recover Transoxiana, the '*gorkhana*' (cemetery of their ancestors). The Mughals also constantly emphasized their ancestral relationship with Chingiz even though Babur always called himself a Turk. The Mongol invasions of India during the thirteenth century and the emergence of a few Mongol settlements in the country had made them a familiar though fearsome people. The Mongols, as feared and as depicted by the people whom they subjugated, were perhaps the most misunderstood creatures. Western and Eastern chroniclers alike have condemned them.[29] As elsewhere, in India also the Mongol acts were equally exaggerated. Although the famous saint Nizamuddin Auliya had expressed his appreciation of Chingiz's sense of 'universal generosity,[30] and a few favourable comments are also found in *Tabaqat-i-Nasiri*,[31] the early medieval chroniclers have generally expressed their resentment against the Mongol invaders in harsh words and have painted them in the most horrid hues. Nevertheless, an ideational transformation in our understanding of the Mongols occurs gradually with the new trends of a favourable depiction of the Mongols in the Mughal sources of the sixteenth-eighteenth centuries. By thus elevating and glorifying the Mongols, the Mughals sought to add prestige to their own dynasty. Extending their hereditary claims over the Indian territories by virtue of having the blood of Chingiz and Timur in their veins was, therefore, logical and expedient. Babur's dynasty in India was given the names of 'Chaghatai', 'Mughal', and 'Qarawanah', disregarding the genealogical differences between these groups and their relationship to Chingiz 'through females—the snares of Satan'.[32]

The significance of this relationship was not only fully realized but was equally utilized by the Mughal rulers and their court chroniclers. Abul Fazl, the court historian and deputy to Akbar, was eager to place the families of Chingiz and Timur on an equal footing. 'They were', says he,

> the descendants of two cousins who were similar and equal even in the acquisition of extraordinary conquests and magnificence ('*Ibn-i am and o dar kishwar kushai qarin ham and*'). This relationship was reported to have been further strengthened by the ratification of a covenant executed between Qachuli Bahadur and Qabal Khan (the ancestors of Chingiz and Timur respectively). Chingiz Khan is said to have 'established' another bond of fatherhood and sonship between them through the marriage of Qarachar to a daughter of Chaghatai.[33]

Although the kindered relations or kinship between the families of Chingiz and Timur cannot be disputed, there is a difference of opinion among the Central Asian and Indian Mughal chroniclers regarding the political significance of Qarachar Noyon[34] According to a Central Asian chronicler like Hafiz Tanish and an Arab historian like Ibn-i-Arab,[35] the covenant between Chingiz and Qachuli Bahadur confirms that kingship was to be the monopoly of the family of Chingiz. The emirate was to be the privilege of Qarachar Noyon. The family of Chingiz enjoyed a 'golden sanctity' attached to it since it was the 'Quraysh of the Turks'.[36] The Indian Mughal sources, however, differ on this point. Abul Fazl informs us that Chingiz Khan instructed Chaghatai not to depart from the sage counsels of Qarachar Noyon (an ancestor of Timur) and should regard him as his 'partner in rule and realm'.[37] This innocuous contradiction brings to the surface the Mughal desire to claim a close relationship and establish terms of equality with the ruling family of Chingiz Khan on the basis of their genealogy, whether real or fictitious.

Such was the pride that the Mughals deliberately cultivated in their genealogy that the text of Akbar's letter to Shah Abbas (sent in November-December 1594 from Lahore) is followed by a description of Akbar's seal fully narrating his genealogy which was traced back to Timur. The inscription of the *muhr* (seal) is followed by the remark, '*muhr ra dar kaghazi kharij zada darmiyani maktub nihadand*' ('The seal was affixed on a separate sheet of paper which was placed in the midst of the letter'). Even some *farman-i-sabti* (letters patent) of the Mughals contain the claim of genealogy all the way back to Timur.[38]

Even in paintings, the Mughals highlighted this relationship. Milo C. Beach rightly points out that the illustrations of the *Timur Nama* were prepared because the

> Mughals continually proclaimed themselves Timurids . . . . The text and illustrations for this history of Timur's life describe briefly his descendants as well,ending with Akbar. The legitimacy of that emperor's power, and his direct continuation of Timur's accomplishments and heritage, could not be more clearly stated, nor the political uses of artistic imagery more clearly understood.

The seventeenth-century portrait 'Shahjahan Riding with Dara Shikoh' (prepared by Govardhan in 1638) depicts the emperor and his eldest son as 'minute figures in the landscape'. Incidentally, 'this stylistic self-consciousness extends to the facing page' from the same *Minto Album* which depicts 'Timur Riding with an Attendant'. This double image not only proclaimed Shahjahan's links with his dynastic predecessor but also the image of Timur was presented in a deliberately archaistic and recognizably Timurid (i.e. in the fifteenth-century) style.[39]

Notwithstanding Babur's occasional outbursts against the Mongols, he held Chingiz Khan and his family and followers in high esteem. Immediately after his conquest of India, he is reported to have declared, 'Whoever there may be of the families of Sahibiqiran and Chingiz Khan, let them turn towards our court. The most high has given us Sovereignty in Hindustan. Let them come that we may see prosperity together.' He doled out assurances of favours, promising that 'if such will come to us, they will receive fitting benefits'.[40]

Akbar's attitude towards his ancestors is appropriately reflected in the comments of his biographer Abul Fazl. Abul Fazl, the wise deputy to Akbar, evaluates Chingiz Khan in his characteristic manner:

Though this great man (Chingiz Khan) be in the eyes of the vulgar and even to the elite (probably this refers to historians like Minhajus Siraj, Juvaini, and Fazlullah), at first glance, a leading exponent of Divine wrath yet to the far-reaching view of the wise, elite of the elite, he is an emanation of Divine blessings. For in the Kingdom of Divine Justice, of which human government is a ray, there can be no injustice or oppression, and everything which comes into existence in the world of evil is based on certain spiritual principles, the real nature of which the superficial cannot perceive and which cannot be comprehended save by the intellects of the far-seeing and awakened hearted.[41]

Presumably, the reference in the passage could be attributed to the Prophet's words which have been stressed by saints of different times in many ways, for example: 'As you are so shall be your rulers', that 'no misfortune shall befall you except what your hands have earned', or 'the sultan is all soul and the people all body and if the soul is impure the body too will be impure', thus placing the responsibility of good government on both the rulers and the ruled. 'If the people are righteous, the just king rules over them.' Such an attitude is clearly seen in the words attributed by Juvaini and Rashiduddin to Chingiz Khan where Chingiz describes himself 'as the flail or scourge (*azab-i khuda*) of God, sent to punish the people of Bukhara for the sins they had committed', though Barthold discounts this characterization.[42]

In one of his letters addressed to Abdur Rahim Khan-i-Khanan, Abul Fazl exhorts him and his companions to interest themselves in works such as the *Zafar Nama,* the *Shah Nama*, and the *Chingiz Nama* and to avoid reading books such as *Akhlaq-i Nasiri* and *Maktubat-i Shaikh Sharaf Maneri* which 'breathe of asceticism.'[43] The visit of Jahangir to Kabul in 1508-9 was commemorated by installing a huge wine basin engraved with the names of Jahangir and his 'ancestor' Timur.[44] To a great extent, the Timurid rulers, therefore, retained their expedient if nostalgic spirit to match with their measures.

## Central Asian Traditions and their Survival in India

Surprisingly, it remains yet to be proved whether the Indian Mughals, after their conquest of India, had given up their Central Asian traditions completely or even partly or whether they had preserved their rich legacy even while ruling over India and, if so, to what extent. The subject will make an interesting study and therefore, requires a detailed examination of its various aspects. The study is only being initiated here.

## THE IMPACT OF THE *TURA* (YASAI-CHINGIZI)

It is possible that many Turco-Mongol traditions might have survived in the Timurid polity in India even though their appearance may have been occasional. While describing the grandeur and royal pomp and fanfare of Jahangir's court, Niamatullah records that it was a 'replica of Timur's court'.[45] In the earlier years of Mughal rule, certain Chingizi traditions were observed. It is interesting to note that there is no reference to the *tura* in the letters of Akbar and Jahangir written to the Uzbek Sultans of Transoxiana (who happened to be the descendants of Chingiz Khan). In this context, it may also be pointed out that, notwithstanding their faith in Hanafite law, the Uzbek Sultans adhered to some of their tribal norms and to the clauses of the *tura* in certain respects (for example, the court arrangements, at least till the end of the seventeenth century).[46] While discussing the survival of the *tura* in the Mughal Empire in India, two basic facts have to be borne in mind. In the first place, the Mughal sources refer to the *tura* not always in the sense of Chingiz's *Yasa* but rather to the Turco-Mongol customary practices and royal traditions. The contents of the Chingizi *tura* include such matters as hunting, military organization, social norms, moral conduct, religious principles, religious toleration, attitudes towards the divines of all religions, the theory of absolute surrender to the sovereign, and so on. But the sources do not contain these references.[47]

The first direct evidence of the *tura* and its application in the Timurid Empire is found in the *Babur Nama*. Of the two references in Babur's autobiography, one certifies the observance of the *tura* by the Mongols in their military system: 'Precisely as Chingis Khan laid down his rules so the Mughals (Mongols) still observe them. Each man has his place, just where his ancestors had it; right, right—left, left—centre, centre.' The second reference relating to the application of the *tura* in the Timurid empire of Central Asia is also significant and is reproduced here. Babur asserts:

> Our forefathers through a long space of time had respected the Chingizi *tura* (ordinances), doing nothing opposed to it, whether in assembly or

court, in ceremonies and feasts, in sitting down or rising up (*majlis, divan, toi* and *ash*). Though it has no Divine authority so that a man obeys it of necessity, still good rules of conduct must be obeyed by whomsoever they are left; just in the same way that if a forefather has done ill, his ill must be changed for good.[48]

Babur's assertions with regard to the Central Asian Timurids are by and large also applicable to the Indian Timurids, and these are corroborated by other contemporary and later historians. In this context, the evidence supplied by Babur's daughter, Gulbadan Begam, is of consequence, particularly because her statements were made without any political motive. Timurid historians such as Babur, Bayazid, Mir Khond, and Gulbadan Begam vouchsafe the continuity of the *tura* in Mughal India without giving any further information about it. Even Abul Fazl, who so lavishly entertains his readers with sundry details regarding India, ignored or has perhaps consciously and deliberately avoided a reference to the *tura* and its clauses.[49]

In the Mughal chronicles, the treatment of the *tura* has three distinct shades. In the first place, the information pertaining to the *tura* and its application in the Mughal empire as supplied by the court chroniclers is meagre and is confined mostly to the sphere of ceremonials and customary practices. During the three centuries of Mughal rule in India, only Babur and Humayun claimed to follow or actually adhered to certain precepts of the *tura*, either as a matter of habit or for reasons of political expediency. References to the *tura* are found more frequently during the first few decades of Mughal rule. It was also observed during the reign of Akbar. In the first few years of the seventeenth century, one feels a deliberate resurgence of the *tura* and the Chaghatai traditions. The *tura* figures in Jahangir's autobiography and is seen in some of his measures. The impact of the *tura*, however, faded away gradually in the reign of Shahjahan and was finally replaced by Perso-Islamic tenets after the religious revivalism in the reign of Aurangzeb.

In the opinion of Erskine, the laws of Chingiz Khan were 'probably merely traditionary' and were a 'collection of old usages of the Mughal tribes'. Erskine reiterates that in Babur's days they were still respected among the wandering tribes but did not form the law of his kingdom since they had been introduced before the advent of Islam and were in many respects inconsistent with the Koran. Abdur Rafi finds the Mongols, customs somewhat incompatible (*na sazgar*) with the precepts of Islam.[50] Although a full text or a complete record of the *Yasa's* clauses may or may not be extant, at least enough fragmentary information is available in various Arabic, and Persian chronicles and travelogues.[51] This material was collected by Riasanovsky[52] and was later presented thematically by Spuler.[53] These clauses do not seem to be at variance with the *Sharia* though the same compliment may not be true in the context of Chingiz's *Yasa*.[54] Juvaini, a Muslim chronicler *par excellence*, stresses that Chingiz Khan 'established such usages as were praiseworthy from the point of view of reason. . . . There are many of these ordinances that are in conformity with the Shariat.'[55] Juvaini also condemns the measures of Chaghatai. The simultaneous adherence to orthodox Islam and the *Yasa* was considered to be incongruous by the medieval historian, Haidar Dughlat.[56]

Certain customs were continued by the early Timurids, a practice which reflects the remnants of their past connection to Central Asia. Gulbadan Begam avers that the ceremonials, etiquette, and norms of Humayun's court were in conformity with the Mongol *tura*. Even the gifts were presented in the Mongol fashion, namely, all sorts of stuff in ninette (*tuquz*). Elsewhere, Gulbadan Begam recounts how in the assembly of the Timurid princes (Humayun, Kamran, Hindal, and Sulaiman) at Kishm[57] (or, if Abul Fazl is to be believed, at Ishkmish), Babur had 'enjoined certain *tura* (regulations) which are fixed for interviews with kings'.[58] Gulbadan Begam describes how Babur's arrival in June 1506 at the call of Sultan Husain Mirza, followed by the latter's sudden death and Babur's subsequent march for condolence, led to a controversy among the Timurid princes. On hearing about the arrival of Babur, all the princes marched to meet him except Badi-uz Zaman who was dissuaded by Burunduq Beg and Zulnun Beg on the grounds of his (Badi-uz Zaman) being older than Babur. The matter was resolved when Qasim Beg Quchin asserted, 'Younger he (Babur) is by years but by the *tura* he has precedence because he has more than once taken Samarqand by force of the sword.'[59]

Several other sources confirm that the prescribed norms and the Turco-Mongol customs and practices were often followed 'in the fashion of Chingiz Khan' during the reigns of Babur and Humayun. Bayazid Bayat also refers to a certain Mongol ruler, Chaghatai Sultan, for whom Humayun had a deep affection. Humayun is said to have practised certain Chingizi regulations. Haidar Dughlat constantly refers to the Timurid rulers of India as 'Chaghatai'. At one place, he records that 'Emperor (Humayun) and myself had become friends (*dust*) after the Mongol fashion.' He stresses that in the councils and in the *farmans* Humayun always addressed him by this name. Presumably, the reference is to the Mongol custom of *anda*.[60]

On another occasion, when a hunting excursion was in progress in the orange gardens of the mountain passes and Hindal was in attendance before Humayun, the latter 'went towards where Mirza Hindal was hunting and had made a very good bag. Following the rules of Chingiz Khan, the Mirza preferred his game to the Emperor for it is a rule of Chingiz Khan that inferiors should so act towards their superior.' The principle of seniority and superiority emphasized here is reminiscent of Chingizi sources like the *Secret History*, and the works of Juvaini and Fazlullah. However, this concept had originated from the Turco-Mongol customs.

Similarly, the importance attached to the *tura* by the early Timurids was not unknown in contemporary Persia. Even Shah is reported to have appreciated the Timurid sentiments by showing due regard to the *tura*. Masum Bhakkari reports that in 1511 Shah Beg of Qandahar was graciously received at the Shah's court and was exempted from performing the *sijda* in the Persian fashion. Instead, he was ordered to kneel on his knees and to offer respects 'in conformity with the Chaghatai Tura' (*ba ain-i tura-i chaghataiya*).[61]

In an account dated 1548, Abul Fazl clearly states that when Kamran came to pay his respects to Humayun, the latter observed 'the ceremonials of reception in accordance with the Tura' (*didan-i Tura*).[62] Similarly, Badauni records that Akbar also 'revised an old Chaghatai custom' in Rajab 983 on the arrival of an old Timurid prince, a cousin of Babur, namely, Mirza Sulaiman (then the ruler of Badakhshan). On this occasion, the royal table was placed in the audience hall and the officers of high ranks collected the soldiers together and took upon themselves the trouble of arranging the customary food. All these measures were taken 'in order to exhibit it to Mirza Sulaiman. But when the Mirza departed, these customs departed too'. Incidentally, no other contemporary chronicler refers to the 'revival' of these Chaghatai traditions, though the arrival of Mirza Sulaiman is described in detail.[63] Again, another reference to the *tura* and to the *tuzuk* is found in Badauni in connection with

Akat Khan's accession, when *amirs* 'in accordance with ancient customs (*Tura o Tuzuk*) gave their allegiance' to him as the rightful king.[64]

Notwithstanding such stray references to the *tura* and to the Chaghatai traditions as found in the sources of the mid-sixteenth century, the reign of Akbar may safely be called a watershed in Mughal history. Akbar was proud of the Mughals, Central Asian connections and traditions as these had stood them in good stead and were likely to enhance their prestige further if exploited properly; yet the fact that Humayun had been thrown out as an 'outside element' by the Afghan potentates was bound to make Akbar's prospects in Central Asia rather grim. It is no wonder, therefore, that Akbar became anxious to build an empire within India itself which was basically cosmopolitan though essentially 'native born' and indigenous in its complexion. Attempts were, therefore, made at amalgamation. The exotic aspects of the Mughal empire were gradually transformed to suit the emperor's outlook and his political needs. In the wake of assimilation, the extra-territorial traits of cultural and social life were not entirely obliterated but were adapted to the existing local conditions. In this process of creating a composite culture and a syneretic civilization, the purely Central Asian traditions became the first casualty, unconsciously though naturally. A fine blend of Central Asian and Indian traditions, with a varnishing of Perso-Islamic principles is noticed in various spheres of Mughal politics and administration under Akbar. Strangely enough, a revival of Turco-Mongol traditions, howsoever temporary, is noticeable in the first few years of the seventeenth century.[65] Apart from Jahangir's 'intentional record' in the form of his autobiography, there are several other sources which contain references to the *Tura-i-Changizi* and the Chaghatai traditions.[66]

The information provided by Qazivini[67] shows that in India also the clauses of the *Yasa* were sometimes used for political purposes to beat down rival claimants to the throne. While referring to the accession crisis soon after Akbar's death, Qazivini (the author of *Halat-i Asad Beg*) describes the proceedings of the consultative assembly in which Khusru's candidature was under consideration along with that of his father.

The two senior nobles of Akbar's court, namely, Man Singh and Khan-i-Azam Aziz Kuka (the maternal uncle and father-in-law respectively of the ill-fated Khusru), argued that Akbar was in favour of placing Khusru on the throne and that Salim's candidature had not received much favour from the emperor. It was at this juncture that Said Khan Chaghatai, a 'simple-minded Turco-Mongol' and a senior Akbari noble (*az Umra-i Kabbur*) who had very close and brotherly relations with Akbar, interrupted. He demanded to know how such a strange formula could be put into practice whereby Sultan Salim could be superseded by his own son, Khusru. It was also unthinkable that both father and son should simultaneously be asked to rule over the empire. Such a practice, he pointed out, was not in conformity with the prevalent traditions and the *tura* of Chaghatai.

The incident reminds one of the accession crisis following the death of Chaghatai, and Qaan Guyuk's subsequent ruling: 'Why should the grandson succeed when there was a son?' Guyuk discarded the claims of Chaghatai's grandson (a son of Metiken) and successfully pleaded the cause of his favourite, Yesu. It should be noted here that Chingiz's verdict had favoured the accession of capable persons of Chingizi blood, be he son or grandson.[68] Even Timur had nominated his grandson Pir Muhammad Sultan though his son Shah-Rukh was still alive. Similarly, the example of the dual government of Sultan Husain Mirza's two sons, namely, Badi-uz Zaman and Muzaffar Husain, in Herat, was also a noticeable precedent. Nevertheless, the Indian Timurids used the *tura* with as much wisdom as their predecessors.

In his autobiography, Jahangir refers to Chingiz Khan's *tura* several times. Like Babur, Jahangir also persuades us to believe that the Mughals in many respects followed this canon. While expressing his desire to benefit Akbari and Jahangiri nobles by converting their birth-places into their *jagirs*, he invited their representation to this effect 'so that in accordance with the Chingizi *tura* the stage might be conveyed to them by Altamgha'. On another occasion, when the rebel Prince Khusru was brought before him in chains, Jahangir describes that Khusru stood weeping and trembling 'with a chain fastened from his left hand to his left foot (or "with his hands tied and chains on his legs from the left side") after the manner and custom of Chingiz Khan'. Similarly, during his meeting with his mother, he asserts that 'I had the good fortune to be received by her. After the performance of obeisance and prostration and greeting which is due from the young to the old, according to the custom of Chingiz Khan, the rules of Timur and common usage, and after worship of the King of the world (God); and after finishing this business, I obtained leave to return.'[69]

A new era in the history of Indo-Central Asian relations begins with the accession of Shahjahan. The diplomatic embassies of Jahangir emphasizing friendly relations with the Uzbeks were subsequently replaced by military adventures and the expansionist policy of his successors. Mughal contacts with the Chaghatai regions had considerably increased, particularly after the conquest of Balkh and Badakhshan. Interesting information is available in the Persian chronicles and in the travelogues of the seventeenth and early eighteenth centuries regarding the geography, political conditions, revenue affairs, military organizations, customs and traditions of the Uzbek Empire and its people, and even about the weaknesses of their sultans which led to their downfall. The genealogy of the Mughal rulers of India tracing their lineage from Timur and his successors, with particular reference to their close connections with the royal family of Chingiz Khan, can also be found in the sources for the later Mughals. Nevertheless, the occasional references to the 'Chaghatai traditions' found in the early Mughal sources are conspicuously missing here. Presumably, the gradual changes taking place in the religio-political arena and the new trends emerging in the second half of the seventeenth and the early eighteenth centuries were strong enough to put down even occasional revivals of the *Tura-i-Chingizi*.

Although the *tura* may have lost its relevance in the later centuries of the now well-entrenched Mughal rule, the Turco-Mongol norms and practices seem to have lingered on, such as the custom of *tuquz* (presents in ninette) which is mentioned in the *Alamgir Nama* and other sources.

As has been discussed elsewhere, the principles of the *tura* and the Chaghatai traditions had limited relevance and utility in the Indian context. In an agrarian society, the norms and traditions framed for a military state and economy were naturally incompatible. A *coup d'oeil* of the Mughal sources shows that the emphasis on the *tura* was motivated by the realpolitik of the Mughal emperors who wanted to highlight their links with the two former conquerors of India and to the great empire builders, Chingiz and Timur. It may, however, be pointed out that the *tura* was preserved and at best its traditions continued to linger in the Mughal empire only in the manner of *kanun-i tashrifat* (the law of ceremonies and etiquette).

## THE ECCLESIASTICAL PILLARS OF THE EMPIRE: THE *LASHKAR-I-DUA*

It is interesting to note that the Mongols believed in individual's freedom in the choice of personal religion (a kind of anabaptism which became popular among certain groups in sixteenth-century England). A child was not given the religion in the cradle. Instead, he was allowed to grow up without being branded as the follower of any one religion. He was thereafter expected to decide for himself after fully understanding the texts of religion. Even Shamanism, the hereditary religion, was not imposed upon them. Chingiz had conquered a vast and multi-religious empire where adaptation and adherence to one particular religion could be politically disastrous. All the sons of Chingiz followed a different style of worship. Juji the eldest was very favourably inclined towards Islam and Muslims, and his son Baraka was a deeply religious and staunch Muslim (hence Dasht-i Qipchaq was renamed Dasht-i Baraka) and so was his descendant Uzbek Sultan. Similarly, Guyuk, son of Ogedei and grandson of Chingiz, was an orthodox Christian and so were his successors. Chaghatai was anti-Muslim and resorted to the suppression of many Muslim practices. Toulou's children were most enterprising in religious ventures. Some of his descendants changed their religion three or even five times. Even Ghazan Khan who won the title of 'Padshahi Islam' was originally a staunch Buddhist who built several pagodas. He converted to Islam to ensure a strong and popular rule over his Muslim subjects as advised by one of his ministers. The only sphere in which the clauses of the *Yasa* were perhaps faithfully followed was in matters of religious tolerance and liberal attitudes towards saints and sages of all religions. Not only did Chingiz recommend and propagate religions and religious tolerance, but he also practised it himself. Juvaini informs us that he (Chingiz) eschewed bigotry, and the preference of one faith for another and the placing of some above others; rather he honoured and respected the learned and pious of every sect, recognizing such conduct as the way to the court of God. Juvaini further asserts that the successors of Chingiz 'do not swerve from the *Yasa* of Chingiz Khan namely, to consider all sects as one and not to distinguish them from one another'.[70]

The concept of the divine theory of sovereignty was another common feature. As in medieval India, this too had always been a political necessity in ancient India. Romila Thapar writes:

The centrifugal forces of the post-Mauryan polity were sought to be counterbalanced by the association of divine elements with the ruler. In earlier periods the gods were often compared with princes; now the kings came to be compared with the gods. In a Satvahana record Gautamiputra Shatakarni is compared to several gods in prowess. The analogy emphasises the divine aspects of kingship which received even more emphasis during the time of the Guptas. The Kushana rulers also tried to deify themselves, as is clear from their title 'devputra' (son of God).

Thapar continues:

The divine nature of kingship was an established idea. It was reinforced from time to time by means of elaborate ritual sacrifices which the king initiated. After the coronation, when his legal status as king had been established, he began the year-long royal consecration (rajasuya) which invested him with divinity brought from the gods by the magic power of the presents. The ritual was highly symbolic, the king undergoing purification and mystical rebirth as a divine.

While commenting on his father's religious attitude, Jahangir notes with appreciation that:

The professors of various faiths had room in the broad expanse of the incomparable sway of his Empire, as in the wide expanse of the Divine compassion there is room for all classes and the followers of all creeds, so, on the principle that the shadow must have the same properties as the light, in his dominions which on all sides were limited only by the Salt Sea, there was room for the professors of opposite religions, and for beliefs, good and bad, and the road to altercation was closed.[71]

Timur and his successors in Central Asia and India continued this practice. Babur's will describes religious tolerance as one of the four ingredients of a lasting and stable empire.[72]

While discussing the *sifat-i-qudsi* (holy qualities) of divinely appointed sovereigns, Abul Fazl emphasizes that the king must be above religious differences. In an age when religious persecution was not unusual, Akbar proved himself to be an exception. In a letter to Shah Abbas of Persia, he condemns the sectarian genocide going on elsewhere in Turkey and Persia.[73]

'The Divine graciousness and Mercy attaches itself to every form of creed . . . hence it is only proper that Kings who are the shadows of God on earth should not give up this practice.'[74] In his *Ains*, he instructs the officials specially to desist from interfering in the religious beliefs of ant one. When Kudaidad Barlas killed Mullah Ahmad of Thatta for his Shia heresy, he was tied to the feet of an elephant and paraded through the city.[75]

The showering of lavish grants on religious groups and the tradition of maintaining them as an 'army of prayers' (*lashkar-i-dua*) were as common in the Central Asian Turco-Mongol empires as in Timurid India.[76] The patronage of saints and the exemption from taxes granted to the holy men were attributed even by contemporary writers to the Mongol traditions.[77] Niamatullah criticizes Jahangir for his puzzling deviation from the 'Chaghatai traditions' of extending respect and honour to the saints and wonders how Jahangir could be so callous towards Saiyid Ahmad Sun. This saint had impressed Jahangir by his own popularity and large following. When Jahangir invited him to Agra, however, no prostration, regard, or respect was shown to him though these were 'binding upon him (Jahangir) in accordance with the Chaghatai order'. The saint was imprisoned and released only through the intercession of Khan-i-Zaman, whom he accompanied as far as the Deccan.[78]

As in the case of Timur, contradictory accounts have been given by chroniclers regarding Akbar's religious attitude.[79] Badauni seems to have a counterpart in Ibn-i Arab Shah who depicts Timur as 'faithless' and 'irreligious' and who alleges that he was not an orthodox Muslim and was an individual who acted upon the principles of *Yasa*, disregarding the Sharia completely. An Arab traveller of the fourteenth century, however, relates the views of Timur on religion at length. According to him, Timur believed in one God but he respected all religions alike—an attitude adopted by most of his successors in Mughal India, particularly Akbar.[80]

Like his predecessors, Chingiz and others, Timur frequently held religious discussions regarding the problems of the *sharia*, partly because of his keen desire to equip himself with the knowledge of Islamic traditions so as to guard against the tricks of the religious classes. Similar considerations of state craft and political expediency can be seen in Akbar's attitude towards mullas such as Shaikh Abdunnabi and Abdullah Sultanpuri. Akbar's quest for religious understanding, his 'search for the truth' and, his quest for self-appraisal accompanied by discourses on various themes ranging from ecclesiastical and philosophical to physical and metaphysical issues finally paved the way for the foundation of the Ibadat

Khana—a process which reminds one of Qubilai's religious discussions and subsequent attempts to organize a religious council.[81] The controversy over Akbar's personal faith—heightened by his own comments at various stages—finds a parallel in Timur's attitude. In the same way, Akbar's image is similar to Ibn-i Khaldun's depiction of Timur: 'Some attribute to him (Timur) knowledge, others attribute to him heresy because they note his preference for the members of the house of Ali (*ahl-i bait*), still others attribute to him the employment of magic and sorcery, but in all this there is nothing; it is simply that he is highly intelligent and very perspicacious, addicted to debate and argumentation about what he knows and about what he does not know.[82] The same inquisitive approach made Akbar complain,[83] 'Discourses on philosophy have such a charm for me that they distract me from all else, and I forcibly restrain myself from listening to them, lest the necessary duties of the hour should be neglected.[84]

In response to Abdullah Khan's charges of heresy levelled against himself, Akbar asserted that his religious discussions had higher motives, that is:

> For a proper comprehension of the subtle intricacies of religious questions, he was examining the interpretations of the jurists, investigating, clarifying and evaluating the objectives of theologians and deducing the sources of the statements and the arguments, the beliefs of the past and present generations, and the many divergent views which had sprung up during the preceding millennium and whose details were available in various works. These discussions resulted in the deterioration of the market of such people and a disfavour of those ignorant persons who were by hypocrisy appearing in the garb of intellectuals and had gained favours. The deliberations over these matters have brought into the limelight certain capable persons who had till then remained in oblivion due to the depravity of the pseudo-theologians who had acquired an important position among the people in the guise of wise men and who had pushed these persons into the background.[85]

According to his own professions, Akbar was 'always anxious to secure the pleasure of God. But since there had been a great deal of difference of opinion in practically all religious matters, he had sought for proof and justification regarding each argument in matters relating to knowledge and action.' Such was his love for rational thinking and research (*tahqiq*) in religions that in 1582 he ordered 'explicitly that the rational contents of different religions and faiths should be translated from the language of each and that the rose garden of the traditional aspects of each religion should, as far as possible, be cleared of the thorns of bigotry. His interest in the *Razm Nama*, therefore, perfectly balanced his wish to learn about traditional India and his waning concern for fantastic or mythological narratives.[86]

Similarly, his desire to learn about Christianity is evident from his letter to King Philip II of Spain.[87] The subsequent confusion is quite interesting as the Jesuit priests found Akbar 'drifting hither and thither', like a ship without a rudder. Notwithstanding the suspicion that this 'search for the truth' could emanate only from agnosticism or even eclecticism, the optimism and hope of the Christian priests 'to reap a great harvest of heathens and commence the conversion of the continent of India' is clearly reflected in their letter.[88] Like Chingiz who had invited Chang Chun the Taoist saint to guide him in administrative affairs, Timur too had once invited the mullahs to come forward to assist him in the task of state management but this amiability of Timur towards the saints and the mullahs was entirely transformed whenever Timur noticed even the slightest high-handedness or suspected an encroachment upon his absolute rights of sovereignty. In this regard, he never hesitated from taking action against the theologians.[89]

The Turco-Mongol rulers held the religious divines and mystic saints in as much high esteem as they were held by the Timurids in Central Asia. In his *Yasa*, Chingiz decreed that: 'No taxes or duties should be imposed upon the descendants of Ali-Bek Abu Taleb without exception as well as upon fakirs, readers of *Al Qoran*, lawyers, physicians, scholars, people who devote themselves to prayer and asceticism, muezzin and those who wash the dead bodies.'[90] A group of religious personages almost always accompanied the army. The Mongol sources pointedly refer to these two classes, namely, the *lashkar-i-zahir* (the apparent army) and the *lashkar-i batin* (the concealed army), denoting the army of the warriors and the army of prayers respectively. Both seem to have equally served as the pillars of the pavillion of their power.[91] It was no wonder then that the ambitious Timur was also kind to these saints and often visited mystic saints to seek their blessings. Timur's devotion to Shaikh Baraka, 'who supported with his prayers what Timur did with his sword',[92] his attachment to Shamsuddin Fahur-i reminds us of Akbar's attachment to Shaikh Salim Chishti and other saints. Timur's relations with Baba Sanku, the *wali* and *sahib jazba*,[93] may have inspired Jahangir to bend his knee before Jadrup Gosain. The construction of the tombs of divines was certainly a matter of devotion and courtesy, or expediency, both in Central Asia and in India. Not only has Akbar's gesture of generosity towards the four classes of men been recorded by Abul Fazl in his *Ain* 19 on Suyurghal, but Jahangir also mentioned the significance of this *lashkar-i-dua* (army of prayers) in his memoirs.[94]

While discussing the active socio-cultural contacts between the two countries, it is also worthwhile to examine the relations between the Sufi saints and Indian social groups. Sufism, which played an important role in spreading humanistic principles, social harmony, and the message of love in India, was mainly a Central Asian import. Abul Fazl's *Ain* includes a separate section on this subject. The Sufis trickled into India at regular intervals and were well settled in the country even before the Sultanate of Delhi was established. In Central Asia, each of the Timurid rulers had spiritual guides from among the Naqshbandi saints who seem to have generally monopolized this privilege. In India, Babur performed the *rauza dashtan* (circumambulation of the religious precincts) and Akbar visited Salim Chishti's tomb.These measures indicate the continuing influence of the Mughals' ancestral faith in the Sufi saints.

During the invasions by Timur and the Mongols, a large number of Saiyids fled from Central Asia and settled in Kashmir and other places. Such fugitives included Bulbul Shah Saiyid Sharafuddin of the Suhrawardia order of Sufis who came to Kashmir during the reign of Suhadeven from Turkestan along with thousands of others. Prominent saints like Qazi Hamiduddin Nagauri and Qutubuddin Bakhtiyar Kaki hailed from Central Asia. The latter's father Kamaluddin Musa came from Ush to Delhi during the reign of Iltutmish. The process of emigration continued till the fall of the Sultanate. During the reign of Sultan Sikandar (1398-1413), poets like Saiyid Muhammad from Khwarazm and saints like Saiyid Jalaluddin from Bukhara along with his followers, Baba Haji Adham and his disciple Baba Hasan of Balkh, arrived. Saints like Hazrat Makhdumi Nura are exceptions, who came to India but left immediately out of disgust on account of the favours shown by Humayun to Shiakh Pul and Muhammad Parghari and an utter neglect of the Khwaja himself. Husain Shah Chak though himself a Shia Muslim by faith had appointed Saiyid Habib, a Sunni jurist from Khwarazm, as *qazi* of Srinagar and a preacher of the Jarna mosque and allowed the practice of the Hanafite law. The Kashmiris who wanted to study jurisprudence were usually acknowledged as 'full-fledged jurists' only after they had studied at Samarqand, Herat, or Mecca, after finishing their initial education in Srinagar. Many outstanding scholars from Kashmir went to Central Asia for further studies and all the famous madrasas of Bukhara kept their names on their rolls. For example, Shaikh Yaqub Serfi, a renowned scholar and Sufi statesman, studied in Khwarazm under Shaikh Husain. After his meeting with the learned men of Central Asia, he was recognized as an accomplished jurist. Similarly, Mohsin Fani acquired advanced education in Balkh and at other places, and served under Nazr Muhammad. In the sixteenth century, the Naqshbandi saints acquired much influence in the Uzbek court. It is generally believed that the Naqshbandiya order was popularized in India by Babur. In the early part of Akbar's reign, some of the Naqshbandi saints migrated to Agra. They comprised two factions, those who criticized Akbar's religious views and those who joined his service and received high posts.[95]

The relations between the Juibari Shaikhs and the Mughal court also form an important part of this cultural affinity. Muhammad Talib refers to the exchange of letters between Akbar and the Central Asian Khwajas and asserts that Akbar wrote to Khwaja Saad (popularly known as Khwaja Kalan of Juibari) several letters in which he addressed him with high-sounding titles. He notes that Khwaja Saad was particularly kind towards Akbar's envoy Hakim Humam during his stay in Turan, that in return Akbar assigned the *wilayat* of Nishapur (which was interestingly not included in the Mughal empire) to him so that he succeeded his father as Shaikhul Islam. Incidentally, the envoy of Jahangir, Mir Baraka, remained for several years in the service of Khwaja Tajuddin. He went to India with Abdur Rahman Khwaja. When Mir Baraka wrote to Jahangir about the proposed arrival of the Khwaja, the Mughal emperor was delighted and allocated for the Khwaja a *mansab* of *haftsadi* (700).

The arrival of Abdur Rahman Khwaja in India was necessitated by political reasons. His son, Abdul Khwaja (b. 1568) was received by Akbar with much fanfare. He was even taken to the royal treasury to pick for himself whatever he wanted. The author of *Matlabut Talibain*, however, boasts that the Khwaja just selected a *Kaukabi tali* and after coming out of the treasury he gave it to a *dervish*. In addition to the Juibari Shaikhs other spiritual guides and theologians also came to India very often. Jahangir writes in his memoirs that he received from Khwaja Dehbadi some arrows and bows as a mark of consideration. In his letters, Khwaja Hashmi cites the poems of Babur addressed in his times to the Khwajas. In response to Khwaja Hashmi's queries Jahangir records his regard and love for the Khwajas in a quatrain. Khwaja Abdul Ghaffar sent several letters to Aurangzeb and in return received Indian goods worth twelve thousand rupees. The Khwajas were always given a warm and very elaborate welcome. Khwaja Abdul Shahid (son of Khwaja Ahrar) lived in the court of Akbar for twenty years and enjoyed a following of 2,000 persons. Another descendant of Khwaja Ahrar, Ashrafuddin Husain, was also given the Sarkar of Nagaur and the hand of Akbar's sister Bakhshi Banu Begam. This policy of special consideration towards the Khwajas was particularly maintained by Akbar and Jahangir, probably to compensate for the lack of enforcement of the Sharia in their empire. Even the Central Asian Khwajas sent presents to the Mughal rulers and received in return goods of equal value.

## The Central Asian Nobility: The Founding Fathers of Mughal Rule in India

The Timurid dynasty in Central Asia had four tribal pillars, namely, Qauchin, Arlat, Jalair, and Barlas. In Timurid India, we frequently hear of who were nobles the descendants of the above-mentioned tribes, particularly during the early years of Mughal rule. From the very beginning of Mughal rule, the Turani nobility had proved its martial capabilities. The Turani nobles enjoyed high-sounding titles (like Safdar Jung, Khan-i Zaman, and Khan-i Alam), high *mansabs*, and posts. They were frequently assigned difficult and challenging campaigns and assignments and more often than not they succeeded in accomplishing even the most troublesome jobs. In many other ways, they enjoyed considerable share in the glories of Akbar's reign though not with adequate appreciation.

Mughal sources seem to suggest that the Mughals and particularly Akbar had inherited a 'turbulent' Turani nobility which stirred up rebellions and continued to disrupt the peace and prosperity of Akbar's empire. Nevertheless, the same sources also confirm that Akbar continued to recruit and induct new forces and talent from the lands beyond the Hindukush even though he had to pay larger amounts as salaries to the Turanis and the Persians notwithstanding the fact that cheaper military personnel were available in India.[96] The praises showered and the criticism heaped upon the Uzbeks further accentuate this anomaly. The Central Asian chroniclers also have not spared the Uzbeks. Even the travellers in India and Central Asia frequently criticized the Uzbeks. Like the Mongols, their descendants the Uzbeks also faced unabated condemnation for the characteristics which were in general a nobility syndrome—the practices customary in the community of the nobles. The so-called 'opportunism' and 'faithlessness' of Uzbek nobles have been commented upon by the Persian chronicler Iskandar Munshi. He cites the instance of the Safavid noble Durmesh Khan who refused to betray his masters (the Persians) for the sake of a promised Uzbek *jagir* because he was not a Turani noble capable of such an unholy alliance. Jahangir also declared that 'no one can be more faithless than a Badakhshi'. According to Shahnawaz Khan, Turani evidence on a question of Shariat law was discarded by Yar Ali Beg simply because 'little reliance could be placed on it as it was Turani evidence'.[97]

Abul Fazl, the celebrated sixteenth-century chronicler of Akbar's reign, criticizes the unitary composition of the Uzbek nobility, saying that 'one class of people if employed to the exclusion of others would cause rebellion as in the case of the Uzbeks and Qizilbashs who used to dethrone their kings'. Abul Fazl's opinion echoes the ideas of Tusi and Nakhchiwani both of whom had, centuries earlier, warned their emperors against employing 'one class (*yak jins*) of people' in an army as 'it was a sure signal of danger (*khatarha khezand*) for they stop working hard and indulge in conspiracies (*takhlit*)'. Abul Fazl's comments may (mis)lead the readers to assume that the Qizilbash or the Uzbek nobility and army were not heterogeneous, multi-racial, or multi-religious and that they were habitually seditious. The Persian nobility comprised Georgians and Circassians who were rivals, in addition to the Qizilbash nobility, even as early as the reign of Shah Tahmasp. The Turani nobility also comprised various factions, namely, the Chaghatai (comprising usually Barlas, Jalair, Qauchin, and Arlat), the Uzbeks (consisting of the Ulusat, Salsa, i.e. the pure and core Uzbek group comprising Qushchi, Naiman, and Durman), Turcomans, Badakhshanis and many others of Central Asian origin. Even the Uzbeks claim to have consisted of ninety-two Turco-Mongol tirbes, sixty of whom were mentioned by Ubaidullah in his letter to Sultan Salim of Turkey.[98] Thus, the Turani and the

Irani nobility were neither homogeneous nor essentially treacherous.

In India also, the Turani nobility at Akbar's court comprised various factions. Apart from the major divisions, namely, the Chaghatai (comprising the Barlas, Jalair, Qauchin, and Arlat), the Uzbeks (consisting of tribes like Qushchi, Naiman, and Durman) and finally, the Turcomans, there were many others of Central Asian origin. It is asserted that there is sufficient evidence to prove that the Turanis lived in India even before the advent of the Mughals. After his invasion, Timur had left behind Qurluq tribesmen to guard the country. One of these, Sultan Husain Khan (the ruler of Pakli) fled after paying homage to Akbar. These poor creatures almost always lost favour allegedly due to their 'presumption' and 'immodesty' as much as due to the 'jealousy and hatred of their enemies'.

In addition to their martial prowess, the Turani nobility also exhibited its talents in the fine arts. Many of them were good poets, painters, writers, philosophers, physicians, wrestlers, and scribes. Qazi Khan Badakhshi, popularly known as 'Qazi Nizam', was a remarkable authority on traditional and rational knowledge. He was the author of many important books. According to Abul Fazl, 'His courage made illustrious his wisdom and his sword exalted the dignity of his pen.' Examples of such talented individuals can be multiplied and are found in the accounts of Abul Fazl, Nizam-uddin, and Badauni. The Turanis were pitted even against their own compatriots. The Barlas *amirs* too chastized the Uzbek rebel, Abdullah Khan Uzbek. Some of them even gave up their life for the sake of duty so that their 'devotion will be told to the king'. People like Shakli Farid Murtaza Khan Bukhari accomplished efficient administrative services and acted not only as *mir bakhshi* and *vizir* but even drew himself the charge of *diwan-i-tan* due to the incompetence of the *divan*. Apart from these duties, says Shahnawaz Khan, he also performed 'two good services' which 'raised him above his peers or rather above all the officers and pillars of the Empire', i.e. nipping in the bud the conspiracy of Man Singh and Aziz Kuka and ensuring the safe accession of Jahangir and the final suppression of Khusru. It was an occasion when 'the Saiyids of Baraka and Bukhara distinguished themselves and devoted their lives'. In this context, the following comments may be quoted: 'His Majesty during the fifty years of his reign increased the number of Chaghatais (Turanis) and Rajputs (among nobles) for these people are not seditious.'[99] Regarding Khan-i Zaman Shaibani's services, Abul Fazl comments: 'Next to Bayram, the restoration of the Mughal dynasty may be justly ascribed to him.' While receiving Nawab Mirza Ghazi Beg Tarkhan (a descendant of Timur's noble, Isa Tarkhan Mir Zulnun), even a statesman like Abul Fazl was obliged to say: 'We are also the lord masters (*makhadim*) and native friars (*hamshahri mulk-i shuma*) of your own country.' Necessity had further brought them closer. Humayun's death let loose all rebellious elements. All territory except Punjab was lost. The Afghans raised their heads and Mirza Sulaiman recited the *khutba* in his own name in Kabul. In this hour of crisis, even the Chaghatai officers 'were not well affected towards staying in India' and were advising a departure to Kabul. Abul Fazl categorically says that the arrival of the families of the nobles had improved the situation but Akbar could hardly rely upon one class of people particularly when a better alternative was available.[100]

The mass exodus of people from Transoxiana was an immediate answer to this problem. While describing the march to Punjab (December 1556), Abul Fazl wrote: 'There were both munificence and pleasures. Turks and Tajiks came in crowds attracted by the fame of benevolence and the lights of justice. Especially there was not a day when large numbers did not come from Kabul, Badakhshan, and Qandahar and pay homage.'[101] The emigrants from Persia mostly included the Sunnis who feared the Persian Shahs and the retaliatory genocide in that country. Economic motives played a limited role, as peaceful and prosperous conditions prevailed in Persia following the end of the wars with the Ottomans after the peace of Amasya (1955) and the Uzbek invasions had been suspended ever since the death of the mighty Ubaidullah Khan Uzbek in 1539. With all its commercial and agrarian potential and the security provided by powerful rulers such as Shah Ismail (1502-24) and Shah Tahmasp (1524-76), the Persian empire flourished to the extent of binding its inhabitants to its soil. In contrast, the situation in Transoxiana had worsened. After the death of Ubaidullah Khan in 1539, Transoxiana was engulfed in civil wars. Mutual rivalries and chaos continued until the ascendancy of Abdullah Khan. Both Sidi Ali Reis and Jenkinson describe the situation of anarchy, political chaos, and financial crisis. Hafiz Tanish says that during the Balkh campaign in 1572-3, a large number of people left their homeland and went to India. The emigration continued even in the later years.

The Turani nobility was, therefore, more numerous than could be surmised on the basis of the suffix (Turani or Uzbek) attached to their names. The Timurid dynasty in Central Asia had four tribal pillars, namely, Qauchin, Arlat, Jalair, and Barlas.[102] In Timurid India, we frequently hear of the nobles descending from the last three tribes named above, particularly during the sixteenth century. Apart from the members of the royal family who later on became the *mansabdars* or provincial governors, like Mirza Shah-Rukh and his sons, there were many Turanis who added neither Turani nor Uzbek to their names. Instead, they preferred their specific tribal or particular town identity to replace the identities based on racial groups or general geographical area. Nizamuddinov claims that the Central Asian emigrants took pride in their descent and continued to call themselves Indarabi, Bukhari, Samarqandi, Tirmizi, Badakhshi, all identities based on specific regional and geographical areas.[103]

Based on his 'happy sayings',[104] Akbar appears to be a person who did not believe in the nobility of birth and origin though his letters sometimes signify his trust in *noblesse oblige*. Mirza Wali Turani, a descendant of the Khwajas of Naqshband, however, found favour with Akbar only due to his *nijabat-i-izati*, and was married to Sultan Daniyal's daughter notwithstanding his wickedness and lack of wisdom. Many of the Turani nobles preferred to remain unidentified. For instance, we have the cases of Alif Khan Beg, a Chaghatai Barlas whose ancestors had served the Timurid dynasty both in Transoxiana and India, and Shah Budagh Khan who belonged to the group of the *miyankal-i-aimaqs*.

Frequent matrimonial relations established with many of these Turani nobles prove that the ruling dynasty at least admitted a degree of open affinity with them. Many Turani nobles at Akbar's court were hereditary beneficiaries of Timur's dynasty.[105] Some of these Turanis were of mixed origin. Sometimes even the nobles of Central Asian origin preferred to adopt an Indian identity. For instance, we have the case of Shah-Rukh's son, Badi-uz Zaman, popularly known as Mirza Fatehpuri.[106] Ali Quli Khan Zaman, the son of Haider Sultan Uzbek Shaibani, was of the Uzbek race but both his mother and his wife were Persians. He spent a large part of his life in Persia, had Shia leanings and preferred Persian culture. He had even fought on the side of the Persians in the battle of Jam.[107]

Similarly, Mirza Fulda (or Fulad), a descendant of Kudaidad Barlas whose family had 'served the Timurid family generation after generation', is described by Shahnawaz Khan as 'Faruqi Hanafi in religion' who 'came from Iraq to Thatta'.[108] While certain Turani officials managed to acquire high ranks and high-sounding titles, some of their compatriots failed to attain the heights of eminence. Nevertheless, they served as the supporting pillars of the Turani pavillion of power. Abul Fazl clearly mentions that at the time of Akbar's accession: 'Agra, the capital of [the] Caliphate and adjoining districts, flourished under Iskandar Khan Uzbek. Sambhal was in the charge of Ali Quli Shaibani; Sarkar Kalpi under Abdullah Khan Uzbek, while the servants of Tardi Beg of Turkestan gave security to Mewat.[109] Qiya Khan Gung in Kol Jalali and Haider Muhammad Khan Akhta Begi in Biyana.'[110] Looking back, Abul Fazl defended Akbar's so-called partiality for the Turanis by saying that these appointments were made 'on a trial basis'. Due to its significance, the entire passage is reproduced here:

> We have left all in possession of their estates as heretofore, so that the sincerity and good service of everyone may be brought to light. Thereafter they shall be advanced to high degree and positions in accordance with the lofty intelligence of the Shahinshah. For the present time the world-adorning judgement of H.M.—the Shahinshah was insisting upon his remaining for some days under the veil of concealment. Either the cause of this far-seeing and right-choosing design was that, by being in the guise of indifference to the world, he might make trial of men and fix in the antechamber of his holy mind the most accurate estimation of each individual or it was the narrow capacity of those men and their not possessing the power to appreciate his perfections, which compelled him for the sake of coming humanity to adopt this line of conduct or it was that black-hearted and crafty forces might engage in their evil acts free from any apprehensions of eminence of holy elements.

Other passages highlight Turani high-handedness and pride. The rebellions of Turani chiefs were frequent occurrences. Khan-i Zaman Ali Quli is blamed for his 'arrogance' due to which he 'did not recognize the rights of his master' and 'in concert with the Uzbek chiefs raised the standard of rebellion'.[111] In this commotion, many Uzbek nobles (including his brother Bahadur Khan Shaibani) took part. It is interesting to note that the intervention of Khan-i Zaman's mother and the subsequent drama of the appearance of the rebel with his sword and a shroud around his neck, though earned for the Khan the required pardon, he along with his fellow tribesmen soon relapsed into a state of opposition and stirred up rebellion. When Khan-i Zaman and Bahadur Khan died, Iskandar Khan had recourse to fraud and strategem and proposed peace. Such activities are often attributed to the 'evil practices of Transoxiana'[112] or to the fact that 'ease and comfort make the turbulent and opportunists seditious' or to the lack of 'real nobility' among them. Even lesser mortals like Bahadur, son of Said and a collector of Tirhut, joined the Bihar rebels, 'spent the revenues of the crown lands on the soldiers and hoisted the standard of disaffection and struck coins and read the *khutba* in his own name'.[113]

Racial rivalry and notions of tribal and ethnic superiority also played an important role. Even in Transoxiana, these white, black, and blue bones separated *aq* (white) Khwajas from *qara* (black) Khwajas and created dissensions between the people of Tashkent and Samarqand. The Chaghatai officers were reportedly 'unwilling to submit to a Qizilbash (Persian)'[114] and fight under his leadership in India, which further aggravated the problem. Sectarian bigotry—a sixteenth-century form of malice—was also a factor which widened the gulf between the Chaghatais, the Turanis, and the Iranis. Bairam Khan killed Tardi Beg allegedly from envy and sectarian motives after obtaining 'a sort of permission' from Akbar, which only aggravated the mutual distrust between these groups. Akbar even punished certain miscreants in his later years for such sectarian killings.

The Turani nobility had a peculiar and unique cohesion and unity among themselves, with a 'greybeard' to defend their interests and fight for them in an alien land. When the rebellion of Khan-i Zaman and Sikandar Khan occurred and Ashraf Khan Mir Munshi brought a 'gracious farman' to Sikandar Khan, the latter arrogantly retorted, 'Ibrahim Khan is the *aqsiqal*, that is, white bearded. He is a near neighbour. I shall go and see him. We shall come together to the court.' Accordingly, he first went to Khan-i Zaman and the turbulence continued.

Escheat was taboo among the Mongols. The *Yasa* of Chingiz decrees: 'If an official or a peasant dies, they (Mongol rulers) do not interfere with the estate he leaves, be it much or little, nor may anyone else tamper with it. And if he have no heir, it is given to his apprentice or to his slave. On no account is the property of a dead man admitted to the treasury, for they regard such a procedure as inauspicious.' The Timurids of Central Asia often avoided it. In one of his *dastur-ul-amals* (regulations), Akbar criticized the Ottomans for practising *ankari* (escheat) and advised his officials to abstain from it. Yet the Mughal rulers seem to have sometimes followed this practice to fill their empty coffers during periods of financial crises.[115]

## THE CONSULTATIVE ASSEMBLY—*KURULTAI* OR *KANGASH*

The similarities in the Eurasian polity have seldom revealed themselves so consistently as in the institution of the consultative assembly. In every part of Asia, the counsellors may not have enjoyed an extraordinarily effective voice but their existence itself, in some form or another, was apparently a sign of a sober and balanced government.[116] In India, for example, Manu, Brihaspaty, and Kautilya stressed that 'all kinds of administrative measures are preceded by deliberations and a well-formed council'.[117] This view is also echoed in the later Persian chronicles written in India.[118]

Most Central Asian chroniclers emphasized the need of the consultative assembly. Nakhchwani,[119] in the early Middle Ages, devoted one entire chapter to the blessings of holding consultations. Samundar Tirmizi[120] endorsed the same views in the eighteenth and nineteenth centuries. Mahmud bin Wali described this group of counsellors as an 'antidote to all dangers.'[121]

After his ascendancy in Central Asia, the Mongol ruler Tuva commented: 'The greatest word wherever it was (said) depends upon (or was in accordance with) the consultations with relatives' (*ulugh qaul har ja ki bashad bur qarar ka ba mashawarat o kangoj aqa o ini*).[119] Abdullah Khan Uzbek also considered consultations to be 'God's signal—a revealed truth and the safest exit from difficulties'. He is said to have never undertaken any special task or campaign without first holding proper consultations in the special assembly (*majlis khas*) with his own confidants (*ahl-i-ikhtisas*). Although freedom of expression was granted, Abdullah could reject the opinion of the majority in favour of his own deputy's suggestion without creating any displeasure among the others.[122]

The traditional significance attached to the holding of consultations on all important occasions in pre- and post-Mongol Central Asia is clearly see in the comments of different chroniclers and the utterances of many sovereigns. It is, however, interesting to note that the Timurid and Uzbek historians like Yazdi, Samarqandi, Hafiz Tanish, and others, feeling probably the pulse of their age, always stressed that these assemblies were in pursuance of Islamic principles. They sought to give it an Islamic colour by insisting that the *kangash* was a kind of assembly giving practical form to the concepts of *ijma* and *shura*, i.e. the Islamic injunction to build consensus.[123] Such comments are found even during the Mongol period. In his *Siyar-ul-Muluk* (*Siyasat Nama*), Tusi[124] praised and recommended *mushawarat* (consultations with the wise and the aged) since the 'deliberations with ten was always better than that with the two'. Tusi considered the institution of then *ijma* or the *shura* as being 'the wisest of all the Prophet's revealed directions'. To abstain from consultations was, in his opinion, a clear proof of a weak mind and such a person was self-willed. Hence, all business undertaken without holding consultations was bound to end in utter failure.[125]

Unlike the Turkish, Persian, and Arabic sources, which stress the significance of the consultative assembly, the available text of the *Yasa* of Chingiz Khan contains no direct and specific ruling on this subject. Nevertheless, there is an implicit suggestion to this effect: 'A point on which three wise men agree can be repeated anywhere—otherwise it cannot be trusted. One's own words should be tallied with those of other wise men. If in agreement, they should be uttered—otherwise not.'[126] It was only on the issue of *Yarghu pursidan*[127] (bringing defaulting nobles to the book and punishing them) that Chingiz forewarned against any wilful or arbitrary judgement in dealing with the defaulters and emphasized the need for *kangamesh*' (consultations) with *aqa o ini* (relatives). He, however, emphasized the need for an annual or biennial assembly of the *amirs* of Tuman and Hazara for listening to the *biliks* of Chingiz. The custom seems to have[128] continued till the very end of the Mongol rule in Central Asia. Apart from the information available in the Persian chronicles,[129] Ibn-i Battuta also gives a detailed account of this annual *toi*. Ibn-i Batuta writes that it was the 'accepted code' among them to assemble once a year. The day is called *toi*. On this occasion, the descendant of Chingiz Khan, *begs*, generals, and the ladies arrive. Apart from the feasts and festivities, the actions of kings and nobles are judged and scrutinized. That a statesman of Chingiz's stature did not feel the need to hold consultations is not at all surprising for it reflects and confirms his love for absolute power. It should, however, be noted that in matters of war, he never hesitated in organizing consultative assemblies. The sources contain many details of such discussions, though no particular council or specific counsellor seems to have existed. Before the campaigns, *kurultai* were held to discuss the feasibility, planning, and strategy of warfare, for example, before the war against Tayauk Khan (year of the rat, Jumad II 600) or another *kurultai* (in Zilqada 615) for the war against the Tajiks. But quite in conformity with his independent outlook, the nomination of his heir apparent was accomplished in a private assembly of the princes (*dar khilwat nashista*) in Safar 613, in the year of the dog. His successors also organized such assemblies. During a span of seven years (Jumad I 632, the year of the sheep, to Shabaan 638), Ogedei organized two *qurulti-i buzurq,* one in Mauza Tallan Disang in the year of the horse and another in the year of the sheep, the purpose being that they should listen to the *Yasa* and its rules once again. All the invitees came to enjoy the *toi* for a month. The tasks performed during the *kurultai* were (apart from the bestowal of *Suyurghameshy* and the distribution of the treasure accumulated during these years) the organization of the affairs of the state and the army (*batartib-i maham-i mulk o lashkar*) and discussions about the proposed conquests of hitherto unconquered lands and the nomination of commanders for this purpose.[130]

The holding of consultations was an important part of the conduct of state business by the rulers in Central Asia. Different names have been given to this state assembly, such as *qurultai* or *kurultai*, *kangash*, *janqi*, *chanqi*, *mashwarat-i-majlisiaali*, and so on in the Central Asian region. In the *Akbar Nama* one comes across the word *kangash*, *janqi*, and *mashwarat*.

In the modern Uzbek language, the *qurultai* denotes 'congress'. In the *Farhang* of Wassaf,[131] the term *kurultai* had been rendered as a 'Turkish word denoting *majma* (assembly), *kangash*, *shura*, or *jashn*'. Due to the loose usage of these terms by the chroniclers, the above-mentioned terms have frequently been treated as synonyms notwithstanding the fact that the *kurultai* had a specific meaning, that is, a 'parliament', whose members were nominated by the ruler. Similarly, the word *kangash* was used to describe both an informal discussion with one person or an entire consultative assembly.[132] Rashiduddin[133] himself occasionally uses the two words (*kangash* and *kurultai*) as synonyms. For example, after the burial of Chingiz, at his real Yurt Kuluran, the princes and the nobles held a *kangash* relating to the settlement of the affairs of state (*bab-i-mulk*), unanimously highlighting the need for an immediate accession of the nominee as the throne had been lying vacant for the past two years and there was a danger of an outbreak of commotion and disturbances. The messengers were sent and a *kurultai* was organized.

The *kurultai* was of two kinds—the grand (*buzurg*) and the ordinary. The word *kurultai* has occasionally also been used in the sense of consultation. From the account of Rashiduddin, it appears that the *kangash* could range from an ordinary, off-hand, casual discussion to a formal or special consultative meeting on any important matter such as war, peace, accession, or administrative affairs, grievances, pre and post-war planning, etc. Any consultation by princes or nobles, both separately or together, was termed as *kangash*. The *kurultai*, however, was a more official, formal, and celebratory affair. It was attended by all the princes and members of the ruling families from every nook and corner of the empire, nobles of all categories, representatives from foreign lands (usually on the accession ceremony), the military aristocracy, and the administrative bureaucracy.[134] The *kurultai* was by no means a *vox populi*, as the decision-making powers, lay entirely in the hands of the Khan, and giving counsel was the privilege of the military aristocracy and the administrative bureaucracy. The common folks, if any, were only the artisans and petty shopkeepers who had to sell their goods at less than the market rates to the participants of the assembly during the sessions of the *kurultai*.

Controversy surrounds the *kurultai* as the functions and the extent of authority vested in this institution have been variously interpreted. Not only has Cohen 'overevaluated' the powers of the Mongol people's assembly but certain other historians have also echoed the same views. Weikwei Sun more moderately underplays the fact that Chingiz, in his later days, assigned to the *kurultai* the highest of all functions, that of electing his successor. The subjects brought before it were delicate and important; and if some of its decisions, such as the final election of the Khan, had to be published immediately, other decisions such as plans of military campaigns were strictly confidential.[135]

On the other hand, Barthold and other Central Asianists considerably downplay the position of the *kurultai,* comparing it with the German Reichstag or describing it simply as a parade in which all the grandeur and brilliance of the Khaqan's power was on display. In Barthold's opinion, the *kurultai* was not a representative assembly (created for deciding affairs of state, important issues, or the election of a new ruler) nor a mouthpiece, a *vox populi* in the strict sense of the term. The *kurultai* held for the accession of a ruler was just a formality as the task performed in this assembly was not that of election but only of proclamation, followed by ceremonial and festive acclamation and the accession of the Khaqan. After the taking of the oath of allegiance, celebrations continued for a month or so. Barthold further contradicts Cohen's view that frequent wars of succession were 'due to the electoral system' or were 'due to old Mongolian privileges and rights'.[136]

In view of these contradictory opinions, a *coup d'oeil* of the Persian sources is necessary. Owing to the significance of the subject, detailed passages from the Persian sources are quoted here, and various incidents and examples pertaining to the *kurultai* have been reproduced. The various duties and functions of the *kurultai* are also examined, including the latent influence of this institution, if any.

The most important function of the *kurultai* is said to be the selection or election of the Khan. Almost all the Persian sources deal extensively with the *kurultai* of accession or coronation, which helps us to understand the procedure. To be precise, the Khans were not 'elected' in these *kurultais*. The decision in favour of a Khan was taken much earlier and the session of the *kurultai* was conducted under the same Khan himself. These *kurultais* began with oath-taking by the princes and nobles, all expressing allegiance to the Khan. This was followed by merry-making, the distribution of awards, the making of plans for new campaigns, the nomination of commanders, the awarding of punishment to defaulters, the confirmation (*imza*) of old and new rulers, and the adoption of regulations and *nishans*. The *kurultai* held at *mauza* Kukanauwar (in Rabi II 643, in the spring of the year of the horse) for the accession of Guyuk is one example. At this assembly the participants were: the princes, nobles of the right and left wings, *amirs*, officials (*arbab-i-ashghal*), and local governors, officers of the revenue department (*ashbab-i-amal*); dignitaries and representatives from other countries such as China, Lur, Iraq, Garjistan, Shervan, Rum, Azerbaijan, Helb, Mosul, Fars, Kiram, Firang, Baghdad, Armenia, Alamut, Aleppo, the Georgia. About 2,000 *kharghahs* (felt tents) were erected for the participants. Due to the flood of human beings, there remained no place vacant in the Urdu Mauza and a sudden spurt in the prices of grains and drinks was noticed. 'For one continuous month', says

Juvaini, 'in unison with the like-minded relatives and with the assistance of kinsmen without compare, he joined dawn to dusk and morning to evening in contrast . . . to bowls and goblets and the handling a round of cups by the hands of beauteous cup bearers.' After the 'enjoyment of all kinds of wanton pastimes' for one month, rewards were scattered upon the small and the great as the 'spring cloud rains upon the grass and trees', so that all might have their share of the gifts of his goodness and liberality. Each new Khan in his *kurultai* of accession confirmed the old and the new *Yasas* and ordinances of his predecessor. In the campaigns to be undertaken, the armies were nominated and despatched. The crimes and offences of defaulters were also brought to the attention of the family and the amirs, and punishments were determined.[137] The details given about the other kind of *kurultai*, that of coronation, are more or less the same. A careful study of the Persian and Arabic sources shows that the *kurultai* was not an 'elective' body, but simply a place for public acknowledgement and acceptance of a particular candidate. This formal ceremony was as much a matter of sentiment and benefits as of politics.

Vladimirtsov and Krader confirm that Chingiz Khan was 'elected' emperor in the 'traditional manner of electing a clan chief according to Mongol custom'. Both assert that he enjoyed 'unlimited and absolute power',[138] a fact reiterated by Barthold.[139] Since Chingiz was 'tied to a consanguineal tradition' and realized the significance of a stratified society and a hierarchical order of the aristocracy only too well, the *kurultai* was allowed to continue as a shadow of the Khan and not as a power behind the throne. The sources (including the *Secret History*) do not refer to any election but to a coronation. The *Yasa* 'affirmed . . . the duty of service in absolute terms' and there was 'no thought of a mutual set of obligations in the code'.[140]

It should, however, be noted that the kings who believed in *l'etat c'est moi* (it is I who am the state) seldom added any weightage to the counsels of their subordinates. Both the formulae *le roi le voult* (the king wills it) and *le roi s'avisera* (the king will consider, the polite way to reject a bill) were applied by such potentates. The famous work *Qabus Nama*[141] in a chapter on 'Regulations and Conditions of Sovereignty' (*Dar ain o shart-i badshahi*) recommends that opinions should always be subjected to and made subservient to the sovereign's own wisdom and stratagems as 'the best Grand Wazir (*Wazir-ul-Vuzara*) for a King is his own wisdom and brain'. Deliberative and consultative bodies found in other Muslim states seem to have the same pattern, for example, in the state of Mahmud of Ghazna, the consultative body hardly played a significant role.

In the early years of his struggle, Timur emphasized the significance of consultations, in the words quoted by Yazdi. The verdict of wealthy and powerful men (*arbab-i-dawal*) is the Divine Commandment (*tafsir-i-qaza*) and nothing occurs except in conformity with what they say. It is interesting to notice that after attaining power Timur ceased to be so enchanted by the *kangash* the *kurultai* and adopted the same causal attitude towards the *kurultai* for which he had earlier criticized his rival Sultan Husain. Yazdi states this in the following words:[142]

> One of the specialities of His Majesty is that, though he always held discussions following the principle of *Sunnat-i Sunniya Mashwarat* and the custom of Kurultai and Janqi which is the rule of sovereignty, he never based his decisions on the opinion nor was he guided by the suggestion of any living being. In every affair of the state, he was solely directed by the revelations and also by secrets divulged to him through his own mind. According to the ideas alighted to him, he performed every work. Each contrivance or politics whether trifle or high was thus accomplished quite in conformity with the prescription of Destiny and the will of God and without any error. Since he was firm, all the matters of state and millat, affairs of administration, war and peace . . . were all quickly or slowly disposed of only through his own judgement.[143]

A similar view is expressed by Ibn-i Arab Shah.

Timur and Abdullah Khan disregarded the opinion of the majority and either accepted those opinions of their confidantes which echoed their own ideas or openly discarded the majority opinion if it conflicted their own assessment by cleverly manoeuvring the acceptance of their own views. In his *Tuzukat*, Timur records his views about *kangash*, which are reproduced here in view of their significance. 'I entered on every measure with counsel and advice . . .', he writes:

> And by experience, it be known unto me, that counsel and deliberation, and skilful measures are only to be found with the wise and the sagacious. There are only withstanding the conclusion of every worldly event is covered by the curtain of Fate. Yet according to the holy word of Muhammad (on whom the blessings of the Almighty) in every enterprise which I undertook, I acted from counsel and deliberation.

But he also adds:

And when my counsellors and my advisers were assembled together, I demanded their opinions on the good and on the evil, and on the advantages and disadvantages of undertaking, or relinquishing the enterprise before us. And when I had heard their opinions thereon, I myself examined both sides of their opinions. And I duly weighed the advantages and the disadvantages; and I considered the perils thereof with the eye of attention. And every plan, in which I discovered a two-fold hazard, I rejected; and chose that in which the peril was single.

At another place he specifically says:

And I asked counsel from all: but I considered the good and the evil of every opinion; and from each I selected those things which were just and expedient, that whichever of the advices appeared most profitable, and I preferred and approved . . . . But in every action of my life on which I had deliberated, I drew an omen from the sacred Koran and I actecd according to the direction thereof. . . .[144]

Ibn-i Arab Shah confirms the above statements of Timur: 'In his judgement, he saw openly the vicissitudes of things, as one sees with a keen eye a thing perceived by the senses.' 'When he has spoken his opinion or indicated his will, presently his command is counted as an oracle.'

Regarding Timur's *kurultais* before campaigns, Ibn-i Arab says that Timur

excelled in various arts of leading others into error and in a profundity of actions which could scarcely be penetrated. . . . When he was making for any place or wished to descend into any plain and intended to hide his purpose and involve it in an enigma and sought to inspire error and doubt . . . he used to summon great men and leaders of his kingdom and his counsellors (*arkan-i daulat wa ayan-i mamlakat wa sahiban-i andesha*), so that none of them was left out or a son admitted in the place of the father or the father instead of the son, then he expounded to them the secret of his affairs and sought from them advice about the regions against which he should move and gave them full permission to speak, saying: By no means shall he be blamed who discusses it, whether noble or simple, observing future events from day to day and year to year, but let each one debate freely and it shall not be counted to him for a fault, whether he falls into the bottomest pit of error or climbs to the peak of right judgement; if he has missed the mark, he shall win reward; therefore let each one exert his strength and employ his zeal and labour and show his diligence until someone said that point which was agreeable to Timur's desire and so let opinions conspire to mark out a place. Then he immediately dismissed that assembly. He would thereafter collect and consult his ultimate friends such as Sulaiman Shah, Qamari, Saifuddin, Allahabad, Shah Malik and Shaikh Nuruddin.[145]

The scene does not seem to be any different from the other *kurultais* held on the eve of campaigns. Similar artfulness and chicanery are noticeable in the *kurultai* of 732 held by Timur at Aqyar in connection with his administrative decision to increase the number of soldiers attached to every official in proportion to his increasing wealth. This assembly was attended by all the *amirs* from Iuman, Hazarajat, and Sadjat and by other rulers from Mauza and Wilayat but no one could dare to raise his voice against this new burden.[146]

The Timurids in India followed the same traditions. Like his predecessors Chingiz and Timur, Babur consulted his begs on matters of war though only in situations of expediency. As is well reflected in his memoirs, Babur had a patronizing and scornful attitude towards his nobles, whom he considered his inferiors. Deviating from the continuing Timurid practice of mighty sovereigns who maintained a distance from their nobles, Babur advised Humayun to hold regular consultations. The sources confirm that Babur specifically recommended 'counselling with prudent and experienced begs', and to 'act as they say'. In a letter to Humayun, Babur advised him 'to summon his younger brothers and the begs twice daily to his presence, take counsel and settle every word and act in agreement'.[147]

Babur was overly protective of Humayun whose weak, irresolute, and vacillating nature was not unknown to him. These precautionary measures could hardly help Humayun as he had to confront the rivalry of his own brothers and the mutual jealousies of the Turani and Irani nobility which further complicated matters, giving new dimensions to the political conflicts at this time.

Ibn-i Hasan[148] gives an insightful account of the transaction of state business at various levels, though no reference is found to any consultative assembly being held by Akbar. In the *diwan-i khas o am, ghusal khana* (private chamber), and the Shah Burj, administrative affairs and state business were attended to by the Mughal emperor without the help of any other 'constitutional body' or consultative assembly. Akbar seems to have appreciated the value of consultation, though following in the footsteps of Chingiz and Timur, overly he too was not dependent on them. Nevertheless,

Akbar's views on holding consultations are clearly recorded by Abul Fazl in the emperor's *Dastur-ul-amal*, that officers:

should not rely upon their own wisdom in dealing with the affairs and should always consult the wise men. Even if such men are not available, consultation in itself is a useful thing and, therefore, should not be avoided though the adviser may not be a wise person. 'Often a foolish person can solve the problems of the wise.' At times, suitable advice may not come from a wise old man while sometimes an ignorant child could accidentally hit an arrow at the target. Nevertheless, should not discuss the affairs and consult everybody as a correct understanding and capacity for comprehension are the gifts of God. These cannot be acquired through study or long experience for, in making consultations with many people, there is always a danger that a group of foolish persons might oppose the venture (an otherwise right one) and cause undue embarrassment. Such people also prevent a person from using one's own wisdom and from consulting the wise and experienced who are always rare.[149]

## NOTES

1. Bamzai, *Kashmir and Central Asia*, New Delhi, 1980, pp. 20-40.
2. For details, see *Studies in Asian History*, Delhi, 1969.
3. *Studies in Asian History*, p. 44 and see A.K. Bag, 'Exchange of Ideas between India and Central Asia', paper read at Indo-Soviet Conference, Moscow, 1989; Krishna Chaitanya, *A History of Indian Painting*, New Delhi, 1976; see plates 33, 34, 36 and pp. 33, 52-53; Sanders, *Tamerlane or Timur the Great Amir*, London, 1936, Appendix, p. 333; Ishwari Prasad, *History of Medieval India*, Allahabad, 1925, pp. 25-40.
4. Kosambi, *An Inroduction to the Study of Indian History*, Bombay, 1975, pp. 71, 82, 83,145.
5. Ibid.; Sanders, *Tamerlane or Timur the Great Amir*, London, 1936, Appendix, p. 333; Ishwari Prasad, *History of Medieval India*, Allahabad, 1925, pp. 25-40.
6. Ibid.
7. Romila Thapar, pp. 107-8, 120.
8. Ibid., also see Kosambi op. cit., pp. 19, 45, 119-20.
9. Ibid.
10. *Indian Architecture*, p. 8; Romila Thapar, op. cit., pp. 107, 108, 120.
11. D.N. Jha, *Ancient India, An Introductory Outline*, New Delhi, 1990, pp. 57, 80-1.
12. Ibid.
13. Romila Thapar, pp. 74, 97-8. Bag, op. cit.
14. Al Beruni Abu Rehan, *Kitab-ul-Hind*, p. 18; also see *Studies in Asian History*, op. cit., p. 208.

15. Abul Fazl, *Ain-i-Akbari*, vol. III, Eng. tr. by Sarkar and Jarret, New Delhi, pp. 2-7.
16. See *Majma-ul-Ruqqat wa Munshaat*, MS 296, ff. 179-80; *Babur Nama*, New Delhi, 1979; Eng. tr., p. 534; also see Hasan Askari, pp. 225-37.
17. Banarsi Prasad Sexena, *History of Shahjahan of Delhi*, Allahabad, 1976, p. 248.
18. Askari, op. cit., pp. 225-37. Abul Fazl, *Insha-i Abul Fazl* (hereafter *Insha*), Harsi Daftar, Lucknow edn., pp. 1-18; or see Eng. tr. by Mansura Haidar, New Delhi, 1998, also see letters of Babur, Humayun and Akbar. *Indo-Persian Documents*, Eng. tr. by Riazul Islam, 2 vols.
19. Ibid.
20. Ibid.
21. Aurunbaev, *Pisma Autograph Abdul Rahman Jami-iz Albuma Navoi*, Tashkent, 1982, p. 8.
22. Mir Husain Shah, 'Role of Aghanistan in Movement of People and Ideas', *Studies in Asian History*, op. cit., pp. 49-61; Illiyas Nizamuddinov, *Iz Istori Sredni Aziatsko-Injiskikh Otnoshenija*, Tashkent, 1969, pp. 5-28.
23. Ibn-i Batuta, *Travels in Asia and Africa*, tr. and selected by H.A.R. Gibb, London, 1963, p. 181.
24. *Insha*, pp. 1-18.
25. Zainuddin Mahmud Wasifi, *Badaiul Waqai*, vol. II, Leningrad ed. AH 1350, p. 121.
26. Illiyas Nizamuddinov, pp. 5-28, 41; also Zainuddin, *Tabaqat-i-Baburi*, p. 11.
27. *Insha* op. cit., 26-8, 52-3.
28. Muhibbul Hasan, *Kashmir under the Sultan*, Calcutta, 1959, pp. 72-3.
29. For such comments of Isami and Barni see, Mansura Haidar, 'Medieval Indian Chroniclers and the Mongols', *Perspectives on Mongolia*, edited by R.C. Sharma, New Delhi, 1988, pp. 39-49; also see Mansura Haidar, 'Relations of Abdullah Khan Uzbeg with Akbar', Cahiers du Monde Russe et Sovietique, *Journal of School of Advanced Study in Social Sciences*, Paris, vol. XXII, pp. 3-4, July-Dec. 1982.
30. Amir Hasan Sijzi, *Fawaid-ul-Fuwad*, Newal Kishore edn., text, p. 17.
31. Aljuzjani Minhajussiraj, *Tabaqat-i Nasiri*, Eng. tr. by Raverty, vol. II, New Delhi, 1970, pp. 1079-82.
32. Ibn-i Arab Shah, *Ajaib-ul Maqdur fi Nawadiri i-Timur*, Eng. tr. by Sanders, London, 1936, p.4.
33. Abul Fazl, *Akbar Nama*, Eng. tr. by Beveridge, Delhi, 1972, vol. I, p. 197, also see the account of Al-Hasan the Arab, *Purchas and his Pilgrims*, Glasgow, MCMVI, vol. XI; Barthold, *Sochinenija*, vol. V, Moscow, 1968, pp. 168-9; vol. VI, p. 44; *Four Studies in the History of Central Asia*, Leiden, 1962, vol. I, p. 14.
34. Milo Cleveland Beach, *Mughal and Rajput Painting*, Cambridge, 1992, pp. 48, 142.
35. Ibn-i Arab, op. cit., pp. 12-13; also see M. Haidar's article, 'The Sovereign in the Timurid State', *Turcica*, vol. VIII, 1976, pp. 61-82.
36. Ibid.
37. Abul Fazl, *Akbar Nama*, pp. 197-201; M. Haidar, op. cit., p. 81. Khafi Khan stretches the verdict and refers to the dreams of Qil Khan and Qachuli Bahadur

leading to their concurrence on the point and if one of them becomes the ruler, he would assign full administrative rights (Ziman-i Ikhtiyari Sultanate o ukadai Wikalat, Khud) to the other brother's descendants, Khafi Khan, *Muntakhab-ul Lubab*, edited by Maulvi Kabiruddin Ahmad, vol. I, pt. I, Calculta, 1868, pp. 8-10.

38. *Mukatabat-i Allami*, B.M. Ad. 7688 ff. 11b-14a, also see Babur, *Babur Nama*, Eng. tr., pp. 14, 85, 256, 487. Riazul Islam, *A Calendar of Documents: Indo-Persian Relation*, vol. I, Lahore, 1979, p. 123.
39. *Mughal and Rajput Painting*, Cambridge, 1992, pp. 48, 142.
40. Babur, *Babur Nama*, text, p. 200b; Eng. tr., p. 218.
41. Abul Fazl, *Akbar Nama*, Persian text, Newal Kishore edn., p. 74; Eng. tr. by Beveridge, New Delhi, 1979.
42. Rashiduddin Fazlullah, *Jami-ul-Tawarikh*, vol. I, Tehran, 1338, p. 361; Juvaini, *Tarikh-i Jahan Kushi*, Leiden, 1911, Eng. tr. by A.J. Boyle, vol. I, Manchaster, 1958, p. 81; V.V. Barthold, *Turkestan down to Mongol Invasion*, London, 1958, p. 410.
43. See *Insha-i-Abul Fazl*, letters to Khan-i-Khanan.
44. Jahangir, *Tuzuk-i-Jahangiri*, Eng. tr. by A. Rogers, New Delhi, 1978, p. 23; also see *Faramin-i-Salatin*, no. 47.
45. Khwaja Niamatullah, *Tarikh Khan-i Jahani wa Makhzan-i Afghani*, vol. II, Calcutta, 1962, p. 663.
46. Al Tughri Berdi, *Al Nujum-uz-Zahira*, vol. VI, p. 268; vol. VII, pp. 182-3 for interesting references to Tura, see Badauni, *Muntakhab-ut-Twarikh*, Eng. tr. by W.A. Lowe, vol. II, 1973, pp. 46-7, ibid, pp. 59-60; also see p. 59, fn. 6; Anand Raj, *Farhang-i Anand Raj*, vol. III under words *Yasa* and *Yasaq*, p. 825; also see Ahmad Yadgar, *Tarikh-i-Shahi Salatini Afghan*, Calcutta, 1939, p. 335, fn. 1. Mahmud b. Wali, *Bahrul Asrar fimanaqibul akhiyar*, MS India Office, 1496, f. 44. Juvaini, op. cit., Pers. text, pp. 17-25; Fazlullah, op. cit., pp. 16-35, 434; Yaun Chao Pishi, Eng. tr. by A. Weley, London, 1963, p. 285; Weikwei Sun's tr., Aligarh, 1975, pp. 149-55. Khwand Mir, *Habib-us-Siyar*, III, Tehran, 1338, p. 18; Banakiti, pp. 340-3, 371-2, Mir Khond, op. cit., pp. 63-9; *Chronicum Syriacum*, ed. Paul Bedjan, Paris, 1980, p. 411; Babur, Eng. tr., pp. 155, 298-9.
47. For details on *Tura* see Mansura Haidar, 'Mongol Traditions and their Survival in Central Asia', *Central Asiatic Journal*, vol. 28, nos. 1-2, 1984, pp. 57-9.
48. Babur, *Babur Nama*, Pers. tr. by Abdur Rahman Khan-i Khanan, transcribed by Mirza Muhammad Malik-ul Kuttab, f. 118; Turkish text, p. 168; Eng. tr. Beveridge, pp. 298-9. Gulbadan Begam, *Humayun Nama*, Eng. tr. by Beveridge, Delhi, 1972, text, f. 72, 106, Eng. tr., pp. 87, 187, 197.
49. Erskin, *History of India*, vol. I.
50. Abdur Rafi, *Tarikh-i Nuzhat hai Iran*, p. 328.
51. Banakiti, *Tarikh-i Banakiti*, ed. Jafar Shear, Tehran, 1348 AH, p. 444; Rashiduddin Fazlullah, *Jamiut Tawarikh*, pp. 16-35, 434-6; Juvaini, text, pp. 17-25; *Secret History of Mongols*, Eng. tr. by Cleaves; *Habib-us-Siyar* by Khwand Mir, pp. 44.
52. Riasanovsky, pp. 82-91; also see Mansura Haidar, 'Mongol Traditions and their Survival in Central Asia', *Central Asiatic Journal*, vol. 28, nos. 1-2, 1984, pp. 57-67.

53. Spuler Bertold, Alam-ul-Islami, *History of Mongols*, London, 1972, p. 48, Juvaini; Eng. tr., op. cit., vol. I, p. 272.
54. Juvaini, op. cit., Persian text, pp. 17-25; Fazlullah, op. cit., pp. 16-35, 434, 436; Yuan *Chao Pishi*, Eng. tr. by A. Waley, London, 1963, p. 285, Weikwei Sun's tr., Aligarh, 1975, pp. 149-55; Khwand Mir, *Habib-us-Siyar*, III, Tehran edn.
55. Juvaini, pp. 17-25.
56. Haidar Dughlat, *Tarikh-i-Rashidi*, Eng. tr. by Denison Ross, New Delhi, 1973, pp. 69-70.
57. Gulbadan, Eng. tr., pp. 87, 187, 197.
58. Haidar Dughlat, op. cit., pp. 473-7, 487.
59. Gulbadan Begam, Eng. tr. by Beveridge, Delhi, 1972, pp. 87, 187, 197.
60. Ibid.
61. Masum Bhakkari, *Tarikh-i-Sind* or *Tarikh-i-Masumi*, Hindi tr. by A.A. Rizvi, *Mughal Kalin Bharat*, Aligarh, 1960, p. 652. Khwand Mir, *Habib-us-Siyar*, III, Tehran edn., 1338, pp. 18-20. Mir Khond, pp. 63-9, Banakiti, pp. 340-3, 371-2; *Chronicum Syriacum*, ed. Paul Bedjan, Paris, 1980, pp. 411-12
62. Abul Fazl, *Akbar Nama*, vol. I, Eng. tr. by Beveridge, Calcutta, 1877-8, text, 281, Eng. tr., p. 536.
63. Haidar Dughlat, op. cit., pp. 473-7. Yauan Chao Pishi, p. 67; Gulbadan, pp. 87, 187, 197; Badauni, op. cit., vol. II, text p. 216, Eng. tr., p. 220; Arif Qandahari refers to the warm welcome given by Akbar to Sulaiman on his arrival in 983 AH. He says that the *toi* (feast) in his honour was organized with pomp and fanfare and glitering vessels of gold and silver studded with jewels and Chinese royal cups. Nevertheless, there is no mention of the revival of the Chaghtai traditions in this regard. In another context, however, Arif Qandahari also stresses that Shah Sulaiman, the ruler of Badakhshan 'ruled in conformity with the regulations of Muluk of Turks and Chaghtais', Haji Muhammad Arif Qandahari, *Tarikh-i-Akbari*, Rampur, 1382, pp. 206-8; *Akbar Nama*, text.
64. Badauni, op. cit., vol. I, text, pp. 192-3, Eng. tr., pp. 258-9.
65. Juvaini, op. cit, text, p. 228, Eng. tr., p. 273; *Yaun Chao Pishi*, Eng. tr. by Weikwei Sun, pp. 165-6; *Purchas and his Pilgrims*, Glasgow, MCMVI, XI, p. 464; Yezdi, *Zafarnama*, vol. II, Tehran, 1336, pp. 478-91; Hilda Hookham, *Tamburlaine the Conqueror*, London, 1962, p. 93, Khawand Mir, *Habib-us-Siyar*, vol. III, Khayam, AH 1333, pp. 314-18; *Tarikh-i Shaibani*, MS Institute of Oriental Studies, Tashkent, no. 1505, ff. 17-20.
66. Jahangir, *Tuzuk-i-Jahangiri*, Eng. tr. by A. Rogers, 1978, New Delhi, pp. 23, 68, and fn., also see *Faramin-i-Salatin*, nos. 47-64.
67. Qazvini, *Halat-i Asad Beg Qazvini*, MS BM OR, 1996, f. 53, also see *Ain-i-Akbari*, Eng. tr. by Blochmann, vol. I, Delhi, 1977, p. 505; *Akbar Nama*, text, p. 281; Eng. tr., p. 536.
68. Juvaini, op. cit.
69. Jahangir, *Tuzuk-i-Jahangiri*, see pp. 44, 68.
70. Juvaini, pp. 26-7.
71. Jahangir, p. 44.
72. For a facsimile of Babur's Will see S.R. Sharma's book *Religious Policy of the Mughal Emperors*; also see letter to Humayun, *Babur Nama* for Babur's above views; also Juvaini, pp. 26-7, 44.
73. Abul Fazl, *Akbar Nama*, vol. III, op. cit., pp. 527-8.

74. *Insha-i-Abul Fazl*, Harsi Daftar, Newal Kishore edn., pp. 4-10; also see *Akbar Nama*, op. cit., pp. 527-8; *Akbar Nama*, vol. I, *Ain*, no. 77, Eng. tr., pp. 170-220.
75. Ibid.
76. Abul Fazl, *Ain-i-Akbari*, vol. I, op. cit., p. 46; *Insha-i-Abul Fazl*, op. cit., the *Dastur-ul-Amal*.
77. Abul Fazl, *AN*, III, op. cit., pp. 804-5.
78. Khwaja Niamatullah bin Khwaja Habibullah Haravi, *Tarikh-i-Khan-i-Jahani wa Mkhzan-i-Afghani*, vol. II, Calcutta, 1962, pp. 663, 810.
79. Riasanovsky, *Yasa of Chingiz Khan*, p. 84; also see Juvaini, pp. 21-30.
80. Al-Hasan the Arab, *Purchas and his Pilgrims*, vol. XI, Glasgow, 1906, p. 407; Hafiz Abru, p. 73; Ibn-i Arab Shah, *Ajaib-ul-Maqdur*, Eng. tr., Sanders, Tehran, 1968, pp. 18, 32; Yezdi, *Zafar Nama*, pp. 444, 574-7.
81. Ibid.
82. *Dastur-ul-Amal*, *Insha-i-Abul Fazl*, also see letter to Shah Abbas; *Ain-i-Akbari* under *Ain-i-Faujdar* and *Ain-i-Kutwal*.
83. Michael Brand and Glenn D. Lowry, *Akbar's India*, London, 1985, pp. 17-18.
84. Ibid.
85. *Insha-i Abul Fazl*, letter to Abdullah Khan Uzbek.
86. Ibid.
87. Milo Cleveland Beach, op. cit., p. 48; *Insha-i-Abul Fazl*, letter to Danayani Firang (King Philip II of Spain).
88. Monscrrate Commentarius, pp. 176-82; Goldie, pp. 63-6, also fn. 3, pp. 73-81, 85-6, 90.
89. Yezdi, vol. I, p. 210.
90. Riasanovsky, p. 83.
91. Nakhchiwani, *Dastur-ul Katib fi taiyyan-ul-Maratib*, p. 48.
92. Yezdi, pp. 167, 574.
93. Hafiz Abru, *Tarikh-i-Shahrukh*, India Office, MS no. 171, f. 173; Jahangir, p. 109.
94. Yezdi, pp. 310, 574-9, also see Ibn-i Arab Shah for details on Timur's relations with saints; see Mansura Haidar, 'Timur's Religious Policy', IHC, Calcutta session, 1976, pp. 426-8; Jahangir, *Tuzuk-i-Jahangiri*, vol. I, p. 109.
95. For details see A.A. Rizvi, *History of Sufism*, II, p. 181.
96. Abul Fazl, *Ain-i-Akbari*, vol. I, p. 42.
97. Iskandar Munshi, *Alam Ara-i-Abbasi*, Tehran, 1972, pp. 280-2. Jahangir, *Tuzuk-i-Jahangiri*; Eng. tr., New Delhi, 1973, vol. I, p. 180.
98. Shahnawaz Khan, *Maasir-ul Umara*, vol. III, Patna, 1920, pp. 660-2; Eng. tr., pp. 996-9. Abul Fazl, p. 444; Tusi, *Siyasat Nama*, Tehran, 1942, p. 60. Shahnawaz Khan, *Maasir-ul Umara*, vol. I, Patna, 1920, pp. 432, 458, 520.
99. Maktubat-i-Jahan, *Gwalior Nama*, BM Add. 16, 859, f. 19.
100. *Calendar of Persian Documents*, no. 122, pp. 262, 279, 323, 324, 390-1.
101. *Akbar Nama*, vol. II, pp. 75-6; Shahnawaz Khan, op. cit., pp. 432, 458, 520.
102. Ibn-i Arab Shah, 44.
103. Nizamuddin, *Tabaqat-i-Akbari*, New Delhi, 1973, pp. 64, 102.
104. *Ain*, I, see chapter on 'Happy Sayings'.
105. *Maasir*, I, pp. 204-5, 389. *Maasir*, II, p. 745.
106. Ibid.

107. For examples see *Maasir-ul-Umara*, I, pp. 156, 389, 565, 620, 743; *Zakhirat-ul-Khawa*, vol. II, pp. 201, 346.
108. *Akbar Nama*, p. 400; *Maasir*, I, p. 377. Ibid., II, pp. 75-6.
109. *Maasir*, I, pp. 177-204, 265-8,
110. Ibid., I, pp. 337, 706.
111. *Akbar Nama*, vol. II, pp. 25-6.
112. *Maasir*, I, pp. 197-202, 348-50.
113. Ibid., p. 660.
114. *Maasir*, pp. 197-202, 337, 691; *Akbar Nama*, vol. II.
115. Ibid., vol. I, p. 648; Maasir, vol. I, pp. 197-203, 432, 457, 520-6, 583-6, 660, 769; *Ain*, I, p. 185; Badauni, vol. III, p. 153; *Ain*, no. 31, p. 364; *Akbar Nama*, II, p. 126.
116. The Holy Sura 3, Ali Imran, *ayat* 159, 1; For details regarding *shura see* Levy, Reuben, *The Social Structure of Islam*, Combridge, 1962, pp. 168-82, 287-90; Muhammad Asad, *The Principles of State and Government in Islam*, Berrkeley-Los Angeles, 1960, p. 48; *Muhammedon Jurisprudence*, pp. 82-97, Duncan B. Macdonald, *Development of Muslim Theology, Jurisprudence and Constitutional Theory*, New Delhi, 1977, pp. 101, 105; Ibn-i Hasan, *The Central Structure of the Mughal Empire*, New Delhi, 1970, p. 235.
117. Kautilya's *Arthashastra*, pt. III, ed. by R.P. Kangle, Delhi, 1986, pp. 134-5; also see 5th edn. of *Arthashastra*, ed. Shamasastry, Mysore, 1956, Chaps. IX and XV, pp. 14-15, 26-9.
118. *Insha-i-Abul Fazl,* Harsih Daftar, Newal Kishore edn. under *Dastur-ul-Amal*; Haji Khairullah, *Dastur-i Jahanqusha*, Aligarh MS. Abdus Salam Collection 328/98, ff. 28-32; Ghayusuddin Ali, *Ruz Namaih Ghazawat-i-Hindustan*, SPB 1915, vol. I, p. 110; *Four Studies*, vol. II, p. 23-4.

    Ziauddin Barani, *Fatawa-i-Jahandari*, Pers. text, advice III, Eng. tr. *The Political Theory of the Delhi Sultanate*, Aligarh, 1957, p. 8.

    Barani categorically records:

    '. . . Even to our Prophet, inspite of his perfect wisdom and the continuity of Divine revelation, God gave the order,

    'And consult them in your affairs'. How then can kings, who receive no Divine inspiration and whose judgement is vitiated by their passions, succeed in administering the affairs of their governments without consulting their experienced officers and sincere well wishers? It has been know to all wisemen, ancient and modern that eradicating the evils of the kingdom-suppressing, disturbances, undertaking great enterprises, making state laws (*zawabit*) and discerning the ultimate consequences of state policies – is not possible without the advice of wise and experienced men, who are the well-wishers of the government and the chosen people of the kingdom.'

    Babur, *Baburnama*, Turkish text 349, Eng. tr., p. 627; French tr. by Bacquet Grammont, *Livere de Babure*, POF, 1980, p. 44, Eng. tr. by Beveridge, New Delhi, 1973, *Sar-i-Pasha, the Dafterdar*, Turkish text, *Nasaih-ul-Vuzere vel Umera*, Princeton, 1935, p. 148; Eng. tr. by Walter Livington Writght, p. 129, also records.

    'They should not refrain from consultation over very matter. Yet they should not consult with every one. They should deliberate with those who have seen service and been present in war and battle, with well-wishers of the state who hide secrets, and to those only should they disclose secrets. But to the rest of the crowd they should not divulge secret matters as they actually are; through symbols and comparisons they should explain and consult with them. For it sometimes happens that from an ignorant child or from a woman of imperfect understanding there comes forth a correct opinion or a wise answer which brings about good results.'

119. Nakhchiwani, *Dastur-ul-Katib fi taiyunul maratib*, Moscow, 1962, Chap. XI.
120. Samundar Tirmizi MS, IOST, Tashkent, pp. 1-8.
121. Mahmud bin Wali, *Bahrul Asarar fi Manaqibul akhiyar*, ff. 34, 198a, 259a, 277b, 282a, 283b, 284a, 302a, 305a.
122. Wassaf, Abul Fazl, *Tarikh i Wassaf-ul Hazrat*, Newal Kishore edn., p. 518.
123. Hafiz Tanish, *Abdullah Nama*, MS India Office Library, Ethe 574, ff. 214, 225-36, 242, 262, 281-2, 392.
    Yezdi, *Zafar Nama*, Calcutta edn., 1888; also see *Zafar Nama*, ed. Muhammad Abbasi, 1336 AH, p. 163.
124. Nizam-ul-Mulk Tusi, *Siyar-ul-Muluk* or *Siyasat Nama*, ed. Jafar Shear, 1348 AH, pp. 138-40.
125. Ibid.
126. Rashiduddin Fazlullah, *Jami-ut-Tawarikh*, Tehran, 1338 AH, pp. 435-6; also see, Riasanovsky, *Fundamental Principles of Mongol Law*, pp. 80-98. Like the canon of Catholic truth enunciated by Vincent of Leins ('Quod Ubique quod Semper, quod ab omnibus'), the Mongols also believed in *vox populi*.
127. Ibid, also see *Defremercy*, pp. 2-43.
128. *Defremercy*, pp. 2-43.
129. *Jami-ut-Tawarikh*, pp. 425-6, 432-3; *Secret History of the Mongol Dynasty*, Eng. tr. by Cleaves, pp. 164-6.
130. *Jami-ut-Tawarikh*, pp. 471-3; Ibn-i Battuta, Rihla edn. by Muhammmad Ali, 3rd edn., Tehran, 1361, p. 240.
131. See Wassaf, *Farhang*, p. 641. *Allughat-ul nawait*, Paris, 1880; *Uzbekcha Inglizcha Lughat*, 1959, p. 632, also see: Burhaonov, Akabir Khwaja Khanov et al., Tashkent, 1963, p. 178.
132. Farhang-i Anand Raj, Lucknow edn., 1889-92, see under *Qurultai*. See *Al Lughat-ul Nawait* under *Qurultai*.
133. *Jami-ut-Tawarikh*, p. 452. The Chinese Chroniclers, however, have given a slightly changed version as the date and place (*Kuluran*) is different.
134. *Jami-ut-Tawarikh*, pp. 507-8, for ordinary consultative sessions called *kangash* see *Jami-ut-Tawarikh*, pp. 452-5, 457, 472, 476, 547, 549, 550.
135. Cahun, Claude, *Introduction al historie del Asia*, 1896, pp. 44, 48; also see *Secret History of the Mongol Dynasty*, p. 107, fn. 1.
136. Qutadgu Bilik Izd. Radlov I, p.L III III; *A Vaprosu ob Oiughurakh*, p. 69; Barthold, *Sochinenija*, Moscow edn., 1963-73, vol. V, pp. 247, 510, 742.
137. Juvaini, Ataul Mulk, *Tarikh-i-Jahankusha-i-Juvaini*, Persian text, Leiden, 1911, pp. 154-5, Eng. tr. A.J. Boyle, pp. 196-8, 242, 248-2; *Jami-ut-Tawarikh*, pp. 568-70.
138. Vladimirtsov, Feudalni stroi Mongolski Khanstova, p. 80; Krader, *Peoples of Central Asia*, Hague, 1966, pp. 85-6; Barthold, *Turkestan down to Mongol Invasion*, 1928, pp. 381-92; see *Muzzakira-i-Ahbab*, Eng. tr.

139. Barthold, *Turkestan down to Mongol Invasion*, pp. 381-92. Krader, p. 86, *Jami-ut-Tawarikh*, pp. 480, 513, 523, 567-72.
140. Ibid., pp. 581-2; Khwand Mir, *Habib-us-Siyar*, vol. III, Tehran, Khayyam, 1954 AH, Bombay, 1857 pp. 58-60.
141. Ghulam Husain Yusufi, *Qabus Nama*, Tehran, 1352 AH, p. 227.
142. Yezdi, vol. I, Tehran edn., p. 94.
143. Yezdi, vol. II, Tehran edn., p. 520.
144. *Tuzukat-i-Timuri*, pp. 1-20, 24-89.
145. Ghayasuddin Ali, *Ruz Nama-i-Ghazawati Hindostan*, Russian tr. by Zimin Dnevnik, SPB 1915, vol. I, p. 110; *Four Studies*, II, pp. 23-4.
Ibn-i Arab Shah, *Ajaib-ul Maqdur fi nawadiri*, Timur, Pers. tr., Tehran, 1960, pp. 25, 44, 77-9, 91, 92, 93, 182, 188; Barthold, *Schinenija*, IV; Al Hasan the Arab, pp. 445, 464, 547.
146. *Zafar Nama*, Tehran edn., Eng. tr. by Sanders, p. 201.
147. See Babur's letters to his sons in *Babur Nama*, Turkish text, p. 349, Eng. tr., p. 627; French tr., p. 44.
148. Ibn-i Hasan, pp. 65-91.
149. See *Dastur-ul-Amal* in *Insha-i Abul Fazl*, Harsih Daftar.

# Turco-Mongolian Heritage in the Mughal Polity

The Mughal rulers were not new to the art of governance since they possessed experience gained from almost two centuries of dynastic rule. They brought with them well-tried and already established principles of administration. The need to adapt to a new land made them flexible enough to absorb the customs and traditions of their surroundings. Thus, the general administrative structure of the Mughals and their policies appear to be a conglomeration of Indo-Islamic trends though the rich heritage of the Turco-Mongol legacy in the form of practices, institutions, loan words and terminology does appear occasionally. Even after almost a century of the use of Persian as the official language, the Mughals did not discard Turkish altogether. Jahangir proudly declared, 'Notwithstanding that I grew up in Hindustan, I am not ignorant of Turki speech and writing.'[1]

The Mughal administrative structure, whose foundations were laid mainly during the reign of Akbar, seems to have a varnishing of Mongol customs. In the *Akbar Nama* and other sources, we find the appearance of Turko-Mongol terms such as *janqi*, *kangash*, *jildu*, *sawurin*, *yirligh*, *souyurghameshi*, *souyurghal*, *kukaltash*, *ulka*, *ulja*, *tugh*, *jagir*, *tankhwah*, and the designations for posts like *wakil us sultanate*, *divan*, *tuvaji*, *ichki*, *sauchi*, *qurchi*, *yasawul*, *bakawul*, *qurchi bashi*, *aishik aqasi*, etc. A Central Asian influence discernible in all these terms.

The dominance of the notion of Plenitudo potestatis and the recurrence of mutual conflicts between the spiritual and the temporal authorities which were so common in Europe were not noticed in the Islamic world by Grunnebaum. However, the fact that the divine theory of sovereignty was evolved in the Muslims kingdoms also proves beyond doubt that such a tug of war must have existed. It is significant that the traditions of absolute sovereignty and the notion of the conjunction of spiritual and temporal rulership were developed at many courts as defence mechanisms against the undue encroachment upon the king's authority by lesser mortals. The philosophy and the spirit behind the concepts of *farr-i-ezdi*, *kiyani khwarah*, and *mubad-i-mobadan* are the same, that is, their intention is to guard against any direct or indirect share in or encroachment upon the king's authority. Akbar's *mahzar* was a comparatively harsh step necessitated by the increasing authority enjoyed by the *mullahs* in the neighbouring Islamic countries of Turan and Turkey, a development which loomed large over the Mughal political sphere. The *mahzar* reminds one of Chingiz's attempts at combining within himself both spiritual and temporal authority. Unlike the Muslim rulers (all over the Islamic world) whose autocracy was limited by the *sharia* and the *urf-o-ada* (holy law and customary practices), Chingiz tried to assume unlimited powers. By eliminating Kokchu Shaman, he had appropriated to himself the powers of a spiritual head and had given a death blow to the very institution that posed a potential threat to his absolute power.[2] Like the Parsi concept of *mobidi mobidan*, he combined in himself both temporal and spiritual authority, and was described by the chroniclers as a 'scourge' or the 'flail'[3] of God, on the one hand, and as the epitome of 'universal generosity',[4] on the other. He was given the title of '*Ssuto Bogdo*' (high lofty god) and his image was hung on all camp doors. Badauni records this fact and due to the significance of the passage, it is quoted here:

> In this year (987) His Majesty was anxious to unite in his person the powers of the state and those of the church; for he could not bear to be subordinate to any one. As he had heard that the Prophet, his lawful successors, and some of the most powerful kings, as Amir Timur Sahib i Qiran and Mirza Ulugh Beg Gurgan, and several others had themselves read the Khutba (the Friday Prayer), he resolved to do the same, apparently in order to initiate their example, but in reality to appear in public as the Mujtahid of the age. Accordingly, on Friday, the first Jumad I 987, in the Jama Masjid of Fathepur, which he had built, His Majesty commenced to read the Khutba, but all at once he stammered and trembled, and though assisted by others, he could scarcely read three verses of a poem, which Shaykh Faizi had composed, came quickly down from the pulpit, and handed over the duties of the Imam (leader of the prayer) to Hafiz Mohammad Amin, the court Khatib. These are the verses:
>
> The Lord has given me the Empire,
> And a wise heart and strong arms,
> He has guided me in righteousness and justice,
> His praise surpasses man's understanding,
> Great is his power, Allah o Akbar.

With all his prejudices against Akbar, Badauni informs us that in 985 *kufr shayi shud* or 'heresy became common'. Further, Badauni writes that in 988 'mean fellows who pretended to be learned but in reality were fools collected evidences that His Majesty was the *Sahib-i Zaman* who would remove all differences of opinion among the seventy-two sects of Islam'. Badauni writes: 'This year the Emperor has claimed prophetship. Next year, if God wills, he will be God.'[5]

The divine theory of kingship was influential in shaping the notions of Perso-Islamic and Turco-Mongol sovereignty from the earliest times to the seventeenth century. Not only does Firdausi refer to this '*farr-i-izadi*' in his *Shah Nama* but even Abu Hamid Muhammad al-Ghazali (1058-1111) highlights the importance of this *farr* (effulgence) in his *Nasihat-ul-Muluk*. The well-known authorities Bernard Lewis and Athar Abbas Rizvi[6] have discussed the origin and evolution of this concept, which hardly needs further elaboration. The only possible addition to their valuable discussion could be from two sources, i.e. the views of Ruzbihan Isfahani as expressed in his *Suluk-ul-Muluk* on the concept of kingship and the ideas of Shaibani as recorded by him in his *Mehman Nama-i-Bukhara* regarding the discussion held by the *ulama* in the court of Shaibani on this subject. These notions, however, echo the views expressed by earlier political thinkers of the Islamic world. The *sifat-i-qudsi* and the rule of 'shepherding and doing the work of watch and ward' are expounded by Shaibani Khan and his associates with the same fervour and passion in the first half of the sixteenth century as by Akbar in the second half of the same century.

In his letter to Abdullah Khan, Akbar wrote the fact:

> During the thirty years which he (Akbar) had spent on the throne by the celestial succour, he had always kept this ideal in view that all this conquest of the world and sovereignty, swordsmanship and clime-conquering was for the shepherding and care-taking of the people and not for the accumulation of treasures, gold and silver or for decorating the crown and the throne, or even for giving oneself up to short-lived pleasures. He had consequently nothing else in his heart other than a simple goodness and good-will towards friends and foes, kinsmen and strangers, and had consistently tried for the prosperity of the people, whether small or great, and had adopted an attitude of kindness towards people from afar or near. God was his witness to the fact that the clearing of the four corners of India, which is surrounded on three sides by the ocean, was not out of self-indulgence or selfishness but only for comforting human beings and for exterminating the oppressors.

In his discussions at Kanigul, Shaibani also confirms that the king ought to be just, a 'redressor' who should not accept kingship merely for the opportunity to indulge in worldly pleasures. A king should do the work of watch and ward and should always behave like a *dafa-i-aziat* (a protector from tyranny and torture).[7]

The concept of divine kingship and the deification of sovereigns in West Asia, Central Asia, India, Mongolia, and other places had existed perhaps from the dawn of monarchy. Although the literature of ancient and medieval Central Asia supplies plenty of information regarding these concepts, the other fine arts do not reveal much evidence of such a symbiotic relationship between God and king. Medieval architecture and painting did not clearly illustrate or indicate such expressions though literary texts devote considerable attention to this subject. The *Dharmashastra* of Manu, the *Mahabharata*, and the *Arthashastra* of Kautilya also provide brief accounts of these concepts. The five clauses in Chapter VII of The *Laws of Manu* relating to the duties of a king throw light on the following subject:

> how a king should conduct himself, how he was created, and how he can obtain the highest success. A kshatriya, who has received according to the rule the sacrament prescribed by the Vedas, must duly protect this whole world, for when these creatures, being without a king, through fear, dispersed in all directions, the Lord created a king for the protection of this whole (creation), taking for that purpose the eternal particles of Indra, of the Wind, of Yama, of the Sun, of Fire, of Varuna, of the Moon, and of the Lord of wealth (Kubera) because a king has been formed of the particles of these lords of the gods. He, therefore, surpasses all created beings in lustre.

Kautilya also in his Book VI discusses the qualities of a sovereign,[8] which are similar to the ones prescribed by various Persian sources. In almost all the states of the Orient, faith and kingship are said to be interdependent, a belief that is well certified by the Persian sources. In West Asia and Central Asia, the concept of kingship evolved by the Sassanids was appreciated and adopted in India by Balban as the Sassanids were said to be the best administrators. In his *Manaquib-ul-atrak*, Jahiz (d. AD869) writes: 'The Sassanid Persians surpassed all other nations in the art of governance and the administration of states as the Chinese excelled in handicrafts, the Greeks in science, and the Turks in the art of war.'[9]

Under the Sassanids, the ruler was a 'despot—absolute and autocratic—who was answerable only to God'. The chroniclers often called the ruler the 'commander of the faithful'. The autocrat was expected to be a good *katkhuda* (landlord) who also supervised all agrarian activities. The Sassanids believed that 'the rightful rulers are endowed with divine effulgence or *farr-i-izadi*'. The ideal ruler was supposed to have the following qualities: 'intelligence, knowledge, sharpness of mind, ability to perceive things, perfect physique, literary taste, application to work, horsemanship, boldness, deliberation, good temper and courage, impartiality towards the weak and the strong, friendliness, magnanimity, tolerance and moderation, judgement and foresight in business, frequent study of his predecessors' work to distinguish between good and evil'. These qualities of the perfect ruler are also found in Akbar's conception of the kingly ideal.[10]

In *Adab-ul-Harb wa Shujaat* and *Adab-ul-Muluk*, Fakhri Mudabbir also prescribes a code of conduct for the ruler, who 'should in the first place be well acquainted with the plight of his subjects and should never be oblivious of the conditions prevailing in his country and must always be vigilant'. He writes:

*Mobid-i Mobidan* says that the excellent rulers and amirs are the ones who possess certain qualities: generosity (in giving the *mal*); truthfulness (in anger); kindness (to the subjects); graciousness (towards the good and the righteous); harshness (towards evil doers). He should not be quarrelsome, jealous, should keep the army under full control so that they may not harass the subjects, agriculturists and artisans. Similarly, the subjects also should not be allowed to exploit or live upon the soldiers. The reis should be alerted so that the hoarding of silver does not create an imbalance and hamper transactions. The king should maintain law and order, ensure the prosperity of the state, encourage the development of trade. Ribats which are the . . . destination (*marhala* and *manzilgah*) of the poor and the Caravans should be well organized and populous (*abadan*). The taxes both in cash and kind should be realized in accordance with the *farmans*, customary *Sharia* rules and regulations (*farman*, *shariat-i maahud*, *qanun*) or else it reduces the subjects to the state of *dervishi* and causes devastation of the *mamlakat*. The destruction of a *wilayat* is caused by two factors: *sitam* (tyranny) and *susi* (laziness and laxity). *Mobid-i Mobidan* is said to have advised the rulers in Persia that the secret of the honour and popularity of a king lies in 'showing to and gaining the love of all greater ones and showing justice to commoners' (*bar Khwas tawaddud namudan bar awam adl kardan*).[11]

These views are also reflected in Abul Fazl's *Ain-i-Akbari* and *Akbar Nama*:

Kingship is a gift of God and is not bestowed till many thousands of grand requisites have been gathered together in one individual. Lineage and wealth and the backing of a mob alone are not enough for this great position. It is clear to the wise that a few of the holy qualities (*sifatiquadsi*) are necessary. These are: magnanimity, lofty benevolence, wide capacity, abundant endurance, exalted understanding, innate graciousness, natural courage, justice, rectitude, strenuous labour, proper conduct, profound thoughtfulness, laudable overlooking of offences, and acceptance of excuses.

Abul Fazl's political thought was a fine admixture of the ideas of Farabi, Ibn-i Arabi, Jali, and several others. Plato's philosophy guided both Farabi and Abul Fazl so that 'the ideal of the philosopher-king is to become like God so far as this is possible; to become like God is to become righteous, holy and wise'. Similarly, Ardashir Babak comments: 'Religion and kingship are twins, neither being complete without the other.' Ghazali also says:

As you will hear in the Traditions, the Sultan is God's shadow on earth, which proves that he is high ranking and the Lord's delegate over his creatures. It must, therefore, be recognized that this kingship and the divine effulgence have been granted to them by God and that they must accordingly be obeyed, loved and followed.

Imam Ghazali's king was to follow the 'right religion' as 'kingship and religion are like brothers'. For Abul Fazl kingship was a blessing. Abul Fazl's king is not only subservient to the Sharia but also possesses the capability of receiving divine illumination more than any of his contemporaries. To him the word '*padshah*' denotes the Lord of Stability. Abul Fazl asserts:

No dignity is higher in the eyes of God than royalty; and those who are wise, drink from its auspicious fountain. A sufficient proof of this, for those who require one, is the fact that royalty is a remedy for the spirit of rebellion, and the reason why subjects obey. Even the meaning of the word *Padshah* shows this; for *pad* signifies stability and possession and *shah* means origin, lord.[12]

The opinion of Douglas E. Streusand that the concept of kingship or the theory of the state as perceived or conceived by Ghazali (or for that matter by any of his predecessors and successors) 'involves no contract'[13] needs reconsideration. According to the Islamic theory of the state, the amir was 'divinely appointed', 'divinely guided' and 'divinely protected' and his term of appointment continued 'during the pleasure of the Almighty', as *farr* (effulgence) symbolized divine favour which kings possessed as long as God did not deprive them of it due to their own failings and frailities. Naturally, His 'choice' falls only on 'what is the best'.

Tusi sums up the divine concept of sovereignty and the condition of '*farr*' in the first chapter of his famous work *Book of Politics, Siyasat Nama* (which deals with rulers), in the light of the Holy Book. He writes:

> In every age, God selects a 'chosen' one from amongst the people, embellishes him with all the good qualities befitting to a ruler and bestows upon him the art of administration. The awe of his dignity and magnificence (*haibat-o hashmat*) sets in the hearts of the people and dazzles their eyes. The subjects then spend their days in complete peace and prosperity. If, however, disobedience to God, deviation from the Sharia or some defects appear (in the sovereign), punishment follows and the one time good sovereign is removed from amongst these sinners. Then wars, bloodshed, the drawing of swords, devastation and destruction of human beings follow in a way as fire breaks out in a jungle. Then God again chooses one from amongst the people and this '*taufiq-i izadi*' brings good fortune, prosperity and ascent to him, providing him with all the wisdom, knowledge and intelligence so that he may give to each what he deserves.

Tusi further stresses that the king should value this gift of God, and as a thanksgiving for this favour the king should be kind and just towards his subjects whose prayers and good wishes will keep the empire and its ruler safe and sound. Similarly, the concept of the much-publicized and so-called 'collective sovereignty' (attributed to the Seljuqids, Ayyubids, Mongols, Timurids and Aq Quyunlus) also does not hold water as each of these dynasties had its own direct system of administration where the supposed co-sovereignty of the princes and the autonomous provincial regions did not exist.

The roles of Askari and Hindal find their parallels in almost all the Muslim states, that is, in Safavid Persia where Shah Tahmasp almost constantly fought against his brothers and could, therefore, better appreciate Humayun's difficulties. Even in the Ottoman empire (one of the most highly centralized domains of the Islamic world), the attitude of princes like Jem is noteworthy since he arrayed various external foes against Bayazid. While the Safavid rulers often threw their rival brothers in prison or confined them the harems, thus depriving the Safavid empire from having capable successors in case of the sudden demise of the ruler, the ambitious Ottoman Sultan Muhammad II even went to the extent of evolving the rule of fratricide (to get rid of unwanted rival claimants) which continued to be observed in the empire for about a century.[14] Thus, the genesis of this strife may be sought in the absence of any definite custom of succession and not in the non-existent notion of 'collective sovereignty'. Similarly, if the plunder acquired from imperial campaigns was not presented to the ruler, this almost always invited a retaliatory invasion, even in Central Asia.

Timur preferred to call himself *Amir*—a term usually adopted by Muslim monarchs in conformity with the then prevalent Hanafite law. Babur was not the first Timurid who took the title Padshah nor did the 'earlier Timurids continuen with the use of the title Mirza'. Shah-Rukh adopted the title '*Alsultan ul muazzam*' from the very beginning of his reign. Incidentally, the *Awimaq-i Mughul* of Mirza Abdul Qadir explains the term '*mirza*' as superior to the status of *shahzada* since the word '*mirza*' is an abbreviation of *amirzada*.[15] Attempts to locate points of difference between the administrative structures of the two states will prove to be an exercise in futility if the Central Asian state system is not viewed in its true perspective.

Barthold states that 'Throughout the whole system of the eastern Muslim political organization there runs like a red thread the division of all the organs of administration with two main categories, the *dargah* (palace) and *divan* (chancery).' This assertion challenged by Ibn-i Hasan.[16] He argues that Barthold's view 'applies to India only as far as the Delhi Sultanate is concerned' and explains that the Mughals departed in their organization not only from the Delhi Sultans but also from the Sassanids and Abbasid governments since 'their entire administrative machinery was divided into central and provincial'. Still, Barthold's conclusion is supported by the sources of Islamic history in general and by those of Central Asian history in particular.

The two well-known phases of Akbar's early regnal years, namely, 'Bairam Khan's regency' and the 'petticoat government', seemingly repeat the history (as depicted in the earlier sources) of the period after the death of almost every Turco-Mongol Khan. After the death of the Mongol and Turco-Mongol Khans, usually two to three months elapsed between the selection of the Khan (followed by the ratification of the choice in a *kurultai*) and his accession. During this interval, the queen mother as regent looked after the administrative affairs of the state. The features of this '*turakina* regime' are all found in the period known as the 'petticoat government'.[17] In the Seljuqid and Uzbek empires, the term '*ataliq*' (lit. Turkish *ata*, father; *liq* designate; or *ata beg*, father chief), denotes a 'father figure' nominated and appointed by the central ruler (the Khan). Occasionally, the recommendation of the prince in the context of the nomination of his own *ataliq* could be considered. The *ataliq* was sent along with the prince to the assigned area. Certain nominated nobles and a detachment of the central army also accompanied the *ataliq* and the prince. The *ataliq* was appointed ostensibly to assist the prince in the cumbersome task of administration. But the real purpose of his presence in the provinces was to safeguard the interests of the central ruler, realize the imperial share of the revenue, keep the ruler informed of the happenings in provincial politics, and influence the policies and divert them into the prescribed channels. These *ataliqs* were appointed as deputies to the princes who were not minors but who had come of age and more often than not were past middle age. These *ataliqs* were powerful *amirs* who excited the jealousy of their less fortunate counterparts, i.e. the provincial chiefs, and sometimes even engendered feelings of rivalry in the prince lord whom they were supposed to assist. Bairam Khan thus seems to fall in the long line of the Turco-Mongol *ataliqs*.

The custom of allocating a definite number of *amirs* with a detachment to accompany the princes to the provincial governorship had continued in Central Asia under the Timurids. Babur also adhered to this principle after his conquest of India, leaving modern historians puzzled as to how and why the armies accompanied the assignee to an already subjugated territory.[18] The practice seems to have been partially continued by Akbar, presumably in connection with the Central Asian potentates. In his letter to Shahbaz Khan, sent probably in September 1594, Akbar informs him that he (Shahbaz) has been appointed as the *ataliq* of Shah-Rukh Mirza in Malwa. The letter is significant as it provides the information that Shahbaz was given, in Central Asian fashion, the title as well as the powers of a governor though no other reference to this effect is available. As the *Sahib-i-suba*, Shahbaz was given full control over civil and financial matters.[19] In the *Akbar Nama*, the appointment of Shahbaz Khan as *ataliq* has been mentioned. Badauni, however, says that Shahbaz was appointed to manage the affairs of Malwa and to serve as *vakil* to Shahrukh. Nevertheless, the *farman* under discussion bestowed upon Shahbaz Khan extensive powers and extended advice to him which were usually given to the *ataliqs* of the princes at the time of their appointment in the provinces in

Central Asia. This letter had been drafted on the pattern of the Timurid letters of appointment issued to *ataliqs* which described such privileges.[20] In India, such pronouncements were probably no more than literary flourishes. It is possible that the incompetence of Shah-Rukh as reflected in his performance in Badakhshan and also his intention to participate in the Deccan campaign might have necessitated such an arrangement.

Posts like *diwan-i-kul*, *vakil-us-sultanate*, and *diwan-i-mushrif*, and the subsequent changes in their powers and positions indicate the process of experimentation which Akbar had resorted to before finally evolving his own administrative structure. Once the lofty office (of the head) of the *divan* came to virtually hold the position of the prime minister (*diwan-i-ashraf* and *vakil*), everything was referred to him, including 'a choice ordering of administrative and financial matters'. On another occasion, the separation of revenue and financial affairs was accomplished and the *vakils* were thus eclipsed by the *diwan*. In the list of commanders, several persons were appointed as *vakils* (rendered by Blochmann as prime minister) or as *wazirs* (translated by Blochmann as minister of finances).[21]

In the Mughal empire, the *vakil-us-sultanate* was the head of the nobles of the state and was said to be the 'Emperor's lieutenant in all matters connected with the realm and the household'. Abul Fazl says:

> He is the one who graces the council by his wisdom, and settles with penetration the great affairs of the realm. Promotion and degradation, appointment and dismissal depend on his insight. Although the financial offices are not under his immediate superintendence, yet he receives the returns from the heads of all financial offices and wisely keeps the abstracts of their returns.

The qualities required in a *vakil* as enumerated by Abul Fazl are exactly the same as described by the Central Asian sources.[22] A thorough adaptation of the Central Asian terms and institutions in accordance with the needs and circumstances as well as the surroundings of India is also noticed. The post of the *qazi-i-lashkar* in the Mughal empire seems to be a continuation of the Central Asian office of the *qazi-i-askar* though the latter enjoyed much more power and a higher position than the former since the Indian subcontinent could ill afford military adventures on the Central Asian magnitude and pattern.

In his *Ain-i-Akbari*, Abul Fazl describes several officers without mentioning their duties or privileges though the nomenclature of these officers seems to be exactly the same as that found in Central Asia. Blochmann provides their probable portfolios: the *mir mal* (perhaps the officer-in-charge of the emperor's private purse, the keeper of the seal) and the *mir bakhshi* (paymaster general of the (army/ court). In Central Asia, however, the connotation of *bakhshi* was different though the term '*bakhshiyan*' appeared in the list of military officials. The *barbegi* was an officer who presented people at the court of public audience and handled their petitions. He was also called *mir-i-arz* or *mir-i-ariz*.

It is interesting to note that several institutions and posts were introduced in the Mughal empire with or without any change. In this context the offices of the *vakil-us-sultanate*, *divan*, *vizir*, *diwan-i-mushrif*, *mustawfi*, *sahib-i-tawjih*, *awarja nawis*, *nazir-i-buyutat*, *diwani-i-buyutat*, *mushrif*, *waqia nawis*, *amil*, *munshi*, *khwansalar*, *qushbegi*, and *akhtabegi* may be mentioned. The offices of the *vizir* and the *vakil* were 'the two pillars of the edifice of the state'. As in Central Asia, the posts of *vizir* and *vakil* were synonymous in Mughal India. Likewise they remained to be the lieutenants of the emperor in financial matters and served as the overall incharge of the imperial treasury and of all state accounts. They were the bankers of the cash of revenue, the cultivators of the wilderness of the world, and 'in reality book keepers'. The *diwan* or *vizir* used to

> explain all matters which appear too intricate for the *mustawfi* and whatever is beyond his own ability he refers to the *vakil*. The *mustawfi*, the *sahib-i-tawjih*, the *awarja nawis*, the *mir saman*, the *nazir-i-buyutat*, the *diwan-i-buyutat*, the *mushrif* of the treasury, the *waqia nawis*, the *amil* of the domains, were under his orders and act by the force of his wisdom.

Sometimes, the office of the *vizir* seemed to be an extension of the office of the *vakil*, both in medieval India and in Central Asia. If an extraordinarily talented person befitting the rank of the *vakil* was not available, a man who had 'some of his qualities' was appointed as the '*mushrif-i-diwan*', an office which was 'higher in rank than that of the divan but lower than that of the vakil'.[23]

Similarly, the post of *sahib-i-taujih* (military accountant) was found in both the Indian and Central Asian Timurid states, though in Central Asia he had a higher position (somewhat equal to the *mir bakhshi* in Mughal India). Both empires also shared similar administrative posts particularly in relation to high-ranking and low-ranking officers like *mustaufi*, *diwan-i-buyutat*, *bitikchi*, *mir bakawal*, *amalguzar* and others. The title '*nuyian*' was continued, though the word '*beglarbegi*' was replaced by *amir-ul-umara* and the term '*oughlan*' by *khanazad*.

There were a number of terms and institutions which were similar in nomenclature though different in their connotation. In this context, the most obvious example is that of *souyurghal*. In Mughal India, it stood for the subsistence allowance granted to the four categories of people. However, the term was used in Timurid Central Asia in the sense of a conditional or military grant. The term '*souyurghal*' appeared in Central Asia with the arrival of the Mongols and further continued under the Timurids to indicate the provincial governership accompanied full administrative and financial powers which were granted to princes or nobles. Under the Uzbeks, however, the term '*souyurghal*' was used in the sense of a subsistence allowance.

Another such term is '*bakhshi*'. In the *Zafar Nama*, the word '*bakhshi*' has been used in the sense of a scribe or a writer. Babur informs us that the Mongols called a surgeon a *bakhshi*. In the Kirghiz and Uighur languages the word '*bakhshi*' denotes a shaman; and in the Uzbek language it stands for a folk musician, a story teller, and a sorcerer.

Since the Uighur script was adopted by Chingiz Khan's chancellary in 1204, it is probable that the higher term '*bitikchi*' (secretary) (who was appointed by the court) was corrupted through use into *bakhshi*. Some scholars are of the opinion that the term '*bakhshi*' was a corrupt form of *bhikshu*. These *bakhshis* performed manifold duties, ranging from writing the monarch's edicts to composing the *tamgha* (seal), the heraldic emblem, and the inscriptions on coins and the tablets of authority (*paiza*) in Mongolian and Turkish. Apparently, the term '*bakhshi*' in the Timurid empire was not used exclusively in the sense of a paymaster general or military officer. The office of the *bakhshi* (paymaster general or adjutant general) in the Mughal system of administration, however, had its parallel in nineteenth-century Bukhara where an officer of the same name was responsible for money transactions concerning armaments. Ali Shir Nawai, the famous poet of Sultan Husain Baiqra's court, described the *bakhshis* as 'the secretaries of the kings of Turkestan who know no Persian at all'. But the *bakhshis* did well in Turkish.[24] Their duties were similar to those of the scribes who were also attached to the court. Abul Fazl merely mentions the personal names of the individuals who held this post without referring to the duties and nature of their assignments.[25] The terms '*iqta*', '*tankhwah*', and '*khalsa*' continued with the same connotations in both the empires. The term '*milk*', however, varied in its connotation. Momin's view that terms like '*idarat*', '*milk*', '*aimma*', and '*wazifa*' were replaced by *souyurghal*[26] needs re-examination. The cash granted as a subsistence allowance was called *wazifa*, whereas the lands given for the same purpose were called *milk*.

The powers of the *sadr* were curtailed by Akbar, though in similar circumstances the Central Asian rulers, while ordering their replacement, still permitted them to continue with their privileges, presumably due to religious constraints.

Like Chingiz, Akbar too was a good physiognomist and assessor of human nature. In *Ain* 7, it is stated that:

> His Majesty (Akbar) discerns the value of a man by the lineaments of his forehead; he also distinguishes a tradesman by the look of his face from a soldier, so much so that experienced people are astonished and refer to His Majesty's power of discernment to hidden knowledge.

Abul Fazl thinks that it is 'necessary for just kings to make themselves first acquainted with the rank and character of men, by the light of insight and penetration, and then to regulate business accordingly. He further informs us that

> the exalted monarch of our time is so endowed with these laudable disproportions, that it is no exaggeration to call him their exordium. From the light of his Wisdom, he discerns the worth of men, and kindles the lamp of their energy; whilst ever clear to himself, and without an effort, he adorns his Wisdom with the beauty of practice.[27]

Additionally, there was Akbar's *Anjuman-i-Dad o Dihish* or assembly of expenditure, especially organized in which a large number of men were introduced. On these occasions, senior grandees and *amirs* brought their acquaintances to be introduced to Akbar in order to solicit appointments for them.[28]

The Mughal military organization and the *mansabdari* system do not seem to be exact replicas of the military system of Chingiz Khan. The similarity appears to be in the structure of the decimal system which was basically not an innovation of Chingiz Khan. It existed in almost all the Turco-Mongol nomadic tribal societies, including that of the Uighurs. Under Chingiz Khan, 'the reviewing and mustering of the army has been so arranged that they (Mongol rulers) have abolished the registry of inspection (*daftar-i-arz*)'.[29] Timur had, however, skilfully tried to evolve a composite military institution combining within its purview the Mongol system of *dim* (muster and counting of all the army) with the Perso-Islamic office of the *diwan-i-arz*. Babur says that in the military sphere 'just as Chingiz Khan had laid down his rule so the Mughals still observe them'. [30] The Chingizi custom of *dim* may or may not have been continued during the reign of Babur in India. Nevertheless, one of the paintings in the *Babur Nama* by a Hindi (Indian) painter of Akbar's court depicts the review of troops (*dim*). This shows a line of flags (*tugh*) pushed into the ground while the counting was supposed to start.[31] It is interesting to note that terminology which had existed since the time of the Sultanate period was discarded in this respect. The titles *amir*, *sipahsalar*, *malik*, and *sarikhail* were replaced by the Turco-Mongol terms '*tumanbegi*' (commander of 10,000), '*mingbashi*' (commander of 1,000), '*yuzbegi*' (commander of 100), and '*unbegi*' (commander of ten) as given in the *Ain-i-Akbari*.[32] The *mansabdari* system introduced by Akbar had brought many new features in its wake while accommodating some of the remnants of the Central Asian system of military organization. Certain practices were completely transformed while others were abandoned and some others were retained with slight modifications.

In the early years of his reign, Akbar seems to have followed the Chingizi principle of expecting each horseman of his standing army to bring his own horse and accoutrements with him. In an agrarian society like India where the martial races did not play as important a role as they did in Central Asia, this measure was not likely to materialize without causing some inconvenience and inefficiency. Akbar therefore discontinued the practice. A horse was provided thereafter to each recruit on joining the army for which he was considered responsible, and only men appointed to the post of an *ahdi* were to bring a horse.[33]

The granting of increased emoluments to soldiers fighting wars in distant places was a Mongol tradition continued by the Mughals in India. When the expedition to Balkh and Samarqand was being planned by Shahjahan, imperial orders were issued that 'on account of the distance of those countries, as long as the expedition should last, each mansabdar should only muster one-fifth'.[34] The awarijas (registers) and the *taliqa* (descriptive rolls) were common to the armies of both countries. In both kingdoms the officer *bitikchi* made out descriptive rolls of the soldiers and registered their peculiarities.

The word '*dafter*', derived from the Greek word '*dapter*', had the same connotation in both the places. The *sanads* for cash payment (written statement of accounts) had its parallel in the *barat* (draft), which was a voucher for payment given to officers and was known by the same name. The three *dafters*, namely *abwab-i-male* (details of revenue, income); the *arbab-i-tahawil* (details of debits and credits, accounts of expenditure): and the *tawjih* (military accounts) were Perso-Islamic and a legacy of Central Asia.[35] Akbar had maintained the Mongol custom of military organization in his kingdom though he gave it the name of the *mansabdari* system.

Abul Fazl writes:

> Whenever His Majesty rides out, or at the time of the *Bar-i Am* or levee, the sons of the amirs, and other m ansabdars and the Ahadis carry the *qur* in their hands and on their shoulders. Every four of them carry four quivers, four bows, four swords, four shields and besides, they take up lances, spears, axes, pointed and all properly arranged.

In the Chingizi fashion 'the flag was hung round with *qutas* (tail of the Tibetan yak) like a *togh*'.[36] The Central Asian *mihaffa* (a sort of wooden turret suspended from two poles between two camels used at the time of travelling was also common in India.

The word '*otbegi*' (in charge of all the royal horses) is again a Mongol-Turkish term; in Turkish it means horse and *begi* refers to the chief.[37] Mongol sources frequently refer to the twelve *kurans*. Although the Mongol dictionary does not have such a word, Steingass renders the term 'as a herd or troops' even though the language from which the term originated is not given. The Uzbek dictionary, however, explains this word as 'appearance, presence, exhibition or show'. To this also belongs the word '*kurnish*', meaning 'appearance, presence'. The context in which the term appears in the Mongol sources also supports the conjecture that these detachments appeared for inspection and presented themselves for one month in a year. Akbar's imperial army was likewise divided into twelve parts, each of which mounted guard for the period of one month; this gave all the troops an opportunity to come to the court.[38]

*The Secret History of the Mongol Dynasty* refers to the various types of camps, dwelling places, and felt houses which are also mentioned in the Persian sources. In his *Ain* 21 on '*farrashkhana*', Abul Fazl gives a similar description, presenting a somewhat improved version of those of the by-gone days of Chingiz Khan.

These included: the *bargah* which could hold more than ten thousand people; the *chubin rawati* which was a replica of the royal *yurt*; the *zamindoz khargah* which was 'the folding tent made in various ways, some with one, others with two doors'. This last item was used very frequently during journeys both the Mughals and by the Turco-Mongols. The walls of the *khargah* were fastened together with leather straps, so that it could be folded together when the camp broke up.[39]

Similarly, the *sarapardah* was common to both regions, the only difference being in its adaptability to Indian weather conditions. Abul Fazl's view that 'in former times' it had been prepared of coarse canvas, but that in later days the quality of its manufacture was improved, particularly under Akbar who had caused it to be made of carpeting, and thereby improved its appearance and usefulness,[40] seems to be based on a misconception about the nature of the so-called nomadic camp court. The description of these camp courts as found in the contemporary sources and (in paintings also) shows that all kinds of silks, velvets, brocades, and several types of gold and silver ornamentation were used in the furnishing of these camp courts and movable dwelling houses.[41]

It appears that the Mughals adhered to the chancellery practices of Central Asia and Persia. The *Mughal ahkam-i-diwani* and appointment orders have the same conventional style and forms of expression, and the same phraseology, tone, and rhythm which characterize Central Asian documents of the same kind. These were introduced by Babur and Humayun to Indian Presumably the drafting of the *Nama-i-Nami* by Khwand Mir was undertaken to provide specimens and models for the Mughal chancellery.[42] The term '*barat*' (meaning draft, also the *farman* issued for financial grants), which was extensively used in Turco-Mongol transactions, also gained currency in the Mughal empire, though at times with a difference in its connotation.

Similarly, Abul Fazl informs us about two seals which display the direct impact of the Timurid style. The round small seal (prepared by a certain Tamkin and improved upon by Maulana Ali Ahmad) continued to be called by its Chaghatai name, *uzuk*. It was generally used for *farman-i-sabti* (for appointments to higher posts only) and kept in the safe custody in the women's apartments of the palace or with some very highly placed, favourite noble man of the emperor. The large seal had the names of Akbar's Timurid ancestors inscribed on it. It was earlier used only for letters sent to foreign rulers, but later it was also used for other purposes. Akbar's *mihrabi* seal (for judicial transactions) inscribed with the couplet—*rast-i mujib-i rizayi khuda ast kasnadidam ki gum shud az rahi rast* ('uprightness is the means of pleasing God; I never saw any one lost on the straight road')[43]—reminds one of Timur's official seal with which all the papers in the judiciary were stamped and which carried the inscription *rast-i-rusti* (i.e. truth is safety). Even Aurangzeb's seals had the same pattern. In the middle of some of the seals was the name 'Aurangzeb, Conqueror of the Worlds'. Manucci says[44] that the Mughal rulers attested all their *farmans* and the grants which they rewarded with the seal that carried the names of Timur Lang, Miranshah, and Abu Said; this practice was prevalent in almost all the contemporary empires, including that of the Ottomans.[45] As in the Chingizide and the Timurid courts, there also existed a separate staff in Akbar's court whose duty was to record in a diary the day's proceedings and the emperor's orders, activities, and sayings in the *durbars*.

In the Mughal chronicles, the word '*aimaqs*' is frequently mentioned in different contexts. Jahangir presented these *aimaqs* with *jagirs* and herds of Iraqi and Turki horses. Rogers renders the term '*aimaqs*' as cavalry. It should be noted that in Mughal India the concept of a tribal cavalry on the Central Asian pattern did not exist. In Central Asia the word '*aimaqs*' denoted a tribal unit. Sometimes such groups took refuge in India; the *aimaqs* of Badakhshan had fled from Central Asia to escape the tyranny of Abdul Momin, who demanded their return from Akbar.[46]

As discussed elsewhere, certain customary practices of Central Asia such as *tuquz*, *sawurin*, and *peshkash* continued to be followed in India. In the Chingizide fashion, the distinctions bestowed upon the *beglar begi* or the *amir-ul-umara* included the yak tail, the *tuman tugh*, and drums. The *tuman tugh* was exclusively a Chingizide standard. On the days of festivity, we hear about the existence of the *damama*, *nafir*, Khwarazmian tunes, and the *surna-i-qurnai* in the Central Asian fashion. The Indian *jhanda* was accompanied by the Turco-Mongol *qur* (a collection of flags, arms, and other insignia of royalty which followed the king wherever he went). The *Ain* 19 refers to the *tuman tugh*, certainly a Chingizide remnant though there are descriptions of the *chatra tugh* (a kind of *alam* but smaller than it and adorned with tails of the Tibetan yak). Both the *chatra tugh* and the *tuman tugh* were 'flags of the highest dignity' though the *tuman tugh* was bestowed only upon great nobles. The standards and ensigns of royalty had their importance in the Turco-Mongol courts. Not only did the Sassanids and their ardent follower Balban emphasize the grandeur of the court which was awe-inspiring but the Mongols and the Mughals also followed it because the 'Shamsa of the arch of royalty is a divine light, which God directly transfers to kings without the assistance of men, and kings are fond of external splendour because they consider it to be an image of Divine glory'. The ensigns of royalty were also the same as those found in Chingiz's empire. These were the *sayabans* or the *aftabgirs* and the *kawkabas* which were hung up before the assembly hall. The *qur* was a Mongol insignia of royalty which always accompanied the *alam* or the royal standard. Whenever the ruler rode out, at least five of these were carried wrapped in scarlet cloth bags. They were unfurled on special and ceremonial occasions. The word *'tugh'* in Mongolian denotes banner. Another Mongolian standard found in Mughal India was the *tuman tugh* which was longer than the *chatra tugh*. The *qur* necessarily contained 'a flag of each kind; but on great occasions, many are displayed'.[47] The sources also refer to the *Sho-tu* which was used either in the sense of a 'raised standard' or in the sense of 'spear and standard'. The word '*tu*' (Turkish *tughi*) was a standard consisting of a long pole surmounted by a receptacle containing a yak's tail. This standard was one of the insignia of the relatives of the khan and istinguished military officers. A detailed account is given in *The Encampments of Journey*.[48] The Central Asian *damama*, *naqqara*, *duhul*, *kanai kurnai*, *surnai*, *nafir*, *sing* and *sanj* were played in the *naqarakhana* in the same manner as in the Turco-Mongol court. Similarly, there were the 'seven performances' which were a daily feature, with musical bands playing the *gharis*. The playing of the four tunes called the *ikhlati*, *ibtidai*, *shiraz-i-qalandari*, and the *nigar qatra* or *nukhud qatra* occupied almost an hour, after which began the playing of the old Khwarazmian tunes of which Akbar had reportedly 'composed more than two hundred (and), which were said to be the delight of young and old, especially the tunes Jalalshahi, Mahamir, Karkat and the Nawarozi'. The Khwarazmian tunes were played by the *mursil* before he began playing his specialized musical tunes. Abul Fazl describes 'the tent containing forty divisions over which twelve awnings are spread, each of twelve yards, and separated by canvases. This place, in every division of which a convenient closet is constructed, is called *ichki*—which is the Chaghatai name used by His Majesty.' The term has been described by both Blochmann and Rogers as *ibachki*. It is a variation of the Chaghatai Turkish (Uzbek) word '*ichki*', which denotes inner apartment.[49]

Ibn-i Tiqtiqa criticizes Chingiz's penchant for the time-consuming recreation of hunting. Ibn-i Tiqtiqa wonders how a king like Chingiz could develop a craze for hunting in a *nirgha* whose extent was spread over a journey of three months' duration.[50] The criticism is made in complete disregard of the fact that the hunting excursion was a necessary measure undertaken for purposes of administrative checking and to collect provender for the winter in a region that was *natura maligna*. Under the Timurids also, hunting was an important occasion for the reconnaissance of various fiefs and their administration. Like Chingiz and Timur, Akbar was also enamoured of the chase and hunting for the 'highest reasons'. Abul Fazl says that Akbar made

> hunting a means of increasing knowledge, and besides, he used hunting parties as occasions to inquire, without having first given notice of his coming, into the condition of the people and the army. He travels incognito and examines into matters referring to taxation, or to souyurghal lands or to affairs connected with the household. He lifts up such as are oppressed and punishes the oppressors.[51]

Sometimes the uncritical adoption of and unquestioning adherence to certain elements of the Central Asian legacy became troublesome. On such occasions, Abul Fazl the court chronicler did not hesitate to condemn these practices. The custom of *tarkhani* (a special hereditary privilege granted to the nobles) became a target of his attack. Abul Fazl comments that to his mind the privilege of not enquiring into the faults of privileged nobles until nine generations had passed 'does not appear to be consonant with propriety'. He writes:

> If farseeing princes are engaged in testing men, and take care that no evil deed be committed by them, and if such orders have been issued for the exaltation of some persons, then it is something comprehensible. But as for that provision that no inquiry is to be made for nine generations, it would look as if the Almighty had given him (the Khan) the power of knowing the future.[52]

According to Beveridge, Abul Fazl went into such details about the custom of *tarkhani* because Akbar had nominally revived this tradition and had conferred this privilege on Maulana Nuruddin, the guardian of his father's tomb.[53] But the context in which this criticism appeared seems to point to the rebellion of Muhammad Jani of Thatta, who happened to be a descendant of one of Timur's *tarkhani* nobles, namely, Atku Timur. The criticism seems to emanate from imaginary fears as much as from proper reasoning.

Contradicting his own professed superiority to the begs, Babur had to adopt a policy of 'comradeship in arms' towards his followers in the days of the adversity. Before the empire could acquire strong foundations, Babur lost his life. Being conscious of the weak position of his newly founded kingdom.

Although several references are found to the consultative assemblies held by Akbar in the *Akbar Nama*, administrative affairs and state business were attended to by the Mughal emperor without the help of any other 'constitutional body' or consultative assembly.

However, the following inscription written by Abul Fazl for a temple in Kashmir and cited in Askari Husayni Bilgrami's *Durarul Manshur* is noteworthy: 'Polytheism and Islam feel after Thee. Each religion says, "Thou art one, without equal."' This confirms the eclectic approach which both Abul Fazl and Akbar adopted.

In his *Ain*, Abul Fazl noted that the 'people of the world may be divided into four classes', and describes them as the warriors; the artificers and the merchants; the learned, the philosophers, the physicians, etc.; and the husbandmen and the labourers.[54] Although Abul Fazl does not mention that these social groups had existed earlier, the entire paragraph seems to have been a reproduction of what one finds in the chapter '*Dastan-i Jamshid*' in Firdausi's *Shah Nama*. The same categories are mentioned in the *Akhlaqi Muhsini* (Chapter XV '*dar adl*') and also in the *Akhlaqi Jalali* and the *Akhlaqi Nasiri*. Both Akbar and Abul Fazl repeatedly recommended the study of these three *Akhlaqs* to their nobles, as is evident from the epistolary records.

It is also significant that Akbar called Salim by the name of Shaikhu, a Turkish term of affection, written as *Ye-hu* and read as *Shehu*. The term '*Shehu*' frequently occurs in historical works on the Turks, and is generally interpreted as meaning '*ta-chen*' (high official); it denoted the highest rank of Turkish officials under the Khan, and the person bearing this title was usually a son, brother, or other near relative of the Khan. He was commonly the *satrapor*, governor of a province, but we also read of the right and left Shehu at the Khan's court. Since Indo-Central Asian contacts owe much of their origin to Buddhism and Sufism, the lingual affinity between these two regions had begun at an earlier period. This point has been discussed elsewhere. Even a cursory dance at Yasin's *Glossary* and other such works shows that revenue officers and taxation terminology were given the same Perso-Islamic and Turco-Mongol terms which had existed in the region ever since the days of the Sassanids, the Chingizis, and the Timurids. These names and terms include: *amin*, *awarya nawis*, *tahwildar*, *tawgih nawis*, *shahna*, *amil*, *qanunge*, *qazi*, *mustjir*, *nazir*, *mushrif*, *tamassulk*, *tumar*, *tughara mustaufi altamgha* (red stamp) (which has been described at length in Jahangir's *Tuzuk* and other sources), *taufir*, *taliqa zabti*, *zabita*, *talibana*, *qunalsha*, *qurq*, *qabz*, *malikana mahal*, *muhassilana*, *salami*, *wajibul arz*, etc.

The treatment meted out to the clan of Atka Khan, about whom Akbar boasted that he had 'brought out the clan of Atkas from Lahore and like stars dispersed them, giving to each one of them a *jagir* in various corners of Hindustan',[55] reminds one of the Chingizide practice of *Kuchanidan* in which the unruly or rebellious tribes were divided dispersed, and sent to different directions of the empire to weaken their collective strength.

Yazdi refers to the record office maintained at the court of Timur where the Turkish, Uighur, and Persian officers were appointed to record the daily proceedings of the cout.[56] Abul Fazl informs us that the idea of the 'great institution of the record office'[57] had occurred to Akbar 'so that the officers might have valuable assistance and that the administrative orders might be preserved'. In his characteristic manner, he omits to mention the fact that this was a common practice not only in the Central Asian courts but also elsewhere.

## NOTES

1. Jahangir, *Tuzuk-i-Jahangiri*, Eng. tr. by A. Rogers, New Delhi, 1978, vol. I, p. 109.
2. Abul Fazl, *Ain-i-Akbari*, Eng. tr. by Blochmann, New Delhi, 1965, vol. I, pp. 2-6. See *Ain-i Rahnamuni*, *Ain*, no. 77, pp. 170-4. Also see *Ain*, Eng. tr., pp. xl, 1v, *Ain*, no. 2, Eng. tr., pp. 12-16, 52, 59, 167-79, 195-9, 256; *Ain* II, Eng. tr. Badauni, *Muntakhab-ut-Tawarikh*, *Bib. Indica*, Calcutta, 1865, 1868; Eng. tr.,

I, pp. 167, 199; Badauni, II, pp. 44, 200, 256, 268, 270-6; *The Secret History of the Mongol Dynasty*, Eng. tr. by Cleaves, p. 144; Mohd. Asad, *The Spirit of Islam*, 1979, p. 10.
3. Juvaini, *Tarikh Jahankusha-i-Juvaini*, Leiden, 1911, pp. 1-30.
4. Hasan Sijzi, *Fawaid-ul Fuwad*, p. 86.
5. Badauni, vol. II, pp. 268, 288, 301.
6. Athar Abbas Rizvi, *Sufis in India*, vol. II, pp. 348-84.
7. F. Ruzbihan Isfahani, *Mehman Nama-i-Bukhara*, Tehran, 1985, pp. 7-41; *Insha-i-Abul Fazl*, Har Sih Daftar, Newal Kishore edn., pp. 1-17.
8. Abul Fazl, *Insha-i-Abul Fazl*, pp. 1-15. *The Laws of Manu*, Eng. tr. by G. Buhler, Delhi, 1964, pp. 216-17; Kautilya's *Arthashastra*, Eng. tr. by Shamashastry, Mysore, 1956, pp. 287-90.
9. Aliahiz, *Manaqibul Atrak*, published under the title *Risalat fi fazailulatrak*, ed. Van Valten, 1903; Eng. tr. by Karley Walker, *JRAS*, 1915, pp. 631-97, also see passages on p. 682.
10. Mohd. B. Mansur b. Said Fakhri Mudabbir, *Adabul Harb wa Shujaat*, Tehran, 1336 AH, pp. 112-19, 166-7.
11. *Ain*, pp. 2-4; Imam Abu Hamid Al Ghazali, *Nasihat-ul-Mulk*, edited by Jalal Hurnari, Tehran; Eng. tr. F.R.C. Begtey, Council for Kings, London, 1964, pp. 45, 73-4; A.A. Rizvi, *Religious and Intellectual History of the Muslims*, New Delhi, 1975, pp. 352-62.
12. Douglas E. Streusand, *The Formation of the Mughal Empire*, Delhi, 1989, pp. 1-50.
13. For more details, see *Cambridge History of Islam*, Cambridge, 1977, pp. 303, 430-44.
14. Abdul Qadir, *Tarikhi-i-Awimaqi Moghul*, Amritsar, pp. 1-7.
15. *Ain*, Eng. tr., I, pp. 4-5, 595; Ibn-i Hasan, *The Central Structure of the Mughal Empire*, London, 1936, pp. 127-37, 148, 227, 244-93; Khwaja Khanov, *Uzbekski-Ruski Slavar*, Moscow, 1959, p. 57; Ibn-i Arab, *Ajaib-ul Maqdur*, p. 4; *Akbar Nama*, text, p. 381; Eng tr., pp. 560-623; *Ain*, p. 60.
16. For the Turakina regime, see examples in Juvaini's *Tarikh-i-Jahankusha*; for criticism of the Petticoat Government, see Athar Abbas Rizvi, *Wonder that was India*, p. 105.
17. See Ahsan Raza's article, 'Babur's settlement of his conquest in Hindustan', Proceedings of the 9th Session of the Indian History Congress, Patiala.
18. See *Insha-i-Abul Fazl*, Daftar I, 'Farman to Shahrukh'.
19. Ibid. Badauni, p. 44; For *farmans* of the *ataliqs*, see Abdussalam Kashmiri, *Rauzat-ur-Rizwan*, MS, Institute of Oriental Studies, Tashkent, p. 444.
20. *Ain* I, Eng. tr., pp. 4-5, 595.
21. Ibid.
22. Ibid., pp. 1-9.
23. Basil Gray, *The Arts of the Books in Central Asia*, p. 32.
24. *Ain* I, Eng. tr., pp. 7-10, 265.
25. Momin Muhiuddin, *The Chancellary and Persian Epistolography under the Mughals*, Calcutta, 1987, pp. 80, 180.
26. *Ain*, no. 19, p. 278.
27. *Ain*, nos. 7-10, p. 256.

28. Juvaini, op. cit., p. 31; *Ain-i-Akbari*, nos. 29 and 76. Eng. tr., pp. 169-70. Also see p. 75, fn. 5.
29. *Babur Nama*, p. 100.
30. *Babur Nama*, compiled by Hamid Sulaimanvo, Tashkent, 1970, painting no. 20.
31. *Ain* 76, Eng. tr., pp. 169-70.
32. Juvaini, p. 31; *Ain*, nos. 29 and 76. Eng tr., pp. 169-70. Also see p. 75, fn 5.
33. Lahori, *Padshah Nama*, I, p. 113.
34. *Ain* no. 11, pp. 269-72.
35. *Ain* no. 35, Eng. tr., pp. 115-16.
36. *Ain* no. 53, Eng. tr., p. 145.
37. *Ain* no. 9.
38. *Ain*, no. 21, Eng. tr., pp. 55-7.
39. Ibid.
40. Ibid.
41. Momin, op. cit., pp. 67-8, 75; also see Cleaves, 'A Chancellary Practice of the Mongols', *Harvard Journal of Asiatic Studies*, Dec. 1951, pp. 494-521. Also see Khwand Mir's *Nama-i-Nami*.
42. *Ain*, op. cit.; no. 20, pp. 54-5.
43. Manucci, *Storia De Mogor*, vol. II, Eng. tr. by William Irvine, Delhi, 1990, p. 364.
44. Clavijo, *Embassy to Tameslave*, ed. by Derison Ross and Eileen Power, Eng. tr. from the Spanish by Lestrange, London, 1928, pp. 295-6; Yuvan Chao Pishi, Eng tr. by A. Waley, London, 1963; Yazdi, *Zafar Nama*, Calcutta, 1889, p. 18; *Ain*, op. cit., p. 193.
45. *Insha-i-Abul Fazl*, pp. 1-17.
46. *Ain*, no. 19, Eng. tr., I, pp. 52-4, 153; Thomas Walters et al., *On Yuang Chwang's Travels in India*, Delhi, 1961, pp. 77-8.
47. See *Ain* 16.
48. Jahangir, *Tuzuk*, pp. 23, 68, 76, fn. 1; also see *Faramin-i-Salatin*, nos. 47-64.
49. Ibn-i Tiqtiqa, *Alnujumuz Zahira*, Persian tr. by Muhammad Wahid Gulpaegari, Tehran, 1350 AH, p. 71.
50. Abul Fazl, *Ain*, no. 27, pp. 292-8.
51. Abul Fazl, *Akbar Nama*, Eng. tr. by A. Beveridge, vol. III, Delhi, 1973, pp. 973-7, Pers. text, pp. 635-7. Also see *Babur Nama*, text, p. 542, tr., pp. 975-6, fn. 1; Badauni, *Muntakhab-ut-Tawarikh*, vol. III, p. 198; *Maasir*, I, p. 480.
52. Abul Fazl, *Ain-i-Akbari*, vol. I, p. 42.
53. Kautilya's *Arthashastra*, 5th edn., edited by Shamashastry, Mysore, 1956, Chapters IX and XV, pp. 14-15, 26-9.
54. *Ain*, II, p. 332; Bayazid Bayat, *Tazkirat Humayun wa Akbar*, p. 253.
55. Yazdi, vol. I, p. 14.
56. *Akbar Nama*, III, Chapter XXII, text, p. 118; Eng. tr., p. 167.
57. Ibid.

# Indo-Central Asian Exchanges and Interactions in the Spheres of the Fine Arts, Handicrafts and Technology

A proper study of the history of medieval Central Asia is essential for a proper understanding of medieval Asian history. A variety of people (fortune-seekers, militiamen practitioners of the fine arts, invaders, traders, exiles and refugees) who had trickled from far-off lands into Central Asia or who had emerged from its own soil contributed in their own ways to the making of Asian civilization.

A study of the history of the Turco-Mongol invaders and their rich heritage in a proper perspective is also needed. Glimpses of the Turco-Mongol institutions and terminologies are seen in the Mughal empire, though these are often misunderstood and misinterpreted for want of adequate knowledge of the languages and customs of the Central Asian region. Similarly, the studies undertaken in Mongolia and Central Asia with regard to the spread of Buddhism in these regions still have some lacunae pertaining to its sociological aspects and its impact on the local society.

From its Turco-Mongol rulers (fourteenth-seventeenth centuries) Central Asia has inherited a rich legacy of various administrative and agrarian records, manuals, *souzomiz*, and *yirlighs*. A detailed study of these documents, royal proclamations, orders pertaining to various forms of land grants, papers relating to legal proceedings of the *qazikhana*, and administrative manuals will misconceptions greatly help to correct as well as fill in the gaps in our information, enabling us to understand the social structure, agrarian systems, functions of ministers and various departments, system of delegation of power, agrarian and social relationships, and commercial transactions. Such studies can also help Indian historians to understand and appreciate the medieval Indian institutions and traditions which had been borrowed to a considerable extent from Central Asia.

It must be kept in view that a study of this nature is likely to have its own problems. In the first place, the non-availability of source material in India and the problems arising from their being in different languages (i.e. Mongol, Arabic, Persian, Russian, Chaghatai, and Osmanli Turkish) make it difficult for a scholar to undertake this study. Besides, the sources often have a more mythical than a historical character, suffering at times from distortions due to personal or religious grievances, or because they present facts tainted by subjectivity or 'centrism'. Discrepancies are also noticed in various chronicles either due to lack of proper and detailed knowledge or even due to the usual urge to include colourful material and juicy details so characteristic of the medieval period. A comparative study of sources in various languages is, therefore, essential to verify and ascertain the facts. If these prerequisites remain unfulfilled, the historians knowing only the Persian language along with English will tend to misinterpret the terms or will study the institutions necessarily within the framework of Islamic history in general. It goes without saying that incorrect assessments of the less-known subject matter or the thorough misconceptions created by the misinterpretation of data and inaccurate chronologies can make a mockery of the study of history.

Owing to frequent interactions and the continuous movement of peoples and ideas among Kazakhistan and the Kirghiz steppes, Mongolia, China, India, Afghanistan, Turkey, and Persia, there developed certain elements common in the culture and ethos of these regions. The socio-economic and religio-political spheres in Central Asia present an amalgam of many cultures and civilizations.

Central Asia has influenced and shaped the developments in the surrounding regions. Scholars need to examine its history, physical features, accounts of the various routes connecting Central Asia with its surrounding regions, the changing political borders of the states, commercial relations, and economic systems.

Although some valuable work has been done in certain European languages (Russian, French, and German), a planned effort has yet to be made to refer exclusively and extensively to sources available in the Persian, Uzbek, Arabic, and Russian languages. One who is not sufficiently equipped to interest and study the original sources in these languages cannot be expected to give a proper interpretation of the terms used in the region; he or she is most likely to study the institutions of Central Asia within the frameworks generally prevalent in the Islamic lands or in Mughal India. A loose usage of terms by medieval historians or a drastically different connotation of one and the same term existing in Central Asia and elsewhere in the Islamic world can mislead one. Again, most of the institutions and customs existing in Central Asia long before the advent of the Mongols and the practices which were prevalent elsewhere have been attributed to the reign of Chingiz Khan, presumably due to a lack of proper familiarity with the laws and systems introduced by him. Consequently, the study of the Central Asian civilization is indeed a much needed venture. The sources available in certain languages contain valuable information about Central Asian history and the institutions and movements which affected the neighbouring regions. They throw light on commercial contacts, the exchange of ideas pertaining not only to the fine arts but also to those events which influenced historical developments and the processes of interaction between the various regions.

The continuous exchange of ideas and technical and artistic skills between India and Central Asia is nowhere more clearly seen than in the sphere of the fine arts. Medieval Indian architecture is an amalgam of several traditions from different cultures. While Central Asian invaders (such as Mahmud of Ghazna and Timur) had carried away as captives all the skilled men, including architects, masons, carvers, sculptors, and engineers, along with building materials from India, voluntary fortune-seekers and invitees emigrated from Iran and Central Asia to implant Central Asian styles and enrich Indian architecture. Indian architecture exhibits the fusion and harmonious synthesis of concepts, techniques, styles of ornamentation, and decoration, all of which seem to bear the imprint of Iranian, Central Asian, and Turkish architectural features. The colourful tile ornamentation and mosaic designs used in the Shah-i Zindah complex at Samarqand had their replica in Jamali's tomb at Delhi, and a striking resemblance is noticed between the square Samanid brick mausoleum at Bukhara (ninth-tenth centuries) and the square marble tomb of Sultan Hoshang at Mandu (fifteenth century). The Central Asian style is visible in the mausoleum of Humayun (constructed by the architect Mirak Mirza Ghayas), in the Nila Gumbad, and the Sabz Burj. Even the architecture of the provincial dynasties of Bengal, Jaunpur, Malwa, Gujarat, and the Deccan present a fine blending of regional and indigenous workmanship, inspired by the styles of Persia and Central Asia (Saiyid tombs, Lodi Bara Gumbad Mosque, 1494, by Abu Amjad; the Bidar monuments of Gulbarga,

Golconda, and Bijapur). Similarities are also noticed in the Agra and Fatehpur Sikri mosques and palaces and the Sarai Nur Mahal in Punjab.

Central Asian architectural features were extensively adopted and adapted in India (such as the *panjara*, *girikh*, *kundal*, *ouimakr*, *kashikari*, *peshtaq*, *guldasta*, *gumbad*, *manara*, *jaimir*, *jal*, *taq*, *suq-samanzar*). Details regarding their names and the exact techniques involved in their making are also available in various treatises. Certain other important features (carpet technique, flat arcuate roof decorated with stucco-deep niches, squinches, pendentives, spandrels) or different kinds of minarets (angular, circular, fluted, stalactite, tapering, attached, stunted), varied types of decor (arabesque patterns, abstract articulation, vegetable and geometric designs) also have been borrowed from Central Asia. Horticulturists from Iran and Turan contributed to the art of gardening. The mural paintings on the buildings of Agra and Fatehpur Sikri reflect the influence of Turanian art. The art of book-making and the eight styles of *belles letters* and intricate *kufi*, *nask*, *sulls*, *riga*, *tauqi*, *parkam*, *dobar* and *nastaliq* decorated Indian buildings. The most astonishing were the underground and underwater structures.

Evidence of a brisk and continuous exchange of ideas, knowledge, and expertise is also seen in the fields of vocal and instrumental music and dance. The process of artistic amalgamation is said to have started with Amir Khusrau or a little earlier and was carried further by patrons of the art like Sultan Husain Sherqi of Jaunpur, Zainul Abidin of Kashmir, the Sur rulers, Akbar, Burhan Khan of Khandesh, and the Nawabs of Awadh. Several treatises and general works written both in India and Central Asia confirm the longstanding contact between the two regions in the field of music and dance. Nearly twelve Perso-Arab airs (like *aiman*, *qawl*, *hawa*, *basit*, *galbana*, *gul*, *zilaf*, *sarpardah*, *ghanam*, *sazzari ghara*, and *sanam*) were introduced in India by Amir Khusrau, whose name is associated with the emergence of *khayal*, *tarana*, and *tappa*. Sultan Zainul Abidin's close contacts simultaneously with the Gwalior School, and the centres of art in medieval Transoxiana further facilitated a fusion of two different systems of musical notation. Even the revelries of Muizuddin Kaiqubad contributed immensely to this sphere. The Sur rulers (particularly Ibrahim Sur, Adil Khan Sur, and Sikandar Sur) were themselves good musicians and patrons of the art. Ali Quli Qutab Shah introduced *Nauroz* and Akbar is said to have composed over 200 of the Khwarazmian tunes (such as *Jalashahi*, *Kurat*, and *Mahamir*), absorbing Iranian and Turanian rhythms into the Indian systems. Similarly, tunes like *Ilahiya* (sung in the later part of the evening), *Husaini Shabana* (sung in the later part of the evening), *Husaini Karna*, and *Todi*, Jampuri, *ahang*, *bazgoi*, Ramdasi, *Malhar Bazkhani*, and *Bahadur Todi* are said to have their origins in Central Asia. The airs, namely, *Shubai Mukhalif*, *Dar-i Israr*, *Maghlub*, *Nihawand*, *Ashiran*, *Nawa*, *Rihawi*, *Biyat*, *Gushai Ajam*, *Iraj*, *Qandahari*, *Fraq*, *Nauroz*, and *Chahargarh* had evolved their equivalents in *Ramkali*, *Purbi* and *Malwa Vibhas*, *Sughrai*, *Jaitsri*, *Jaijaiwanti*, *Dhamosri*, *Kanra Darbari*, *Suddhi Todi*, *Bhairwan*, *Malkaus* and *Purba*, *Lalit Pancham*, and *Gujri* respectively. The new tals like *Sawari*, *Pahlwan*, *Jat*, *Poshtu*, *Ara Chautali*, *Qawwali*, *Jald*, *Sul*, *Sul Fakhta Ferodast*, *Jald Titala*, and *Jhumra* were the homogeneous forms of the blending of the Perso-Arab, Central Asian, and Indian musical notes. Apart from a number of well-known mixed *ragas* (such as *Eman*, *Junylah* and *Hijj*, a corruption of the Perso-Arab airs of *Zangulah* and *Hijaz*), various other products of indigenous, Central Asian, and Perso-Arab scales are mentioned in the sources, with detailed descriptions of the intricacies of each of these specialized versions. Incidentally, similarities are noticed in the tenor, content, and form of Abhinav Gupta's *Natya Shastra* and the treatises of Abdurrahman Jami and Kaukabi. In the *khiyal*, Indian mythological themes sung in the Islamic style, brought a completely new grace and embellishment to this old art. Although Kashmiri music is composed of diverse elements, its chief components came from Persia and Turkestan. Even the main schools of music in the valley were initiated by Irani and Turani musicians during the time of Zainul Abidin. The seventeenth-century musician Darvesh Ali is acknowledged to have extensively benefitted from Amir Khusrau's musical contributions while compiling his *Risala-i Mausiqi*.[1]

A number of stringed and other instruments such as the *kanun* (dulcimer), *qabus*, *tambur*, *dutar*, *sitar*, *nafir*, *surnai*, *kurnai*, *rubab*, *chang* (harp), *ghichak*, *shahrud*, *ud*, *nai*, *naqqara*, *aobuz*, are found both in India and Central Asia. Their antecedents, genesis, and functions need further study. Surprisingly, the Kirghiz folk tale '*Manas*' refers not only to the *duff* but also to the *dhol*. The Siddi dance of Andhra Pradesh seems to have elements of Turkish dance movements whereas the Kashmiri dances (such as the *Rouf*, *Hafiza*, *Bachcha*, and others) reveal the influence of Central Asia. In this synthetic blending and commingling of Indian and Central Asian schools, the original identity of many of the specialized arts in music and dance were entirely or partially lost, coalescing to assume altogether different and new forms. This fact is amply borne out by a number of works, including *Mauji Mausiqi* and the works of Safiuddin, Ladiki, and others. Valuable information can be gleaned even from paintings and travelogues and through certain valuable works (like *Mamak*, *Lahjat-i Sikandar-Shahi*, *Nishat Ara*, *Mirat-i Aftab Numa*) compiled in medieval India. An extensive study of Indo-Persian and Central Asian works remains to be undertaken. If the relevant portions in each work are efficiently translated they can help a great deal in furthering our knowledge about such arts.

Central Asian industries exercised as great an influence on Indian handicrafts as Indian industries had influenced Central Asian fine arts. The origin and growth of the carpet, shawl, and paper industries is attributed to Central Asian lands. There is a striking resemblance in the production techniques of chintz printing, jewellery, ceramics, metalware, and inlay work of the two lands. The lustrous glazed patterns which characterize the ceramics found in the excavations in Afrasiyab had a striking similarity to the artifacts found in the Purana Qila (New Delhi) and Andhra Pradesh excavations. Firearms, the preparation of ink, and other forms of technological expertise were borrowed by the Indians from Central Asia.[2]

Indian medical sciences and products were highly valued and widely appreciated in Central Asia. Avicenna greatly admired the excellence of Indian medical practitioners and medicines. The shopping lists of travellers like Samarqandi almost always included medicines.[3] In literature also, the Indian style known as *Sabak-i Hindi* was occasionally adopted in Central Asia.[4] Astronomy, mathematics, and philosophy were other fields in which Indo-Central Asian cultural and ideological exchange is clearly seen.

Mughal paintings have been examined by many scholars and valuable studies on this subject have been produced. There still remains much scope for a deeper study of the relationship between Indian and Central Asian paintings not only on an individual basis but also in the context of cultural interactions. Most scholars of Mughal paintings have ignored the Persian and Uzbek (and Turkish) sources and have instead relied secondary sources. Consequently, even these studies remain incomplete.

Some of the travelogues pertaining to the two regions are of immense value. The accounts of Abdurrazaq Samarqandi (1411) and Jamali are available though the word paintings of 'wandering souls' like Tahir Ghani Kashmiri (d. 1666 or 1668), Sirajuddin Bukhari, and Haider Lahori (*Ganj-i-Tarikh* compiled in 1885) are not easily available in India. Both Abdurrazaq Samarqandi and Jamali stress the fact that in India the rulers of Vijayanagar and certain other places were keen to know about Samarqand and its environs. Similarly, Mutribi confirms that Jahangir was inquisitive about the unseen ancestral lands of Central Asia. The examples can be multiplied.

In medieval Central Asia, the love of the fine arts was not confined to the elite or to the ruling class. Even ordinary people such as artisans, workers, and labourers appreciated them. After a hard day's work they assembled at night to 'earn their night's sport'. Whether on the crossroads of the city, under the street lamps, or on the planks of the shops, poets and literary figures recited their new poems, discussed new trends, and tried to keep active contacts with men of letters in distant lands. Even traders who went on trade missions to various parts of the world often managed to kill two birds with one stone.[5] Thus, Tarzi Samarqandi, a merchant, when in India enjoyed the company of learned men and had his 'cup of knowledge filled to the brim by the waters of their wisdom'.[6] Those involved in literary pursuits struggled hard to achieve excellence and perfection and each such attempt was proudly proclaimed as a breakthrough. For example, Khwaja Husain Mervi[7] composed a long *qasida* of a hundred couplets in which cardinal numbers were used appropriately. Its first line gave the same number as the year of Akbar's accession and the second line yielded the date of Prince Salim's birth. He called this poetical performance *Asar-i Karnam* and sent it to Bukhara, obviously as a challenge to the Bukhara poets. Not only did Khwaja Hasan Nisari Bukhari compose in return an imitative poem of the same length and rhyme but this experiment of metres also found favour with other Akbari poets of foreign origin like the poet Nuruddin Tarkhan.[8]

In India, talented men from Central Asia were always valued. Not only the kings but also the nobles had their own galaxy of accomplished men. Both Sahmi Bukhari and Fahmi Tehrani were attached to the court of Khan-i Azam Aziz Kuka and lived mostly in Delhi. Sarwi Samarqandi was associated with the court of the Mirzas of Qandahar for whom he wrote a *Fath Nama* to commemorate their victory in Bharooch. Manzari Samarqandi was in the service of Bairam Khan. During his three visits, Haider Tabrizi enjoyed the patronage of no less than three lovers of the fine arts.[9]

The two highest recipients of Akbar's generosity emerged from the Central Asian literary firmament. The first, Maulana Qasim Kahi, a student of Maulana Jami, was an extremely talented person. He was a man of many parts, who excelled as a poet, mystic, musician, philologist, athlete, and wit. In Badakhshan, Prince Askari was said to have showered his treasures on Kahi. When Kahi reached Akbar's court, he was also much appreciated. Akbar gave him an award of 10,000 *tankas* for one of his poems, the second highest award ever given to a poet; the highest award of 20,000 *tankas* had been bagged by Khwaja Hasan of Merv. Kahi's lyrics were sung in the assemblies of kings. These lyrics composed and set to music by Kahi himself were 'famous throughout the world'. Kahi was a 'protege' of Khan-i Zaman, while 'retaining his affiliations with the court of Akbar'. Kahi was popular among his contemporaries and there existed mutually cordial relations and exchanges of friendly correspondence between Ghazali Mashhadi and Kahi. Nevertheless, Abul Fazl does not seem to be very highly impressed by Kahi's talents, and asserts that 'he knew something of the ordinary sciences', and well-meaning people upbraided him because they did not know the circumstances; he developed 'spiritual attractions' and was a 'member of Akbar's Divine Faith and a panegyrist of the Prophet'.

Other important areas in which fruitful exchanges took place included astronomy, medical sciences, and arithmetic. The father of Ibn-i Sina (980-1038) instructed him to learn Indian arithmetic in particular. The system of Aryabhatta as presented in the *Ardha Ratrika* was also studied and followed by scholars like Alkhwarazmi and Abu Mashar Balkhi.

Not only were Indian mathematicians, scholars, and physicians honoured by extending invitations to them but their works were also translated into Central Asian languages. The *Charak Samhita, Bhel Samhita* and the works of Nagarjun and other Indian specialists were very popular.[10]

During the reign of Caliph al Mansur (AD 755-75), Indian mathematical and astronomical works were translated. Presumably, at this juncture Hindu numerals were also introduced among the Arabs. Alkhwarazmi (AD 800-50) wrote a book on Indian numerals. Although its original Arabic manuscript is not extant, its Latin version is available. Ibn-i Sina writes that discussions were held on philosophy, geometry, and Indian arithmetic among his circle of scholars. The Indian method of computation was equally appreciated and used. After a careful survey of nineteen important Arabic texts, and particularly through the comments of al-Uqlidisi (AD 952), Saidan is said to have concluded that words like *takht* (computing board), *ghubar* (numerals), *turab* (numerals), and *al-Hind* (Indian or Indian way) were widely used by Arab scholars who got their ideas from the Indian practice when the knowledge of the Hindi arithmetic found its way to Arabia. The Arab appreciation for the Rule of Three (*Trairasika*) is borne out by Al Biruni's remarks. Al Biruni had himself independently compiled a treatise entitled '*Fi rasikat al Hind*' (The Rasika of the Hindus) and even used an example of *Vyasta Trairasika* in his *Kitab-ul Hind*.[11]

In the field of astronomy in particular a fruitful exchange of ideas is noticed. Some Uighur texts discovered in Turfan and dealing with the lunar mansions were utilized in Indian astronomy. Abu Mashaar Al-Balkhi studied astronomy from Indian, Persian, and other sources, and was highly influenced by Aryabhatta's system of *Ardha Ratrika*.[12] Al Biruni, who possessed knowledge of Sanskrit, studied astronomical works during his thirteen-year sojourn in India, and in turn he blessed Indians with the advanced knowledge acquired by the Greeks, Romans, Muslims, and Sufis. Tusi (1259) and Ulugh Beg (1420) built their observatories at Maragha and Samarqand respectively. The work done by Uzbek Khan Kuchikunji Abdul Latif and others in Samarqand in the field of astronomy was also of much significance, though this has remained largely unappreciated.[13]

In the field of the medical sciences also a regular exchange of ideas took place. Much has already been written on this subject. Sanskrit is said to have 'played the same role in Khotanese medicine as did Latin in Europe'. Buddhist monks carried with them Indian drugs (like *navantika*) to their destination and brought back important drugs from Central Asia. Abdurrazaq Samarqandi expressed his appreciation of Indian drugs and brought some of these for use to Central Asia.[14]

Abu Mansur Muwafaq, a famous physician from Herat, adopted the Indian way of learning as he found the Indians to be 'more sharp-sighted in the medical sciences than any other people and [who] were accurate in medicinal researches'.[15] Bernier refers to 'the Mogal and Mahometan physicians who follow the rules of Avicenna and

Averroes'.[16] If Wasifi is to be believed, an Indian, Hamara Pal, served Avicenna and wished to be taught *ilm-i tibb*. Although Avicenna later manumitted him, he never included the Indian among his forty slaves who were inducted for medical training. The dejected Hamara Pal returned to India and learnt *ilm-i tibb* from Indian physicians, and returned to Transoxiana as a *tabib-hakim* and *jarrah*; at the request of Avicenna he cured one of his slaves of an eye ailment through Indian medicine and later on also treated the ruler.[17]

Indian handicrafts found their way into Central Asia through various routes. As revealed by his own records and in accordance with his usual practice, Timur 'spared all artisans and clever mechanics, who were masters of their respective crafts, including all builders and stone masons' and ordered that 'these should be set apart for my own special purpose to await my commands . . . and no craftsman of whatever craft he be, shall be found any more in this.' Thus, like Babylon, Delhi was left desolate. The captives of war were often carried away. Babur, however, appreciated the many Indian workmen and artisans of every kind but complained that in Indian handicraft work 'there is no form or symmetry, method or quality'. He referred to wick lamps and lamented the lack of 'candles, torches or candlesticks'.[18]

Babur wished to remedy the 'lack of running waters' and to ensure that 'water should be made to flow by means of wheels erected' where ever he settled down. He looked for garden lands (even if ugly and displeasing). The land was converted into a *chaharbagh* with tanks, *talar* (audience hall), garden, hot baths, and private houses. Thus, the plots of gardens were laid out in an orderly and symmetrical way with suitable borders and partings in every corner, with perfect arrangement of rose and narcissus. Although gardens had earlier been built by Firuz Shah Tughlaq (1351-88), the Mughals were the first to introduce 'formal watered oasis gardens'. The extension of irrigation and the custom of building tombs within a garden was also their contribution. Abul Fazl echoes the complaints of Babur regarding the lack of iced or cooled water, the excessive heat, the scarcity of grapes, melons, carpets, and camels, and proudly proclaims that Akbar had 'remedied these deficiencies'. Not only had saltpetre become popular due to its cooling properties, but also under Akbar's supervision, trellised chambers of the slender fragrant root called *khus* (*odoriferens grass*, *andropogon muricatum*) were constructed (presumably in line with the traditions of the *yurt*). 'If water be sprinkled, another winter arises amid the summer heats.'[19]

Abul Fazl notes that 'the horticulturists of Iran and Turan have settled here (in India) and the cultivation of trees is in a flourishing state'. Under Akbar's patronage, 'skilled hands from Turkestan and Persia sowed melon and planted vines'. Traders 'introduced in security the fruits of those countries, each in its season, which occasioned an abundance here when they were not procurable in their own.' The technique of grafting had its origin in Central Asia. The concept of animal zoos or bird sanctuaries is said to be of Central Asian origin. Foods of many kinds were also introduced. Abul Fazl's *Ain* includes the recipes of Central Asian food seasoned with Indian spices. Even today 'Mughlai' food attracts gourmands. Tea is said to have been introduced in Kashmir by traders who came into the valley from across the Pamirs. Mirza Haidar Dughlat is credited with having introduced the drink into Kashmir, though its use was limited till 1878.[20]

The evolution of Mughal miniature painting owes a great deal to the art of the Central Asian masters. Here the mutual exchange of ideas is clearly visible. Delhi was enriched by the arrival of Muhammad Murad Samarqandi, the famous miniature painter of his times, whose 115 illustrations of Firdausi's *Shah Nama*, preserved in the Tashkent Library, bear witness to his skill. After he came to India, he produced such masterpieces as 'Portrait of a Young Man Studying a Book' and 'A Princess' in the style of the Indian school. His miniatures, though of a 'provincial trend', possessed 'democratic tendencies representing the peoples' struggles'.

In sixteenth-century Central Asia, a desire for classical literature and increasing religious fanaticism demanded an 'official ceremonial style' which Muhammad Murad reluctantly adopted. The Indian style of miniature painting, especially those of the Delhi masters, was followed in Central Asia by some Central Asian miniaturists in the seventeenth century. In Hatifi's *Timur Nama*, copied in 1560, Indian life is rendered with great skill and realism in the Samarqand illustrations of the *Zafar Nama* copy of 1628. Similarly, in the illustrations made by Avaz Muhammad and Mulla Bihzad for the *Hamza* (1668-71), the volume modelling of figures, the arrangement of the landscape scenes, and the many minor details all bear the mark of Indian art, although in essence the miniatures preserve Central Asian traditions.

Muhammad Nadir remained in India from 1590 up to the mid-seventeenth century. He not only introduced a volume of plastic face portraits done in Indian ink but also excelled in genre compositions: his 'Merchant Pulling Yusuf Out of the Well' is said to be a blend of Central Asian and Indian styles.

Another renowned 'master of the Herat groups' was Mahmud Muzzahib who is said to have enriched the well-known classical devices of the Timurid trend by introducing new ones. He was the first of the Bukhara school to introduce a light chiaroscure model to depict his figures in profile, a tendency almost entirely alien to the conventions of Central Asian miniature painting. The new features introduced in the painting 'Mystery Treasury' possibly 'anticipated the style typical of the Mughul miniatures in India'.

Some miniature painters of the seventeenth century are said to have followed the Indian style of painting, particularly that of the Delhi masters. In this context, Hatifi's *Timur Nama* (British Museum, Add. 22703), copied in 1560 and illustrated at the turn of the sixteenth century, was a unique example of the Indo-Turani style. While Indian life is treated with, a great depth of feeling precision, and knowledge, there was also an unmistakable style reminiscent of the Samarqand illustrations of the *Zafar Nama* (copied in 1628). The historical episodes illustrated in Indian manuscripts depict Indian architecture, flora and fauna, and ornamentation. These elements are also found in Central Asian paintings, which suggests Indian influence on Central Asian painting. Such paintings are seen in the *Zafarnama* illustrations of Timur's campaign in India. The Herat manuscript *Mantiqul Tayir* (1456) includes miniatures which are simple and balanced in composition, with a 'primitive concept of space and puppet-like figures', indicating that 'they have been illustrated in India as they had certain affinities with Sultanate paintings'.[21]

Towards the end of the sixteenth century, Uzbek painting is said to have lost its 'wholeness' and acquired certain features from the Iranian and Indian styles of painting. In this context, the portraits of the personages depicted on the margins of Jami's *Salman and Absal* (1581), with all their ethnic characteristics, and distinctive costumes, appear to be an 'eloquent reflection of the fusion and blending of Indian, Iranian and Turanian (of Transoxiana) styles'.

Farrukh Beg, a Qalmaq of Central Asia, joined Akbar's service in 1585 and brought with him 'a style of painting which was not only reminiscent of Mongolia and China but which also showed a marked individuality'. Farrukh the Qalmaq is included by Abul Fazl among the list of painters who had 'attained fame'. Although his influence on the school of Akbar would be felt only in the later period, his work made a distinct impression on the art of painting as a whole. During Jahangir's reign, Farrukh Beg became the leader of the school of painting and in Jahangir's own words he was 'unrivalled in the age'. Farrukh Beg was not the only Central Asian painter. Muhammad Nadir and Muhammad Murad were also two excellent portrait painters from Central Asia. Muhammad Nadir Samarqandi worked in Delhi from 1590 to the mid-seventeenth century and was renowned particularly for his portrait painting, both of single and group portraits. Muhammad Nadir is thought to be the founder of 'a special graphic manner' (*siyahi-i qalam*, plastic face portrait) done in Indian ink. He is also said to be a master of genre compositions. His miniature 'Merchants Pulling Yusuf Out of the Well' is a blend of Central Asian and Indian styles; it was prepared in Kashmir in 1616 where he had accompanied Jahangir. It can safely be surmised that the style of Bukhara art was very well known to the Mughal miniature painters and many of these had been used by them in the preparation of their paintings. Ashok Das says that even the 'Herati idiom, so often encountered in Mughal works, was in many cases imitated from the Bukhara versions'. The architectural style of the Hindu temple at Somnath with all its details as painted by an Indian seems to correspond with a similar form of architecture depicted by Mirak in a miniature of the *Khamsa-i Nizami* (1523-4), though the latter had no chance to look at it. In Ali Sher Navoi's *Lisanal Tair*, prepared at Bukhara in 1553, and in the *Baharistan* of Jami, prepared for Abdul Aziz in 1547, 'a miniature with an exactly similar composition' is noticed.[22]

Indian scholars are often puzzled by the similarities noticed in these paintings. Ashok Das says that six out of the thirteen miniatures of the *Gulistan* of Saadi, prepared at Bukhara in 1567 by the famous calligrapher Mir Ali Husain al Husaini, are painted in the contemporary style of Bukhara. Strangely enough, two of these bear the name and titles of Akbar while four of them bear signatures of Shamim Muzzahib and 'show familiarity with Indian costumes, especially the typical Akbari painted Jama'. Das adds that the *Bustan-i Saadi*, prepared at Bukhara for the library of Uzbek Sultan Abdul Aziz of Bukhara (1540-50), was acquired by Jahangir. Out of the three miniatures which were added to it at the orders of Jahangir, two are said to be 'very close to the Bukhara School'—a definite sign that 'contact between Bukhara and Mughal India was very close indeed'.[23]

Although the closeness of Indo-Uzbek contacts cannot be denied, it should also be remembered that many of the manuscripts from Bukhara were somehow smuggled into India soon after these were transcribed or illustrated. Either the international traders in manuscripts or the artists seeking patronage or employment in India could have done the trick. The *Bustan-i Saadi* was copied in Bukhara in 1531-2, with its 'three miniatures retouched by artists working for Jahangir in the early years of the seventeenth century'. Jami's *Tuhfat-ul Ahrar* was another manuscript copied in Bukhara in the 1540s, also with three miniatures. In this connection, two facts should be borne in mind. Sometimes, the illustrations in the Central Asian manuscripts were retouched or one or more scenes were added. Second, more illustrations were also added to the manuscripts.[24]

Daulat Muhammad records that he added the golden hills in a mid-sixteenth-century Bukhara copy of a fifteenth-century hunting scene attributed by Mehdi Bahrami to Mahmud Muzzahib. Two of Mahmud Muzzahib's works were repainted by Jahangiri artists. The illustrations of *Gulistan* (British Library, no. 59) contain thirteen miniatures out of which six were painted in the Bukhara style in 1567-8 (as the colophon suggests), while the remaining seven were added to it by Mughal artists during the first decade of the seventeenth century. The artist Shaham Muzahib (the illuminator) who is less known in India painted these 'in a manner that clearly belies the artist's Bukharan origins'. In the opinion of Brand and Lowry, 'This Mughal intrusion, along with the fact that all the paintings are larger than the text panels, allows one to conclude that the seven Bukhara miniatures were actually added after the manuscript arrived in India.' Shaham's paintings are also detected in the *Anwar-i Suhaili*. The *Anwar-i Suhaili* comprises twenty-seven illustrations out of which two are in 'almost unadulterated Bukharan style although the rest are in the most advanced, imperial Mughal style of the time'. Braud and Lowry, however, conclude that since Shaham did not receive patronage later on, the Bukhara paintings 'had virtually no effect on the development of Mughal art'. A reversal in this trend is noticed in the nineteenth century when Indian influence on Central Asian painting is clearly visible.[25]

Sometimes Indian themes were dealt with much proficiency as in the case of the 'Governor of Kashmir and his sister Mihro Naz'. Commenting on, the Indo-Turanian art of painting, Sulaimanov says that a comparison of the Khokand miniatures of Navoi's '*Hamzah*' with designed manuscripts of the nineteenth century (USSR Collection of Manuscripts) leads one to an amazing conclusion, that Indian elements appear in the Central Asian miniatures of the nineteenth century. As is generally known, cultural ties between India and Central Asia became stronger in the seventeenth and eighteenth centuries. There was an exchange of artists and calligraphers. The result of this development was to foster a closer resemblance between the miniatures produced in the eighteenth and nineteenth centuries in India (Kashmir in particular) and those of Bukhara. This is seen in the great likeness between the miniatures of Jami's *Yusuf and Zuleikha* painted in Kashmir in 1228/1813 (Institute of Oriental Studies, Uzbek Academy of Sciences, no. 791), and Ashik's *A Divan*, copied in Bukhara in 1221/1806-7 (Institute of Oriental Studies, Uzbek Academy of Sciences, no. 1454).[26]

There is a great deal of similarity in the composition and colouring in the portrayal of human images, garments, episodes illustrating Prophet Solomon's flight while sitting on the throne, and the 'Ascension' of Muhammad. These miniatures embraced the subjects of Jami's *Yusuf and Zuleikha*, which was copied in India in the eighteenth century, Hafiz Shirazi's *A Divan*, produced in India in 1194/1780 (Institute of Oriental Studies, Uzbek Academy of Sciences, no. 10042), and '*Hamzah*' (Inventory no. 23). The last two episodes are the most typical in both miniatures, Solomon's throne has brown *devas* who are followed by two *parees* fanning the Prophet. In the 'Ascension' (as depicted in the miniatures of both the manuscripts), there is no image of Prophet Muhammad on the legendary Burak; the composition depicts angels with a flame in their hands, on page 30b of the poem. The likeness of these manuscripts is so great that it suggests that they were painted by one and the same artist. There are grounds for assuming that the miniatures of 'The Language of Birds' from the '*Hamzah*' (which are in the possession of the Institute of Manuscripts) were pasted into the manuscript at a later period.[27]

One cannot help agreeing with Beach that the 'roughmanship' of certain miniatures in India was due to the fact that the sources from which artists in Iran had obtained their pigments and papers—zinc white came from Kashghar, for example, and many of the finest papers from Samarqand—were simply not available initially to the Mughals in India, and this obviously affected the way they could paint.[28]

Calligraphy and the art of bookmaking further facilitated mutual interaction as the regular and constant transcription of works continued. Thus, the *Masnavi* of Jalaluddin Rumi was prepared by Khwaja Abdur Rauf, the calligraphist, in 1690 in Ahmedabad. It was later transcribed in 1813 by Rasul Baba Katib Kashmiri. Similarly, the work of Abul Husain al Ansari, *Ikhtiyarat-i-Badi*, was copied under Ahmad Shah (1748-75). The *kitas* of calligraphists like Murad Kashmiri, Mir Saiḍ Ali Khan Jawahar Raqam, Hidayatullah Mir Muhammad Mumin Ali Arshi, Bala Pandit, Muhammad Musa Husaini, Muhammad Baqar, and others are preserved in the various libraries of Turan. The famous work *Tazkirat Khattatan-i Bukhara* includes the work of many such calligraphists who had worked in both the places and thereby exchanged artistic skills. Calligraphists and painters continued to come to India. Haji Sabir, the well-known calligraphist of his period, came to India on his way back from Mecca where he had accompanied Imam Quli Khan. In the Mughal chancellery, he worked as a scribe for twenty years and returned to Balkh only in his later years. Another calligraphist, Saida, renowned for his skill throughout India, Iran and, Transoxiana, arrived at the Mughal court at the beginning of Shahjahan's reign. Here, he initially copied the books of the chancellery and later on engaged himself in *tillanavisi*.[29]

Exchange of books was a common practice. Almost all the Mughal works like the *Ain-i Akbari*, *Akbar Nama*, Jahangir's autobiography, the three *Badshah Namas*, and the like were available in Central Asia. Similarly, Central Asian works were available in India. Even the illustrated manuscripts were found in different libraries of India.

Some Central Asian sports also found favour with the Indian Mughals. In his *Ain* 29, Abul Fazl gives details of the games played by Akbar. The game of *chaugan* is mentioned by all the Muslim historians. Akbar took much interest in the game not simply 'as a mere amusement' or 'play' but for higher purposes.[30] In the early Middle Ages, it was a favourite game of the elite. Qutubuddin Aibek died in 1210 while he was playing *chaugan*. Sultan Husain Baiqra is also said to have been extremely enchanted with the game of pigeons. When Abdullah Khan Uzbek sent Akbar a gift of excellent pigeons,

Akbar recorded his appreciation for these Farghanian fairy flying pigeons sent with the able pigeon flier Habib, whose despatch was a token of their friendship. Some people may take these small birds as a handful of feathers or as a mere play or sport. But to someone with a deeper insight, flying them, sweeping them, and playing with them resembles the ecstasy of the dervishes which reminds one of the source (i.e. the Creator). That is why Akbar takes an interest in this activity. He is assured that God the omniscient knows that his casual occupation with such pleasures is simply a veil over his devotion to the Almighty and his soul is not satisfied only with apparent and outward things (i.e. wings and feathers). In the *Ain*, Abul Fazl also expresses the same view and adds that Akbar had even used the activity of pigeon flying 'as a way of reducing unsettled, worldly-minded men to obedience and avails himself of it as a means productive of harmony and friendship'. In Abul Fazl's *Ain* there are two separate notes on *ishqbazi* (pigeon flying) and the colours of *khasa* pigeon, both of which throw light on Akbar's deep interest in pigeon flying. Abul Fazl maintains that although in his youth Akbar had been fond of this amusement, he discontinued the hobby when he grew older. Afterwards, on 'mature consideration' he again adopted 'obviously from higher motives'. Apart from these activities, animal fighting and wrestling were equally popular in both the regions.[31]

The arts of paper-making and book-binding are also said to have been borrowed from Central Asia, where, after the Battle of Talas the Chinese prisoners of war, in AD 751, introduced the art of manufacturing rag paper; this technique was improved particularly due to the invention of the transfer mould. Some say that Sultan Zain-ul Abidin (1420-70) sent two persons to Samarqand for training at state expense, who on their return taught this art to others. It is also opined that Sultan Zain-ul Abidin brought paper makers to establish the industry near Ganderbal where waterpower was developed to pulp the rags and at Naushehr to the north of Srinagar where vats were erected to turn the pulp into paper. Surprisingly, the industry remained here 'without any improvement or advance over Central Asian methods which have remained intact in their entirety'. During the reign of Zain-ul Abidin, a number of calligraphists came to the valley from Persia and Turkestan and were given *jagirs*. Maulana Mir Ali 'brought his art of calligraphy to perfection by initiating the writings of Sultan Ali Meshedi'.[32]

Al Biruni states that 'paper was first invented by the Chinese. The Chinese captives introduced it in Samarqand whence it diffused to other parts of the world.' On the other hand, Bag asserts that 'the paper mills at Khurasan also came up during this time' and that Khurasani paper was introduced in India by the Arabs in the early eighth century AD when they conquered Sind. The paper-making industry thereafter spread to Kashmir, Sialkot, Zafarabad (Jaunpur, Oudh), Azimabad (Patna, Bihar), Arwal (Gaya, Bihar), Murshidabad Hoogly, and other places.[33]

Akbar's desire to acquaint his sons, principal nobles, and courtiers coming from Turkestan, Afghanistan, and Persia with the Indian way of life, culture, and literature is seen in his policy of recruiting scholars capable of translating the Hindu religious texts (such as the *Atharva Veda*, *Ramayana*, *Mahabharata*, *Harivamsa*, and *Yoga Vashishtha*) into the Persian language. Literary works like the *Singhasan Battisi*, *Katha Sarit Sagara*, *Nala Damyanti*, *Yoga*, and *Vedanta*, mathematical works like *Lilavati*, and historical works like *Rajtarangini* were also translated. In the same way, a large number of Central Asian and Persian works were produced in the atelier during this time. These included works like the *Zafar Nama*, *Tuti Nama*, *Nafhatul Uns*, and the *divans* of Jami, Anwari, and Shahi. Philologists were constantly engaged in translating Persian works into other languages. Thus, a part of the *Zichi Jadid-i Mirza* was translated under the guidance of Amir Fathulla Shirazi; the *Babur Nama* was translated from the Turkish into Persian; and chronicles like the *Chingiz Nama* and the *Zafar Nama* of Yezdi were also illustrated. Abul Fazl translated the *Kalilaah wa Dimnah* under the title *Iyar-i Danish* from of the Arabic into Persian. This was the well-known ancient '*Panch Tantra*'. The *Mahabharata* was rendered into Persian under the title *Razm Nama*. Badauni translated the *Ramayana* in 1591.

The exchange of technology between Central Asia and India is also traced back to ancient times. Needham says that four-wheeled vehicles, horizontal windmills, water-raising arrangements like the *nasba* of Iraq or the *mote* of India had their origin in Central Asia and Persia.

Although swords were sometimes 'damascened with gold and silver, the blades were almost always imported from outside the Islamic world such as from China, India and Malaysia'. The *teghaha-i-Hind* (Indian swords) were much 'esteemed in Central Asia for their high quality'. Fakhri Mudabbir says that these were the 'best and most lustrous' and considers the *Chachi* and *Khwarazmi* bows to be inferior to the *Lahori* and *Ghaznavi* bows. The superiority of Indian swords, bows and arrows is also supported by other sources.[34]

Many scholars believe that gunpowder technology was an 'important invention' of the Chinese, from whom the Mongols learnt it and transmitted it to Central Asia, from where it spread to India. On the other hand, the Europeans claim that it was their contribution. This controversy is discussed elsewhere. The fact, however, remains that this technology was known to both Timur and Babur. In his memoirs Babur describes his use of the Ottoman style of *Taburi Chengi* as the casting of artillery by his Rumi expert while in India.[35]

It was only through Central Asian immigrants in the thirteenth century that the Indians learnt the use of lime mortar. Undoubtedly, 'this was by all standards a great feat of engineering' because this facilitated the construction of waterproof walls and floors for pavilions and mausoleums within lakes.

The transmission of the spinning wheel, 'which had become the poor women's companion in Central Asia and Iran as early as the twelfth century', must be reckoned as a crucial step in the development of India's textile technology, more so since India was the home of the cotton industry.

Irfan Habib has argued that the stirrup and the horseshoe were introduced by the Turkish invaders into India. However, Simon Digby contends that the toe stirrup and probably the full foot stirrup were in use in northern India centuries before the diffusion of the stirrup in Arabic lands and the Mediterranean world, although he concedes that both the devices (toe stirrup and full foot stirrup) were probably introduced by the north-western route.[36]

References to India and Indian people, Kashmiri shawls, and Indian towns like Lahore are found in Ali Sher Navoi's *divans*. Navoi and Jami often expressed feelings of affection and love for India in their letters. Sometimes versified letters were exchanged between Tajalli Hindi, Tash Khwaja Asiri, and Furqat. The revolutionary poets of later centuries further strengthened these ties. Tursun Zada's poem '*Mihman-i Maghribi*' (Guest from the West) shared the sorrow of the colonized Indian people, asking the *zarparast* folk (devotees of gold, the British) to 'leave a place where they had lived like strangers for full two hundred years'. On the occasion of the sixth anniversary of India's independence, a poem 'Great India' was written by the famous revolutionary Uzbek poet Ghafur Ghulam, who describes India as a 'land of ancient culture of thousand years'. This 'great land', says he, 'favourably compares with the ancient civilizations of Egypt, China and Mesopotamia where the treasures of knowledge of *maarifat* were discovered even earlier than the wisdom of Confucius and works like Taurit'. India is said to have 'a bright heart', and own a 'jewel like the *Mahabharata*'. 'Through its wealth and charm alone, it had attracted invaders.'[37]

Similar expressions and picturesque descriptions of the magic world of India are found in other works. The affinity and closeness of these two peoples is clearly reflected in parallel historical developments. One is surprised to find similar views among the poets of these two regions. Habib Yusufi Samarqandi's poems, particularly *Rahbari-i Janan*, reminds one of Faiz and Faiz's poems. Habib's poem *Husn-i Tu* is an echo of Majaz's address to women. Even in lyrics, the same expressions are noticed. Abdul Salam Dehati's poems share similar meanings to those of Arif Abbasi Baliyawi. Amin Zada Muhiuddin's poem, '*Arzu-i Man*', contains the same ideas as Iqbal's '*Ek Arzoo*' and Ghalib's *ghazals*. It will thus be seen that the friendly relations established between the two great ancient lands several centuries ago have continued with the same fervour to this day.

To give an example: the technique of batik printing had all along been extremely popular in India. In Khwarazm Khoqand and other places the same kind of printing is noticed on cloth. Similar designs are sometimes visible in the cloth covers used for book binding. Emil Esin writes: 'The Turkish tradition of the art of the book developed in Inner Asia as shown by its history and terminology.' Gabain concludes that the word '*bitiq*' designated a book or any written record, and was derived from the Chinese character *pi* which indicates the scribe's brush, which had possibly been initially used by the Turks when the runiform Kok-Turk characters were predominant, perhaps for the preliminary tracing of lapidary inscriptions.

Underground sepulchral vaults and cupolas round the central dome often remind one of the Central Asian excellence in art. Similarly, the Kashmiris were known to the outside world as *shastra silpina* or architects for their skill in this art. Glimpses of Kashmiri sculpture and art are also found in Central Asia.[38] Timur carried away with him all kinds of artisans. Both Ghiyasuddin Ali and Babur refer to the fact that in the walled city of Samarqand, near the iron gate, Timur had built a Friday mosque of stone which was constructed by some excellent stone cutters brought from Hindustan. Not only were Indian craftsmen in demand but 'in order that there should be no deficiency', the spoils of war also included the consignments of stone. According to an eye witness account, 90 captured elephants had carried the stone. In the sixteenth century, there were 200 Indian slaves working in the Kahriz built by Miri Arab.[39]

The architectural features of Central Asia are seen at several places in India. The exotic academy complex (including a mosque, lecture halls, and a library), constructed in 1472 by Mahmud Gawan, is said to 'have been moved . . . from the Registan at Samarqand'. Similarly, the *manara* of Mir Masum at Sukkur (Pakistan), which was erected in 1594, resembles several towers in Turkestan, such as the Kalyan *manara* of Bukhara built in 1127 and the *manara* of Vabkent built in 1196-7, in their tapering outline and decorative work and also in the disproportionately small pavilion on the top, though the complicated stalactite gallery so common in Turkestani towers is missing here. According to Husain, the origins of the flutings of the Qutab *manara* as well as the Mughal corner turrets, whether octagonal or round in design, lofty and extremely decorative, all of them appear to have been derived from the *manaras* of Herat and Samarqand.

Nevertheless, the introduction of new arts and crafts and the renewal of old ones in Kashmir are attributed to Timur. When Sikandar Butshikan sent his son Shahi Khan (Zainul Abidin) to his liege lord Timur, in Samarqand, the latter did not allow him to return to Kashmir. Shahi Khan remained in Samarqand for seven years and observed the various arts and crafts there. When Timur died in 1405, Shahi Khan returned to Kashmir with his experiences and tried to introduce similar handicrafts and arts in Kashmir. Haidar Dughlat refers to all these arts and crafts (of Kashmir) which are in most cities uncommon, such as stone polishing, stone cutting, bottle making, window cutting, gold beating, etc. In the whole of Mawaraunhar, except in Samarqand and Bukhara, these are nowhere to be met with, while in Kashmir they are even abundant. The parcel gilt silver work of Kashmir 'is an art imported by the Mongols but influenced by the natural superiority of the Kashmiri people. The silver gilt and jewelled coffee pot is said to have been 'evidently derived from a Mongol (Turkoman) original'. The art of enamel practised every where in India is 'probably a Turanian art'. Similarly, the enamelled pottery so popular 'in all imperial Mughal cities of India was introduced from China through Persia by the Afghan Mongols through the influence of Timur's Chinese wife'.

Any artist or specialist from Khurasan, Iraq, or Turkestan was not allowed to leave the borders of Kashmir unless he taught the Kashmiris whatever he knew. Presumably, in this way the *sultan* introduced the use of the weaver's brush and the loom, as well as the wearing of silken cloth with such patterns as had made the stuff unique; and from the famous valley in India, the silkworm was carried northwards and spread in Khotan, Persia, and other states of Central Asia. Kashmiri silk was popular in Damascus, Bukhara, and Issidons. The Khotan natives were the main agents in the silk trade, carried on through Western Asia and Europe by the Oxus river over the Caspian Sea and the Black Sea.[40] Haidar Dughlat says that among the wonders of Kashmir were the mulberry trees, 'cultivated for their leaves for the production of silk'. The Tibet *baqqals* bought shawls, *namdas*, and other goods in exchange for raw wool and sold them at higher prices in the various markets of Central Asia.[41] Abul Fazl says that through Akbar's 'favour all products of art and manufacture of woollen and silken carpets and of brocades' were extensively 'encouraged' since velvet tufts of wool on the strings of the warp of the carpets and the manufacture of pile carpets' too is supposed to be a Turkestani gift. In his *Ain* 32 on shawls, stuffs, etc., Abul Fazl does not refer to the origin of this industry though in *Ain* 21 on the *Farrashkhana* under the subheading of carpets, he does refer to the fact that the *gilins* of Iran and Turan are no longer thought of as all kinds[42] of carpet weavers have settled here and have a flourishing trade. They are found in every town, especially in Agra, Fatehpur Sikri, and Lahore. Nevertheless, the local traditions of Kashmir in the nineteenth century confirm that the first Kashmir shawls were produced by Turkestani weavers who were invited by Sultan Zain-ul Abidin to settle in the valley. Another supposed founder of the shawl industry is said to be Saiyid Ali Hamdani. Since the *Rajtarangini* does not refer to any such industry, it is deemed that the Turkestani and Persian weavers introduced new patterns and new techniques like the twill tapestry technique which is said to have a parallel in Persia and Central Asia and not in India or Pakistan. In Kashmir particularly the dress of the upper classes was the same as that of the rich people in Turkestan, Persia, and Arabia; it is said to have been introduced by Saiyid Ali Hamdani during the reign of Sultan Qutubuddin and by the time of Sultan Sikandar even the Brahmins had started using it. The cloth *buckram* is said to be derived from Bukhara. A coarse cloth *khada* (lit. woven) was in great demand in the markets of Kabul and Turkestan and in other towns between Bengal and Central Asia through which the Paracha merchants passed.

Multan was a great meeting centre of the Povinda merchants who traded in chintzes, printed fabrics, and in all the articles exported from India to Central Asia. Velvet and the famous Andjani silk called the *rumal Andjani* were also imported. At Peshawar, silk was largely made for sale in Kabul and Merv.[43]

In other spheres too the same impact is seen. Abul Fazl writes that 'Irani, European and Mongolian articles of wear were in abundance' in his times as 'skilful masters and workmen have settled in this country to teach people an improved system of manufacture'.

## NOTES

1. *Tarikh-i-Rashidi*, p. 434; Krishna Chaitanya, *A History of Indian Paintings: The Mural Tradition*, New Delhi, 1976, see Plates 33, 34, 36, 52, 53.
2. Birdwood, *The Industrial Art of India*, Delhi, 1974, pp. 149, 151, 167, 193, 206, 220, 320-1, 343.
3. Muhibbul Hasan, pp. 92-3; Bamzai, pp. 29-31.
4. For details see Kabir Ahmad Jaisi, *Jadid Tajiki Shaeri*, Aligarh, 1990, pp. 47-51, 95-112, 128-34, also see *Armughani Tashkent*, Selected Poems of Ghafur Ghulam, tr. Qamar Rais, Tashkent, 1968, pp. 61-3.
5. For such descriptions see Mansura Haidar, *Central Asia in the Sixteenth Century*, Delhi, 2002, chapter on 'Cultural Life in Shaibanid Times'.
6. Mutribi, *Tazkirat-ush-Shuara*, MS no. 2253, IOST 119a; also see, *Khatirat-i-Mutribi*, ed. Abdul Ghani Mirzaev, Karachi, 1977, pp. 3-8.
7. Hasan Nisari, *Muzzakkira-i Ahbab*, text, pp. 447-50; Eng. tr., pp. 58-60.
8. Ibid., *Mirat-ul Alam*, f. 376b for Ghazali Meshedi's imitative performance see *Muzzakkira*, Eng. tr., p. 64.
9. *Muzzakkira*, pp. 447-50.
10. See *Ain-i-Akbari*, vol. I, pp. 106-13; also see Mansura Haidar, 'The Exchange of Ideas in the Medieval Period', paper read at Indo-Soviet Conference, 23-6 May 1988, Moscow; *Muzzakkira*, pp. 447-50, Eng. tr., pp. 58-60.
11. Ibid.
12. A.K. Bag, 'Exchange of Ideas between India and Central Asia', paper read at Indo-Soviet Conference, Moscow, 1989.
13. *Muzzakkira*, p. 434.
14. Abdurrazaq Samarqandi, II, p. 80.

15. Bag, op. cit.; also see Mansura Haidar, 'Exchange of Ideas'; and Introduction supra.
16. Bernier, *Travels in the Mughal Empire*, New Delhi, p. 338.
17. Wasifi, op. cit., vol. II, pp. 38-88.
18. Ghayasuddin Ali, *Dnevnik Pokhoda Timura Va Injii*, pp. 189-91; *Babur Nama*, text, pp. 456, 2291; Eng. tr., pp. 77, 531.
19. *Ain-i-Akbari*, III, pp. 10-11; also see *Babur Nama*, text, p. 299; Eng. tr., p. 531; *The Gardens of Mughal India*, London, 1972, pp. 35-56.
20. *Ain* 28; *Babur Nama*, Turkish text, p. 299, Eng. tr., p. 531; *Ain-i-Akbari*, III, pp. 10-11; *The Gardens of Mughal India*, pp. 35-47, 56; *Ain*, III, op. cit., pp. 10, 11, 14, 114; Percy Brown, *Indian Paintings under the Mughals*, pp. 26, 64, 65, 81; *Ain*, I, p. 28. see MS no. 1811, IOST, f. 105.
21. B.G. Dalinskaya, Khudoshjnik Miniaturist Muhammad Murad Samarkandi, Izvestia AN Uz SSR Tashkent, 1955, no. 9; also see Pugachenkova and O. Galerkina, *Miniature Sredni Azi*, Moscow, 1979, pp. 40-50; Percy Brown, *Indian Paintings . . .* , pp. 64-5, 81. Asok Kumar Das, *Mughal Paintings*, Calcutta, 1978, pp. 80-1, 126-7, 185; Milo Cleaveland Beach, *Mughal and Rajput Paintings*, p. 29; Braud and Lowry, op. cit., pp. 94-6; Sulaimanov Hamid, Alisher Navoi, *Asrarlariga Islangan Rasmlari*, Tashkent, 1982, pp. 31-6. *Ain*, I, Blochmann, p. 114, Percy Brown, *Indian Paintings under the Mughals*, New Delhi, 1981, pp. 64-5.
22. Pugachenkova, p. 45.
23. A.K. Das, op. cit., pp. 80-1, 126, 127, 185.
24. Pugachenkova, p. 60; Sulaimanov, pp. 31-6.
25. Braud and Lowry, op. cit., pp. 94-8.
26. Sulaimanov, pp. 31-7; Pugachenkova, p. 48.
27. Ibid.
28. Beach, p. 29.
29. *Muzzakkira*, p. 83.
30. For details on the subject see Mansura Haidar, *Insha-i-Abul Fazl,* Har Sih Daftar, New Delhi, 1998, letters of Akbar to Abdullah Khan Uzbeg and Khan-i Khanan.
31. Ibid., also see *Ain on Sports;* Wasifi, p. 129.
32. Mansura Haidar, 'Exchanges', op. cit., p. 17.
33. Bag, op. cit., p. 20.
34. Adab-ul Harb wa Shujjaat, p. 48.
35. For interesting details on the subject see *Babur Nama*.
36. Simon Digby, *War-Horse and Elephant in the Delhi Sultanate—A Study of Military Supplies*, Oxford, 1971, pp. 12-14; Irfan Habib, 'Technological Changes and Society: 13th-14th Centuries', Presidential Address, 31st Indian History Congress, Dec. 1969; Separatum, 1970.
37. Ghafoor Ghulam, p. 17.
38. A.A. Rizvi, *Wonder that was India*, p. 36; also see Muhibbul Hasan, p.108.
39. Wasifi, vol. II, p. 220.
40. Sheolkovi Puti (The Silk Road), op. cit., p. 25.
41. See *Tarikh-i Rashidi* for description of Tibet and Kashmir.
42. *Ain-i Akbari*, *Ain* 21 on *Farrashkhana*.
43. See Muqminova, op. cit., p. 34.

# Central Asian Contribution to Indian Culture

The study of history reveals many parallels in different regions of the world, particularly between which places are interlinked due to geographical proximity and a common cultural heritage. For example, similar trends in literary and artistic activities in India and Central Asia were reinforced through the exchange of ideas. Significant contributions have been made by Central Asian, Iranian, and India scholars, painters, and other artists to the enrichment of Asian culture and civilization. Active relations and the continuous exchange of ideas between the two regions led to the opening of many new avenues of cultural creativity in literature and art, often producing a blend of two or more styles or even leading to the emergence of a unique pattern. Timur brought with him a group of artisans, architects, and artists; from the tenth of the seventeenth centuries scholars continued to visit India at regular intervals and settled in the country or made a temporary sojourn there. India appeared to be a country of gold, riches, and strange wonders and secrets, a hospitable land offering protection to refugees, poets, artists, and even embracing foreign invaders. The country was renowned for its philosophy, religions (like Buddhism), medicines (which were in great demand), its strange customs (where the bride paid the dowry to the bridegroom), its beautiful arts and crafts, and its commonly available opportunities for work, employment and patronage. In addition, the route to Mecca through India was both safe and comfortable as compared to the passage through Iran, which was bedeviled by sectarian rivalries.

Mutribi, a seventeenth-century Central Asia poet, said that one must behave like a pawn in a game of chess, whose ascent is possible only through continuous travelling. Mutribi's assessment represents the typical views of a medieval man; he found travelling advantageous and fruitful and particularly essential for philosophers and scholars. The purpose of travelling is not to accumulate wealth and satiate one's animal desires but to acquire and spread knowledge.[1]

The emigration of artists of every kind was most frequent during the early decades of Akbar's reign. Under Abdullah Khan (1583-8), the situation became favourable for the development of the fine arts. Not only did Bukhara, the capital, emerge as a centre of cultural life but several other towns like Samarqand, Tirmiz, and Balkh also emerged as noteworthy centres offering patronage to facilitate the enrichment of culture and hence to discourage talented individuals from leaving their homeland. Even after Abdullah Khan, the favourable conditions continued for various reasons. With the appearance of Imam Quli Khan (1611-42) and Abdul Aziz Khan (1647-80) on the political scene, there was a lull before the storm. Quite in conformity with Ibr-i Khaldun's definition of the five stages in the evolution as well as the degeneration of an empire, the time of peace was conducive to the development of the fine arts.[2] During the period of Abdul Aziz, the number of court poets reached thirty, including poets such as Mulla Nakhil, Mulla Qatli, Yagana, Yakta, Hasan Beg Rafe, and Khwaja Sabir. The accession of Subhan Quli (1680-1702), however, resulted in the destruction of the tradition and put an end to court poetry (as is evident from the comments of Saida).[3] Once again, poets were forced to flee in different directions in search of patronage.

During the reigns of Jahangir (1605-27) and Shahjahan (1628-58), therefore, Central Asian poets and artists arriving in India were fewer in number as compared to the days of Akbar, though the successors of Akbar did extend all kinds of patronage to attract outside talents. Mutribi, the author of *Nuskhai Zebai Jahangiri*, writes about the excessive riches offered to him. Not only did Jahangir give him money, *khalats*, a horse, and a slave but almost everyday he received a thousand rupees (each of which was of the weight of one *misqal*), and also a sum of five hundred rupees from Nurjahan Begum. Mutribi had dreamed of paying a visit to India since 1612, though he was constantly prevented from achieving his goal due to financial reasons. He finally came in 1626. Jahangir was unwilling to allow him to leave for his motherland and when he pleaded that his relatives needed him, assurances of full maintenance and allowances for his relatives in India and Transoxiana were given. In view of Mutribi's anxieties, the emperor finally agreed to his departure on the condition that he would return after a year.[4] The poet, however, failed to keep his promise for reasons not known so far.

In the meantime, a number of Indians also started arriving in Central Asia Mirza Masum Razmi (popularly known as Mirza Aqbi Qushchi) was one such person; he was born in India and spent some time in Bukhara. Mutribi describes his poems as difficult but in the 'Indian style'. Par Badi was born in Kashmir but served Juibari Shaikh Hasan Khwaja in Bukhara. Par Badi was a good poet and scholar and finally returned to India. There were others also like Karimi and Zahir Kabuli. Since the subject deserves a separate discussion, only the Central Asian contribution to Indian art and culture will be our focus.

The exchange of ideas often took several forms. Manuscripts and other works were frequently exchanged. Mutribi refers to the exchange of letters between Faizi Faiyazi and the Shaikh of Juibar and the famous poet Khwaja Hasan Nisari of Bukhara over the style of Indian poetry and even about new *ghazals*.[5] Another Indian poet, Sanai Mashhadi, once sent his *Karnama*, a *qasida* of a hundred verses, to Transoxiana. Often answers were given through the medium of the *ghazal*. Once Mutribi wrote a *ghazal* in answer to Aazmi. Thus, the parallel development of Persian literature presents many new facets. The biographies of poets included the names of many talented persons from both countries. References are available about the active contacts between the poets in the two countries in the writings of Hasan Nisari, Mutribi, Sami, Maliha, Badauni, Nizamuddin, and Abul Fazl.

Before his sojourn in India, Mahmud Ibn-i Wali had been a student of Saiyid Mirak Shah Husaini under whose influence he became a scholar of skepticism and was engaged in the study of religious questions; he prepared his first work, known as the *Rawaihi Taiyyiba*. Later, he broadened his pursuit of knowledge and travelled from one end of the region to the other in his search for learning. About his yearning to visit India, he wrote: 'The author of these lines wished to see the wonders and marvels of the world. Since India is full of rare diversities, fine monuments and secret openings, in July 1625, I started from Balkh for the said country.'[6]

The route chosen by him ran through Kabul, Peshawar, Lahore, Agra, Delhi, Allahabad, and Banaras, from where he went to Vijayanagar and Serendip. In Ceylon, he stayed for twenty-one days and returned to India by sea. The vessel in which he was travelling was wrecked and Mahmud and a few of his companions swam their way to Cuttak with great difficulty. During his three years' stay in Orissa, he worked as the official interpreter at the court of the sovereign of a province, Baqar Khan Ibn-i Mustafa, and developed friendly relations with Mirza Husain, the brother of the ruler. Mahmud participated in all literary and scientific discussion held in the evenings at the court. In 1628 he reached the court of Shahjahan at Agra; Shahjahan gave him a *khalat*, a horse and also an elephant.[7] After a brief stop there, he returned to his motherland. During his stay in Punjab, Mahmud Ibn-i Wali wrote his poetical work *Akhlaq-i-Husaini*, which he dedicated to his friend Mirza Husain. On his return to Balkh he finally engaged himself with the preparation of his work, *Bahr-ul-Asrar*. In his voluminous work *Bahr-ul-Asrar*, Mahmud Ibn-i Wali devotes forty pages to the description of the customs, traditions, religious beliefs, medicines, culture, and art of the Indians. He was enchanted by the beauty of the temple in Surat, which consisted of sixty yards of gardens and had a height of 150 yards; he wrote, fascinating poetry about it. About the *madrasa* of Golconda built by Muhammad Qutub, Mahmud says that 4,000 *tumans* were spent on its construction. His descriptions of the people and animals of Bengal, about Indian in general, and about Indian pearls is fairly interesting. Mahmud found the people of Ceylon and India 'cordial, amicable and considerate towards foreign travellers'. He held Indian thinkers in high esteem. He also visited the tombs of Khusro Dehlavi, Hasan Dehlavi', Shaikh Nizamuddin Auliya, and Humayun Shah. He befriended saints, government officials, and others and won them over with his friendly gestures and his profound knowledge of the arts and sciences. Mahmud Ibn-i Wali liked the people of Bengal and also showered praises on Nizamuddin Auliya and Amir Khusrau. He described his three years' stay in Orissa in candid detail.[8]

Maulana Ghazanfar Sabri Mervi served under Jahangir as secretary and was closely associated with the renowned Indian thinker, Taqi Auhadi. Similarly, Yar Muhammad Islam, who was born in Herat and educated at Bukhara, became a close associate of Jahangir. He enjoyed the title of *Amir-i-Kalan* and was made the Qazi of Kabul. After some time, he was recalled to the court. The post subsequently held by him for the next thirty years, up to 1650, was termed *Qazi-i-Lashkar*,[9] which was probably only an ornamental title since such a post did not actively exist in India. He died in Lahore and was buried there. Qazi Ghazanfar Samarqandi, the famous scholar and thinker, lived in Gujarat for a long time till he left for Mecca.[10] Maulana Abdul Rahman Waiz, the scholar-theologian, was invited by Akbar to India in 1572. He stayed in Fatehpur Sikri and participated in several sessions with Akbar during which they discussed matters of jurisprudence.[11] Other scholars included such persons as Maulana Said Turkestani, who came to India in 1561,[12] delighted Akbar with his knowledge, and died the same year. Hafiz Kuki Tashkandi was a disciple of Mulla Asmatuddin Ibrahim. Mirza Muflis Samarqandi, a scholar and poet, came to India in 1571, and taught in the *madrasa* of Khwaja Moin at Agra, and went to Mecca.[13] Meraji Tashkandi, a poet famous for his *qasida* '*ada*', died in 1554 in Agra.[14] Ghayuri Hesari stayed initially with Mirza Hakeem at Kabul and later joined Akbar's service.[15]

The men of arts at the court of Abdul Aziz Khan frequently visited India. Thus, among the scholars and poets who visited the court of Aurangzeb were: Nasir (the *Qazi-i-Askar* of Abdul Aziz Khan who left behind his *diwan*); Khairullah Beg Shamim (an ordinary officer in the court of Abdul Aziz Khan) who visited India during the reign of Subhan Quli and introduced the Indian style in poetry; Mirza Afzal Munshi Wali (a secretary in the court of Abdul Aziz Khan who came to India and died there in 1663); Lami Nasafi (the court poet of Abdul Aziz Khan with whom the poet went to Mecca from where he came to India and died there); Mir Said Jalal (librarian of Abdul Aziz Khan who went to Mecca and from there went to India; Dastur Nasafi (the court poet of Abdul Azia Khan who returned from Mecca to India and served as Qazi of Kabur for some time. Later on, he was recalled to the centre from where he returned to his home town and died there in 1691. Khwaja Same Sadat, the court poet of Abdul Aziz, went to Meshed with Khan who appointed him to fetch Khwaja Yaqub, the Juibari Shaikh (then staying in India). The former Bukhara Khan Sadat was cordially received at the court of Aurangzeb. Another court poet of Abdul Aziz, Nasim Nasafi Mahram, who visited India in the second half of the seventeenth century, is credited with the work of popularizing the Indian style of poetry among the Central Asian poets, particularly the Indian style followed by Shah Tughra, Nasir Ali, and Qasim Beg. Maliha, the author of *Tazkirat-ul Ashab*, wrote: 'In these days (1688-9), Nasim Mahram goes to India. Thanks to his visits the prose of Shah Tughra Kalandar, the poems of Nasir Ali Hindi, and the *divans* of Qasim

Qasim Beg *Divana* have become famous in Balkh, Bukhara and Samarkand.' Maliha describes Maulana Ibrahim Mesari as 'a man of many parts and a multifarious genius', who came to India and taught in the *madrasas* of Yalangtush and Juibar in Bukhara, where he died in 1684.[16]

Muhammad Ishaq Shaukat Bukhari, a philosophical thinker and a talented person born and educated in the environs of Bukhara, migrated to Khurasan and from there to Isfahan for the same familiar reasons, i.e. his inability to adjust to the times and his failure to restrain himself and his thoughts which did not suit the ruling clique. Shaukat came to India and served under Muhammad Ali Gauhar Shah. He died in Isfahan in 1665 after spending some insignificant and uneventful days there. Shaukat prepared a book in collaboration with a famous Indian philosopher and poet, Bedil and had adopted the Indian style. Shaukat's deep love for India is reflected in his poem in which he expresses his desire to see the land though its glamour was fast fading.[17]

Manba Samarqandi (born in Bukhara in 1681) came to India on his way back from Mecca. He received a *mansab* of '*Hazart*' at the court of Aurangzeb and prepared his lyrics in the form of a *masnavi* entitled *Sarvo Qamar*.[18] Mulla Mufid Balkhi (born in Samarqand) was exiled first from Samarqand and then from Balkh for his satire and criticism of the ruling clique and was exiled to India in 1660, where he resided in the valley of Kashmir.[19] Certain poets had migrated to India and settled there, although they constantly suffered from homesickness. Sadiq's poems speak of his 'vagrant heart' and give assurances to his motherland that though Destiny had taken him away from his home, his heart had always remained with it. The famous poet, Shaida, from Khej, who had migrated to the Deccan, echoes the same feeling and sends his good wishes through the breezes to his friends in Tashkent: 'Sharing with them the secret that though in collusion with seclusion, he manages to be there in his homeland in a flash, he still missed it, yearned for Khujand.' The other exponents of the Indian style of poetry in Central Asia were Nasafi, Shaukat, and Mashrab. While fighting against scholasticism, they used the weapon of their poems to propagate their pantheistic views and humanistic ideas; they persuaded the people to love life and reactionary influences to reject.[20]

Ikram has rightly pointed out that 'out of the several strands which provided the warp and woof of Muslim civilization in India, the most dominant was the influence of Central Asia'.[26] This has greatly influenced each and every sphere of religio-political and socio-economic life in India.

The Urdu language, which is the best example and most visible sign of active Indo-Central Asian link, was greatly influenced by the Uzbek language. In conversational north Indian languages, the word *gap* (conversation, chatting) is frequently used. In Indian dictionaries the word is nowhere to be found except for the somewhat similar word *gal* in Punbaji. In the Uzbek language, the word *gap* means chatting. A contemptuous phrase '*Turam Khan*' is used frequently in Uttar Pradesh to denote someone bloated with self-importance and egotism. This word cannot be traced anywhere except in the Uzbek language in which it means 'Your Excellency' or 'My Sacred One' (i.e. *Tura* means sacred, high; *am* means 'My Great Lord').

Abul Fazl says that there were in Iran, Turan, India, and Turkey 'eight calligraphical systems current'. He includes the names of Arghun of Kabur among the famous copyists. Sultan Ibrahim, son of Mirza Shah-Rukh, was also a well-known practitioner of this art. Maulana Abdul Hayy, the private secretary of Sultan Abu Said Mirza, wrote Taliq well. A number of works written by him are still extant. The literary style famous as *Sabaki Hindi* also had a deep impact on the development of Indian literature, particularly during the reign of Akbar. Its early features are seen in the works of Jami and Fughani. The famous phase of *Sabaki Hindi*, which followed the two earlier phases of *Sabaki Iraqi* and *Sabaki Khurasani* in the different stages of the development of *ghazal* composition, originating in all probability in Iran, was also an example of Indo-Central Asian cultural syncretism.[21] This pattern became popular under the Timurids and dominated Persian poetry during the age of Akbar. Many poets in Transoxiana showed their skill in this particular art. Certain other features are briefly discussed here.

In the days of the Delhi Sultanate, Bukhara, Samarqand, Balkh, and Khwarazm were widely recognized as the 'centres of Muslim learning' and attracted those who wished to acquire knowledge in the Muslim arts and sciences. Maulana Badruddin Ishaq visited Bukhara to discuss certain intellectual and religious questions with the scholars of that region. Sheikh Bahauddin Zakaria (pp. 1182-3) visited Khurasan and Bukhara to complete his study of the traditional sciences under the Samanids. Bukhara and Samarqand far surpassed Baghdad as centres of culture and learning. Shaikh

Muinuddin Chishti received his education and learning in the seminaries of Bukhara and Samarqand. Due to the Mongol invasions, these centres of higher learning suffered a setback at least temporarily and many scholars and divines left Central Asia for India.[22]

The courts of the Sultans of Delhi and the Mughals, particularly that of Iltutmish, Muhammad bin Tughlaq, and Akbar, were meeting places for various men of talents. Khwaja Husain of Merv was attached to the court of Humayun. When Akbar started his bureau of translation, a number of Persian, Sanskrit, and Turkish works were translated. The translation of the *Mahabharata* was also ordered. If Abul Fazl is to be believed, the task was assigned to

> Maulana Badauni and Shaikh Thanesar. The book contains nearly one thousand verses; His Majesty calls this ancient history *Razmnama*. The same learned men translated also into Persian the *Ramayana*, likewise a book of ancient Hindustan which contains the life of Ram Chandra but is full of interesting points of philosophy. Haji Ibrahim of Sirhind translated into Persian the *Atharban* which according to the Hindus is one of the four divine books. The *Lilawati*, which is one of the most excellent books written by Indian mathematicians on arithmetic, lost its Hindu veil and received a Persian garb from Shaykh Abul Fayz Fayzi. The *Majmaul Buldan*, an excellent work on towns and countries, has been translated from Arabic into Persian. The *Haribas*, a book containing the life of Krishna, was translated into Persian by Maulana Sheri. By order of His Majesty Abul Fazl composed a new version of *Kalilah Damna* and published it under the title of '*Ayar-i Danish*'. The Hindi story of Nal and Daman which melts the heart of feeling readers has been metrically translated by Fayzi in the *masnawi* in the metre of the *Layla Majnun*. At the order of Akbar, Mukammal Khan of Gujarat translated into Persian the *Tajak*, a famous work on astronomy. The memoirs of Babur, 'which may be called a code of practical wisdom, were translated into Persian by Mirza Abdurrahim Khan-i Khanan.[23]

Khwaja Husain of Merv was attached to the court of Humayun and served him for many years. He was one of his intimates and was also a member of his 'heavenly assembly'. Since he was the son of Shaikh Ruknuddin Alauddaula of Simnan, a *vazir*, he had no difficulty in acquiring higher learning and

> was distinguished among his fellows by a high degree of intelligence and the sharpness of his understanding. In those branches of knowledge which exercise the reasoning faculty he was a student of Maulana Isamuddin and Mulla Hanafi and in the study of Holy law, he was the disciple of the last

and the best of the sages and traditionalists—Shaikh Banu Hajar-i Sani. He was renowned for his facility in verse, his elegance in literary style, his rhetorical flourishes and his fine delivery. His copiousness of diction and his wit were unrivalled. He composed a *divan* and his poetry though not of the first rank was of respectable quality.[24]

Syed Najmuddin Muhammad Abul Qasim, whose pen name was Qasimi-i-Kahi, was born in Turkestan and brought up in Kabul. In 1493-4, at the age of fifteen, he met the famous Sufi poet Jami and also Hashimi of Kirman. On his arrival at the Mughal court, he was given a warm reception by Humayun. After spending a long time in Banaras, he moved to Agra where he died in 1580. Badauni wonders how 'all his life was spent in heresy and infidelity' when he 'had the advantages of associating with the Shaikhs of former days, particularly Maulana Jami and others'. Varied estimations of his verses have been offered by different biographers. Badauni is critical as usual and says that 'his verses are crude and his ideas are all stolen from others', though Badauni found them 'to be written in a connected style' and concedes 'that Kahi had no equal'. He is said to have set two odes to sweet music 'so that they have become known throughout the world and are sung in all assemblies enlivening alike the banquets of kings and the gathering of mystics. He wrote an excellent *qasidah* on the astrolabe which runs on into an encomium on the late Emperor Humayun. His copiousness of diction is well exemplified therein.'[25] The standard of his scholarship was equally controversial. Abul Fazl says that he knew something of the ordinary sciences. Nizamuddin in the *Tabaqat* adds that 'he had many accomplishments and was especially distinguished in the art of music'. Badauni found him 'well versed in astronomy, rhetoric and the mysticism of the Sufis and he wrote a treatise on music' and that in short, he had no equal in his time in the knowledge of the mysticism of the Sufis, 'the art of composing enigmas, history, elocution, and various other arts'. Most chroniclers agree that he 'lived a free and unconventional life, following no creed or doctrine and was a pugilist and runner'. He often foretold future events. He possessed liberality and generosity; he was open handed; and his bounty was extreme. Badauni says that he was always surrounded by a crowd of *qalandars* lewd fellows, and courtesans.[26]

Khanjar Beg, an old Chaghatai noble related to Tardi Beg, has been praised by his biographers who write that 'he had no equal in his time'. He was endowed with multifarious talents. Badauni acknowledges him as a versatile man, unequalled in the art of war, in calligraphy, in poetry, in the composition of enigmas, in general knowledge in the use of the astrolabe, in astronomy, and in handling figures. He was the author of several works. He composed *masnavis* of three hundred couplets on his own circumstances and also eulogized Akbar. His 'poetic genius' and personal qualities are dearly seen in his well-known *masnavi* on '*dancing girls*' and his famous *divan*. He is said to have 'excelled specially in music'. He had collected information regarding the Persian and Indian systems of music, particularly the six modes of Hindu music (namely, Bhairav, Malav, Sarang, Hindal, Vasant, Dipak, and Megh). Although it was a great contribution and an 'undertaking which was impossible except for wealthy men of high rank and exalted position, but unfortunately there was even in his own times no trace of that information left in the land'.[27]

Mir Abul Ghais Bukhari was given a *jagir* in the vicinity of Lakhanauti. His praise was beyond the power of the tongue or the pen 'and had rendered the chronogram of his death also with the same words: The Mir of praiseworthy disposition', and declares him to be 'Bukharai through whom Dihli became the qubbatul Islam'. Mir Abul Ghais of Bukhara was said to be a 'high-minded man' of 'pure religion' and 'angelic qualities', described as one of the noblest of Gods' works.[28] Sahmi Bukhari is said to have chosen his pen name 'Sahmi' from the profession of his own father who was an arrow maker. Since Sahmi was 'addicted to poetry' from the first decade of his life, he became well versed in it and became famous throughout the world.[29] Amongst other well-known poets may be mentioned the names: Fahmi of Samarqand, the son of Nadiri of Samarqand, who 'was a jovial man and an expert at composing enigmas'.[30] Mirza Lal Beg Lali, the son of Shah Quli Sultan of Badakhshan, was highly praised by Badauni for his 'exceeding nobility of disposition, purity of nature, beauty of form, good manners, humility, amiable disposition, courtesy and modesty', which undoubtedly made him 'one of the intimate associates of the Emperor'.[31] As against this, Mirza Muflis, the Uzbek, a disciple of Mulla Ahmad Jand, who came from Transoxiana to India and taught in the Juma mosque of Khwaja Muinuddin Farankhudi in Agra, 'was not eloquent and when engaged in teaching behaved grotesquely'. His figure was ungainly and he spent his time in religious retirement. He was one of the disciples of Mulla Ahmad Jand, an able mulla 'quick and ready in controversy'.[32]

Mulla Sadiq Halwai of Samarqand left an indelible imprint upon his age by the sheer dint of himself. He was 'too honourable to be placed among the poets and reckoned along with the poets of his age. So to place him thus is a disgrace to him and a disgrace to me.' He was described in contemporary sources as a 'Mulla of good understanding, of pleasant speech and full of apposite learning. After many vicissitudes he came to India, and having devoted himself to the succession of self-styled saints in this country, set most of them by the ears.' He had good taste in poetry and a sublime imagination. While on his return to his native country Jurjan in 1570-1, Mirza Muhammad Hakim detained him at Kabul as he wished to study under him (Mulla Sadiq). Even after his return, Mulla Sadiq continued his busy schedule of teaching and learning and led a respectable life.[33]

Maulana Mirza of Samarqand was described by Badauni (who had studied *Shamsiya*, a commentary on logic, and other works under his able guidance) as 'an angel in the form of a man' and 'one of the best men of his times'.[34]

Mulla Niyazi of Samarqand was 'well skilled in the arts of poetry and prosody, as a compositor of enigmas, in history and all minor branches of knowledge and has written treatises on these subjects'. Badauni, however, says that 'he was quarrelsome and impudent and confirmed by his behaviour the general belief regarding the character of poets'. If Badauni is to be believed, the reason for Niyazi 'being turned out of Transoxiana was an ode which he wrote, of which the closing verses were as follows: I am a debauchee swilling the lees, and the goblet of the sky is my cup. Since Niyazi has become the king of the age in the kingdom of eloquences, the name of Jarhi has been obliterated, and that of Niyazi is in its place.'[35] Qazi Abdus Sami of Miyankal (a province in Transoxiana) was appointed as Qazi-ul Quzzat. If Badauni's account can be trusted, Abdus Sami:

> used to play chess for a wager and to give great odds, this cup draining was notoriously a congenial habit and in his sect bribery and corruption were considered as a duty for the moment, and making profit on bonds for debt and on signing judicial decrees a positive command. But verily since there was no reference to faith or religion left, even this amount was something towards the removal of opprobrium.

Many Turanian poets possessed extraordinary talent in composing poems. Mulla Subuke of the Chaghatai tribe possessed 'great skill in poetry' though he is said to have lived a very unrestrained and licentious life, hence the words 'Subuke the wine bibber' was the chronogram of his death in 973 (1565-6) at Agra. Generally, the Begs of Kolab had a natural talent for poetry. A kind of competitive spirit and the urge to exchange patterns and ideas almost always encouraged and inspired the talented men on both sides to enrich each other's work, capacity, and quality. Manzari Samarqandi, described by Badauni as a 'pleasing poet', was in the service of Bairam Khan and 'designed an epic book of kings (*Shah Nama*); he completed the versification of several incidents included in it, particualry relating to the battle against Sikandarpur. When he presented it to the emperor, he made some detailed suggestions for correcting it. Manzari managed to incorporate these into three or four hundred couplets during the one night and received a notable reward for his achievement the very next morning.[36]

This competitive spirit often took an ugly and acrimonious turn. A Central Asian poet named Bayazi criticized Kahi and Ghazali. 'Kahi and Ghazali, those two drunkered foolts, have put hand to open to belittle Jami and Navoi. There has been nobody like them in the world for Kahi is naught but straw and Ghazali is naught but a dog.' The trading of such insults reveals that this competitive spirit often turned into rivalry leading to mutual hostility.[37]

Qasim Khan of Badakhshan, one of the well-known nobles of Humayun, 'was well acquainted with the art of poetry and wrote poetry well'. He composed a *masnavi* of six thousand couplets in imitation of Jami's *Yusuf Zulaikha* and also wrote a poem 'Laila u Majnu'.[38] Mir Mudami of Badakhshan had 'good taste in poetry' and was for some time in the service of Mirza Aziz Kuka.

The continuous inflow of Sufi ideas along with spiritual flourishes was a common phenomenon in the Middle Ages. Sufis and scholars came from Iran and Turan. Qazi Abul Shahi (the son-in-law of Shaikh Azizan) performed the *Zikr-i-Arra* after his prayers with his companions; he had disciples and taught books like *Shash-i Waqayat* to men like Badauni who found him to be a boundless sea of learning.

Maulana Said Turkestani came to India in 1560-1. He has been described as 'the most learned of the sages of his time'. Being a disciple of Mulla Ahmad Jand, Mulla Muhammad Surkh, and Mulla Isamuddin, he had acquired great learning and possessed all the qualities of a true religious man; though lonely minded he was of a most generous disposition. It is stated that in understanding and quickness of perception no *mulla* of Turkestan who had appeared in this country had ever equalled him. He was an eloquent and charming speaker and as a teacher was kind and gentle towards his pupils. He joined the service of the emperor who is said to have delighted much in his company. Yet he could not remain longer in India as he was homesick, frustrated, and unhappy owing to the blindness of its people. He died after his return from India to Kabul in 1560-3.[39]

Shaikh Husain of Badakhshan carried the flag of the Kubrawiah order in Akbar's time. Everyday after morning prayers, Shaikh Rashid's *Misbah* was recited in his assembly in accordance with the Kubrawiah practice. He was 'well versed and firm in the path of the most pure law' and delivered speeches full of spiritual knowledge which had a deep impact on the people. Some of his Turkish disciples lived in Badaun, and Badauni says that the Shaikh as their spiritual leader 'made that place resplendent with the light of his presence and the bounty of his blessed companionship reached the inhabitants of that district. He was one of the spiritual successors of Shaikh Husain of Khwarazm. Religious ecstasy, overpowering him, used to reduce him to a state like inebriety.'[40]

The theological knowledge of Shaikh Azizan has been highly praised. Badauni writes that the Shaikh was so 'learned a chronicler of law and divinity that if we may suppose that all the books on the theology of the Hanafi school disappeared from the world he would have been able to write them afresh'. It is also said that Abdullah Khan 'had put a stop to the study of logic and dialectics in his dominions, and expelled Mulla Isamuddin of Isfahan, along with his pupils from Transoxiana. Badauni describes the circumstances which led to such a situation: when the study of logic and dialectics had gained ground in Bukhara and Samarqand and students looked into the frequently repeated fallacies, Shaikh Azizan 'wrote a treatise on divinity, meeting and urging Abdullah Khan to banish this school and adducing clear proofs of the unlawful need of teaching and studying logic and philosophy. He also recorded his opinion that there was no harm in using . . . paper on which logical exercises had been written and wrote much more to the same purpose.'

Qazi Abul Maali, the son-in-law, disciple, and spiritual successor of Khwaja Abdul Shahid, the 'orthodox successor of Khwaja Ghani

Khwaja (who was the true successor of Khwaja Akbar)', came to India from Samarqand and lived in India for seventeen years. He was perfect in exoteric and esoteric knowledge and 'practised severe austerities' and was 'a compendium of all such perfection as man can attain to. The people acquired grace from the precious utterances of that model of virtuous man. . . .' On the eve of his death he felt a strong desire to go back to Transoxiana, in 1574-5. While in Kabul, he requested Mirza Shah-Rukh who was there carrying captives from Kabul to release the unfortunate souls. Nearly ten thousand persons were set free.[41]

Khwaja Muhammad Yahya, the fourth in the line of descent from Khwaja Ahrar, was 'well acquainted with the seven styles of penmanship and was a professor of that art. He had a great practice and wonderful skill in medicine and theraputics. His excellent qualities and disposition were an inheritance which he had received from his forbears and although he was little given to discourse he exercised hospitality and whatever he received from his jagir was spent in furnishing the table of friendship. He was the benefactor both of high and low.' Badauni says that when the 'new heresy was introduced and the influence of the vilest of man waxed great, he withdrew from the society, was made *mir-i-haj* and was sent on the pilgrimage'.[42]

Mir Hisamuddin (son of Ghazi Khan Badakhshi) was so intensely 'seized by the tumult of the divine companionship' that he was 'drawn away by attraction (*jazba*), he decided to forsake the world' and threatened 'to become mad' if he was not allowed to go to Delhi to spend the rest of his life at the shrine of the Sultan of the Great Shaikhs. It is said that he 'smeared his body with mud and clay and went about in the streets and lanes. When this was reported to Akbar, he allowed him to go to Delhi. For thirty years, he lived in complete abstinence and observance of the law.' Having renounced the world, he laid aside all the sciences he had acquired. He concentrated on 'meditating on the Koran and in the practice of Sufism'. He was also a disciple of Khwaja Baqi Billa from whom he received permission to guide travellers on the path of piety. Mir Hisam's wife was a sister of Abul Fazl. It is recorded that she distributed all her gold and jewels to the poor as she 'had cleansed her skirt from the defilement of worldliness'. Every year, she sent a large sum for her husband's monastery.

Qazi Nizam, popularly known as Ghazi Khan Badakhshi, was

another important scholar who 'studied the sciences under Mulla Islam and was . . . unique of the age in traditional and rational knowledge'. Being a pupil of Shaikh Husain Khwarazmi, he acquired a thorough knowledge of Sufism. He was the author of several important works. Abul Fazl commented that 'his courage made illustrious his wisdom and that his sword exalted the dignity of his pen. Though sunk in the field of ordinary learning, he worshipped along with the pure Sufis, and so, though outwardly fettered, he achieved liberation. He always had a weeping eye and a burning heart.'

Qazi Nizam of Badakshan was the disciple of Isamuddin Ibrahim Maulana Said Turkestani and Shaikh Husain Khwarazmi. Hence he had a great taste and proficiency in Sufistic studies. He was a noble associated with the court. When he came to India, he received 'unbounded honours' and the titles of Qazi Khan and Ghazi Khan. He excelled in the art of pleasant delivery and wrote several 'standard works', among which was a 'treatise on the proof of the word of God and an account of the religion of truth and verity'. He also wrote marginal notes on the commentators on the dogmas of the faith and numerous treatises on Sufism. He died in Awadh in 1584.[43]

Another poet 'Akbari' (whorthless, designed) of Badakhshan is best described in Badauni's words: 'His assumed name accords well with his nature. He had committed to memory, parrot like, some phrases from the *Futuhal* and the *Fasus ul Hikam* and had striven hard in a polemical treatise to establish the faith of Pharaoh for which reason he has been nicknamed Pharaoh's advocates.'

Another disciple of Maulana Isamuddin was Hafiz Tashkindi who was also a 'professional scholar', especially in Arabic, and who acquired proficiency in all branches of knowledge. All the learned men of Transoxiana 'concurred in acknowledging his superiority'. He came to India in 1569 and joined the services of Akbar. When he went to Turkey, it is claimed that he received ten times more honours and attention than he had received in India; even the office of the grand vizir was offered to him but he declined the offer and returned to his motherland Transoxiana where he died. Whenever he rode abroad he had a quiver in his felt, after the manner of the Turks, and was therefore known as 'Kumaki'.[44]

Many Turanians excelled in the art of war and distinguished themselves not only as good fighters but also as capable and efficient administrators. The salary paid to the warriors from Turan was higher than that received by non-Turanians as the soldiers from Turan were said to be superior. The soldiers who showed bravery were richly rewarded. Those who lost their lives in war did not go unwept and unsung. The debts of Shaikh Muhammad of Bukhara and of Saif Khan, who died in the battles of Patan and Ahmedabad respectively, and Khusru Be, an Uzbek Quruqchi who belonged to an influential and wealthy family of Turan, were posthumously rewarded by Akbar out of public treasures. He was brave and marks of sense and ability were apparent in him, 'hence he was made faujdar of Delhi and Narnol which were hotbeds of strife . . . '. He was said to have 400 plumed *qarquadar* Uzbek troopers mounted on Turkish horses who were all brave men. 'In carrying out the duties of this magistracy, he did not neglect one iota of what was necessary for putting down the disturbers of the peace. He cleared the country of the weeds and rubbish of rebels and was applauded by the court.' He excelled in his auxiliary service to Shahjahan who recommended him to his father. When Shahjahan established a *thana* in the hilly country of Rana, Khusru Be was appointed as *thanedar*. He appreciated this 'magnanimous disporting and every day he had food prepared for the soldiers and every one who did not appear at his table was put down as absent. He was very liberal with gifts and rewards. He changed nothing of what had been his customs and habits in Turan.'

Maulana Ali Ahmad Nishani of Delhi acquired great fame and proficiency in the art of seal-cutting. Badauni says that 'coins of which the dies have been cut by him are taken as talismans and relics to Iraq, Khurasan and Transoxiana'.[45]

## NOTES

1. Mutribi, *Tazkiratush shura*, MS no. 2253, Oriental Institute Library, Tashkent; also see *Khatirat-i-Mutrabi*, ed. by Abdul Ghani Mirzaev, Karachi, 1977, pp. 3-8; *Ain-i Akbari*, vol. III, Eng. tr. by Sarkar and Jarret, New Delhi, pp. 2-7.
2. See Ibn-i-Khaldun, *Muqaddamah*.
3. Iliyas Nizamuddinov, op. cit., pp. 130-1.
4. Mutribi, op. cit., pp. 3-8, for a similar story of Akbar and poet Mulla Qasim see Abdullah Kabuli, *Tazkirat-ut-Tawarikh*, Institute of Oriental Studies, Tashkent, MS no. 2093, ff. 185, 282-3. See also Mutribi, op. cit., pp. 61, 115, 187, 203;

204, 232; also see Bori Ahmedov Gasudarstova Kochevikh Uzbekov, Tashkent, 1966, p. 4.

5. Mahmud Ibn-i Wali, *Bahrul Asrar fi Manaqib ul akhiyar,* MS no. 1375, Institute of Oriental Studies, Tashkent, f. 283.
6. Ibid.
7. Ibid.
8. Ibid.
9. Ibid. See MS no. 10018, Institute of Oriental Studies, Tashkent.
10. Bakhtawar Khan, *Mirat-ul Alam*, MS no. 2097, Institute of Oriental Studies, Tashkent, f. 617.
11. Nizamuddin, *Tabaqat-i-Akbari*, p. 315.
12. *Tarikh-i-Akbar Shahi*, vol. II, p. 26.
13. Badauni, op. cit., p. 38.
14. *Tabaqat-i-Akbari*, p. 314.
15. *Nafais-ul Maasir*, p. 156; Iliyas Nizamuddinov, p. 124; also see Mirzaev Abul Ghazi, *Role va mesta Syed Nasaffi va Tajikski Literature*, vol. XVIII, Dushambe, pp. 28-30.
16. Ibid.
17. Ibid.
18. Z.G. Rizaev, Shaukat Bukhari, Tashkent, 1961, pp. 20-2; also see Nizamuddinov op. cit., pp. 124-6.
19. Maliha Samarqandi, *Tazkirat-ul Ashab*, MS. no. 2613, Institute of Oriental Studies, Tashkent, f. 120; also see S. Sami, *Kamis-ul Alam*, Istambul, 1314, vol. IV, f. 2881.
20. Mutribi, 119; *Tarikh-i Khatatan-i Bukhara*, f. 5; Jaisi, pp. 47-134; Nabi Hadi, 89. Nizamuddinov, pp. 120-31, See Hamid Sulaimanov, *Ali Sher Navoi's Ellek Divan*, Tashkent, 1968, pp. 71a, 137a, 566; also see *Asiri Khujandi Ashaar-i Muntakhab*, ed. by Sadullah Asadullaev, Moscow, 1982, text, pp. 85, 195; tr. pp. 6, 13, 77, for details see Kabir Ahmad Jaisi, *Jadid Tajiki Shaer*, Aligarh, 1990, pp. 47-51, 95-112, 128-34, also see *Armughani Tashkent*, Selected Poems of Ghafur Ghulam, translated by Qamar Reis, Official Publication House, Tashkent, 1968, pp. 61-3. Hasan Nisari, pp. 58-60.
21. See *Ain-i-Akbari*, I, pp. 106-13; also see Mansura Haidar, 'The Exchange of Ideas in the Medieval Period', paper read at Indo-Soviet Conference, 23-6 May 1988, Moscow; Khwaja Hasan Nisari Bukhari, *Muzzakkira-i-Ahbab*, text, pp. 447-50, Eng. tr., pp. 58-60; *Mirat-ul Alam*, f. 376b, *Muzzakkira*, pp. 58-60; for Ghazali Meshedi's imitative performance see *Muzzakkira*, Eng. tr., p. 64.
22. Ibid.
23. *Ain*, 106-13.
24. See Badauni, vol. III under Khwaja Husain of Merv, pp. 248-51, 401.
25. Ibid., pp. 240-7, 271, 276.
26. Ibid.
27. Ibid., pp. 310-15, 384.
28. Ibid., pp. 182-3, 500.
29. Ibid., pp. 336-7.
30. Ibid., p. 405.
31. Ibid., p. 441.
32. Ibid., p. 218.

33. Ibid., pp. 354-5.
34. Ibid., pp. 209-10.
35. Ibid., pp. 496-8.
36. Ibid., pp. 469-70.
37. Ibid., pp. 240-7, 270-6.
38. Ibid., pp. 448-50.
39. Ibid., pp. 212-13.
40. Ibid., pp. 151-2.
41. Ibid., pp. 210-11, 472.
42. Ibid., pp. 148-9, 345, 439 n. 4.
43. Ibid., pp. 214, 374, 375, 409 n. 2, 410.
44. Ibid., pp. 213-14.
45. Ibid., pp. 480-93.

# Central Asian Impact on Indian *Madrasas*

Although a detailed description of *madrasas* is already available in many valuable works,[1] a comparative study of the *madrasas* found in different countries and their mutual contact and impact upon each other is yet to be undertaken. An attempt is being made in this paper to discuss Central Asian *madrasas* and their impact on various aspects and spheres of Indian centres of learning (e.g. their architectural pattern, curriculum).

When the Arabs and subsequently the Turks arrived in India, the land of Vedas, Upanishadas, and centers of learning like Nalanda and Takshila, they found a well-organized system of education here. To the existing Indian traditions of learning and erudition, the new entrants 'made tangible contribution'. In 93 AH Muhammad bin Qasim got a Jama mosque constructed which was not only used for congregational prayers but served the purpose of a place of learning also, ever since 133 AH the mosques in Mansurah continued 'more or less on the pattern of self contained educational institution' till fourth century of Hijrah. A *madrasa* was constructed at Mansurah where Qazi Abu Mansuri delivered lectures.[2] Thus side by side with the political hegemony of the Arabs, entered their educational system in Central Asia, India and other places. The custom of mosque cum *madrasas* had continued even later. Such traditions not only influenced Central Asia but gradually crept into Medieval Indian educational system. Yusuf Husain has rightly pointed out that 'under the Abbasids, all the important cities in Persia and Central Asia vied with Baghdad in the magnificence of their educational institutions, established by royal personages or munificence of private individuals. Through these institutions the highest spirit of culture and investigations flourished.'[3] Mahmud Begrah is said to have maintained a mosque like 'Paradise' (*khuld-i-barin*) and a *makatib* on the pattern of Bihisht.

Shahjahan had described the eastern part of his domain as 'Shiraz of his Empire and upto 1120 AH the place was thronging with the *ulama* and blooming with the florescence of learning (which had its impact on its soil).'[4]

Ghulam Ali Azad's famous comment confirms this fact:

> The Eastern lands (*sar zamin-i-Purab*) had all along been the repository of learned men and reservoir of erudition. Although all the provinces of India are distinguished for their scholars, the province of Oudh and particularly most of the province of Allahabad in which the noble and respectable population spread over five to ten *krah* are dedicated to learning. Since they received *jagirs*, scholarship and subsistence allowance from rulers, they built mosques, *madrasas* and *khanqahs*. The scholars and teachers opened the gates of knowledge to the students who moved from place to place for acquisition of knowledge. The men of high standing and wealthy men (*Sahib-i-taufiqan*) always patronized and looked after the students and service to this group was considered to be good fortune (*Saadat-i-Uzma*).[5]

Seemingly, the Central Asian educational system and *madrasas* were a replica of Perso-Islamic and Turkish traditions. Nizam-ul-Mulk, the Seljuqid *wazir* (456-85 AH) is erroneously credited with the introduction of this institution. Since Nizam-ul-Mulk had taken keen interest in spreading the education, it is not surprising that people mistook him for being a founder of the *madrasa*. The mosque cum *madrasas* are said to have existed in the entire Muslim world where all branches of Islamic sciences were taught. The academies like *Bait-ul Hikma* in Baghdad, *Khazinat-ul Hikma* (for astronomy) where Abu Mashar Balkhi studied, *dar-ul Ilm* or *dar-ul Hikma* of Egypt, the *madrasas* founded by scholars like al-Bayhaqiya, al-Saidiya and several others were there where people not only took interests in the study of Koran, *hadis* and *fiqh* but also in *al-ulum-al-qadima*, the Hellenistic sciences like logic philosophy, mathematics, astronomy, medicine, music and alchemy. Nizam-ul-Mulk had, therefore, opened numerous *madrasas* named after him as 'Alnizamiya' in Nishapur, Balkh, Musil, Hernt and other places. The most famous Nizamiya was established in Baghdad.[6] Although Badauni had divided the subjects into two broad groups (i.e. sciences and non sciences). Abul Fazl had classified the subjects into three major groups namely *Ilahi* (divine science or theology); *Riyazi* (music, medicine, mathematics, astronomy) and *Tabiqi* (all physical sciences). There are various subjects of Arabic curriculum which are included in the *Dars-i-Nizamiyah*. Evén the suggested books and bibliography then prevalent is found in the *Khulasat-ul maktib* (1688). Central Asian and Perso-Islamic traditions had a deep but very far reaching impact on Indian educational system.[7]

## Influence on Madrasa Architecture

### CENTRAL ASIAN *MADRASAS*

The main features of the *madrasa* architecture usually included

a vaulted portal with domed halls designed for the mosque and the auditorium on both sides opening to the yards, its portals on the main axis, encompassed by two stories of vaulted hujras (students cells) which were opened through the facades through a number of arches. The main façade had circular towers or at the corners; the arches, arranged in two stories, occupied the space between the portal and the towers. The façade was adorned with tiled mosaics and majolica, and the arch of exterior portal was unframed by a rope, a characteristic of 15th century architectural decor. A massive decor out of inlaid bits of wood was remarkable for the carving on its lids, in which geometrical elements were combined with vegetable motif with inscription.

In the fifteenth century the enlightened ruler Ulugh Beg erected three big *madrasas*. One of them, was reared up in 1417 in the Centre of Bukhara. Its shape 'set a standard for all larger development of the kind in other areas which presented, therefore, various degrees of approximation to the Bukhara prototype'.[8]

The Central Asian *madrasas* certainly surpassed the Indian *madrasas* in finesse of execution and delicate designs in architecture, though most of the Central Asian architectural features like domes of all kinds and varying types of minarets, the stalactite well decorated could be seen in the *madrasas* of India. But the tall auditoriums, sparkling cupolas, the massive mural surfaces, geometrical, vegetable and floral designs on the minarets and walls, the *kundal*, chaspak, panjara and mosaic décor, the rope winding around airy arches or glazed arches inserted into rectangular frames, marble panels, the recessed painted walls, majestic vaulted portals with decorated pendants were all missing in the architecture of Indian *madrasas*. A short description of *madrasas* found in Central Asia and India as given below would prove the point. From amongst the *madrasas* of Samarqand the following are famous and still in good shape.

Unlike Timurids the Uzbeg rulers never wasted their resources in building mausoleums of dead kings. The utilitarian architecture constructed by them included mosques, *madrasas*, *sardabahs*, *sarais*, *ribats*, public bath houses, bridges market places, hospitals and *khanqahs*.

Madrasa-i-Ulugh Beg (1420) is said to be 'a new word in (the then) contemporary architecture. This building 62 × 90 yards in size had a square yards with all four flanking portals opened into the yard. These portals, modest in size and flat were a hall mark of Madrasa-i-Ulugh Beg in striking harmony with portals of the flanking facades likewise looking out side. An impressive entrance portal consumed two thirds of the front façade. At the corners of the building were four minarets but on the whole, its composition departed from a typical *madrasa* plan for its end plans had equal width and there was a cross auditorium and an elongated half in the rear of the yards. Partitions between the main on either side of entrance portal and the corner minarets received planner solutions without the customary and deep cut arches. The geometrical designs of light and dark blue gazed brickwork against yellow background burnt brick looked strikingly beautiful. The Madrasa-i-Tillya Kari (Tillikari?) was built in 1646-7 though the ornamentation of it continued till 1660 and even then it could not be fully completed. The *madrasa* had the characteristics of the Bukhara *madrasa*. It is said that Mirza Ulugh Beg was so keenly interested in getting it constructed in the most artistic manner that he personally visited the *madrasa* then under construction every day and even lifted the bricks and handed it over to the architect (*ustad*). Once Maulana Khwafi was sitting amidst the brick load and heard someone asking Mirza Ulugh Beg that hence *madrasa* is nearing completion who would be appointed as its *mudarris*. Mirza Ulugh Beg's enthusiastic comment that 'the *mudarris* of this *madrasa* would be the one who was (*dar jami ulum mahir wa dar tamam funun kamil o Mutabahhir bashad*)'. Maulana Muhammad of Khwaf who had for quite a long time struggled in the city to get a footing recommended himself.

Madrasa-i-Shir Dar was started in 1619 and completed in 1635-6. It was 'across the square from Ulugh Beg Madrasa which it replicated both in façade composition, huge portal and minarets and two turquoise ribbed cupolas on either side of the portal on the one hand and in being of equal width and interim square space. There was however some difference in that the Shir Dar had in its plan a usual outline with a mosque and an auditorium in the frontal part. The glazed facing of Shir Dar though of high quality was inferior to fifteenth century mosaic styles. A distinguishing feature of the *madrasa* were the images of a lion attacking a doe and the sun with human features. Minarets in both the décor and ornamentation in the building of mosques and *madrasas*. *Madarsa* were dispossessed of their clerestory and had only a stalactite crown to top them. Madrasa-i-Miri Arab (1535-6) was a 'magnificent ensemble in the heart of Bukhara', with its large double storeyed buildings of the *madrasa* having hundred and ten cells for students. Due to its beautiful décor and splendid lay out, it seemed to be far ahead of the fifteenth century architectural designs of *madrasas*. The chopped corner yards provided access to the rooms and the niched entrance. In front of the façade were two crossed halls, an auditorium mosque and a sepulcher covered by twin domes. The tiled mosaic décor of main and flanking façades seems to be a fourteenth century legacy but with certain novel features, e.g. Majolica inserts into the alabaster moulded semi-cupolas and decorative flat cupolas, raised over the corridors leading into the yard and made out of ground bricks with turqoise-like seams filled with tiled bans.[9] The Madrasa of Burraq Khan had a mosque also attached to it.

With the accession of mighty and more pragmatic Abdullah Khan, the earlier style, excessive decoration and unique grandeur was replaced by a more 'mass character', which was economically feasible with revised old patterns, design, approach to plan and volume; broader connotation and 'diversified' décor. The already developed engineering and construction skill was further improved as the 'daring innovators and slayers of frozen architectural canons in their refusal to make do with cumbersome exterior cupolas'. Consequently, 'the aseismic qualities of the building enhanced and architecture regained its once abandoned form and structure'. It was a period of the rapid development of forms with criss-cross arches and shield shaped pendants which multiplied gradually to form a smooth web-like traditions to the calot of the dome. Other novel features were: broad variety of decorative cupolas with herring-bone pattern of ground brickwork, and five and exquisite facets and tiled mosaic inserts (such cupolas and semi-cupolas were installed in the entrance hall and the niches of the yard). In larger buildings there were 'blank interiors without tiles and murals but with plastic form of the roofing with a highlighting clerestory in the summit of the dome. *Chaspak*, a two colour stuccoe mosaic was successfully applied to decorating the interior surface of the cupolas. Majolica, previously a component of the façade décor gave place to new decorative styles such as sectional mosaics either tiled or of ground brickwork with glazed dark or light blue seams'.

In Central Asia the largest *madrasa* known as Kukultash spreading over an area of 95 × 76 yards and consisting of 130 *hujras* was constructed in 1568-9. Although its lay out, and somewhat crude finish had nothing to recommend them but its majestic cupolas in attached mosque and auditorium gave its 'blank interior' enough impressive look and an altogether different form in its domes. After fifty years, Nadir Divan Begi had built a *khanqah* mosque and a caravan *serai* infront of this *madrasa* but the same buildings were converted to a *madrasa* and the entire complex came to be known as Labi Hauz.[10]

There were two *madrasas* constructed in the western part of Bukhara and being in one place were called *qush madrasas*. One of these was Madrasa-i-Madari Khan (Abdullah Khan's mother) which was constructed in 1566-7 when Abdullah Khan was an ordinary provincial king hence the building lacked grandeur. Another *madrasa* again built by Abdullah Khan in 1588-90 when he had become the king carries the splendour and décor of earlier centuries. With its nicely carved doors, numerous *hujras*, octagonal domed hall facing the niches, two storeyed building, criss-cross arches supporting the cupolas, star shaped ornamentation on the relief and its 'complex lay out reflected a strenuous search for new solutions' and made it a 'typical example of contemporary *madrasa* style'.[11]

The Madrasa of Abdul Aziz Khan (1651-2) stood facing the *madrasa* of Ulugh Beg, lacked the symmetry and proportion though distinguished itself in excellent majolica décor, and 'exuberant polichrome ornamentation of the stalactite facings and fine landscape motifs and was planned by architect Muhammad Salih of the murals'.[12]

The Madrasa of Shaibani Khan was constructed in the *chaharsuq* (market place) of Samarqand. The height of it was very impressive. There were five teachers (*mudarris*) appointed here, one of whom was Maulana Khwajagi a descendant of Maulana Khwafi.

## *Madrasas* in India

A cursory look at the style of construction of the *madrasas* in India proves that the Perso-Islamic and Central Asian pattern had been followed. For some reason, the simplicity was a distinctive feature minus the ornamentation. Apart from Masud's (1240-6) school at Lahore Sultan Muhammad Ghauri's (1175-1206)' *madrasa* at Ajmer and the first ever *madrasa* of Iltutmish at Delhi. Sultana Razia had also founded the Muizzi College at Delhi. Balban had established Madrasa-i-Ali Nasiriya at Badaun when Nasiruddin Mahmud was the ruler. Alauddin Khilji (1296-1316) also built a *madrasa* at Delhi. In 1346 Mahmmad bin Tughlaq's (1325-51) *madrasa* was constructed at Delhi. Badr Chach had in a chronogram on this building highly praised its garden, pillars, engravings, edifice. It is surmised that Firuz Shah Tughlaq's *madrasa* at Delhi 'became a model for the *madrasas* established later on—in medieval India' with many lecture rooms, a mosque, some hostels for the students and quarters for *imams* and other servants of the mosque. There were thirty other *madrasas* established by Firuz shah. Sultan Ahmad Shah (1411-41) had established innumerable *maktabs* and *madrasas* in the town of Ahmedabad which was established by him. To Sikandar Lodi (1489-1517) goes the credit of establishing *madrasas* at Mathura, Narwar and Agra.[13]

A sum of Rs. 36 lakhs was disbursed by Firuz Tughlaq on the monthly salaries of teachers.

In his *madrasa*, the teachers and students enjoyed free board and lodging.

Firuz Shah's *madrasa* at Siri and Firozabad, had a 'nice surrounding and superb building'. In his valuable work *Alshafi-sinat-al-Insha* compiled in India during the reign of Tughlaqs, Al-Qalqashandi says that there were one thousand educational institutions and seventy hospitals in Delhi alone. These *madrasas* belonged both to the Shafaites and Hanafites. For the upkeep of these *madrasas* large scale grants, and stipends were given.[14]

Several *madrasas* were constructed during the reign of the Mughal emperors. Humayun had provided generous grants from the royal exchequer for building of educational institutions. At the order of Humayun one *madrasa* was built at Delhi which was headed by Shaikh Husain and another was established at Agra which was headed by Shaikh Zainuddin Khwafi.[15]

Sher Shah's *madrasa* constructed at Narnaul in 927 AH in the memory of his grandfather Ibrahim Sur was named as Madrasa-i-Sher Shah Sur. Other *madrasas* were Maham Begam or Khair-ul Manzil, called by Badauni as Begum Madrasa.[16] Innumerable *madrasas* for learning Arabic language were constructed by Badauni at Agra and Fatehpur Sikri.[17] Jahangir rejuvenated several dying educational institutions. Under him the *Ankari* was practiced for the benefit and development of education. Under Shahjahan there was a *madrasa* constructed which was attached to the Jama Masjid of Delhi and named as *Dar-ul-beqa*. A maid servant of Shahjahan called Lado had established a *madrasa* and a mosque at Lahore. Dara Shukoh also constructed a *madrasa* in 1661 at Thanesar in Punjab.

Abdurrahim Khan-i-Khanan's *madrasa* had a library attached to it. The *madrasas* built in India were not so sumptuously constructed as in other Central Asian states as there was more emphasis on other kinds of buildings like mausoleums, palaces, gardens, etc. Besides, the building material and the indigenous architectural pattern also made the difference.

## Teachers and the Curriculum

While discussing the educational system of medieval Central Asia, one has to differentiate between *maktab* and *madrasa*, the former was for primary education while, higher learning was accomplished in *madrasas*. Where, apart from teaching, the tradition of discourses by eminent scholars followed by discussions was a regular feature. Usually *maktabs* were attached to the mosques but sometimes they were separately established for learning of Arabic, Persian or any other subject. The teachers were called *maktabdar*, *maulavi* or *muallim*. The salaries were given to them from the income of *auqafs*.[18]

Elementary education imparted in *mektabs* included the learning of alphabets and also reading, writing and arithmetic. Nice paintings are available which depict the scenario in an average *maktab* though erroneously the compilers had presented them as *madrasas* in the captions.

Mirza Ulugh Beg was particularly anxious to get the most talented and learned men appointed in his *madrasa*, a tradition which continued even several centuries later. When maulana Khwafi had enquired about the appointment of a *mudarris* in that *madrasa*,

Mirza Ulugh Beg had stated that in this *madrasa* only that person will be appointed as *mudarris* who had full command over all sciences (*dar jami i ulum mahir o dar tamam funun Kamil o mutabahir*). Maulana Khwafi Muhammad presented his own candidature for the post. Mirza got necessary information collected about him and called him later before him and asked innumerable questions on all branches of knowledge. Since he received satisfactory answers on whatever he asked, Mirza was satisfied and sent Maulana to the *hamam* for a bath and awarded him a special dress. He was taken by the Mirza to Qazi Zada-i-Rumi where he showered many praises upon him and made him his fellow scholar (*ham sabaq*). Wasifi recorded that on the day of court assembly (*ijlas*) Maulana Khwafi was delivering his lecture and *mujassati* and there were ninety *danishmands* present there. (Such was the learned talk that) except Mirza Ulugh Beg and Maulana Qazi Zada-i-Rumi none could understand a word of it. Mirza is said to have commented that the expertise and extent of Maulana's depth of knowledge was such that if the books and *risalas* on all the sciences (*ulum*) are drowned in the river, the Maulana was the one who could reproduce the entire lost treasure (through his effort and memory) and none of them would be missing.[19]

In the Madrasa of Mirza Ulugh Beg which had no equal in the world, ten teachers (*mudarris*) were appointed, one of whom was Maulana Amir Kalan. Maulana was extremely knowledgeable in *ulum-i-yaqinia*, *dinia* and *ulum-i-shariat*. He also knew the canon of *Kanun-i-shifai-imrazo haw-i-kuliyat-i-araz*. In the *suffa* of *shart-i-waqff* the condition for appointment was that the teacher appointed in the *madrasa* ought to be *alam ul ulama*.[20] Wasifi had highly appreciated the Madrasa of Mirza Ulugh Beg which was constructed by the Mirza in *chaharruq*, the market place of Bukhara where men of excellence like Saiyid Shamsuddin Muhammad, used to teach.[21] The names of *mudarris* of Samarqand who assembled at the *waz* at Juma mosque have been enumerated by Wasifi which included luminaries of the age like Maulana Ibrahim Shirvani, Maulana Khwajji, Maulana Mahmud Bukhari. It should also be noted that there was constant exchange of knowledge between the scholars of Central Asia and other countries. The extent and depth of knowledge of *savants* of that age may therefore be gauged from various events described by Wasifi, one of which is being described here:[22]

When the Safavids had conquered Persia many like wasifi had migrated to Khurasan. In the hour of acute poverty and adversity he had met Khwaja Abul Wafa Khwarazmi, a disciple (*talamiz*) of Saiyid Zain-ul Abidin, Amir Mustaz and one of the friends of Ikhwanussafa and Khulanalwafa. He had acquired *istehzar* over most of the *ulum-i-ghariba*. Since both of them were faced with a financial crunch and were desperately looking for better prospects, they decided to approach a great saint named Abuljud who had come from Andalus, was well versed in all kinds of *ulum-i-ghariba* and fine arts (*funun-i-badia*) for his prophecy about themselves. Abul Wafa was certain that such was his extensive knowledge and habits and *Rhawariq-i-adat* that whenever any one entered his house, he could tell the name of the stranger alongwith the details of his father, tribe, nation, profession and points of excellence. The saint excelled in whatever *ulum* come under the *Kama-i-kala-i-sirran*.

He had mastery over *Ilm-i-kimia* (art of converting metals into other metals: alchemy), *ilm-i-limia* (which stands for *ilm-i-adad*, *hindisa*, *ilm-i-haiyat* and *ilm-i-mausiqi*), *ilm-i-himia* which means *ilm-i-jabr*, *muqabala*, *ilm-i-masahat*, *jarri saqil*, *ilm-i-zijat*, *taqawim*; *ilm-i-simia* which is well known; *ilm-i-rimia*, *tilisamat* and *nairi-i-rijat*. If Wasifi is to be believed, the saint not only called him by his full name immediately after he entered the door but gave him all details regarding his future prospects. The forecast of imminent political events was also truthfully broadcast.[23] A careful study of the sources shows that even the princes were experts in varied kinds of subjects of exact sciences and fine arts as skilfully as the ordinary folks.

There was a continuous exchange of ideas men and commodities under the Sultans of Delhi, the tradition of inviting learned men from surrounding and far off regions continued. The scholars came from Balkh, Khwarazm, Samarqand, Bukhara and other places. Since *Fiqh-i-Hanafi* was the binding factor between India, Central Asia and Turkey, the exchange was brisk and regular. It is recorded that many educational institutions were established by Sultan Shahab-uddin Muhammad Ghori and the most prominent scholar and 'famous exponent of Islamic theology' was Kamaluddin a Saiyid from Tirmiz.[24] In the court of Qutubuddin Aibak also there were men like Maulana Bahauddin of Ush (who wrote a *qasida* in praise of Aibak).[25] Barani refers to Maulana Burhanuddin Balkhi also.[26]

Sikandar Lodhi had sent an open invitation to men of letters and learned men from Arabia, Persia and Central Asia 'to take charge of education'. Several scholars trickled into India even without invitation. Mahmud Gawan the famous *wazir* of Bahmanis had invited Maulana Abdurrahman Jami the renowned Sufi scholar of Central Asia to accept the offer of Principalship of his *madrasa* at Bidar. Jami had refused to accept the offer due to his old age.

Under Shahjahan scholars assembled from different quarters. The centres of education at Delhi, Jaunpur, Ahmedabad provided excellent teachers.

Many Indian scholars went to Central Asia to acquire learning. While appreciating the *ulama* of Alauddin's period, Barani emphasises that they were past masters excelling in their fields to an extent that they could not only be compared favourably with Central Asian scholars but had no parallel to them available in Samarqand, Bukhara, Khwarazm and other places. The very fact that Barani compares them with Ghazali and Razi in the field of fiqh[27] shows that during this period Central Asian scholars and men of jurisprudence were considered to be still superior. Moreover, the list of the scholars and men of jurisprudence who had the place name attached to their personal names (e.g. Multani, Bhakkari, Badauni, Zafarabadi, Amrohi, Koli, Beyani, Barani, Akbarabadi, Panipati, Thanavi or the professional status (like *Jauheri*, *Tajir*), shows that already a large number of indigenous scholars well versed in various sciences and jurisprudence did exist.

During the sultanate period, the traditional pattern of curriculum continued which was inherited by the Lodis. There were subjects collectively called *manqulat* and *maqulat*. Rational sciences included the former like *tafsir* (exegesis), *hadith* (traditions) and *fiqh* and the latter comprised the *sharh-i-shamsiah* and *sharh-i-shafia* in addition to subjects like grammar, logic, literature, mysticism (*tasawwuf* ) and scholasticism (*Kalam*).

While describing the educational development during the reign of Alauddin Khilji, Barani refers to various branches of knowledge including logic, philosophy, *usooliden* or its allied subjects, literature, grammar, history, geography. Usually the books like *Gulistan* and *Bostan* of Sadi, *Shah Nama* of Firdausi, *Khumsah* of Nizami and Amir Khusro, Minhaj-us Siraj's *Tabaqat-i-Nasiri*, *Sikandar Nama*. *Chingiz Nama*, *Qabus Nama*, *Zafar Nama* of Yezdi were taught in the *madrasas*.[28]

The education started with reading of the Holy Koran and *ahadis sarf* (conjugations and rules of grammar), *nahb* (syntax) in both Persian and Arabic languages.

Akbar is said to have particularly patronized and encouraged the subjects like astronomy, mathematics, medicine and philosophy.[29]

Sikandar Lodi is credited with the introduction of annual examinations and award of *Hun*.[30] Later on *Ejazat Nama* or *sanads* were provided with the details of the subjects studied and the standard of the students and the teachers under whom educated.[31]

The discourses and discussions so frequently held in India were attended by a large number of scholars/*ulama* who took part in the debates and conventions.

Abul Fazl's long discussion over the changed pattern of education introduced by Akbar shows how the outside influence had transformed the system of education prevalent in India. He records:

> In every country, but specially in Hindustan, boys are kept for years at School, where they learn the consonants and vowels. A great portion of the life of the students is wasted by making them read many books. His Majesty ordered that every school boy should first learn to write the letters of the alphabet, and also learn to trace their several forms.

'No one should be allowed to neglect those things which the present time requires.' Further, these regulations shed a new light on scholars, and courses.[32] In the new curriculum introduced by Akbar, the Central Asian courses and *madrasa* features were distinctly present:

> Every student was supposed to study works on morals, arithmetic, the notation peculiar to arithmetic, agriculture, mensuration, geometry, astronomy, physiognomy, household matters rules of government, medicine, logic, physics, mathematics, sciences and history (*ikhlaq*, *siyaq*, *malahat*, *masahat*, *hindisa*, *nujum*, *raml*, *tadbir-i-manzil*, *siyasat*, *tib*, *mantiq*, *tabii*, *riyazi*, *ilahi*, *tarikh*). From Indian System of Learning, they were expected to study grammar (*vyakaran*), *vedant*, Patanjali's work.

Now the reading and writing were taught to the child simultaneously. There was particular emphasis laid on *amokhta* or recapitulation of lessons.

The boys were expected first to learn alphabets, their shape and name and practice its writing within two days. The joint letters may be practiced for a week. After this identification of alphabets and words, the knowledge and memorization of the prose and verses in praise of God or moral sciences were taught. The teacher was expected to look after five things, knowledge of letters, meaning of words, the hemstitch, the verse, the previous lesson. If this method of teaching is adapted, a boy will learn in a month, or even in a day, so much so that people will be astonished.[33]

According to Abul Fazl, on experimental basis this curriculum proved to be successful. Mir Fathullah Shirazi is said to have 'greatly influenced the educational policy of Akbar'.[34] But the Central Asian influence on the medieval Indian curriculum was far more deep than the Indian educational system.

It is indeed very interesting that the teachers who were appointed for the princes usually hailed from Persia and Central Asia as the place-name added to their name suggests. It is also interesting that in earlier stages there is no mention of indigenous teachers whereas in the later period certain Indian scholars are also included in the list of teachers of princes.

Humayun's teachers included Khwaja Kalan, Shaikh Zainuddin. The tutors of Akbar were Bairam Khan, Mulla Islamuddin Ibrahim, Abdul Latif Qazwini, Mulla Bayazid, Mulla Mir Kalan Haris, Qutubuddin Khan, Abdurrahim Khan-i Khanan. Faizi and Ahmad Nishani supervised Jahangir's education. Shahjahan had following teachers: Qasim Beg Tabrizi, Hakim Dawai Gilani, Shaikh Abulkhair and Wajihuddin Gujrati. Similarly, Mulla Abdul Latif Sultanpuri, Mir Muhammad Hashim Gilani, Maulana Syed Muhammad Qanauji, Mulla Shaikh Ahmad and Danish Khan were teachers of Aurangzeb. Even a hurried look at the courses taught to the princes in the Timurid and the Uzbeg courses would show and prove the similarity existing between Indian and Central Asian sphere of education.[35] It should not be therefore, very surprising that all sorts of works on jurisprudence, *fiqh*, Central Asian *malfuzat* literature, classical works, manuscripts on medical sciences, *diwans*, *risalas* on various arts are extant in Indian libraries. The continuous import of books by the Mughals is recorded in the sources and the epistolary records. The subjects generally taught in the *madrasas* included epistolography, calligraphy, astronomy, astrology, physiognomy, botany, physics, chemistry, music, medical sciences.

Turkish language continued to be taught to the princes throughout the Mughal period perhaps because the Mughals prided in their Turkish descent and did not want the children to be ignorant of their father-tongue. Jahangir asserts that he was not ignorant of Turkish speech and writing. While discussing the curriculum and education imparted to Prince Bahadur Shah, Maasir-i-Alamgiri's author also confirms that alongwith Arabic and Persian, Turkish language was also taught.[36] There are numerous bilingual (Turkish-Persian), trilingual (Persian-Turkish-Mongolian) and atr-lingual (Arabic, Persian, Turkish—Mongolian) dictionaries available which were prepared under the Mughals to facilitate the study of Turkish. Similarly, Babur, Mirza Haidar Dughlat, Shahjahan and Aurangzeb were good calligraphists. Shahjahan's writing pad was decorated with his own beautiful script but Shahjahans's signature on various manuscripts, e.g. 'Majalis-i-Khamsa', 'Tuzukat-i-Timuri', on the painting of Abdurrahim Khan-i-Khanan and on numerous works preserved in the Library of Asiatic Society, Calcultta[37] are a fair proof of his expertise in calligraphy. Princes were particularly taught the culture and morals. Similarly nobles also learnt and practised varied forms of sciences and arts. Abulfaiz Faizi was well versed in all forms of learning and particularly excelled in *sher* (poetry) (muamma), *uruz o qafiya*, dictionary (*lughat*), (*tafsir*) history (*tarikh*), *tibb khat o insha inshapardazi*[38] was another subject. Abul Fazl's *Insha-i-Abul Fazl*, *Har Sih Daftar* was recommended in *madrasas* of India.

The recitation of Holy Koran (*qirat*) and *hifz*, the art of the *tajweed*, *tartil*, were also part of the syllabi. The vocational training was provided in a different manner. The Central Asian rulers had always ensured that the services of prisoners of war were used in a constructive manner. Before plundering, imposition of *mal-i amani* and general massacre experts in every field (fine arts, learning, handicrafts) were selected and carried to the land of conquerors where their expertise was used in the royal court and regal workshops. In India Firuz Shah had, therefore, used these captives of war in the royal *karkhanas* for imparting and receiving vocational training.[39]

Apart from the teachers of the *madrasa*, there were *moayyids* who were the students of higher classes and assisted their teachers by giving them relief from teaching the lower classes. There were peripatetic teachers as well as those enthusiasts like Mir Fathullah Shirazi who visited the homes of their students to teach them.

According to Perso-Islamic and Central Asian tradition, the *Tasmi a Khwani* and *Bismillah* was organized at the age of four years, four months, four days. The ceremony for Humayun, Akbar, Jahangir and Shahjahan was performed at the same age. Babur's education was started at the age of five in Samarqand where he pursued varied kinds of academic and artistic pursuit for six years.[40]

Since the Central Asians drew their lineage from Alonaqova—a female, it is presumed that the women enjoyed extra ordinary privileges amongst Turco-Mongols and also amongst the Turks—a fact confirmed by Ibn-i-Arab Shah as well as by Abu Talib Isfahani. They not only acquired learning but also the art of warfare. They rode the horses, sat in the court, took part in political affairs, and worked with the men folk on all fronts. The women in medieval India were also the off shoot of these very people. Sultana Razia's educational qualifications and the training imparted had been discussed by Barani. Shad Khanam, the daughter of Muhammad Sultan Mirza (son of Jahangir and grandson of Humayun) was an excellent calligraphist and transcribed the holy book in *Khat-i Raihan* and at the end of it she had written her name and genealogy in *Khat-i Riqa*. Gulbadan Begum enumerates the various arts in which the royal ladies excelled.[41] Salima Sultan Begum has been highly appreciated by the contemporary chroniclers. Gulbadan Begum's charismatic personality was proverbial. Mulla Ashraf Mazandarani had been appointed as the teacher of Aurangzeb's daughter Zebun Nisa.[42] The ordinary women had their *otin bibis* to teach them at their homes. It is interesting to note that these *madrasas* used to have large *waqf* lands granted to them for their maintenance. Several *Waqf Namas* are extant which indicate how vast domains were allotted to them. One example is being quoted here: 'The Madrasa-i-Aliya which was situated in Chaharsu in the Mohalla of Baba Khudaidad and is famous throughout the world for its *darsgah-i-ulumi sharia*, numerous *hujras*, *qaraq qariyans*, *mutawajjihin mutaqqin*, *mutahajjidin*, *hifaz*, *sulha* was built by Shaibani Khan (and known as Madrasa-i Khan also).' Muhammad Salih records that Shaibani had constructed this *madrasa* to commemorate his victory of Samarqand and also to establish something in the memory of Muhammad Sultan who died in 1504. As per information given by Maliha Samarqandi it was repaired in seventeen century by Muhammad Nadir bi Ataliq and later on by Shah Murad (1785-1800). If Abu Tahir Khwaja is to be believed the *madrasa* was given the name of Madrasa-i-Shaibani Khan from the time when both father and son (i.e. Shaibani and his son Timur) died on 29 November 1510 and 17 March 1514 respectively. Mihr Sultan Khanum, the daughter-in-law of Shaibani Khan, thought of building a *madrasa* near the Madrasa-i Khan and her own place of burial so that her head was near the feet of her husband Timur Sultan. In the *Waqf Nama* of the *madrasas*, the first part of this document was compiled by the name of Mihr Sultan Khanam the daughter-in-law of Shaibani Khan with all the legal formalities and mentioning all the movable and immovable property and immense wealth in the document for this *qush madrasa* with all the *haqqut tauliya* and other such expenses (*sarfa-i-waqf* ), *islah o istihkam*, *wazaif*, *rawatib* and *ikhrajat* as mentioned in the document. The *mahsulat* from the agricultural lands were to be spent as the *mutawwali* wanted (*mahsulat-i-aanra Khwah Khud Khurad o Khwah poshad o Khwah bahar kas ki Khwahad dehed*). Several other privileges were granted to the *mutawwali* though his appointment and removal was subject to the will of Shaikhul Islam and the Aqzi-ul Quzzat. The *mudarris* were also to be appointed with care and their salaries were to be disbursed by then from the *quqaf*. Several such *waqf* documents do exist indicating that *madrasas* were by and large nicely funded.[43]

There were other sources of income for these *madrasas*. To quote an example both Shami and Yezdi record that Timur used to visit the *madrasas* before and after the campaigns and distributed stipends, money, etc., among the students. This was not an isolated incident. Each Sultan used to perform such charitable activities. In India the situation was not different.

Apart from the *waqf* endowments assigned to every *madrasa*, there were other sources of income both for the students, teachers. The *madrasas* in India also, had this provision. Sher Shah considered it to be the duty of the monarchs to provide financial assistance to scholars and teachers. There were generous donations and *jagirs* offered by rulers for upkeep of educational institutions. The students were given stipends. Aurangzeb had established innumerable *madrasas* and had fixed scholarships both for the teachers and the students so that they could pursue their studies without financial worries.

Ali Muhammad Khan, the author of *Mirat-i-Ahmadi* says that Aurangzeb had circulated orders to all the provincial *diwans* in his domain that all the students from the highest to the lowest who studied *kashshaf* and *mizan* should be given financial assistance from the provincial treasury with the sanction of the provincial *sadr*. The assistance was given in proportion to students' proficiency. Thus the students who studied *mizan* received 1 *anna* daily, those who studied *munshab*, received 2 *annas* and upto *sharh-i-waqayah* 8 *annas* daily.[44] It is also described that Akramuddin Khan, the *sadr* of Gujarat established *madrasa* at Ahmedabad bearing an expense of Rs. 1,24,000 and requested for some financial assistance from Aurangzeb for running it. The Emperor had allocated the village of Sondrah (Sanoli) and Sibilah and sanctioned the stipend of Rs. 2 daily to the poor. Without citing any source, Ashfaque says that 'Like other Muslim countries, in India also education was free and within the reach of every one.'[45] He himself cites later on 'considerable sum of money was laid aside' by the Mughals for 'extension' of education and 'properties were bequeathed' and stipends were given. However, a closer look at the sources shows that these occasional benefits were not sufficient as the plight of the students was not very good if they were not well-connected. Wasifi says that in 919, there was a severe cold, frost followed by famine and inflation. The students in Khurasan who had neither any scholarship money nor any acquaintance were further distressed as a thief had broken open the lock and stole whatever was there. The ten *talib-i ilm* were in a state of acute poverty and penury approached Wasifi that if he does not come to their rescue they would die of starvation and cold. Although Wasifi had written letters and the students were given the *pustin-i barra*, *pairahan* and *tanbani* and were invited to a feast by Amir Kai Shah, but the condition of the poor students could hardly improve with such meagre assistance. Two of them were so starved that they were compelled to sell their coat (*pustin*) and died of cold. The event compelled Wasifi to write a eulogy to extract some favour from Uzbeg ruler Sultan Abu Said who provided him ten (*ras*) of fat sheep, twenty maund flour (of *arad* ), 100 *khani* and 4 trees for fuel. At least that winter the students could live comfortably thanks to Wasifi.[46] Muhammad Salih had complained that some of the poets and learned men had never seen gold.

There are numerous episodes given by scholars which confirm that there did exist envy, jealousy and rivalry between the scholars which often took the form of acrimonious exchanges.[47] A few examples may be cited here:

After Persian occupation of Khurasan, the famous Maulana Haji had migrated to Samarqand. Babur who could see his worth, extended a warm welcome and appointed him as *mudarris* in the Madrasa of Ulugh Beg. When Samarqand was conquered by the Uzbegs and given to Kuchikunji Khan, Maulana Haji was suspected of his affiliations with the Qizilbash. Although the intercession of wasifi had saved him from Uzbeg wrath and his honour was retrieved, another person Haji Tabrizi cultivated good relationship and close amity with the group of Uzbeg Shaibanids. Such was the trust on the mulla's scholarship that Shaibani had appointed him as *mudarris* in the Madrasa of Ulugh Beg where the *alim-ul-ulamai* was the first condition of teaching (shart-i-tadrisi). Once there arose a misunderstanding between Mir Khwarazmi and another teacher of his time and the former always came earlier than the fixed time and occupied the place while the other teacher waited impatiently for his turn in vain. He therefore, sent Wasifi and certain other *talib-i-ilms* to request him to allocate the time so that there should be no clash of their timings. When Mirza Khwarazmi heard this request he was irritated and burst out that Haji Tabrizi had lost his senses. He does not know that in this *suffa* the condition is that *Mard-i Ghurbai 'Alamtar Shartast*. He should be asked not to overstep his authority and utter such absurd comments. When these sentences were conveyed to Hafiz Tusi the *sadr* of Kuchikunji Khan, he initially laughed but immediately after he started crying and said 'just imagine how the teaching Nadir and that standards and the level of teachers had reached to its *ulema* and the scholarship had gone so low that such men have occupied such high places and uttered such absurd words. There is none who could dare to tell him why and what kind of utterances he come forth from him. When the dignitaries of Samarqand heard about it they took pity and got him appointed in the Madrasa of Khwaja Ahrar.[48]

It is indeed a very interesting feature that whenever the intellectuals felt insecure, they thought of leaving for India. Wasifi quotes several such examples, when there was the onslaught of a large force of 18,000 Qazilbash under Najm-i Sani in Rabi II 918 and there was the despair, dejection and fear in Samarqand Maulana Haji Tabrizi alongwith a group of *tulba* (students) thought of turning towards India. Similarly, when there was some misunderstanding among the Uzbeg princes over the letter of Mir-i Arab and Saiyid Shamsuddin Muhammad Kurti (who was the *mudarris* of Madrasa-i-Ubaidullah Khan) expressed the fear that the in stay in that place was not safe and Wasifi also thought of leaving for India as the students of *madrasa* had also dispersed.[49]

## Patronage to Ulama

In central Asia, almost all the royal in the assembly the *sadat*, *naqib*, *ulama*, *quzzat*, *ashraf* o *aayan* were all present and usually the kings used to preside over such assemblies.

Response to the lectures determined the intelligence of the audience which comprised an assorted lot. There were certain intelligent persons who established their position by one sentence or the dunces who failed to impress the audience. The performance of scholars invited both praises and condemnation while appreciating the intelligence and the eloquence of Maulana Kamaluddin Haji, the Shaikh-ul Islam of Tabriz had commented that during past twelve years when the Shaikh delivered his *dars*, Maulana Haji was always present and never had shirked from commenting when it was essential and always abstained from speaking whenever it was uncalled for.[50]

When Kuchikunji Khan ascended the throne of Samarqand, he 'extended the patronage to the learned men (*ulama* and *fuzala*) in compliance with the injunction min *akram alima faqad akramni*'. During his regime many *madrasas*, *khanqahs*, mosques, cells and charitable institutions (*baqa-i khair*) which had earlier been shelved (*indaras yafta bud*) again started thronging with life, as it had been repaired and decorated. The Madrasa of Mirza Ulugh Beg was again repaired and his astronomical researches and teaching progress was also ensured. While the Ottoman Government did not directly deal with the administrative planning and management of education which was the responsibility of municipality, the Uzbeg kings themselves took keen interest in the construction of *madrasas* and appointment of teachers. Frequently, assemblies were held and the high and low of the cities were invited for discussions and exhibit their worth.[51] Kuchikunji Khan had invited Wasifi in his assembly of scholars and men of pen.[52]

In the night assemblies (*majlis-i shabana*) held at Madrasa-i Khania, the scholars gathered and Khan Ubaidullah himself presided over these sessions, other such assemblies were held by Souyunch Khwaja Khan. There are many episodes given by Ruzbehan Isfahani and Khwandmir about the assemblies in this *madrasa farmans*, *nishans* to princes and provincial rulers always carried the instruction to offer patronage to the *ulama*, *sulha*, etc. Even under the Mongols, there was an additional grant allocated for the purpose. The sultans of Delhi were keen to decorate their courts with brilliant talents. The Mughals too had instituted the *suyurghals* (subsistence allowance) and excessive rewards to attract the foreigners. In Central Asia, the practice of holding literary assemblies was a regular feature. In such assemblies, there was the possibility of rising to the heights of ones' career if the kings or their *wazirs* had noticed and appreciated the works of such fortune seekers as happened in case of several such ordinary folks. The scholars took pride in their knowledge and looked down upon the less qualified and less knowledgeable dignitaries. The learned men could even challenge the scholarship of higher officials with ease. Khwaja Yusuf Malamati, the *wazir* of Khan-i Azam Kuchikunji Khan was freely criticized by Wasifi in the *Manazara* and presented a *zam ba ma yashabbahul midh*. To save his honour Khwaja was advised to tactfully handle the situation and bestow upon Wasifi a *saropa*, 100 *khani* which was immediately sent to him. When an ashamed Wasifi really praised him in a euology of 35 verses another reward of 350 *tangcha-i khani* were given to him.[53]

## NOTES

1. Md. Ashfaque Ahmad, *System of Education in Medieval India 1526-1761*, New Delhi, 1987; Krishna Lal Ray, *Education in Medieval India*; Yusuf Husain, 'The Educational System in Medieval India', *Islamic Culture*, vol. XXX, no. 2, April 1956, Hyderabad, pp. 106-20; Josh Pedersen, 'Some Aspects of the History of the Madrasa', *Islamic Culture*, Oct. 1929, pp. 525-37; P.N. Ojha, 'Some Aspects of Education in India under the Great Mughals', Indian History Congress, 1950, pp. 234-33.
2. *Futuh-ul-Buldan*, vol. II, pp. 187, 443, Md. Ashfaque Ahmad, *System of Education in Medieval India 1526-1761*, New Delhi, 1987, pp. 2-8.
3. *Maasir-i-Kiram*, vol. I, pp. 221-2.
4. Ibid.
5. *Ain-i-Akbari*, vol. I, Blochmann, pp. 25, 278-79; Krishna Ray, pp. 44-5; also see Pedersen, op. cit., pp. 525-37.
6. Padersen, op. cit., pp. 525-37.
7. *Ain-i Akbari*, vol. I, Blochmann, pp. 25, 278-9; Krishna Ray, pp. 44-5.
8. Varonina, V, *Arkhitectural Pamitniki Sredni Azi* (*Architectural Monuments of Middle Asia*), Leningrad, 1969, p. 28.
9. Ibid., p. 29.
10. Varonina, pp. 29-30.
11. Ibid., pp. 28-30.
12. Ibid.
13. *Tarikh-i Farishta*, vol. I, Bombay, 1831, pp. 464-5; *Tarikh-i Firuzshahi*, Badr Chach had in a chronogram on this building highly praised its garden, pillars, engravings, edifice, Calcutta, 1862, pp. 562-66; Eng. tr., vol. III, p. 441.
14. *Tabaqat-i Nasiri*, London, 1873, p. 667, Eng. tr. by Raverty; *Tarikh-i Farishta*, vol. I, Eng. tr. Briggs, p. 461; Elliot & Dowson, vol. III, pp. 316-17, 343; *Nuzhat-ul Khawatir*, vol. I, p. 11, quoted by Ashfaque, p. 10; Barni, pp. 460, 564; Al Qal Qashandi, vol. V, pp. 68-9.
15. Ibid.
16. *Tuzuk*, p. 5, *Farman*, no. 3.

17. Ashfaque, p. 15.
18. *Tabaqat-i Akbari*, vol. II, p. 276, *Mirat-i Ahmadi*, vol. I, p. 272.
19. Wasifi, vol. I; Tehran edn., pp. 40-1.
20. Wasifi, 38-9.
21. Wasifi, I, pp. 164-5.
22. Wasifi, p. 325.
23. Wasifi, *Badai-ul Waqai*, pp. 4-8.
24. Ashfaque, p. 5
25. Ashfaque, p. 5
26. Ashfaque, p. 6
27. Barni, 352-3.
28. Barni, 352; see Abul Fazl's Letters of Khan-i Khanan in Har Sih Daftar, *Insha-i Abul Fazl*.
29. *Muntakhab-ut Tawarikh*, vol. I, p. 357.
30. *Bustan-al Salatin*, p. 162.
31. *Maasir-ul Kiram*, vol. II, pp. 227, 345, 529.
32. *Ain-i Akbari*, vol. I, p. 143; Ashfaque, pp. 33-8.
33. Ibid., I, p. 143; *Akhbar-ul Akhyar*, p. 294.
34. Yusuf, p. 113.
35. *Shahjahan Nama*, vol. I, p. 31.
36. Maasir, p. 535.
37. *Shahjahan Nama*, vol. I, p. 31.
38. *Tazkira-i Ulema-i Hind*, p. 3, quoted by Ashfaque, p. 78.
39. Afif, pp. 268-73; *Muntakhab-ut Tawarikh*, vol. III, p. 105; *Maasir-ul Kiran*, vol. I, p. 150.
40. *Muntakhab-ut Tawarikh*, vol. I, p. 342; vol. III, p. 201; *Akbar Nama*, vol. I, p. 201; *Tabaqat-i Akbari*, vol. II, p. 311; *Tuzuk-i Jahangiri*, p. 6; *Shahjahan Nama*, vol. I, p. 31.
41. *Siyar-ul Mutakhirin*, p. 263.
42. *Maasir-ul Kiram*, vol. I, p. 116.
43. *Waqf Nama-i Shaibani Khan*, 1969, pp. 4-43.
44. Yusuf, p. 117
45. Yusuf, pp. 117-18; Ashfaque, pp. 11, 83.
46. Wasifi, I, ed., pp. 62-78.
47. Wasifi, I, ed., pp. 41-4.
48. Wasifi, pp. 58-9.
49. Wasifi, pp. 113-14, 294.
50. Wasifi, I, p. 56.
51. Wasifi, pp. 38-9.
52. Wasifi, pp. 254, 310.
53. Wasifi, I, ed., pp. 44-55.

# Indo-Central Asian Trade Relations

Central Asia which had earlier been one of the important regions on the old Silk Road is said to have become commercially a 'subdued phenomenon' during the sixteenth century.[1] During this period the Ottomans made feeble overtures to establish an alliance with Central Asia against the increasing challenge posed by the Portuguese and the Russians. This was countered by the Russo-Persian coordination against the allies and the subsequent disturbances and conflicts created alternately by the Kazaks and the Persians in the region. European travellers observed with dismay that in the sixteenth century there was no hope of good trade in any part of the country and that the trade in Persia and Tartaria alike was of 'little utterance and small profit'.[2] To an early medieval Persian chronicler, however, the brisk commercial transactions at the various entrepots of Central Asia seemed to show no decline. In Ibn-i Hauqal's estimation, the wealth of the people of Khwarazm (in the absence of mines of gold, silver, and precious stones) depended mainly upon two things: cattle breeding and trade in slaves from Saqlab, the Caspian Sea and its vicinity, and in the trade of ermine furs and skins.[3] Writing in 1405 Clavijo comments: 'Every year to Samarqand much merchandise of all kinds came from Cathay, India, Tartaria and from many other quarters for in the countries round the Samarqand territory commerce is very flourishing'.[4] Ibn-i Battuta refers to the nice Khwarazm melons which were sweet and syrupy and dried in the sun; these were carried to India and China and nothing among the dried fruits seemed better. The merchants brought these to Delhi. Similarly, Ibn-i Battuta refers to the '*alu*', dried and carried to India and China. Later on in the fifteenth century the trade with China[5] was hampered. Clavijo[6] also found each corner of Samarqand thronging with crowds of people from diverse sects, creeds, and races and speaking many languages—Mongols of Central Asia; turban-clad Iranians, and Indians, Russians, and Chinese. The caravans on camels with the loud noise of ringing bells, and loads of merchandise (*kala*) passed through the city. They disembarked and placed their luggage in the vestibule or inner yard of the caravansarais. The shops were full of Chinese goods (*parandi chini*), as it was just six months' journey. Leather and cotton goods from Russia and Central Asia, medicines, swords, armour, cuirasses, and precious stones from India which were in abundance. Babur refers to the dried plums of Bukhara, the best paper on the world manufactured in Samarqand, excellent wood *tabulghu*, and *cramoisy* velvet being taken from one place to another.[7]

Isfahani notes appreciatively that Andijan was 'perhaps developed exclusively for trade purpose'. Uruganj and Arquq were the two famous entrepots in the Khwarazm region.[8] Rarities were brought from different places to Sighnaq, which happened to be a 'junction of traders' (Mahall-i Tujjar),[9] from Transoxiana, Kashghar, Khutlan, and Turkestan. In the sixteenth century Yasi was also said to be a centre of brisk trade where novelties from the Uzbek countries (in Dasht) in the north and from Andijan up to Khitai (China) in the east were brought by traders.[10]

From Dasht and Haji Tarkhan, traders used to carry away sheep, horses, camels, and other rarities like furs and skins (*samur* and *sanjab*), strong arrows and bows, and fine silken cloth.[11] Several articles like shoes, cotton cloth, saddles, arms, and a number of consumer goods were supplied by the Central Asian traders to the steppes. In return they received wool, skins, slaves, and cotton.[12]

In the presence of a great variety of handicrafts, internal trade flourished. Several trade routes were established connecting Samarqand and other towns and villages of the Shaibanid empire. Caravan *sarais*[13] were built on these routes. In certain areas, bridges were built over rivers, and reservoirs and wells were also provided on the routes. Internal trade was carried on between distant towns and villages. For example, wheat and barley had been brought from Tirmiz to Khwarazm since Ibn-i Battuta's time as during the summer the river Amu was navigable as far as Tirmiz, the journey down-stream taking ten days between Khwarazm and Tirmiz.[14] When there was a shortage of grain during the Herat campaign, Abdullah Khan requested Khwaja Juibari to send 1,000 camels laden with 10,000 *mans* of barley from the stocks of Andkhud. If, however, the grains were not available in Andkhud, supplies were to be brought from the *sarkar* of Merv.[15]

The market relationship between the city and the village had always existed. Fruits, corn, and other rural-based products were brought to the city for sale, while certain manufactures were taken from towns to the villages. The sources refer to the sale of melons and grapes at the city gates.[16] Metal vessels, clothes, saddles, and cheap jewellery were most in demand from village consumers. The cloth imported from one town to another carried the name of its place of manufacture. The caravans, comprising a number of camels, transported goods from one city to another. Each magnate used to own several hundred camels. The Juibari shaikhs had more than 60 *qatars* (rows) of camels, each consisting of twelve camels.[17]

In the fifteenth and sixteenth centuries, monetization developed to some extent in the countryside. During the first three quarters of the sixteenth century, small-scale retail trade was carried on in copper coins. As discussed elsewhere[18] the opening of temporary mints in big and small towns, suburbs, and even villages for the exchange of coins shows the expansion of money use.

Apart from generating commercial trade for its own products, the role of Central Asia in international commerce as an intermediary region was also important. India's commercial relations with Novgorod and the Baltic during eighth to the eleventh centuries 'carried down the Oxus and up the Volga' by the Russians of the steppes has been confirmed by Le Conte d'Alveilla on the basis of his numismatic studies.[19] The Sughdian centres of the Chinese silk trade were at Samarqand, Kash, and Paykand which functioned as intermediaries between the East and the West. Suq as Sughd (the market of Sughdians), was one of the most ancient quarters of the city of Merv.[20] According to Bento de Goes, 'Even in the very earliest periods of history, it was through Turkestan that China and the West were in touch with each other.'[21] It seems that no direct contact between India and Russia had been established.[22] It is reported that the Bukharan envoys to India in 1671 were asked about the products of Russia that could be acquired directly from Central Asia and which ones were available in Central Asia. The envoy gave the entire list mentioning such things as fish bones, sables, shelves, vixen, and so on which could be supplied from Russia through Central Asia to India.[23] Similarly, an Indian merchant Mail Baqqal who was in Moscow in 1675 along with his companions is said to have reported that several Russian things like sables, vixen of varied colours, fish bones, mirrors of different sizes, velvet, grey falcons, and greyhound dogs were in much demand in India.[24] It can be inferred that the trade relations between Russia and India could be pursued indirectly through Central Asia. Although a Russian envoy is said to have come to Aurangzeb in 1696, the Russian traders do not seem to have had free, consistent, and direct access to the Indian market.[25]

Clavijo found the markets of Samarqand 'amply stored with merchandise imported from distant and foreign countries'.[26] Indigo brought from India and sold in the markets of Samarqand and Bukhara by the *neelfarushan* (indigo sellers) was also exported from Central Asia to Moscow. *Ruyan* (madder) was one of the export items to Russia brought by the Khivan traders along with cotton cloth since the Russians sold madder to the *Kazan* manufacturers of red calico.[27] Traders from various countries, including Arabia and Persia, assembled in the two large stone caravansarais built by Khwaja Juibari in the Charasui and Sarrafan areas in and outside Bukhara.[28] Another *sarai* was built by Khwaja Qutub-ul Akbar. Samarqand served as a trans-shipment centre for *baqam* (Brazilian wood) brought here from other countries.[29] Samarqand was the centre for the production of azure, golden dye, and other paints, though Jenkinson mentions that these colours were imported from India.[30]

The role of the Bukhara traders in the Russo-Persian trade is evident from the documents of the 'secret deals' containing the lists of items traded between the two lands.[31] To Astrakhan came caravans from Central Asia, Iran, the Caucasus, Armenia, and India. The Ottomans also played an intermediary role in the caravan trade between the countries of East Asia and West Asia through Central Asia.[32] The traders from Persia, Arabia, Turkey, and Kazan lived in Samarqand and Bukhara and carried on trade in Central Asian handicrafts through Bukhara. The Tartar merchants from Kazan were called 'Bukhara Yurtchi'.[33]

The cotton-growing areas of Turkestan exported fabrics to Iraq.[34] From Merv *abresham* (silk thread) was exported to other countries.[35] Bukhara woollen carpets were especially in demand. Although there are references in the historical records to exports from Central Asia to Egypt in earlier centuries, there is little evidence of trade relations between the areas in the sixteenth century. However, stray references to *katani misri,* Egyptian *katan* (cotton), and (*teghi misri*) Egyptian sword do occur.[36] Zendani cloth was much in demand in Iraq, Fars, Karmina, and India from the seventh to the nineteenth centuries.[37]

The arrival of Central Asian merchants in Asia Minor is mentioned by Ibn-i Battuta.[38] The role of the Ottoman empire in Central Asian commerce needs to be discussed separately. Throughout the sixteenth century, the Ottomans tried to find an ally against Russia and Persia among the Shaibanid rulers by establishing direct relations with the Khanates. Trade was to be revived along the route stretching from Khwarazm through Astrakhan to the Crimea, a route that was then under Ottoman control. Ibn-i Battuta describes the coastal town of Azaq (Azov) as a 'well-built' town, visited by the Genoese and other merchants.[39] Bayazid Bayat refers to the place 'Tokhta' as the 'bajgah of Balkh'.[40] In Ibn-i Battuta's time, Hormuz was a 'well-provisioned' market from where the products of India were exported to the two Iraqs, Fars, and Khurasan. Abbé Raynal found it 'an agreeable city in the east'[41] where 'persons from all parts of the globe exchanged their commodities and transacted their business with an air of politeness and attention seldom seen in other places of trade'. A number of letters were exchanged between the Ottoman rulers and various Uzbek sultans, the latter pleading for Ottoman intervention against Persian 'high handedness'.[42] Almost simultaneously the rulers of Shirvan and Gilan also asked for the intervention of the Sultan of Turkey against the Persians. The Ottoman *wazir,* Sokollu Muhammad Pasha, was thus 'planning to solve the Persian and Muscovite problems in one stroke and the Czar and Persia hastened to draw together'.[43] The conquest of the Khanate of Siberia (1598) by Russia also had long-lasting effect. Apart from facilitating the penetration of Russia into Central Asia at a later stage, it also caused traffic between Eastern Europe and Eastern Asia to move over to Siberia in the following centuries, thus bypassing Central Asia. Consequently, the importance of Turkestan declined considerably.[44]

## Trade with India

In Babur's time, there were two trade marts on the land routes between India and Khurasan, namely, Kabul and Kandahar. The caravans to Kabul came from Kashghar, Farghana, Turkestan, Bukhara, Samarqand, Balkh, Herat and Badakhshan, and the merchants made higher profits in Kabul as it was an excellent trading centre.[45] Clavijo says that from India were brought to Samarqand the rarer spices which were the most costly such as nutmeg, cloves, mace, and cinnamon.[46] Every year caravans of ten, fifteen, or twenty thousand heads of horses carrying slaves, white cloth, sugar candy, refined and common sugar, and aromatic roots came to Kabul from Hindustan. Many traders were not content with a profit of 30 or 40 on 10 (i.e. 300 to 400 per cent).[47] Over three hundred years later Burnes (1837) tells us of Luhani merchants carrying precisely the same articles of trade.[48] Hafiz Tanish[49] refers to a *sarai* situated on a transit route (Peshawar) where a large crowd of people was always engaged in commerce (*sud o sauda*). Hafiz Tanish[50] also refers to a multitude of traders from Khurasan, Turkestan, and Transoxiana who had spent quite a long time in the countries of 'India, the Deccan, and Gujarat'. While returning to their country, they brought with them the rarities of various places in India, and stopped in Peshawar, then a dependency of Kabul, to obtain local supplies.

According to Babur, Abul Fazl, Hafiz Tanish, and Jenkinson, the chief commodities of export from Central Asia to India in the sixteenth century were almonds (also called *kandi badam*), apples, pears, raisins, Khwarazm melons, Russian furs, hunting birds, red hides, raw silks, slaves, and horses.[51] Abul Fazl gives a long list of Central Asian fruits (both fresh and dried) along with their growing seasons and prevalent rates.[52] Bernier found Central Asian fruits in Indian markets and observed that Indians consumed an immense quantity of fresh fruits from Samarqand, Bukhara, Balkh, and Persia, including melons, grapes, and pears which were eaten in Delhi and purchased at very high prices throughout the winter.[53] Likewise dried fruits, such as Bukhara prunes (*alubukhara*), almonds, pistachio, plums, apricots, various small nuts, and white and black raisins were also available the whole year round.[54] Indian merchants brought fewer goods to Central Asia, exporting fine whites for turbans and other whites made of cotton and *crasca* for apparel, tea, spices, pearls, and dye colours.[55]

One of the most important and profitable trades of Central Asia to India was the export of horses.[56] Babur,[57] Manucci,[58] Bernier,[59] and others refer to the continuous import of horses from the Uzbek regions of Balkh, Bukhara, and Kabul to India. Babur claimed that the number of horses coming down to Kabul annually ranged between 7,000 and 10,000.[60] Even in Yuan Chwang's time, Samarqand was 'yielding many fine horses'.[61]

Abul Fazl reports that 'droves after droves of horses arrive from Turan and Iran' and in his time there were 12,000 in the stables of Akbar. The horses were usually brought from Iraq, Turkey, Turkestan, Badakhshan, Qirghiz, Sherwan, Tibet, Kashmir, and other countries.[62] Ibn-i Battuta found the horses in the Uzbek empire of Dashti Qipehaq. According to the classification given by Abul

Fazl, the horses 'imported from Turan, though strong and well formed', belonged to the fourth class. The best horses were the Arab breeds, the second were Persian, the third class were Mujannas (Turkish or Persian), and the Uzbek.[63] Manucci says:

> Most of the horses used by the Mughals came from the regions of Balkh, Bukhara, and Kabul and thence came every year more than, 1,000,000 horses and on them the king maketh a great profit by the duty he imposes, the usual number taken being 12,000. The horses called Turki are courageous in war, can stand much fatigue and never forsake their masters unto death.[64]

Manucci probably exaggerated in his estimate of the number of horses. Bernier says that India received 25,000 horses from the Uzbeks.[65]

Indian traders were seen in Astrakhan and Haji Tarkhan by Barbara Contarin in the fifteenth century, and by Jenkinson in 1558.[66] Indian merchants and Moncylenders lived in one of the quarters of Bukhara.

During Timur's time[67] the two prominent and profitable points of the trade routes were said to be the two iron gates (*darband-i ahinin*).[68] Babur says that there were seven roads in the Hindukush mountains.[69] Abul Fazl also mentions seven routes used by the people of Turan to travel from Balkh and Badakhshan to reach Kabul and five practicable roads to Turan from India, namely, Karapati, Khyber, Bangash, Naghar, and Farmul. While Karapati was not used in Babur's time, travellers from Turan and India took the Khyber route in Akbar's time.[70] This fact is corroborated by the accounts in the *Abdullah Nama* as Hafiz Tanish refers to the caravans of Indian traders from the Deccan, Gujarat, Multan, and other regions of India who carried goods in 1584 through Peshawar for Khurasan, Transoxiana, and Turkestan.[71] The same routes were used at least until the eighteenth century. Chandra Bhan Brahmin (1230 AH) also mentions the same seven routes between Kabul, Badakhshan, Balkh, and the Hindukush through which the Turanis travel to and from India.[72]

### Trade with Russia

The trade of Central Asia with Russia had considerably developed after the conquest of Astrakhan and Kazan. The Russian sources speak of 'friends' (merchants) from Urganj who came to Astrakhan in July 1557 from Hajim Khan as envoys and reached Moscow in

October 1558 along with the Bukhara envoy.[73] The Jenkinson mission was also an attempt to promote commercial relations between Central Asia and Russia.[74] In Moscow itself there was a Tajik colony engaged in trade.[75] Abul Ghazi refers to the exchange of a number of embassies and trade missions between Russia and Central Asia.[76]

Soviet scholars describe a special pattern of trade existing between Russia and Central Asia. According to Baikova and Yuldasheva, individual trade was not encouraged. Individual traders who could manage to send or take their goods by any route did so at their own risk. All sorts of taxes (sale, custom, etc.) were imposed on them in addition to the *zakat*. Generally, the Russo–Central Asian trade was of three categories, i.e. (1) the usual trade in cheaper wares for common use such as cotton fabrics; (2) the sale of the goods of the Khan or the Czar through his own personal representatives, merchants coming with the envoys. No custom duty was imposed upon these. They comprised an assortment of cheap as well as expensive objects; and (3) custom-free trade between the first merchants of the two states called 'amateurish feast' or 'disguised trade', consisting of the exchange of the rare goods of both countries (in which gifts exchanged between the rulers were valued by the experts and gifts of the same value were returned).[77]

An important feature of Russo-Central Asian trade in the sixteenth century was the beginning of state trading though in a rudimentary form. Due to Abdullah's efforts to combine diplomatic assignments with commercial responsibilities for his ambassadors to Moscow, trade relations with Russia progressed further.[78]

Khwaja Qutub-ul Abrar is said to have sent a certain Maulana Jan Muhammad from Bukhara to Moscow for a year. He returned after enjoying the hospitality of the Czar and conducting commercial transactions[79] and concluding favourable agreements. Hafiz Tanish refers to the return of an envoy whom Abdullah Khan sent to Moscow to bring back falcons (*shunqar*), armours, and coats of mail (*zirah*, *joshan*).[80]

In 1557, the Uzbek Khans sent an embassy to Czar Ivan IV (1530-84), congratulating him on his victory in Astrakhan and requesting him to widen the route to south-eastern Europe with a grant of free trade to Central Asian merchants in Moscow. Free trade in this context meant 'the freedom to carry on trade in any place, commodity; to sell your goods at your own price and buy whatever you want'. The Caspian Sea region became especially advantageous for Central Asian traders as the Khivan Khans, as their documents reveal, often requested for permission to increase the trade between Astrakhan and Karaghan haven (on the eastern bank of the Caspian Sea) where twice a year in spring and autumn merchants gathered and even the Czar's pearl (boat) came with Eastern and Russian merchants. Astrakhan *voivode* (governor in ancient Russia) supervised the trade, provided *strelets* (soldiers) for safety, verified documents, checked merchandise, and sent information through the *khabarshik* (messenger) to Khiva and Bukhara. The striking of commercial transactions continued for a month on the shores of the Caspian Sea. At the end of the period, officials came to write down the details for imposing taxes.[81] The distance between Karaghan and Astrakhan was traversed from between two to eight days, depending on the weather. In Astrakhan, Kazan, and Samarra, envoys and merchants stayed back and waited till the Czar received the king's *yirligh* and allowed them an audience. Nevertheless, Jenkinson found 'this island of merchants' near Kazan completely 'forsaken'. Although 'earlier merchants from Russia, Kazan, Crimea, Nogailands and from other countries did resort to keep mart for buying and selling here, the place was now (1558) without any such resort thither or at any place about it from Moscow until . . . Caspian.'[82] Jenkinson also notes that there was no trade worth the writing, nor was there any hope of trade in all those parts worth the following. Ibn-i Arab Shah writing in the mid-fifteenth century refers to the 'convoys of travellers' from Khwarazm to the Crimea earlier which had stopped during his own time: 'none moves or rests and nothing ranges there but antelopes and camels'.[83] Similarly, Jenkinson found that Astrakhan had 'beggarly and small trade though Russian, Persian and Tartar traders'.[84]

The main items of export from Russia were red hides, sheepskins, woollen garments of various kinds, falcons, armlets, vests, sugar, hardware, tin, mercury, candles, kerosene, paraffin, armaments, wooden vessels, metal goods, bridles, and saddles. In exchange Russia imported cotton wool, varied types of silk, *crasca*, and dye stuff.[85] Narshakhi says that many villages near Bukhara, particularly Zandan, prepared nice cotton fabrics called *zandanchi* which were not only used by the local people but which were also sent to Iran, Fars, Kirman, India, and other regions.[86] Writing in 1552, Rhode reports that the Russians, particularly the common people, could not do without *alacha* and *shai*. These were light, inexpensive but durable textiles and good for caftans.[87] Bukhara cotton in Moscow had no competitors due to its cost and quality.[88] Thus, the main items of export from Bukhara to Moscow were textiles, raw cotton, Karakul skins (Astrakhan or Persian lamb), wool hides, carpets, and silks like *atlas* which, in the words of the Bukhara envoy Mulla Farrukh, 'was not available at all in Bukhara or when available was of coarse quality'. Even in the nineteenth century, Shergul Afghan says that cotton and dry fruits were quite profitable for the *dihqans* in their trade with Russia and Siberia for these fetched them cent per cent profit (*yaki bar sad faeda midihand*).[89] Shergul Afghan also refers to the commerce in cotton, fresh and dry fruits, dried grapes, apricots and apples especially sent to Russia and Siberia from Tashkent.[90] In 1585 alone there were 4,200 *zendani* pieces among the 5,000 pieces of material sent for sale to Russia.[91] After the fall of Kazan and later Astrakhan to the Russians, Russia had its own ships in the Caspian Sea in the sixteenth century. These ships (called the Czar's Bussi or pearls) were sent at least twice a year, mainly to obtain animals, horses, and other such merchandise for the Czar. Owing to the extortionate demands made by the feeders and rowers (on the Czar's boats) from the Central Asian merchants, there often arose serious trouble between them whenever Central Asian merchants boarded the Bussi. In a petition to Czar Ivanovich in May 1589, a certain Muhammad Ali complained that rowmen and feeders had taken away 5 *caftans*, 6 *zendani* silk pieces, and 60 *sash*, all of which even in the lowest estimate cost 22 roubles and 20 kopeks. The merchandise was always opened for the Czar's 'first pick' by his trusted servants who usually thought themselves entitled a 'second pick'. When the tax collectors came to see the merchants at the latters' first halting place, wanting them to declare their goods sold to the Khan, they charged a fee before declaration on each good or by weighing the merchandise. Over and above these were the Czar's taxes. These merchants again paid a number of other taxes like the *tamgha* fees and the charges of tax collectors, 'main', ordinary and 'fives'.[92]

There were two main trade routes between Central Asia and Russia in the south-east and Siberia. The first was called the 'Karaghan haven', being the Caspian Sea route via Astrakhan, and the other was the land route along the Volga from Astrakhan to the interior of Moscow. The voyage from Karaghan to Astrakhan lasted between two to eight days depending upon the weather. The Siberian land route ran from Tobol via Irtish, Ishim to Turkestan, and then to Bukhara by a relatively safe road; from Bukhara to Siberia a trade route also ran through Kazakstan.[93]

Official documents of tax collectors in Siberia and *aul* orders (issued to nomadic regions) show that a number of petitions were submitted by Siberian and Bukharan merchants. For example, Alim Sulaiman petitioned with his companions, demanding from Russian officials the restoration of their right to carry on trade. Such documents offer evidence of competition between the merchants settled in Siberia and the local merchants. It appears from the Bukhara petitions that for the Bukharians it was beneficial to stand by the privileges given to them by Moscow. The *yirlighs* of the Khans and others of the Czars contain continuous reassurances for respecting the protection of free trade 'as existing earlier'. There is, however, no mention of the agreed upon terms in clear words. One thing is certain: that trade, with whomsoever it was conducted, its chief beneficiaries were the exchequers of only the Czar and the Khan. The regulations were tilted consistently from one side to another to serve the Czar's interests. The permission for free trade (excluding furs and other forbidden things) was given among others to Jenkinson's Moscow Company of Englishmen for twenty years on the Volga–Caspian Sea route.[94]

The privileges granted to the English merchants in 1569 by the Czar authorized them 'to be and abide freely, to barter and bargain freely all wares of sale without custom of people', not only in Russia but also 'to pass through our land to Boghar, Persia, Caspian and other countries'.[95] They were also asked to bring 'fine wares out of England or from Bukhara, Persia, etc.'. The first pick was done by the Czar whose 'Chancellor' had a look at them and selected those 'needful' for him. The remaining articles would then be bartered or sold. Similarly, these 'Russian adventures' were to serve these English merchants in trade. They were not to be checked at Astrakhan and Kashan and 'our authorized people were to quietly let them pass, not viewing their wares nor taking any toll or custom of their wares'.[96] These privileges were exclusively for the English merchants. Two more documents were issued in August 1596 and December 1609 by Feodore Ivanovich (1584-98) and Ivan. An order dated 10 February 1596[97] issued from Moscow ordered the opening of trade between the local inhabitants and the coming Bukhara and

Nogai traders, who could also go forward without hindrance to Tobol and other Siberian towns. Another order of 31 August 1596 allowed the Bukhara and Nogai traders to carry on the free trade of 'forbidden things' like Siberian fur, saddles, axes, etc., and also free of custom duty. The Bukhara traders could move with their merchandise in the north as a result of the Moscow document of 1600.[98]

During the years 1620-30, the Kalmuk invasions from the east disrupted trade, and the indifferent attitude of the Czar towards the high-handedness of his officers, the harassment of Central Asian merchants, and the complaints of the Khans further aggravated the situation. Things came to such a pass that Isfandyar Khan (1623-42) of Khiva wrote a letter to the Czar complaining that while Russian merchants travelled and traded comfortably in his territory, the Khivan merchants were harassed by Russian captains and were compelled to sell their goods at less than the cost price or were denied passage and that officials in Astrakhan levied heavy illegal duties upon them. Notwithstanding the Czar's reassurances, the harassment of Central Asian merchants continued and the Khiva and Bukhara ambassador—merchants in 1623 received a very impolite reception at the Czar's court.[99]

The kings often had a share in the commercial enterprises. It is said that Ulugh Beg gave money to the merchants to engage in trade and in return received a share of the profit.[100] A merchant of Turkestan named Fazil, who had been coming to Shaibani, received the status of Tarkhan, and was even assigned the task of supervising the defence of the gate of Samarqand.[101] Hussain Alauddin, a trader from Bukhara, used to have many transactions with the Sultans. The Uzbek Khan Ubaidullah is reported to have been in his debt.[102]

Sometimes the kings sent their representatives to buy luxury goods for their personal use as these were not produced indigenously.[103] A *souzomiz* (order) of Imam Quli dated early June 1633 orders the *hukkam*, *ummal*, *alighdaran*, *qarawuls*, and *rahdars* of the *wilayat* of Russia not to demand any *rahdari* or *kharj*, *baj*; to allow the merchant to travel along which ever route he wished without any interference, and to let him buy the goods, grains, spices, and rarities (*asbab*, *ajnas*, *masaleh*, *aqmasha*, and *ajnasi-nafisa*) by way of trading (*ba tariq i saudagari*) to purchase for the imperial needs (*ba'aze az zaruriyat i sarkar i khassa*) from India, Iraq, Kazan, and Moscow.[104]

The merchants themselves were entirely dependent on the ruling class, and only a few privileged persons could carry on trade on favourable terms. Alkashifi refers to a number of Khwajas like Khwaja Kalan, Khwaja Maulana Sa'aduddin, Shamsuddin Muhammad Ruhi, Khwaja Juibari, and Khwaja Qutubul Islam who travelled far and wide for commercial transactions and who sent their representatives to Moscow and other places for profitable trade (*sud o sauda*).[105] The Tarkhan traders continued their commercial activities in indigenous and imported goods. In their own vested interests, the elite supported this privileged merchant class, shifting the share of collections from them to the shoulders of those who were expected 'to pay *zakat* at the proper time and avoid appropriation of others' property'.[106] Unlike the Tarkhani granted to the landlords and other such magnates, the trading Tarkhans were completely exempt from all forms of taxes, state dues, customs, *padnashini*, and even voluntary formalities to the local and central rulers. One such trader, though not himself of Samarqand, received Tarkhani privileges in lieu of his services from Shaibani Khan.[107] The Tarkhani privileges could be given to the foreign traders as well, and exemption from some taxes were granted to them. One such person, Haji Ilyas Chelebi, was given the Tarkhani or exemption from the *tamgha*, *kharaj*, as well as an exemption from the fulfilment of the *ulagh* in the territory of Transoxiana. Certain *nishans* exempting the grantee from all taxes and obligations refer to 14 such taxes.[108] Another *nishan*—a specimen of Tarkhan grants refers to the order of the ruler exempting the holder from *darughagi*, *rahdari*, *khidmatana*, *kishtibani*, and unforeseen demands. Still another such *nishan* issued to a merchant refers to exemption from *baj*, *kharaj*, *tamgha*, *zakat*, and *ulagh*.[109]

The internal market apparently suffered from a shortage of supplies of various commodities. Wasifi drafted two letters, one on behalf of Sultan Ali Muhtasib and addressed to Khwaja Shaikh Muhammad Diwan, requesting him to release some peas and pulses (*mash-i-gurinj*) from his store as the petitioner was unable to acquire them from the market. A letter of Maulana Fathullah Haravi addressed to a candlestick maker (*shamma'a*), Khwaja Husain, asks him to provide some candles as these were not available in the Samarqand market for the past several days.[110]

The trading communities in Central Asia were Sarts, Tajiks, and Jews.[111] In later centuries the wholesale trade in silkworms in the Khanates was controlled by the Bukhara Jews.[112] Although the existence of credit operations, letters of credit (*suftah* or *suftaja*), pay orders within a time limit and *khatt-i-sarraf* (cheques for local transactions) in the form of 'dumb bartering' are mentioned in the sources, no detailed information about the working of these is available. Muqminova says that the wholesale trade was carried on not only in ready money but also by promissory notes (*tamassuk*). One such legal document signifying the receipt of goods was prepared at a *qazikhana* in Samarqand. The document refers to the delayed payment for textiles. In the list of goods received there are mentioned 14 names of textile articles, most of them being of Indian origin.[113]

## Reasons for the Decline in Trade

The Central Asian trade followed an erratic pattern throughout the sixteenth century. This was undoubtedly due in part to lawlessness and civil wars which threatened peaceful commerce in and around Central Asia. The strained relations of Central Asian rulers with certain neighbouring countries also caused commercial blockades.[114] For example, Shaibani issued a *farman* that the people of Turkestan should not have any contact with the merchants from the Kazak lands and that the Kazak traders should be harassed, deprived of their belongings, and even killed, if they were found in Turkestan and Khwarazm.[115] During the period (1586-98) the import of Central Asian goods to Siberia declined considerably owing to wars between Abdullah Khan and the Kazak ruler, Tawwakkul. Consequently, Moscow merchants replaced Bukhara traders in Siberia. The death of Tawwakkul and the conquest of the Khanate of Siberia (1598) by the Russians further restricted Siberian trade with Central Asia.[116]

Commercial relations with Persia and China also fell on bad days due to recurring hostilities in the case of the former and disorders in the intervening zones in the case of the latter. During the wars in Qandahar, a group of Hindustani traders in Kalat 'fell a prey to Babur's followers who wanted to plunder them as they were coming to an enemy's country'. Babur, however, persuaded his men to accept *peshkash* instead.[117]

While recounting the twenty years of 'most perfect peace and security' under Mansur Khan, Haidar Dughlat says that anyone could travel alone from Kamul in Khitai to Andijan without having any duties levied upon him and would be taken every night as a guest into some house on the road at that time.[118] Similarly, Clavijo describes the peaceful atmosphere and opportunities provided for trade under Timur. But the accounts of Sidi Ali Reis (1553-6) and Jenkinson (1558) present a very different picture of Central Asia. Sidi Ali Reis speaks of the Nogai tribe 'committing violence' against travellers and the roads being 'swarmed with robbers and highwaymen'.[119] Jenkinson was harassed by thieves on his return journey and even his hundred well-armed escorts, supplied by Abdullah Khan, could barely protect him. Jenkinson also mentions 'certain field people as well as Gentiles and Muhammadans living between Bukhara and China on the borders of the cities of Tashkent and Kashghar who had made it almost impossible for any caravans to pass unspoiled'.[120] The tribal population (Manghits, Turcomans, Hazaras, and Baluchis) inhabiting the area between Central Asia and India, on the one hand, and Central Asia and Persia, on the other, also caused much trouble. Babur calls the Afghans of Kabul and Lamghan (Ning Nahar) 'thieves and abettors of thieves even in quiet times'.[121] Hafiz Tanish refers to the perpetual danger from the Raushanais.[122] In his letters to Abdullah Khan and Shah Abbas of Persia, Akbar repeatedly refers to the many Afghans entrenched in the hills of Bajaur Swad, Tirah, and Bangash who 'intercepted the caravans proceeding to Turan' and who were a 'stumbling stone to travellers to Turan'. Similarly, Abul Fazl refers to the 1,00,000 Yusuf Zai tribals who 'caused much injury to traffic and intercourse'.[123] Bento De Goes (1603-7) also found the area 'infested with robbers who lie in wait for caravans and commit many atrocities'.[124] He speaks of the 'perils' and 'encounters' which confronted travellers, necessitating 'eight months compulsory rest' besides the 'loss of companions'. He recounts how they had to take shelter for a 'full weary month in Taliqan due to the Calcian revolt against the Khan of Bukhara' and their 'ravaging and plundering'. When they departed, they were 'attacked' near Taliqan, then under Abdullah Khan, and 'escaped complete ruin' only by paying a tribute on their merchandise. He was harassed by the rebels also. In Badakhshan even the escort of Goes 'made common cause with the populace' and fell upon the traders.[125] Such experiences often deterred a 'number of travellers from continuing the journey'.[126] The caravans from India and Persia were once looted and the travellers were massacred by robbers while on their way to Bukhara. Not only that, the trade with Astrakhan, Mongolia, and Persia suffered due to unsafe routes; the caravans could not travel safely even through Kashghar and Tashkent.[127] Shergul Afghan says that after the accession of Yunus Khan as the Khan of Tashkent, the Kirghiz and the Kazaks who were busy in 'plundering (*yaghmagari*) feasts' were taken to task and severely dealt with, resulting in the complete suppression of such troubles. Nevertheless, the routes remained unsafe even when Burnes travelled in these areas.

Civil wars too were a continual feature of Central Asian political life in the sixteenth century. Both Sidi Ali Reis and Jenkinson describe the horrors and evil effects of these wars on commerce. While in Central Asia, both of them were asked to leave as a civil war was imminent and they would be in danger of losing their lives and goods.[128] Such wars, whether long or short range, must necessarily have diverted capital and manpower from trade investments to mutual non-productive military enterprises internally. Inter-state trade also received a setback. In a letter to the Naqshbandi saint, Khudai Pirdi, a brother of Sultan Said urged him to ensure that those who brought grain into the province or exported whatever they deemed proper (for sale elsewhere) should not be obstructed.[129] Jenkinson describes how civil wars led to an increase in highway robberies in Urganj:

> When there are wars between these brethren (as they are seldom without) he that is overcome if he be not slain fleeth to the field with such companie of men as will follow him and there liveth in the wilderness resorting to watering places and so robbeth and spoyleth as many caravans of merchants and others as they be able to overcome continuing in this sort his wicked life until such time as he may get power and aid to invade some of his brethren again.[130]

This evidence cannot be brushed aside as the exaggerations of a prejudiced traveller. Haidar Dughlat himself refers to such 'desperadoes'.[131] According to him, Vais Khan, the Mongol ruler, took to the life of a robber because he found the 'science of his uncle (rulership?) irksome'. Many youths volunteered to follow him, including Haidar Dughlat's grandfather, Mir Ali.[132] Even the reigning kings of Khwarazm are alleged to have indulged in such activities.[133] Abdullah once received a petition from his special envoy returning from Russia, asking for protection against the high-handedness of the Khwarazm Sultans to ensure the safe conveyance of goods brought from Moscow. Abdullah accordingly appointed Tinash Haji to escort the envoy and warned the Khwarazm rulers through a *farman*.[134] Again, on the arrival of another envoy from India, special measures were taken to thwart the attempts of the plundering tribes and rulers to harass him and his companions.

But such imperial protection was not always effective. Jenkinson and his party had to face the danger from robbers at every step, notwithstanding the 'letters of safe conduct' issued to him by the various kings and the detachments appointed as escorts.[135] Jenkinson complains that though one of these groups 'consumed much of the victuals', they escorted them to a certain point only, after which they demanded a fabulous amount for the journey ahead and, on being refused, returned to their master, the Sultan of Urganj, who was 'privie to the conspiracie'. Jenkinson and his party fought bravely against the robbers for two hours. These robbers were again 'banished princes' and their followers. Ultimately, Jenkinson and his companions had to buy their safety by giving them 'twenty times nine several things and a camel for carrying it'.[136] Some of the companions were even kidnapped later[137] during the journey. Jenkinson says that peaceable travellers usually 'go in a caravan with camels', whereas all those 'horsefeeting travellers without camels were to be doubted'.[138] Bento De Goes, who was in Central Asia in 1602-7, also says that 'the country between Cialis and the Chinese wall' was notorious for Tartar raids so that:

> the traders always crossed it in the greatest fear, sometimes even in the strictest silence and under the cover of the night. One often came across the dead bodies of Muhammadans who have attempted the journey unaccompanied though, on the other hand, the Tartars were not wont to kill the native population, considering them as their servants and herdsmen who they occasionally rob of their flock.

Goes himself travelled at night.[139] Similarly, near Astrakhan, Thomas Bannister and Geoffrey Ducket, the agents for the Moscovie Company, met Nogai Tartars in 1568 who were 'thievish and cruel' and who attacked them with swords, spears, and bows and arrows.[140] It seems that the trade between Russia and Central Asia was frequently disturbed by the inroads made by the Turcomans, Khivans, and Kalmuks on the western routes, by the Kalmuks, Kazaks, and Qara Qalpaqs in the east, and by the Afghans and Turcomans in the south. In the seventeenth century Uzbek Khan even looked for support from the Czars in his struggle against the Kalmuks.

Apart from highway robberies there were other difficulties as well.

Jenkinson had to cope with 'bad and brutish' people whose fighting, stealing, begging, and raising the prices of horses, camels, and victuals forced him and his party to buy even drinking water. They were forced to sell provisions 'so that for every camelload 1,400 weight of our three hides of Russia and four wooden dishes'; they were forced to pay tributes to princes and governors ('one-ninth and two-seventh: namely nine several things and twice seven several things'). Jenkinson's caravan was detained at another place in the name of the Menguslav prince, Timur Sultan. The Tartars took the choice things again from him as *tuquz* (gift for the king) without paying any money. Even Timur Sultan did not give Jenkinson any money. Jenkinson complains that Abdullah Khan 'showed himself a . . . Tartar', as he went on an expedition without paying the money for the purchases he had made from Jenkinson; the merchant had to come back to recover the debt; moreover, Jenkinson was, very 'ill satisfied' when he was paid in kind and was forced 'to rebate part', which compelled him to observe that he could expect no 'better payment from a beggar'.[141] At the gulf of the Caspian Sea, the 'customers of the king of the Turcomans' levied a custom duty for the king.[142] The system of *silao* (offering presents before being allowed to cross the frontier without let or hindrance) continued upto the nineteenth century and those found to be recalcitrant 'were beaten up'. Repeated experiences of this kind were naturally great irritants to traders.[143]

Then there were the taxes. Jenkinson gives a long list of custom duties, 'a custom of every five and twenty one and seven-ninth for the king and his brethren'[144] at Urganj, a custom 'as well for our own heads as for our camels and horses' and 'petty custom' at the river Ardock and later at Kait. He also paid custom for every camel besides petty gifts to the officers. At Bukhara a fortieth part of merchandise was to be paid on goods as toll.[145] The Central Asian merchants had to pay *baj*, *kharaj*, and *tamgha* at Peshawar.[146] Bento De Goes records as a strange fact that while passing through Jilalabad and Aliabad on the Kunduz river, 'the Brahmins had the right of exacting tribute given to them by the king of Bucarate[147] (Bukhara)'. The caravan of Burnes had to pay at Sighan 'a Nankeen Pelisse with eight or nine rupees (the usual tax on a caravan) to its chief Ali Muhammad Uzbek. At Khulm also the ruler Rahmatu'llah Khan claimed a tax on the traveller though he is but a tributary of Kunduz.'[148] The imposition of heavy duties by the Central Asian sultans at their provincial borders[149] restricted the free movement of traders with a resultant increase in the price of commodities.

The custom officers could detain merchants and artisans not holding immunity grants and could even inflict physical punishment. The documents given to the privileged few specifically enjoin officials 'to allow the merchants to go safe and healthy' and 'to give them cooperation and assistance in all dangerous spots'. Such merchants must have been closely associated with the Khan and presumably might be carrying even the king's own goods. The attempts of the Khans and rulers to subjugate trade (particularly international trade) and to exploit the traders is borne out by the order contained in the *Maktubat was asnad* directing the traders 'from wherever they may be' to bring their valuable goods and precious things for an inspection by the king's nominee who could acquire the goods at set rates for the Khan. The traders were asked 'not to conceal anything' and 'no one could buy anything from the merchants till the inspection was over'.[150] Generally speaking, in the sixteenth century there were no guarantees of immunity and safety in respect of the personal property of artisans and traders. Barthold rightly concludes that the absence of all guarantees from new and unforeseen taxation was partly responsible for the stagnation of the economy. The decline in general prosperity also restructured the market for commodities. Enumerating the causes of the poor trade, Jenkinson says 'the few ships upon the Caspian Sea, the want of mart and port towns, the poverty of the people and the ice maketh the trade nought'.[151]

## NOTES

1. Cf. Spuler, *The Muslim World*, pt. III, Leiden, 1969, p. 243. For the Silk Route, cf. Map 16 in *The Art of Central Asia*, p. 9. For details about early trade, cf. *The Silk Road*, pp. 149-63; C.G.F. Simkin, *The Traditional Trade of Asia*, London, 1968, p. 58; Khuda Bakhsh, *The Renaissance of Islam*, pp. 468-79; Barthold, *Sochinenija*, VI, pp. 368-72, III, pp. 54-8; Bretschneider, I, p. 269; Shaban, *The Abbasid Revolution*, Cambridge, 1970, p. 15.
2. Jenkinson, pp. 15, 30; also see *Hakluyt*, ser. II, pp. 108-9.
3. Ibn-i-Hauqal, pp. 209-10; also see Al Jahiz, p. 35.
4. Clavijo, p. 278.
5. Ibn-i Battuta, Persian tr., pp. 411-14.
6. Clavijo, p. 278; *Nuhzatha-i Iranian*, III, pt. II, p. 725.
7. *B.N.*, pp. 4, 48-9; Eng. tr., p. 81; also see *The Renaissance of Islam*, pp. 468-79.

8. *Mehn*, 85; *Fsi*, p. 50.
9. Ibid., p. 200.
10. Ibid., 256. Ibn-i Battuta describes the fine port of Karsh in Dasht, 'which was a magnificent harbour with about 200 vessels in it, ships of war and trading vessels, small and large, for it is one of the most notable harbours in the world'. (Ibn-i Battuta, pp. 142-3).
11. Ibn-i Hauqal, p. 195. He also notes that cotton and silken cloths were produced in Khwarazm and were sent to various places. Ibn-i Hauqal, p. 209; *Mehn*, pp. 85, 199-200.
12. *G.K.U.*, p. 151.
13. For a detailed and interesting description of *sarais*, cf. Obruchev.
14. Ibn-i Battuta, Persian tr., p. 406; Eng. tr., p. 168.
15. *Rauzat-ur Rizvan*, pp. 260-1.
16. *Badain-ul Waqai*, p. 201.
17. See *Rashhat*, p. 221.
18. See infra, Currency, Wages, and Prices.
19. Sourin Roy, 'From the Ganga to the Volga: The History of an Ancient Trade Route', *Studies in Asian History*, New Delhi, 1969, pp. 171-2.
20. Shaban, *The Abbasid Relations*, Cambridge, 1970, p. 15.
21. Under the Abbasids, the Sughdanians were famous for their commercial enterprise and were highly interested in the Chinese silk trade, the centres of which were at Samarqand, Paykand, and Kasht; they worked as intermediaries between the east and the west. Suqhd (the market of the Soghdanians) was one of the most ancient quarters of the city of Merv. Shaban, *The Abbasid Revolution*, Cambridge, 1970, p. 15. Dobson says that Bukhara has always served as the depot and agency for distributing Indian teas as well as Russian wares throughout the surrounding countries (*Russian Railway Advance*, p. 374); also see Bento De Goes, p. 30.
22. The 'horrifying tales of bitter experiences narrated by Nikitin discouraged the direct future commercial relations between India and Russia' (E.P. Magudovitch, *Ocherki pa istori geograficheski atkriti*, Moscow, 1957, pp. 81-4), in addition, the political circumstances also seem to have contributed to freezing such contacts.
23. *Russko Injiski atnashenija*, vol. V, no. XVII, p. 48, Collection of Documents, Oriental Institute, Moscow, 1958, p. 171. The Mughal sources, however, do not refer to any such queries.
24. *Russko Injiski atnashenija*, vol. XVIII, B.M., 1956, p. 5.
25. Spuler, p. 243. The Mughal chroniclers, however, do not seem to have recorded this event.
26. Clavijo, p. 288.
27. Cf. Muqminova, p. 88. The other items brought to Bukhara were copper, steel, iron, blue paper, mercury, painted stones, pens, cloth (*parcha-i udraing*, *fulful*, *wrilte*), coral, gold threads, etc. For details, see *Manzil-i Bukhara*, pp. 13-15.
28. *Rauzat*, p. 295.
29. Ibid., p. 157.
30. Jenkinson, p. 22, *Istorija Samarqand*, p. 277.
31. Baujiva, pp. 108-15; Ziaev Kh. Urta Azia va Siberia, Tashkent, AN uz SSR, 1962, pp. 68-70; M.V. Plickner, p. 8.

32. Targovliya Russkovo Casudarstova sa stranami Vastoka va XVI vekov, trud, State Historical Museum, issue 31, M. 1956. Also see Obruchev, p. 37.
33. Robert Mantran, 'Le Empire Ottoman et Le Commerce Asiatique', *Islam and the Trade of Asia*, pp. 169-79.
34. Ibn-i Hauqal, pp. 204, 362.
35. Ibid., pp. 246, 362.
36. Ibn-i Hauqal, pp. 246, 316. *Islam from the Prophet Muhammad to the Capture of Constantinople*, ed. and tr. by Bernard Lewis, vol. II, 1974, USA, p. 155. Even the cotton-growing areas of Turkestan exported fabrics to Babylonia. For details, cf. Ibn-i Hauqal, p. 362. Al Jahiz (p. 35) says that paper from Samarqand; sweet grapes and ghawshana, truffles from Balkh; zither players, carpets and fur suits from Merv; musk, ermine, marten, foxfurs, and sweet sugar from Khwarazm were exported to Iraq.
37. Narshakhi, Russian tr., p. 18.
38. Ibn-i Battuta, vol. I, Pers. tr., p. 365; Eng. tr., p. 144.
39. Ibid.
40. *Tazkira-i Humayun wa Akbar*, Calcutta, 1941, pp. 227-8. See Nicola A. Ziadeh, 'Change of trade centres in the Persian Gulf in the Middle Ages', *Studies in Asian History*, New Delhi, 1969, pp. 296-301.
41. Ibn-i Battuta, vol. II, p. 314; also see V.A. Gardlevski, *Izbraniyi Sochinenija*, Moscow, 1960, p. 145.
42. *Munshaat-us-Salatin*, pp. 17, 88, 99, 108.
43. *Cambridge History of Islam*, I, A, p. 335.
44. Ibid., p. 469.
45. *BN*, pp. 129-30, Eng. tr., pp. 202-6; also see Spuler, *Islam and the Trade of Asia*, pp. 16-19.
46. Clavijo, p. 289.
47. *BN*, text, pp. 129, 149, Eng. tr., pp. 202, 235.
48. Ibid., for Indian merchants in medieval Azerbaijan and Shirwan, cf. S.B. Ashurben, *Injiski kuptsi va sredni vekovikh goradakh Azerbaijan e Shirwan*, pp. 92-6, Narod Azi e Afriki 4, 1964; Burnes, pp. 238-88.
49. *Abdn*, f. 456.
50. *Abdn*, p. 456 for interesting details on Armenian traders in India, cf. Surendra Gopal, *Central Asia*, New Delhi, 1970, pp. 200-14.
51. *BN*, text, pp. 129, 149; Jenkinson, pp. 24-5; *Tuzuk-i-Jahangiri*, I, p. 350.
52. *Ain*, I, *Travels in the Mughal Empire*, pp. 118-19, 203-4.
53. Francisco Bernier, Eng. tr., *Ain*, Blochmann, pp. 65-9, Delhi, 1968, pp. 118-19, 203-4.
54. Bernier, pp. 118-19, 203-4. Marco Polo witnessed the export of white salt and fruits from Central Asia to foreign lands. The almonds and pistachio nuts from the southern hills of Taliqan were carried to distant lands (Marco Polo, pp. 57-9); also see Maqdisi, p. 234; Adam Mez, *The Renaissance of Islam*, Eng. tr. by Margliouth and Khuda Bakhsh, Delhi, 1979, pp. 438, 442.
55. Jenkinson, pp. 24-5. *Ajaib-ul-Gharaib*, MS 47, Ouseley, Bodleian Library, ff. 55. If Soviet accounts are to be believed, gold was also an important object of export from Central Asia to India and was exchanged for cheaper silk and cotton material. For details, cf. Davidovich, *Monetnovo dela*, pp. 194-6.
56. In Marco Polo's time, this trade was in the hands of the Persians. Marco Polo

found in Turkomania an excellent breed of horse called Turki and also fine mules sold at high prices (Marco Polo, *Travels*, pp. 24, 40, 61, 194, 288, 322). Ibn-i Battuta (p. 167) refers to the cheapness of the horses in Saraichik as he sold his exhausted horses there at the rate of 4 silver dinars per head or even less.

57. *BN*, p. 129; Eng. tr., p. 202.
58. Manucci, pp. 390-1.
59. Bernier, pp. 203-4.
60. *BN*, p. 129; Eng. tr., p. 202.
61. *Watters*, p. 94.
62. *Ain*, p. 49, *Ain-i-Akbari*, Eng. tr. by Blochmann, vol. I, New Delhi, 1977, p. 140.
63. Ibid. *Ain*, I, pt. 2; *Ain*, II, pp. 243-4.
64. Manucci, pp. 390-1.
65. Ibid.; Bernier, pp. 203-4.
66. For details, cf. Baikova, pp. 102-10.
67. Clavijo says that the first was where the eastern spur of the Caucasus range comes down to the Caspian Sea, a narrow pass between the mountains and the sea in the kingdom of Shirwan which was a gateway between Persia and the Golden Horde. The other was situated in the mountain range between Samarqand and Balkh called 'the guard house of the imperial city' through which all who travel up to Samarqand from India, Leh can come, nor can those who go down from the imperial city, voyaging to India travel by another route. (Clavijo, pp. 204-5).
68. For interesting details about Darband, cf. Bretschneider, II, pp. 115-19; Hilda Hookham, pp. 165-7.
69. *BN*, pp. 129-30, Eng. tr., pp. 202-6. Babur says that these seven roads separate Kabul from Balkh, Kunduz and Badakhshan (namely, three leading to Pajshir Khwak, Tul and Bazarak) and four other roads leading Kabul from India.
70. *Ain*, II, pp. 405-6; *BN*, p. 206.
71. *Abdn*, p. 451.
72. Chandra Bhan Brahmin, *Chahar Gulshan*, Abdus Salam Collection, Maulana Azad Library, MS no. 292/62, ff 93.
73. Soch, III, p. 90.
74. Allworth, *Central Asia: A Century of Russian Rule*, pp. 23, 31, 38, 40.
75. Ghaffurov, *Tajiki*, pp. 538-42.
76. Abul Ghazi, II, pp. 293-4; Soch, III, p. 90; Abulghazi, III, pp. 293-8, 338-43.
77. Baikova: *Role Sredni Azi va Russko*, Injiskish targoirkh svyazi, Tashkent, 1964, pp. 51-2; Yuldasheva, *Kistori targovikh e pasolskikh svyazi sredni Azi c Russie*, Tashkent, 1964, pp. 1-70.
78. *Abdn*, p. 378.
79. MS Oriental Institute, 77, no. 2094, f. 90.
80. *Abdn*, p. 378.
81. Yuldasheva, pp. 60-2.
82. Jenkinson, *Hakluyt*, I, p. 440; *Purchas*, XII, pp. 3-4.
83. Ibn-i Arab, Eng. tr., p. 77.
84. Jenkinson, *Hakluyt*, I, p. 44.
85. Jenkinson, pp. 24-5, Ghaffurov, pp. 538-42; Wheeler, p. 44.

86. Muhammad Narshakhi, *Istorija Bukhara*, Russ. tr. by Likoshima, Tashkent, 1897, p. 23; Frye, *Bukhara, the Medieval Achievement*, Norman, 1965, p. 31.
87. Baikova, pp. 100-8.
88. Ibid.
89. Shegul, p. 137. The value of exports to Russia between 1827 and 1837 is said to have exceeded that of imports by 2,000,000 roubles (Wheeler, p. 44; Lyashehenko, pp. 54-60, 605-18; Becker, pp. 170-6).
90. Turkestan, pp. 136-8. Spuler includes satins, bludgeons, metal goods, axes and firearms, silver needles, nails, and dishes among the exports from Russia to Central Asia though he does not cite his source. Central Asian exports to Russia comprised Karakul pelts, carpets, and even precious stones and ornamented weapons (Spuler, *The Muslim World*, p. 243. Also see *Cambridge History of Islam*, I, A, p. 483). Both Krader and Allworth believe that the slave trade, being remunerative, was one of the prime sources of Russia's wealth. Allworth, pp. 30-7; Krader, *Peoples*, p. 98. Also see Belk, 'Turkestan: Russian Mennonites' promised land', *Studies in Islam, Journal of Indian Institute of Islamic Studies*, New Delhi, Jan.-April 1973, pp. 58-62, 95.
91. M.V. Fahner, *Targovlya Russkovo Gasudarstova*, p. 75.
92. Baikova, pp. 75-98.
93. There exists a controversy regarding the location of Kabakal. For details, cf. Chuloshnikovo, *Targovlya Moskovski gasudarstova kistori targovikh pasoskikh svyazi sredni Azi c Russia va XVI-XVII vekov*, Tashkent, 1964, pp. 56-64; Baikova, p. 98.
94. Baikova, pp. 108-15.
95. Hakluyt Soc, ser. II, pp. 85-7.
96. Ibid., pp. 88-93, 324; Baikova, pp. 108-15.
97. G. Miller, *Istoria Siberia*, Moscow, 1937, p. 201. Also see *Puteshestivya Ispafaria Zapiski Russkovo Geographicheskova Obsnestva pa otdel ethnografi*, vol. X, SP 1182, p. 43.
98. Ibid.
99. Yuldasheva.
100. *Material pa istori uzbekskoj, Tajikskoj Turkmenskoj SSR*, Leningrad, pt. I, 1923, pp. 428-31, also fn. 178; Allworth, pp. 23-4.
101. *Tarikh-i Shaibani*, pp. 8-9.
102. *Muzzakkira*, pp. 166-7.
103. For examples of similar exchanges and purchasing missions, see Riazul Islam, *A Calendar*, pp. 159-60, 164-6, 178-9, 184, 186.
104. For original document, see Yuldasheva, p. 75.
105. *Rashhat*, ff. pp.130, 221; also *Rauzat*, f. 9; *Muzzakkira*, pp. 164, 484-5.
106. *Vazliubleonni Sirdsa*, p. 31; *Ocherki pa remesla*, pp. 189-90.
107. *BN*, Eng. tr., p. 132.
108. *Makwasnad*, p. 171; *Ocherki pa remesla*, p. 190.
109. *Makwasnad*, pp. 77, 170; *Ocherki pa remesla*, p. 190.
110. *Badaiulwaqai*, pp. 114-19.
111. *Waqaitassalut i russiya bar Asiya*, pp. 13-14, Shergul Afghan. Obruchev, p. 63; *Cambridge History of Islam*, I, p. 483; *Islam and the Trade of Asia*, pp. 13-17.

112. Imamuddin, '*Bait-ul mal* and the Banks in the medieval Muslim world', *Islamic Culture*, XXXIV, no. 10, 1960. Spuler, 'Trade in the Eastern Islamic Countries', *Islam and the Trade of Asia*, pp. 13-17.
113. Muqminova, pp. 190-1.
114. *Mehmannama*, p. 156.
115. Ibid.
116. For details, see *Cambridge History of Islam*, I, p. 469.
117. *BN*, text, p. 207; Eng. tr., p. 331.
118. *TR*, Eng. tr., pp. 126-7.
119. Sidi Ali Rais, pp. 72-3.
120. Jenkinson, p. 25.
121. *BN*, p. 213, Eng. tr., p. 341.
122. *BN*, pp. 159, 213; Eng. tr., pp. 341, 251; *Abdn*, pp. 456, 475, 489.
123. *Insha*, pp. 7, 20; *AN*, III; Eng. tr., p. 1010; *Rauzat*, p. 156.
124. *Jahangir and the Jesuits*, p. 146.
125. C. Wessels, *Early Jesuit Travellers in Central Asia*, pp. 16, 19, 20.
126. Ibid.
127. Jenkinson, pp. 20-1, 23-6; Sidi Ali Rais, pp. 66-7, 72. Even Ibn-i Battuta records how the armed and well-built Turks near Herat used to invade the environs of India almost continuously, plundering and capturing slaves (cf. Ibn-i Battuta, Pers. tr., p. 437).
128. Jenkinson, pp. 14-15, 18-26, Sidi Ali Rais.
129. *Rauzat*, pp. 157-8.
130. Jenkinson, p. 15.
131. *TR*, Eng. tr., pp. 60, 63-4.
132. *TR*, Eng. tr., pp. 60-4.
133. Jenkinson, pp. 23-4; *Abdn*, p. 378.
134. *Abdn*, p. 378.
135. Jenkinson, pp. 10-14.
136. Jenkinson, pp. 18-20; *Hakluyt*, I, pp. 445-6, 451-5.
137. Ibid., p. 21.
138. Ibid., pp. 18-20.
139. Bento De Goes, pp. 37-8.
140. *Hakluyt's Voyages*, II, pp. 27, 119; also see Boies Penrose, *Travel and Discovery in the Renaissance* (1420-1620), Cambridge, Mass., 1955, p. 193.
141. Jenkinson, *Purchas*, pp. 11-12, 22-3. *Hakluyt*, pp. 446-8. The non-payment for the purchases made by the king seems to be common among the medieval Asian sovereigns. Thomas Alcock and Richard Cheini both had the same complaints against Abdullah Khan, a provincial ruler in Persia. It was after a long stay and with much trouble that Cheini 'recovered' some of his money. Arthur Edwards also did not receive payment for certain debts while Thomas Alcock's debts were 'past hope of recovery' (*Hakluyt*, II, pp. 31-2, 35-6).
142. Jenkinson, p. 15.
143. Jenkinson, *Purchas*, pp. 11-12; *Hakluyt*, I, pp. 446-8. Marco Polo, pp. 57-87.
144. Jenkinson, pp. 13-14; *Hakluyt*, pp. 448-52.
145. Jenkinson, *Hakluyt*, I, p. 464.
146. Hafiz Tanish, p. 456.

147. *Early Jesuit Travellers*, pp. 19-20.
148. Burnes, p. 194.
149. Soch, V, p. 208.
150. *Maktubat wa asnad*, p. 30.
151. Jenkinson, pp. 15, 30. The same situation prevailed elsewhere. See also *Hakluyt*, pp. 108-9.

# Indo-Central Asian Scenario in Present Times

Events in the recent past in Central Asia have brought in their wake instability and uncertainty almost to every nation in this region. As it was at the turn of the nineteenth century, Central Asia is once again at the threshold of a new phase in its history, a period of 'reconnaissance' or 'looking back'—perhaps even a 'renaissance' or 'rebirth'—which includes an earnest search for its identity, a desire to solve its problems, and an equally zealous but circumspect search or quest to locate and identify with its friends. The joy of a recently won independence is mingled with an understandable concern, anxiety, and fear about the future of this region.

The complexities of the situation make one wonder how the hopeful nations will carve their paths to their desired destinations and how at this stage of uncertainty India would perceive its role in regional politics, particularly when a scramble for Central Asia is going on and the newly emergent Central Asian states are being drawn into new and at times difficult and (sometimes even) doubtful commitments. The centrality of the region adds to its significance to the extent that happenings in this part of the world cannot be ignored. There are indeed many possibilities and enormous potential for establishing and pursuing wide-ranging cooperation in various spheres between India and Central Asia. For developing a mutually beneficial relationship, therefore, ways and means will have to be devised after a careful study of the rapidly changing situation in Central Asia.

Among the Asian nations, India is in the foremost position to benefit from the present-day policy of globalization and can, therefore, play a leading role not only in matters of socio-economic development but it can also influence the Central Asian republics to ensure a lasting peace in the region. For a really beneficial and cooperative venture among the various countries, a careful understanding of the region is the first requirement. An indepth study is, therefore, necessary for a proper understanding of political and economic issues confronting the region today.

In the past few years, many conferences and seminars on Central Asia have been held. In many ways, however, these discussions have only touched the surface of the problem. Unless we study the problem more closely and try to feel the pulse of the people, the danger is that most of our suggestions will remain theoretical while the need is to offer some practical suggestions based on a serious examination of the ground reality. Central Asian culture has its own historical continuity from the medieval period to the present day and has to be studied against this background. Even today the influence of the medieval institutions, ethos, and cultural trends is visible. Although Central Asia had remained under foreign domination for over two centuries, first under the Czarist rule and then under the communist regime, the vestiges of its old culture survived, just as we in India have preserved our own heritage and culture despite British domination for two centuries. A proper understanding of the history of Central Asia is necessary to determine present-day policy and to plan for the future.

The countries of Central Asia have now come of age as full-fledged nations. The important questions connected with this development include: whether pan-Turkism which was once a 'national chauvinistic ideology' would dominate, creating certain zones of Turkish power, or whether a political pan-ethnolingualism will result in a unitarian state where all ethnic groups would ultimately merge and the country would emerge as a national Turanian state. Whether religious revivalism would necessarily, result in stagnation and retrogression or whether the newly found cultural freedom, self-rule, and rational outlook would give a positive boost to Central Asia. Whether religion would be used as a tool to gain power, or whether it would simply be a source of moral strength or even a tool to secure certain limited political objectives. Whether the new Central Asian states would opt for Turkish laicism or for an Iranian style fundamentalism or whether they would follow Pakistan's pattern. It is also worth examining whether freedom of religion and freedom of expression are being enjoyed as they are in a democratic country like India, or whether there still operates an unseen remote control, which engenders fears in people's minds and chokes their voices. It is interesting to examine how the *madrasas* are being run and whether the offering of prayers in mosques is a voluntary or an organized affair and whether these activities are under state control even now.

The recent reforms and their impact on the economy and on the general standard of living have to be estimated. The people's own assessment based on their experiences of the changes in the economic sphere and their subsequent impact on the social milieu will have to be judged and analysed. The instruments of authority and power have evidently not changed much as the half-masters of yester years continue to dominate in the corridors of power. What is the position regarding supply and demand? Are they adjusting to each other or not? In addition, the Indo-Central Asian tie-ups and political relations after the recent shift in the balance of power have to be reviewed; these events were not confined to one particular region and, their impact also extends to the surrounding areas. People's woes, grievances, and complaints (for example, those relating to the controversial cotton-picking traditions), their expectations and aspirations should also form an interesting part of the study. The rapidly changing ideologies, tensions during the period of transition, the metamorphosis from a nation of pan-Turkists and pan-Islamists to materialist Marxists and then back to a world of medieval religious fervour, and that too all within a hundred years must have added to the confusion. The reactions and responses of different generations to such sudden and super imposed social convulsions, the societal implications of this confused ethos, the undercurrents of mutual suspicions leading to frequent civil dissensions—whether in Ferghana or in Tajikistan or even in far away Kazakhstan—are questions which deserve attention. These social eruptions and resurgences, confrontations and outbursts, must be studied in their proper perspective. Are there economic, religious, or political reasons which result in the eruption of trouble or is there a foreign hand manipulating every upheaval. What are the people's views about such eruptions? How do the people think these can be tackled and controlled? Each of the newly emerged Central Asian states faces an identity crisis but each is eager to be acknowledged as a progressive, rapidly developing, self-sufficient nation. And hence ironically they find themselves drawn consciously or unconsciously into a mixed world of myth and reality. Unable to recognize their friends, confused about distinguishing between exploiters and helpers, surrounded by those who merely wish to make hay while the sun shines, they live in the midst of hopes and fears. The intelligentsia, a progressive force in most developing nations and in the vanguard of revolutionary trends, seems to be simply receding into the background, over whelmed by two totally different assignments, yet eager to face challenges and meet the demands of this new system. But to what extent will they be successful? Will they continue to accept this pattern of life? Some have taken to the toy trade. The sudden rise of the business class and increasing opportunity to make money fascinate the younger generation more than the rigours of studies. Have the old moral values changed? Do they continue to drink to the same extent as they did under Russian rule? Have the partially permissive ways of the Russians made a deep impression? Or have Uzbek moral and ethical values, which had all along lingered started reasserting themselves more vigorously?

In the present-day circumstances and in view of the growing political importance of Central Asia, a deeper study of the existing situation in all aspects is urgently needed. An assessment of its external involvements and internal wrangles (whose repercussions could affect the neighbouring regions) and the patterns of its new alignments (which could shape the course of history in the long run), also need careful examination, particularly because the time is ripe for giving an appropriate form and foundation to Indo-Central Asian relations. Such investigations will cover the geo-political, historical, and physical features of the region, examine the routes connecting Central Asia with its surrounding regions, assess its commercial potential and assets, and look at its socio-economic and religio-political conditions. Despite the crucial importance of these considerations, these have received comparatively less attention in recent studies on the present-day situation in Central Asia.

A detailed study of these new socio-economic and religio-political conditions will greatly help us to better appreciate and understand contemporary bilateral relations. The main purpose of this indepth examination would be to prepare a really authentic, first-hand assessment of the present-day socio-economic and religio-political dimensions in Central Asia, highlighting the direction, nature, and pattern of the exchange of ideas which would benefit bilateral negotiations.

Recently, there have been many scholarly works on Central Asia. Some of them are not based on authentic original sources, some have explicit and implicit political purposes and dimensions, some propagate certain interpretations, while some others add to our knowledge considerably. These have to be seen in their proper perspective. Hence, these recent writings from Central Asia and other parts of the world have to be critically examined; these analyses should not be accepted at face value. Critical inquiry becomes necessary as certain scholars (like G. Wheeler) have dubbed the period of pre-Russian. Central Asian history as the 'Dark Ages' while others have excessively and unrealistically glorified the independent nations of Central Asia. A balanced study, without any preconceived notions or ideological compulsions, based on an analytical approach is urgently needed.

A closer appraisal would reveal the ground realities of the situation in Central Asia. Motivated by a sense of patriotism, many Central Asians are often reluctant to disclose the dismal conditions in their newly emerged nations. For example, if certain plans have not been implemented or have failed to materialize these nationalists would sometimes describe these to a foreign as accomplished successes. Thus, while the desire to glorify their country's achievements within the short span of self-rule is temporarily fulfilled, the reliability and accuracy of such statements remains suspect. Similarly, important issues are camouflaged and various reasons for the frequent uprisings are put forward. The historical irony of the loss of a nation's united old world and replacement by separate fragmented states through division of people and the reduced resources—a direct consequence of their subjugation by an alien power and a vindictive culmination of their forced departure—have left scars which would take a long time to heal.

It is necessary to survey various sources in order to examine the breaks and continuities in the history of Central Asia and to assess how the past will affect the nature and direction of its future. The changing internal conditions in the Central Asian states which have brought in their wake newly discovered connections collaborations and affiliations deserve very careful study and handling, as these fragile connections may snap, leaving sharp differences resulting in permanent disparities and inequalities. Since Indians have already suffered through the painful breakup of their country, they are in a position to better appreciate the attendant risks faced by the Central Asian States.

A few examples will prove the point. As a friend of both Uzbeks and Tajiks with whom I have shared moments of joy and sorrow, I can say even while sitting here thousands of miles away that I am constrained to observe that the situation, if not checked in time, could lead to disaster. The origins of the Uzbek-Tajik conflict are usually traced back to the mid-1940s. Bobojan Ghaffurov was appointed the first secretary of Tajikistan in 1945 and Usman Yusuf was appointed the first secretary of Uzbekistan. There was general discontent at the time fueled by the widespread belief that all the Tajiks then residing in Samarqand, Bukhara, and Khiva were included in the category of the Uzbeks and were identified as such on their passports. Whether this was a voluntary effort to avoid a cumbersome adjustment to the new conditions dictated by necessary emigration or whether it was merely a matter of convenience for over-worked officials eager to take short-cuts is yet to be determined. Another much stressed point of discord was that Samarqand and Bukhara were traditionally said to be in the 'Tajik zone' where people continued to speak the Tajik languages. In this context, the following facts may be noted. Strangely enough, no one cared or dared to study thoroughly the process of denationalization, where the script was also immediately replaced, in order to cut down the very roots of the people's connection with their heritage and to make them aliens to their own history and culture, removing thereby the symbols around which any future resistance might be organized. Originally, all the ethnic groups were governed by the homogenous application of a uniform nomenclature, i.e. Turks, Turanis, or Muslims. The division of the people according to linguistic differences was done deliberately to weaken their strength and unity. Even today there are frequent misapprehensions, mostly misplaced and unjustified. Recently, a new device to divide the two friendly nations (i.e. the Uzbek and the Tajiks) has been seen. There are undercurrents of persistent displeasure over certain newly invented hot ideas on the agenda, i.e. the states of Samarqand and Bukhara had earlier belonged to the Tajiks and are now seemingly lost to the Uzbeks or, to put it more bluntly, have been usurped by the Uzbeks.

Even in medieval times such pretexts for provocations were thoroughly understood, and the anticipated dangers were averted cleverly. When Abdullah Khan Uzbek wrote to Akbar, asking him to wrest his ancestral territory Qandahar from the Persians, the wise Mughal emperor hinted that certain other territories (i.e. Transoxiana) had also belonged to his ancestors but he was a follower of the dictum of 'peace with all' and hence he did not want to involve himself in extra-territorial wars which were bound to destroy the peace and prosperity of the nations in the region. A similar answer, in a different context, was also sent to the Persians when they requested help from Akbar.

The proxy or indirect war is conducted through multi-channel media; sometimes a volley of charges and counter-charges further embitters the relationship between these young nations. Attention is cleverly diverted by trouble shooters (who are the real culprits and who are keen to fish in troubled waters) from the mischief makers to those who have nothing to do with the problem though these latter individuals are capable enough of reacting against false accusations and causing damage to the already shaken state through internal dissensions and external threats. In the long run, these serve the interests of those very 'real culprits' behind the scene who wish to see each state tottering to its fall through internal wars. In this same way, the Tajiks and the Uzbeks developed a hidden misunderstanding when in northern Khujand troubles arose in October-November 1998, and at the instigation of those with vested interests one state started blaming another for minor matters.

From India, however, each of these states has an open offer of friendship. Both the Uzbeks and the Tajiks, for example, are old and trusted friends of India. Bobojan Ghaffurov was as close to the hearts of the Indian intellectuals as Ghafur Ghulam and Zulfia were at one time close to Indian academic circles. This close relationship with the Indian intellectuals continues with the same fervour as before providing sound intellectual foundations for the edifice of co-operation and friendship in the future. In the present circumstances, both of the recently separated nations should be alert and not be swayed by the inflammatory and provocative comments of their enemies and should guard against divisive tendencies.

Tajikistan's borders are contiguous to the lands of Qazaqs, Qirghiz, Turkmen, and Uzbeks. In the early sixteenth century, Babur had expressed his view in the *Babur Nama* that the borders of his motherland Farghana were secure from all but one side, that is Khujand, from which an enemy could enter into his otherwise safe domain. The state of Khujand (earlier named Leninabad) is the capital of northern Tajikistan. It is located on the Silk Road, and its borders touch the state of Qazaqs, Qirghiz, Turkmen, and Uzbeks. If Khujand is separated from Tajikistan, it would naturally go to Uzbekistan, which lies at a distance of a four-hour journey by car. This geo-political proximity may not have heightened mutual suspicions as much as the instigations by external elements to create a conflict as the one in Azerbaijan and Armenia. If a political crisis breaks out at any time, the entire Central Asian region will be affected. In particular, Tajikistan has to play its cards with great care. The *World Drug Reports* of recent years have placed it in the category of a 'much sought after haven' unlike Uzbekistan and other places where such dangers have been eradicated or minimized. The place is already torn apart by the internal strife between Quliyab and Khujand which continues even after the death of Nabiev. In the region of the Pamir in southern Tajikistan, Quliyab and Dushambe have their own problems. Any political upheaval may sweep away regional peace and concord. The question naturally arises whether the cities of Samarqand and Bukhara, which enjoy relative peace and prosperity, would now seek (due to a lingual affinity) re-unification with Tajikistan, which suffers from insecurity, anarchy, and economic troubles, howsoever temporary the political and socio-economic crises may prove to be. Despite having to battle centrifugal and separatist tendencies, these newly emerged states have tried their best to realize their goals. In Turkmenistan, President Niyazov, the Turcomanbashi, and in Uzbekistan, President Karimov have managed to control their affairs properly and have become 'living symbol' of the unity of their people. These men have assembled their people under one banner, notwithstanding the charges of encouraging 'personality cults' and of misusing the threat that 'democracy is in danger'. In some places (such as Uzbekistan), the multiparty system has been replaced by the Yakta (unitary) party system. In short, the present-day conditions only emphasize the truth that nations in their infancy need better care but greater discipline and stronger control.

Thanks to its abundant natural and mineral resources and its skilled labour force, Uzbekistan has now entered into another phase of its history, new, independent, and free from the restraints of a totalitarian regime. However, it faces a serious two-fold problem: first, how to evolve a mechanism to convert a command economy into a market-oriented economy, and second, how to integrate the hitherto isolated small-scale economy with the global economy, and how to survive in the new financial setting and establish inter-state regional economic relations.

In the closed system of the past regime, the Uzbek region merely served as the main supplier of cotton, gas, gold, non-ferrous metals, fruits, and vegetables. The sale was at a minimal price (fixed by the state) in which even labour charges were not included. The discriminatory attitude adopted by the over-centralized economy of the previous decades can be gauged from the fact that in Uzbekistan the deep processing and manufacturing of the finished products made of caprolactame (extracted from gas or from the processing and manufacturing of nitron products at Chirchik and Navoi Chemical Plants) were not allowed simply because Russia, Ukraine, and Belorus had built similar plants and were in need of raw materials.

The previous regime had reduced the republics to neo-colonies, whose main task was to supply raw materials only, thus contributing to the deeply entrenched territorial and economic disparities and to outdated and largely unproductive assets. The bitter reality is that the very foundations of the then prevailing legal systems were in conflict with the realization of the economic plans of the republic. The laws and acts mainly served the interests of the earlier lords. Since its independence, however, the enactment of a number of legal and economic regulations has helped to put in its place a new economic policy which should transform the economy and the society.

For each reform, whether popular or not, an intellectual foundation and some degree of acceptance is essential. A multi-dimensional relationship with a multi-faceted financial system (not limited to official exchanges alone) is needed to gear up fiscal activities. More extensive and frequent exchanges of views among economists and intellectuals of the participating countries is required for which the setting up of an infrastructural arrangement is a pre-requisite.

Some sort of a theory of relativity for the economy should be followed. Mutual cooperation should not merely aspire to establish separate productive units; inter-related and inter-sectoral complexes covering the extraction of raw materials, primary and secondary processing, production of machinery and equipment for industries, provision of research, consultancy, and design services, training of personnel, etc., should also be part of the plan.

In order to take maximum advantage of the existing economic programmes and to better implement inter-state agreements, it is necessary to have a comprehensive knowledge of the new economy and a deep understanding of the complexities involved while formulating future plans.

Although perceptions regardomg economic problems including

trade protocols are (and should be) exclusively concerned with finances in all its outward formulations and appearances, they are usually influenced (and often even camouflaged) by the analyst's political or ideological predilections. Since such non-economic elements of perception carry the danger of confusion and misguidance, the choice of economists and intellectuals who have to deal with and be at the helm of these affairs should be very carefully made. Other impediments to ventures of production cooperation include delays in communication, receipt of inquiries, finalization of contracts, non-availability of information on product costings, frequent changes in technical specifications, etc.

Another major constraint to the expansion of economic cooperation is the lack of adequate and precise information about technology, production, capabilities, economic analyses, and details of policies and procedures in the present context of the rapidly changing policies in Uzbekistan.

Indian know how, experience, and expertise can be of some assistance to Uzbekistan mainly in the spheres of technology and equipment. Some potential areas of cooperation are: (a) the production technology for computers, printers, graph plotters, memories for magnetic disks of the 'Winchester' type, sound synthesizers, electronic musical instruments, laser printers, peripheral units for computers; (b) the techniques of manufacturing modern, ready-to-use medicines, including special medicines for children (microgranules, capsules, air sprays, syrups, suppositories, capsuled solutions, tube syringes, plastic coverings); (c) manufacturing amorphous belts; (d) water or gas spraying of metal alloy powders; (e) technology and equipment for injection casting of ceramic blanks of complex configuration out of oxides, nitrides, and carbides.

India can also help Uzbekistan in the spheres of textile processing, electronic goods, agricultural experimentation, and training personnel in business administration, banking, and finance. Cooperation is also possible in the electro-technical industry, the civil engineering and road-building machinery industry, in the manu facture of various instruments in the spheres of telecommunications, computers, automatic central systems for specialized field applications, etc.

Some of the important commodities of export from India could be: tea, coffee, tobacco, fruit juices, jute articles, chemical products, spices, castor oil, mica, hides, consumer goods, cosmetics, perfumes, pharmaceuticals, leather goods and garments, shoe uppers, black and white metals, readymade clothes, luxury items, wooden stuffs, and textiles, some specialized items of machinery such as automobile batteries, machine tools, etc. The establishment of joint ventures for the manufacture of leatherware and footwear, newsprint, cellulose making, jute articles, agricultural products, and synthetic rubber production could also be rewarding and productive areas.

Uzbekistan has immense potential to emerge as a strong, self-reliant country. Its large population and strong prospects offer an excellent market for India's consumer goods. Uzbekistan's deposits of oil and natural gas (40 per cent of natural gas in the CAR, 31 per cent crude oil, 74 per cent gas condensate) and radio-active elements like uranium and thorium could be useful for Indian nuclear power stations. Uzbekistan claims to hold the eighth place in the world in the total production of gold. There are 30 deposits of uranium, and the annual production of copper is 80,000 tons. With its developed power base and already explored reserves of gas (constituting about 2 billion cubic m), coal (more than 2 billion tons), more than 140 deposits of oil, a production of 75 per cent of all the cotton grown in Central Asia, and as the fourth largest producer of cotton in the world, Uzbekistan has the potential to become a rising power among the developing nations within only a few years of its existence as an independent notion, Uzbekistan has already established more than 7,600 private firms, 460 stockholder companies, and 1,300 enterprises given on lease. All that Uzbekistan now needs is to secure cooperation and assistance from its closest neighbours like India and Iran to fend off exploiters and to share the burden of Asianism with its immediate neighbours on an equal footing. On its own, Uzbekistan can play a significant role in strengthening bilateral ties at different levels as it enjoys the confidence and friendship of its neighbours (Uzbekistan made its presence felt in the Afghan-Tajik confrontation and had a say in matters of the ECO and the OIC). Due to its strategic and central position, its contiguous borders with all the CAR, and its vibrant and active contacts with the main administrative and economic centres of the former Soviet Union through a network of roads, railways, and airways, the region can serve as a politically reliable, materially advantageous, and sincerely cooperative neighbour for both India and Iran.

# Some Aspects of Indo-Turkmenistan Relations

In the long history of the relations between India and the lands beyond the Hindukush, Indo-Turkmenistan relations have largely escaped the attention of scholars and historians alike. Undoubtedly, the material on the subject is not extensive though sufficient information can be gleaned from the sources[1] to fill up the lacunae in the historical record. Ancient myths and Indo-Persian sources affirm this close relationship to an extent that both Indians and Turcomans are supposed to have originated from one common stock. They are said to be the descendants of the Prophet Noah. Ham, one of the nine sons of Noah, was supposed to be the ancestor of the Indians. Noah's grandson Kamari (the son of Noah's third son Yafis Oglan) was said to be the ancestor of the Turcomans. There are several names under which the Turcomans are mentioned or described in the sources, such as Tarakuma, Turkmen, and Turkoman. The word Turcoman seems to be a diminutive of Turk-Manand (Turk-like). Abul Fazl, the deputy of Akbar, writes:

> The term Turcoman did not exist in old times but when their posterity came to Persia (Iran) and propagated there, their features came to resemble the Tajiks. But as they were not Tajiks, the latter called them Turcomans. Turk-manand, i.e. the Turk-like which was through use corrupted or diminuted into Turcomans. But some say that the Turcomans are a distinct tribe and are not related to the Turks.[2]

The Turcomans are said to be an admixture of Turks and Tajiks and are supposedly not of pure Turkish origin, hence the name. The word Turkoman is a 'compound of the proper name Turk, and the suffix men (corresponding with the English suffix ship, dom); it is applied to the whole race, conveying the sense that the nomads style themselves pre-eminently as Turks'.[3] Presumably, the Turcomans were the people who were involved in the seventeen marches and who ultimately gave rise to the Ottoman empire, a speculation or conjecture supported by legends. The Turcomans proudly declare that Ertughral who led the five thousand emigrants from Merv to reach Erz Rum and who assisted Kaikhusru against his enemies and who subsequently built their state on the ashes of those of the Seljuqids of Konya were their own kith and kin, i.e. the Turcomans. Since the place from where the emigrants reached the Seljuqid domain is more or less the present-day abode of the Turcomans, this myth of origin cannot altogether be brushed aside. The word in use with us, i.e. Turkoman, is a corruption of the Turkish original and the Turcomans or Turkmen as they style themselves, inhabit for the most part that tract of desert land which extends on this side of the river Oxus, from the shore of the Caspian Sea to Balkh and from the same river to the south as far as Herat and Astarabad.[4]

The Turcomans played a leading and important role in the history of Central Asia. Sometimes they emerged like a tempest to overrun the entire area and sometimes they rose like kings, for example, Aq Quyunlu and Qara Quyunlu. Occasionally they were king makers, the real prop and pillars of the empire as in the case of the Safavids. The Turcomans contributed much to the turkicizing of north Persia, during the period when the family of the Atabegs ruled in Iran, and beyond all dispute, it is they who contributed the largest contingent to the Turkish population on the other side of the Caucasus, to Azerbaijan, Mazendaran, and Shiraz.[5] Vambery asserts: 'The Turcoman is without any possibility of contradiction next to the Kipchak the most war-like and savage race of Central Asia; in his rear, in the cities of Khiva, Bukhara and Khoqand, we find the seat of cowardice and effeminacy. . . .'[6] The last risings of the Turcomans in masse occurred under Nadir Shah and Aga Muhammad Khan. Nadir Shah, 'helped by their tribes and by the Afghans at the commencement of the last century shook Asia out of her slumber; and the second conqueror above mentioned availed himself of the sword of the Turcomans to found his dynasty'.[7] Apart from being bellicose warriors, the Turcomans proved themselves to be men of the pen and were excellent writers. The *Tarikh-i Alam Ara-i Abbasi* written by Iskandar Beg Turcoman gives certain details about the history of the tripartite relations in the region which are not available elsewhere. Hasan Beg Rumlu's book *Ahsan-ut Tawarikh* is another valuable source for the study of history.

Interestingly enough, these Turcomans, like their counterparts, spread far and wide in the region and in each place they had a different set of tribal entities. Vambery describes their tribal organization at length, though Schuyler ignores their existence. Krader and certain other historians describe their tribal structure under varying names.[8] In a letter of Nadir Shah, sent in 1740 to Muhammed Shah, the Turcomans of Dasht have been mentioned. Riazul Islam says that these were perhaps the Turcoman of Khwarazm.[9] The Turcoman tribes who supported the Ilbar Khans of Khiva included: Qazaq, Aral, Tekke, Yamut, Shariq, and Ersari.[10] The nine Turcoman tribes which formed the backbone of the Safavid dynasty of Persia were: Rumlu, Takkalu, Shamlu, Istajlu, Afshar, Qachar, Zulqadr, and Warsak. They hailed, it is said, from places like Rum, Sham, Takla Makan, and hence the names of the tribes were derived from their place of origin.[11]

In geographical works also there are references to the Turcomans. The cities of Turkmenistan have not been properly described, probably because these Turcomans still did not have a highly urbanized culture in the medieval period. Although Qazvini describes the region, he merely makes a passing reference to the place Ashkabad as Shikabad. Other such names included Sakabad, Sikmabad, Sakmomabad, and Shaklabad, signifying perhaps present-day Ashkabad.[12] The inhabitants of the region have been described as Ashkanian, Ashkidban or Ashkidabad in certain Persian sources.[13] Etymologically the word Ashkabad had varied origins. Presumably it was the corrupted form of Ashkanian or Ashkahan. Ibn-i Hauqal refers to Ashkahan where the Jews exiled from Isfahan and its vicinity took shelter and which in Ibn-i Hauqal's time was commonly called 'Yahudia'. The Jews themselves called this place as 'Ashkahan', a Hebrew word Since the original inhabitants of the place who were cattle breeders disliked this infiltration, a confrontation took place. After prolonged warfare the Jews were destroyed and the place was turned into a prosperous and populous city where, Muslims and rich peasants lived. Here most of the people were friendly, righteous of and nice.[14] Another traditional Turcoman version regarding the history Ashkabad is that it may have originated from the word *'ishq'*, i.e. Ishqabad (the abode of love), though this claim has no historical basis.

In India, the Turcomans were known not by their tribal suffixes but mostly (rather always) by their racial name, i.e. the Turcomans. In the biographical notes available in the sources, however, their *taefas*, etc., have been explained. They participated in various campaigns and won laurels for the Mughals. Apart from their martial feats, they greatly contributed towards the enrichment of the cultural life in Mughal India. As will be discussed later, the traces of Indo-Turkmenistan relations are not only preserved in the pages of the annals of history but they are also visible on the face of the earth even today. In many big and small towns of India (for example, in Delhi and Aligarh) there are majestic gates especially named after the Turcomans, i.e. the 'Turkman Gate' in northern Delhi. These were evidently the commercial portals through which horses and other commodities were brought into India. These also served as the centres where the Turcomans lived and sold their rare and exotic products. Turcoman carpets decorated the palaces and houses in India and the Turcoman jewellery added to the beauty of Indian women. The Turcoman soldiers swelled the ranks of the Mughal army and increased the number of the Mughal nobility.

Indo-Turkmenistan relations were further deepened and strengthened by men like Bairam Khan and his son Abdurrahim Khan-i Khanan. Like other medieval Central Asians, Bairam was a fine admixture of the qualities of the head and the heart. He was endowed with both the graceful and creative capacity of the pen and the furious ferocity of the sword. Badauni, the chronic and habitually bitter critic of human souls, credited Bairam Khan for being 'a poet of no mean pretensions'.[15] Bairam Khan's love for India was as deep as his attachment to his motherland. He played a key role in successfully bridging the gulf between India and Central Asia and also initiated and maintained friendly relations with other countries. His court was equally open to men of talents from Central Asia, India, Persia, and other places. Many Turcomans were inducted into the Mughal court. Many worthy people came from Central Asia and served Bairam for quite a long time.

Due to his military prowess, political sagacity, and extraordinary courage, Bairam attracted the attention of Indian magnates like Raja Mitra Sen, Sher Shah, and others who offered patronage to him. However, Bairam's love for the Mughals, did not allow him to desert his patrons. 'The reconquest of India may justly be ascribed to Bairam Khan.' He proved himself to be 'the best of all the leaders—a forefather in the battle', who thereafter won many lofty titles for his selfless service. His wisdom saved the Mughal dynasty from extinction as his timely suggestion to seek help from Persia and his subsequent continuous and dedicated support to Humayun and Akbar assisted tremendously in firmly rooting the Mughal empire in an alien land. It was this dedicated service to the family that endeared Bairam Khan to Humayun and Akbar. After his preliminary conquest of India, Humayun sent messages to all (including Khan Bairam Khan). On the *fathnama* sent to Bairam Khan in Qandahar, Humayun himself wrote a few lines. In this particular *fathnama* the day of victory over the Indian forces was described as 'the day of *nauruz* of Bairam' (*ruzi nauruz-i Bairam ast imroz*). There are two couplets addressed to Bairam in the same document by Humayun expressing his deep love for his friend and supporter:

This translates as: 'All the arrangements for the gala celebrations of the victory are ready and my heart is yearning for a meeting with you so that my ears could be delighted to hear your voice and my eyes could be brightened by the visibility of your face.' In the same letter, Humayun wrote: 'Oh, thou who is the friend of mine in the sorrowful moments, when my mind is free and well adjusted, not a single moment I am without your remembrances. Are you also so love stricken as I am?'[16]

As a Shia perhaps Bairam's love for Iran and Iranians was not unusual. To several persons who fled from Iran he offered protection, posts, rewards, and titles. For example, Bairam assisted Muhammad Qasim Khan of Nishapur, Sadiq Khan of Herat, and Haji Muhammad Khan of Siestan.[17] Shah Tahmasp, the Safavid King of Persia, 'admired the abilities and loyalty' of Bairam. 'As that sovereign', writes Shahnawaz Khan, 'sometimes feasted with Humayun for the sake of enjoyment, and sometimes had a hunting party with him, he one day, when there was a display of polo and of tilting (*qabaq andazi*) gave him the title of Khan. After the return from Persia he was sent with a letter of royal advice and a *farman* in favour of Mirza Kamran.' When Humayun captured Qandahar 'by force' from the Persians, he assigned it to Bairam Khan as a measure of safe play. In his apology to the Shah, Humayun convincingly justified his action: 'Bairam Khan is the trusted servant of both of us. We have made over the fort to him.'[18] Bairam proved to be a safety valve for Humayun. Whenever the embassies arrived from Persia, Shah Tahmasp always sent separate presents to Bairam Khan. In 1552 when Tahmasp sent a few horses of good breed and nice pieces of cloth from Yazd and Kashan to Humayun, he did not forget to send horses and a *saropa* to Bairam Khan. When the rubies, diamonds, and jewels were presented by Bairam Khan on behalf of Humayun, the Shah bestowed upon him the title of Khan and one drum.[19] Out of nine horses to be given to

Humayun after his arrival in Persia, one was allocated by name to Bairam Khan by the Shah of Iran in his letter to Humayun: 'Let all nine horses be produced for his auspicious inspection and mention which of them are for the fortunate nawab and also mention which is for such and such an officer'.[20] Nahawandi says that it was in Iraq that Bairam Khan received the title of Khan-i Khanan from Shah Tahmasp. Besides, many grand actions emanated from him which won him favours and honours. 'He was an excellent archer. In Persia he had shown his skill when archery was keen (lit. *the qabaq bazaar hot*). Bairam Beg received the title of Khan'. Even the Shah of Iran wistfully declared that he would like to have a *sipahsalar* like the Khan-i Khanan on whom he could rely and leave the entire burden of management and administration, while himself enjoying all kinds of luxuries and freedom. While admiring the Khan-i Khanan, the Shah often commented that such a wise, brave, and experienced person could never be found in the entire family of Qarayusaf of the Qara Quyunlu dynasty.

Nurullah Shustri writes about Bairam Khan: 'Although apparently, the Khan was wearing the crown of official authority and enjoyed all grandeur and majesticity, he was in fact in the garb of poverty and carried the mystic rings in his ears.' Commenting on the Khan's generosity, he adds: 'In these days of real difficulty, anybody who entered India safely and directly reached Bairam Khan and got the patronage without any recommendation, invitation or prior permission.'[21] Scholars from all over the region flocked to Bairam. His connections with the Central Asian lands were never severed. In Bairam Khan's time came several reputed poets like Kandi, Manzari Samarqandi, Sahmi, Bukhari, and Mahwi. Maulana Alauddin was one of the most famous of the learned men; he was for sometime among the companions of the Khan-i Khanan by whom he was highly regarded and much honoured. Mulla Pir Muhammad of Shirvan was also a mulla of good standing and great pretension, and gathered round him a cheerful company. He arrived from Shirvan and joined the service of the Khan-i Khanan in Qandahar and 'received advancement.' After the conquest of India he received the title of Khan and afterwards that of Nasir-ul Mulk; he lived for three or four years in the greatest honour and consideration. Tazarvi of Abhar came from Turkey to India during Bairam Khan's ascendancy and is said to have 'profited much by his generosity'.[22] Manzari Samarqandi was in the service of Bairam Khan at Agra and designed an epic Book of Kings (*Shahnama*) on the model of Firdausi and completed the versification of several of the incidents to be included in it. . . . He presented it to the Khan at Patyali and the Khan made some corrections in it and told him the whole story of the fight in proper order from the beginning to the end. Manzari in one night, as it was the Khan's wish, corrected those three or four hundred couplets and read them at his level the next morning, and received a notable reward.

Another famous poet Maulana Mansur, who originally belonged to Sawah (though he was commonly known as Tabrizi), often visited various countries for the sake of trade or merely for recreation. He lived in India for quite a long time and took up service with various persons. He was very close to Bairam Khan, and shared his deep-seated love for India. Commenting on India, Maulana Adham once recited, in response to Bairam Khan's verse, the following: 'The country of Hind abounds in damsels with black eyes who are found everywhere. They are both a catastrophe to our faith and a cataclysm to the life'.[23] In India, Bairam Khan's court was open and his munificence also extended to talented men form in India. It is indeed very commendable that even when the Khan-i Khanan

had nothing in his treasury, the gave at one sitting a lac of *tankah* worth in money and goods to Ram Das of Lakhnau (father of the famous poet Surdas) who was one of Ashim Shah and one that in music and song you might term a second Miyan Tan Sen. This man used to be the Khan-i Khanan's companion and intimate associate and by the beauty of his voice continually brought tears to his eyes.[24]

Sometimes his patronage of Indians brought charges of nepotism against Bairam Khan. Bairam patronized Shaikh Gadai who had

perfected himself in exoteric learning and enjoyed the society of the learned men of the age, being benefited from their companionship. By means of the claim which intimate friendship gave him on Bairam Khan, he obtained the appointment of sadrussudur in India and was for several years resorted to as an authority on religion by the sages and principal men of Hindustan, Khurasan, Iraq, and Transoxiana. He was a born poet and used to compose and sing hymns and religious songs after the Indian manner to which pursuits he was passionately addicted.[25]

Thus, Bairam Khan spent most of his time in the company of men of learning and excellence (*ahl-i fazl-o kamal*). The men of letters, poets, and boon companions were all prosperous and flourished during his time. 'He held this group of learned men in high esteem.

He squandered silver and gold on them without even weighing them. The musicians, singers and other artists were all freed from the sorrows in his assembly.'[26]

Bairam Khan often extended patronage to and showered rewards generously on all leaned men. Hijaz Khan Badauni, an Afghan *amir* who had a standard, a kettledrum, and a pennon, towards the end of his life retired from military affairs; with the enjoyment of a very trifling pension the pursued rectitude by following the path of asceticism and devotion. To him in return for a *qasida* which in the *maqta* he dedicated to the Khan, Bairam gave a lakh of *tankahs* and made him superintendent of the government of Sirhind and caused him to be appointed to that province. Badauni comments that the saying of Khwaja Kalan Beg came true, viz., 'Heaven above is of course a good judge of poetry. The sum of the whole matter is that 100,000 were to the liberal mind of the Khan as one.' Comparing this with his own times, Badauni remarks: 'How different indeed to these base ones, who now have come to the surface of the water: If the odour of fidelity thou perceivest from any one, His foot thou shouldst kiss much more than that of kings.'[27]

Badauni records that learned men came from all parts of the world to visit Bairam Khan and departed happy 'in the possession of gifts bestowed by his hand, as open as the ocean itself, and his court, lofty as the sky, was the resort of the lords of learning and had perfect qualities'. There were some poets and scholars who were said to have suffered at his hands but their number was not large and they had their own or some other reason for not remaining in India. For example, Ashraf Khan Mir Munshi, a Saiyid of Sabzwar, who was a 'renowned calligrapher, a clever writer, exact in his style', took part in the battle against Hemu. He was imprisoned by Bairam but escaped and went to Mecca. Hakim Saif-ul Mulk of Damawand (a place to the east of Tehran) was 'held in much honour in India for some years during the time of Bairam Khan and afterwards but according to his own statement he received neither patronage nor honour and returned to his country disappointed'. Badauni, who was usually very critical about his contemporaries, for some reason, greatly applauds Bairam Khan's period, saying: 'The time of Bairam Khan was that best of times, when India was as a bride. . . .' Badauni wistfully and frequently recalls the time 'when Bayram Khan was in power' and often refers to events 'during Bayram Khan's regency'.[28]

In addition to having an extremely talented Central Asian wife of the stature of Salima Begam, Bairam Khan also married an Indian lady. After Humayun had reconquered India and 'established himself at Delhi, he, in order to give assurance and encouragement to the *zamindars*, instituted marriages with their daughters. Jamal Khan, the cousin of Husain Khan of Mewat who was one of the influential *zamindars* of India, waited upon Humayun. He had two daughters. Humayun married the eldest and gave the second to Bairam. From this Indo-Turkmenistani union was born the world-famous scholar and poet Abdurrahim Khan-i Khanan on 17 December 1556. Abdurrahim further strengthened the ties of love between the two countries. Well versed in Turkish, he translated Babur's autobiography into Persian which facilitated its world-wide spread and study. He was equally proficient in Indian languages and wrote excellent quatrains and couplets (*duhas*) which are widely acknowledged as the pearls of wisdom.

Abdurrahim was only three or four years of age when his father Bairam Khan died. He was taken to Akbar (in 1562), who 'notwithstanding the insinuations of malicious courtiers, took charge of him'. The post of *otbegi* (the in-charge of all horses belonging to the government, and who directs all the officers charged with the management of the horses), which was 'one of the highest of the state and was only held by grandees of high rank', was also held by the Khan-i Khanan.[29] He was given the title of Mirza Khan and later on that of *farzand-i barkhurdar Khan-i Khanan sipahsalar*. Several letters written by Akbar and Abul Fazl to him testify to the exclusive position which he deservedly enjoyed at Akbar's court.

The Khan-i Khanan is said to have been a brave soldier and a good paymaster. When the Deccan wars were going on, Dowlat Khan who was perturbed by the numerical strength of the enemy approached him and said: 'Their numbers are immense and victory rests with heaven. Point out a place where we can find you should we be defeated.' 'Under the corpses', replied the Khan-i Khanan. Such an attitude presumably infused a new spirit among the men because victory was attained and the Khan-i Khanan distributed 75 lakhs of rupees among his soldiers. He received the highest dignity, that of *amir*, the *mansab* of 5,000, the highest available in those days, and the title of Khan-i Khanan, a horse, *khalat*, etc., in recognition of his two victories at Sarkhij and Nandot in Gujarat. He was himself so pleased with his success that he gave away his entire property to his soldiers, even his inkstand which he gave to a soldier who came last and said he had not received anything. During his thirty years' stay in the Deccan, Abdurrahim showed his diplomatic skills to such an extent that the 'four *duniyadars*' (the rulers) of the Deccan became his subservients.

Such was his magnetism that every *Tabqa* and *Taefa* left his homeland to join his service. Not only did he hold students (*danishmands, ahl-i ulum, tulaba*) in high esteem but he also made every effort to extend all possible help to them. He richly rewarded them. Many incidents are quoted in the chronicles to prove the extent of his generosity. Once a *piyadah* made a mistake in the records and put his signature on a thousand rupees (instead of a thousand *tankahs*). This error was not corrected but immediately accepted and the money paid. Similarly, whenever a *qasida* (eulogy) was written for him, he gave one assload of *zar*. Mulla Nawai was weighed in gold. Mulla Shakibi was given one thousand *asharfis*. Mulla Shauqi was allowed to carry as much red gold in his shirt as he could. When Abdurrahim saw his shirt, which was in a bad shape, he gave him a fine new dress also. Mulla Hayati was taken to the treasury to carry as many *asharfis* as he could. Mulla Naziri Fazili is said to have told the Khan-i Khanan that he had never seen a sum of one lakh rupees. It was not only shown to him but was also bestowed upon him. Mulla Urfi was sent a similar amount every year to relieve him from the anxiety of deprivation. Shah Hisamuddin of Delhi received thirty thousand rupees for his expenses. The Khan-i Khanan went to the cells of the dervishes to offer *nazr* and *futuh*. In fact, he had full faith in the nice disposition, fine taste, and good nature (*saliqa wa tabiat*) of these men of learning. The *pargana* of Dholqa in Gujarat which yielded annually a sum of 5-6 lakh of rupees and which measured 30,000 *bighas* was given as subsistence allowance and scholarships to the dervishes and the poor. No doubt there were volumes compiled in praise of the Khan-i Khanan. It is also recorded that in intellect, far-sightedness, understanding, and affairs of administration he was incomparable. He possessed almost all the qualities which a human being could and should have.[30]

Nahawandi depicts Abdurrahim as a deeply religious man. Keeping in mind the medieval ideals of excellence, he has been described as a righteous person and a strict follower of the Sharia who abstained from all kinds of temptations and dedicated himself to the service and fulfilment of the desires of his subjects—the deposits of God. In Sufi ways, studies, and *tazkira*, he was like his contemporaries Junaid and Bayazid. Such burning passion compassion asceticism, and content men were never seen in any Sufi. He kept himself engaged in the recitation of the Koran and in the study of religious and intellectual works. He had mastered the Koranic verses. He was educated by the most competent, knowledgeable, and intelligent teachers like Muhammad Amin Andijani, Ghazi Khan Badakhshi, Fathullah Shirazi, and Hakim Ali Gilani. Such was his intense liking for and inclination towards studies that even when he was bathing, his servant stood alongside with a book which he continued reading. On hunting excursions too, he was engrossed in reading while riding his horse.[31]

Abdurrahim was also an excellent administrator. After the death of Raja Todar Mal, all the arrangements and management of the *wizarat* were assigned to him. Despite his busy schedule and his involvement in administrative affairs, he always sought and looked forward to the company of the *dervishes* and recluses. At night, he went out to *khanqahs*, mosques, *madrasas*, and cells to meet them all, thinking perhaps that without their blessings the management and leadership of the kingdom could not be attained. In the shepherding of people and in the imparting of justice, he had no equal and tyranny found no place in his state. Although he was a military commander, which is an essential requisite for politics, he continued to be most forgiving and often overlooked and pardoned offenders. He had many good qualities like modesty, amiability, and abstinence from any kind of revengefulness, tyranny and callousness. He was a *dervish* in the form of a sultan and an angel in the form of a human being. In the acquisition of learning he had reached the pinnacle, and had distinguished himself as a scholar at the global level. Having closely studied all the current and customary sciences, his own self had turned into a tablet or encyclopaedia of Arabic and Persian literature and learning.[32] He solved many problems of a scientific nature, and being an intellectual endowed with reason and having expertise in technical, traditional and historical knowledge, he had equally excelled in logic, mathematics, physiognomy, astronomy, *fiqh*, *tafsir*, *kalam*, and *hikmat*. His dialectical spirit was so intense and penetrating that this quality surprised many. In the art of letter writing he had no equal and drafted even the *manshurs* and the *ahkams* in the most efficient manner. Some of the letters written by him in Turkish and Persian were collected by Nahawandi. One of the wonders of his intelligence and skillfulness, says Nahawandi, is that lengthy letters in the Devanagari script are instantly read and translated into Persian and the Persian letters are read and translated into Hindi with as much ease as Arabic letters are translated into Hindi and Persian. Such is the accurate 'uninterrupted' and fluent eloquence that those present could never even imagine that he was interpreting it. In writing letters to the rulers of Iran and Turan and in drafting *firmans* to provincial rulers, he had such an exclusive expertise that none could excel in this art better than him.[33]

Abdurrahim's court included men of learning, and art. Pir Abdulbaqi of Tabriz was a popular *danishmand* of Iran and Iraq, who excelled in Sufism and was acknowledged as an accomplished master (*sar-amad*) of art. Other luminaries of his court were: Shaikh Jamaluddin Muhammad of Astrabad, M. Raza-i Taj Meshedi, Yulqul-i Beg, Anis-i Shamlu, Maulana Navai Khurasani, Muhammad Shariq, Wuqui of Nishapur, Mir Muhammad Hashim, Muhammad Husain Nasiri of Nishapur, Mahwi, Nuvaidi Turcoman, Shakibi Isfahani, Urf-i Shirazi, Kami of Qum, Mir Dust-i Samarqandi (a disciple of Mushfiqi Bukhari), and others. Mirza Shukrulla of Shiraz distinguished himself in literary attainments, accounting, etc. There were others like Qazi Abdul Aziz Hamdani and Muhammad Baqar of Tabriz.[34]

Sujan Rai, a bitter critic of Bairam Khan, nevertheless praises his son Khan-i Khanan Abdurrahim. He writes:

> Khan-i Khanan who is renowned in India for his extraordinary genius, elegance of temperament, unique and unusual couplets, innate generosity and personal bravery is the same Abdurrahim. He had exhibited his talents in poetry from the age of eleven and his poems carried both the spirit of love and the aura of mysticism. He never had to adduce or caused to produce a poem as it was spontaneous. He had many disciples from far and near.[35]

His expertise in chronogram was also exceptional.
Often he wrote the *Tarikh* in five languages in one couplet.

These lines in praise of Abdurrahim were written in the Kashmiri language. He wrote good quatrains. Abul Fazl says: 'People by a happy comparison called him Mir Ali Sher', and notes that 'his court was like that of Mirza Sultan Husain Baiqra—full of scholars'. He made an immortal name for himself as a poet. He adopted his personal name Rahim as his pen name also. The poems written by him in Hindi, Turkish, and Arabic are equally exquisite specimens of his poetic genius, but his Hindi couplets are indeed superb and like a bright lighthouse. In the Hindi language, he contributed very commendable and pleasing (*Ashaarimatino abiyat-i dilnasin*) couplets (*duhas*).[36] Nahawandi says that India is a multilingual country where different languages and dialects are spoken and the urban and rural languages are also different. The Khan-i Khanan was well versed in all of them and fluently conversed in and understood these languages.[37] His ancestral language being Turkish, he was very well acquainted with the intricacies of this language, had translated the *Babur Nama* from the Chaghatai Turkish into Persian, and acquainted the non-Turkish people with that document of the utmost importance, 'so that its exquisite bounties might moisten the lips of the thirsty and its hidden treasure might be seen by those with empty hands'. Although the Turkish language is not commonly understood in India, some of its inhabitants like the Rumis, the Chaghatais, the Uzbeks, the Turks, and the Qizilbash know this language well. He not only composed poems in all the three languages but also explained and interpreted the poetry in several other languages. He was equally knowledgeable about the customs and traditions of his ancestral home in Central Asia and also those of India. Before going to bed, he used to listen to Hindi, Turkish, and Persian stories and folktales in order to closely familiarize himself with the social milieu and ethos of a country and the people with whom he came into daily contact. While managing the affairs of the *diwan khana*, the Khan-i Khanan used to converse with the people in their respective languages. For example, if there came an Arab, he would talk to him in Arabic. If an Arab had some financial and administrative problem, the Khan-i Khanan used to talk to him in his own tongue. With Indians, he relied upon Hindi. With every group he maintained the same style of exclusive closeness so that no gap in communication was likely to occur. Since in India there were many Christians who had close contacts with the Emperor and since there were exchanges of embassies between the Mughals and the European rulers, Akbar ordered him to learn the language of the *firangis* and acquire the art of writing letters in that language. The Khan-i Khanan was so intelligent that he learnt this art within no time after brief meetings with the Christian specialists. He spent time occasionally with the traders and the Christian elite in the court and became such an expert that he could teach these skills to his own servants and children. None of his contemporaries, had such a command over so many languages. Like Shah Abbas who knew all the dialects (Gilani, Shirwani,

Mazandarani, Garzi, Qiyafa, Chirkis, Turcoman, etc.) of his country and who conversed with his subjects in their own languages, the Khan-i Khanan also won over the people with his gift of lingual affinity.[38] He spent a fortune in enriching his library. After his death a book in Hindi was discovered in his library, the cost of which amounted to 50,000 rupees as it was studded with gold, silver, and precious stones. He was generous in distributing knowledge and books. Once he bestowed 700 valuable books in one day on the *ulama* (learned men) of Burhanpur.[39]

A group of Indians received subsistence allowances and scholarships from Bairam Khan. Their rights were confirmed by the Khan-i Khanan and orders were issued for their renewal on a permanent basis. Half of the amount was paid in cash on the very day when the matter was first brought to his notice. Such was his munificence that once, when the news of a shipwreck reached him, he gave one lakh *mahmudis* to be divided equally between the victims and Maulana Shakibi. He used to help many learned men who found it difficult to make both ends meet. The *Maasir-i Rahimi* is a 'splendid testimony to his generosity; it shows that he was the Moecenas of Akbar's age'.[40] He was a very largehearted and generous man. His two confidants, Gobardhan Das and his brother Anand Das, betrayed him and opened negotiations for better prospects with Adil Shah. When the latter refused to oblige them on the plea that they had let down their former master and their faithfulness could not be trusted, the duo again approached the Khan-i Khanan, pleading for mercy from him. They were forgiven and assigned fresh jobs. He had many loyal Hindu officials whom he valued greatly. Gobardhan Das was appointed as *diwan*, Anand Das became his *diwan-i kul*. In 1615 when Shahnawaz Khan won the war in the Deccan, many brave men like Maha Singh, Lal Bir Singh, and several others were rewarded and precious gifts were given to them. In the celebrations that followed the conquest of Gujarat, he bestowed upon 1,200 commanders and *sardars* (like Baz Bahadur, Tilak Bahadur, Rai Durga, Rai Lonkorn, Manohar Sher Dil, Ram Chandra, Udai Singh, Sanku Rajput, Tulsidas, Raja Singh, and others) belts, swords, *saropas*, special *khalats*, Iraqi horses, elephants, etc.[41] In an order (*hukm*) dated 11 Muharram, 995, the Khan-i Khanan exempted Gobardhan Das from taxes like *qurnaq*, *gao*, *shumari*, etc., from his own grazing grounds in Sawi, Lahar and Bari.[42]

The Khan-i Khanan was broad-minded and had no feelings of religious chauvinism. He had many Hindus in his retinue and always showered unadulterated love on them, yet he was balanced in his outlook and never allowed the overplay of religious fanaticism which trampled human beings and their feelings. Badauni presents the story of Haji Sultan of Thanesar, who was:

> employed for four years alone and without any coadjutor, on the translation of the *Mahabharata* which is known as the *Razm Nama* and what was begun by Naqib was finished by him. He was so proud of the fact that he answered to one of the queries, 'I am translating what was well known ten thousand years ago into the modern tongue.' Yet on account of the crime of cow killing which was brought against him by the Hindus of that *pargana* (Thanesar) an order was issued for his banishment to Bhakkar and the Khan-i Khanan, who was in those days in charge of the *suba* of Multan, fully cognizant of his innocence treated him with great consideration and kindness. After conquering the provinces of Asirgarh and Burhanpur, he prayed in one of his petitions for the reversal of the sentence against him. His request was granted . . . so that the Emperor privately ordered Sh. Abul Fazl to appoint him Karori of Thanesar.[43]

The chroniclers say that though the Khan-i Khanan's father had been a Shia, Mirza Abdurrahim was a Sunni, but people also said that he was a Shia who practised *taqiyya*.[44] Shaikh Farid Bhakkari also confirms that Bairam Khan followed the *mazhabi aimma asna ashr*, i.e. Shiism. No evidence can be more authentic in this context than that of Shustri who describes him as a follower of this very faith. Like his father Bairam Khan, Abdurrahim was also a true representative of his age, at a time during which the Bhakti and Sufi movements spread the message of love and harmony. He was eclectic and pantheistic in his views. His visits to the places of Hindu pilgrimages and shrines such as Haridwar surprised many of his contemporaries.

He was justice loving and used to sit every Thursday on a platform in the *kotwali* which was situated in the Nakhas of Burhanpur *maidan*. It was widely circulated that those desirous of seeking justice should come to him. The feeble, down trodden, and old men expressed their problems and sought solutions without any fear or hesitation. If any gate keeper interfered with the free entrance he was suspended and lashed. The Khan-i Khanan always assisted in fulfilling the demands of the needy. On the three days, namely, Saturday, Monday, and Wednesday, he used to sit in the *diwan khana* to deal with the affairs of administration and the management of the state.[45] He was so keenly interested in the current affairs of the court and of people that he appointed men like Mahmud Khan Wakil, Uttam Chand, and Babu Miyan Kalal, each of them separately to send through the *dak chauki* instant news on a day-to-day basis. *Harkaras* were also employed in the *adalat khana*, *chabutra*, and *kachehri* to note down the details happenings in these places. In lanes, markets, and *gudri* informers were dispatched to collect rumours and views of the commoners. The reports thus collected were all read by him and then thrown into the fire.

Apart from a ship *Jahazi Rahimi* named after him, the Khan-i Khanan had three boats in the port of Surat which were named *Rahimi*, *Karimi*, and *Salari*. These were launched for the benefit of pilgrims going to Mecca, learned men, teachers, and traders. The money for the salaries of pilots and workers was paid as *ulufa* by the Khan-i Khanan.[46]

Nahawandi says that in India the construction of *hamams* (bath houses) was said to be 'forbidden'. Besides, running water in the plains was a rarity and only wells, lakes, and *talabs* existed. The Khan-i Khanan built the Kariz Talab near Lal Bagh for the benefit of the commoners. Many lakes (*nahrs*) were also properly constructed. Muhammad Ali Gurg Khurasani got *hamams* built for which grants were provided by the Khan-i Khanan. This measure helped the poor and the needy in maintaining personal cleanliness. The Lal Bagh *talab* was quite deep and measured 200 m × 200 m. In the *talab* grew *kamal* (lotus) in great profusion. Prior to the Khan-i Khanan's arrival, none had seen the *kamal* growing in Khandesh. A *suffa* in the Juma mosque was also constructed. The construction and beautification of the place known as Jahangirpura by the Khan-i Khanan's own money was another feat of that noble soul; he persuaded several persons to settle down there and make the place populous and prosperous. During his stay in Gujarat, the Khan-i Khanan ordered that a garden and a house should be constructed in the palace of Mahmud Gujarati which became a place of excursion for Indians. A garden was laid out near the river. While he was in Lahore, the Khan-i Khanan ordered that gardens, buildings, and *dehkadas* (villages) should be constructed and established. In Agra, the famous Iranian architect Ustad Baruli designed and constructed beautiful buildings. Several buildings were constructed in Delhi on which over 2 lakh of rupees were spent but these provided halting places for the poor and the deserving.[47] During his governorship of Khandesh, Berar, and the Deccan, the Khan-i Khanan ordered that the garden palaces which the rulers of Khandesh had started building and which were now in a dilapidated state should be reconstructed. He insisted on employing excellent gardeners, engineers, horticulturists, and builders. Here Iraqi, Khurasani, and Indian fruits and dry fruit trees were planted. If Nahawandi is to be believed, the melon (*kharbuza*) was totally unknown to the people in India who thought that this was either some kind of a medicinal herb or was something connected with dresses. The planting of melons for the Indians was an uphill task. The Khan-i Khanan summoned Iraqi and Khurasani horticulturists and selected the village of Balkwara, the climate of which suited the cultivation of melons. The variety of this fruit produced in India was sweeter and better than was found elsewhere and this lowered the value of mangoes and sugar.[48]

In the sphere of Indian music, his mind and artistic talents combined to produce a miracle. Even the masters of this art depended on him for deciphering difficult musical compositions and works and looked to him to resolve complicated matters. He compiled famous works on music. It is widely acclaimed and appreciated that the expertise which the Khan-i Khanan acquired in Indian music was never attained even by an Indian. In the knowledge of harmony, musical rhythm, and melody, including that of the Iranians, the Khan-i Khanan was unique.[49]

The third volume of Mulla Abdul Baqi Nahawandi's work *Maasir-i Rahimi* contains many references to the family of Bairam Khan. The volume begins with the chronograms of the birth of Airij Darab Rahmandar and the victories of Mirza Airij Shahnawaz Khan. Apart from the descriptions of the men of the pen (who were either invited by the Khan-i Khanan or who were indirectly or directly connected with his or Akbar's court), there are numerous *qasidas* in praise of Abdurrahim Khan-i Khanan. Some of these are quoted here. They evidently echo the feelings of many of his admirers.[50] Nahawandi was not the only panegyrist of the Khan-i Khanan. Another famous work, *Nawab Khan-i Khanan Charita* was composed at the instance of Pratap Saha, the ruler of Salasaila and Mayur Parvata. Certain Rajput works of this nature are also extant. The deep appreciation and lavish praise showered by the chroniclers on Abdurrahim Khan-i Khanan has provoked certain later historians to argue that since the crown or the ruling authority is necessarily doomed to commit errors and become involved in disputes, they look forward to exploiting elements of human weakness. If the historians fail to find such references in the historical record, they dismiss the history of that individual as a eulogy or hagiology. But sometimes the hagiological and panegyrist accounts do actually reflect the reality, as in the case of Abdurrahim Khan-i Khanan.[51] The available sources seem to confirm his outstanding qualities.

In his later years the Khan-i Khanan had to face some disgrace, just as his father had done earlier while in the service of the Mughals. He was denounced as a partisan. He became covetous and pursued worldly acquisitions. His higher values were given in to vicious changes as now he frequently uttered that acts of hostility with an enemy should be performed in the guise of friendship. Due to his bad experiences for which he had not bargained, he must have lost faith in human beings with whom he had all along been nice. Perhaps the last days of the Khan-i Khanan were not very pleasant and his death (1036 AH) was equally painful which surprised Shaikh Farid who asked how the Khan-i Khanan, who was an *insan-i kamil* (perfect man), had become so restless and tense. Shaikh Farid's query was met with the reply that for fifty years he had lived like a Khan-i Khanan, but now his spirit and body were being separated, hence the physical trauma. The Khan-i Khanan was buried in Delhi under the same dome where his wife had earlier been laid to rest. This was, ironically, again near the tomb of Humayun.

## Abdurrahim Khan-i Khanan: A Patron of Fine Arts

Abdurrahim Khan-i Khanan was a true representative of his age, a man of many capabilities, an apostle of communal amity and fraternity, and a symbol of India's emerging composite culture. In his preface to Samar Bahadur Singh's book on Abdurrahim Khan-i-Khanan, Jadu Nath Sarkar describes him 'as superior to Massiness', at least in one respect that he had in his court two distinct streams of culture—Muslim and Hindu, with Persian and Sanskrit both merging into one *sangam* (the confluence of two or more rivers), irrigating and nurturing the heart of India and its environment.[52] Abdurrahim Khan-i Khanan inherited the best traits of his parental lineage from his father's side, the qualities of far-sightedness, gallantry, generosity, love of literary and artistic pursuits, and skill in administration. The heritage of Turcoman bravery, the gift of Persian cultural standards, and the legacy of Mewati Khanzada's military prowess and courage adorned his personal character. He was large-hearted and broad-minded, and was influenced by the eclecticism and pantheistic movements of his age. His father was a follower of the Shia faith and his mother belonged to the Sunni sect. As a result, his own views about religion were far from orthodox. In an age when the orthodox Badauni and conservative Brahmins translated the *Atharva Veda* into Persian, such was his faith in the principle of co-existence that many authors believed that he was a devotee of Krishna and a follower of other Hindu traditions. It is interesting to note that all those poets who wrote eulogical accounts of Rahim did not shower similar praises on any other ruler. Rahim extended his patronage to poets like Gang, Prasidh, Mandan, Sant, Lakshminarayana, and Ban. Once he bestowed a reward of 36 lakh of rupees on Gang for his *chhappay*. Rahim developed very close relations with contemporary poets like Tulsi Das, Raskhan, Shri Vyasji, Bihari, Ahmad Sur Das, Mati Ram, and others. The well-known poet Keshav dedicated his book *Jahangir Chandrika* to Rahim's son Erij Bahadur. Surajmal, the author of the Rajasthani *granth Vansh Bhaskar*, compares the Khan-i Khanan with Bhoj in his knowledge of the *Shastras*, who could easily and ably participate in such scholarly and religious discussions. Samar Singh rightly calls him 'Bhartiyon ke Bhartiye', i.e. 'Indian of Indians'.[53]

It was on 24 November 1589 that Abdurrahim Khan-i Khanan completed the translation of Babur's *Tuzukat* (*Waqiat-i-Baburi*) and presented it to Akbar, who ordered that at least four copies of the volume should be illustrated.[54]

Krishan Daivajua, the renowned astrologer and author of *Jatak Padheti Udaharan* who was also a contemporary of the Khan-i Khanan, showers lavish praises on him for his knowledge of different Indian and non-Indian languages, a fact confirmed by the famous Hindi poet Rudr-i-Ravi in his work *Nawab Khan-i Khanan Charita*. The Khan-i Khanan knew Arabic, Persian, Turki, Rekhta (Khariboli), as well as provincial dialects like Braj, Dingal, and Awadhi. Naik gives a valuable account of his attainments and accomplishments in different spheres. Abdurrahim's works included *Shrangar Saurtha*, *Rahim Kavya*, *Khet Kautakam*, *Barvai Naikabhed*, *Madanashtka*, *Nagar Shobha*, *Raspanchadhyay*, *Phutkar Padas*, and *Phutkar Barwais*. It is generally believed and widely acknowledged that

Tulsi das had composed his *Barwe Ramayana* on the pattern of Abdurrahim Khan-i Khanan whose diction in *Barvai Naikabhed* was adopted by him. Baba Beni Madhav specifically mentions in his *Gosai Charit* that Abdurrahim had not only inspired but also goaded and prompted Tulsi to compose this extraordinary work. The poems of Mati Ram also seem to carry an imprint of Abdurrahim Khan-i Khanan's poetry and Mati Ram owed a great deal to him as is well proved by Krishan Bihary Mishr in his *Mati Ram Granth*. The art of mixed poems initiated by Amir Khusrau in 1382 and adopted by Kedar Bhatt in his *Virit Ratnakar* and later on by Narayan Bhatt in his Sanskrit *tika* was further developed by the Khan-i Khanan. He has been described as '*har fan maula*', 'master of all trades and Jack of none'. Like his father, he also had a liking for astrology and is said to have written a book exclusively on the subject. The *janm kundli* of the Khan-i Khanan discovered by Munshi Devi Prasad was included in the book *Rahim Ratnawali*. The Khan-i Khanan was an expert in the art of playing chess. He compiled a book on the intricacies of this game, though it is not extant. Abdurrahim was 'the one shining orb in the horizon of literary patronage at the Mughal court and in the whole empire of Asia'. He deserves the foremost place as a supporter of Persian art and literature among the contemporary rulers of Persia, India, Central Asia, and Turkey. Akbar among the Asian monarchs was undoubtedly eminent but his court noble. Abdurrahim was pre-eminent. He is said to have drawn his inspiration from three major sources, i.e. the universal element, devotion, and nature. Some of the couplets of Kabir Das and Rahim are said to convey similar thoughts and words, which has led certain scholars to conclude that Rahim had stolen Kabir's couplets. Yaghaik has pervasively argued that these couplets under discussion were wrongly attributed to Kabir, most of whose couplets (*sakhir*) were recorded 150 years after his death. Many poets borrowed Rahim's ideas, words, and expressions but they failed to reproduce the spirit and lively presentation of the original.[55] Rahim's *Dohawali* had not yet been published. The two works *Dahasar Sangrah* and *Gurgani Nama* comprise certain *dohas* which are attributed to Rahim and Kabir both.

Due to Akbar's deep passion for paintings, an imperial workshop already existed at the court. The Khan-i Khanan was perhaps the only other connoisseur of art who possessed his own production centre though many others could only venture to build their own libraries. Pratapaditya Pal thinks that the *Ramayana* and the *Razm*

*Nama* (*Mahabharata*) were the two manuscripts illustrated for the Khan-i Khanan and belonged to the school of 'sub-imperial' or 'non-imperial' Mughal paintings.[56] The Khan-i Khanan has been portrayed as 'a man of action as well as of culture'. This avid bibliophile and poet 'maintained a library well stocked with books some of which were produced in his own workshop'. The *Ramayana* was completed in 1598 (now in the Freer Gallery, Smithsonian Institution Washington, D.C.) and the *Razm Nama* prepared after two decades. Pal says that the Khan-i Khanan had borrowed 'Akbar's copy to be used as a model by his artists'. The style of his copy of the *Razm Nama*, prepared between 1615-20, looks back to the Akbari *Ramayana* and reflects little awareness of contemporary Mughal painting that was being done for Jahangir. Clearly, the Khan-i Khanan was not as passionately keen about painting as were Akbar and Jahangir. This seems to have been generally true of most sub-imperial Mughal patrons. Since most of the talented artists were attached to Akbar's atelier, many of the Khan-i Khanan's own artists were perhaps not 'eminent', as they mostly emerged from the 'local talent'. Yet the Khan-i Khanan's contribution in the sphere of painting and calligraphy was noteworthy. Pal writes:

> In fact, many compositions of the *Ramayana* are based on the imperial copy, but the styles of paintings differ considerably. His *Razm Nama*, however, seems not to have been dependent on the imperial copies. It has been surmised that the manuscript may have been prepared while the Khan-i Khanan was in the Deccan and hence had no access to the imperial library. In fact, he travelled widely while the manuscript was under preparation.

Pal asserts that the mode of the distribution of text panels and illustrations in both prove that the *Razm Nama* was prepared on the model of the *Ramayana*. Still Pal is of the view that the

> pictures in this copy of the *Razm Nama* are less polished and sophisticated than the illuminated manuscripts done for both Akbar and Jahangir. This difference is attributable to the Khan-i Khanan's needs rather than his purse. It seems that he was more interested in the text than in the illustrations. He was less discriminating than both Akbar and Jahangir in selecting his artists and probably less demanding a patron as well.[57]

The library of Abdurrahim Khan-i Khanan had a large staff, including a *nazim* or *mutamad* (director) and a *darogha* (manager) with 95 people working under him producing and preserving several thousand manuscripts. On a flyleaf of the manuscript *Ramayana*, there is an inscription written by the Khan-i Khanan himself which shows that Mulla Shakibi Imami, the famous artist, was then holding the charge of the illustration work at the Khan-i Khanan's library. Since the atelier was usually a part of the library establishment in those days, the Khan-i Khanan's library also had gilders, painters, illuminators, bookbinders, and calligraphers.[58]

Nahawandi says that Muhammad Amin (from Mashhad), the marbler of the Khan-i Khanan, invented marbled paper, but this view has been contradicted by Porter who asserts that marbled paper was already much in vogue in India towards the end of the sixteenth century. While discussing 'other decorated papers', Porter notes that 'coloured stencils' (*aksi haftrang*), which had been invented by Muhammad Amin Mashhadi, Junior for the Khan-i Khanan, were used for paintings in which 'seven stencils are required—one per colour'.[59]

The latest and most probable date for the founding of the Khan-i Khanan's library was fixed by Naik as 1583. The library was constantly shifted from place to place, following its master in accordance with the assignments he received. He was fond of reading books and needed them continuously. The Khan-i Khanan's personal library came into existence during his stay in Ahmedabad as the Subahdar of Gujarat. While he was in Sironj (Malwa), the library became large enough to require a *darogha* (superintendant) of the stature of Aqa Muhammad Shirazi, with Maulana Baqai also employed in it. He was a talented person of many abilities and had full command over the then prevalent sciences.[60] They worked there for over seven years. Nahawandi says (in 1617) that Mulla Muhammad Husain Harawi had been serving in the library for the past thirty-five years. There were several persons connected with the management of the library, its income, expenditure, and appointment and dismissal of the staff. A well-organized administrative system and a properly planned and efficient scheme for its maintenance were in place. According to Nahawandi,[61] a capable and highly accomplished person, Maulana Ibrahim Naqqash, held the charge of *nazim* and *mutamad* (chief librarian or registrar), with full authority over matters concerning income, expenditure, and appointments and dismissals of the personnel of the library. In the supervision and management of internal and external affairs, he was assisted by a number of subordinate officers who helped him in the classification, cataloguing, purchase, and proper placement of the books. There were separate section in charges who took care of their own sections. Mir Baqi Nahawandi was at one time employed in the library and later he gradually rose to the position of *darogha*. Shaikh Barhami of Bahraich, a well-known poet of Brajbhasha, once held the rank of *darogha* of the library. When he moved away from India, his son Abdus Salam was brought up by the Khan-i Khanan and was later appointed as the *darogha* of the library. The preservation of books and their transcription was as much a difficult task as was their illustration. Well-trained calligraphers were appointed to write on smooth, fine paper which was already perfumed and decorated with gold dust and designs. The Khan-i Khanan was an extraordinary calligraphist and could write *belles-lettres* in both Hindi and Persian. In his employment were such highly competent calligraphists like Shuja of Shiraz who excelled in *naskh* and *souls* and who was brought to the Khan-i Khanan while the latter was residing in Thatta. He created such a good impression that he was appointed as *darogha* of the library. The famous calligraphist Mulla Abdurrahim of Herat who was honoured with the title *Ambarin Qalam* due to his expertise in *naskh* and *nastaliq* enjoyed the patronage of the Khan-i Khanan for quite a long time. There were also efficient gilders, bookbinders, painters, paper cutters, calligraphers, and illuminators. Muhammad Amin Khurasani was a famous gilder in Khurasan from where after the Uzbek invasion. He was given a high salary of 4,000 per mensem. The shining paper (*abri*) is said to be his invention. Mulla Muhammad Husain Harawi and his brother Mulla Muhammad Mumin were skilled bookbinders. Manda was an excellent painter and prepared illustrations and decorated the manuscripts. Maulana Sufi was proficient in calligraphy and wrote a number of books. Mian Nadim the brother of Mian Fahim and Maulana Ibrahim Naqqash, was a very talented painter. Mulla Mushfiqi, Bahbud, and Madhav were other important artists in the Khan-i Khanan's library. The most noteworthy feature of the Khan-i Khanan's library was that most of the original manuscripts were written by the authors.[62]

Several poets realized the significance of the Khan-i Khanan's deep interest in literature and considered it to be an honour to present their own works for his library. In 1590 Urfi Shirazi sent the rough copies of his own 14,000 quatrains, *ghazals*, and eulogies to the Khan-i Khanan, who corrected and edited them and later ordered Siraj Isfahani to compile these in the form of a *diwan*. The *diwans* of Nuruddin Muhammad Zuhuri and Muhammad Sharif Waqui were also prepared. Hasan Sani Khurasani's work was also sent for correction to the Khan-i Khanan, who later on retained a copy of it for his own library.[63]

Verma rightly raises 'the vexed question of the identity of the painters'[64] who worked in the establishment of Abdurrahim Khan-i Khanan as most of the contemporary sources like the *Ain* and the *Maasir-i-Rahimi* do not mention their names exclusively in connection with the atelier. Certain painters like Madhav, Qasim, Mahan, Dhanno, Banwari, and Ibrahim Naqqash were also mentioned in connection with the imperial atelier as 'these artists could move from one atelier to another'.

Several portraits of Bairam Khan are available. One of them in a group prepared by Govardhan in 1630, depicts Timur seated between Babur and Humayun. Standing before the three are their respective *vizirs*, Mirza Rustam, Mirza Shahrukh, and Bairam Khan.[65] Another portrait (signed Govardhan, illus. from the *Akbar Nama*, dated 1604, British Library, London) shows Akbar learning to shoot under the guidance of Bairam Khan. The painting 'The arrest of Abul Maali', designed by Basawan and painted by Shankar, from an *Akbar Nama* manuscript, Mughal, *c.* 1585, is said to be the 'finest'. This painting shows Abul Maali being held in open court by servants of Bairam Khan, who is standing just in front of the newly enthroned Akbar.[66]

One of Farrukh Beg's paintings, 'Turcoman Prisoner', *c.* 1590-1600, carries the inscription 'Amal-i Farrukh Beg—Shabihi Bairam Ughlan' (i.e. the work by Farrukh Beg, the picture of Bairam Ughlan). But Amina Okada describes this identification as 'erroneous' and 'fanciful'. This painting depicts a man whose neck and hands are clapped in a wooden congue. In Central Asia, rebels and victims of the king's wrath were always tortured by hanging *dushakha* (congue) around their necks.[67] The denigration of Bairam Khan in the later decades of the sixteenth century, as presented in the sources, is well proved by the painting. It is quite likely that the painting, as per the inscription, depicts the fallen regent of Akbar, Bairam Khan. The assumption is supported by two facts. Akbar's keen interest in getting the 'likeness taken of all the grandees of the realm' was emphasized by Abul Fazl in his *Ain-i-Akbari*. The writes: 'An immense album was thus formed. Those who have passed away have received a new life, and those who are still alive have immortality promised to them.' Hence, it is clear that the portraits of even the dead grandees were painted. Second, the inscription cannot be ignored, particularly when the name of the painter accompanies the information. There is another painting in a private collection in Jaipur carrying the inscription 'the work of devoted disciple Aqa Reza' and depicting Yildirim Bayazid (erroneously mentioned as the ruler of Dasht-i-Qipchaq) who is shown wearing a congue. The only difference between the two paintings is that Bayazid is wearing a royal cap, richly embroidered, and embellished and a ring on his right thumb, both showing ensigns of royalty, whereas Bairam Khan is shown in an ordinary flat cap. The painting is entitled 'Turcoman Prisoner',[68] and dated *c.* 1590-1600. The most poignant painting of Bairam Khan is the one in which he is shown sitting in a boat while the Afghans are engaged in totally attacking him.

A painting of the Khan-i Khanan as a child is available in one of the most beautiful and emotionally expressive and exciting paintings of Akbar's period prepared for his *Akbar Nama*. This famous painting 'Akbar at court receives the child Abdurrahim' was the *amal* (work) composed and painted by Anant. After the death of Bairam Khan, the child Abdurrahim had been brought to the Mughal court and a 'gracious order was issued', says Abul Fazl, for the attendance of Abdurrahim to the court in Agra in the middle of the sixth regnal year, i.e. in September 1561, by 'several true men such as Babai Zambur, Yadgar Husain and His Majesty the Shahan Shah in spite of evil speakers and evil thinkers, received the child of lustrous forehead with inborn kindness and reared him in the shadow of his own supervision'.[69] Geeti Sen rightly notes that 'this splendid court scene' introduced the event which 'became significant thirty years later' Akbar is depicted in 'translucent' clothing and a person (perhaps Ataqa Khan wearing an ochre and white *khalat*) presents the child who greets the emperor by performing the *sijda* (prostration). The grandeur and splendour of the court is seen in the bright and glittering brocades, carpets, awnings, magnificent throne, fabulous decorations, and regal pomp and show. Nevertheless, 'the tremendous restraint of colour' was 'the master stroke in suggesting the emotive quality of this scene, and of Akbar's reception of the child'.[70]

Many other portraits of Abdurrahim Khan-i Khanan are available, though most of them adopted the 'formalist tendency' of 'courtly portraiture'. One of these is signed by Hashim (*c.* 1626) and appears on a page from the Kevorkian Album, Freer Gallery of Art,

Smithsonian institution, Washington, D.C. The portrait of Abdurrahim with the inscription by Hashim is mentioned by Beach. Another portrait carrying the inscription '*amal-i-Manohar*' (produced by Manohar), is said to be unauthentic. There are many paintings carrying the impressions of the 'Turcoman court' style paintings. These include Capture of Afrasiyab, late fifteenth century; Naushirwan resting in a landscape, *c.* 1470; Courtiers in Attendance, late fifteenth century; Rustam and the White Demon, late fifteenth century. Hunting Cheetah; Defeat of Kaykaus in Hamawaran (1494); Rustam and the Mad Elephant; Commercial Turkmen (1475); Gushtasp and the Dragon (1475); Prince at Archery Practice (1488); Majnun Brought to Layla's Tent (1475); Landscape (1490); Bahram Gur seated with Shangul; and Prince Riding with Attendant.'[71] Geeti Sen rightly concludes that Abdurrahim Khan-i Khanan 'grew to be a genuine exponent of the cultural synthesis bred at the Mughal court'.[72]

## NOTES

1. Mir Khwand, *Rauzat-us-Safa*, vol. II, Tehran, 1339; Badauni, *Muntakhab-ut-Tawarikh*, 3 vols., Delhi, 1973; Kewal Ram, *Tazkirat-ul-Umara*, MS Aligarh, *Farsiya Tarikh*, 32/57; Nizamuddin, *Tabqat-i Akbari*, *FT.*, 32/57; Abdul Qadir Khan, *Awimaqi Mughul*, 1902. Abul Fazl, *Akbar Nama*, Persian text, Newal Kishore edn., Eng. tr. H. Beveridge, New Delhi, 1972; Abdul Baqi Nahawandi, *Maasir-i Rahimi*, Calcutta, 1925; Abul Fazl, *Ain-i-Akbari*, I, Eng. tr. Blochmann, Calcutta, 1977, pp. 329-32; Shaikh Farid, *Zakirat-ul-Khawanin*, Karachi, 1961; Nurullah Shustri, *Majalis-ul-Muminin*, Ahsan Collection.
2. *Akbar Nama*, op. cit., text 58-61; tr. pp. 167-72.
3. Vambery, *Travels in Central Asia*, New Delhi, 1996, pp. 301, 326-7.
4. Ibid.
5. Ibid., pp. 326-7.
6. Ibid.
7. Vambery, p. 327; Lockhart, *Nadir Shah*, Jalandhar, 1993.
8. Krader, *Peoples of Central Asia*, 1966, vol. 26; Riazul Islam, *Persian Documents*, pp. 65-75, 81-5, 288.
9. Lockhart, *Nadir Shah*, p. 67.
10. Ibid.
11. For details on these tribes, see Iskandar Beg Turcoman, *Alam Ara-i-Abbasi*, pp. 1085 onwards.
12. Mir Khawnd, *Rauzat-us-Safa*, vol. 9, p. 277; Hamdulla Mustaufi, *Qazvini Nuzhat-ul-Qulub*, Leiden, 1913, p. 183.
13. Syed Ibn Muhammad Ibn-i Yaqub Al Haravi, *Tarikh Nama-i Harat*, Tehran, 1973, pp. 319-20, 328-9, 417; *Rauzat*, p. 728.

14. Ibn-i Hauqal, *Surat-al-Arz*, Tehran, 1345, p. 110.
15. *Ain*, pp. 379, 382, 405.
16. *Awimaq-i Mughal*, p. 404.
17. For details see biographical notes given in *Ain-i-Akbari*; also see C. Naik, *Abdur Rahim Khan-i Khanan and his Literary Circle*, Ahmedabad.
18. Iskandar Turcoman, p. 99; Shahnawaz Khan, *Maasir-ul-Umara*, III, Eng. tr., p. 173; Sujan Rai, *Khulasat-ut Tawarikh*, p. 345.
19. Bayazid Bayat, *Tazkira-i Humayun wa Akbar*, Calcutta, 1941, p. 370; Jauhar Aftabchi, *Tazkirat-ul-Waqiat*, Urdu tr. by Hidayatullah, Karachi edn., p. 102; Nahawandi, vol. II, p. 2; Nurullah Shustri, *Majalis-ul-Muminin*, Ahsan Collection 940/21, Maulana Azad Library, MS Aligarh, ff. 459-61, Kewal Ram, ff. 32-3.
20. *AN*, III, p. 423.
21. Shustri, p. 460.
22. Badauni, *Muntakhab-ut-Tawarikh*, vol. III, Eng. tr., pp. 217-18, 437.
23. Hasan Nisari Bukhari, *Muzzakkira-i-Ahbab*, Hydrabad, 1969, pp. 458-9, 472; Badauni, III, pp. 344, 351, 361, 473, 495, 508.
24. Ibid.
25. Badauni, vol. 3, pp. 76-122.
26. Nahawandi, pp. 6-7.
27. Badauni, II, text, pp. 33, 43, 109, 148, 182; Eng. tr., pp. 37, 127, 162, 185, 209, 227, 255.
28. Ibid.
29. *Maathir-ul-Umara*, Eng. tr., p. 50; *Tazkirat-ul-Khawanin*, p. 31. *Ain*, Eng. tr., vol. I, no. 53, p. 145 and no. 29, pp. 354-7; Badauni, p. 336, Eng. tr., p. 346.
30. Badauni, I, p. 336, tr., p. 346; Kewal Ram, *Tazkirat-ul-Umara*, Farsiya Tarikh, ff. 32, 157, Maulana Azad Library, Aligarh, 48b-51b; *Zakhirat-ul-Khawanin*, p. 45.
31. Nahawandi, *Maasir-i Rahimi*, pp. 530-40, 590, 596, 608-9; *Zakhirat-ul-Khawanin*, I, p. 62.
32. Nahawandi, pp. 546-9.
33. Nahawandi, pp. 540-57.
34. Nahawandi, pp. 21-4, 27-30, 61, 63, 64, 517, 635, 687, 726-32, 736-50; Badauni, III, pp. 188, 253, 262, 344; Eng. tr., pp. 344, 351, 361, 376, 473, 495, 508.
35. Sujan Rai, p. 345.
36. Nahawandi, pp. 555-65; *Ain* 29, p. 360; Shustri, pp. 60-1.
37. Nahawandi, p. 590.
38. Nahawandi, p. 592; *Zakhirat-ul-Khawanin*, pp. 60-3.
39. Ibid.
40. *Zakhirat-ul-Khawanin*, pp. 572-5, Abul Fazl, no. 29, p. 360.
41. Nahawandi, pp. 572, 576-8.
42. Ranchhodji Naik, *Abdurrahim Khan-i Khanan and his Literary Circle*, Ahmedabad, 1966, p. 500.
43. Badauni, III, p. 118; Eng. tr., pp. 173, 174.
44. *Ain-i Akbari*, biographical note 29, Eng. tr. by Blochmann, p. 360 and also p. 332; Badauni, III, p. 190; Bhakkari, pp. 62-3; Nurullah Shustri, *Majalis-ul-Muminin*, Ahsan Collection, 940/21, ff. 459a-461b.

45. *Zakhirat-ul-Khawanin*, p. 63; Nahawandi, pp. 610-15.
46. Ibid.
47. Nahawandi, pp. 600-12.
48. Nahawandi, pp. 598-604.
49. Nahawandi, p. 590.
50. Arif Qandahari, *Tarikh-i Akbari*, Rampur, 1962, pp. 122-38, 183-9, 192-213, 325, 371, 385-93, 424-46, 450-69.
51. *Contribution of Muslims to Sanskrit Literature*, vol. II, p. 59.
52. Samar Bahadur Singh, *Abdurrahim Khan*, Jhansi, V. 2018, 'Prakathan'.
53. *Vansh Bhaskar, Madhya Patika*, vol. III, pp. 2373-4; Mishr Bandhu Vinod, p. 30. Samar Singh, pp. 12-13, 306; Munshi Debi Prasad, *Khan-i-Khanan Nama*, Mathura, 1892, p. 48.
54. Amina Okada, *Imperial Mughal Painters*, tr. by Flammarion Deka Dusinberre, pp. 20, 23, 150, 153.
55. Balkrishna Ankichan, *Bhartiye Niti Kavya Parampara aur Rahim*, pp. 333-62, 502; Mohd. Abdul Gham, *A History of Persian Language and Literature at the Mughal Court*, Allahabad, 1930, p. 221; C.R. Naik, *Abdurrahim Khan-i-Khanan and His Literary Circle*, Ahmedabad, p. 228; *Contributions of Muslims to Sanskrit Learning*, II, p. 57; also see M. Shankar Yagnik, *Rahim Ratnavali*, Varanasi, 1879, pp. 20-38.
56. Pratapaditya Pal, *Indian Painting*, vol. I, *1000-1700*, Ahmedabad, pp. 30, 179, 188, 189, 07, 293, G.G.18, also illus. 83, 85.
57. Ibid., pp. 106, 188, 293; Beach, 1986, p. 106; S.P. Verma, *Mughal Painters and their Works*, Delhi, 1994, pp. 8-9.
58. Nahawandi, *Maasir-i-Rahimi*, vol. III, p. 1668; also see Yves Porter, Eng. tr. by Mrs. S. Butani, *Painters, Paintings and Books*, New Delhi, 1994, pp. 46, 52, 170.
59. Nahawandi, *Maasir-i-Rahimi*, vol. II, p. 888; vol. III, pp. 1680, 1686; *Ain-i-Akbari*, vol. I, p. 461.
60. Nahawandi, vol. III, pp. 1675, 1680-8.
61. Khalifa Shaikh Ghulam Muhammad Haft Qalam-Dehlawi, *Tazkira-i-Khushnavisan* (RASB, 1910), quoted by Naik, pp. 272-3; Nahawandi, vol. III, pp. 118, 298-9, 637, 888, 1355, 1358, 1681, 1688; Shibli Nomani, *Sher-ul-Ajam*, vol. III, p. 97.
62. Ibid.
63. S.P. Verma, *Mughal Painters and their Works*, pp. 8-9, 17, 78-9, 172, 175, 253, 255.
64. Amina Okada, p. 30, Fig. 30, *Paintings from the Minto Album*, Victoria and Albert Museum, London.
65. Ibid., p. 185, Fig. 219. Geeti Sen, op. cit., *Paintings*, p. 4; Milo C. Beach, *The New Cambridge History of India*, Cambridge, 1992; *Mughal and Rajput Paintings*, p. 63, illus. 44, p. 65.
66. Amina Okada, *Imperial Mughal Painters*; Flammarion, *Artists in the Imperial Atelier, Persian Aestheticism at the Mughal Court*, pp. 120-3, Fig. 130. Also see Stuart C. Welch, *The Art of Mughal India*, House Gallery Publication, Japan, p. 30.
67. Ibid., Asoka Kumar Das, pp. 8-9.
68. Ibid.

69. Abul Fazl, *Akbar Nama*, II, Eng. tr. Beveridge, pp. 203-4.
70. Geeti Sen, op. cit., p. 61, Plate 15. Amina Okada, pp. 150, 153, also Figure 180. Verma, *Mughal Painters and their Work*, p. 172, no. 14, p. 175, no. 44. See *Reproduction*, Beach (7) 183, Cat. no. 18, a colour pl., p. 84, detail on p. 74.
71. Robinson et al., *Islamic Painting and the Arts of the Book*, London, 1976, illus. 35m, III, pp. 128, 130, 142, 159, 160, 176, 179, 192, 194, 197.
72. Geeti Sen, *Paintings from the Akbar Nama: A Visual Chronicle of Mughal India*. New Delhi, 1984, p. 61.

# A Vindication of Bairam Khan and a Reappraisal of His Role in Mughal Court Politics

In the sixteenth century, persons with multifarious talents were not uncommon. Bairam Khan was also a man of many parts. His proverbial courage, kind disposition, skill in physiognomy, excellence in administration, political wisdom, and martial capabilities have rightly been admired by medieval[1] and modern historians alike. During his chequered carrier he was involved in very trying situations from which he came out with flying colours, though, undoubtedly, he was often caught in the whirlpool of circumstances and the uncertainties of political situations. Yet there are few episodes in Mughal history so confused and controversial as the regency of Bairam Khan or the period of his *vakalat*. Similarly, Bairam Khan is perhaps one of the most maligned, misunderstood, misrepresented, and controversial figures in Mughal history. Despite his extraordinary achievements and rare talents, he was continuously denounced as being 'arrogant in manners, somewhat narrow in outlook, dictatorial by temperament and vindictive by nature. He possessed diplomatic shrewdness but lacked the vision of a man. He was at best a successful military leader'. He was also denounced for 'unconcerned barbarity', 'unseemly doings', 'womanish jealousy', and 'intellectual bankruptcy'.[2] To be fair to Bairam Khan, he was far from owing or exhibiting any such petty characteristics. As will be discussed subsequently, it was neither his Irani origin (which had in fact assisted and supported him and his Mughal patrons) nor his Shia leanings which made him unpopular with his compeers. It is also a fact that Bairam Khan never attempted to grab power which came to him easily and automatically by virtue of his being the regent.

The controversy emanates from two basic factors: the lack of proper understanding of the Turco-Mongol institutions, customs, and traditions and also because Bairam Khan's dilemma has not been properly appreciated, particularly at a time when the Mughal rulers were alienated from their kith and kin, both in India and in Central Asia, and largely depended upon the good will and sympathy of the regional rulers.

Another factor that contributed in deepening this confusion was the raw material provided by contemporary sources which suffers occasionally from distortion of facts, subjectivity, and intentional interpretations. The variations in the medieval accounts, therefore, added considerably to the already existing confusion. Abul Fazl does not seem to be very favourably inclined towards Bairam Khan. While Erskine describes Abul Fazl as 'Bayram's warm panegyrist', Amir Haidar Bilgrami, the author of the *Sawanihi Akbari*, asserts that Abul Fazl 'does not show much friendliness to Bayram'. The account of Arif Qandahari, who had remained with Bairam Khan till his last breath, offers a more reliable and detailed version of the fluctuating fortunes of Bairam though he wrote his book after the death of the latter at the court of Akbar. Another work the *Massir-i-Rahimi* written by Abdul Baqi Nahawandi at the court of Abdurrahim Khan-i Khanan, presents a concise but more objective assessment of the family of the Khan-i Khanan though he is a confirmed hagiologist. Surprisingly, Badauni is not so fiercely critical of Bairam Khan and the information given by him is by and large illuminating. There is a controversy regarding even the date and year of birth of Bairam Khan, as well as the exact chronology of the various stages of his life.[3] The sources are rich in information but most of it is contradictory.[4] Modern historians also did not neglect various important issues and valuable work has already been done on Bairam Khan's life, his achievements, and the different aspects of his political career. Various scholars have ably presented and analysed the facts, which can hardly be overlooked or challenged. Yet there is a need for a slight reinterpretation and reconsideration of certain factors which need to be seen in a more precise and proper perspective. This chapter has only a simple aim—to reassess Bairam Khan's role as regent and to re-examine his tarnished image both as a man and as a loyal Mughal magnate.

The chapter first deals with the reasons given in the sources for Bairam Khan's unpopularity and presents a vindication of him by offering justifications and well-founded and well-grounded explanations based on original sources for his much criticized actions.

The second part of the chapter deals with the later developments in Bairam Khan's life which prove beyond doubt that his loyalty and faithfulness were exploited by the Mughal rulers to their own advantage. The third and last section shows that Bairam was not only a fighter but also a man of unique capabilities in other spheres and had a larger share in the glory of Mughal rule than has been recognized or admitted.

## Bairam Khan as an *Ataliq*

In the lifetime of Humayun, Bairam Khan had been made Akbar's *ataliq* and sent to Mankot to exterminate Sikandar. Another large force was sent under Abul Maali. After the death of Humayun, the opponents and enemies started raising their heads. It was only out of his sincerity that Bairam Khan got the *khutba* of Akbar read and acquired the ranks of *madar-ul-mamalik* and *vakil-us-sultanate* in order to save the newly established state. All the affairs of state, the untying (*hall-i-uqda*) of administration, and the control and expansion of affairs were brought under his control. Chroniclers say that during five years of Akbar's young age, the 'Khan-i Khanan fulfilled this gigantic task with such excellence that it would be repeated till the day of judgement'. It was perhaps this excessive talent which empowered the Khan-i Khanan to maintain the position assigned to him by Humayun. Farid Bhakkari echoes the views of many when he writes that, 'It was due to his (Bairam Khan's) magnificence that this grand Empire received strong foundations.'

The court historian tried to enhance the position of the sovereign to be who was then merely 13 years, 8 months, and 28 days old. Abul Fazl writes:

> In November 1555 in an auspicious hour which befitted the accession to the throne of the seven climes, His Majesty, the Shahinshah, the divine nursling, was appointed to the Punjab, according to the rules of sovereignty and splendour. Bairam Khan was nominally appointed as guardian of His Highness but in fact the education of that support of dominion was committed to the fortunate auspices of His Majesty, the Shahinshan. A number of loyal and faithful followers attended on his stirrup.[5]

It was in Punjab that the news of Humayun's death reached Bairam Khan and Akbar. Nevertheless, Badauni says that Akbar—with the approval of Bairam Khan—began to honour and adorn the throne of the Sultanate in 1556, which shows the supreme authority then enjoyed by Bairam Khan. Yet the Turco-Mongol custom of holding formal consultations with the nobles was not ignored by him. It is clearly written in the *Tarikh-i Akbari* that on Friday, Rabi II 963 Nawab Khan Alishan Muhammad Bairam Khan Khan-i Khanan, who at that time held the *mansab* of *ataliqi* which is one of the highest *mansabs* of the state, placed Akbar on the throne in consultation with the *amirs* and officers of the state while he was only fourteen years of age.[6] Bairam Khan's position was further strengthened due to the young age of Akbar. Shahnawaz Khan reports:

In the year 963/1556, when he was made the guardian of Prince Muhammad Akbar and was appointed to suppress Sikandar Khan Sur and to manage the affairs of the Punjab in the same year on 2 Rabi 11/ 14 February 1556, when Akbar sat upon the throne in the town of Kalanur, Bairam was made *vakil-us sultanate*. He had the control of affairs and had the title of the Khan-i Khanan and was styled in correspondence Khan Baba.[7]

Almost all the contemporary, near contemporary, and later sources confirm that

Bairam Khan became all powerful in the affairs of the state and finances. This was due to the fact that the young prince after the death of his father spent his time in the pleasures of hunting excursions, watching elephant fighting and other such recreations. The bridle of all the important transactions (*zimam mahamm*) and the fate of various sections of people, both commoners and special ones, rested in the hands of Bairam Khan. His Majesty Akbar had bestowed upon him all kinds of blandishments, solicitude, and bounty every moment and said that matters should be accomplished in such a way that they may relieve him of administrative worries so that he could personally be free to busy himself in his own way. This had made Bairam the sole authority.

Another factor in Bairam's fall was the concentration of power in his own hands. Badauni says:

And in fact the Emperor himself (because he had not absolute power in his own kingdom, and sometimes had no voice in some of the transactions relating to the expenses of the exchequer, and because there was no privy purse at all and the servants of the Emperor had but poor fiefs and were kept in the depth of poverty, while the Khan-i Khanan's men were in ease and luxury), wished that the circle about him should be put on a different footing. But he had no power to accomplish this until, in accordance with the saying, 'When God wills a thing, its causes are at hand,'[8] circumstances combined to bring about the desired result.

Hsan Rumlu also confirms that 'Bairam Khan kept all powers in his own hands, and Akbar naught but the name of the king'. Even Abul Fazl says that, 'This exoteric . . . king gave all affairs of state and finance to Bairam Khan and busied himself in things which acted as complete veils of His Majesty and were impenetrable by the superficiality of his age.'[9] Abul Fazl further confirms that:

All this time His Majesty Jahanbani enjoyed sensual and mental recreations (*tannazzuhat*) and pleasures, spiritual and temporal, and had feasts and entertainments and visited the hermitages of dervishes and the cells of pure religionists, and distributed largesse in accordance with their conditions. Among others, he frequently visited Maulana Zainuddin Mahmud Kamangar (the bow maker) who was one of the determined opponents of sensuality, and holy words were spoken on both sides. There were conversations about the attainment of desires in time and eternity.[10]

Immediately after his accession to the throne, however, Akbar took only two historic decisions. The one who was favoured first was Munim Beg who had been earlier appointed as his *ataliq* in Kabul. He was not only given the place of Kabul as *darubast* but also *jama daghu*, elephant, *tumantugh*, *naqqara*, and the title of Khan-i Khanan were also bestowed upon him. On the contrary, another person, Abul Maali, was suspected of opposition and was captured and imprisoned. Shahnawaz Khan, however, says: 'When Akbar mounted the throne, Bairam Khan perceived in him the marks of rebellion and arrested him in the assembly on the third day after the accession and sent him to Lahore. His brother Shah Hashim who was the ruler of Ghorband was thrown into prison at Kabul till he died.'[11] Apart from these two steps, Akbar continued to bask in the sunshine of Bairam Khan's glory till the fall of his revered tutor.

Despite gaining such extraordinary power and pelf, Bairam Khan was initially very popular among the nobles. When Munim Khan enquired about the situation in India, Bayazid Bayat says that 'Qul Muhammad Ughuluq had started praising (Kalanihai) Bairam Khan to such an extent that these cannot be included in the *Tazkira*.'[12] Badauni also appreciated Bairam: 'In wisdom, generosity, sincerity, goodness of disposition, submissiveness and humility he surpassed all.'[13] His prestige and position began to gradually decline along with his popularity. Varied reasons are given for Bairam Khan's fall after his meteoric rise. Badauni holds the conspirators among the nobility responsible for this fall. He says: 'At last vile hypocrites poisoned the mind of His Majesty against him until his affairs fell at length.'[14]

In this context it is highly interesting to read the following comment in the *Ain*: 'In 1557, Bairam married Salima Sultan Begam and soon after the estrangement commenced between Akbar and him'. The fact that after the death of Bairam Khan Akbar married Salima Sultan in 1560 should not mislead one to see mundane emotional causes behind this act though it cannot be denied that, like Nurjahan Begam, Salima Sultan Begam was also a talented person. Jahangir greatly admired her talents. He says: 'She was adorned with all good qualities. In women this degree of skill and capacity is seldom found. As a poetess she was famous under the pernname Makhfi—a name adopted later on by Auranzeb's daughter Zebunnisa also.'[15] The reason could be the fact that Salima Sultan Begam was a daughter of Gulrukh Begam (daughter of Babur) and Mirza Nuruddin Muhammad, a Naqshbandi saint. It was perhaps due to Bairam Khan's continuous faithfulness and services that he was given the rank of *gurgani* (son-in-lawship). Abul Fazl reports: 'Humayun had destined her (Salima Sultan Begam) for Bairam Khan who married her in the beginning of Akbar's reign.' Jahangir also confirms that it was 'by way of kindness to Bairam'.[16] Bairam Khan's connections with the royal family through the female line could, as per the Turco-Mongol fashion, facilitate his claims to the throne—a fact bound to be distasteful to any prince, to say nothing of Akbar.

Commenting on Akbar's change of heart (*taghayy Yaftani-i mizai-i ahraf*) towards Bairam Khan, Arif Qandahari records two main factors which in his view were responsible for this. The first was that Bairam Khan enjoyed the post of *vakalat* though he already held the high position of *ataliqi*. The second reason was that certain activities of the enemies of the state who had apparently become the friends of the Khan-i Khanan caused much displeasure to Akbar who thought that the Khan-i Khanan was brought up, honoured, and kindly treated by his own family and that this gracious attitude shown to him during the past forty years had altogether been forgotten by him. He had instead given ear to trouble makers who wanted him to throw away the burden of gratitude and rise in rebellion.[17] Bairam Khan was also blamed for high-handedness in fiscal matters though, he did enjoy financial freedom under Humayun also. In honour of

Humayun, 'Bairam Khan neglected no punctilio of civility.' For example, the whole winter was spent in Qandahar in enjoyment. And during this time whatever was necessary for the king's privy purse was all defrayed by Bairam Khan. He had all the court servants brought into the houses of his own servants, where their entertainment was provided for.'[18]

Badauni attributes the fall of Bairam to the ill-treatment of Pir Muhammad and the influence of Adham Khan and his mother Maham Anga (Akbar's nurse), and Siddiq Muhammand Khan Shihabuddin Ahmad Khan who effectively complained of the wretchedness of their *jagirs* and the emptiness of the treasury while Bairam Khan's friends lived in affluence.[19] It cannot be denied that Bairam was benevolent in rewarding those who supported him in his endeavours to carry out his missions. Nahawandi records that in the battles of Machiwara and Sirhind, the fighters of every class, noble, sharif, slave, lord chamberlain, footman, Turk, and Tajik who had played some role were generously benefited. Their names were noted down and they were given high *mansabs*. Even *farrash* (chamberlain) and *sarban* (camel driver) reached the rank of the sultanate, some became khans, and others acquired eminence.[20] But that goes in favour of Bairam.

Sujan Rai Bhandari does not refer to Bairam Khan's role in persuading Humayun to go to Persia or to help him in making him comfortable there though the other contemporary and later sources stress the fact. Nevertheless, Sujan Rai Bhandari took pains to give a long list of the unjust acts (*be etedalihai*) of Bairam Khan which led to his ejection from India. He writes:

> As Hazrat Khaqan-i Zaman, due to his young age, busied himself much less with the affairs of Kingdom and all the matters concerning the administration and finances of the state were left open for the Khan-i Khanan, the power (*iqtidar*) in the hands of the Khan-i Khanan increased considerably. Having passed through and enjoyed the status of *wikalat* and *amirul umarai*, his hands of authority extended up to all the workshops and over all the affairs his might was established. He did not value this and committed certain improper and displeasing acts. He had, with high-handedness, assigned all the rich and prosperous *jagirs* and lots of *mansabs* to his own adherents. He treated the servants of His Majesty unfavourably. Imagining that the prince was young (*Khurdsal*), he attributed all the victories over his opponents and excellence in the management of affairs of administration to himself.

The other 'extraordinary' and 'audacious' acts attributed by Sujan Rai Bhandari to Bairam Khan included: the assassination of one of the Umarai, Kabbar Tardi Beg Khan, without the royal orders, and the killing of Musahib Beg (who was a royal serfant). Maulana Nasirul Mulk, who was a dependent of Akbar who loved him tremendously and sought his company, was suspended from his *mansab* and sent to Kaaba. Likewise, with many royal servants he behaved in a rough and fierce manner. He captured an elephant from the royal stable and handed it over to his own servants. Similarly, he occupied other workshops, etc. When an elephant went berserk and out of the control of the elephant keeper, Bairam Khan did not observe courtesy and put to death the elephant keeper though the elephant had been killed instantly. Once when Bairam Khan was sitting in a boat during an excursion in the river Yamuna, one of the royal elephants in a frenzied rage rushed towards Bairam's boat in the river. Although the elephant keeper tried his best to hold him, Bairam Khan got suspicious that it was a deliberate attempt to endanger his life. Some say that Bairam Khan even thought that it was the handiwork of Atka Khan or the result of Akbar's planning. Sujan Rai, however, avers that since the days of Bairam Khan's ill-luck of falling off from allegiance (*ayyam-i-idbar*) he gave up obedience and adherence to the *Tura* and put the elephant keeper to death and behaved in a disrespectful manner.[21] The commentator of the English version of Badauni's work *Muntakhab-ut Tawarikh* holds Shihabuddin Ahmad Khan responsible and instrumental in bringing about the fall of Bairam Khan. Shihabuddin was described as a 'relation and friend of Akbar's foster mother—and a commander of Delhi from the beginning of Akbar's reign'. Naik attributes this to Akbar's 'trammels of tutelage' which became galling due to Bairam transgressing the bounds of decency and equity.

A vindication of Bairam Khan, seems essential to bring to light the bare fact that he was neither arrogant by nature nor a power maniac as depicted by modern historian, though he was indeed a victim of his own circumstances. Torn by the conflicts of his own emotional nature, beset by the vicissitudes of fortune and faced by harsh realities, Bairam fought against heavy odds throughout his life. The reasons for the 'conceit' and 'behavioural disorder', if any, afflicting Bairam should be sought in the uncertainties and insecurity of his life. He lost his father at an early age and faced unforeseen hardships. His patrons were themselves in a state of acute danger and uncertainty. To Bairam Khan's own personal problems were added the difficulties arising from the disintegration of the Timurid state, the exile of Babur and Humayun, the search for support from all possible quarters, and the anxiety and concern regarding relatives and nobles. Bairam Khan's attitude towards his compeers was determined not so much by the demands of his own interests or wilful attitudes as it was dictated by the pressures of political expediency which best suited his masters. The nobility was not necessarily a nuisance as depicted by certain historians. Bairam Khan has been blamed for being ruthless towards some of his contemporaries without rhyme or reason. In almost each case, a thorough examination of the information and the circumstantial evidence, and a careful, analysis of the available data proves that the Khan-i Khanan's actions were justified.

The absence of a strong central ruler and the elevation of a noble to the position of an almighty *atabeg* who assumed the airs of an independent sovereign must have irked the *amirs* who were used to seeing an *ataliq* merely as a primus inter pares and that too within the ambit of a particular region. On the eve of Akbar's accession to the throne the Mughal state was in a nebulous form—a young sapling that was likely to die rather than grow. At the time of Humayun's death, Sidi Ali Reis happened to be at the Mughal court. He recounts how 'the khans and sultans were in the greatest consternation. They did not know how to act'. It was at this juncture that Sidi Ali claims to have

> encouraged them and told them how at the death of Sultan Salim the situation was saved by the wisdom of Piri Pasha, who managed to prevent the news of his death from being bandied abroad. He suggested that by taking similar measures they might keep the sovereign's death a secret until the prince should return. This advice was followed. The *divan* (council of state) met as usual, the nobles were summoned, and a public announcement was made that the emperor intended to visit his country seat, and would go there on horseback. Soon after, however, it was announced that on account of the unfavourable weather, the trip had to be abandoned. On the next day a public audience was announced but as the astrologers did not prophesy favourably for it, this also had to be given up. All this, however, somewhat alarmed the army, and on the Tuesday it was thought advisable to give them a sight of their monarch. A man called Molla Bi, who bore a striking resemblance to the late Emperor, only somewhat slighter of stature, was arrayed in the imperial robes and placed on a throne especially created for the purpose in the large entrance hall. His face and eyes were veiled. The

chamberlain Khoshhal Bi stood behind and the first secretary in front of him, while many officers and dignitaries as well as the people from the riverside on seeing their sovereign made joyful obeisance to the sound of festive music. The physicians were handsomely rewarded and the recovery of the Monarch was universally credited.[22]

This eyewitness account is further confirmed by Badauni's words: 'Before the decrees for the accession (of Akbar) went forth Bairam Khan had by all the arts of finesse sent for Pir Muhammad Khan Sherwani so as not to allow the news of the death of the late Emperor to be spread abroad.'[23] Vambery was really struck with surprise by this 'very striking want of reserve wherewith this news that the Emperor was alive was spread to serve a political purpose'.[24] The wisdom of Bairam Khan has been widely appreciated by modern historians who note that he managed to avert the troubles, if any, by concealing the news. It should be noted here that Bairam was simply following the Turco-Mongol principle of suppressing the news of the death of the sovereign till the new ruler was appointed. It was a widely practised custom under Chingiz and his successors. Before the formal election of the Khan, a lot of hobnobbing took place and alignments had to be made, hence the process of the selection of the Khan often took not merely weeks but several months. It goes to the credit of Bairam Khan that he never thought of usurping the throne of his ward though circumstances favoured him. His control over the military and the treasury made him powerful enough to take the leap. Bairam Khan was not devoid of support till his last days when he arrived at Pattan in Gujarat. Musa Khan Fulad, governor of Pattan, and Haji Khan of Alwar received him with the greatest respect and gave themselves up to the necessary duties of hospitality.[25] As against this, Akbar's position was still very weak. India was yet to see stability and Akbar was still far from initiating a process of reconquest. The nobility, the army, and the *nukars* did not recognize a lad of fourteen whom Bairam Khan had allowed to enjoy the pleasures of regal adolescence. The following of Bairam Khan was not negligible and the comradeship in arms and the loyalties to Bairam Khan were enough to sustain him, as will be shown here. It was Bairam Khan's loyalty which brought him again and again into the clutches of Akbar. His relations with Shah Tahmasp were cordial and with the Turcomans a bit more amicable due to racial affinity with them. He was neither weak nor personally timid.

What made him helpless and tied him to the foot of the Mughal throne was his sense of faithfulness and devotion.

The administrative system under Bairam Khan also won the appreciation of the chroniclers. Such was his administrative excellence in Qandahar that the place had been converted into *dar-ul-qarar.* Nahawandi says that Bairam Khan had striven hard (*dar tarbiyat-o aini sultanate*) and excelled in the art of management and the maintenance of its rules, and that he knew the methods to decorate the kingdom and run it well.[26] The aura of his grandeur and magnificence was very impressive. Arif Qandahari was in his service and all the *sarkars* were attached to him. He had noticed good qualities (*ausafi hamida*) in him though only one per cent could be presented here. He says: 'Howsoever I dived deeper into the river of thought, I could not get a pearl befitting the description of his good qualities.'[27] The Khani-i Khanan used to 'come two days a week to the court, and in conjunction with the nobles used to settle the important affairs of the kingdom'.[28] Being an excellent administrator and an imaginative and thoughtful person, Bairam Khan immediately started introducing reforms. It seemed that some of the traders and travellers were overburdened and restless due to taxes like the *tamgha*, *sarana*, *jihat*, and *matalibat*. Since the emperor intended to do away with such irreligious demands and also because he wanted to give some relief to the people, Bairam Khan presented the problem before Akbar, saying that the abolition of such taxes would provide comfort to the subjects, encourage the arrival of traders, and the remission of *hawalat*, *magasamat*, and *awarizal* would leave people in ease. It was, therefore, ordered that in the *balda*, *pargana*, *qasbat*, and *wilayats*, the *tamgha*, *jihat*, *rahdari*, *salamana*, *peshkash*, and *sarana* would not be demanded and that no *hawala* would be issued. This declaration greatly relieved and delighted the people. The matters which were in a disorganized state were brought to order.[29]

The personal qualities and capabilities, the successful career, and the services of Bairam Khan to the Mughal emperor excited the jealousy of other nobles. Even during the later days of Humayun, certain miscreants had created confusion and misunderstandings, between Humayun and Bairam Khan, who was then governor of Qandhar. Abul Fazl writes:

> In the beginning of the winter of this year (1553), His Majesty determined to go to Qandahar rather than to India, as a number of strife mongers had

made false representations about Bairam Khan. Accordingly, he went there: Bairam Khan recognized the advent of the King as a great favour and returned thanks for it. With a heart full of loyalty, he did homage—and His Majesty was convinced that the reports about him were not true.[30]

In his descriptions of the 'splendid feasts' held in Qandahar, Badauni records that,

> Some malevolent speakers, who were jealous of the absolute authority which the Khan-i Khanan enjoyed as the Vakil and especially Adham Khan (who on account of his being the son of Maham Anga held the post nearest to his person) and Sadiq Muhammad Khan and others, seized the opportunity of misrepresenting to the Emperor certain words of the Khan-i Khanan.[31]

While discussing Bairam Khan's regency, it should be noted that the imprints of a culture are seldom erased and the vestiges of customs and traditions are not so quickly obliterated, particularly in the short span of three decades (1526-56), and that too in the midst of wars, continuous rebellions and uncertainties and, also when the numerical strength of the conquerors was much less than that of the conquered. The assimilation which usually follows such external conquests is gradual and bilateral. Many Turco-Mongol customs had, therefore, crept into the Mughal polity. The misconceptions regarding Bairam Khan's regency occur because the term '*ataliq*' had been misunderstood in the context of the regent or tutor of a minor which was common in the East and the West alike. The post of the *ataliq* in Central Asia had a totally different connotation and function. *Ataliq* or *atabeg* means father like or father chief. The *ataliq* was a full-fledged officer—the second in rank in the provinces, the first being the ruler or chief of the province. The *ataliqs* in the Turco-Mongol or the Timurid empire were like the governors (of present-day India) who checkmated the provincial rulers and streamlined the administration in accordance with the centre's guidelines given in the *manshurs* of the assignments. The post of *ataliq* or *atabeg* carried with it sufficient powers to outweigh and outmanoeuvre the provincial rulers. Being the nominees of the centre, they ensured that the provincial ruler was bound by the orders of the central ruler and did not go astray or devour the revenue of the crown lands situated in the provincial ruler's domain. The *ataliq* was nominated by the central ruler with or without the consent of the provincial ruler and the conflict between the provincial ruler and the *ataliq* was also not uncommon. To deal with unsavoury situations in the provinces, the *ataliqs* accompanied the princes. A group of loyal nobles and army detachments always followed the prince and his *ataliq* in the Turco-Mongol as well as in the Timurid-Mongol states. The authority and status of the *ataliq* was quite high. In one of his orders to Shahbaz Khan Kambuh who had been appointed, like Bairam Khan, as the *ataliq* and *vakil* of Shah-Rukh, 'full control over the management of the civil and financial affairs' and the extensive powers of a *sahib-i subah* were given to him.[32] Due to the excessive powers enjoyed by the *ataliq*, the post was described in the sources as 'most coveted'. When Abdurrahim Khan-i Khanan 'had been selected for the high honour' of being the *ataliq* of Jahangir, the latter was also given the same status and authority, showing that the post of the *ataliq* was considerably important. When the Khan-i Khanan came from Burhanpur to receive the post, Jahangir writes:

> Delight and happiness had so overpowered him that he did not know whether he came on his head or his feet. He threw himself bewildered at my feet. By way of favour and kindliness. I lifted up his head and held it in an embrace of kindliness and affection and kissed his face. He brought me as offerings two strings of pearls and some rubies and emeralds. The value of the jewels was 300,000 rupees. Besides these, he laid before me many valuable things.[33]

The *ataliq* or *atabeg*, therefore, was neither the regent of a minor nor merely a tutor. Bairam Khan's authority as an *ataliq* or *atabeg* should be viewed in the Central Asian institutional and administrative perspectives (which gave him excessive power) and not in the light of the usual concept of the regent of a minor prince.

## A Reappraisal of Court Politics: Bairam Khan and His Contemporaries

Due to the instigation of his near and dear ones, Akbar himself was afraid of the growing power of Bairam Khan and felt himself relieved and 'free from the care of the Khan' (*az Karobari Khan Said Shaheed Khan-i Khanan Farigh Shud*),[34] only after the latter's death. The other nobles were jealous of Bairam Khan's talents and his extraordinary position at the Mughal court. It should be noted that the galaxy of nobles punished by Bairam Khan consisted of those who later proved to be a cause of trouble for Akbar himself. A few examples may be given in this context. Adham Khan's mind, which was always engrossed in planning the extermination of Bairam Khan, was put at rest after Bairam Khan's departure to Gujarat. Almost immediately, Adham Khan concentrated his attention on the removal of Shamsuddin Muhammad Atka Khan who had become extremely powerful (*Sahib-i Ikhtiyar*) after the removal of Bairam Khan. The rest of the *amirs* who were keen for the removal of both (Bairam and Shamsuddin) 'as a requisite and expedient action (*wajibat*) ignited and provoked Adham Khan as he was the most courageous and recklessly fearless'. Arif Qandahari states that 'a group of Khans and amirs were envious of Atka Khan as the rays of the sun of the king's kindness were concentrating upon him'. Adham Khan was, therefore, also thrown down from the ramparts of the Agra Fort.[35] Bairam was blamed for putting to death a certain Musahib Beg. Commenting on the incident Badauni says that Musahib 'was not free from evil qualities and inward vice'.[36]

Bairam Khan's relations with some of his other contemporaries were soured but the punishment meted out to them was certainly justified and was not due to personal animosity. A short description of the events would confirm the point. There was some resentment on the part of Bairam Khan against Atka Khan on account of one of the Emperor's elephants having run into the Khan-i Khanan's tents; but Atka Khan came to Lahore and, bringing all his sons with him to the Khan-i Khanan's tent, took an oath on the Holy Book (that the affair was a mere accident), so all suspicion was removed. The incident of the elephant has been properly explained in the *Tarikh-i Alfi*. During their stay in Lahore, Akbar had suddenly become interested in the strange game of elephant fighting. These fights took place frequently. Once when the two elephants Tauhafi and Lakhna were fighting, there was much clamour. Bairam Khan saw in this incident much more than was real and his imaginary fears were confirmed by the calumnies of his detractors. Despite Maham Anga's assurances that it was just by chance, Bairam refused to believe it.[37]

The differences between Bairam Khan and Tardi Beg had begun much earlier. After Bairam Khan's successful expeditions against Nasib Khan Afghan, he came near Jalandhar when the Afghans 'thought it prudent to fly and owing to the dispute which occurred in the victorious army they were able to save their lives and the rest of their property'. It was then that a difference of opinion arose. Tardi Beg wanted to pursue the dispersed Afghans and Bairam Khan did not give him the permission. When Tardi Beg sent Baltu Beg to

Bairam Khan to insist upon his undertaking this mission, Khwaja Muazzam Sultan 'spoke harshly and abused him. Baltu Khan retorted and the Khwaja used his sword and wounded Baltu Khan in the arm. When His Majesty heard of this he wrote a letter of admonition and sent Afzal Khan to explain matters. He conveyed His Majesty's counsels to the officers and brought about a reconciliation.'[38] Another dispute occurred when Sikandar Khan was appointed to Machiwara. He went and thinking he had it in hand advanced further and took possession of Sirhind. Much property fell into his hands.

Meanwhile, Tatar Khan, Habib Khan, Nasib Khan, Mubarak Khan, and a number of Afghan soldiers arrived from Delhi. Sikandar Khan did not think it prudent to remain in Sirhind and came to Jalandhar. Bairam Khan did not approve of this and was angry. He said that Sikandar Khan should have kept his ground at Sirhind and should have sent only word to him. After much discussion the great officers took hold of the saddle straps of the royal house fortune and advanced from Jalandhar. When they came to Machiwara, Tardi Muhammad Khan and many officers did not think it advisable to cross the Satlaj. As the rainy season was near at hand the proper thing to do, they said, was to secure the ferries and to halt. When the violence of the rains was over, and the air had become temperate they could cross the river. Bairam Khan and the far-sighted perceived that it was right to cross the river and spoke properly in this sense. At length by the exertions of Mulla Pir Muhammad, Muhammad Qasim Khan of Nishapur, Wali Beg, and Haidar Quli Beg Shamlu, Bairam Khan crossed the river. Tardi Beg Khan and other officers were obliged to do likewise.[39] But the scars remained which must have widened the gulf between the two.

Another author says that the reasons for Tardi Beg's murder were altogether different though the people said that Bairam Khan was offended by Tardi Beg as he was at that time a *muhrdar* of Humayun and Tardi Beg happened to be the ruler of Itawa when the latter did not allow the former to sit on his carpe.[40] Shahbaz Khan, however, blames Khwaja Sultan Ali 'who gave way together with Ashraf Khan Mir Munshi and Maulana Pir Muhammad Shirwani' for seeking an opportunity for ruining Tardi Beg, the Commander in Chief. The defeat of Tardi Beg and the flight of the soldiers was in itself both humiliating and frustrating. Bairam Khan's reaction was interpreted by many as an act of vendetta, though to him the awarding of an exemplary punishment was the need of the hour. Bayazid Bayat writes:

Since Nawab Bairam Khan had an old grudge and enmity (*niza-i qadim bud*) he made this defeat a pretext to invite him to his own house. He himself disappeared pretending to go for ablutions. Some men were held in readiness for the purpose. He ordered a group of people appointed for the task to take Tardi Beg to the *diwan-khana* and kill him on the surface of blankets and carpets.

The wrath of Bairam Khan against Tardi Beg was so well known and dreaded that even the friends of Tardi Beg like Mir Asghar Munshi, Khwaja Sultan Ali, and others had fled to Mecca. Jahangir also stresses that 'As Bairam Khan disliked Tardi Beg, he made this defeat an excuse to put him to death'.[41] Apparently, Akbar's loyalists were afraid of revealing the skeletons in his cupboard and had to condemn Bairam Khan in order to defend Akbar. Sujan Rai indirectly speaks the truth:

Tardi Beg, having been defeated by the enemy, reached Sirhind. Since Bairam Khan thought him to be his equal (*ham chashm*) and due to the vagaries of fortune, defeat was inflicted upon him. Bairam Khan by artifice and deceit (*makro firib*) brought him to his own station and assassinated him. Afterwards, it was conveyed to the Emperor that the victory of Hemu and the defeat suffered by the nobles was due to the recklessness of Tardi Beg Khan and his execution was essential so as to serve as a warning (*ibrat*) for other coward nobles. Khaqani Zaman ignored it and did not utter a single world.[42]

Elliot, however, does not agree with the accusations made by Bairam Khan against Tardi Beg.[43]

Tardi Beg's defeat and subsequent flight from the battlefield compelled the other nobles also to run away. Ali Quli and others admonished and condemned (*malamat-i bisyar kardand*) Tardi Beg. The Khan-i Khanan who happened to be a pillar of the state (*Rukn-i Khani in daulat*) was much (*baghayat azurda Khatir shud*) perturbed. Since in the very beginning of the emperor's reign this big catastrophe had befallen the victorious army owing to his cowardice (*baddili*) and since signs of rancour and enmity were reflected through his words and deeds, he was brought to Bairam Khan's home and put to death while Humayun had gone on a hunting excursion.[44] Arif Qandahari gives a similar account of the murder of Tardi Beg Khan. Due to the significance of the information, the passage is translated here:

Tardi Beg Khan, who happened to be the chief of Khans of Delhi, due to his negligence and slothfulness (*susti*) in the war (against Hemu) was put to death after interrogation and deliberations in a consultative assembly (*janqi*) with Pir Muhammad Khan Shirwani.[45]

In this context the following points may be noted. The Turco-Mongol custom of bringing to book a defaulter (particularly in a war) was duly observed by Bairam Khan before resorting to capital punishment. Besides, the decision was not taken by Bairam Khan alone as it was properly discussed, in accordance with the custom, in a *janqi*. In conformity with the Turco-Mongol tradition, the victim was rolled and killed on a blanket. All those who had colluded with him were also put to the sword. Relatives of Tardi Beg, Khanjar Beg, and Khwaja Sultan Ali Mir Munshi were thrown into prison to buy peace. The Khan-i Khanan had also taken care to send one of his special persons to convey to Humayun before his departure that the courage to undertake the murder of Tardi Beg without the permission of the king emanated from a desire to seek the betterment and peace of the state and was done out of acute tension and restlessness. It was certain that Hazrat out of mercy and kindness would be reluctant to kill him notwithstanding such a big crime on his part. It was not in the interest of the ever-increasing position of the king and for the protection and security of the emperor from his (Tardi Beg's) enmity to leave him alive. This should be tantamount to the sincerity and good wishes of the emperor's loyal nobles and hence the words of the selfish persons should not be heeded.[46] Badauni also confirms that:

The Khan-i Khanan who, although he was in disposition alienated from Tardi Beg Khan, still in spite of this used to call him Toqan, i.e. Elder Brother, perceiving the cause of the defeat of that army to have been the treachery of Tardi Beg Khan and having succeeded in impressing this on the Emperor's mind by bringing the Khan-i Zaman and many others as witness to substantiate his accusation and obtained a sort of permission to put him to death.[47]

Abul Fazl also criticized Tardi Beg for his disloyalty and shows no inclination to mourn over the 'injustice', if any. His comments are as follows: when Mirza Askari 'with his evil intentions' approached Mashtang, Tardi Beg Khan and the other faithless servants came and paid their respects to the Mirza who made them all over to trusty men of their own. Abul Fazl further records:

A short-sighted man who does not reflect on the evil day or on a bad end and who enters on the path of wicked designs and of shamelessness in reality strikes an axe into the foot of his own well-being and prepares for himself misfortunes and heaven-sent adversities. He (Askari) alighted at the door of His Majesty Jahan Bani's residence and had all the men one by one, small and great, arrested. He made over Tardi Beg Khan to Shah Walad and he put all the unfaithful servants in charge of his men and took them off to Qandahar. Many of them he destroyed by hardships and torments and from Tardi Beg Khan he took all his board so that he soon got the retribution of his deeds.[48]

Bairam Khan's attitude towards Abul Maali was not bad. He escaped from the prison in Lahore and subsequently failed in a futile invasion of Kashmir, and took shelter in Dipalpur where he was discovered and sent to Gujarat. Having committed another murder in Gujarat, he was imprisoned in Biyanah. He was released by Bairam Khan when the latter fled from the court. Ironically enough, 'he left Bairam Khan and joined Akbar but having treated the emperor with disrespect, he was sent off to Makkah'.[49] The *Tarikh-i Alfi* states that Mir Abul Maali who had been sent to undertake the extermination of Sikandar Khan was not very kindly disposed towards the nobles who accompanied him on the expedition and consistently maltreated them (*ba umra-i Kumak neku suluk nami kard*), devoured their *iqtas*, and appropriated even the crown treasury (*dar iqtaat-i ishan tassarruf namuda ba khazana-i Khalsa nez dast andaz-i mi Kunad*). Sikandar grew stronger everyday. The emperor thereupon elevated Bairam Khan to the rank of the *atabeg* of the prince and appointed him to remove Sikandar Khan. It was also ordered that Abul Maali should come to Hisari-i Firuza.[50] Even before his arrival in Lahore, Shah Abul Maali had become reckless and proud. This news had reached Humayun also, along with a request that if he himself came to that side he should arrange affairs in such a way that Abul Maali should be appointed in his own service. Accordingly, Humayun sent Akbar, Bairam Khan, and certain *amirs*. A group of nobles—Muhammad Quli Barlas, Khwaja Jalaluddin Mahmud, Farhad Khan, Muhammad Tahir, Mir Khurd, Mihtar Timur Sharbati—who were with Shah Abul Maali came and met the Khan-i Khanan. Shah Abul Maali had written to Bairam Khan that the enemies had been ejeted.[51]

Since the position of Pir Muhammad had been elevated, and his importance increased, and his control over affairs, power, and privileges (*itbar-o ikhtiyar*) had been greatly enhanced, he became so proud and haughty that even the members of the court, the pillars of the state, i.e. the nobles and the eyes of the king, i.e. ministers or princes (*arkan-i daulat-o ayan-i hazrat*), the amirs of the *Chaghatai Ulus* had to wait for long hours and often did not get an audience and had to return dejected. Bairam Khan's relations with Pir Muhammad became somewhat strained and embittered in 1558. In 1558-9 the Khan-i Khanan dismissed Pir Muhammad who had become a pillar of the state (*rukn-i-azam*) by now from service and exiled him (*mazul karda ikhraj namud*). He proceeded to Gujarat on a Haj pilgrimage. Haji Muhammad Khan was appointed in his place as the *vakil* of the Khan-i Khanan. Shaikh Gadai, who had maintained a friendship with the Khan-i Khanan and who had performed good services during the Khan-i Khanan's stay in Gujarat, was appointed on the *mansab* of *sadarat*. Pir Muhammad stayed on in Gujarat, waiting perhaps for a proper opportunity to retaliate. Badauni, however, justifies the treatment meted out to Pir Muhammad. He says:

> Pir Muhammad Khan from being a mulla had become an amir, and, as has been related, he had become the closer and opener of every important affair of state and finance as vicegerent of the Khan-i Khanan. His opulence had reached such a pitch that one day in the course of going from Delhi to Agra, when the Khan-i Khanan went on a hunting excursion with Pir Muhammad Khan, the Khan-i Khanan asked his private purveyor: 'Is there no provision in store for we are hungry?' and Pir Muhammad Khan on the spur of the moment said, 'If you will be pleased to alight, whatever may happen to be at hand shall be served.' So the Khan-i Khanan with his suite alighted under a tree and 3,000 drinking cups, and 700 porcelain dishes of various colours were brought out from the travelling stores of Pir Muhammad Khan. Although the Khan-i Khanan was astonished, he let no signs of astonishment escape him but great jealousy found its way into his heart.[52]

When they reached Agra, Pir Muhammad fell ill and the Khan-i Khanan came to visit him. Servants who were in the habit of keeping off people, both great and small, came to stop him and said, 'Be pleased to wait until your request has been made known. When you have made application you may come in.' An enraged Bairam Khan wanted to terminate his authority. Although Pir Muhammad came running and begged for forgiveness, saying, 'Forgive me, for my porter did not know you', the Khan-i Khanan replied, 'Nor you either.' Although Pir Muhammad Khan had been quite close to

Bairam Khan during the latter's *vakalat* days, later developments brought about a complete rupture in their relationship. The Khan-i Khanan sent a message to Pir Muhammad which reflects his thoughts and in a way reveals his concept of the code of conduct and morality.

You will remember that you came to Qandahar in the position of an unfortunate student and that when we found that you possessed ability, the quality of fidelity, and when also some worthy services had been performed by you we raised you, a mere student and beggar, from the lowest step among the degraded to the highest grade among the exalted in the sultanship and Khaqanship, and to the post of amir of amirs, but since the carrying of a high position is not in your capacity, nothing but suspicion, rebelliousness and baseness remains in you. So we will take away from you for a time the insignia of your pride that your base disposition and inflated brain may come to their senses. Now it is right that you should surrender the standard, and kettledrum and the paraphernalia of pomp.

So Pir Muhammad Khan, in accordance with this command, surrendered on the spot to some of the Khan's people those accessories of conceit. Soon after this, they sent the *mulla* to the fortress of Biyanah and there he was confined. After some time, he was sent from Biyanah on a pilgrimage to the sacred Makkah. Nizamuddin writes:

The sudden rise in Pir Muhammad's fortune was too much for him who displayed over-weening arrogance towards his patron by whom he was deservedly dismissed and exiled. It is ironical that Pir Muhammad was still in Gujarat when the decline of the Khan-i Khanan's power began. Pir Muhammad safely returned to the Emperor and having won the title of 'Nasirul Mulk', he was appointed to go in pursuit of the Khan-i Khanan. Another person was Shaikh Gadai Kambuh who won over the confidence of the Khan-i Khanan to such an extent that he put him over the heads of all the magnates of Hindustan and Khurasan, and appointed him to the high office of *sadi*.[53]

Some chroniclers say that Bairam Khan had started ignoring even the duties towards Akbar and had made his own servants his confidants, promoted them to high *mansabs*, his orders alone carried the imperial effect, and his *amirs* became like senior potentates. The *amirs*, therefore, collectively thought of removing and exterminating him. Adham Khan, who by virtue of being the son of Maham Anga and also due to certain other reasons had come closer and become dearer to Akbar, was keen to remove Bairam. His mother Maham

Anga was afraid that Bairam Khan might come to know of Adham Khan's intentions and might decide to punish him. She, therefore, took special care and calculated steps to continuously utilize any available opportunity to malign Bairam Khan to an extent that cannot be imagined. Besides, it was ensured that whosoever got the time and the opportunity should convey something or the other against Bairam Khan. Such an incessant campaign of vilification fell heavy upon Akbar who finally ordered the Khan-i Khanan, on 20 Jumad II 966, to stay on in Agra to perform the required duties and he himself proceeded on a hunting excursion towards Sikandarabad in the environs of Delhi. In his letter to Bairam Khan, written in 966, Akbar maintained all the norms and forms of courtesy and sending him the *salams* of kindness and messages of affection, he assured the Khan-i Khanan that

> though there may occur some vexation between the father and son, a complete rupture or indifference (*bezari*) is not possible. As you are my Khan Baba that very relation has to be observed and guarded. Despite this indignation and grief and improper and inopportune acts, I still hold you dear and have a feeling of affection and love. Since at present I am not favourably inclined towards you and have some displeasure, it seems inadvisable that you should come to me. Instead be at your own and fulfil your duties. Our meeting is likely to be delayed. You should proceed towards Mecca and send someone to this side for the *nazr*.

The hopes of the Khan-i Khanan were belied. In a shattered state of mind and like an insane person, the remained alone as his army was dispersed. All khans and sultans who were with the Khan-i Khanan deserted him and joined Akbar. Bairam Khan cried bitterly. His entire luggage and every thing was looted. A kind of fear overtook him Badauni writes: 'Akbar's trick resembles exactly that which Sultan Abu Said the Mughal adopted towards his Minister Amir Chuban.'[54]

Bairam Khan had in his service and company Arif Qandahari who gives an eyewitness account of the last few months of Bairam Khan's life and his subsequent death. If Arif Qandahari is to be believed, Akbar was not very kindly disposed towards Bairam Khan from the end of Jumad I 977 due to certain incidents (*baaze umur inhiraf yafta*) and grew angry. Leaving him in Agra, he himself proceeded with the entire army towards Delhi. Since the Khan-i Khanan had always been keen to go to Mecca, the permission was granted. By sheer chance Queen Mariam Makani was in Delhi, and Shihabuddin Ahmad Khan, the ruler of the place, was closely connected with and amicably related to the (*Khweshi wa dosti*) Maham Anga. The latter persuaded Akbar to see the Dowager Queen Mariam Makani, 'who had fallen suddenly ill', in Delhi. It was at this juncture that Maham Anga and Shihabuddin Ahmad Khan 'in concert made mountains of mole hills and prejudiced the mind' and poisoned the ears of Akbar saying that the power and authority of Bairam Khan was increasing and that this fact was very well known. Now, when Bairam Khan learns that this royal cavalcade had arrived in Delhi at Maham's 'instigation' but not at the Khan-i Khanan's suggestion,

> he will be sure to wish to avenge himself, and she (Maham), having no power to resist, requested to be sent to Mecca. It was also stressed that those who were in the service here were aggrieved and revengeful as Musahib Beg and others had been killed for very minor defaults. The servants of the king notwithstanding the long time of their service and dedication did not have a claim even on one *dinar* while the servants of the Khan-i Khanan Bairam Khan squandered away the entire revenues of Akbar's domain. Whereas we all shudder and tremble like a leaf, the only alternative we have is to convey our problems to His Majesty.

Akbar reacted to this very sharply, saying that a messenger should be despatched to Bairam Khan immediately to convey that those who had come with him had no say in the matter of the visitation to Delhi and that it was Akbar's own wish. A further directive was that agreements with instructions for Maham Anga and those who were with Akbar should not be despatched. When this reached the ears of Shihabuddin, it was spread to men far and near that a kind of vexation against Bairam Khan had set in the heart of the emperor and that the cause of his arrival in Delhi was also the same. On reaching Delhi, Shihabuddin Khan started uttering things loudly against Bairam Khan. All those who looked forward to receiving favours and whose words carried some influence told such details against the Khan-i Khanan that it gradually and greatly affected Akbar.

As luck would have it, the envoys for securing the *ahdnamas* (agreements) were despatched and benumbed the spirit of Bairam Khan, who got worried and came to know that he had lost his authority. He sent Haji Aminuddin Muhammad Khan Gilani and Qurban Beg to apologize on his behalf with the request that an ill-will against those who had always striven for strengthening the threshold of His Majesty should not be given way.[55] Bairam claimed that he had not till now entertained any feeling except good will and good wishes. By the time the Khan-i Khanan's envoys reached Delhi, the affair had reached beyond redemption. His messengers were not even allowed to return, what to say of securing an audience with Akbar. At this point of time the anger of the emperor against the Khan-i Khanan became known to all and sundry. All the *amirs* who had been anxiously waiting for this day, wherever they were, turned their reins towards Delhi. The first entrant was Qaba Khan, an old servant of the family, who fled from Agra to Delhi. Others also followed and received kind treatment. Shihabuddin Khan, in consultation with Maham Anga, fulfilled the duties relating to the people's affairs. Each enemy of Bairam Khan received *mansabs* and rewards. Bairam Khan was dejected as his men did not return and became increasingly perturbed on hearing the news of the developments at Akbar's court Initially out of fright and confusion, he thought of conquering Malwa and subsequently of suppressing the Afghans but such ideas appeared and passed away. In an assembly, Bairam Khan discussed the matter with the handful of *amirs* who had not yet deserted him and thereafter left for Nagaur. The news of the departure of Bairam Khan added to Akbar's apprehensions to such an extent that he decided to go to Nagaur to prevent Bairam Khan from reaching there. The news of Akbar's march frightened the remaining followers of Bairam Khan, all of whom now deserted him and joined the emperor. Even the old servants of Bairam Khan did not stand by him.[56] Akbar sent Abdul Latif Qazvini to the Khan-i Khanan with a clear message that until this day, the affairs of administration and the state had been run in consonance with Bairam Khan's sage counsel as the king had been enjoying hunting excursions and recreations. Now Akbar said that he wished to claim and to return to the affairs of the people who are the deposits of God personally, that it was now befitting for the Khan-i Khanan to withdraw himself from worldy affairs and leave for the Haj pilgrimage. Whichever *pargana* he wanted would be assigned to him as a subsistence allowance. Bairam Khan expressed his allegiance, reassured Akbar that he had no intention of creating mischief or opposition and nor would he do it in future. All the insignia of royalty, *alam*, *naqqara*, elephants, etc., were sent through Husain Quli Khan Zulqadr, and he himself proceeded towards Mecca. All the faithful followers and confidants of Bairam Khan (like Wali Beg Zulqadr, Ismail Khan, Wali Beg, Shah Quli Khan Mahram, and Husain Khan) were not allowed to accompany him.

The large detachments of *amirs* who had deserted Bairam Khan joined Akbar. Mulla Pir Muhammad Shirwani, who had been exiled by Bairam Khan, reached the court at once and received the title of Khan with an *alam* and *naqqara*, etc., and was despatched along with a large group to pursue Bairam Khan. If Bairam Khan proved to be reluctant and resisted going to Mecca, he was to be sent (*jabran wa Qahran*) nolens volens. Arif Qandahari, however, says that they had been sent to persuade Bairam Khan, to allegiance as desired. Bairam Khan had foreseen the imminent danger and, having sensed this peril, he did not find it feasible to stay on in the region and proceeded towards Jalandhar after having suffered prolonged and excessive hardship and agony. His mental trauma increased as it was also ingrained in his mind that if he had any idea of enmity or rebellion then he should know the grave consequences of going astray. The royal army would be out to exterminate him. At this juncture endurance, submission, and surrender were the only options, which out of expediency he accepted. In this hour of crisis, some of his belongings, his luggage, and his associates were left with Sher Muhammad, the *jagirdar* of Tabarhind, an old friend and 'adopted son' and beneficiary of Bairam Khan. That 'ingrate extended his hands of the entire luggage and additionally caused much torture of varied sorts though he got the retribution thereafter'. In desperation, Bairam Khan sent Muzzaffar Khan to Dervish Khan Uzbek, the ruler of Dipalpur, who sent the envoy along with his companions to Akbar. Anger overpowered Akbar who sent a number of Khans along with Shamsuddin Muhammad Atka Khan-i Azam to suppress this commotion (*ba dafa'in Kar*) and to put the Khan-i Khanan down with a heavy hand. In the battle which followed in the Mauza Gayaur, Bairam Khan was defeated. Many of his men like Wali Beg Zulqadr, Yaqub Hamdani, and Murad who were the cause of this commotion and several others fell into captivity. Arif Qandahari pleads that, 'This war was fought by Bairam Khan not out of any animosity or defiance but merely because of necessity (and self-defence which compels a person to hold the sharp blades of a sword in hand when there is no escape).' When Akbar reached Lahore, the Khan-i Khanan regretted the action which he had performed out of necessity (*ba jihat-i zarurat*) and proffered his services and offer of peace. Immense booty fell into the hands of the royal army.[57] When the news of the defeat of Bairam Khan and his desperate efforts to secure help from the rajas of the hills reached

Akbar, he personally rushed to the scene. Bairam Khan was perplexed and in a state of acute poverty. His agony and discomfiture increased as Munim Khan was awarded the title of the Khan-i Khanan and the *mansab* of *vakalat*. Some of the captives of Bairam's army were taken to the court. Wali Beg succumbed to his injuries and his head was taken to Delhi and Agra. The army started for the Shiwalik Hills where again a battle ensued in which the hill people fought with bravery and courage. The royalists overcame the forces of Bairam Khan. A bewildered Bairam Khan who was already totally worn out by extreme worries, depressing circumstances, and the fatigue of the journey, surrendered and sent his reliable servant Jamal Khan to Akbar, begged for forgiveness, referring to his past rights as the intercessor of his sins. The pleas were accepted. It should be noted here that Akbar could not recount even one single fault of Bairam Khan to enable himself to entangle his *ataliq* and exile him. In 1560, Makhdum ul Mulk brought about a reconciliation, and appeased Bairam Khan who was given a warm reception at the court, and was brought to the Urdu *ibuzurg* with all honour. In that assembly excessive efforts were made to remove Bairam Khan's shamefulness, hence the kindness shown to him knew no bounds. These exaggerated expressions of affection satisfied Bairam and banished his fears. A few persons who had accompanied the Khan-i Khanan kissed the threshold. With sincerity, hopefulness, and repentance for his audacity, the Khan-i Khanan fell at Akabr's feet. Abul Fazl defends his master by saying that 'Bairam Khan arrived in September 1564 and His Majesty, for the sake of giving greater pleasure and out of the affection he bore him, had the feast repeated and gave an entertainment more splendid than that of the Id.'[58] Other sources report that Bairam Khan was very ashamed and, in a state of acute repentance, sent his petition to Akbar, requesting him to send his confidant to fetch Bairam and present him before the emperor. Initially, Maulana Abdullah Sultanpuri Makhdul Mulk and afterwards Munim Khan were appointed to soothe and encourage Bairam Khan. They brought him to the court with a towel kerchief (*ru-pak*) around his neck and presented him before Akbar. Bairam Khan wept bitterly and Akbar out of deep affection removed the kerchief from his neck and ordered him to sit as before. When the assembly came to an end, Bairam Khan received permission to go to Hijaz. The royal cavalcade proceeded towards Delhi and Bairam Khan started for Mecca in the sixth regnal year.[59]

Another version is also available. Apologists for Akbar say that having heard all improper and unapproved facts, Akbar became worried and gave up the usual courtesy (*tark-i madara namuda*) and sought some remedy. After some time, Akbar accompanied by some *amirs* came out of Agra on the pretext of hunting. On reaching Delhi, Akbar discussed this secret with the *subahdar* of the place, Shahabuddin Ahmad Khan. *Farmans* were issued to the *amirs* of the outlying regions that the cogitations of Akbar and his favourable attitude towards Bairam Khan had changed and that he had decided to take over the responsibility of all state affairs personally and that each of them should come and attend the court. Mir Shamsuddin Muhammad Atka was summoned from Bhira and the *alam*, *naqqara*, *tumentugh*, and *mansab* of Bairam Khan were bestowed upon him. Most of the nobles from the surrounding regions arrived Those *amirs* who were close to Bairam Khan also deserted their master and reached Akbar's court. When this became known to Bairam Khan, he resorted to submission and tendered apologies. But the emperor sent him a message that it was not proper for him to come to the court. It would be much beter if he started for Mecca. On his return from there, he would certainly be the recipient of immense favours. Apparently Bairam Khan took the permission for his departure for Hijaz, and came out of Agra. Having reached Mewat, he allegedly sent the sons of Sikandar Afghan and Ghazi Khan Sur (both of whom were with him at that time) to create confusion in the protected dominion (*mamalik-i mahrusa*). Bairam Khan himself planned to proceed towards Punjab. Having heard this, Akbar sent him a *farman* full of wise counsel. But Bairam Khan ignored this and went to Bikaner. He spent some time with Kalyan mal Zamindar and then went towards Punjab where he raised the curtains of secrecy from his activities and became rebellious.

It is highly interesting to hear the other side of the story, according to which Bairam was still very submissive and had no intention of raising a rebellion. While in exile near Darwaza-i Kafiran, Bairam Khan wrote a letter to Munim Khan and sent it through Muhammad Husain Nazir. The contents of the letter showed Bairam Khan's acute agony and complete surrender. He wrote:

> I have taken shelter with the kafirs out of necessity. If you can come and take me out of this place, I am willing to accompany you. Today my fate is like that of Sultan Husain whom someone had killed. How can I reconcile with such a type of depravity and sedition which is not requisite (*fasad-i*

*bezururat*). If, however, the monarch and his pillars of the Empire are keen to have a spoonful of my blood, I would be willing to this remission.

Having read this letter, Akbar asked Munim Khan to extend all sorts of mind-assuaging reassurances and bring him to the court. Whatever agreements were reached, these were to be respected by Akbar. When Lashkar Khan took this *parwana* to the Khan-i Khanan, Khwaja Jahan, Ashraf Hasan, Haji Muhammad Khan Siestani, and Bayazid Bayat who were the servants of the Khan-i Khanan came out from the gate of Qala-i Kafiran. The Kafirs were standing on both sides with naked swords. There was only very limited place to move about and only three horsemen could enter at one time, probably to provide safety to Bairam Khan, who was sitting under a tree surrounded by a hundred well-equipped Mughals. When he saw Munim Khan, he stood and walked ahead. They embraced each other and cried at the reunion and also at the sad demise of Humayun. When Bairam Khan repeated what he had written in the letter, Munim Khan took a vow on the Holy Book (which he had taken with him) that as long as he was alive no harm would be caused and no injury done to Bairam's property or life. Whatever Bairam desired would be conveyed to and fulfilled by the king.[60] All the others also repeated the same oath. They all started for the court. Once again Bairam Khan had been entrapped.

Bayazid who was among the nobles was then sent ahead to inform the others about the arrival of Bairam Khan. He records how every one in the camp of Akbar was worried over the situation and how they all delighted at the news of Bairam Khan's arrival and he then knew that 'falsehood had reached them and that the group would be caught inside'.[61] Bayazid had been very richly rewarded both by the ladies in the harem and by the servants and the Khans. When Bairam Khan came before Akbar the emperor showed him such friendship and extra encouragement as though no vexation and misunderstanding had ever occurred between them. While Munim Khan told Akbar that he had spoken to the Khan-i Khanan about his own proposed departure to Mecca along with Bairam Khan and asked for the permission of the emperor, Akbar answered that he wanted Munim Khan to stay with him alone. After the arrival of the royal cavalcade in Sirhind, the case of Bairam Khan was again taken up. He was sent to Mecca after three or four days. Munim Khan sent Bayazid with money and luggage to accompany Bairam Khan for a few yards. Perhaps Bairam Khan was aware of his doom as he wrote a letter in which he bequeathed all his belongings, property, and whatever he had in India to Munim Khan as private possession (*ba tariqi-milkiyat*). Bayazid sent this letter to Munim Khan on his return. Accordingly, Munim Khan received the *manzil* (house) of Bairam Khan as he had no abode of his own in Delhi, in addition to other things. Bayazid, however, still had to face the consequences of having maintained loyalty to Bairam. Once even Khwaja Jahan demanded that Bayazid be put to death as during his service to Bairam Khan many injuries and harm had been caused to the people. If he was still allowed to be at large again harm was likely to reach the people.[62]

The treatment meted out to Bairam Khan perhaps was not liked by the army and the people. Bayazid records that after the arrival of Bairam Khan at the court, the people in the army (*mardum-i Urdu*) slept comfortably and with ease under their *chadars* and all commotion (*fitna-o-fasad*) which had taken root in the hypocrisy of the people was extinguished.[63] Through the intercession of Abdullah Makhdum-ul-Mulk, Bairam Khan was satisfied and came to kiss the royal threshold. The same day he was allowed to go to Mecca. In Rabi II 968, he received Rs. 50,000 as his allowance for the journey. Bairam Khan went from Hansi to Pattan. The Afghans who had been exiled from India after its reconquest by the Mughals and who had settled in Gujarat out of fear of Bairam Khan now collected together to seize this opportunity. The enemies of the Mughals (whom Bairam Khan had earlier destroyed) now treated Bairam as their enemy. They fell upon him, and surrounded him from all sides while he was coming from Kulab after an excursion. One of them, known as Mubarak Khan, came forward and wounded the Khan-i Khanan with his dagger. It was propagated that Mubarak's father had been killed by one of the soldiers of Chaghatai Ulus in a confrontation and he had decided to take revenge. The martyrdom of Bairam Khan took place on Friday, 14 Jumad 968. The entire baggage and Urdu of the Khan-i Khanan was plundered and put to naught. His followers were dispersed. Abdurrahim Mirza, who was an infant, was brought to the court by M. Aminuddin and Baba-i Zambur. Arif Qandahari who had accompanied Bairam Khan saved his life with great difficulty.[64]

For obvious reasons, mainly to do with his disenchantment with the Mughals, Badauni offers a very far-fetched explanation for Bairam Khan's repeated submissiveness:

Although the Hindus of that place supported the Khan-i Khanan, fellow feeling with the Moslem religion seized his skirt so that turning his thoughts to the world to come and purifying himself in the path of religion, he with a view to obtaining forgiveness for his shortcomings sent without delay, and with the greatest humility, a message by the hand of Jamal Khan, a *ghulam*, craving an audience with the Emperor.

The moral and military support received by the Khan was enough for him to muster up courage to face the challenge. The Talwarah fort where the Khan-i Khanan had shut himself up was a very strong and almost inaccessible place in the mountains of Kushmal (Siwalik) on the banks of the river Biyah, the government of which belonged to Raja Gobind Chand. But Bairam Khan was perhaps unwilling to raise arms against his benefactors. The unhappiness of Shah Tahmasp over the issue of Qandahar and Akbar's indifference to his embassy and his arrogance might have provided an anchor and an opportunity to Bairam to sail through his own tempestuous days. Yet he refrained from adopting any such attitude. The Turcomans in general and Bairam Khan in particular detested the supremacy of any leader as they were believers in the motto '*Biz Bibash Khalq Bolamiz*' 'We are a people without a head' and their beliefs that 'We will not have one. We are all equal. With us every one is king.' The tribes have their *aksakals*, yet 'they are liked and tolerated only so long as they do not make their supremacy felt by unusual commands or extravagant pretensions'. Bairam Khan, therefore, could hardly tolerate any high-handedness on the part of the nobility,[65] though with the kings who were the shadow of God on earth the matter was different.

Bairam Khan does not seem to have been overambitious to throw overboard his loyalties for the sake of petty worldly gains. His explanation given below of the Koranic verse, 'Thou exaltest whom thou will (by contentment) and thou humblest whom thou will (by continued craving)', shows his attitude towards life. For him 'a contented mind is a continual feast' and so the contented man is always exalted. On the other hand, the discontented man is always asking for more and always considers himself as ill-used.[66] It is also stressed that such was Bairam's faith in his patrons that even in his last moments he summoned his son who was still a minor and instructed him not to ask for help from anyone but to go to the court before Akbar. In accordance with Turco-Mongol practice, the female sovereign took over. After the fall of Bairam Khan, 'Maham Anga, by whose machinantions that result was brought about, became *de facto* (if not *de jure*) prime minister.'[67] It is interesting to note that despite his political strength, Bairam lost without grudge his authority which even in his last days he was quite capable of defending. Bairam Khan lost on the political front despite a long, arduous, and extremely bitter fight against heavy odds which he had to face for the sake of his masters. Nevertheless, he had many good points in his career which ought not to be neglected while assessing him as a human being. He had completely destroyed himself in the service of the Mughals though his original connections and good character continued to sustain him throughout his life.

## Assessment of Bairam Khan's Achievements

If *noblesse oblige* has any significance, Bairam Khan certainly belonged to a noble family. Bayazid Bayat caustically mentions that Bairam Khan Baharul traced his connection and lineage (*Khudra Asilsilah Migoyad*) to Jahanshah. The genealogy of Bairam Khan as recorded in detail in various sources confirms his lineage from the noble family of Qara Quyunhu.[68] Nahawandi dedicates several chapters of his book to Bairam Khan's ancestry. The *taefa* of Baharul was one of the *tabqas* of the Qara Quyunlu Turcomans who were Shias. Bairam Khan's great-grandfather, Pir Ali Beg (son of Alisher Beg Baharul), had been driven out by Sultan Husain Turcoman and came to Hesar to join the services of Mirza Sultan Mahmud (Babur's paternal uncle). Due to the internecine warfare among the Timurid Mirza brothers, he could not stay there and went to Kabul and from there to Fars and Shiraz where he met the *amirs* of Hasan Beg. Being defeated, he returned to Khurasan. On the way he fought against the servants of Sultan Husain Baiqra. Pir Ali Beg was killed and his followers dispersed. His son Bairak Beg came to Qunduz and joined the services of Khusru Shah, the famous noble of Babur. When Khusru Shah was defeated by Babur, Bairak Beg and Saif Ali, the two sons of Pir, entered the service of Babur. Saif Ali, the father of Bairam Khan, died in Qazvin and the infant Bairam lived in Balkh where his early education was completed. He came from Balkh to Badakshan and reached Babur's court while still in his teens. Here he learnt the various arts (*iktisabi fazail-o kamalat*). At an early age Bairam Khan served Babur and 'in middle age he obtained advancement' in the service of Humayun and received the honourable title of the Khan-i Khanan and added Babam to his titles. His gallantry, courage, and endurance won for him the favours, royal patronage, and appropriate *mansabs*. He suffered considerably during his stay in Sind, Gujarat, and in the house of Rai Mitrasen. Yet his determination and resolute courage withstood him in times of crisis. Bairam Khan had seen difficult days with Babur during the latter's days in exile at Kabul and stood firm in the hour of need for his patrons Humayun and Akbar.

Due to his personal qualities and talents Bairam attracted the attention of Sher Shah who also discerned in him extraordinary excellence. The Mughal sources record how, 'after exposing his life in the unfortunate affairs of Qanauj he went to Sambhal' to seek refuge. The news of Bairam's reception by Raja Mitrasen, great and important landlord of Lucknow, prompted Sher Shah to send for him and the Raja, being helpless, sent the Khan who had a meeting with him on the road to Malwa. Sher Shah rose up and embraced him and sought to attract him by enticing words. Abul Fazl says that Sher Shah 'spoke crafty words to him. Among his remarks was this 'Whoever keeps his loyalty stumbleth not.' 'Yes', replied Bairam Khan. 'Whoever keeps his loyalty should not stumble.' Shah Nawaz Khan says that Sher Shah remarked, 'Whoever acts sincerely does not err.' Bairam answered, 'So it is. Whoever acts sincerely shall not go astray.' Near Burhanpur he, after a thousand difficulties and with the help of Abul Qasim, Governor of Gwalior, made his escape and went off to Gujarat. On the road Sher Shah's ambassador sent men and had him and Abul Qasim, 'who was remarkable for the beauty of his person', arrested. Abul Qạsim said heroically, 'This is my servant and he wants to devote and sacrifice himself for me; beware and withdraw your hand from him.' They withheld their hands from him. 'Out of nobleness and generosity, Bairam Khan stoutly asseverated that he was Bairam Khan. Not recognizing Abul Qasim, they put him to death.[69] Sher Shah often used to say that 'When Bairam Khan said "Whosoever is sincere shall not go astray" (or "Whoever keeps his loyality shall not stumble"), I perceived that he would not arrange matters with us, and would not come to terms with us.' Bairam Khan escaped and went to Sultan Mahmud Gujarati. Sultan Mahmud Gujarati also tried to win over Bairam and tried to induce him to stay with him but could not succeed. He got leave to go on pilgrimage and came to Surat and from there he came to the feet of his master Humayun.[70] The loyalty of Bairam was valued highly and he was held in high esteem by the royal family of the Mughals under whose banner he saw the light of growth and development as he had lost his father in infancy. It is clearly recorded that, 'The conquest of India may justifiably be ascribed to Bairam Khan.' In the Indian expedition, Bairam proved to be 'the best of all the leaders and was a forefather in the battle and was victorious. Especially, in the battle of Machiwara, when with a few men he attacked a numerous army of Afghans and defeated it'. He received the *pargana* of Sirhind, etc., in fief and the lofty titles of *yar wafadar* (the faithful friend), *Baradur Neku Siyar* (well conditioned brother), and *Farzand Saadatmand* (auspicious son).[71]

Like other medieval Central Asians, Bairam was a fine admixture of the qualities of the head and the heart. He was endowed with the art of simultaneously using the graces of the pen and the ferocity of the sword. Bairam's fight against the Arghunians and in favour of Humayun showed his military prowess and skill to such an extent that the soldiers thought he was 'as heaven-sent ally'. In the expedition to Persia, he was the best and most faithful servant.[72] The Khan-i Khanan showed valour and martial excellence in several wars. In the battle of Garhi, Bairam Khan showed his valour. Abul Fazl records:

> Bairam Khan turned several times and attacked the enemy, and dispersed them. He made gallant efforts, but from want of management he was not properly supported, and things did not go satisfactorily. While in another fight with the Arghunians, Tardi Beg Khan was remiss in fighting, Sher Ali stood firm and in that battlefield which is the banquet table (*bisatibazm*) of the brave quaffed with unaltered mien the sherbet of martyrdom. The heart of Humayun was grievously wounded by the fate of so faithful a follower and some other untoward circumstances and he determined to go to Qandahar. Just then on 13 April 1543, Bairam Khan arrived alone from Gujarat and laid a balm on the wounded spirit of His Majesty and was a cause of cheerfulness and joy. One of the wounderful things was that as he was coming to the camp, he had first to pass over a battlefield. Before he could make his obeisance or reveal himself, he had to prepare for war and to fight bravely. The victorious soldiers were amazed and thought, 'He comes from the secret army of God.' When it transpired that he was Bairam Khan a shout was raised by those standing in battle array and the heart of His Majesty rejoiced.[73]

When Bairam Khan was despatched to Kabul as an ambassador, many Hazaras blocked the way in the Rughni Pass and the Ab Istada. Mughal forces chastised them. Bayazid Bayat refers to the contribution made by Bairam Khan in this respect. Badauni also says that, 'The conquest of Hindustan and the building of the Empire were due to his strenuous efforts, his values and his own wise policy.'[74]

Bairam Khan has also been appreciated for his physiognomy. Bairam's rare 'gift of selecting proper men'[75] is proved by several facts; for example, no less than twenty-five of Bairam's friends reached the dignity of *panjhazaris*. The choice of Muzaffar Khan Turbati as *diwan* also speaks of Bairam's extraordinary intelligence. Although Sher Muhammad Diwan had sent Muzaffar Khan Turbati in chains to Akbar, and several countries had advised the emperor to put Muzaffar to death, Akbar first made him only *amil* and then appointed him *diwan-i Buyutat* (Collector of Imperial Stores). The case of Muhammad Qasim Khan is also noteworthy.[76]

As compared to his compeers like Munim Beg, Tardi Beg, Tursun Mirza, and others, Bairam's role was much more constructive. Bairam's arrival from Gujarat on the eve of the Sehwan campaign infused a new spirit in the Mughal forces. Humayun was so pleased with the news that he not ony thanked the Almighty but uttered the words: 'One who shares our sorrows and agonies has arrived.' It was Bairam Khan who was asked to lead the group that pursued Shah Husain. Tardi Beg's folly in mistaking the robbers left the royal loyalists in extreme difficulty. On the way to Qandahar when robbers had already plundered much of the luggage and the acute cold was unbearable, Humayun tore apart his woollen coat and ordered that the upper portion be given to Bairam Khan who must have caught cold and the lining should be handed over to Mahqar Khan. Bairam Khan's far-sightedness is further proved by the fact that when Mirza Askari's forces were approaching to attach Humayun's small force and the latter was keen to fight (he was confident as he had two *qarabins*, *kaman-i-hizb-i-jang*, and several *banduqchis* who could resort to incendiary warfare), Bairam Khan insisted that they should depart immediately as Askari's forces were numerically superior and hence they could easily overpower them. Even at this hour of need, Humayun's request to Tardi Beg to lend his horses was cruelly turned down by the latter. Although Humayun, on reaching Garmsir, decided to relax for a few days, Bairam again intervened to tell him out of far-sightedness that the stay in the vicinity might be misconstrued by Tahmasp. A letter was despatched to inform the Shah about Humayun's arrival. *Farmans* were instantly issued to receive Humayun. It is interesting to note that when Humayun reached the fort of Dars, Shah Tahmasp summoned Bairam Khan first. In Qazvin, Bairam Khan was ordered by the Shah to get his hair cut and wear the crown. Bairam Khan protested, saying that he was subservient to some other persons whose orders alone he would abide by and act accordingly. Shah Tahmasp was offended and advised Bairam that he should be his own *tabe* (follower). Certain *chiragh kush* who were already in prison were brought and put to death in order to overawe Bairam (*bar binai siyast*) and out of expediency.[77] Some may take this frank refusal to wear the Persian cap as evidence of Bairam's hatred for Shiism. In fact, the Turcomans were by nature very independent in their thinking and attitude. Sidi Ali Reis notes that one may decipher the martial demeanour amongst the Kirghiz, the Karakalpaks, and the Uzbeks, but 'it was only in the Turcomans that I always found an absolute independence and absence of all constraints'. Nevertheless, the Shah was so highly impressed by Bairam Khan's talents that he wanted to discourage him from going back to Humyun's service and offered to appoint him as 'Amirul Umarai Turcomans', chief of the entire Turcoman tribe, which also Bairam declined.[78]

On the eve of the reconquest of India, the importance of Bairam Khan in the Mughal hierarchy may be gauged form the fact that Bayazid gives the list of the nobles and servants of Humayun, Akbar, and Bairam Khan only. While recording the 'names of the officers who served the state during their exile',[79] Abul Fazl writes: 'The head of the faithful servants was Bairam Khan who throughout waited on the stirrup of His Majesty as if he were his good fortune.'[80] Arif Qandahari notes that despite a galaxy of nobles and princes around Humayun, the latter chose Bairam Khan for the governorship of Qandahar. When in 1553 Humayun started for the conquest of India, Bairam Khan again accompanied him. The same favour was shown to him when Akbar was sent to Punjab to drive out Sikandar.[81] Such special favours did not go unnoticed.

Bairam's loyalty to the Mughals was beyond doubt. Stray instances prove that he seldom cared for his own life or interests if the interests of his masters were at stake. After the return from Persia, Bairam was sent to Mirza Kamran 'with a letter of royal advice and a Farman of favour'. To ensure that this royal letter would be given a properly respectful reception by the haughty Kamran, Bairam took a copy of the Holy Book with him as a gift. When he presented it to Kamran, the latter stood up in reverence, and then at once these two letters were given to the prince. Nevertheless, this devotion made Bairam Khan suffer tremendously. He was 'kept under surveillance' and after hundreds of solicitations let go after a month and a half. During the siege of Qandahar also Mirza Askari only 'outwardly assumed the airs of a suppliant, but secretly excreted himself to strengthen the fort and when Bairam Khan came he renewed his opposition. After the victory and in accordance with royal orders, Bairam Khan hung the sword round M. Askari's neck and introduced him. When in 1554 some nobles fed the king with untrue things about Bairam Khan, he came to Qandahar and ascertained that the reports were false. He treated him graciously.'[82]

Abul Fazl further informs us:

> When the excellent loyalty of Bairam Khan was made clear and it became apparent to all that his foot was firm in the path of obedience and good service, His Majesty confirmed him in the Government of Qandahar which it had been his recent intention to give to Munim Khan. He gave leave of absence to Bairam Khan in order that he might make preparations for this expedition and join him as soon as possible. His Majesty took Wali Beg and Haji Muhammad Sistani with him because people were continually telling tales of them and putting together the materials of a strike.[83]

Although Abul Fazl made it out to be a virtuous gesture, the assignment of Qandahar to Bairam Khan was made out of expediency. Not only do the Mughal sources mention it but contemporary Persian chroniclers also affirm that Bairam Khan was assigned this territory because he was a well-wisher of both (*chun daulat khwahi tarfain ast*). Even the family (*urugh-o sahi*) had been left in Qandahar in such uncertainties. Nevertheless, the placement of an important fort under Bairam Khan was resented by the nobles who had in a *kangash* suggested to Humayun that he should wrest it from Bairam Khan, but he did not agree to this. The nobles who were with Humayun at this time included Qasim Husain Shaibani, Haider Sultan Shaibani, Haider Muhammad Khwaja Muazzam, and others. Although the fort could not be taken from Bairam Khan, steps had to be taken to assuage the feelings of the nobles. No other sources so candidly records the change as Abul Fazl, who mentions the appointment of Munim Khan as the *ataliq* in place of Bairam Khan in an apologetic tone:

> Towards the end of the year 1554, Munim Khan was raised to the office of guardian of His Majesty, the Shahin Shah. Though, from use and wont His

Majesty gave the name of guardian (*ataliq*) to the elder man, yet in reality he sent him, like a child, to learn wisdom from that exhibitor of universal reason. Munim Khan returned thanks to heaven for this great gift and prepared a glorious feast. He also tendered fitting gifts and arranged the materials of his own exaltation. In early November 1554 the services of the ladies and the affairs of the provinces of Kabul were entrusted to Munim Khan. BairamKhan, in the meantime, obtained leave to go for the purpose of settling some royal matters, and of arranging his equipment and remained in Kabul. In December 1554, Bairam Khan arrived from Kabul.[84]

Bayazid Bayat says that the post of *ataliq* was given to Munim Khan only temporarily (*bachand waqt*) as he had to look after the *amirs* of Hindal who had been appointed to serve Akbar.[85]

The Mughals owed much of their success in India to Bairam Khan's support, constructive role, and towering personality. The moral and material support given personally by Bairam Khan or procured from outside was considerable. Bayazid Bayat clearly states that in 1551 Humayun had resolved to appoint Munim Khan in Qandahar. Perhaps Munim Khan did not have the courage to take up the assignment and advised Humayun to desist from removing Bairam Khan as people might think that since Bairam Khan had not agreed to leave Qandahar, Humayun was forced to come to the place only to eliminate him. He suggested that since Humayun was leaving for India in the winter of 1551, it would be more befitting and convenient to take Bairam Khan at that time with the royal army and instead appoint him (Munim Khan) or some other person in his place. It was also found that Qandahar was a pivotal station and a crucial boundary town and that the Qizilbash might come to this side. Moreover, Humayun had himself told the Shah that he was leaving Qandahar to Bairam Khan. It was also suggested that Bairam Khan should be appeased, pleased, and rewarded with rich commodities and horses. This advice appealed to Humayun, who left Qandahar after a few days. Accordingly, perhaps the volume on astronomy and the dry fruits brought for Humayun were sent as *alash* to Bairam Khan.[86]

It is interesting to note that Bairam Khan himself was least concerned about the reactions of people and never tried to weigh or compare his position with those of others. Oblivious of the undercurrents of political machinations, he concentrated only on one objective: the reconquest of India for those whom he loved and served. Bairam Khan stood through thick and thin with Humayun and continued to be his close associate and sole friend throughout adversity at a time when Humayun's brothers and nobles had deserted him. The list of 24 nobles who were with Humayun's *ordu* when he conquered Qandahar and Kabul in AH 942 place Bairam Khan only next to Khwaja Muazzam, who is described as the *naffahi* of Jalaluddin Akbar.[87]

Bairam Khan's services were requisitioned whenever Humayun had to send some important embassy to the Shah of Iran or on some other serious mission. In many ways, Bairam was an asset to Humayun's retinue of servants. It was only through Bairam's good offices that the support of the Turcomans could be acquired. A few examples may prove the point. When Humayun ordered the Turcomans to plunder the fort of Madain where Mirza Askari's Amir, Mir Khalj , was stationed, the Turcomans took the plea that this would be a contravention of the Shah's orders. After the conquest of Qandahar, the affairs of Mirza Askari were to be settled. If Jauhar Aftabchi is to be believed, the Turcomans were somewhat suspicious of Humayun. Mirza Askari's treasures, in Humayun's view, were to be sent to the Shah. Since the Turcomans suspected the intentions of Humayun, they decided to take the emperor, Mirza, Askari, and the treasures to the Shah of Iran so that the Shah's decisions could be carried out in this regard. The news reached Humayun who ordered that all the *amirs*, the *topkhana*, and the well-equipped cavalry should be summoned. When the *amirs* were collecting from all sides, the Turcomans apprehended some more trouble and the intentions of Humayun seemed to them to be pernicious. They recalled how Babur had got Najm Beg killed at the hands of the Uzbeks and the Turcomans and it was a possibility that Humayun might kill them also.[88] It was Bairam's influence alone that kept them under full control.

There exists a controversy regarding the religious and sectarian views of Bairam Khan. Some scholars think that the information given in the sources that he was a Shia is absolutely baseless and that Bairam Khan was a Sunni. To be sure, Bairam was not orthodox in his religious beliefs. He is said to have 'always had a sympathetic heart and was devoted to the words of the great Shaikhs and in his noble company, the talk was ever of the word of God, and the word of the Prophet.' Moreover, having been born in the medieval age, he was a practising Muslim and he never neglected his Friday prayers and attendance at the mosque.[89] Nurullah Shustri, who happened to be an orthodox believer in Shiism, stresses this fact in the following words: 'He (Bairam) was the standard bearer of the Millat of Nabi and one who fixed the verses of the highway to Hazrat Murtuza, (*rafi rayat-i Millat-i Nabwi wa nasibi ayat-i Minihaji Murtuzvi bud, arqam-i muhabbat-i aal-i aba chun naqsh bar nagin-i Khatim-i drakash muntaba*). The love of posterity of the Prophet is strongly inscribed in his perception like an inscription on a ring'. Elsewhere Shustri states clearly: 'Bairam was a follower of the religion (*tab mazhab-i haqq-i aimma asni-o ashr*) of the Twelvers and the rights and Truth of *aimma*. He was a sincere *ghulam* of Hazrat Ali whose praises (*manqabat*) he wrote in a *qasida*. The same was inscribed on the tablet of his tomb.'[90]

Although he was said to be a Shia, even an orthodox Sunni Muslim like Badauni had 'a great admiration' for him. Many have conclusively described Bairam Khan as a *tafzeeli*. The argument of Ray that Jahanshah, the ancestor of Bairam Khan, 'is not regarded anymore as a zealous Shiah' because 'twice he banished Shaikh Junaid (grandfather of Shah Ismail I) from Ardabil as the Shaikh was charged with Shiah views' does not hold ground. The political ambitions of the Safavids and their increasing strength and popularity were a bigger threat for the Quyunlus than their religious faith, which they adopted much later (as the Safavids too were originally Sunnis) and that too as a political gimmick to be used as a countervail against the Sunni hegemony in the region. There are, however, several proofs to indicate that he was favourably inclined towards Shiism.

Although Badauni was most critical and ruthless towards other Shia men of talents in the court of his Mughal patrons, his attitude towards Bairam Khan was not as critical. In the 'irreligious' atmosphere of Akbar's court, a practising Muslim would have been dear to Badauni's broken heart. Badauni records that Bairam was a great friend to religions, was subject to fits of religious ecstasy, and was a benevolent man. There are several facts which indicate his inclination towards Shiism. Badauni records two facts. Bairam Khan obtained martyrdom at Pattan in 1561 and his bones were, in accordance with his will, taken to Mashhad. Once Bairam Khan sent a sum of Rs. 7,000 through his servant Sayyafi 'as an offering to the shrine of his holiness, Imam Raza'. Since the servant spent all this money, he was there called to account by Shah Tahmasp (in 1556-7) and was released from torture by death. Bairam wrote a *qasida* in praise of Imam Raza which has been reproduced by Nahawandi. It is also said that Bairam Khan 'displayed the banners of the Imam of the Shiah before his troops'. After the defeat of Bairam Khan in the battle of Kanur Phillour, immense spoils fell into the hands of Atkah Khan. Among them was a standard worked with pearls and gems which the Khan-i Khanan had made, and intended to have sent to the most holy sepulchre. They say that the banner nearly cost a crore of gold. A person like Sidi Ali, hailing from a Hanafite Sunni background could not appreciate the Shia faith and would highlight such factors which go against this sect, particularly when sectarian bigotry was at its peak, leading to imperialist wars and when a common sectarian faith could further ensue the much needed closeness and solidarity with India.[91] Ray's comment that 'the new orientation that Akbar gave to Indo-Muslim history was beyond his (Bairam Khan's) vision and power'[92] emanates from his own familiarity with the Central Asian ethos. Bigotry crept into Central Asia only in the sixteenth century when sectarian wars were at their peak. In the fifteenth century, Sufism had so completely engulfed the social milieu that the religious faith of potentates such as Baisunghar Mirza, Sultan Husain Mirza Baiqra, Ali Sher Nawai, and several others was suspected of having a Shia varnish. Spiritualism and dedication to dead or living saints became widespread practices. Bairam Khan was also a Sufi by nature of his religious beliefs. These pantheistic and eclectic views were brought by the Mughals to India from Central Asia. Akbar's religious ideas were not his own innovations as he basked in the borrowed glory of Bairam Khan, who also had the same approach. Bairam Khan had composed an ode in praise of his holiness, Ali, the commander of the faithful. The '*Munajat*' and its opening couplets particularly reflect Bairam Khan's deep love for the son-in-law of the Prophet Muhammad: 'Though a king be so great that his crown towers over the nine heavens, if he be not the slave of Ali let dust be cast upon his head. Hope not for love for the king of men from one who knows not his own fathers, *cujus matris ignominiam discooperitu alienus*.'[93] Many scholars who are well versed in the history of Sufism know that Ali was considered to be the 'First' Sufi (apart from Imam Jafar-i Sadiq, or Caliph Abu Bakr). *La fata illa Ali la saif ullah Zulfiqar* and many persons in the Middle Ages were in these regions also devoted to the fourth Caliph. Bairam's visit to Haridwar for a pilgrimage may indeed by very surprising for people like Shahnawaz

Khan but the seeds of this Indo-Muslim unity were sown by Bairam Khan and later more extensively, be his son Abdurrahim resulting in a cultural amalgam of the two regions.

It is also suggested that 'Bairam Khan owing to the machinations of malevolent and perverse persons, the chief of whom was Shaikh Gadai, became puffed up with pride on account of his transient high position. He began to regard the holy Shaikh with disfavour and summoned him from Uch. The Shaikh was much displeased, and declared that the order augured ill for his persecutor and there happened to Bairam Khan what did happen.' Shaikh Muhammad Ghaus attributes the subsequent confusion in the affairs of Bairam Khan to his own journey to court (in obedience to a summons). Shahnawaz Khan says that the Sadr Shaikh Gadai had brought to the notice of Bairam Khan the treatise which the Shaikh had written in Gujarat called *Mirajiyya* which gives an account of his own *miraj* (ascent) and which the learned men of Gujarat had denounced. In 1558-9, this famous saint of the Shattari Silsilah, Shaikh Muhammad Ghaus Gwaliary, travelled from Gujarat to Agra. Although Humayun had the 'greatest faith in and attachment to this Shaikh' who had, if Badauni is to be believed, 'with much exhortation and persuasion, availing himself of the influence of those about the court, enrolled the Emperor Akbar, then a youth, among his disciples, but the emperor soon rejected his teaching, and since Shaikh Muhammad's companionship was distasteful to the Khan-i Khanan Bairam Khan and to Shaikh Gadai, he withdrew, ill pleased, to Gwalior.[94] Like Central Asian potentates, each of whom had a spiritual guide, Bairam Khan too had his own circle of dervishes. Bairam was closely attached to Shaikh Fakhruddin and though the Shaikh was a Sunni and Bairam Khan was a Shia, the latter 'used generally to recite his Friday prayers in the Shaikh's masjid and the effects of this companionship with the Shaikh were seen in his increased tenderness of heart'. Bairam Khan was well acquainted with the social milieu of Transoxiana and knew the evil effects of the *sarbadar* and *akhi* movements for the state, hence he did not even entertain the Shattari saint.

Bairam Khan's intelligence and quick-wittedness were also noteworthy. It is said that once Humayun was in conversation with Bairam Khan, who was overcome by drowsiness. His Majesty reprovingly said, 'Ha, Bairam Khan, it is to you that I am speaking.' He replied, 'Yes, sire, I am attentive but since I have heard that in the service of kings a watch should be kept over the eyes; and among dervishes a watch should be kept over the heart, and among learned men a watch should be kept over the tongue, I was just pondering over which I should keep a watch, for your Majesty is a king, a dervish, and a learned man.' Humayun was delighted at this seemly reply, and expressed his approval of it.[95] Such was Bairam Khan's regard for Humayun that when a letter of Humayun was brought to him unawares, he dropped himself from his horse (*khudra az asp andakht*) and performed the *taslimat*.[96]

Bairam also had some knowledge of astronomy and cosmography as Humayun had once ordered him to select and supply books to him on the subject. He had even written a *qasida* in praise of the astrolabe, the commencing couplets of which are as follows:

What globe is this whose axis rests on the centre (of the universe), this full moon across whose midst the meteors dart? Though it vaunts itself the equal of both sun and moon, it gladly enrolls itself among the Emperor's slaves. The sun's resplendent orb looms not so largely in our eyes. As the crescent which surmounts the banners of the world-famed king of kings—both sky and earth are ever subjects to his authority, like the seal of a ring on the hand of a monarch as powerful as Jamshid. This globe brings with it a golden tray full of *ashrafis* to scatter before the feet of great kings, the feet of the Emperor of exalted dignity, Humayun, before whom, in order to obtain honour, the sky itself places the head of humility on the threshold of the court.[97]

Bairam Khan was also an innovator in many ways. He prepared a *harba* (implement of war, a javelin or dagger) from the wood of bitter almonds with which he often rushed and fell upon the enemy. Another quality which added lustre to Bairam's personality was the Central Asian trait of giving freedom of expression even to the have nots so that the evils of administration could be detected and cured. Bairam Khan's administrative talent was beyond doubt but he always welcomed reports against his men, if any. Nuvaidi Turbati composed a poem 'satirizing Kuchik Beg, the accountant of Bairam Khan, the letters of whom a hundred storms like that which occurred in the days of Noah would not wash from the pages of this age.' He writes:

I have a word to say: I will expound it to the Nawwab. I have difficulty: I will represent it to his servants. Thou has given the high post of accountant to Kucik Beg. Say for what reason, o boast of mankind. Thou art perhaps ignorant of his reprehensible acts. Although inquiry into the characters of servants is a duty incumbent on Governors. He was an infamous boy, and conceited, wine-bibbing libertine. A lad ever hankering after gold—soft and self-willed. Other things are known about him from a certain source. But I feel ashamed to reveal them before his honour, the Khan. To cut a long story short and to make an end quickly, I will come to my tale. And I will tell a tale regarding that mutilated wretch. Wherever he has been, his conduct has been such that he has brought upon himself the hatred of all, both gentle and simple.[98]

Nahawandi says that he was unique in his times (*be nazir-i zaman*), (*nadir-i dauran*) and well versed in all the likable and favourite arts. The men of eloquence (*arbab-i balaghat-o fasahat*) liked his couplets in Turkish and Persian. He had a nice complete *diwan* in Persian. Even a bitter critic like Badauni credited Bairam Khan for being 'a poet of no mean pretensions'. He is said to 'have composed a *divan* in Persian and Turki which is in every hand, as his verses are on every tongue'. No one could ever imagine that a warrior-statesman like Bairam could also experience such finer sentiments and suffer the pangs of mundane feeling of love:

> Oh! Thou whose street is the Kabah of our happiness, whose face is the point towards which we turn in prayer, blest will be the tie when thou graciously drawest us to thyself, freeing us from the bonds of ceremonialism and conventionality.[99]

Bairam Khan once 'composed an excellent ode' on Akbar's *qabaq*-shooting and presented it at the feast, though it is said that he borrowed certain features from somewhere. Another episode undermining Bairam's position as a poet has been mentioned by Badauni, who records that he paid a sum of 60,000 to 100,000 *tankas* 'by way of compensation' to Muhammad Hashim for the latter's ode which 'Bairam afterwards palmed off and published as his own'.[100] Yet undoubtedly Bairam Khan showed his skill in the composition of poems. Bairam Khan wrote an acrostic in twenty-four verses, of which the rhymes were '*azim*' and '*qadim*', and the rhyming letter was *mim* in such a way that the initial letter of the first hemistiches composed the words 'Hazrat Muhammad Humayun Padshah Ghazi' and the initial letters of the second hemistiches composed the 'Shahizada Jalaluddin Muhammad Akbar' and the final letters of the first hemistiches the words 'Mirza Shah Abul Maali' together with some other epithets, and the sum of 24 *mims* which closed the verses gave 24 × 40 = 960, the date of the composition of the acrostic.[101] He wrote such poems, both in Persian and in Turkish: 'Who am I? Who has given up the bridle of my heart from my hand, from the hand, the heart through the path of agony fell down from my feet.' His Turkish poems and *ghazals* were like honey-coated words.

Hasan Nisari appreciated Bairam Khan's multifarious qualities. He says: 'Bairam was one of the confidants and trusted *amirs* (*az umra-i Mutabar*) of Humayun. He held the *mansab* of *Amir ul umarai* and had in his power the entire kingdom of the king'.[102] A group of people were in his service. He had been widely admired, particularly for his expertise in the laws of governance and administration. He had extended patronage, kind and honourable treatment, and likeable arrangements for the distinguished men of learning and talents. His generosity was unique and his munificence rarely comparable while the beauty and excellence of his socialization and friendship was very agreeable and soothing.[103]

Bairam Khan was awarded with royal favours and titles like *yar-i wafadar* (loyal faithful friend), *baradar-i neku siyar farzand-i saadatmand Khan-i Khanan*, Khan Baba, and *ataliq*. Yet the end or rather the doom he met is no fair commentary on the kind of patronage the poor loyalist of Akbar received. Whatever be the reasons, the disgrace inflicted upon Bairam Khan cannot be justified. The contemporary and later men of letters were much more generous and benevolent in evaluating Bairam Khan's talents. Nuvidi of Turbat, who was for a long time at the court of Bairam, writes: 'O, thou in whose glorious days time glories—Khan, son of a Khan, chief, and high officer of the King—Bairam. The steed of perception cannot traverse the valley of the understanding. The noose of imagination cannot reach the settlements of the place of thy glory.'[104]

Arif Qandahari, who remained in the service of Bairam Khan till the last days, called him saint-like (*dervish sirat*); (*parhezgar*), sober, careful and a friend (*Raiyyat parwar*), a nourisher of his people, who was 'so high and lofty (*alim-i-qadari*) that even the sun from his high place seemed to be non existent (*napaida*) like a very vague and minor meteor (*qutub-i sifli*) through the microscope. In the commandership, he was like Rustam and Isfandyar. In grandeur, magnificence, courage and justice, he was the shelter for all sultans of his times. Bairam Khan's own quatrain best exemplifies his personality:[105]

The masters of self-effacement are both high and low. It is they who are ever drunk with draughts from the cup of immorality. Whatever there may be in the plane of non-existence, know for certain that it is they who truly exist.

No assessment of Bairam Khan could be more appropriate and better expressive of the exact situation than Badauni's comments that 'His (Bairam's) existence was, indeed, an honour to the age in which he lived.'[106]

## NOTES

1. Nurullah Shustri, *Majalis-ul-Muminin*, MS, Aligarh, Maulana Azad Library, Ahsan Collection, no. 940/21, ff. 459-61; Nahawandi Abdul Baqi, *Maasir-i Rahimi*, 3 vols, Calcutta, 1923-5; Arif Qandahari, *Tarikh-i Akbari*, Rampur, 1962; Badauni, *Muntakhab-ut-Tawarikh*, 3 vols., Eng. tr. by Lowe, Delhi, 1973; Farid Bhakkari, *Zakhirat-ul-Khawanin-i Karachi*, 196; Kewal Ram, *Tazkirat-ul-Umara*, MS, Aligarh, *Farsiya Tarikh*, 32/57.
2. Sukumar Ray, *Bairam Khan*, Karachi, 1992, p. 222; Qazi Mukhtar Ahmad, 'Was Bairam Khan a Rebel'?, '*Islamic Culture*, Jan. 1947, p. 59; C.R. Naik, *Abdur Rahim Khan Khanan*, Ahmedabad, 1966, p. 13.
3. Sukumar Ray, op. cit., pp. 12-18.
4. Nahawandi, op. cit., pp. 3-4; Arif Qandahari, op. cit., p. 25. Sultan Rai Bhandari, pp. 337-8; *Zakhirat-ul-Khawanin*, p. 11.
5. Abul Fazl, *Akbar Nama*, vol. III, text, Newal Kishore edn., p. 355; Eng. tr. by H. Beveridge, Delhi, 1972, p. 640.
6. Badauni, *Muntakhab-ut-Tawarikh*, op. cit., vol. II, text, p. 8; Eng. tr., p. 1.
7. Shahnawaz Khan, *Maasir-ul Umara*, vol. III; Eng. tr., p. 371; Arif Qandahari, p. 28.
8. Abul Fazl, *Akbar Nama*, Eng. tr., III, pp. 610-11; *Maasir-ul Umara*, p. 371; *Tarikh-i Alfi*, account of 967 and 970.
9. Abul Fazl, *Akbar Nama*, III, Eng. tr., pp. 610-11.
10. Ibid.
11. Bayazid Bayat, *Tazkirat Humayun wa Akbar*, Calcutta, 1941, pp. 195-6; *Maasir-ul Umara*, vol. I, Eng. tr., p. 133.
12. Bayazid, pp. 220-1.
13. Badauni, Eng. tr., 365; text, p. 190.
14. Badauni, III, text, p. 190; Eng. tr., p. 266.
15. Salima Sultan Begam's following verse is very famous: 'In my passion, I called thy lock the thread of life. I was wild and so uttered such an expression.' *Maasir-ul Umara*, p. 371.
16. Abul Fazl, *Ain-i Akbari*, Blochmann's Eng. tr., vol. I, no. 30, pp. 321-2, 331; Jahangir, *Tuzuk-i Jahangiri*, Delhi, 1973, p. 232; Badauni, II, p. 13.
17. Arif Qandahari, pp. 56-7.
18. *Akbar Nama*, III, text, p. 333; Eng. tr., p. 610.

19. Badauni, II, p. 36; *Ain-i Akbari*, p. 331.
20. Nahawandi, p. 3.
21. Sujan Rai Bhandari, *Khulasat-ut-Tawarikh*, pp. 306, 342-3; also see Naik, *Abdur Rahim and his Literary Circle*, Ahmedabad, 1966, pp. 13-16.
22. Sidi Ali Rais, *The Travels and Adventures of the Turkish Admiral*, London, 1899, pp. 56-7.
23. Badauni, II, text, p. 9; Eng. tr., p. 2.
24. Sidi Ali Rais, *The Travels and Adventures of the Turkish Admiral*, London, 1899, Eng. tr., pp. 56-8.
25. Badauni, II, text, p. 45; tr., p. 40.
26. Nahawandi, pp. 6-7.
27. Arif Qandahari, pp. 32-3.
28. Badauni, II, text, p. 20; Eng. tr., p. 13.
29. Nahawandi, pp. 6-7.
30. *Akbar Nama*, III, text, p. 333; Eng. tr., p. 610.
31. Badauni, text, pp. 35-6; Eng. tr., pp. 29-30; Hasan Rumlu, *Ahsan-ut-Tawarikh*, p. 392; also *AN*, II, p. 26.
32. *Mukatabat*; Allami, *Insha-i Abul Fazl*, Har Sih Daftar, I, ed. Mansura Haidar, New Delhi, 1998, pp. 89-91.
33. Jahangir, *Tuzuk-i Jahangiri*, Eng. tr., A. Rogers, Delhi, 1968, p. 147.
34. Arif Qandahari, p. 66; *Tarikh-i Alfi*, pp. 607-8.
35. Arif Qandahari, pp. 69-70.
36. Badauni, II, text, p. 26, Eng. tr., p. 19.
37. *Tarikh-i Alfi*, p. 131.
38. Ibid.
39. *Akbar Nama*, III, pp. 343-4, Eng. tr., p. 625.
40. Bayazid, Bayat, Calcutta, 1941, pp. 212, 218, 220-1, 228-9; Badauni, II, 14, tr. p. 7.
41. *Maasir-ul Umara*, vol. I; Eng. tr., p. 149; *Tuzuk*, p. 39.
42. Sujan Rai, pp. 338-9, 342-3.
43. Elliot and Dawson, *History of India*, vol. II, p. 251.
44. *Tarikh-i Alfi*, pp. 121-4.
45. Arif Qandahari, p. 50.
46. *Tarikh-i Alfi*, pp. 121-3; Arif Qandahari, pp. 50-1.
47. Badauni, II, text; Eng. tr., p. 7.
48. *Akbar Nama*, pp. 192-3; Eng. tr., pp. 392-3.
49. Badauni, II, p. 248; Eng. tr., p. 344; Arif Qandahari, however, says that Bairam Khan himself sent him to the Emperor, *Tarikh-i Akbari*, p. 59.
50. *Tarikh-i Alfi*, f. 589b.
51. Jauhar Aftabchi, *Tazkirat-ul Waqiat*, pp. 175-9; Badauni, II, text, pp. 26-9; Eng. tr., pp. 18-25.
52. *Tarikh-i Alfi*, pp. 56-135 in the events of the year 966. Badauni, II, pp. 26-9, Eng. tr., pp. 18-22.
53. Badauni, II, pp. 26-9, Eng. tr., pp. 18-22; Nizamuddin, *Tabaqat-i Akbari*, II, p. 139; *Zakhirat-ul Khawanin*, p. 13; Arif Qandahari, pp. 55-6. Also see C.R. Naik, *Abdur Rahim Khan-i Khanan and His Literary Circle*, Ahmedabad, 1966, pp. 526-7.
54. *Zakhirat-ul Khawanin*, pp. 11-15.

55. *Ain*, I, op. cit., p. 33.
56. *Tarikh-i Alfi*, pp. 967-70; Badauni, II, p. 36; Eng. tr., p. 30.
57. *Tarikh-i Alfi*, pp. 599-609.
58. *Zakhirat-ul-Khawanin*, pp. 11-18; Arif Qandahari, pp. 3-4, 60-4; Sujan Rai, pp. 342-4.
59. Ibid.
60. *Tarikh-i Alfi*, pp. 602-3, 607; Arif Qandahari, pp. 60-4; Sujan Rai, pp. 342-4; *Akbar Nama*, III, text, p. 335, Eng. tr., p. 613.
61. Ibid.
62. Bayazid Bayat, *Tazkira-i Humayun wa Akbar*, pp. 228-30.
63. Ibid.
64. Bayazid Bayat, pp. 230-9; *Maasir-i Rahimi*, II, pp. 2-6; Arif Qandahari, pp. 64-5; *Maasir-ul Umara*, I, pp. 371-84; Sujan Rai, pp. 342-4; Badauni, II, text, pp. 43-4; Eng. tr., pp. 38-9.
65. Sidi Ali Rais, pp. 309-10.
66. Badauni, II, text, 46-7; Eng. tr., pp. 41-2, 49 fn. 4. Farishta, *Tarikh-i Farishta*, Eng. tr. by Briggs, II, p. 211.
67. Bayazid Bayat, p. 41; *Maasir-ul Umara*, I, Eng. tr., p. 145.
68. *Ain*, I, Eng. tr., pp. 329-32; Bayazid, p. 41; *Maasir-i-Rahimi*, II, pp. 1-60. *Zakhirat-ul-Khawanin*, pp. 11, 20; Badauni, text, p. 190; Eng. tr., p. 265. Nurullah Shustri, *Majalis-ul-Muminin*, Ahsan Collection, no. 940/21, AMU, Azad Liberary, ff. 459-61.
69. *Akbar Nama*, text, pp. 185-6; Eng. tr. pp. 381-3; Shahnawaz Khan, *Maasir-ul-Umara*, vol. I, Eng. tr., H. Beveridge, Patna, 1979, p. 369.
70. Ibid, also *Ain*, p. 330.
71. Ibid.
72. Shahnawaz, p. 370.
73. *Akbar Nama*, pp. 152-3, 185, 230; Eng. tr., pp. 334, 380-1, 460; Nahawandi, pp. 9-12; Jauhar Aftabchi, pp. 160-5, 169-79; *Ain*, pp. 330-1, 373, 379.
74. Badauni, text, p. 191; Eng. tr., p. 266; *Akbar Nama*, Eng. tr., pp. 474-89.
75. *Ain-i Akbari*, Eng. tr., pp. 330-1.
76. Ibid, pp. 330-1, 373, 379.
77. Jauhar Aftabchi, pp. 81, 86-7, 96, 102; *Akbar Nama*, pp. 190-1, Eng. tr., pp. 390-2. Nurullah Shustri, *Majalis-ul-Muminin*, f. 460. *Ahsan-ut-Tawarikh*, pp. 114-17.
78. A. Vambery, p. 315.
79. Shustri, p. 460. *Tazkirat-ul-Umara*, p. 60.
80. Bayazid Bayat, pp. 176-7.
81. *Akbar Nama*, p. 221, Eng. tr., p. 447.
82. Arif Qandahari, pp. 22-3; Nahawandi, pp. 2-3.
83. *Akbar Nama*, III, pp. 231-6, 462-8; Iskandar Beg Turcoman, *Alam Ara-i Abbasi*, Tehran, 1314, p. 92; *Zakhirat-ul-Khawanin*, p. 12.
84. *Maasir-ul-Umara*, p. 370; Jauhar, p. 159.
85. *Akbar Nama*, pp. 334-5, 340-1, Eng. tr., pp. 612, 620, 622; Arif Qandahari, pp. 22-3; *Maasir-ul Umara*, p. 370; Jauhar, p. 159; Bayazidm Bayat, pp. 51-4, 165.
86. Bayazid Bayat, p. 165.
87. Bayazid Bayat, pp. 170-2.

88. Ibid., pp. 4, 32, 44, 48.
89. Jauhar Aftabchi, pp. 113-18.
90. Shustri, pp. 460-1.
91. Badauni, III, p. 190; Eng. tr., p. 265. Also fn. 4. Badauni, II, text, pp. 40-1; Eng. tr., pp. 35-6; *Darbar-i-Akbari*, p. 192; Shahnawaz, p. 369.
92. Badauni, II, pp. 40-1, Eng. tr., pp. 35-6. Badauni, III, p. 190, Eng. tr., p. 265, also fn. 4; Shahnawaz, p. 369.
93. Sukumar Ray, *Bairam Khan*, pp. 234-6.
94. Badauni, III, text, p. 191; Eng. tr., p. 266; Shahnawaz, p. 369; vol. I, p. 89.
95. Badauni, p. 141; Badauni, III, pp. 8-9; Eng. tr., pp. 13-14.
96. Badauni, III, text, p. 192; Eng. tr., p. 267.
97. Bayazid Bayat, pp. 172-3.
98. Badauni, text, p. 191; Eng. tr., p. 267; Bayazid Bayat, pp. 171-2.
99. Bayazid Bayat, p. 42.
100. Badauni, III, Eng. tr., pp. 475-6.
101. Badauni, III, p. 190; Eng. tr., p. 266.
102. Hasan Nisari Bukhari, *Muzzakkira-i-Ahbab*, Hyderabad, 1969, pp. 248-50.
103. *Akbar Nama*, III, pp. 335-6; Eng. tr., pp. 613-14.
104. Badauni, II, text, p. 41; Eng. tr., p. 36; Badauni, III, text, p. 388; Eng. tr., pp. 524-6, also fn. 1.
105. Arif Qandahari, pp. 50-1.
106. Badauni, II, text, p. 9; Eng. tr., p. 2.

# Central Asia and Indo-Iranian Relations: Historical and Cultural Perspectives

Indo-Iranian cultural relations have a pleasant past and a long history. It is interesting to note how the multi-dimensional contacts from the pre-historic period down to our own times had brought the two different regions of India and Iran so close to each other. In the letters exchanged between the Mughal emperors and the Safavid rulers, the formal and the spiritual (*suri wa manavi*) friendship, amity, and concord between the two royal houses had been consistently emphasized. Such expressions of mutual friendship and warmth are found not only in the various letters exchanged between Abul Fazl and Mir Sharif Amuli but also in the notes that the poets and calligraphists sent to each other. The *tazkiras* of poets, biographical sketches of men of talents (scholars, physicians, architects, painters, musicians, calligraphers, and other artists) available in chronicles like the *Ain-i-Akbari, Muntakhab-ut Tawarikh*, *Tabaqat-i Akbari*, and *Muzzakkira-i Ahbab, Tuhfa-i Sami* confirm the continuous presence of the Persians at the Mughal court and the continuous exchange of ideas, men, and commodities between the two lands. The Persian influence on the origin and growth of literary and Sufi traditions in India have been examined in various valuable works. The Persian style of history writing influenced the pattern of historiography in India. The Persian poetry of Sadi, Rumi, Nizami, and Hafiz accomplished with far more subtle overtures what straightforward politics and war could not. There was a continuous inflow of extra-territorial talents into India. Some of the Sultans of Delhi like Iltutmish, Muhammad bin Tughlaq, and others were particularly kind, generous, and large-hearted towards the foreigners. During the reign of Sikandar Lodi, 'nobles, shaikhs and men of learning from the lands of Arabia, Persia, Hind and Bukhara induced to do so by his favour and benevolence took up residence at Agra where the king himself generally dwelt'. In his *Guldasta* or *Chahar-i Chaman*, Chandra Bhan Brahmin rightly points out that:

> Since this (Mughal) Empire was a rendezvous where the heartfelt wishes were fulfilled, a large number of men of sword and pen, the people of excellence, quality and learning, men of letters, poets and writers, skilled artisans and eminent persons from the cities of the world around like Istanbul, Aleppo, Egypt, Syria, Basrah, Baghdad, Hamdan, Shirwan, Sumakhi, Gilan, Mazandaran, Astarabad, Gunjah, Burdah, Tabriz, Ardabil, Qazwin, Qum, Sawah, Kashan, Tehran, Yezd, Isfahan, Shiraz, Kirman, Suman, Damghan, Bustam, Sabzwar, Nishapur, Merv, Mashhud, Tus, Tis, Qain, Tun, Isfarain, Jam, Herat, Khawaf, Bukhara, Siestan, Farah, Qandahar, Balkh, Badakhshan, Bukhara, Samarkand, Andijan, Tibet, Kashghar and countries of Turkistan and various kinds of people of other places came to this splendid Empire with great hopes and anticipations. They entered with the service of this bountiful kingdom, which was an asylum for the people of the world.[1]

But this galaxy of meritorious men could not overshadow the radiance of Iranian eminence. The learned men, poets, scholars, painters, calligraphists, men of science and technology distinguished themselves in the medley and left an indelible stamp on the cultural history of India. India's link with Iran go back to the pre-historic period. The emergence of the Aryans was as much a great event in the early history of India as was their rise in Iran. The common features found in the languages of the *Rig Veda* and the *Zend Avesta* also support claims of this affinity. Whether it was Darius or later on Shah Abbas, close relations had always existed between the two countries. Since the present cannot be delinked from the past and the future, the emerging perspectives will necessarily also indicate future prospects. An earnest endeavour is, therefore, made here to touch upon each sphere and to cover the various aspects of political, economic, social, and (mainly) cultural relations between India and Iran in order to determine the contribution to the culture and civilization of the two countries.

In the first place, geographical proximity, contiguous borders, and racial consanguinity had brought the two different peoples together. The Iranians are neither Semitic nor Turkic by origin. They belong to the Aryan stock, confirming the authenticity of the famous legend that Persians, Indians, and Central Asians are the branches of one family tree.

Iran's contribution to the world of Islam in general and to Mughal India in particular have been nicely summed up by G.M. Wickens who writes that 'the dominant function of the Persian mind has long been recognized as part-solvent and part-catalytic'. As will be discussed later, political events paved the way for closer collaboration. Cultural interchange inevitably followed as the political interests of the two regions were interlinked. Geographical proximity and political amity played a very vital role in the maintenance of cordial relations and the brisk exchange of men, commodities, and ideas. The geographical location further added to this cohesion as Persia had all along been accepted as a 'land bridge' between Europe, Turkey, and the Mediterranean world, on the one hand, and Central Asia, South-East Asia, and India, on the other hand.

Global and regional events further united the two peoples. The Safavid dynasty had created a somewhat different military and political structure, with the Shia creed as the state religion and the Iranicization of Persian Islam, which led to the emergence of a new cultural entity, i.e. a Persian Shia state. The Safavid state emerged from a religious-cum-political nucleus. Thus, the intertwining of religion and politics, which is noticed at the outset, seems to have kept pace with the sectarian bigotry noticed in the Hanafite, Sunni, Ottoman, and Uzbek states. The rising power of the Shia Safavids (a new contender for supremacy in the Muslim world) startled the Ottomans and the Uzbeks who could have otherwise easily incorporated Persia into their domain or who could have at least established their dominance over the maritime trade routes, particularly Hormuz, despite the Portuguese menace. As always, religion was exploited for political purposes.

Political amity and mutual understanding were carefully preserved and the balance of power in the region was accurately maintained by a series of rather strange and non-commital 'friendly embassies' between the Mughals and the Persians. When Ubaidullah Khan Uzbek wrote to Sultan Salim (1508-20) about his proposed campaigns against Persia with a view to avenge the martyrdom of Shaibani Khan, the Ottoman sultan expressed his agreement with the Uzbek ruler over his criticism of Persia though no keenness for a joint military venture is noticeable in his reply. Similarly, Sultan Salim's campaign of Chaldiran was preceded by a similar indirect appeal which culminated in the same negative answers.[2] When the Uzbek ruler Abdullah Khan requested help from Akbar, the latter not only emphasized his policy of *sulh-i-kul*, non-alignment, and non-imperialism but also reminded him of the relationship of the Safavids with the Prophet. The pleas for ensuring the safety of travellers to Mecca was met with an equally convincing reply that a shorter and cheaper route was then already available through Gujarat.[3] Thus, regional politics and local interests prevented the rulers from forging any military alliance, which was then neither possible nor feasible in view of the balance of power which changed frequently in the region and which was so assiduously maintained by the rulers, until a confrontation became inevitable. The Persians were alternately befriended by the Russians and the Portuguese who had a common enmity against the Uzbeks and the Ottomans respectively. The only power which could really be of some help to the Persians in the region was Mughal India. The Mughal rulers were the beneficiaries of the generous assistance which the shahs offered to them right from the outset. Babur received military support from Shah Ismail I in his hour of need though at a very high price because his alliance with the Persians, his appearance in Persian attire, and his reading of the *khutba* in the name of the twelve Imams and the Shah of Persia coupled with the minting of coins with the Shah's name created a furore in Central Asia.[4] Wasifi and Haidar Dughlat give a picturesque description of the ensuing hue and cry followed by mourning in the mosque.[5] The ultimate eviction of Babur from his motherland was, therefore, expedited by this alliance with the 'heretics'.

Like Timur, who is said to have valued the 'Khurasanis' more than the others, Babur also appreciated them but with certain reservations. In his hortatory letter of April-May 1526 (*Nasihat Nama*) to Kamran, Babur warned him against placing undue reliance and faith in the Khurasanis for he was conscious of the sectarian susceptibilities of his kinsmen and compatriots. Yet he also admired them while at the same time trying to deliberately dissociate himself from such dangerous attachments. He wrote:

> I hear that those Chaghatais who stayed in Herat after the death of Sultan Husain Mirza became yet more allied with the people of Khurasan, and so became alienated (from their old ways in Transoxiana). They developed much ability and acquired graces, (but) though the Khurasanis are a pleasant folk and there can be no question about their cleverness, there is doubt about their religions and their principles, and they are a nation of . . . and agitators. The sons are alienated from the fathers, and the fathers from the sons. Do not be deceived by their plausible ways and for your own safety's sake, do not let them get out of control.

The comments were not only in response to some 'enthusiastic expressions of Kamran' about the Persians but were meant also to clarify his own position *post facto* in order to pacify his kinsmen and followers. Babur's criticism of the Persians is understandable as he had to pay the price for his expedient alliance in accepting the exacting terms of Shah Ismail which had led ultimately to his eviction from Central Asia. Babur's desperate attempts to dissociate himself from the Persians is also reflected in his criticism, contained in the *Babur Nama*, of Baisunghur's faith.[6]

In the case of Humayun, however, the story seems to be somewhat different as Shah Tahmasp found Humayun sailing in the same boat, grappling with the atrocious activities of his scheming brothers and their intriguing nobles. Contrary to the expedient assistance accorded to Babur by Shah Ismail, political exigencies did not play a role in the warm welcome accorded to Humayun. The anxiety of the Shah to accord a regal reception and hospitality to the royal refugee is apparent in Shah Tahmasp's letter and is amply supported by the accounts given in the *Tazkirat-ul Waqiat* and the *Akbar Nama*.[7] The authenticity of Humayun's supplicatory letter to the Ottoman Sultan Sulaiman II (1520-66), dated 13 October 1548, and sent through Amir Saiyid Ahmad Shah, which requested him 'not to put faith in the Qizilbash' has been challenged by Riazul Islam. Yet the same historian highlights the 'ill treatment' allegedly meted out to Humayun by Shah Tahmasp.[8] Still the military assistance given to Humayun was enough to enable him to recover his lost domain—a fact not denied by any source, and which is in itself sufficient proof of the friendly attitude of the Persians towards the Mughals. Yet Qandahar continued to be the bone of contention between the two dynasties and the loss and gain of this region determined the nature of the relationship between the two rulers. Akbar's attitude was rather cold towards Shah Tahmasp, whose capture of Qandahar had soured Mughal-Safavid relations. The attempts of Khudabanda and Shah Abbas to seek help from Akbar failed miserably and even the embassies sent by them remained unanswered till Qandahar was recovered by Akbar.[9]

It is interesting to note that Badauni also bitterly criticized the Persians whom he held responsible 'for turning the Emperor from Islam'. In his opinion, it was under the influence of the Persian heretics, whom 'Islam casts out as people cast out hair which they find in yogurt, that the observance of the five prayers and the fasts, and the belief in everything connected with the Prophet were put down by the Emperor as *taqlidi* and man's reason was acknowledged to be the basis of all religions'. Such condemned and misguided souls included men like Hakim Abulfath (whose 'manners and address were exceedingly winning' and who 'obtained in a short time great ascendancy over the Emperor'—a fact well proved by Akbar's letter of condolence over the former's death) which is included in the *Insha*; Abul Fazl; Mulla Muhammad of Yazd (who 'got the nickname of Yazidi' for 'reviling the Sabaha'); Sharif Amuli (running 'from country to country, like a dog that has burnt its foot, and turning from one sect to the other, he went on wrangling till he became a perfect heretic'). Although Badauni moans that the 'heretical ideas had certainly entered Hindustan from Persia', he himself was convinced of the cosmopolitan ethos of India and conceded that 'Hindustan, however, is a nice large place, where anything is allowed, and no one cares for another, and people go on as they may'[10]

Shah Abbas too was no stranger to diplomacy. His friendship with Jahangir, the consistent exchanges of gifts, the showering of expensive presents on the young prince, and warm assurances of assistance and moral support offered even during Salim's rebellion were sufficient. The calculated civilities finally made Jahangir so confident and trusting that he fearlessly withdrew the forces from Qandahar during Khurram's rebellion, leaving the ground open for the Shah to occupy the land.[11] The loss of Qandahar enraged the Mughals once again and the search for gullible allies was initiated. New methods were invented and Akbar's policy of *sulh- i-kul* was doomed to be abandoned.

The bogey of religion was once again raised and sectarian similarity was frequently exploited in the search for political alliances. In his letter to Sultan Murad IV (1623-40), sent from Akbarabad (Agra) sometime between 18 November 1636-January 1637, Shahjahan was all set to exploit the 'strong bonds of the Hanafite faith and sect (*din-o mazhab*) existing between the Mughals and the Ottomans, and was determined to persuade them to undertake the 'extirpation of heretics and innovators in religion (*mazhab tarash*)' that is, the Persians, as it was an obligation on the kings.[12] Although Sultan Murad wholeheartedly supported Shahjahan in his move 'to protect the pure faith of the Holy Prophet' to fulfil this righteous mission of cleansing the earth of their existence', and also to strive to make it safer for pilgrims from India and the lands of the Uzbeks to proceed to Kaaba; and enable the traders and the travellers to move freely to all ports and places, he totally ignored the intentions of a joint venture. The contacts existing between the Shahs and Dara Shikoh and Murad Bakhsh are also recorded.[13]

The issue of Qandahar was not the only reason which engendered mutual rancour. The bitterness was often also aggravated due to the Deccan factor. On the one hand, the persistent expansionist policy of the Mughals and, on the other, the sectarian affinity of the Persians with Bijapur and Golconda contributed immensely towards the growing Perso-Deccani relations. These contacts ran smoothly as emigrants from Persia trickled in on a regular basis and held high positions at the Mughal and Deccani courts. The regular exchange of embassies between the rulers of the Deccan and the Shahs of Persia and the latter's readily available intervention in Mughal-Deccani affairs always annoyed the Mughals who hated these mutual, extra-territorial, ambitious relations of their neighbouring rulers.[14]

In early 1637, Shah Safi appointed Ahmad Quli Beg Qurchi to proceed on a mission to Adil Shah. When Abdullah Qutub Shah sent Hakim-ul Mulk in 1641 to the ruler of Persia, the Mughal authorities objected and tried to stop these exchanges. It is interesting to note that in addition to the regular exchange of embassies, Qutub Shah used the good offices of his nephew (who was then attached to the Persian court) also to initiate the talk of his own safe flight to and asylum in Persia if ever the need should arise.

In 1650 a Persian envoy arrived in an English boat as now the Shah had conquered Qandahar and was in a position to bargain. A diamond merchant Muhammad Said Mir Jumla maintained his connections with his homeland and continued correspondence with Shah Abbas II, Khalifa Sultan, and other friends. Abdullah Qutub became jealous of his 'over mighty subject' and Mir Jumla was therefore driven to the Mughal court. A confrontation ensued, compelling Qutub Shah again to seek the intervention of Shah Abbas II, who was particularly moved by the clause regarding 'military assistance on a payment basis' as contained in the former's request for help.[15]

Letters were also exchanged between the ladies of the two royal families. The aunt of Shah Abbas wrote a letter to Miriam Makani and a number of letters were also written by the royal ladies during Jahangir's reign.[16]

The Mughals thought of recovering their ancestral lands of Transoxiana though in the case of Persia they never thought of proceeding beyond Qandahar.

Perhaps the latent but strong desire to maintain a permanent peace with the Persians was responsible for the creation of certain miniature paintings depicting Jahangir seated next to the Safavid Emperor Shah Abbas I and attended to by a Persian confidant and the emperor's brother-in-law, Asaf Khan, and the Mughal ambassador designate to Persia, Khan-i Alam. The Persians distinguished themselves in amicable relations, amiable attitudes, and pleasant disposition. Consequently, their position in the Mughal court was almost always secure not only as boon companions but mainly as sober and sincere scholars and careful and efficient administrators.

Ghiyas Beg (the father of the famous Nurjahan Begam), who was a poet, a clever correspondent, and an expert in the beautiful *shikasta* hand, was highly praised by Jahangir for his social qualities. Jahangir is reported to have 'confessed that his society was better than a thousand *mufarrih-i yaqut* (exhilarative garnets)'.[17]

It would not be out of place here to say a few words about the Persian ladies who had won the admiration of travellers and nobles alike. While Marco Polo is full of praises for Iranian beauty, Mirza Aziz Kuka particularly appreciated these beauties with brains for their expertise in the art of conversation. The fact that the Iranian women possessed a super magnetism is clearly evident by the fact that the above-mentioned Ghiyas Beg's daughter Mehrunnisa first became the 'light of the palace' (Nurmahal) and then the 'light of the world' (Nurjahan) and cast such a spell over Jahangir that the emperor writes in his autobiography that he wanted nothing except some meat and wine for the rest he had left to his Persian wife Nurjahan Begam. The political influence enjoyed by Nurjahan (who was virtually the ruler, with orders issued and coins struck in her own name) had no parallel in the annals of Indian history. In the wake of this extra-constitutional authority arose a '*junta*' of Nurjahan's confidants which controlled the body politic and administrative structure. Mirza Aziz Kuka bitterly criticized Jahangir for patronizing the Persians to such an extent that the Chaghatais and the Turks were completely ignored. Another beauty of Persian origin, Mumtaz Mahal, a niece of Nurjahan, had impressed her husband Shahjahan so much by her charm that the emperor ordered the construction of the Taj Mahal at Agra to commemorate his love for his Persian wife after her death.

The ecclesiastical experiments of the Middle Ages, however, provided reasons for Perso-Mughal closeness. The ever-increasing spell of orthodoxy, which had sharpened sectarian bigotry to serve political ends, could only be counteracted through an indirect patronage of the Sufis who could be turned into convenient mediums for orchestrating the messages of love, peace, and universal brotherhood. Although relations with the ruling family may not be expediently cordial, the attitude towards the Sufis and the *dervishes* of Persia was *pragmatically ardent*. While expressing his paternal affection for Shah Abbas, Akbar advised him to pursue a policy of religious toleration and moderation and cited his own example and policy of making no distinction among his subjects on the basis of cult and creed and his ideal of *sulh-i-kul*. Although Shah Abbas appreciated Akbar's 'pleasant advices' (*nasayihi dilpasand wa pand-i sudmand*), he did not forget to criticize Akbar's policy of *sulh-i-kul* and was equally vociferous in justifying his actions on the plea that 'each one of the Prophets urged war on the "*ashqiya*" (cruel criminals)'.[18] Akbar's religious experiments had already created a furore in the orthodox Muslim elitist world and the Sufi saints were his only hope. The relationship with the ruling class may not be cordial but the connections with the saints vouchsafed close and amicable relations. The attitude towards the saints seems to be more placating. In his *farman* to Mir Saiyid Safiuddin Ahmad Kashi, Akbar states: 'Love for the people of Iran (*tabaqa-i Iraniyan*) is deeply embedded in the imperial heart of Akbar and it is his desire that this exalted community (*guruhi-i wala*) should come close to him spiritually and materially, and the high and the low (that is, of all classes) thereof should partake of imperial favour.' This 'spiritual relationship' with the Iranians, however, was continued by Akbar through these Sufis. The *farman* sent to Mir Safiuddin Kashi in November 1584 is a good proof of Akbar's indirect approach:

> It is therefore fortunate that Amir Ahmad is present there so that he can guide the community on the right path. The Mir should constantly report his spiritual experience to and seek guidance from him (Akbar) who is indeed the solver of problems spiritual and universal, *hallal-i mushkilat-i rumuz-i anfasi wa afaqi*).[19]

Akbar further instructed the Mir 'to assure Sadiduddin Darvesh Khusru whose excellence has been brought to royal notice by Abul Fazl, of royal honour and favour' and added that 'it would be good if Rashiduddin Ishaq could also come in person to the imperial court'. It is further 'expected from Mir Kashi that he will keep the writer well informed about (the members of) the *tabaqa-i illiya-i umana* in Iran. Blessed is he who comes to his (Akbar's) sacred presence. If for some reason the Mir is not able to fulfil this *umniyat*, he will still be remembered in the august assembly of Akbar'. Akbar's faith had generally excited controversy. In this context, the Persian chronicler Iskandar Munshi concludes that Abul Fazl (who was called the 'Jonathan' of Akbar even by the Jesuit fathers) had influenced Akbar's mind so much that the emperor had become a latitudinarian (*nuqtavi*) and since Mir Kashi was also a disciple of Darvesh Khusru Qazvini, the 'ring leader' of the *nuqtavis*, Abul Fazl and Akbar both were in correspondence with the Mir.[20]

Indo-Iranian cultural relations were further strengthened due to lingual affinity which hastened the process of amalgamation. Persian culture and language were eagerly adopted by the medieval elite, and Persian continued to be an official and spoken language of the ruling class not only under the Sultans of Delhi (who were said to be Turks) but also under the Mughals. Originally both Persian and Sanskrit (with its versions in Bengali and Hindi) belonged to the Indo-European group of languages; hence a certain commonness is noticeable between the *Rig Veda* and the *Zend Avesta*. During the medieval period the lingual closeness bridged the gulf and paved the way for a quick assimilation, culminating in total submersion. It is interesting to note that the Mongols after their arrival in Central Asia had forsaken their past cultural links. The commingling with the indigenous Turks once again made them a part and parcel of their old stock, confirming Rashiduddin Fazlullah's statement that the Turks and the Mongols were '*minjinsi wahid*' a (homogeneous lot). The Timurid rulers of India were also Turco-Mongols (being related to the Mongol dynasty of the 'Jetahs' of Semireche from the mother's side and to the 'Qaraunah' Turks of the Sughdian region from the paternal side) though they took more pride in their Turkish descent than they did in acknowledging their ties to the Mongols.

The Safavids spoke Azari Turkish and Persian. The keenness of the Mughals to acquaint the princes with the Persian and Turkish languages simultaneously is clearly seen in the compilation of bilingual dictionaries, glossaries, and directories of phrases which are still extant. The chronicles, *farmans*, *manshurs*, epistles, and *dastur-ul-amals* were all written in Persian though they also included Turkish terms. The adoption of Persian in India and its synthesis with Prakrit and other dialects finally contributed to the emergence of a soldier's and trader's dialect, Urdu, a noteworthy example of lingual fusion. Indo-Persian literature was produced in the medium of the Persian language but with Indian ideas and an Indian background. Amir Khusrau made a significant contribution in shaping this lingual fusion and his contribution to the development of the new medium of expression, Urdu, is noteworthy.

The view that emigrants merely and essentially went to India 'to make their fortunes' is belied by the deep and sincere feelings expressed in many verses. A number of reasons necessitated this brisk movement of people between the two lands. In the first place, the desire and the need for the exchange of ideas was as strongly felt by the political savants of the day as was felt by the bibliomaniacs of earlier centuries.[21]

This is well reflected in Saib's verse:

> Happy that company who are intoxicated with each other's speech.
> who through the fermentation of thought are each other's red wine.
> They do not break on the stone of criticism one another's pearls (i.e. verses)
> but rather strive to give currency to the wares of one another's shop.
> When their genius tends to become blunted
> they are each other's whetstone.

Abul Fazl in India presents the same viewpoint.[22] Rudaki believed that 'there are many hardships and difficulties on the way to India but it pays'. Ali Quli Salim's echoed the sentiment: 'There exists not in Persia the means of acquiring perfection. Henna does not develop its colour until it comes to India.' Badauni enumerates 170 poets of Persian descent living or born in India, and Shibli gives a list of 51 poets who came to India from Persia. Some confess that they are 'captives of India', Sayid Tabrizi (d. 1677-8) says: 'There is no head wherein desire for thee danceth not, even as the determination to visit India is in every heart.'[23] Abu Talib Kalim expresses a similar thought: 'Though longing for India, I turn my regretful eyes backwards in such fashion, that even if I set my face to the road I do not see what confronts me.' Occasionally the poets 'had a fling' at this exodus of poets. Qasim Kahi once objected to this: 'O Kahi—you are a nightingale in the garden of Kabul—you are not a cow or a kite to flock to Hindustan.' Yet Kahi was attracted towards India and moved by his yearning to improve his knowledge of mysticism and to meet the famous mystic Mir Hafiz Kirman Shah Jahangir of Sind. Political unrest, wars, and economic pressures also forced many to leave their homeland. Culture shock and homesickness often spoiled the pleasure of intellectual pursuits. There were men like Shaikh Ali Hazin whose nature 'had no agreement with the fashions and manners of this country (India) nor any power of patiently enduring them' as the sight was 'hateful', leading to his intense desire to and continuous hope of 'escape'. Yet he had to live in India for forty years—though he refused to reckon this (time of his residence) as a 'portion of his real life'. Perhaps it was the magnetism of the Indian social milieu which seized and nurtured these talents to their full bloom, receiving in turn a cosmopolitan outlook.[24]

Mir Masum of Bhakkar (a Saiyid from Tirmiz settled in India) was not only a poet and a good historian but was 'also skilled as a composer and tracer of inscriptions'. If the author of *Riazush-shuara* is to be believed, 'on his travels Masum was always accompanied by sculptors'.[25] Abul Fazl adds that from 'India to Isfahan and Tabriz, where he was presented to Shah Abbas, there are numerous mosques and public buildings which he adorned with metrical inscriptions'. Shah Abu Turab one of the great Saiyids of Shiraz, was the 'counsellor of the Sultan of Gujarat'.[26]

The talented men who were with Humayun during his exile included such luminaries as Khwaja Ghazi of Tabriz, a skilful accountant who was also acquainted with histories and chroniclers; he was appointed *Mushrif-i Diwan*. Khwaja Amiuddin Mahmud of Herat is said to have 'surpassed all the world in the science of accounts (*fann-i siyaq*); he also wrote in *Shikasta* admirably. He was very subtle (*mu shigaf*, lit. hair splitting) in matters of business and had a deep knowledge of arithmetic.' He was appointed as *Bakhshi* and even received the title of *Khwaja Jahan*. Baba Dost Bakhshi was distinguished for his knowledge of accounts and always displayed great aptitude in the affairs of the *diwani*.[27] Maulana Nuruddin was acquainted with mathematics, astronomy, and the astrolabe.

On ceremonial occasions (particularly on *Nauroz*), Hakim Fathullah (d. 1589), the renowned philosopher, scientist, and astronomer from Shiraz, always showed his newly invented mechanical devices. His books contain discussions on mechanical concepts and inventions and the force of movement. Inspired by the works of Nasiruddin Tusi and Bahauddin Amuli (1547-1621), Ustad Ahmad (d. 1649) and his three sons wrote a treatise on mathematics.

Shaikh Abulqasim Jurjani and Maulana Ilyas of Ardabil, who were 'adorned with external and internal knowledge', also joined

Humayun's service. During his sojourn in Meshed, the Mughal ruler in particular discussed the '*Durrat ul Taj*' with these two scholars. He held regular and long discussions with the learned and the eloquent who waited upon him and who were 'benefited by the alchemy of his companionship'. Maulana Jamshed, who was an 'aggregate of excellencies', repeatedly had the honour of getting an audience.[28]

During Akbar's reign Mir Fathullah of Shiraz (who 'had been with great efforts brought to the court of Adil Khan of Bijapur') also received a *farman* 'requiring his presence' at the Mughal court in 990 AH after the death of his patron. The Mir was an expert 'in the regions of theology, mathematics and physics and in all branches of science both logical and traditional and in talismans and incantations, and discovering treasures—he was without his equal in that age'.[29] Mir Fathullah was described by Abul Fazl as 'the wise man of the age', who was elevated to the rank of *Bakhshi* and who received the title of *Azdu-daula* (arm of the empire). The Mir was described as 'singular for theoretical and practical knowledge' and was a 'compendium of ancient sages'.[30] Khwaja Shah Mansur Shirazi, 'an adept at the mysteries of accounts' was raised to the high office of *Vazir*.[31]

The Iranian bureaucrats (the *ahl-i-qalam*) were known in Asia for their administrative efficiency and were frequently employed in various offices as scribes. A number of letters inviting the men of learning and talents to the Mughal court by emperors and their nobles are still extant. One such letter sent from Herat by the famous chronicler Mir Khwand to Babur in response to the emperor's invitation shows how the talents were sought after and valued. In many ways, the Mughals adopted the chancellery practices of Central Asia and Persia. The *Name-i nami* drafted by Mir Khwand seems to have had this simple justification.[32]

Interesting information regarding Indo-Iranian cultural contacts can be gleaned from several *farmans* despatched to various persons in Persia. Akbar's *farman* to Mir Sadruddin Naqib sent through Khwaja Chalebi Qazwini on 23 October 1590 from Lahore appreciates the Mir's 'high scholarship, excellence of disposition and piety and his sincere devotion to the Emperor'. It was, therefore, recommended that 100 *tuman-i raiji Iraqi* be immediately given to the trader Khwaja Chalebi Qazwini to be conveyed to the Mir as his travelling allowance so that the Mir could come to the court at once.

In case the money was not sufficient, an additional sum could be requested from the Khwaja or even from the traders engaged in business transactions in India.[33] Another *farman* sent by Akbar in 1591 to Chalebi Beg of Shiraz also refers to the praises of The Beg which had reached Akbar, who invited him to join his court and issued instructions to Fattahi Shirazi to make the necessary arrangements for the scholar's comfortable arrival.[34]

Akbar's claims in the above-mentioned *farman* that 'this court's patronage of men of learning, especially of the nation and tribe (*aqwam-o ashair*) of the Mir is well known' is borne out sufficiently by his *farmans* despatched to various persons. Such was the alertness of Akbar's men in the search for men of talent that Abulfaiz Faizi who had been sent to the Deccan on a political mission did not forget to look for men of excellence. Faizi's letter to Akbar sent from Ahmadnagar in 1591 further indicates the various kinds of contact which Akbar wished to maintain with Persia. In this letter Faizi gives information regarding the learned men and poets of Persia and the surrounding regions who could embellish the court of Akbar.[35] The same letter refers to the arrival of three ships from Chaul (a port to the south of Bombay, in *Nizam-ul-Mulk's* territory). Some of the travellers were the Qizilbash (comprising men like Husain Quli Afshar and Hasan Beg Lashkar Nawis) who had fled Iran. Having suffered considerably in Persia, they had decided to seek service under Akbar. They lacked enough resources and were keen to receive Akbar's help. Faizi extracted from them valuable and relevant information not only about Shah Abbas and Persia but also about the neighbouring countries.[36]

A full-fledged department where philologists were constantly engaged in translating books from Persian into Hindi (and vice versa) was instituted by Akbar. Valuable works like a part of *Zich-i Jadid-i Mirzai* was translated under the superintendence of Amir Fathulla of Shiraz; Kishan Joshi; the Gangadhar; Mohesh Mahananda were translated from the Sanskrit into Persian. The *Mahabharata* was translated from Hindi into Persian under the superintendence of scholars like Naqib Khan, Maulana Abdul Qadir Badauni, and Shaikh Sultan of Thaneshwar and was named the *Razm Nama*. The *Ramayana* was also rendered into Persian by the same scholars. In Abul Fazl's view, it not only contained the life of Ram Chandra but it was also 'full of interesting points of philosophy'. Haji Ibrahim of Sirhind translated into Persian the *Atharban*. Similarly, *Lilawati*, one of the most excellent works written by Indian mathematicians on arithmetic, 'lost its Hindu veil and received a Persian garb' at the hands of Shaikh Faizi. In compliance with Akbar's orders, Mukammal Khan of Gujarat translated into Persian the *Tajak*, a famous work on astronomy.[37]

*The History of Kashmir*, which covers the period of the last four thousand years, was translated from the Kashmiri language into Persian by Maulana Shah Muhammad of Shahabad. The *Mu'jamul Buldan*, an excellent work on towns and countries, was translated from the Arabic into Persian by several Arabic scholars such as Mulla Ahmad of Thatta, Qasim Beg, and others. The *Haribas*, a book on the life of Lord Krishna, was translated into Persian by Maulana Sheri. A new version of *Kalilah Damnah* was published under the title *Ayar Danish*. The Hindi story of Nal and Damyanti, which 'melts the heart of . . . readers', was metrically translated by Faizi. The translation of the Upanishads and other important works by Dara Shukoh into Persian immensely strengthened the pantheistic trends.[38]

In his *Ain 34*, 'The arts of writing and painting', Abul Fazl mentions several Persian calligraphists, some of whom had also served the Mughals in India.[39] These luminaries included Maulana Sultan Ali of Qayin, Maulana Mir Ali who 'brought his art to perfection by initiating the writing of Sultan Ali of Mashhad', Shah Mahmud of Nishapur, Maulana Muhammad Husain of Tabriz, Shamsuddin of Kirman, Maulana Hasan Ali of Mashhad, Mir Muizz of Kashan, Mirza Ibrahim of Isfahan, Nizami of Qazvin, and several others.

Mahmud Gawan the efficient administrator of the Bahmanis an excellent mathematician and a grand scholar is said to have remitted annually valuable presents to several learnedmen in Khurasan, some of whom apparently were associated with Ulugh Beg's *madrasa*. There were Khurasani merchants in Delhi who supplied books and other valuable goods for sale in India.

It is generally believed that the basis of theoretical knowledge in Unani (Greek) medicinal art was borrowed by the Indians from the Persian works of experts like Abu Muhammad Ibn-i Zakariya ar Razi (d. 925) and Ibn-i Sina (980-1037). Persian contribution in treatment and pharmacy (not diagnosis) is commonly acknowledged. Humayun's secretary Yusuf Ibn-i Muhammad of Herat is credited with compilation of prescriptions and remedies for all diseases. Muhammad Riza of Shiraz dedicated his work on hygiene and health entitled '*Riyaz-i Alamigiri to Aurangzib*'.[40]

In India, the knowledge concerning astrolable was mainly drawn from Persian works of Nasiruddin Tusi (e.g. *Bist Bab dar asturlab*) and Qutubuddin Mahmud Shirazi. In Tabriz a funny event occurred due to Humayun's penchant for astronomy and keenness about astrolabes, spheres (*kura*) and other instruments of observation. The emperor ordered his equerry Paik Muhammad 'to search diligently' in the city for (*kura*). That 'simpleton' brought some colts (*karra karra* = mares).[41] The Ilkhanid envoy Rashiduddin Fazlullah is said to have come to India in search of Indian herbs and medicines. The gifts Abdurrazzaq Samarqandi the envoy of Shah-Rukh bought in plenty from Indian soil consisted of medicines in bulk. The story of Hamara Pal and Avicenna given in Wasifi's *Badaiul Waqai* further confirms the regard Avicenna had for Indian medicines and practitioners. The *Charak Samhita* was translated in Persian and is still extant. In the Mughal court the Persian physicians were held in high estimation and Persian diagnosis and medicines were also appreciated. In *Ain-i-Akbari* and other biographical sketches detailed information about Persian physicians and medical practitioners is available.[42]

In Akbar's Irani, European and Mongolian articles of wear were 'in abundance'. Skilled workmen and masters of this art were also settled in India to teach people an improved system of manufacture so that 'the imperial workshops furnish all those stuffs which are made in other countries'. The *gilims* (carpets) were imported from Goshkan, Khuzistan, Kirman, and Sabzwar. Takya *namdas* or woollen coverlets were also brought from Persia. The Persian carpets and textiles were superior in quality perfection of colours and design. During Akbar's time also this import continued though Abul Fazl asserts that the carpets of Iran and Turan are no more thought of' as 'all kinds of carpet weavers have settled here and drive a flourising trade'.[43]

Akbar looked upon fruits as 'one of the greatest gifts of the Creator' and used to pay much attention to them'. The horticulturists of Iran and Turan had, therefore, been settled in India and the cultivation of trees was in a flourishing state during Akbar's time. Melons, grapes, water melons, peaches almonds, pistachios, pomegranates were plentiful, excellent and could be found everywhere. Similarly, many flowers from Iran and Turan were also found in

Mughal India, e.g. *gul-i surkh nargis*, violet, *yasmin-i kabud*, the susan (iris), the *rayhan* (sweet basil), the *rana*, the *zeba*, *shaqayiq*, the *taji khurus*, the *qalgha*, the *nafarman*, the *khatmi*, and so on.[44]

A Khurasani horticulturist was entrusted with the task of laying out the garden of Sultan Mahmud I of Gujarat at Champanir, the remains of which were excavated only recently.[45] Horticulturists from Iran and Turan contiributed a great deal to the art of gardening. Not only did Akbar invite the horticulturists of Iran but, on the other hand, Shah Abbas also requested Jahangir to send him horticulturists who specialized in dressing plants, indigo planters, indigo dye makers, etc.[46]

The continuous exchange of ideas, technical skills, and artistry between India and Iran is most clearly seen in the sphere of the fine arts. Mughal paintings are an excellent example of Perso-Mughal artistic interaction and cultural amalgamation. During his exile in Persia, Humayun came to intensely admire the Persian style of painting, which led to continuous borrowings from the Iranian art. Despite financial constraints, Humayun was keen to invite painters trained in the Bihzad School. Not only did Humayun bring with him famous painters from Persia, but Indian representations like 'Tree of Buddha' and 'Mountains of India' were also illustrated in the *Jamiut Tawarikh* much earlier. The Persian school of painting left a deep impact on the Mughal art of painting through the influence of experts like Maulana Dust, Maulana Yusuf, Maulana Darvesh Muhammad, Mir Mansur and his son Mir Saiyid Ali, and Aqa Riza. The art of book making and the eight styles of *belles-lettres* and intricate *kufi*, *naskh*, *sulls*, *riga*, *tauqi*, *perkam*, *dobar*, and *nastaliq* decorated Indian buildings.[47]

Abul Fazl mentions that during Humayun's sojourn in Meshed, the exquisite and magical Khwaja Abdus Samad, the Shirin *qalam* who was famous as painter, poet, and calligraphist, came and entered the service of Humayun and 'was much esteemed by that connoisseur of excellence'. Although he could not accompany Humayun immediately 'from the hindrances of fate', he joined him later at Kabul. Abdus Samad hailed from Shiraz. Out of adoration for his own master, Akbar, Abul Fazl says that 'though he had learnt the art before he was made a grandee of the court, his perfection was mainly due to the wonderful effect of a look of His Majesty which caused him to turn from that which is form to that which is spirit. From the instruction they received, the Khwaja's pupils became masters.' One such promising painter, Daswanth, received training under Abdus Samad.

Several Persian books, both prose and poetry, were ornamented with pictures and a very large number of paintings were thus collected. The *Dastan-i Amir Hamzah* was richly illustrated and all its twelve volumes comprising one thousand and four hundred passages of the story were decorated 'with the most astonishing illustrations' by a team of one hundred painters, gilders, and binders under the supervision of Saiyid Ali and Abdus Samad, both of the Bihzad School.[48] Although there were more than a hundred painters who had 'become famous masters of the art', Abul Fazl mentions the names of Mir Saiyid Ali of Tabriz along with twelve others, including Khwaja Abdus Samad. Mir Saiyid Ali had learnt the art of painting from his father and had 'made himself famous in his art and has met with much success'. Abul Fazl says that he 'attained, under the care of His Majesty, the greatest perfection in the art of painting'. He illuminated the story of *Amir Hamzah*. He was also widely known as a poet under the pen name Judai.[49]

The two painters, Muhammad Nadir and Muhammad Murad, cultivated the genre of a completely new style of portrait painting—the *siyah-i qalam* which they could compare to the unique '*espece de Sepia de Camaieu*', for example, the portraits of Muhammad Nadir in the British Museum (1920, nos. 9, 13, 17, 20, 32, 39). The system flourished even during the seventeenth century.

Akbar imported artists from Iran and a combination of the Indo-Iranian style of painting encouraged a totally distinct mode of production. Although there were several painters carrying the name Farrukh, the one who entered Akbar's service in 1585 at Rawalpindi is said to be an 'Iranian emigre'. In *Ain 34* on paintings, however, Abul Fazl's list of painters includes this name as Farrukh the Calmuck.[50]

In the splendour of Mughal architecture the inventive pattern is clearly exhibited as distinct from the novel features which characterize Persian art. In Indian architecture are noticed a fusion and harmonious synthesis of conceptual scheme, technique, ornamentation, and decor which seem to bear the imprint of Iranian architectural features. The most astonishing were the underground and underwater structures. The Persian influence is clearly visible in the painted horseshoe-shaped arch with radiating voussoirs in the Alai Darwaza added by Alauddin Khalji to the Delhi mosque. Certain other imported features (carpet technique, flat arcuate roof decorated with stucco-deep niches, squinches, pendentives, spanudrels), or different kinds of minarets (angular, circular, fluted, stalactite, tapering, attached, and stunted), varied types of decor (arabesque pattern, abstract articulation, vegetable patterns, and geometric designs) seem to be common. The monumentalizing feature of double minarets found in many Indian buildings was also perhaps inspired by an Iranian prototype. Jaunpur, the capital of the Sharqi rulers, was generally known as 'the Shiraz of India'. Deccan architecture also bears the impact of Iranian architecture. Similarly, Persian features are seen in Sultan Zain-ul Abidin's tomb. The decor of the Buland Darwaza, the Chishti monuments, and other buildings in Fatehpur Sikri present a fine blend of Indo-Iranian art. The traditional Indo-Persian foliage design is seen in the *pietra dura* work on the Taj Mahal. Similarities are also noticed in the Agra and Fatehpur Sikri mosques, palaces, and in the Sarai Nur Mahal in Punjab. The architecture of the provincial dynasties of Bengal, Jaunpur, Malwa, Gujarat, and the Deccan also presented a fine blending of regional and indigenous workmanship inspired by styles from Persia and Central Asia (for example, the Saiyid tomb, the Lodi Bara Gumbad Mosque, built in 1494 by Abu Amjad; the Bidar monuments of Gulbarga, Golconda, and Bijapur).

Another sphere which reveals evidence of a brisk and continuous exchange of ideas, artistry, and expertise is the field of vocal and instrumental music and dance. The process of artistic amalgamation is said to have started with Amir Khusrau or a little earlier and was carried further by patrons of the art like Sultan Husain Sharqi of Jaunpur, Zain-ul Abidin of Kashmir, the Sur rulers, Akbar, Burhan Khan of Khandesh, and the nawabs of Awadh. Several treatises and general works written both in India and Central Asia confirm the long-standing contact between the two regions in the field of music and dance. Twelve Perso-Arab airs (*aiman*, *qawl*, *hawa*, *basit*, *golbana*, *gul*, *zilaf*, *sarpardah*, *ghanam*, *sazgari*, *ghara*, and *sanam*) were introduced in India by Amir Khusrau. Ali Quli Qutab Shah is said to have introduced *Nauroz* and Akbar is said to have composed over 200 of the *Khwarazmian* tunes (such as *jalashahi*, *karat*, *mahamir*, etc.), absorbing Iranian and Turanian rhythms into the Indian systems. The new *tals* like *sowari*, *pahelwan*, *jat*, *poshtu*, *ara chautali*, *qawwali*, *jald*, *sul*, *sul fakhta*, *ferodust*, *jald titala*, and *jhumra* were the homogeneous forms of the blending of Perso-Arab, Central Asian, and Indian musical notes.

Apart from a number of well-known mixed *ragas* (such as *Eman*, *Junglah*, and *Hijj*—a corruption of the Perso-Arab airs of Zangulah and Hijaz), various other products of indigenous and Perso-Arab scales have been mentioned in the sources with detailed descriptions of the intricacies of each of these specialized versions. Incidentally, similarities are noticed in the tenor, content, and form of Abhinav Gupta's *Natya Shastra* and the treatises of Abdurrahman Jami and Kaukabi. In this synthetic blending and commingling of Indian, Central Asian, and Iranian schools, the original identity of many of the specialized arts in music and dance were entirely or partially lost, coalescing to assume an altogether different and new form. This is amply borne out by a number of works, including *Mauji Mausiqi* and the works of Safiuddin Latiki, Nishat Ara, Lahijat-i Sikandar Shahi, and others.

It is interesting to note that Akbar abolished the Hijra era by issuing a *farman*. A new era starting from his own first regnal year was introduced under the name *Tarikh-i Ilahi* or Divine Era, though significantly the months in that era had the same names as those during the time of the old Persian kings, and as given in the *Nisab us Sibiyan*. During his religious adventurism, Akbar had specially called the Parsi Ardashir for guiding him into Zoroastrianism. When Akbar was 'informed of the feasts of Jamshed, and the festivals of the Parsi priests, he adopted them and used them as opportunities to confer benefits'. Akbar followed the customs of the ancient Parsis, who held banquets on those days the names of which coincided with the names of a month. Fourteen festivals were introduced, corresponding to the feasts of Zoroastrianism. The festival of *Nauroz* or New Year's Day was celebrated in accordance with the Iranian calendar and custom.

Although the Perso-Indian overland trade is said to have somewhat declined after the adventurous feats of the Portuguese Bartolomeu Diaz (1487) and those of Vasco da Gama, Armenian traders served as the major exporters. The state trading conducted in a rudimentary monetary form, the toy trade, and the purchasing missions confirm the mutual appreciation which the Indian and Persian rulers entertained for the rarities of each other's countries. The letter that Shah Abbas I sent to Prince Salim through Abdul Husain al-Nasiri al-Tusi in 1603 confirms this fact.

A number of purchasing missions also arrived from the Deccan. In this context, Shah Safi's missions are significant. In his letter sent to Shah Abbas I through Miyan Rafiq Tajir, Jahangir profusely thanked the Shah for the rare *Qutub Numa*, a *yadbud* which was 'sure to augment Jahangir's love for the Shah'. In return Jahangir sent him a wine cup of Venetian make (*Kari-vendik*). The services rendered by a lesser mortal like Haji Rafiq in promoting friendship with the Shah earned him the title of *Malik-ut Tajjar* from the emperor.[51]

## NOTES

1. Chandra Bhan Brahmin, *Chahar Chaman-i Brahmin Guldasta*, MS Sulaiman Collection, farsiya 666/44, Maulana Azad Library, Aligarh, ff. 5-6
2. For details see Appendix A infra.
3. *Insha-i-Abul Fazl*, Har Sihdaftar, text, pp. 1-18, Eng. tr. by Mansura Haidar.
4. Mansura Haidar, *Central Asia in the Sixteenth Century*, Delhi, 2002, Chapter 'Struggle with the Safavid', p. 128.
5. Wasifi Zainuddin Mahmud, *Badaiul Waqai*, Moscow edn., vol. I, 1961, pp. 1-20; Haidar Dughlat, *Tarikh-i-Rashidi*, Eng. tr., p. 238.
6. Riazul Islam, *Calendar of Documents on Indo-Persian Relations*, Karachi, 1982, vol. I, pp. 59-60; Babur, *Babur Nama*. Letter to Kamran and Humayun.
7. Ibrahim Hakki, *Hand Hukumdari Humayun Sahim Kanuniya gonderig, bir mektep*, vol. VIII, no. 202, Istambul, 1937, also see A.A.A. letter of Tahmasp.
8. Riazul Islam, *A Calendar of Documents on Indo-Persian Relations*, vol. II, Karachi, 1982, pp. 295-9; Riazul Islam, *Indo-Persian Relations*, pp. 31-40.
9. *Insha-i Abul Fazl*, pp. 1-18, also see Mansura Haidar, Eng. tr.
10. Badauni, *Muntakhab-ut-Tawarikh*, II, pp. 39, 211, 241, 245.
11. For details see Riazul Islam, op. cit., pp. 59-60.
12. For Salim's friendly relations see Riazul Islam's *A Calendar of Documents on Indo-Persian Relations*, Karachi, 1982, vol. II, pp. 312-13.
13. Ibid., pp. 314-15.
14. See *Indo-Persian Documents*, op. cit. under letters of Mughals; also see, *Central Asia in the Sixteenth Century*.
15. *Indo-Persian Documents*, pp. 312-14.
16. *Akbar Nama*, vol. III, p. 25.
17. *Ain-i -Akbari*, I, Eng. tr., p. 573.
18. *Insha-i-Abul Fazl*, see Akbar's letter to Shah Abbas; also see *Akbar Nama*, III, letter to Shah Abbas, for Shah Abbas's criticism of Akbar see *Indo-Persian Documents*, Shah Abbas's letter to Jahangir.
19. *Majmua*, MS 2591, Tehran University Central Library, ff. 152-3.
20. Iskandar Munshi, *Alam Ara-i Abbasi*, pp. 473-7.
21. See Shibli, *Sher-ul-Ajam*, vol. III, pp. 10, 198; Browne, *Literary History of Persia*, pp. 164-8.
22. Abul Fazl, *Ain-i-Akbari*, vol. III, Eng. tr., Sarkar and Jarret, New Delhi, pp. 2-7.
23. Shibli, *Sher-ul-Ajam*, vol. III, p. 10.

24. Hasan Nisari Bukhari, *Muzzakkira-i-Ahbab*, Persian text, pp. 469-70; Eng. tr., pp. 62-3.
25. Browne, III, pp. 278-81.
26. *Ain*, I, p. 579.
27. Badauni, 258.
28. Abul Fazl, II, *Akbar Nama*, vol. I, Persian text, pp. 222-3, Eng. tr. by Beveridge, Delhi, 1972, pp. 448-50.
29. Ibid., text, p. 223; Eng. tr., p. 450.
30. Badauni, II, p. 325.
31. *Akbar Nama*, III, pp. 578, 593.
32. Ibid., p. 273.
33. See Khwand Mir's *Nama-i Nami Mohiuddin*, pp. 67-8.
34. *Munshaat*, MS Bodleian Library, 2711 f. 234, also see *Akbar Nama*, vol. III, pp. 575-85.
35. *Mukatabat-i-Allami*, Lucknow edn. 1280/1863, p. 77.
36. *Latifa-i-Faizi*, Ethe 1479, ff. 17-38.
37. Ibid.; *Ain*.
38. *Ain*, pp. 10-11.
39. *Ain*, p. 34.
40. Farishta, *Tarikh-i Farishta*, Eng. tr. by Briggs, vol. II, p. 510; *Mirat-i-Sikandari*, p. 107; for details see *Ain-i-Akbari*, see also *Indo-Persian Documents*.
41. *Akbar Nama*, I, Persian text, pp. 220-1; Eng. tr., pp. 444-5.
42. *Ain*, Eng. tr., I, pp. 113-15.
43. *Ain*, I, pp. 113-14, also p. 660.
44. *Ain*, p. 114.
45. *Mirat-i Sikandari*, p. 107.
46. *Ain-i-Akbari*, pp. 113-15; Riazul Islam, *Persian Documents*, letter to Jahangir 230.
47. Brand and Lowry, p. 61; Beach, pp. 60-1; Krishna Chaitanya, pp. 56, 81-2; also see A.A. Rizvi, *Wonder that was India*, pp. 305-7.
48. Badauni, II, text, p. 301; Eng. tr., p. 316; *Ain*, I, pp. 204, 286; *Akbar Nama*, Eng. tr., pp. 15-29.
49. *Ain*, pp. 204-5; Badauni, II, p. 301.
50. *Ain*, 34.
51. Muhammad Salih, *Majmui Mukatib-i-Mukhtahfa*, MS 2247, Tehran Majlis Library, ff. 265-6.

# A Constellation of Iranian Talents in the Indian Sky

From the land of Avicenna many good physicians emerged, though most of them also had multidimensional interests and other vocations. Hakim Abul Fath's father Mulla Abdurrazzaq of Gilan was a learned and talented man; he held the post of *sadr* of Gilan and met his death after the conquest of Gilan by Shah Tahmasp. His son Abul Fath came to India with his two talented and eminent brothers, Hakim Humam and Hakim Nuruddin. From the posts of *sadr* and *amin* 'he rose higher and higher in Akbar's favour and possessed an immense influence in state matters and on the Emperor himself. Though only a commander of one thousand, he is said to have had the power of a *vakil.*' He was not only a man of the pen but also a man of the sword; he successfully participated in expeditions against Sawad, Bajaur, Kashmir, and Zabulistan. Both Abul Fazl and Badauni admired the 'vast attainments' of Abul Fath, whose *munshiyat* containing interesting and informative letters serves as a valuable source of history. His closeness to Akbar excited jealousy, and his acumen and quickness of comprehension and his proficiency in all worldly accomplishments (and not merely his 'winning address and open flattery') made him dear to the emperor. Abul Fath's brother Hakim Humam was also a 'personal friend of Akbar and possessed great influence at court'. He held the office of *Bakawal Beg* and the rank of 600. Badauni denigrates Abul Fath as 'no less a byword' for his 'infidelity and all other reprehensible qualities', and blames Abul Fazl and Yazdi (nicknamed as Yazid) for trying hard to convert Akbar to Shiism and for turning the emperor entirely aside from the Sunni faith and leading him to reject inspiration, prophecy, miracles, and even whole law. In spite of all his good qualities and quick wit Hakim Hasan of Gilan did not make much progress as he did not possess learning. Hakim Humam (the younger brother of Abul Fath) was 'better in his disposition than his brother. Although it was not naturally good, yet it cannot be said to have been naturally evil.

Originally his name was Humayun Quli, which was changed by Akbar to Humam (magnanimous prince). Hakim Humam was sent as Akbar's envoy to the ruler of Turan. Hakim Fath Nuruddin Qarari of Gilan and a full brother of Hakim Abul Fath had, like his brothers, many accomplishments and virtues, among them being poetry, penmanship, and studiousness. He was also endowed with the qualities of holy poverty and humility.[1] Although Akbar criticized the Ottomans for their practice of *ankari* (escheat) in his *Dastur-ul Amal*,[2] Badauni says that soon after Humam's death, their property was 'at once put under seal and escheated to the government, so that they were destitute of a decent shroud'. All the wealth which they had amassed 'disappeared in a moment, vanishing as though it had been sunk in the Red Sea and the Arabian Sea and nothing remained with them except regret'. One of the two sons of Humam, Hakim Najati of Gilan, was 'proficient in poetry and in the composition of enigmas'.[3]

Hakim Misri is said to have been a 'very learned man', 'a clever doctor', 'a man of a most amiable and unselfish character' who had full command over the theory and practice of medicine and all traditional and profane sciences such as exorcism, etymology, and the formation of broken plurals. Badauni notes that he 'was a cheerful soul, a good companion whose very approach was a blessing'. He composed 'droll verses' in Persian and also prepared some practical treatises on medicine. He was a good poet. Another 'simple' and 'pious man' was Hakim Masihul Mulk who had gone from Shiraz to the Deccan and served as physician to Sultan Murad. He was 'exceedingly well-skilled in medicine' and 'had the disposition of a religious man and also sound faith'.[4] Hakim Zanbil, a brother of Mirza Najat Khan, was a '*Muqarrib*' (the closer ones) of Akbar, and was 'distinguished for his learning'.[5]

Hakim Fathullah of Gilan knew a great deal of medical literature, and was also well versed in astronomy. He wrote a Persian commentary to the Koran. Hakim Lutfullah of Gilan was also a clever practitioner of medicine, and possessed great learning. His grandson Fathullah was a physician at Shahjahan's court. Interestingly enough, there was a physician, Hakim Saifulmulk Lang, who got the nickname of 'Saiful Hukama' (the sword of doctors) because he helped his patients on their journey to the next world. He came from Damawand to Agra and wrote poems under the *takhallus* of 'Shujai'. Badauni writes that he had 'united a task for writing vilely scurrilous and satirical verses to great learning and knowledge of medicine' though he also mentions the 'ill luck' of Shujai before whose cure, like that of Shaikh Jalal before him, even the messenger of death expressed helplessness, saying, 'Where he kills one this physician kills many.' Although Shujai was 'held in much honour in India', he left the place because, as he himself said, he 'received neither patronage nor honour' and sent back a satirical poem to this effect.[6]

Shamsuddin Hakimul Mulk of Gilan not only surpassed all his contemporaries in the other branches of traditional learning, but 'in medicine and the healing arts, he was the Galen of the age, and was endowed with the healing breath of the Messiah'. Despite Hakim's criticism of Badauni's book, the latter depicts him as a sincere, amiable person with a firm faith in God and as one who was devoted to the welfare of the people. He helped his students generously in their studies as much as with financial resources. Hakim Ainul Mulk of Shiraz, a relative from the maternal side to the renowned logician Muhaqqiqi Davvani, was said to be a 'learned man' and a 'clever writer' who held many important assignments and who also served as the *faujdar* of Sambhal, as *sadr* of Bengal, and as *diwan* and *bakshi* of Agra. He excelled in diplomatic assignments and was sent as an envoy to Chingiz Khan of Gujarat and to Ali Adil Shah of Bijapur. Both Akbar and his critic Badauni liked Hakim and Hakim is said to have been a friend of Badauni. Apart from being 'distinguished by his gracious manners and excellent qualities', he was an excellent physician in his own right. 'In the treatment of opthalmia, his equal has not been seen.' He occasionally composed nice verses and his pen name was 'Davai'. He built a mosque in old Bareli, in Mirzai Muhalla, which is known as Padshahi Masjid or Mirzai Masjid. The inscription shows that the date of its construction was AH 987, when Hakim held the *faujdari* of Sambhal.[7]

Ever since Sultan Husain Baiqra and Ali Sher Navoi had renewed the literary and artistic activities at Herat, the place had turned into a meeting place of talents who eventually contributed to the glory of the fine arts of India. Mirza Beg Sipihri's *divan* and his couplets were the 'fruits of his brilliant intellect'. Muhammad Mirak Salihi of Herat was a descendant of Nizamul Mulk Tusi and had 'good taste both in poetry and in prose composition'. He was studious and a calligraphist with a 'good hand'. Khwaja Husain Sanai of Mashhad, the son of Ghiyasuddin Muhammad, also had his admirers. Badauni asserts that the great men of his country used to secretly assemble at social gatherings to discuss even a single couplet by him and in each gathering his couplets were read by way of a good augury, and all agreed both with his tongue and with his pen, and recognized his preeminence in poetry, and recorded their opinions. Abul Faiz Faizi was Sanai's pupil. Since his arrival in India all his poetic fancy had been frozen by envy, neglect, and a hundred shafts of criticism and 'he wanders distracted in the way of the vulgar'. The author of the *Atashkadai Azar* contradicts this assessment by saying that 'whether no one understands the meaning of his verses or his verses have no meaning is a debatable matter'. This statement was also supported by others. Yet Badauni insists that his *divan* was well known and contained a good *masnavi* and that he had a poetic nature and in all subjects save unity, preaching, advice and direction, he had a wonderful aptitude. However, he does concede that his *divan* was 'for the most part pointless and its style not comparable with that of his loftier odes'. Abul Faiz Faizi died in Lahore in 1591-2.[8]

Saiyid Muhammad Fikri, popularly known as 'Mir Rubai' (because he was 'distinguished for his quatrains'), came to India in 1561-2 and spent many years at the court of Akbar. Although he was a cloth weaver of Herat, 'in the description of poetry, he was like the Umar Khayyam of the age', and his verses were 'well known'. Razi places his date of arrival in India in AH 969. His excellent *rubais* earned for him the title of 'Khayyam of the age'.[9]

Liqai of Astarabad is described as the 'epitome of many accomplishments'. Muradi of Astarabad came to India in 1571-2 and 'is remembered for many verses which he had left behind'. A poetess 'Nihani' who happened to be a 'near one' (*qarina*) of Mahisti of Herat has also been mentioned by Badauni. [10]

Another Heart-born talented person was Mir Dauri (Sultan Bayazid) who received the title 'Katib ul Mulk, (Scribe of the Kingdom) as probably 'nobody in Hindustan has written the *nastaliq* hand better than he' and he is said to have possessed 'good taste in poetry'. His pupil Khwaja Ibrahim Husain was also well known. Mirza Quli, popularly known as 'Mayali' or 'Maili of Herat', was such a master of the political style 'that none of our later versifiers can be mentioned beside him'. Mayali of Herat came to India in 979 AH (according to the *Nafais-ul Maasir* in 983 AH, as recorded by Taqi). He was brought up in Mashhad. After the death of his patron, Sultan Ibrahim Mirza Safawi, he came to India and joined the service of Nawrang Khan. The author of the *Atashkadai Azar* describes him as 'one of his favourite poets'. His works had generally been highly appreciated. Nevertheless, the poet is said to have been poisoned in Malwa due to some suspicion, and that too by his own patron.[11]

Maulana Sani Khan of Herat, an Arlat by origin, was denounced by Nizamuddin as a 'low fellow who was originally a *qalandar* and eventually rose to be an *amir*', though Badauni says that he was 'well known for his ability, scientific knowledge and wit'. He served the Mughals for a long time. He was first in the service of Hindal and after his death (20 November 1551) he entered into Humayun's service. Since his name Ali Akbar was partly similar to that of Akbar, he made this an 'excuse' to address to him 'treatises on heresy, in which agreeably to the system of Nuqtawis, he sets forth both the emperor and himself as that promised person', i.e. Mahdi. He verified the *Kafiyyah* or the *Al-Kifayyat fin nahw* by Shaikh Jamaluddin Ali Umar, popularly known as Ibn-ul Hajib, and a treatise on Sufism.[12] Badauni says that Maulana Mir-i Kalan was 'endowed with both inward and outward perfection and was a profound sage, being especially proficient in the tradition in which respect he was the wonder of the age and his angelic nature was a manifestation of the nine attributes of God'. He was a disciple of Shaikh Jalal of Herat.[13]

There were many good poets from other parts of Iran. Hayati of Gilan, though 'free from the bad qualities of poets', was described as 'a sympathetic friend', who 'excelled in all descriptions of poetry'. He was highly esteemed for his deep learning: 'A stream from the ocean of thought passed by his house; correctness and equity are visible on his forehead. Serenity and truth are in him united.' Having come to India 'to better his circumstances', he 'was liked by Akbar' and got a *jagir*. He lived mostly in Burhanpur where he constructed a villa and a *masjid* named after him.[14] Nasruddin Qarari of Gilan was another 'man of understanding and of lofty thoughts'. He apparently suffered from 'a curious monomania that his elder brother was the personification of the world' and that Hakim Humam was 'a man who represents the life to come'.[15]

Qazi Tawaisi of Khurasan, 'a most trustworthy man', perhaps being carried away by the philosophy of Sarbadran, 'would as far as possible show favour to the poorer party, even though he were in the wrong'. Badauni is of the opinion that Qazi Tawaisi must have suffered much at the hands of the wealthy men of his time and was, therefore, always much prejudiced against them, little realizing that in those days, 'it is generally the wrong doer that cries for justice'. For defending the interests of weaker men and fighting for human rights, Tawaisi met his doom when he gave a verdict after Khan-i Zaman's rebellion stating that 'the seizure of the effects of a rebel was unlawful'. He was deposed and replaced by a more pragmatic person, Qazi Yaqub. Perhaps in a state of shock at this act of injustice, Qazi Tawaisi passed away.[16]

Mir Murad of Juwayn had been in the Deccan for quite a long time and was hence also called 'Dakhini'. Since he was an 'excellent shot', Akbar appointed him as 'rifle instructor' to Prince Khurram. He held the post of *bakhshi* of Lahore. His son Qasim Khan was also an 'excellent poet and rose to distinction' as treasurer of Bengal; two of his sons reduced the fort of Hugli in February 1632 and put down the Portuguese who 'converted natives by force to Christianity'. He built a Jami Masjid in the bazaar of Agra.[17]

Mulla Talib of Isfahan earned a reputation as a 'thoughtful poet' with a 'correct' taste both 'in prose and poetry'. He is also credited with being 'experienced in political matters'. He was sent as an envoy to the ruler of Little Tibet. He spent thirty years of his life in Kashmir under the patronage of the Sultans. He was a 'very sympathetic man' and was 'much liked' in India. Originally he lived like a 'religious mendicant' and later on entered the service of Akbar. He was 'often in the company' of Hakim Abul Fath, Zain Khan Kuka, Abul Fazl, and Shaikh Faizi. He was also appointed as *sadr* of Gujarat.

Another 'well-known poet', a pupil of Taqiuddin Muhammad of Shiraz, was Shakibi of Isfahan. He was 'acquainted with chronology and the ordinary sciences; and the purity of his nature led him to philosophical independence'. Besides, he had acquired good taste and wrote well. Shakibi was the son of Zahiruddin Abdullah Imami of Isfahan. As a young budding talent, he left his homeland for Herat and came into contact with poets like Sanai, Mayali, and Wali Dasht Bayazi. When he came to India, he was attached to the literary circle of Abdurrahim Khan-i Khanan who gave him a reward of 18,000 *asharafis* (or 10,000, according to the *Haft Iqlim*) for his *Saqi Nama*. Another composition which earned a present of 1,000 *asharafis* each from his patron and Jani Beg both was his *masnavi* on the conquest of Thatta. Even after writing a number of eulogies for his patron he fell out with him. Shakibi later sought greener pastures, and through the good offices of Mahabat Khan he got an entry into the Mughal court. Although he wanted to go back to Iran, Jahangir detained him and appointed him *sadr* of Delhi and here he breathed his last in 1023 AH.[18]

Another poet Wafai of Isfahan sojourned in Kashmir and Lahore and finally joined the service of Zayn Khan. According to Badauni, he 'possessed sparks of tastes', while Daghistani writes that his 'impudent flattery was proverbial'.[19]

Sharif Sarmadi distinguished himself as an upright and zealous performer of his duties. His 'rhymes were excellent' and he understood arithmetic well. He held many insignificant posts and participated in many campaigns.[20] Mulla Tashbihi Kashani visited India two or three times. Mir Ali Akbar spent forty years of his life in Hindustan. The *Atashkadai Azar* gives a very favourable account of this poet: a 'decent man', he was 'singular in his manners'. He was not 'widely known', perhaps because (according to Daghistani) he was a 'heretic and led a retired life'. His *masnavi* 'The Atom and the Sun' (*Zarrah-o Khurshid*) is well known. The *Atashkadai Azar* notes that, 'Whilst in Hindustan, he tried to improve the morals of the people, dressed as a fakir and did not visit kings.' Tashbihi's *divan* is also extant. In the biographical sketches of the poets in the *Ain*, he has been described as belonging to the Mahmudi sect and it is also noted that his mind was rather unsettled. Badauni comments that Tashbihi 'attempted to reduce men to heresy and invited them to join the sect of the Basakhwanis'. He even went to the extent of persuading Shaikh Abul Fazl that he was 'an infallible spiritual guide' and managed to present an ode to Akbar and dedicated a treatise 'after the manner of the Nuqtawi sect' to Abul Fazl. Badauni suspects that the sole motive of Tashbihi was to misguide Akbar by inciting him to overthrow the 'self-styled orthodox' so that truth might be confirmed in its central position and pure monotheism might be established.[21]

Mir Rafiuddin Haidar of Kashan, whose pen name was Rafii, 'was a composer of enigmas' whose 'excellent understanding', 'correct taste', and 'unrivalled' competence in the art of composing enigmas and chronograms was well recognized. He is described as being 'well acquainted with the ars poetica' and was also 'distinguished as a writer of riddles and *tarikhs*'. For one of his *tarikhs*, he received an award of 10,000 rupees. Although Rafii wanted to return to his motherland after a sojourn of a few years, the shipwreck near the Makran Coast forced him to come to India. Although the copies of Faizi's poetical works which Rafii was carrying with him were all safe, his own belongings amounting to 2 lakh of rupees were destroyed in the catastrophe. However, his losses were compensated by the rich presents and rewards which were showered upon him. After a stay of two years, he returned home and received rent-free lands from Shah Abbas. Sanjar had come from Persia to India in 1000 AH. For some 'crime' which he allegedly committed, Akbar threw him into prison. Although he was set free and went to Ahmedabad, he found it unsafe to remain there and returned to Ibrahim Adil Shah of Bijapur. Shah Abbas had a regard for his father and insisted that Sanjar should come back to his native land but he died in 1021AH before he could depart.[22] Another person, Khusrawi of Qain (between Yazd and Herat), was in the service of Prince Salim, 'excelled in music', wrote *shikasta* well, and was a good hand at shooting with the bow and matchlock.[23]

Shaikh Hasan Ali of Mausil was a 'faithful' disciple of Shaikh Fathullah Shirazi. He joined the service of Akbar and was given the charge of Prince Salim's initial education 'until the young prince could repeat certain lessons from Persian and other treatises on philosophy'. Badauni gives a very interesting account of the Shaikh's sojourn in India:

> Shaikh Abul Fazl also for some time secretly received instructions from him in the exact sciences and in physics and other branches of philosophy, but notwithstanding this he never attempted to advance the Shaikh's interests, so that while he himself has his place on the carpet in the imperial presence, his master takes his stand on the bare floor. Shaikh Hasan Ali, finding that the conduct of such men was not in accord with his religious views, gave up the allowance which he used to receive and went to Gujarat, where he associated himself for a time with Mirza Nizamuddin Ahmad. The latter and his son, Muhammad Sharif, received much profitable instruction from him in those branches of knowledge which exercise the reasoning faculty, and in secular learning, so much so indeed that they advanced to perfection therein. After the death of Shaikh Fathullah, Shaikh Abul Fazl and others recounted the Shaikh's accomplishments and perfection in Akbar's court assembly. The Emperor invited him and the Shaikh came to Lahore. On reaching the court, the Shaikh was instructed by Nizamuddin Ahmad to perform Sijdah instead of Kornish which so displeased him that he made his release from the obligation of performing the ceremony of his attendance and even in his house he could not bear so many things which were abominations to him and on the pretext of visiting his mother he decided to leave India in 1589-90. When he reached Hormuz, he sent a message to the officers of the Imperial Court saying 'Praise be to God! I am freed from the hypocritical companionship of my friends.[24]

Ghazali of Mashhad left his homeland during the reign of Shah Tahmasp. Badauni says that there was an attempt on his life 'on account of infidelity and intemperance' which forced him to go to the Deccan. Ghazali of Mashhad had been invited by the Khan-i Zaman to Jaunpur; later on he joined the service of Akbar and received the title of Malikush Shuara. The *Muzzakkira-i Ahbab* simply says that 'during those days his poems had acquired fame among the people. They are nice.' He is, however, said to be unrivalled in the depth of his understanding and the sweetness of his language and was well acquainted with the noble thoughts of the Sufis. There are different opinions about the number of books written by him. The *Atashkadai Azar* reports that he compiled sixteen books; the *Mirat-ul Alam* says he had two books to his credit, the *Asrar-i Makhtum* and the *Rushhatul Hayat*; to this list one other name, *Miratul Kainat* was added by the *Haft Iqlim*. Badauni states that the poet had compiled several *divans* and a book of *masnavis*. It is said that he had written no fewer than 40,000 or 50,000 couplets. Nizamuddin gives the number of his poems as 100,000; the *Atashkadai Azar* puts the figure at 40,000; and the *Haft Iqlim* at 70,000. Whatever may be the exact number of his poems, Badauni concedes that 'he had great facility of expression in the language of the mystics'. Although his compositions did not rank very high, his poems 'as regards both quality and quantity are superior to those of many of his contemporaries'. He died in Ahmedabad in 1572, leaving behind a fortune of 20 lakh rupees.[25]

Mirza Jafar Beg Asif Khan of Qazvin came to India in 985 AH, and was initially made the commander of 2,000 and got the title of Asif Khan. He led several successful campaigns against the Raushnais. He also held the following posts: *thanedar* of Swat; *vakil* and commander of 5,000; and *ataliq* to Prince Parvez. Although Jahangir bestowed upon him a pen box studded with jewels as the insignia of the post of the *diwan,* the beneficiary never trusted his benefactor. He was, however, a 'man of the greatest genius, an able financier, a good accountant', so that 'a glance is said to have been sufficient for him to know the contents of a page'. Being a great horticulturist, he planted trees and lopped off over-grown branches with his own hands in his gardens and he often transacted business with a garden spade in his hands. In religious matters, he was 'a free thinker, and one of Akbar's disciples'. He was one of the most eminent poets of Akbar's age, an age 'most fruitful' in great poets.

His *masnavi*, entitled '*Nur Nama*' is ranked after Nizami's *Shirin Khusraw*.[26]

Another person from Qazvin was Khwaja Ghiyasuddin Ali Khan, a man of learning and also a man of the sword as is clearly reflected in his military calibre shown in Gujarat. He was also appointed as *bakhshi* and introduced the branding (*dagh*) system along with Shihab Khan.[27]

Mir Yahya, a Saifi Saiyid of Qazvin, was a 'well-known theologian and philosopher who had acquired such extraordinary proficiency in the knowledge of history that he was acquainted with the date of every event which had occurred from the establishment of the Muhammedan religion to his own time'. Shah Tahmasp was very kind to him. Yahya's enemies soon managed to poison the Shah's ears to such an extent that Yahya along with his sons was to be thrown into prison. Yahya stayed back and died in 962 AH, but his son, Mir Abdul Latif of Qazvin, joined the imperial service and 'was gladdened by the emoluments which he received through the boundless liberality and generosity of the emperor'. Although Badauni says that Akbar took some lessons from him in various passages of the *divan* of Khwaja Hafiz and other books, it is generally accepted that the Mir went to Hindustan at the invitation of Humayun but reached that land just after Akbar had ascended the throne. Akbar extended a very warm welcome to the Mir, who was appointed in the second year of his reign as his preceptor. At that time, Akbar 'knew not how to read and write but shortly afterwards he was able to repeat some odes of Hafiz. The Mir was a man of great eloquence and of excellent disposition and so moderate in his religious sentiments that each party used to revile him for his indifference'. Mir Abdul Latif of Qazvin is said to have tutored Akbar in the precepts of '*sulh-i kul*' or 'peace with all'. Abul Fazl says that 'Abdul Latif was accused in Persia of being a Sunni and in Hindustan of being a Shia'. The Mir died in 981 AH at Fatehpur Sikri. His son Mir Ghiyasuddin was a 'personal friend of the emperor'. Although he did not rise above the rank of a Hazari he possessed great influence at court and was given the title of Naqib Khan. Like his grandfather, Naqib is reported to have excelled in the study of history. It is said that he learnt all the seven volumes of the *Rauzat-us Safa* by heart. Badauni, a school fellow of Naqib claims that, 'No man in Arabia or Persia was as proficient in History as Naqib.' Jahangir praised him for his extraordinary and remarkable memory. Naqib's son Abdul Latif was also 'distinguished for his acquirements'.[28]

Haidari of Tabriz came to India three times. During his first visit, he enjoyed the patronage of Qasim Khan of Nishapur. On his second visit he joined the services of Khan-i Azam Mirza Aziz Kuka who once showered upon him 2,000 rupees merely for an ode. He was later introduced to Akbar by Shamsuddin Muhammad Atka. Akbar liked his ode on the elephant so much that he rewarded him with 2,000 rupees and a horse. For some reason, this payment was delayed and Haidari promptly wrote a complaint in verse against the treasurer. When he visited India a third time he found a patron in Abdurrahim Khan-i Khanan, whom he accompanied on his expedition to Gujarat and received liberal presents for an ode on the victory of Sarkhej. Blochmann notes that 'though he made money in India, he wrote a satirical quatrain on the country, the purpose of which is that in a country in which two men can feast for a rupee, the worth of men is not difficult to guess'. His worth as a poet was not very highly valued. The *masnavis* written by him 'in imitation of' Saadi's *Bustan* were described as 'inspired' and 'remained unknown'. Badauni claims to have seen his *divan* containing 14,000 couplets but with little good stuff among all these, hence the comment that 'his company was more agreeable than his poems'. When Shah Abbas, enraged at the cold behaviour shown to him by the inhabitants of Nazar, is said to have ordered a general massacre, it was Haidari who 'happily prevented' it through his 'influence'. Haidari breathed his last in 1593-4, 'beloved by all'. After his death his son Samiri came to India and took up service with Abdurrahim Khan-i Khanan, who appointed him as Mir Saman of his household. He was 'also a good officer and was killed during the wars in the Deccan'.[29]

Although Maulana Mansur Tabrizi originally belonged to Sawah, he became famous as Tabrizi. Since he loved travelling, he went to India and joined the service of Bairam Khan. He composed *ghazals* and *qasidas* with equal ease and eloquence. Hasan Nisari appreciated his forceful, effective, sweet, and high-sounding (*purzor*, *shirin guftar sukhnan-i balandash*, *paidar*) poetry.[30]

Another poet from Tabriz, Nizami, has not been mentioned by Abul Fazl or Nizamuddin Ahmad. However, Badauni appreciated him in the following words: The lustre of his poetry is vouched for by his trade, which is that of an appraiser of jewels. He has a mind well adapted to poetry and has composed a *divan* which is well known.[31]

Khwaja Saiyidi Muhammad Urfi came from Shiraz where his

father looked after Shari and Urfi matters, being *darogha* to the magistrate of Shiraz. The Khwaja had taken his *takhallus* 'Urfi' from the occupation of his father. Urfi first went gone to the Deccan where he was highly disappointed as his talents were not recognized. Yet Urfi Shirazi distinguished himself as a 'man of sound understanding and composed poetry of all kinds well'. He was attached to the court of Shaikh Faizi for a brief period and then joined the services of Hakim Abul Fath Gilani at whose recommendation he got an entry into the Khan-i Khanan's court where 'both his poetry and the esteem in which he was held made great progress'. Urfi had to his credit a collection of poems and a *masnavi* written in the metre of the *Makhzan-ul Asrar.* His *masnavi Majma-ul Akbar* was often called *Majma-ul Afkar*. Hakim Haziq admired Urfi's *ghazals* to such an extent that he regarded these as better than his own odes. In his characteristic manner, Badauni says that, unlike Shaikh Faizi (who had spent large sums from his *jagirs* in having his works copied and illuminated and even then nobody asked for them—the only copy for which he had any sale was the solitary one which he himself sent abroad), Urfi and Husain Sanai had 'wonderful good fortune with their poetry, for there was no street or market in which the book-sellers did not stand at the road side selling copies of the *divans* of these two poets and both Persians and Indians wished to buy them as auspicious possessions'. Although it is accepted that 'the forehead for his diction shines with decorum and possesses a peculiar grace, self-admiration led him to vanity and made him speak lightly of the older classics. The bud of his merits withered away before it could develop itself', as he died very young.[32]

Khwaja Shah Mansur of Shiraz was another of the several skilful and talented persons who came to India. Azduddaula Amir Fathullah of Shiraz acquired a special name and fame for himself and came to India at the invitation of Adil Shah of Bijapur. He was a disciple of Khwaja Jamaluddin Mahmud, Kamaluddin of Shirwan, and Mir Ghiyasuddin Mansur of Shiraz. He came to the Deccan from where, after the death of Adil Shah (991 AH), he was invited by Akbar who elevated him to the rank of *sadr* and honoured him with the titles Amin-ul Mulk and later Azduddaula. He helped Todarmal and 'rendered good service in working up the old revenue books'. As *sadr*, he could not function personally as he was sent to the Deccan and his servant Kamal looked after the work in his officiating capacity. The Khwaja so excelled in all branches of natural philosophy, especially mechanics, that Abul Fazl said of him: 'If the books of antiquity should be lost, the Amir will restore them.' He introduced many reforms in the monetary system under the Mughals, the details of which are given in the *Ain-i-Akbari*. Under the guidance of Amir Fathullah Shirazi, a part of the *Zich-i Jadid-i Mirzai* was translated. The Mir was bitterly criticized by Badauni not only for his staunch belief in Shiism but also for being, in his view, 'a worldly office hunter and worshipper of Mammon'. He was so confident of his understanding of the medical arts that he turned down the advice of the famous Hakim Ali and tried to cure his own fever by eating '*harisa*' and died.[33]

Mir Murtaza Sharifi of Shiraz was the grandson of Mir Saiyid Sharif Jarjans who surpassed all the learned men of his age in the knowledge of the exact sciences, in various branches of philosophy, in logic, and in metaphysics. He studied the traditions and acquired a teaching diploma under Shaikh Ibn Hajar and 'attained a higher position than most learned and erudite men of former or recent times'. He continued his teaching of the art and sciences till his death in 1566-7. Another poet, Qaydr of Shiraz, distinguished himself in the acquisition of the usual sciences. Initially he was well received by Akbar but soon he fell into disgrace. He kept on wandering for some time as *faqir* in Bayana district and returned to Fatehpur Sikri where he lost his life due to an incompetent quack.[34]

Khwaja Abdus Samad Shirin Qalam hailed from Shiraz where his father Khwaja Nizamul Mulk worked as the *wazir* to Shah Shuja. During Humayun's sojourn in Persia, Abdus Samad, who was by that time already a well-known painter and calligraphist, met Humayun in Tabriz. Despite Humayun's insistence, the Khwaja could not accompany him and only managed to follow him in 956 AH to Kabul. Although the Khwaja held an ordinary low *mansab* of 400, he enjoyed 'great influence' at the court. His various assignments like being in charge of the mint at Fatehpur Sikri or holding the *diwani* of Multan did not hamper his artistic progress. In his characteristic manner Abul Fazl writes: 'His perfection was mainly due to the wonderful effect of a look of His Majesty which caused him to turn from that which is form to that which is spirit.' Such was his skill that he wrote the *Surat-i Ikhlas* (Koran Sur. CXII) on a poppy seed (*danah-y khashkash*).[35]

Miyan Kamaluddin Husain (son of Maulana Hasan) of Shiraz arrived in India during the reign of Sikandar Lodi. Later he come to

Agra with the caravan of Saiyid Rafiuddin the traditionist and Miyan Abul Fath of Khurasan, the father of Miyan Budh, and settled there. Shaikh Zainuddin Vafai praised him because he 'combined in himself the knowledge of the sciences both of reason and tradition'. Since Akbar recognized his worth, he was 'exceedingly desirous that the Shaikh should join the imperial service'. Badauni had known him for forty years. 'With all his excellence and perfection in religious matters, he had the highest ability and perfect eloquence, excellent penmanship, skill in orthography and a masterly style are his by inheritance'.[36]

Khwaja Shah Mansur of Shiraz surpassed many in his administrative talents. He started his career as a *mushrif* (accountant) in the *khushbu khana* (perfume department) and later served as *diwan* under Khan-i Zaman and Munim Khan. In 983 AH when he was appointed as *wazir* he started his ambitious projects which excited the jealousy and anger of the people.[37]

Ghayrati of Shiraz was well acquainted with the history of the *pat* and his diction was also good. Pairvi of Sawah was a skilful painter; he had attained by means of studying the outward form an understanding of the hidden truths and had written as an outward form and hidden essence a political treatise.[38]

It is said that the Persian poet Naziri of Nishapur possessed 'poetical talent and the garden of thought has a door open for him'. Similar ideas were also expressed by Jahangir. Jahangir writes in his memoir early in AD 1611 that he had invited to his court Naziri of Nishapur 'who is well known for his poems and poetical genius, and at present lives in Gujarat as a merchant'. He presented to Jahangir an encomiastic *qasida* on the model of a *qasida* of Anvari, in return for which the emperor presented him with a thousand rupees, a horse, and a robe of honour. Naziri had left his homeland at an early age for Kashan where he attended *mushairas* with poets like Fahmi and Hatim. In India he enjoyed the patronage of Abdurrahim Khan-i Khanan. He went on a Haj pilgrimage in 1012 AH. After his return, he settled down in Ahmedabad where he died in 1022 AH.[39] He is said to have been the 'equal of Shakibi of Isfahan' in 'graceful wit and clearness of intellect'. In India, he was associated with the court of the Khan-i Khanan, and in Badauni's estimation he was 'enrolled in that band of poets who were entitled gentlemen of the suite'. After his visit to Mecca, the poet is said to have become 'very pious'. According to the author of the *Mirat-ul Alam*, Naziri was so generous that he gave away everything he had to his friends and the poor.

Mulla Maqsud of Qazvin, a 'jovial poet of the age', produced a *divan* which was 'properly arranged in alphabetical order'. He wrote 'a *qasidah* in imitation of Khwaja Salman and tacked on to it the name of Qazi Yahya of Qazvin'. Jafar Beg Qazvini was 'a man of profound thought, has learnt a good deal and describes very well the events of past ages'. As an accountant also he surpassed many experts and was 'unique'. He was a disciple of Akbar's *Tauhid-i Ilahi*.[40] He always had a keen desire to surpass others and made attempts to produce better and more innovative work or at least to excel in any art.[41]

Badauni bitterly criticizes Muhammad Sharif Waqui of Nishapur for his religious views.[42] Sharif Waqui also wrote a historical work *Tarikh-i Muhammad Sharif Waqui*. Hasan Nizami Nishapuri (or Bistami)[43] possessed immense knowledge of current sciences, especially literature and lexicography, and had a full command over Persian and Arabic; he was acknowledged as both a good poet and prose writer. Muhammad Sharif belonged to a 'distinguished family' of Saiyids of Nishapur. His mother was a sister of Amir Shah Mir, an assay master of Shah Tahmasp. He had written *qasidas* in praise of the Imams when he was very young. 'In penmanship, letter writing and accounts he had wonderful skill, and although he was not diligent, he had read some Arabic works on history.'

Taqiuddin of Shushtar joined the imperial service, and was 'well versed in those sciences which call for the exercise of the reasoning faculty and in traditional knowledge'. He was also 'well acquainted with poetry and had poetic genius'. He had been assigned the task of 'turning' the *Shah Nama* into prose.[44]

From amongst the lesser-known talented men and poets the names of the following may be mentioned:

Sarmadi of Isfahan who had 'some poetic genius' Mir Sharif Amani of Isfahan 'spent twenty years of his life in India living in religious retirement and wrote charming verses'. Saiyid Shah Saiyyidi of Garmsir who was 'imbued with religious mysticism'. Huzni of Isfahan was 'an inquiring man of a philosophical turn of mind and was well acquainted with ancient poetry and chronology. He was free and easy and good-hearted and friendliness was stamped upon his forehead'. Shuuri of Turbat who was a student and practiced book-keeping was good enough as a poet to be included in the list of Badauni.

Asadullah Khan of Tabriz excelled as a good military man. Maulana

Amani of Herat who spent 60 years in Kashmir was the *az mustaidani zaman*.[45]

He possessed both learning and accomplishments and was a 'man of education'. He belonged to the intimate circle of Akbar and was one of the most 'entertaining' men of his times. Since the climate of India did not suit him and also because he did not receive a promotion in the imperial service, he left India and died in his native place Rai.[46] Amir Qazi Asiri of Rai was a 'man of education' and the best pupil of Hakim Ainul Mulk. He left India after a brief stay partly because he did not find Akbar's patronage and partly because the climate did not suit him.

Fahmi of Tehran, who also had 'some poetical genius', was widely travelled though he visited India for only a brief period. Vidai of Herat who died in India also possessed some attainments. Although Jafar, a Saiyid of Herat, has not been mentioned by Abul Fazl or Nizamuddin, Badauni says he had 'good taste in poetry and in the composition of enigmas'. He also wrote an ode and composed an enigma which he dedicated to Mirza Aziz Kuka containing a list of his titles and prayers for his long life and prosperity. Vafai of Isfahan,[47] Talia of Yazd was a 'pen man' who wrote *nastaliq* well. Ulfati of Yazd was also 'well skilled in the exact sciences' and received one thousand rupees from the Khan-i Zaman for composing a couplet. Mir Waiz Vuquii of Herat who originally belonged to Badakhshan was famous for his preaching and 'held stirring meetings for preaching'. Tahir Muhammad Khwaja Tatar Khan held the posts of *vazir* and governor of Delhi.[48]

Nuvidi of Nishapur was a man of considerable attainments and was highly regarded as a poet. He died in Ujjain in 1565-6. Mirza Mirak Razawi Khan of Mashhad was made the *diwan* of Jaunpur and later on a *bakhshi* of Bengal. Liwai of Sabzwar, Muṡawwir of Mashhad, Mir Muhsin Rizvi of Mashhad, Shaikh Haji Muhammad of Khabushan, 'Naui' and others were also known poets.[49]

A careful study of the Indo-Persian sources reveals that the cities of Iran were famous for producing men of learning and many talents. The province of Khurasan with its capital at Herat was a noteworthy centre for men of excellence. It is said that Herat was 'the best place in Khurasan and seventy apostles had expressed their good will for the place'. Another place which was renowned as the birth place of many scholars and poets was Juwayn—the Arabic word for the Persian Gujan—a small town in Khurasan. The district of Khawaf was 'famous for the kings, ministers and learned men it has produced'. The Ali Muzaffar dynasty—seven of its kings had ruled for 59 years over Fars and Shiraz—were Khawafis. The author of the *Zakhirat-ul Khawanin* records that the inhabitants of Khawaf were bigoted Sunnis though later on they became 'staunch Shias'. Razi gives many anecdotes illustrating the proverbial sagacity and quick wittedness of the inhabitants of Khawaf. Khwaja Shamsuddin and his brother Mumin present a good example of this. Many persons from this revenue district of Nishapur joined the service of the Mughal emperors.[50]

Mir Saiyid Muhammad Jamabaf, a famous scholar of his age, excelled in (*ikhtira, maani-o Ikhtirai Alfaz*) though he was (*dar surato Khilqat tarkib-i Khas buda*). He came to India in 969 AH, was richly rewarded, and spent his time in comfort till his death in 970 AH . Many Iranians were tempted to visit India because 'the seed of wandering was sown in their heart'. Danihi Nishapur wrote poems often in a 'rustic dialect' though sometimes he composed 'odes in more polished language'.[51] Being famous for their penmanship and expertise in accountancy, the Persians worked as scribes and book-keepers. Mir Azizullah, of the Saifi Saiyids of Qazvin, is said to have come first 'among accountants and scribes' and possessed 'some proficiency in those branches of learning which are not treated of in Arabic literature'. He was appointed as *Divan-i Saaddat* (clerk to the *sadr*). Fusuni of Shiraz was also an 'excellent accountant' and knew astronomy well.[52] Inayatullah Shirazi was appointed in the imperial library as a librarian.[53] Nurullah Qasim Arslan hailed from Tus (or Mashhad) and was brought up in Transoxiana. He was a poet, 'sweet of song, welcome to all both great and small for his beauty and graceful wit, open and cheerful disposition, sociability and social amiability'. He was unique in writing chronograms, was a 'renowned calligraphist of the age', and 'possessed some talent'. He wrote the *nastaliq* script well. He was broadminded on matters of religion. He died in AD 1587 in Lahore.[54]

Muhammad Asghar Ashraf Khan Mir Munshi was a Hussaini Saiyid from Mashhad (or Sabzvar). Apart from his 'natural poetical ability' he was well versed in the seven different styles of penmanship and was 'well qualified to instruct the best calligraphists of the world'. He was 'a clever writer, exact in style, was a renowned calligrapher who improved *taliq*. He was perhaps the first of his age to write the *taliq* and the *nastaliq* characters and was well versed in *Ilme Jafar* (witchcraft). Being in Humayun's service, he got the posts of *miriarz* and *mir mal* and the title of *munshi*. He went away to Mecca when Bairam Khan was imprisoned. On his return in 1560-1 he received a *mansab* and the title of Ashraf Khan. He died at Gaur in 1575.[55]

Humayun's court was decorated by the talented duo, Mir Abdul Hayy of Persia[56] and his brother Mir Abdullah. The former held the rank of *sadr* while the latter was a jurist and 'one of Humayun's intimate and specially honoured confidants'. Both men were 'endowed with administrative ability (*nizamat*), piety, sanctity and regularity of life'. The alleged expertise of Mir Abdul Hayy in writing the Baburi script was a controversial issue. Although Alauddaula reports that Mir Abdul Hayy devoted some attention to the study of this accomplishment and that nobody had learnt to write in the difficult Baburi style more quickly or better than he, Mirza Aziz Kuka wrote in the margin of the memoir that Mir Abdul Hayy had no knowledge of any branch of learning and that his one accomplishment was some knowledge of the Baburi script, with which he was very imperfectly acquainted. Badauni agrees with Mirza Kuka who, in his view, was 'better known' to Abdul Hayy and therefore was 'nearer to the truth'. Nevertheless, Mirza Aziz Kuka's prejudices against the Persians are well known and clearly reflected in his letter to Jahangir. Even if we believe his contention that Abdul Hayy was imperfectly acquainted with the Baburi script, the excellence of Abdul Hayy in other forms of calligraphy was very clearly evident in by the books transcribed by him.[57]

Many Persian families attached to the Mughal court exhibited their talents in various forms and in different fields. With their multifarious capacities, they outshone and surpassed their contemporaries in the spheres of the fine arts, management, and administrative talents. As part of his religious innovations, Akbar 'sent money to Iran to bring to India a wise Zoroastrian of the name of Ardsher'.[58] Abul Fazl appreciates Akbar for his 'sagacity that he employed in his service people of all classes—Jews, Persians, Turanis, etc.'. However, his assertion that Shah Abbas 'imitated the practice of Akbar and favoured the Gurjis' (Georgians) is not correct as the Georgians and Circassians had first been inducted in the royal service during the reign of Shah Tahmasp.[59]

Excellent handicraftsmen and artisans hailed from Iran. Maulana Maqsud of Herat, a servant of Humayun, wrote well the *riqa* and *nastaliq* characters. The astrolabe, globes, and various *mistars* which he made were much appreciated by people of experience. Abul Fazl boasts that the 'patronage of His Majesty (Akbar) perfected his art'. Similarly, Maulana Ibrahim of Yazd 'excelled in the art of cutting of cornelians'. He was the brother of Sharaf of Yazd. In the estimation of Abul Fazl, Ibrahim even surpassed the ancient engravers, and it was impossible to distinguish his *riqa* and *nastaliq* from the masterpieces of the best calligraphers. He engraved the words 'Lal-i Jalali', or the glorious ruby, upon all imperial rubies of value. In *Ain* 6, Abul Fazl mentions that there were Persian wrestlers and boxers at Akbar's court. The 'best wrestlers of the age' included Mirza Khan of Gilan, Muhammad Quli of Tabriz (to whom Akbar gave the name Sher Hamla, or lion attacker), Ali of Tabriz, Fulad of Tabriz, Qasim of Tabriz, and Mirza Kuhina Sawar of Tabriz.[60]

Brocade and velvet from Yazd were highly valued and were the most expensive as their prices ranged from 15 to 150 *muhars* whereas the brocade and velvet from Kashan and Herat cost only 10 to 40 *muhars*. The *deba* silk from Yazd was sold at prices ranging from 1 to 1½ *muhars* and the velvet plain silk from Kashan, Yazd, and Mashhad cost between 2 to 4 (or 7) *muhars*, and the Kamkhab cost between 1 to 5 *muhars*; Mushajjar per piece was sold for 1 to 2 *muhars*.[61]

Amina Okada dates the origin of Mughal painting in the reign of Humayun to the arrival of two Safavid painters, Abdus Samad and Mir Saiyid Ali. With the establishment of a *kitab khana* by Akbar, 'the Mughal style' is said to have emerged, which was 'clearly distinct from previous painting traditions proper to Turkey and Iran'. Yet these 'painters from various backgrounds and diverse pictorial traditions' were 'guided' by the Persian masters Abdus Samad and Mir Saiyid Ali; they 'doggedly acquired the art of drawing by attempting to outdo one another in faithfully imitating the work of earlier, primarily Persian masters'. Abdus Samad Shirin Qalam, born in Shiraz and brought up in Tabriz, joined Humayun at Kabul. He 'produced elegant, masterful compositions characterized by superb control and skillful construction in the manner of Persian masterpieces'. Both Abdus Samad and Mir Saiyid Ali were expected 'to teach Safavid artistic canons to Indian painters'. Humayun appreciated Mir Saiyid Ali's skill in miniature painting which he learnt from his father Mir Musavvir and noted that the painter could portray an entire group of riders playing polo on a grain of rice.[62]

Similarly, Sharif Farisi, the son of the renowned painter Abdus

Samad Zarrin Qalam, was also 'unrivalled in the beauty of his penmanship and in painting'. He had a pleasant disposition. He was also a good poet and left behind a valuable *divan*. While his father was famous for writing in a full and legible hand on one side of a poppy seed the *Surat-ul Ikhlas* and on the other side of it the argument of the chapter, his son Sharif distinguished himself in a similar art by boring eight small holes in one poppy seed and then passing wires through them; he also drew on a grain of rice a picture of an armed horseman, preceded by an outrider and bearing all the things proper to a horseman such as a sword, a shield, a polo stick, etc.[63] Payrawi of Sawah was also a good painter.

Another versatile but controversial artist was Mir Saiyid Ali of Tabriz, son of Mir Mansur, whose pen name was Judai. He was best known for his paintings, each page of which was said to be 'a masterpiece' and he himself was described as a 'second Mani'. The sixteen volumes of the *Dastan-i Amir Hamza* were illuminated and completed under his supervision. Each volume fills a box, and each page of it is a yard wide and a yard long, and on each page is a picture. He was awarded the title of Nadirul Mulk.[64]

Controversy surrounded Judai position as a poet. Although Badauni is silent about this aspect, certain others (including a couplet of Mulla Tariqi of Sawah) had alleged that he had stolen Ashki's poems. On his deathbed, Ashki handed over his more than 10,000 verses to Judai to arrange them. Judai selected the best ones and got them published under his own name and the rest of them were thrown into water. Apparently the confusion had been created due to their similar pen names as there did exist another Judai of Sawah whose involvement in the affair seems to be more likely as they both belonged to the same place. Both the *Atashkadai Azar* and Taqi's *Tazkira* mention his name. Yet the allegation quoted by the Daghistani that Ashki died in Mir Judai's house prevents a complete exoneration of the latter from the above-mentioned charge.[65]

Mir Ashki was the son of Mir Saiyid Ali Muhtasib of Qum in Persia. His elder brother Huzuri was also known as a poet. The number of his poems are said to have exceeded 10,000. In Badauni's estimation, 'he displayed a pleasing fertility of imagination' in his poetry though 'he was an imitator of Asafi'. Ashki was interested in coming to India mainly because of Ghazali whose fame was then on the rise, though he could not meet him.[66]

In the list of the 'finest painters of Akbar's court' which had seventeen names, Abul Fazl 'awarded' the first place to Mir Saiyid Ali. Blochmann refers to him 'as the first of the court painters'. Abul Fazl writes: 'Among the forerunners on the right road of art, I may mention first Mir Saiyid Ali of Tabriz who learnt this art from his father. From the time of his introduction at court the ray of royal favour has shone upon him. He has made himself famous in his art and has met with much success.' He illuminated the story of *Amir Hamzah* 'which was represented in twelve volumes and clever painters made the most astonishing illustrations for no less than one thousand and four hundred passages of the story.[67]

The court historian writes that 'Persian books, both prose and poetry, were ornamented with pictures and a very large number of paintings were thus collected.' Many books like the *Razm Nama* (the *Ramayana*), the *Nal Daman*, the *Kalilah Damnah*, and the *Ayar-i Danish* were illustrated.[68]

Tabriz Maulana Yusuf Shah, Maulana Shah and Muhammad Amin of Mashhad, Maulana Ibrahim of Astrabad, Maulana Fazl-i Haqq of Nizami, Munshi Jamaluddin of Qazvin, and Mirza Ibrahim of Isfahan have been described as the famous calligraphists attached to the court of Akbar. Maulana Muhammad of Awbah was said to be 'an excellent writer' of *nastaliq*. Maulana Mir Ali, the 'illustrious' calligrapher, was probably the pupil of Maulana Zaynuddin. He 'brought his art to perfection by imitating the writing of Sultan Ali of Mashhad. The new method which he established is a proof of his genius; he has left many masterpieces.' Abul Fazl says that once someone asked him: 'What is the difference between your writing and that of the Mawahna?' He said, 'I also have brought writing to perfection but yet his method has a peculiar charm.' Maulana Mir Ali was a Saiyid of Herat (d. 924 AH). He excelled in composing poems and 'as a poet his name is often mentioned together with that of Mir Ahmad, son of Mir Khusrau of Delhi, and Bairam Khan-i Khanan as a master of *dakhl* poetry. *Dakhl* or entering is the skilfull art in which a poet makes verses, or parts of verses, from the compositions of another poet.[69]

Akbar was fond of acquiring knowledge. Abul Fazl records that 'among the books of renown, there are few that are not read in His Majesty's assembly hall; and there are no historical facts of the past ages or curiosities of service; or interesting points of philosophy with which His Majesty is unacquainted'. Valuable Persian works like *Akhlaq-i Nasiri*, *Kimia-i Saadat*, *Qabus Nama*, the works of

Sharaf of Munayr, the *Gulistan*, the *Hadiqa* of Hakim Sanai, the *masnavi* of Manawi, the *Jami Jam*, the *Bustan*, the *Shah Nama*, the collected *masnavis* of Shaikh Nizamul, the works of Khusrau and Maulana Jami, the *divans* of Khaqani, Anwari, and several works on history were continually read out to Akbar.

Maulana Nuruddin Tarkhan was born in Jam in Khurasan and received his education in Mashhad. He was first introduced to Babur and thereafter became a friend of Humayun as both of them shared a love for astronomy and the astrolabe. He accompanied Humayun during his exile and remained in his service for twenty years. Afterwards he became the *mutawali* of his master Humayun's tomb in Delhi. Akbar gave him the titles of Khan and Tarkhan and appointed him to Samana. He is described as 'a man of great erudition', a poet with the pen name 'Nuri'. He was known as 'Nuri Safidun' as he had for some time held Safidun as his *jagir*. He was also a good mathematician and astronomer.[70]

Despite his personal merit, Fathullah was criticized by Badauni as a staunch Shia. Even in the state hall he said, with the greatest composure, his Shia prayers—a thing which no one else would have dared to do. His Majesty, therefore, put him among the class of the bigots; but he connived at his practice, because he thought it desirable to encourage a man of such attainments and practical knowledge.[71] There was already deep-rooted jealousy and rancour between the Deccanis and the Abyssinians; the ascendancy of the Persians further inflamed the natives whose interests were thus seriously injured. This often led to conflicts and massacres. Although there were also Deccani, Abyssinian, Turkish and Arab nobles, the Persian nobles enjoyed an extraordinary importance at the court of the Deccan rulers. In the Deccan, many Persian poets flourished. Most of them finally left for the Mughal court.[72]

Malik of Qum, 'supposed to be the king of words', lived the life of a *dervish* in the Deccan. Badauni had seen the copy of his works which Faizi had brought from the Deccan. All of his creations were said to to be 'after the fashion of that of the poets of this age and he had not departed from their set forms. No odour of love, of sympathy, or of any fresh subject has touched his verse.'[73]

Saiyid Muhammad of Najal spent some time in the Deccan where he was 'honoured' for his poems and then decided to leave for Allahabad to join Akbar's court. Since he was 'bold' and 'slovenly' (*Bebak-o Nahamwar*), his comment that in the Decan, he would not have looked at a fellow like Fathullah angered Akbar, who got him imprisoned in Gwalior Fort for ten years and ordered a search of his papers to see if there were any satires written by him on other persons. It was only at the intercession of Prince Salim and some other courtiers that he was set free and summoned to Lahore. But Itabi perhaps continued to annoy Akbar, who then gave him 1,000 rupees and instructed Qalij Khan to send him from Surat to Hijaz, but Itabi managed to return to the Deccan. He was a 'clever Katib' and letter writer and composed excellent poems in Arabic and Persian.[74]

There were many controversial individuals who played an important role in enhancing Indo-Persian contacts. One such person was Mulla Qazi Nurullah of Shustar, who was well known for his learning, clemency, quickness of understanding, singleness of heart, clearness of perception, and acumen. Badauni says that he was distinguished for his justice, virtue, modesty, piety, and such qualities as are possessed by noble men. He wrote several good works and also a monograph on the undotted commentary of Shaikh Faizi which was beyond all praise. He also possessed poetic facility and wrote impressive poetry.[75]

Qazi Nurullah was introduced to Akbar by the instrumentality of Abul Fath Gilani, the physician. When the imperial cavalcade reached Lahore, Qazi Muin was replaced by Qazi Nurullah due to the former's 'feebleness of old age and the failure of his natural powers'. During his qaziship at Lahore, Qazi Nurullah 'reduced the insolent *muftis* and the crafty and subtle *muhtasibs* of Lahore who venture to give lessons to the teachers of the angels, . . . and has closed to them the avenues of bribery and restrained them within due bounds as closely as a nut is enclosed in its shell and to such a degree that stricter discipline could not be imagined'.[76] Nawai of Mashhad was also a 'poet of talent' who 'writes well'.

Khwaja Husain Sanai of Mashhad served at the court of Ibrahim Mirza Safavoi (son of Shah Tahmasp). If the account given in the *Miratul Alam* can be trusted, Sanai had written an ode in honour of Shah Ismail II who suspected that the eulogy was in fact written for Ibrahim Mirza because it did not mention the name of Shah Ismail II. The frightened poet preferred to seek refuge in flight. His scholarship and poems aroused controversy. While Faizi 'looked upon him as a teacher', and Nizamuddin admired his poems, the author of the *Atashkadai Azar* contemptuously recorded that 'either no one understands the meaning of his verses or his verses have no meaning' an assessment also echoed by Abul Fazl. Badauni is more careful in his evaluation of the works of this poet and though he 'did not think much of his verses', he did not deny his poetical genius. Sanai's two works—his *divans Sikandar Nama* and *Saqi Nama*—are still extant.[77]

Khwaja Maqsud Ali of Herat was a servant of Akbar's mother Hameeda Banu Begam. The Khwaja's mother Picha Jan Anaga was one of Akbar's nurses. 'On Humayun's flight to Persia Maqsud was always near the *howdah* of Akbar's mother and remained attached to her in all her misfortunes.' His brother Khwaja Hasan's daughter was married to Prince Salim and was the mother of Parwiz. Khwaja Maqsud Ali's son Zayn Khan Koka undertook the shattering campaigns against the Yusuf Zais whom he put down with a heavy hand.[78]

Yol Quli Anisi Shamlu Turkoman who had served as the librarian of Ali Quli Khan Shamly, the Persian governor of Herat, was not only a good poet but also a gallant warrior. His pen name was changed from Jahi to Anisi by his patron Ibrahim Mirza. When Abdullah Khan Uzbek conquered Herat in 1588-9, Anisi was captured and taken to Transoxiana from where he fled to India and joined the service of Mirza Abdurrahim Khan-i Khanan, who appointed him first as Mir-i Aoz and later promoted him to the post of Mir Bakhshi. His battle against Suhail Habshi won laurels for him. Despite his preoccupation with battles, he managed to write several *qasidas* in praise of the Khan-i Khanan, a *masnavi* in the *Khusru Shirin* metre, and the *divan*[79] was much liked by the people of Khashmi. Mirza Yusuf Khan, son of Mir Ahmad-i Razawi, had served as the anchor of the Mughal rulers in Kashmir where he conciliated Shams Chak, the claimant to the throne, and persuaded him to go to the court, though later on his activities made Akbar suspicious. Yet he was made the *darogha* of Jaunpur, and the *ataliq* of Prince Murad. He distinguished himself in the Deccan wars and is said to have been 'more energetic than other grandees'.[80]

Muzaffar Khan Turbati of Khurasan was well known for his revenue reforms, the abolition of the *Jama-i Raqms*, and the introduction of a new rent roll called *Jami Hasil-i Hall* or the roll of the present actual income and fixation of the numbers of soldiers. He was given important assignments like the *vakilship* of the empire with the title *Jumlat-ul-Mulk*, governorship of Bihar and later of Bengal. He is said to have constructed a Mosque in Agra. In certain respects, the attitude of Muzaffar often enraged Akbar, whose wrath was almost always conquered by Muzaffar through his efficient handling of affairs. Muzaffar's brother Saif Khan distinguished himself in bravery and died while fighting gallantly against Muhammad Husain Mirza. Akbar held him in high esteem and 'having heard that he was heavily involved in debt, he paid, on his return to Agra, every debt due by him'.[81]

Muhammad Qasim Khan, a rich landowner of Nishapur, fled to India after the Uzbek invasion. He had first served Bairam Khan and then joined a group of Chaghatai nobles. Asif Khan Abdul Majid of Herat, a descendant of Shaikh Zaynuddin Tayabadi, served as a grandee and *diwan* of Humayun. After the suppression of Bairam Khan's rebellion, he got the title of Asaf Khan, was appointed governor of Delhi, received a flag and a drum. Later on, he was given the governorship of Manikpur.[82]

Like his forefathers who had served the Timurids with sincerity, a nephew of Mirza Dost Khurasan named Wasim Khan Mir Bahr was also an ardent supporter of the Mughal rulers. When Mirza Kamran was besieged in Kabul and Humayun was yet to conquer India, Qasim Khan and his younger brother Khwajaji Muhammad Husain jumped down the walls of the fort to join Humayun who gave them an honourable reception. Later Qasim Khan enjoyed the rank of the 3,000 and held various other important posts like the commander of Agra and the governor of Kabul, and also led expeditions to Kashmir. He superintended the construction of the fort of Agra at a cost of 7 crores of *tankas* (or 35 lakh of rupees). The fort was built of red sandstone, joined well together and fastened to each other by iron rings which passed through them. On every side, its foundations reached water. Ashraf Khan Mir Munshi held the position of Mir Arz and Mir Asaf Khan of Qazvin.[83]

Mir Muizzul Mulki Musawi of Mashhad was another person who successfully suppressed Khan-i Zaman, not merely because 'the . . . of the Khurasanis towards the Uzbeks decided the matter' but also because his younger brother Mir Ali Akbar had prepared a *Maulud Nama* (history of the birth of Akbar) and presented it to the emperor. Although they both were talented, they rebelled against Akbar and met their doom.[84]

The family of Ghiyas Beg Tehran in particular has been very famous in India. His father Khwaja Muhammad Sharif Hijri served as *vazir* to Tatar Sultan, son of Sharafuddin Taklu, a *beglarbegi* of Khurasan. The Khwaja continued in the office even during the regime of his son Qazaq Khan after whose death, he was made a *wazir* of Yazd by Tahmasp. His two brothers, Khwaja Mirza Ahmad and Khwajaji Khwaja, were not as famous but their sons distinguished themselves in various capacities. The son of Khwaja Mirza Ahmad was the famous Khwaja Amin Ahmad Razi, the author of the excellent work entitled *Haft Iqlim*, the Kalantar of Ray. Khwajaji Khwaja's son Khwaja Shapur was also a literary man. Khwaja Ghiyas Beg was made *diwan* of Kabul and later on *diwan-i buyutat*. He was given a *mansab* of 1,000 and the title of Itimadud Daula. Khwaja Ghiyas Beg distinguished himself as a poet, a clever correspondent and an expert in *shikasta*; he became *vakil-i kul* (prime minister) and enjoyed the rare privileges of the flag, had the drum beaten at the court, and had *mansabs* of 6,000/3,000. But his daughter attained an even higher position as empress of Hindustan. The son of Ghiyas Beg, Asaf Khan Abdul Hasan, held the *mansab* of 9,000 and the titles of Yaminuddaula and Khan-i Khanan Sipahsalar during the reign of his son-in-law Shahjahan. It was in memory of Mumtaz Mahal, the daughter of Asaf Khan, that the famous Taj Mahal was built. Ghiyas Beg's other son, Ibrahim Khan Fath Jang, was governor of Bihar and Bengal.[85]

Farighi of Shiraz (a brother of the famous Mir Fathullah Shirazi) came to India twice and died in the country. His two sons, Mir Taqi who was a man of noble disposition and high aspirations and Mir Sharif who had many excellencies and perfections, were also associated with the Mughal court. Mir Taqi was 'another Shah Fathullah in his knowledge of astronomy and astrology'.

Badauni presented to Mir Taqi a part of the twenty chapters which he had written on the astrolabe. Some of the Salami Saiyids of Shiraz settled in Gujarat. Mir Abu Turab came to Gujarat during the reign of Shah Ismail Safavi; he returned to Gujarat during the reign of Sultan Mahmud Begara and settled in Champanir, set up as a teacher and writer of school books (*darsiya kitab*). The family was attached to the territories of Shaikh Ahmad-i Khattu.[86]

Although the Iranians were more famous as 'men of the pen' (*ahl-i qalam*) rather than as men of the sword (*ahl-i saif*), they had managed to reserve for themselves a special status in the ranks of the nobility and the military aristocracy. They were good politicians and dominated the Mughal court and state as much as they did in the sphere of the fine arts.

As is evident from the preceding description, the Iranians were scattered throughout the Mughal empire and even outside, holding various positions and ranks of all kinds. Surprisingly most of the Persians excelled in several arts though they might be masters of just one trade. With their multifarious capabilities, they could handle different assignments, professions, and creative hobbies with ease and dexterity.

## NOTES

1. *Ain-i-Akbari*, I, Eng. tr., Blochmann, bibliographical notes, nos. 112, 205, pp. 468, 470, 529-30.
2. Abul Fazl, *Insha-i Abul Fazl*, Har Sih Daftar, vol. I, Newal Kishore edn. See *Dastur-ul Amal*. Also see Eng. tr.
3. Badauni, *Muntakhab-ut-Tawarikh*, text, III, pp. 233-5, 312-14, 361, 406; Eng. tr., pp. 432-4, 495; *Ain-i-Akbari*, I, p. 586.
4. *Ain*, I, nos. 230, 231, 251, also p. 550.
5. Ibid.
6. *Ain*, I, no. 86, pp. 612-13. Badauni, vol. III, text, pp. 163, 170, Eng. tr., pp. 226-38.
7. Badauni, vol. III, text, pp. 230-1; Eng tr., pp. 320-2; Badauni, vol. II, p. 403; *Ain*, I, pp. 234, 480, 537-8.
8. Badauni, text, pp. 207-20, 240, 258, 295, 327, 330, 355; Eng. tr., pp. 287-9, 334-5, 358, 360, 406, 451; *Ain-i-Akbari*; Eng. tr. by Blochmann, vol. I, pp. 549 n. 6, 563, 602.
9. Ibid.
10. Ibid
11. Badauni, III, pp. 228, 230, 329, 360-1; Eng. tr., pp. 316, 317, 454, 494; *Tabaqat-i-Akbari*, pp. 354, 596; Sprenger, *Catalogue*, pp. 43, 54.
12. Badauni, III, text, p. 297; Eng. tr., pp. 286-7.
13. Ibid., text, pp. 151-2; Eng. tr., pp. 211-12.
14. *Ain-i-Akbari*, vol. I, no. 10, pp. 574, 644; Badauni, text, pp. 219-20; Eng. tr., pp. 304-5.
15. *Ain*, no. 22, p. 656.
16. Badauni, text, p. 789; Eng. tr., p. 125.
17. *Badshah Nama*, I, pp. 435-7.
18. Badauni, III, p. 265, Eng. tr., p. 367; Badauni, II, text, p. 372; *Ain*, I, p. 607; *Maasir-i Rahimi*, MS Asiatic Society of Bengal, p. 233; *Miratul Alam*, p. 48; *Ain*, I, no. 11, Eng. tr., p. 646.
19. *Ain*, I, Eng. tr., no. 29, pp. 53, 662, 677; Badauni, III, p. 358.
20. Ibid.
21. Badauni, III, text, pp. 204-6; Eng. tr., pp. 283-6.
22. *Ain*, vol. I, nos. 31, 34, pp. 663, 665; Badauni, text, p. 232; Eng. tr., pp. 322-4.
23. *Ain*, I, no. 27, p. 661.

24. Badauni, III, pp. 135-6; Eng. tr., pp. 192-3; *Ain*, I, pp. 606, 638 n. 5; *Muzzakkira*, p. 481; Eng. tr., p. 65.
25. Badauni, III, text, pp. 136-7, 170-2; Eng. tr., pp. 192-3, 239-41; *Ain*, I, pp. 606, 638 n. 5; *Muzzakkira*, p. 481; Eng. tr., p. 65.
26. *Ain*, no. 98, pp. 126, 451-3, 479; *Tuzuk-i-Jahangiri*, pp. 218-19; *Akbar Nama*, II, pp. 23, 281.
27. Ibid.
28. *Ain*, no. 161, pp. 497-8; *Akbar Nama*, II, pp. 23, 281. Badauni, III, pp. 97-8; Eng. tr., pp. 148-50.
29. *Ain-i Akbari*, vol. I, p. 603; Badauni, vol. III, pp. 302-4.
30. *Ain*, pp. 116, 471-2.
31. Badauni, III, p. 377; Eng. tr., p. 511; *Muzzakkira*, p. 471.
32. Badauni, pp. 285-7; Eng. tr., pp. 392-5; *Ain*, p. 639; *Maasir-i Rahimi*, p. 537.
33. *Ain*, pp. 34, 110, 208, 284, also see *Ain*, pp. 34-5.
34. *Ain*, I, no. 40, p. 669; Badauni, I, text, p. 56.
35. *Ain*, no. 266, pp. 114, 554-5.
36. Badauni, III, p. 126; Eng. tr., p. 184; *Ain*, I, no. 122, pp. 475-7.
37. *Ain*, no. 122, pp. 475-7.
38. Badauni, I, no. 32, p. 663; Badauni, III, text, p. 195; Eng. tr., p. 271.
39. Badauni, I, text, pp. 335-6; Eng. tr., pp. 462-3; *Ain*, no. 8, p. 643.
40. Ibid.
41. Badauni, I, text, p. 375; Eng. tr., p. 508; *Tuzuk-i-Jahangiri*, p. 91; *Ain*, pp. 580, 649; Badauni, III, text, pp. 378-9; Eng. tr., pp. 512-13.
42. Badauni, III, pp. 378-9; Eng. tr., pp. 512-13.
    Badauni bitterly criticized Muhammad Sharif Waqui of Nishapur for his heretical views. 'He was not a Basakhwani pure and simple, nor a Sabahi pure and simple, but was betwixt and between these two sects damned by God and cursed by people and believed in cycles, held the doctrine of the transmigration of souls'. In Badauni's words, he did not deserve to be called by this name Sharif (noble): 'Alas that such a noble name should be borne by such a vile fellow.'
43. For controversy regarding his birth place, see Mumtaz Ali Khan, 'Some Important Persian Prose Writing of the Thirteenth Century AD in India', Aligarh, 1970, pp. 70-7.
44. Badauni, text, III, p. 206; Eng. tr., pp. 285-6.
45. Badauni, text, pp. 184, 245, 254, 292, 381; Eng. tr., pp. 258, 340, 353, 403, 405, 516; *Ain*, pp. 471, 635. *Haft Iqlim*, II, p. 162.
46. Ibid.
47. Badauni, III, pp. 182, 1890; Eng. tr., pp. 255, 264; *Ain*, I, p. 599.
48. Ibid.
49. Badauni, III, pp. 266, 356-8, 385; Eng. tr., pp. 440, 447, 468, 519; *Ain*, I, no. 141, p. 485.
50. Amin Ahmad Razi, *Haft Iqlim*, II, pp. 134-58; Sijistan is said to be the worst place, *Ain*, I, Eng. tr., p. 494, also fn. 1.
51. Badauni, text, pp. 229-30; Eng. tr., pp. 319-20.
52. Badauni, I, text, pp. 279-81; Eng. tr., pp. 386-8.
53. Badauni, text, p. 284; Eng. tr., p. 391.
54. *Ain*, I, pp. 103, 609.
55. *Ain*, I, pp. 389, 423 n. 74; Badauni, p. 181, Eng. tr., pp. 254-5.

56. Abul Fazl describes him as a Khurasani whereas Badaúni traces his origin to Mashhad.
57. Badauni, text, pp. 273-4; Eng. tr., pp. 378-80.
58. *Ain*, Eng. tr., pp. 220-1.
59. *Ain*, Eng. tr., p. 221.
60. *Ain*, p. 20; Eng. tr., pp. 54-5, 263.
61. *Ain*, I, pp. 32, 97, 102.
62. Amina Okada, *Imperial Mughal Painters*, France, 1992, pp. 11, 12, 14, 62, 72, 77-9, 93, 106, 117.
63. *Ain*, I, p. 495, nn. 5, 7; *Tuzuk-i Jahangiri*, pp. 6, 113; Badauni, I, pp. 310-11, Eng. tr., pp. 429-30.
64. Badauni, III, text, pp. 186, 211-12; Eng. tr., pp. 260, 291-3; *Ain*, I, pp. 107, 598 n. 3; Amina Okada, op. cit., p. 69.
65. Ibid., *Haft Iqlim*, p. 634; *Ain*, Eng. tr., I, p. 598 n. 3; Badauni, III, p. 186, Eng. tr., p. 260.
66. Ibid.
67. Ibid., *Ain*, I, Eng. tr., p. 114.
68. *Ain*, I, pp. 114-15.
69. *Ain*, pp. 105-8.
70. *Ain*, no. 55, p. 611.
71. Badaúni, II, p. 315.
72. *Haig's Historic Landmarks of the Deccan*, pp. 4-10.
73. Badauni, I, pp. 332-5; Eng. tr., pp. 458-61.
74. *Ain*, I, no. 23, p. 658.
75. Badauni, III, pp. 137-40; Eng. tr., p. 193.
76. Ibid., pp. 136-9; Eng. tr., pp. 192-6.
77. Ibid., pp. 208, 334; Eng. tr., p. 324.
78. *Ain*, no. 34.
79. *Ain*, no. 10, p. 648; *Maasir-i Rahimi*, p. 356.
80. *Ain*, nos. 35, 37, 38, 40, 41.
81. Ibid.
82. Ibid.
83. *Ain*, I, pp. 412-16, 423, also nos. 59, 61.
84. Ibid.
85. *Ain*, I, Eng. tr., p. 76, no. 319, pp. 571-5.
86. Badauni, text, pp. 292-4; Eng. tr., pp. 403-5.

# Index